# PRINCIPLES OF
# ECONOMICS
## Fourth Edition

**Jeff Holt**
*Tulsa Community College*

Boston   Burr Ridge, IL   Dubuque, IA   New York   San Francisco   St. Louis
Bangkok   Bogotá   Caracas   Lisbon   London   Madrid
Mexico City   Milan   New Delhi   Seoul   Singapore   Sydney   Taipei   Toronto

The **McGraw·Hill** Companies

Principles of Economics, Fourth Edition

4 5 6 7 8 9 0   QDB   QDB   15 14 13 12 11

ISBN-13: 978-0-07-812643-7
ISBN-10: 0-07-812643-6

*Learning Solutions Manager: Ann Veith*
*Learning Solutions Representative: Michael Hemmer*
*Production Editor: Carrie Braun*
*Printer/Binder: Quad/Graphics*

# Principles of Economics, 4th Edition   by Jeff Holt

## Table of Contents

Contents - 5

# Introduction:  A Brief History of U.S. Economic Growth

The history of the U.S. economy is a history of remarkable economic growth.  From its humble beginnings in the Jamestown colony, the U.S. economy has achieved almost continuous growth.  Today, the U.S. economy is the largest national economy in the world and produces the highest standard of living of any of the thirty-five largest economies in the world.  This chapter provides a brief historical account of the remarkable growth of the U.S. economy.

## From Jamestown to the Present

This brief history of U.S. economic growth begins in 1607, when the Jamestown colony was established.  The Jamestown colony was the first permanent English settlement in what would become the United States of America.  The original colonists landed on Jamestown Island on May 14, 1607 after a four month journey aboard three small ships.

The Jamestown colonists were drawn to the New World largely by economic motivation.  They hoped to strike it rich by discovering gold, silver, or copper.  The 105 original Jamestown colonists included a number of goldsmiths and jewelers, but not a single farmer.

The original colonists in Jamestown did <u>not</u> strike it rich.  Instead, they confronted the basic economic problem of scarcity.  They had only limited resources to try to satisfy their unlimited wants.  (The basic economic problem of scarcity will be discussed in more detail in Chapter 1.)

Initially, the colonists struggled to produce enough output even to sustain life.  Of the 105 original colonists, only 38 were still alive when the second group of colonists arrived in January of 1608.  There were 214 colonists in Jamestown in the fall of 1609.  By June of 1610, only 60 colonists were still alive.  The Jamestown colony was on the verge of failure.

But in June of 1610, ships under the leadership of Lord De La Warr arrived at Jamestown bringing more colonists and supplies.  In 1612, the Jamestown colony began producing tobacco for export, earning very high returns.  Nonetheless, the Jamestown colony continued to struggle for a number of years, with most of its colonists either dying or returning to England.

> **Example 1:**  Of the approximately 14,000 colonists who arrived in Jamestown between 1607 and 1624, only 1,132 were living there in 1624.

Economic conditions in Colonial America eventually improved.  More people arrived and more colonies were established.  As the population grew, the labor force became more specialized, increasing labor productivity.  Physical capital was built up through savings and investment.  Human capital was developed through education and training and through work experience.  The colonists enjoyed a good deal of economic freedom, even though they were under British rule.  The economy and the population grew dramatically during the colonial era.

By 1790, there were nearly 4 million Americans. They had fought and won a war of national independence. They had established a Constitution that balanced a strong central government with individual freedom. And they had achieved economic growth so that they enjoyed a standard of living higher than most people in the world at the time. Still, their standard of living was extremely low by modern standards.

> **Example 2:** George Washington died in 1799, probably from an upper respiratory infection. He was under the care of three physicians and received the accepted medical treatment of the time. Unfortunately, the accepted medical treatment of the time included bloodletting. Washington was bled a significant amount (by some accounts, over five pints), which may have contributed to his demise.

Economic growth continued in America after 1790. Between 1790 and 1860, per capita output increased by fifty percent. **Per capita output** (or per capita GDP) is a basic measure of standard of living. Per capita output is computed by dividing a nation's total output by its population.

> **Example 3:** In 1940, U.S. Gross Domestic Product (GDP) was $1,034 billion and the population was 132,107,000. Thus, per capita GDP was $7,827 ($1,034,000,000,000 ÷ 132,107,000 = $7,827). In 1950, U.S. GDP was $1,777 billion and the population was 151,660,000. Per capita GDP was $11,717 ($1,777,000,000,000 ÷ 151,660,000 = $11,717). (GDP for both years is measured at the 2000 price level.)

With the fifty percent increase in per capita output between 1790 and 1860, the average consumer in 1860 could consume fifty percent more than the average consumer in 1790. The average worker in 1860 was fifty percent more productive than the average worker in 1790.

The primary economic activity in pre-Civil War America was agriculture. Most of the economic growth between 1790 and 1860 was caused by improvements in agricultural productivity. Agricultural productivity improved due to advances in agricultural technology and due to improvements in transportation.

> **Example 4:** Among the advances in agricultural technology were Eli Whitney's cotton gin (1793), Cyrus McCormick's mechanical reaper (1834), and John Deere's self-polishing steel plow (1837). Improvements in transportation included turnpikes, canals, steamboats, and, by 1860, thirty thousand miles of railroad track. The transportation improvements allowed agricultural production to take place where the land was most fertile, even if this was far from population centers.

Economic growth was disrupted by the Civil War (1861-65). The Civil War was fought at incredible cost to the nation. The war resulted in terrible loss of life and destruction of property. Over 600,000 Union and Confederate soldiers died. Another 500,000 soldiers were wounded. (The nation's population was only about 30 million at the time.)

The total cost of the Civil War, including lost human capital, government expenditures, and destruction of property, has been estimated at $6.7 billion. This was about double the national income of 1860.

After the Civil War, agricultural production continued to increase. Corn production increased from about 730 million bushels in 1866 to about 2,850 million bushels in 1910. Wheat production increased from about 170 million bushels in 1866 to about 625 million bushels in 1910.

The Industrial Revolution caused increased industrial productivity. There were major technological breakthroughs in steel production (the Bessemer process, the open-hearth method), in communication (telephones, radios), and in transportation (automobiles, airplanes).

The increases in agricultural and industrial production meant a higher standard of living. Per capita output doubled between 1860 and 1929. The average consumer in 1929 could consume twice as much as the average consumer in 1860, three times as much as the average consumer in 1790.

In 1929, the Great Depression began. The unemployment rate would average 18% for the decade of the 1930s. (The Great Depression is discussed in more detail in an appendix to Chapter 12.) Nonetheless, since 1929 productivity has grown at an even faster pace than previously.

Continued improvements in agricultural and industrial productivity, continued development of physical and human capital, and continued advances in technology have caused per capita output in the U.S. to more than quintuple since 1929. The average consumer today can consume five times as much as the average consumer in 1929, ten times as much as the average consumer in 1860, and fifteen times as much as the average consumer in 1790.

In the twentieth century, per capita output in the U.S. increased by about eight-fold. This rapid economic growth caused remarkable improvements in the quality of life for the average American.

> **Example 5:** In 1900, the poverty rate was about 90%. In 2000, the poverty rate was about 12%. In 1900, 3% of American households had electricity, 33% had indoor plumbing, and 15% had an indoor toilet. In 2000, among Americans below the poverty line, 46% owned their own homes, 76% had air conditioning, and 97% owned at least one color television. In 1900, there were 8,000 automobiles in the U.S. and 14 million horses. In 2000, there were 5 million horses and 200 million automobiles. Life expectancy for Americans increased from 47 years in 1900 to 77 years in 2000. (Life expectancy increased by another year from 2000 to 2005.) In the twentieth century, the infant mortality rate in America decreased by 95% (from 14% in 1900 to .7% in 2000).

In many ways, even a wealthy American in 1900 would have been at an economic disadvantage compared to the average American in 2000. In 1900, there were no airplanes, no movies, no television, no cell phones, no penicillin, no open-heart surgery, no organ transplants, no computers, and no air conditioning.

Will the rapid pace of economic growth continue in the twenty-first century? The U.S. is off to a good start. Per capita Real GDP increased from $34,759 in 2000 to $38,148 in 2007 (measured at the 2000 price level).

If the rate of economic growth in the twenty-first century matches the rate of growth in the twentieth century, by the year 2100 per capita output in the U.S. will increase to about $290,000 (measured at the 2000 price level).

The U.S. economy is by far the largest in the world, producing over $14 trillion worth of output in 2008.  Per capita output was about $47,000 in 2008.

The table below lists the 35 largest national economies for the year 2007, measured by purchasing power parity.  The information is from the "CIA World Factbook".

## 35 Largest National Economies - 2007

| Nation | Gross Domestic Product (GDP) | per capita GDP |
|---|---|---|
| United States | $13,840 billion | $45,800 |
| China | 6,991 billion | 5,300 |
| Japan | 4,290 billion | 33,600 |
| India | 2,989 billion | 2,700 |
| Germany | 2,810 billion | 34,200 |
| United Kingdom | 2,137 billion | 35,100 |
| Russia | 2,088 billion | 14,700 |
| France | 2,047 billion | 33,200 |
| Brazil | 1,836 billion | 9,700 |
| Italy | 1,786 billion | 30,400 |
| Spain | 1,352 billion | 30,100 |
| Mexico | 1,346 billion | 12,800 |
| Canada | 1,266 billion | 38,400 |
| South Korea | 1,201 billion | 24,800 |
| Turkey | 888 billion | 12,900 |
| Indonesia | 838 billion | 3,700 |
| Australia | 761 billion | 36,300 |
| Iran | 753 billion | 10,600 |
| Taiwan | 696 billion | 30,100 |
| Netherlands | 640 billion | 38,500 |
| Poland | 621 billion | 16,300 |
| Saudi Arabia | 565 billion | 23,200 |
| Argentina | 524 billion | 13,300 |
| Thailand | 519 billion | 7,900 |
| South Africa | 467 billion | 9,800 |
| Pakistan | 410 billion | 2,600 |
| Egypt | 404 billion | 5,500 |
| Belgium | 376 billion | 35,300 |
| Malaysia | 357 billion | 13,300 |
| Sweden | 335 billion | 36,500 |
| Venezuela | 335 billion | 12,200 |
| Greece | 325 billion | 29,200 |
| Ukraine | 320 billion | 6,900 |
| Colombia | 320 billion | 6,700 |
| Austria | 318 billion | 38,400 |

## Appendix: Book Review – "The Progress Paradox"

In 2003, Gregg Easterbrook published "The Progress Paradox", subtitled "How Life Gets Better While People Feel Worse". In the book, he details some of the many ways in which contemporary American life grows steadily better. He also tries to explain why so many Americans fail to appreciate the improvement, or even deny that the improvement is happening.

Easterbrook asserts that the great story of the current era is that average people are better off. Among the statistics that Easterbrook gathers to support this view are:

1. Per capita income in America has more than doubled since 1960, in inflation-adjusted dollars.

2. The median family income of African-Americans is currently rising twice as fast as the median family income for the United States as a whole.

3. In the year 2000, almost 23 percent of American households had an income of at least $75,000. In 1890, less than 1 percent of American households earned the equivalent of $75,000, in inflation-adjusted dollars.

4. Almost 70 percent of Americans own their homes today, versus less than 20 percent a century ago.

5. American housing stock has increased to the point that there are, on average, two dwelling rooms per person. Most European nations still have slightly fewer dwelling rooms than persons.

6. In 1900, 42 percent of men in the labor force were employed in mining, forestry, fishing, and farming. 47 percent of women in the labor force were employed as domestics. Today, the majority of both men and women in the labor force have white-collar jobs.

7. In the middle of the nineteenth century, the typical person spent 50 percent of his or her waking hours over the course of a lifetime engaged in some form of imposed labor. Today, due to shorter work weeks and greater life expectancy, the percentage is less than 20 percent.

8. The world's "proven reserve" of petroleum is larger today that in was in the 1970s.

9. Since 1970, smog has declined by a third, even though vehicle-miles traveled have increased by 143 percent. Acid rain has declined by 67 percent.

10. Despite the 143 percent increase in vehicle-miles traveled, annual auto crash deaths are down almost 20 percent since 1970.

11. In 2000, death by heart disease was 60 percent lower, adjusted for population, than in 1950. Stroke deaths were down 70 percent.

12. Since the early years of the twentieth century, overall IQ scores have risen by about 20 percent.

Despite these and many other examples of progress, opinion polls show that many Americans feel that the country is going downhill. The percentage of Americans who describe themselves as "happy" has not increased since the 1950s.

Easterbrook proposes a number of possible explanations for the paradoxical relationship between the objective progress and the average person's generally negative perception, including:

1. An active preference for bad news.

   a. Political activists achieve more fund-raising success by emphasizing (and often exaggerating) problems than by pointing out past improvements.

   > **Example 6:** Candidates for public office in 2008 spoke often about the need to fix the "broken" U.S. economy. This despite the fact that the U.S. economy in 2008 was the largest in the world and was generating a standard of living (per capita Real GDP) almost 70% higher than in 1980.

   b. To the news media, "bad" news is news and "good" news is not news. Viewers are more likely to "stay tuned" if the upcoming story is about the "latest crisis" rather than about the latest improvement.

   c. The elite have a preference for bad news. A sense of crisis increases the power and influence of the elite. And the elite see a person with a cynical attitude toward the future as "sophisticated", while a person with a positive attitude is seen as a "Pollyanna".

2. The inability of money to buy happiness. Research indicates that a lack of material necessities causes unhappiness. But once a basic level of material well-being has been attained, additional income does not increase happiness.

3. Abundance denial. People strive for higher living standards, anticipating greater happiness. When their higher living standards do not yield greater happiness, they conclude that they have not actually achieved higher living standards. If they had achieved higher living standards, they would be happier. Since they are not happier, they must not have achieved higher living standards.

4. Collapse anxiety. People fear that the current living standards cannot be sustained. Collapse anxiety is triggered by such fears as exhaustion of natural resources, environmental calamity, and political upheaval.


**Questions for Introduction**

**Fill-in-the-blanks:**

1. _____ _____ output is a basic measure of standard of living.

**Multiple Choice:**

_____ 1. The Jamestown colonists were drawn to the New World by:
    a. economic motivation
    b. desire for political freedom
    c. desire for religious freedom
    d. None of the above

_____ 2. During America's colonial era:
    a. there was little economic growth due to British oppression
    b. the population grew rapidly
    c. the rapidly growing population hindered economic growth
    d. All of the above

_____ 3. By 1790:
    a. there were nearly 4 million Americans
    b. the standard of living in America was roughly the same as it is today
    c. Both of the above
    d. Neither of the above

_____ 4. In 1960, GDP for the U.S. was $2,502 billion (measured at the 2000 price level) and the population was 180,780,000. Per capita GDP in 1960 was:
    a. $7,047
    b. $12,700
    c. $13,840
    d. $28,380

_____ 5. Most of the U.S. economic growth between 1790 and 1860 was caused by:
    a. central planning by the U.S. government
    b. the development of computers
    c. growth in industrial productivity due to the Industrial Revolution
    d. improvements in agricultural productivity

_____ 6. Between 1860 and 1929, per capita output in the U.S.:
    a. quintupled
    b. doubled
    c. increased by fifty percent
    d. stayed the same

_____ 7. Compared to 1790, the standard of living today is:
    a. about the same
    b. nearly three times as high
    c. about five times as high
    d. about fifteen times as high

_____ 8. In the 20th century, the poverty rate in the U.S.:
    a. decreased from about 90% to about 12%
    b. decreased from about 50% to about 10%
    c. decreased from about 20% to about 15%
    d. stayed the same

_____ 9. In the 20th century, life expectancy in the U.S.:
   a. remained steady
   b. decreased slightly due to the rising murder rate
   c. increased by almost 10 years
   d. increased by 30 years

_____ 10. Per capita output in the U.S. in 2007 was:
   a. $33,800
   b. $39,000
   c. $45,800
   d. $55,600

_____ 11. Of the thirty-five largest national economies, the one with the lowest per capita GDP in 2007 was:
   a. Pakistan
   b. Egypt
   c. India
   d. Indonesia

_____ 12. Of Japan, Germany, France, and Canada, the one with the highest per capita GDP in 2007 was:
   a. Japan
   b. Germany
   c. France
   d. Canada

_____ 13. In 2007, the sum of GDP for Japan, Germany, the United Kingdom, Russia, and France was:
   a. about triple that of the U.S.
   b. about double that of the U.S.
   c. about one-and-a-half times that of the U.S.
   d. almost as great as that of the U.S.

_____ 14. According to Gregg Easterbrook, the great story of the current era is:
   a. average people are better off
   b. the rich get richer
   c. the poor get poorer
   d. Both b. and c. above

_____ 15. According to "The Progress Paradox", the percentage of Americans who own their homes:
   a. is slightly less than a century ago
   b. is almost twice as great as a century ago
   c. is three and a half times as great as a century ago
   d. is seven times as great as a century ago

_____ 16. In 1900, 47 percent of women in the labor force were employed as:
   a. teachers
   b. domestics
   c. nurses
   d. secretaries

_____ 17. As life expectancy has increased and the population has grown:
   a.  death by heart disease and stroke has been rising, adjusted for population
   b.  annual auto crash deaths have been increasing
   c.  smog and acid rain have been increasing
   d.  None of the above

## Problems:

1.  Describe the initial economic struggles of the Jamestown colonists.

2.  Describe the economic cost of the Civil War.

3.  List, in order, the five largest national economies in 2007.

4. List four possible explanations for the paradoxical relationship between the objective progress and the average person's generally negative perception.

## Answers for Introduction

**Fill-in-the-blanks:**   1. Per capita

**Multiple Choice:**
| | | |
|---|---|---|
| 1. a. | 7. d. | 13. d. |
| 2. b. | 8. a. | 14. a. |
| 3. a. | 9. d. | 15. c. |
| 4. c. | 10. c. | 16. b. |
| 5. d. | 11. a. | 17. d. |
| 6. b. | 12. d. | |

## Problems:

1. Initially, the Jamestown colonists struggled to produce enough output even to sustain life. Of the 105 original colonists, only 38 were still alive when the second group of colonists arrived in January of 1608. There were 214 colonists in Jamestown in the fall of 1609. By June of 1610, only 60 colonists were still alive.

2. The Civil War was fought at incredible cost to the nation. Over 600,000 soldiers died. Another 500,000 soldiers were wounded. The total cost of the war, including lost human capital, government expenditures, and destruction of property, has been estimated at $6.7 billion. This was about double the national income of 1860.

3. The five largest national economies in 2007 were:
   (1) United States
   (2) China
   (3) Japan
   (4) India
   (5) Germany

4. Four possible explanations for the paradoxical relationship between the objective progress and the average person's generally negative perception are:
   (1) An active preference for bad news.
   (2) The inability of money to buy happiness.
   (3) Abundance denial.
   (4) Collapse anxiety.

# Chapter 1  Scarcity and Choices

## The Basic Economic Problem

What is the basic economic problem?  Various problems may come to mind:  poverty, unemployment, inflation, recession, budget deficits, etc.  There are many economic problems.  But...

## The basic economic problem is scarcity.

Imagine that you are stranded all alone on an island.  Maybe you landed on the island after being shipwrecked, like Robinson Crusoe or Gilligan.  Or maybe your plane crashed into the ocean, like Tom Hanks in "Castaway".

But there you are.  On an island.  All alone.  Just you and your economic wants.  What do you want?  Well, you want water, food, shelter, and a way back to civilization.  If you are unable to get back to civilization, you'll soon want new clothing, medical care, recreation, etc.  To meet these wants, you must produce goods and services.  So you use the resources available to produce goods and services in order to satisfy your wants as well as possible.

But how well will you be able to satisfy your wants?  Would you expect to eventually achieve a standard of living that is totally satisfying, where there is nothing else that you want?  Probably not.  Even if you achieved a high standard of living, you would prefer it to be higher.  Even if your island were flowing with coconut milk and honey, you would still long for chocolate.  By your human nature, you will tend to always want more.  This is one side of the problem of scarcity...

## Human wants are unlimited.

> **Example 1:**  Imagine that a person could be transported through time from the America of two hundred years ago to the America of today.  This time traveler would be amazed at our high standard of living.  They would see the average American consuming food, shelter, clothing, transportation, medical care, recreation, etc. in quantities and qualities that would seem incredible to them.  They might assume that most modern Americans are perfectly satisfied with their standard of living, desiring nothing more.  But that is not the case.  We all want more.  And even the time traveler would quickly grow accustomed to the relative abundance of modern America.  Soon they would notice things that they wanted and did not have – a bigger house, a nicer car, a faster computer, membership in a country club, fashionable new eyeglasses, an iPhone, etc.  The list of human wants is unlimited.

Back on the island, how will you go about trying to satisfy your unlimited wants?  You will produce, using the resources available to you.  On the island, your resources are very limited.  You have only your own labor, the land and other natural resources of the island, and whatever capital goods you are able to produce yourself.  And since you are forced to be self-sufficient, specialized resources that might be very valuable in a developed economy (e.g. your computer programming skills) may be of little value on the island.

Forced to practice self-sufficiency, your standard of living is likely to be very low. You may not be able to produce enough output even to stay alive. If only you could get back to civilization, where resources are so much more abundant. Then you could have everything that you want!

Or could you? No. Even in the most productive societies, it is not possible to produce all of everything that everyone wants. Even where resources are abundant, they are limited. This is the other side of the problem of scarcity…

**Resources are limited.**

> **Example 2:** Modern America is blessed with abundant resources. We have a large and highly productive labor force, hundreds of millions of acres of high-quality agricultural land, huge investments in physical capital, etc. Yet, our resources are limited. We could produce more if we had more doctors, nurses, school teachers, scientists, engineers, police officers, highways, airports, refineries, windmill farms, forests, public parks, etc. Our resources are abundant, but also limited.

The basic economic problem is scarcity because human wants are unlimited and resources are limited. So we can define scarcity as:

**Scarcity** – the problem that human wants exceed the production possible with the limited resources available.

Every individual and every society faces this basic economic problem. How individuals and societies attempt to deal with the problem of scarcity is the fundamental focus of economics.

**Economics** – the study of how individuals and societies use their limited resources to try to satisfy their unlimited wants.

The problem of scarcity cannot be solved. Even if individuals and societies achieve much higher standards of living, the problem of scarcity will persist. Yet most individuals and societies continue to strive for higher standards of living. The basic goal in dealing with the problem of scarcity is not to satisfy all human wants. That goal is impossible. The basic goal is to produce as much consumer satisfaction as possible with the limited resources available.

**Categories of Resources**

**Resources** – the inputs that make production possible.

Resources can be divided into four broad categories:

1. **Labor** – the physical and mental efforts that people contribute to production. The productivity of labor depends largely on the amount of human capital that the labor force develops. **Human capital** is developed ability that increases a person's productivity. Human capital is developed primarily through education and training and through work experience.

**Example 3A:** In 1940, about 25 percent of Americans 25 years and older had completed high school and about 5 percent had at least a bachelor's degree. In 1970, about 52 percent had completed high school and about 11 percent had at least a bachelor's degree. In 2007, 86 percent had completed high school and 29 percent had at least a bachelor's degree. (Information is from the Census Bureau.)

**Example 3B:** In 2007, Americans 25 years and older with a bachelor's degree earned an average of $59,365, those with a high school diploma earned $33,609, and those with no high school diploma earned $24,077. (Information is from the Census Bureau.)

2. **Land** - the naturally occurring resources, such as unimproved land, minerals, fossil fuels, forests, water, and weather.

**Example 4A:** In 2002, there were 749 million acres of forests in the U.S. Since the 1950s, timber growth has consistently exceeded timber harvest. (Information is from the U.S. Forest Service, "Forest Resources of the United States, 2002").

**Example 4B:** At the end of 1976, the U.S. had proven reserves of crude oil of 33.5 billion barrels. Over the next 29 years, U.S. crude oil production was 71.7 billion barrels. At the end of 2005, the U.S. had proven reserves of crude oil of 21.8 billion barrels.

**Example 4C:** At the end of 1976, the U.S. had proven reserves of natural gas of 213.3 trillion cubic feet. Over the next 29 years, U.S. natural gas production was 523.2 trillion cubic feet. At the end of 2005, the U.S. had proven reserves of natural gas of 204.4 trillion cubic feet. (Information on crude oil and natural gas reserves is from the Energy Information Administration.)

3. **Capital** - produced goods that are used in the production of other goods. Highways, harbors, airports, railroads, factories, warehouses, office buildings, and machinery are all examples of capital.

**Example 5A:** Railroad mileage in the U.S. increased from about 9,000 miles in 1850 to about 130,000 miles in 1890. The ton-miles of cargo carried by U.S. railroads more than tripled between 1930 and 2005.

**Example 5B:** In 2006, there were almost 4 million miles of highways in the U.S. The interstate highway system, which contains just 1.2% of all highway miles, carries 24% of highway traffic. (Information is from the American Association of State Highway and Transportation Officials.)

4. **Entrepreneurship** - the special skill involved in organizing labor, land, and capital for production. Entrepreneurs start new businesses, develop new production techniques, and introduce new products.

   Entrepreneurs are generally motivated by the goal of profit-maximization. But not all entrepreneurial efforts succeed. Entrepreneurs also bear the risk of loss. Profits (and losses) direct entrepreneurs and the resources that they control into (and out of) different types of production.

**Example 6:** Famous American entrepreneurs include Benjamin Franklin, John D. Rockefeller, Henry Ford, Thomas Edison, George Eastman, Milton Hershey, Ray Kroc, Sam Walton, Fred Smith, Bill Gates, Larry Page, and Sergey Brin.

## Rational Person Assumption

In a market economy, the resources are generally owned by private individuals. Thus, most production decisions will be made by private individuals. Most consumption decisions are also made by private individuals. How do we expect these private individuals to make their production and consumption decisions?

In economics, people are assumed to behave rationally. A rational person will have certain goals (e.g. to stay warm and well-fed, to maximize profit, to find true love, etc.) and will pursue these goals in a rational manner.

Rational people will want to do that which makes them better off and will want to avoid doing that which makes them worse off. Rational people will pursue their own self-interest. In the pursuit of self-interest, rational people will respond to incentives. An **incentive** changes the benefit or cost associated with an action.

**Example 7:** Celle Community College institutes a merit pay plan for its professors. The college administration decides that evaluating the professors on their performance as teachers is too subjective. So the professors' merit is measured by objective factors, such as the number of committees served on and the number of conferences attended. The professors will respond to this new incentive by signing up to serve on more committees and by attending more conferences. Teaching performance may suffer.

For more on the rational person assumption, see the appendix at the end of the chapter.

## Resource Owner Motivation

In a market economy, the resources are generally owned by private individuals. For instance, each person owns his or her own labor. How do private individuals decide the most desirable use for their resources?

Adam Smith addressed this question in his book "An Inquiry into the Nature and Causes of the Wealth of Nations" (published in 1776). According to Smith, "It is not from the benevolence of the butcher, the brewer, or the baker that we expect our dinner, but from their regard to their own interest."

We assume that the basic resource owner motivation is self-interest. Each resource owner will use whatever resources he or she owns to pursue self-interest. But what about the best interest of society? Will the resource owner's pursuit of self-interest also serve the best interest of society?

According to Adam Smith, the resource owner's pursuit of self-interest <u>will</u> generally serve the best interest of society. According to Smith, the resource owner "intends only his own gain, and he is in this…led by an invisible hand to promote an end which is no part of his intention…By pursuing his own interest he frequently promotes that of society more effectually than when he really intends to promote it."

Why does the resource owner's pursuit of self-interest generally serve the best interest of society?  Most resource owners have a self-interest to generate maximum profit from the use of their resources.  In a competitive market, this pursuit of profit-maximization will lead the resource owners toward two actions that serve the best interest of society;

1.  **Resource owners will direct their resources to the use that is most highly valued by consumers.**

> **Example 8:**  Kris opens a donut shop featuring seaweed-based donuts.  Unfortunately, consumers find the donuts unappealing.  If Kris wants to stay in business and have a chance to earn a profit, she will have to change her donuts in response to consumer demand.

2.  **Resource owners will use their resources as efficiently as possible.**

> **Example 9:**  Kris employs only persons with advanced degrees in nutrition at her donut shop.  Unfortunately, the high salaries of her employees make her donuts so costly to produce that they are not competitive.  If Kris wants to stay in business and have a chance to earn a profit, she will have to use her resources more efficiently.  She will have to employ the cheapest available workers who can do an adequate job.  She will have to produce donuts at the lowest cost (with the least valuable combination of resources) that she can.

These actions serve the best interest of society by helping society to achieve the basic goal in dealing with the problem of scarcity; produce as much consumer satisfaction as possible with the limited resources available.

## Opportunity Cost

The basic economic problem of scarcity means that people have to make choices.  How will they use their limited resources?  Which of their unlimited wants will they satisfy?  As they make these choices, they are foregoing other desirable choices.

If resources are used to produce Good A, those resources are not available to produce Good B.  If income is spent on Good C, that income is not available to consume Good D.  The value of the best alternative surrendered when a choice is made is the opportunity cost of that choice.

**Opportunity cost** - the value of the best alternative surrendered when a choice is made.

> **Example 10:**  When Cindy quits her job at the Sonic to join the Army, her opportunity cost is the income she could earn at the Sonic.  When NFL strong safety Pat Tillman gave up his job with the Arizona Cardinals to become an Army Ranger, his opportunity cost was the income he could have earned in the NFL (over $1 million per year).

## Rationing

The basic economic problem of scarcity creates the necessity to ration the limited resources to production and to ration the limited goods to consumption. In the U.S. economy, the primary rationing device is dollar price. Using dollar price as the rationing device means that resources will be rationed to the use that is most highly valued by consumers. And goods will be rationed to the consumers who are willing and able to pay the most for them.

> **Example 11A:** Jessica can earn $8 an hour selling t-shirts at Old Navy, or she can earn millions as a popular singer performing concerts. Dollar price will ration Jessica's labor to the concerts. She generates more consumer satisfaction singing in concert than she does selling t-shirts (as indicated by the higher dollar price she can earn).

> **Example 11B:** Jessica performs in concert at a 15,000 seat arena. If admission to the concert were free, 100,000 fans would be willing to attend the concert. Dollar price rations the 15,000 available seats to the consumers who are willing and able to pay the most for them.

## Marginal Benefits and Marginal Costs

The basic economic problem of scarcity requires people to make decisions. You make many economic decisions each day. Will you attend class or put in extra hours at work? Will you buy a candy bar from the vending machine or spend that money elsewhere? Will you stay up late and study for another half hour or go on to bed?

Economic decisions are made by comparing the marginal (extra, additional) benefits of a choice with the marginal (extra, additional) costs.

> **Example 12:** If the marginal benefit of another half hour of study exceeds the marginal cost of the lost sleep, you study for another half hour. If the marginal cost exceeds the marginal benefit, you stop studying.

Any activity should be continued as long as the marginal benefit of the activity exceeds the marginal cost. The optimal (ideal, most efficient) level of the activity occurs where the marginal benefit and the marginal cost are equal. A more detailed explanation of the optimal level of an activity is given in Chapter 18.

## Thinking Like an Economist

To make sound economic decisions, a person needs to think like an economist. Six aspects of thinking like an economist are discussed below:

1. **Realizing that association does not necessarily indicate causation**. In making economic decisions, we often look for cause and effect relationships. If a person studies more, will this cause an improvement in his or her test grade? Association ("I studied more and my test grade improved") often indicates causation ("My test grade improved <u>because</u> I studied more"). But association does not always indicate

causation ("I painted my toenails blue and my test grade improved"). Many superstitions arise because a person believes that association <u>must</u> indicate causation.

2. **Avoiding the fallacy of composition**. The fallacy of composition is the idea that what is true for one must be true for the group. This is <u>not</u> necessarily true. If one person leaves the football game at the end of the third quarter in order to exit the parking lot faster, that one person will be able to exit faster. If all the fans leave the football game at the end of the third quarter, the group will <u>not</u> be able to exit the parking lot faster. Likewise, an economic policy that benefits one person or a small group may <u>not</u> be beneficial to society as a whole.

3. **Distinguishing between positive statements and normative statements**. **Positive statements** claim to describe the way things are (e.g. "The use of pesticides increases farm productivity."). Positive statements can be tested for accuracy. **Normative statements** propose the way things ought to be (e.g. "Farmers should <u>not</u> be allowed to use pesticides on crops intended for human consumption."). Normative statements express value judgments, and cannot be tested for accuracy.

4. **Assuming ceteris paribus when examining the relationship between variables.** Ceteris paribus (kā´ ter is - pair´ u bus) means "all other things held constant". For example, if we want to know what will happen to the quantity of donuts demanded when the price of donuts increases, we must assume that the change in price is the only change affecting the quantity demanded. If another variable is also changing, such as consumer income, then the relationship between price and quantity demanded will be uncertain. Other variables must be held constant if we are to arrive at the actual relationship between the variables that we are examining.

5. **Realizing that people respond to incentives.** An **incentive** changes the benefit or cost associated with an action. Rational people, pursuing their own self-interest, will respond to incentives. (Refer back to Example 7 on page 1-4. Also, see the appendix on the Rational Person Assumption at the end of the chapter.)

6. **Trying to anticipate unintended consequences.** Actions are taken in hopes of achieving a desired outcome. But unintended consequences may also result.

---

**Example 13:** Imagine that new federal regulations require all automobiles and drivers to be as well-equipped with safety devices as NASCAR racers. The desired outcome is to reduce auto fatalities. But what would happen to the number of auto accidents and to the number of pedestrian fatalities?

---

## Macroeconomics versus Microeconomics

**Macroeconomics** is the branch of economics that focuses on overall economic behavior. Inflation, unemployment, economic growth, budget deficits, and trade deficits are examples of macroeconomic concerns.

**Microeconomics** is the branch of economics that focuses on components of the economy. Households, firms, particular markets, and specific industries are examples of microeconomic concerns.

> **Example 14:** The unemployment rate for the overall economy is a macroeconomic concern. The effect of a new collective bargaining agreement on the unemployment rate in the airline industry is a microeconomic concern.

### Graphs

In the study of economics, we are often interested in the relationship between two variables. If the value of one variable changes, what will happen to the value of the other variable? If the price of donuts increases, what will happen to the quantity of donuts demanded? **Graphs** illustrate the relationship between two variables.

A graph consists of a pair of intersecting number lines. The number lines intersect at zero on each number line. The horizontal number line is called the X axis. The vertical number line is called the Y axis.

> **Example 15:** On a graph, the X axis and the Y axis intersect at zero on each axis.
>
>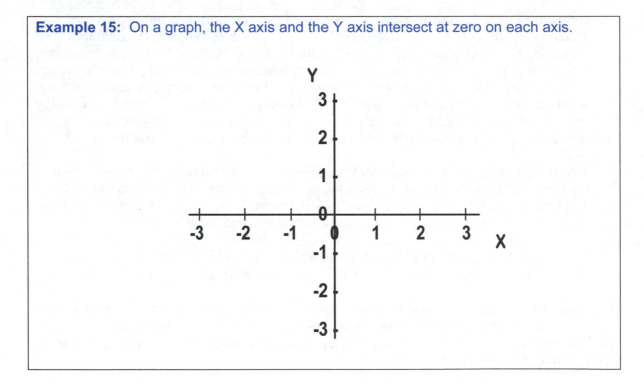

In the study of economics, we usually are dealing with positive numbers. So graphs are drawn without the negative portions of the X axis and the Y axis.

Example 16, on the next page, illustrates the typical set-up for a graph in economics. Only the positive portions of the X axis and the Y axis are shown.

**Example 16:**

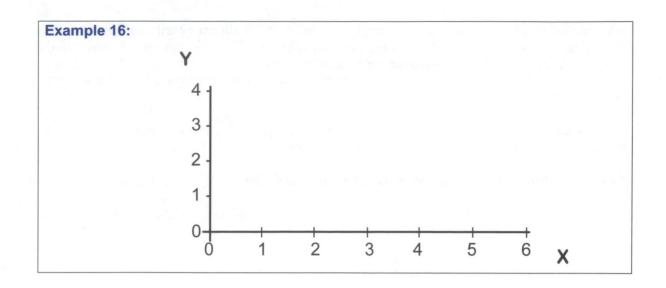

To illustrate the relationship between two variables, points are plotted on a graph based on the numerical relationship between the variables. Then a curve is drawn connecting the points.

**Example 17:** The table below shows five combinations of values for variable X and variable Y. The combinations are plotted on the graph below. Then the points are connected with a curve to indicate the relationship between the two variables.

| Point | X | Y |
|-------|---|----|
| A | 1 | 2 |
| B | 2 | 4 |
| C | 3 | 6 |
| D | 4 | 8 |
| E | 5 | 10 |

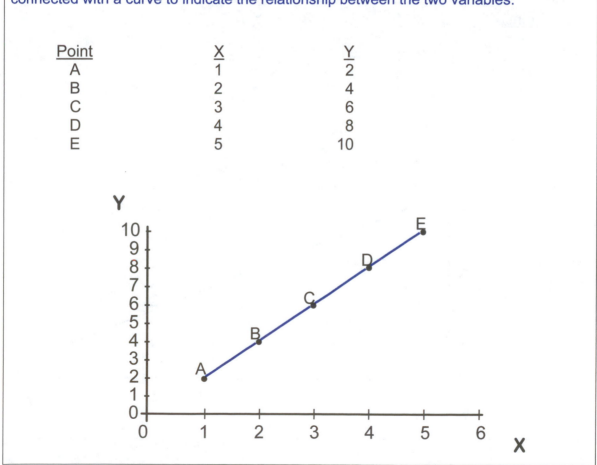

An upward sloping curve (as in Example 17) indicates a **direct relationship** between the variables. As the value of X increases, the value of Y also increases. A downward sloping curve indicates an **inverse relationship** between the variables. A horizontal curve or a vertical curve would indicate that the variables are unrelated to (independent of) each other.

The **slope of a curve** is the ratio of the vertical change to the horizontal change as the graph is read from left to right. Expressed as a formula:

**Slope = Change in Y variable ÷ Change in X variable** $= (Y_2 - Y_1) \div (X_2 - X_1)$

For the curve illustrated in Example 17, the slope could be computed between points A and B as below:

Slope $= (Y_2 - Y_1) \div (X_2 - X_1) = (4 - 2) \div (2 - 1) = 2 \div 1 = 2$

Example 18 below illustrates an inverse relationship.

**Example 18:** The table below shows five combinations of values for variable X and variable Y. The combinations are plotted on the graph below. Then the points are connected with a curve to indicate the relationship between the two variables.

| Point | X | Y |
|-------|---|---|
| A | 1 | 5 |
| B | 3 | 4 |
| C | 5 | 3 |
| D | 7 | 2 |
| E | 9 | 1 |

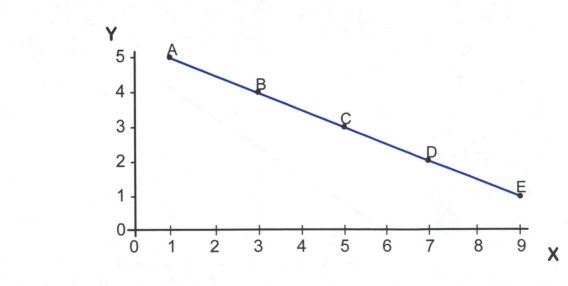

The slope between points A and B is:

$$\text{Slope} = (Y_2 - Y_1) \div (X_2 - X_1) = (4 - 5) \div (3 - 1) = -1 \div 2 = -\tfrac{1}{2}$$

## Appendix:  Book Review – "Robinson Crusoe"

In 1719, Daniel Defoe published his popular novel, "Robinson Crusoe".  The novel is an adventure story with strong religious overtones.  It also illustrates a number of important economic concepts.

As a result of a shipwreck, Robinson Crusoe is cast away on an island near the mouth of the Orinoco River of South America.  As a castaway, Robinson Crusoe has to practice self-sufficiency.  Self-sufficiency is very difficult.  To make it plausible that Crusoe is able to survive alone, Defoe places Crusoe on an island with few dangers (no dangerous wild animals, only rare visits by dangerous humans) and abundant natural resources (goats, turtles, grapes, limes, a climate conducive to growing crops).  Defoe also allows Crusoe to return to the wrecked ship twelve times.  From the wrecked ship, Crusoe salvages food, clothing, guns, gun powder, various tools, some barley seed and some rice seed, sailcloth, a grindstone, etc.

With the resources that he salvages from the wrecked ship, Crusoe attempts to produce what he needs to survive.  Many of his attempts at production fail.  Over time, his experiences increase his human capital and his production efforts become more successful.  With his increased human capital, he is able to build a safe and comfortable shelter, to plant and harvest barley and rice, to bake bread, to manufacture wicker baskets, earthenware pots, and clay pottery, to build a small canoe, to domesticate the goats of the island, to make cheese and butter, and to use a grindstone to sharpen his edged tools.

The novel illustrates the necessity of saving (delaying consumption) and investing in order to increase one's standard of living.  Crusoe spends three weeks enclosing his grain field with a hedge to protect his barley and rice from goats and hares.  He spends a week making a wooden spade so that he can prepare more land for cultivation.  He plants his entire harvest of barley and rice, eating none of the produce, until his fourth harvest.  He digs pitfalls and captures goats to domesticate.  He spends three months building a hedge for an enclosure for his domesticated goats.  Crusoe's diligent saving and investing allows him to survive and to have a reasonably comfortable standard of living during his twenty-eight years on the island.

## Appendix:  Rational Person Assumption

In economics, people are assumed to behave rationally.  Rational people will want to do that which makes them better off and will want to avoid doing that which makes them worse off.  This does not mean that rational people will never make mistakes.  Rational people may make mistakes due to misinformation, erroneous logic, excessive emotional involvement, etc.  Yet, assuming that people behave rationally will better predict human behavior than assuming that people behave irrationally or randomly.

Scarcity and Choices

Rational people pursue their own self-interest. In the pursuit of self-interest, rational people respond to incentives.

> **Example 19:** When bank robber Willie Sutton was asked, "Why do you rob banks?" he reportedly replied, "Because that's where the money is."

> **Example 20:** If all banks begin employing teams of armed security guards, the rational bank robber may turn to robbing liquor stores instead of banks.

### Appendix: Think Like an Economist – Rational Robbers

If the government responds to an increase in the incidence of liquor store hold-ups by passing a law that makes the punishment for armed robbery the same as the punishment for murder, there will be fewer liquor store hold-ups. If you work at a liquor store, will you be happy about this change in the law?

Thinking like an economist (remembering that rational people respond to incentives), how would you expect the behavior of armed robbers who continue to rob liquor stores to change in response to the new law?

### Questions for Chapter 1

**Fill-in-the-blanks:**

1. _____ is the problem that human wants exceed the production possible with the limited resources available.

2. _____ is the study of how individuals and societies use their limited resources to try to satisfy their unlimited wants.

3. _____ are the inputs that make production possible.

4. _____ refers to the physical and mental efforts that people contribute to production.

5. _____ _____ is developed ability that increases a person's productivity.

6. _____ refers to the naturally occurring resources.

7. _____ refers to produced goods that are used in the production of other goods.

8. _____ is the special skill involved in organizing labor, land, and capital for production.

9. A(n) _____ changes the benefit or cost associated with an action.

10. _____ cost is the value of the best alternative surrendered when a choice is made.

11. _____ statements claim to describe the way things are.

12. _____ statements propose the way things ought to be.

13. _____ focuses on overall economic behavior.

14. _____ focuses on components of the economy.

15. _____ illustrate the relationship between two variables.

16. On a graph, an upward sloping curve indicates a(n) _____ relationship between the variables.

17. The _____ of a curve is the ratio of the vertical change to the horizontal change as the graph is read from left to right.

## Multiple Choice:

_____ 1. The basic economic problem is scarcity because:
   a. human wants are unlimited and resources are limited
   b. there are never enough jobs for all the people who want to work
   c. there is never enough money to consume what we want
   d. human wants are limited and resources are unlimited

_____ 2. If the U.S. could triple its per capita income:
   a. all economic problems would be solved
   b. everyone could consume all that they wanted
   c. the basic economic problem would still be scarcity
   d. Both a. and b. above

_____ 3. The basic goal in dealing with the problem of scarcity is:
   a. to produce as much consumer satisfaction as possible with the limited resources available
   b. to decrease human wants until they are consistent with the resources available
   c. to satisfy all human wants
   d. Both b. and c. above

_____ 4. Between 1940 and 2007, the percentage of Americans 25 years and older who had completed high school:
   a. decreased by 25 percent
   b. remained the same
   c. almost doubled
   d. more than tripled

_____ 5. _____ refers to the naturally occurring resources.
- a. Labor
- b. Land
- c. Capital
- d. Entrepreneurship

_____ 6. In a competitive market, the self-interest of the resource owners will cause resources to be directed:
- a. to the use that is most highly valued by consumers
- b. to a use that harms society
- c. to their most convenient use
- d. in a random way

_____ 7. Using dollar price as the rationing device means:
- a. that resources will be rationed to the use that is most highly valued by consumers
- b. that goods will be rationed to the consumers who are willing and able to pay the most for them
- c. Both of the above
- d. Neither of the above

_____ 8. The optimal level of an activity occurs where:
- a. the marginal benefit is maximized
- b. the excess of marginal benefit over marginal cost is maximized
- c. the marginal benefit and the marginal cost are equal
- d. Either a. or b. above

_____ 9. "If I have more money, I will be better off. Therefore, if everyone has more money, everyone will be better off." This statement is an example of:
- a. the association-causation issue
- b. the fallacy of composition
- c. the ceteris paribus assumption
- d. All of the above

_____ 10. Which of the following is a normative statement?
- a. "The unemployment rate in November, 2008 was 6.7%"
- b. "American and European companies employ over 2 million workers at call centers in India"
- c. "The federal government should fine U.S. companies that outsource jobs to foreign countries."
- d. None of the above

_____ 11. Each morning, Homer buys 2 donuts on his way to work. Yesterday, Homer received a salary increase. This morning, the price of donuts was up by 5¢, and Homer bought 3 donuts. Does this prove that people will buy more donuts as the price of donuts increases?
- a. Yes, this is simple cause and effect
- b. No, this only proves that Homer will buy more donuts as the price increases. Applying that to people in general is the fallacy of composition
- c. No, since Homer received a salary increase, we have failed the ceteris paribus assumption. All other things are not held constant

_____ 12. Grandma promises to pay Miki's tuition for the upcoming semester if Miki earns at least a 3.5 GPA. Miki drops her two hardest classes and replaces them with easier classes. This is an example:
- a. that people respond to incentives
- b. of unintended consequences
- c. Both of the above
- d. Neither of the above

_____ 13. If the value of one variable on a graph remains the same while the value of the other variable increases, there is:
- a. a direct relationship
- b. no relationship
- c. an inverse relationship
- d. None of the above

Use the graph below to answer questions 14. through 16.:

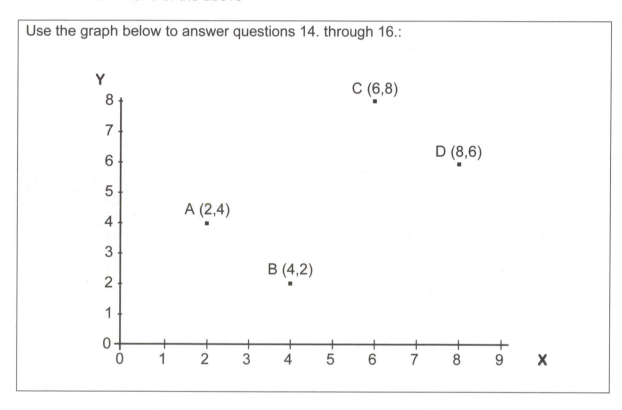

_____ 14. When the value of the X variable is 4, the value of the Y variable is 2. When the value of the X variable is 8, the value of the Y variable is 6. A line connecting the two points just described would run from points:
- a. A to B
- b. B to C
- c. C to D
- d. B to D

_____ 15. The slope of the curve connecting the two points described in problem 14. is:
- a. ½
- b. 1
- c. 3
- d. -2

Scarcity and Choices

_____ 16. The two points described in problem 14. indicate a(n):
   a. direct relationship
   b. inverse relationship
   c. independent relationship

_____ 17. The novel "Robinson Crusoe":
   a. illustrates the difficulty of self-sufficiency
   b. illustrates the development of human capital through work experience
   c. illustrates the necessity of saving and investing in order to increase one's standard of living
   d. All of the above

## Problems:

1. List and define the four categories of resources.

2. Explain the role of entrepreneurs in the economy.

3. Explain why the resource owner's pursuit of self-interest will generally serve the best interest of society.

4. The table below shows five combinations of values for variable X and variable Y.
   a. Plot the combinations on the graph below
   b. Connect the points with a curve
   c. Compute the slope of the curve

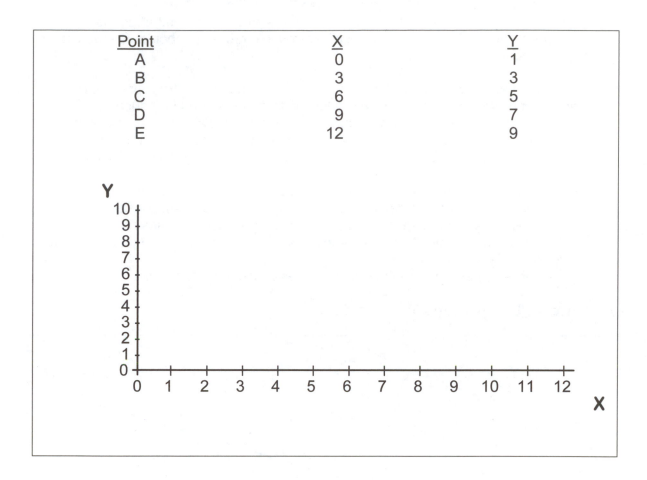

| Point | X | Y |
|-------|-----|---|
| A | 0 | 1 |
| B | 3 | 3 |
| C | 6 | 5 |
| D | 9 | 7 |
| E | 12 | 9 |

## Answers for Chapter 1

**Fill-in-the-blanks:**

| | |
|---|---|
| 1. Scarcity | 10. Opportunity |
| 2. Economics | 11. Positive |
| 3. Resources | 12. Normative |
| 4. Labor | 13. Macroeconomics |
| 5. Human capital | 14. Microeconomics |
| 6. Land | 15. Graphs |
| 7. Capital | 16. direct |
| 8. Entrepreneurship | 17. slope |
| 9. incentive | |

**Multiple Choice:**

| | | |
|---|---|---|
| 1. a. | 7. c. | 13. b. |
| 2. c. | 8. c. | 14. d. |
| 3. a. | 9. b. | 15. b. |
| 4. d. | 10. c. | 16. a. |
| 5. b. | 11. c. | 17. d. |
| 6. a. | 12. c. | |

**Problems:**

1. The four categories of resources are:
   (1) Labor – the physical and mental efforts that people contribute to production.
   (2) Land – the naturally occurring resources.
   (3) Capital – produced goods that are used in the production of other goods.
   (4) Entrepreneurship – the special skill involved in organizing labor, land, and capital for production.

2. Entrepreneurs organize labor, land, and capital for production. Entrepreneurs start new businesses, develop new production techniques, and introduce new products. Entrepreneurs are generally motivated by the goal of profit-maximization. Entrepreneurs also bear the risk of loss. Profits (and losses) direct entrepreneurs and the resources that they control into (and out of) different types of production.

3. Most resource owners have a self-interest to generate maximum profit from the use of their resources. In a competitive market, this pursuit of profit-maximization will lead the resource owners toward two actions that serve the best interest of society;
   a. Resource owners will direct their resources to the use that is most highly valued by consumers.
   b. Resource owners will use their resources as efficiently as possible.

4. Slope = (9 – 1) ÷ (12 – 0) = 8 ÷ 12 = ⅔

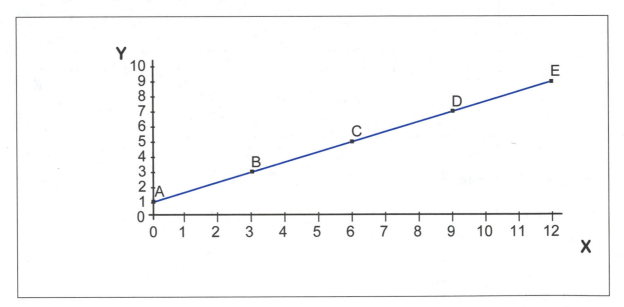

**Answer to Think Like an Economist:**

If the government passes a law that makes the punishment for armed robbery the same as the punishment for murder, there will be fewer liquor store hold-ups. However, armed robbers who continue to rob liquor stores will be more likely to murder their victims since the punishment if they murder their victims is no greater than if they don't murder their victims, and the likelihood of being caught and punished is less if no witnesses are left behind.

# Chapter 2  Trade and Economic Systems

## Self-sufficiency or Trade

The basic economic problem is scarcity.  Human wants are unlimited.  Resources are limited.  The basic goal in dealing with the problem of scarcity is to produce as much consumer satisfaction as possible with the limited resources available.  To achieve this goal, the limited resources must be used as efficiently as possible.  Resource owners must choose how to use their limited resources.

One possible choice is to use the limited resources to practice self-sufficiency.  Self-sufficiency means that you use the limited resources that you possess to produce the goods and services that you want to consume.  You can consume only what you yourself are able to produce.

Self-sufficiency has advantages:  You don't have to worry about unemployment, since you are working for yourself.  You have no need for money, since you are not engaged in trading with others.  Inflation is of no concern to you.

The problem with self-sufficiency is that it yields a very low standard of living.  A lone person will have very limited resources and will be compelled to use those resources in production processes that the resources are not well suited for.  Remember when you were stranded alone on the island (Chapter 1).  Computer programming skills are not well suited for catching fish.  The practice of self-sufficiency is not a common choice.

Instead, most resource owners choose to engage in trade.  You use your resources to produce where you have a comparative advantage, and you trade for everything else.

A person has a comparative advantage when he or she can produce a good or a service at a lower opportunity cost than other producers.  Producing according to comparative advantage leads to a more productive use of resources and a higher standard of living.  A more detailed explanation of comparative advantage is given in Chapter 16.

How does a person know when to engage in a trade?  If a person values what he or she is receiving in the trade more than what he or she is giving, then the trade is beneficial to that person.

But what about the other person in the trade?  Is one person's gain another person's loss?  No.  The second party in the trade must also value what he or she is receiving in the trade more than what he or she is giving.  So when two parties voluntarily engage in a trade, they both expect to benefit from the trade.

## Consumer's Surplus and Producer's Surplus

What is the benefit received by the two parties to a trade?  The net benefit the buyer receives from a trade is called consumer's surplus.

**Consumer's surplus** – the difference between the highest price a buyer is willing to pay and the price actually paid.

> **Example 1:** If a buyer is willing to pay $90 for a concert ticket and the price of the ticket is only $65, the consumer's surplus received by the buyer is $25.

The net benefit the seller receives from a trade is called producer's surplus.

**Producer's surplus** – the difference between the lowest price a seller is willing to accept and the price actually received.

> **Example 2:** If a seller is willing to sell a concert ticket for $50 and the price of the ticket is actually $65, the producer's surplus received by the seller is $15.

The net benefit to both the buyer and the seller in a trade is the sum of the consumer's surplus and the producer's surplus received by the buyer and the seller.

The net benefit to society of having a market available for trading is the sum of the consumer's surplus and the producer's surplus received by <u>all</u> the buyers and sellers in the market.

For a graphical representation of the net benefit to society of having a market available for trading, see Example 12 on page 3-10.

## Externalities

Both the buyer and the seller expect to benefit from a trade. But what about third parties? Will a trade yield benefits to third parties or impose costs on third parties? It might. A trade can cause external benefits or external costs.

**Externality** – a benefit or a cost of an activity that affects third parties.

> **Example 3:** If Pam buys a flu shot, not only does she benefit by avoiding the flu, but others benefit in that Pam doesn't pass the flu on to them. This is an external benefit (positive externality). If Pam buys a new CD, she enjoys the music, but if she plays the music too loudly, others may suffer. This is an external cost (negative externality).

When an external benefit or cost is generated, the private market will underproduce (external benefit) or overproduce (external cost) compared to the economically efficient outcome. The effect of externalities on market efficiency will be discussed in Chapter 27.

## The Production Possibilities Frontier

The basic economic problem of scarcity requires that economic choices be made. Choosing to produce more of one good means choosing to produce less of another good. One way to illustrate the trade-off between two goods is with a production possibilities frontier (PPF).

**Production possibilities frontier** – represents the maximum combinations of two goods that an economy can produce.

**Example 4A:** Assume that a very simple economy can produce only two goods; coconuts and fish. Six possible combinations of the available resources are detailed below:

| Combination | Resources Producing Coconuts | Resources Producing Fish |
|---|---|---|
| A | 0% | 100% |
| B | 20% | 80% |
| C | 40% | 60% |
| D | 60% | 40% |
| E | 80% | 20% |
| F | 100% | 0% |

If all resources are identical, the following quantities of coconuts and fish might be produced with the different combinations of resources:

| Combination | Units of Coconuts | Units of Fish |
|---|---|---|
| A | 0 | 100 |
| B | 20 | 80 |
| C | 40 | 60 |
| D | 60 | 40 |
| E | 80 | 20 |
| F | 100 | 0 |

Realistically, all resources will <u>not</u> be identical. Some resources will be better suited for producing fish. Fish producers will try to utilize these resources first, and less productive resources would be added as fish production is increased.

Some resources will be better suited for producing coconuts. Coconut producers will try to utilize these resources first, and less productive resources would be added as coconut production is increased.

**Example 4B:** The following quantities of coconuts and fish might be produced with the different combinations of resources:

| Combination | Units of Coconuts | Units of Fish |
|---|---|---|
| A | 0 | 100 |
| B | 40 | 95 |
| C | 70 | 85 |
| D | 85 | 70 |
| E | 95 | 40 |
| F | 100 | 0 |

Graphing the possible combinations of coconuts and fish yields the production possibilities frontier. The production possibilities frontier is illustrated on the next page:

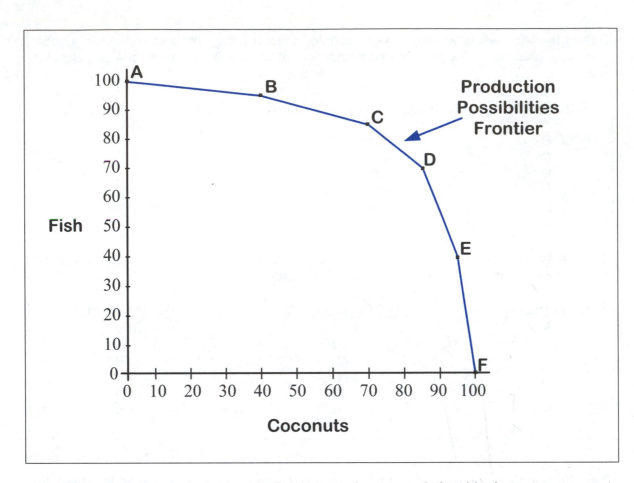

The PPF is downward sloping, indicating an inverse relationship between coconut production and fish production. Choosing to produce more coconuts is choosing to produce less fish, and vice versa. And the PPF is bowed outward (concave) indicating that the opportunity cost of producing each good increases as more units of the good are produced. This is illustrated on the table below:

| Combination | Coconuts | Marginal Units of Coconuts | Opportunity Cost |
|---|---|---|---|
| A | 0 | X | X |
| B | 40 | 40 | 5 units of fish |
| C | 70 | 30 | 10 units of fish |
| D | 85 | 15 | 15 units of fish |
| E | 95 | 10 | 30 units of fish |
| F | 100 | 5 | 40 units of fish |

**Law of increasing opportunity cost** – as production of a good increases, the opportunity cost of producing that good increases.

The opportunity cost of producing a good increases because resources are <u>not</u> identical. The first resources used in producing coconuts would be those best suited for producing coconuts. As more coconuts are produced, resources that are less well suited for producing coconuts (and more well suited for producing fish) would have to be used. This will increase the opportunity cost of producing coconuts.

Another way to understand the law of increasing opportunity cost: Given the basic economic problem of scarcity, people will try to produce any good with as few resources as possible (at the lowest opportunity cost). As production of a good is increased (and additional resources are used), the opportunity cost of producing that good will rise.

---

**Example 5:** Sudha has a paper to write this weekend. She expects the project to take 3 hours. She decides to write the paper on Saturday afternoon between 1 o'clock and 4 o'clock. This is her least valuable (lowest opportunity cost) time of the weekend. When Sudha finishes her paper at 4 o'clock, she discovers that she has a second paper to write. This project will also take 3 hours. Writing the second paper will involve a higher opportunity cost than writing the first paper. Sudha has already used her least valuable 3 hours of the weekend. She will have to write the second paper using more valuable (higher opportunity cost) time.

---

## Economic Efficiency

An economy is operating efficiently when it is producing the maximum output with the available resources and technology. In other words, an economy is operating efficiently when it is producing <u>on</u> its production possibilities frontier. An efficient economy can produce more of one good only by producing less of another.

---

**Example 6:** Assume that the economy in Example 4B is operating on its PPF, say at Combination B (40 units of coconuts, 95 units of fish). This economy can produce more units of coconuts (by moving to Combinations C, D, E, or F) only by producing fewer units of fish.

---

## Economic Growth

An economy's output is limited to an amount on its production possibilities frontier. If economic growth occurs, the PPF shifts outward. **Economic growth** is an increase in the productive capacity of an economy.

There are many possible specific causes of economic growth; increase in the size of the labor force, increase in human capital, improvements in physical capital, improved production techniques, etc. But there are only two general sources of economic growth.

Sources of economic growth:

1. **An increase in the quantity of resources.** An increase in the quantity of labor, land, capital, or entrepreneurship increases productive capacity.

2. **An advance in technology.** **Technological advance** is the ability to produce more output per resource. The increased output per resource increases productive capacity.

Economic growth is discussed in more detail in Chapter 14.

## Economic Systems

Scarcity forces every society to answer economic questions. The way in which a society answers economic questions is its economic system. The two primary economic systems are capitalism and socialism. The two primary economic systems are the product of two very different economic visions; the capitalist vision and the socialist vision. Each vision is summarized below for the following important topics; private property, market prices, and government.

### Capitalist vision:

1.  **Private property is economically and politically desirable.** Private property is economically desirable because it leads to the efficient use of resources. Self-interest (e.g. the goal of profit-maximization) will lead resource owners to use their resources in ways that benefit society. The more consumer satisfaction that a resource generates, the more income the resource owner will receive. Resource owners will direct their resources to the use that is most highly valued by consumers and will use their resources as efficiently as possible. (Remember Examples 8 and 9 in Chapter 1.)

    Private property is politically desirable because it contributes to individual freedom. Resource owners are free to use their private property as they see fit. Collective ownership of resources would require collective decision making instead of individual decision making. Thus, collective ownership of resources would reduce individual freedom.

    The connection between capitalism and individual freedom is examined further in an appendix at the end of the chapter.

2.  **Market prices contribute to economic efficiency.** Prices determined in free markets contribute to economic efficiency by providing information, incentives, and rationing.

---

**Example 7:** If a hurricane knocks out electricity in south Florida, the demand for electric generators in south Florida will increase. The market price of electric generators will rise. This higher price is useful information to potential buyers and sellers of generators. The higher price gives generator sellers the incentive to supply more generators (such as by shipping generators into south Florida from other markets). It gives generator buyers the incentive to look for alternative (and cheaper) sources of power. The higher price rations resources toward the production of more generators, and rations the available generators to the buyers who are willing and able to pay the most for the generators (and thus apparently have the most valuable use for the generators).

---

3.  **Government is inherently inefficient and should be limited.** Government cannot possess as much information as the millions of individual decision makers in the private market. Nor is government motivated to secure the self-interest of the millions of individual decision makers. Government may be more responsive to special-interest groups than to concerns about the general welfare (see Chapter 28). Since the outcome reached in the market is generally efficient, any government intervention is likely to reduce economic efficiency.

### Socialist vision:

1. **Private property is economically and politically harmful.** In a market economy, some people will be more successful in accumulating private property than others. Inevitably, the private property will come to be concentrated in the hands of a few. This control of private property allows the few (the rich) to dominate politically and economically, to the disadvantage of the masses. Instead of private property ownership, most resources should be owned (or controlled) by the government and used to benefit the general public.

2. **Market prices are often manipulated by powerful businesses.** Big businesses often face few competitors and may cooperate with their competitors to manipulate prices and consumer demand. The government should be willing to use price controls to ensure that prices are fair for all.

3. **Government promotes the best interests of the general public.** Government protects the masses from exploitation by the rich and by the big businesses that the rich control. Government should be large and strong enough to protect the weak from the powerful.

The U.S., like other countries, uses an economic system that is a mixture of capitalism and socialism. Most economic decisions in the U.S. are made through the use of markets.


### Three Economic Questions

The basic economic problem is scarcity. Human wants are unlimited. Resources are limited. Scarcity forces every society to answer three questions concerning the allocation of resources and goods. The three questions, and how they are answered in a market economy, are detailed below:

1. **What to produce?** This is determined in a market economy by consumer demand. If there is a stronger consumer demand for candy bars than for rice cakes, then more candy bars will be produced than rice cakes.

   Is this the best way to determine what to produce? Generally, it is. Remember that the basic goal in dealing with the problem of scarcity is to produce as much consumer satisfaction as possible with the limited resources available. The best judge of any consumer's satisfaction is that consumer. If consumers buy more candy bars than rice cakes, then consumers must be getting more satisfaction from candy bars than from rice cakes.

2. **How to produce?** This is determined by the least cost method of production. Producers desire maximum profit. This means that they will try to satisfy consumer demand at the lowest possible cost of production.

   Is this the best way to determine how to produce? Generally, it is. To produce as much consumer satisfaction as possible with the limited resources available requires that everything be produced with as few resources as possible (at the lowest opportunity cost).

> **Example 8:** The Bagelry employs Tanisha, a teenager, to slice their fresh-baked bagels. The Bagelry could employ a surgeon to slice the bagels. Why does the Bagelry employ a teenager instead of a surgeon? A surgeon could do a more precise job of slicing the bagels. But the teenager can do an adequate job and the teenager's labor costs less. The low-cost labor will contribute to the firm's goal of profit-maximization. Employing a teenager for this job instead of employing a surgeon will also serve the best interest of society. Society would not want to employ a surgeon's labor to slice bagels. The surgeon's labor is much more valuable to society when employed to perform surgery.

3. **For whom to produce?** This is determined by the distribution of income. The distribution of income is determined by the markets for resources. If a person owns resources that are highly valued in the marketplace, that person can receive a relatively large share of the income.

Is this the best way to determine for whom to produce? It has two advantages and one disadvantage.

One advantage is that resource owners have the incentive to develop their resources so that they will produce maximum consumer satisfaction. If a person, through education and training or through work experience, develops his or her human capital, that person will be able to earn a higher income.

> **Example 9:** Irina is a janitor. Janitorial labor is <u>not</u> highly valued in the marketplace. Irina attends college at night, eventually earning a degree in computer programming. Irina earns a much higher income as a computer programmer than she could as a janitor. Irina produces more consumer satisfaction as a computer programmer than as a janitor.

The other advantage is that resource owners have the incentive to direct their resources to their most valuable use.

> **Example 10:** If Frank has the skills to be either a gardener or an architect, and architects earn a higher income than gardeners, Frank will probably choose to be an architect.

The disadvantage is that the distribution of income may prove to be very unequal. An unequal distribution of income may mean that the goods and services produced do <u>not</u> generate the maximum consumer satisfaction possible with the limited resources available.

> **Example 11:** 50 coconuts are produced on Gilligan's Island. The Howells consume 45 of the coconuts, and the other 5 coconuts are divided among the rest of the group. The 50 coconuts will yield a certain amount of consumer satisfaction distributed in this way. If the coconuts had been distributed more equally, they would probably yield more consumer satisfaction.

The problem of unequal distribution of income is addressed in more detail in Chapter 31.

## Appendix:  Book Review – "Capitalism and Freedom"

In his 1962 book, "Capitalism and Freedom", economist Milton Friedman presents his viewpoint of the connection between capitalism and freedom.  He also addresses the proper role for the government in a capitalist system.

According to Friedman (winner of the Nobel Prize in Economics in 1976), capitalism is a necessary condition for individual freedom.  Capitalism provides individual freedom in economic arrangements and is also indispensable for achieving political freedom.

Capitalism provides individual freedom in economic arrangements by providing for the coordination of the economic activities of millions of people through the voluntary cooperation of individuals.  In a capitalist system, economic activities are coordinated through the voluntary market exchanges entered into by consumers and producers, employers and employees, etc.  All market exchanges are voluntarily entered into because both parties to the exchange expect to benefit.  No coercion is necessary.

Capitalism is indispensable for achieving political freedom because capitalism removes the organization of economic activities from the control of government.  A government that controls economic activities has tremendous power over individuals.  It can punish dissenters by depriving them of employment (since the government is the only employer in the economy).  It can silence dissenters by withholding the resources necessary for communicating their dissent (e.g. television, newspapers, publishing companies, etc.)

What is the proper role for the government in a capitalist system?  Friedman asserts that the primary function of government is to establish and enforce the rules by which the system operates.  For a capitalist system to operate properly, the government must establish and enforce property rights and contract rights.

The government would also have other functions which cannot be well performed by the market system.  The government would need to provide and control the supply of money.  The government would also need to correct for market failure by promoting competition and by making adjustments to the market outcome for neighborhood effects (externalities).  The government would also need to supplement private efforts to care for those who cannot care for themselves.

Friedman listed a number of activities undertaken by the government (in 1962) that, in his opinion, were unjustified.  Among these were:

1. Agricultural subsidies.  (See Chapter 30 of this textbook.)
2. International trade restrictions.  (See Chapter 16.)
3. Price controls, such as rent controls and minimum wage laws.  (See Chapter 3.)
4. Anticompetitive regulation of industries such as railroads, trucking, and banking.  (Some deregulation of these industries has occurred since 1962.)
5. Social Security.
6. Anticompetitive licensing requirements.
7. Public housing.
8. Military conscription.  (Military conscription was ended in the U.S. in 1973 and replaced with an all-volunteer military.)
9. National parks.

### Appendix: A Movement along a Curve versus a Shift in a Curve

Graphs illustrate the relationship between two variables. When the value of one variable on a graph changes, the value of the other variable may also change. This is a movement along the curve illustrating the relationship between the two variables.

**Example 12A:** Moe Mohwer has a lawn mowing service. The table and the graph below show the relationship between the number of hours Moe works each day and the number of lawns he can mow.

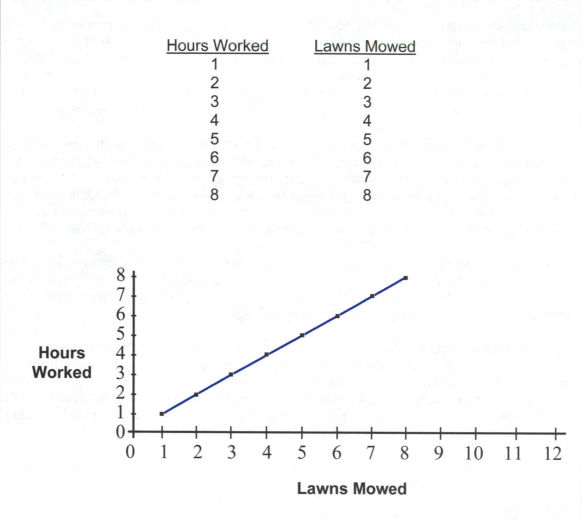

| Hours Worked | Lawns Mowed |
|:---:|:---:|
| 1 | 1 |
| 2 | 2 |
| 3 | 3 |
| 4 | 4 |
| 5 | 5 |
| 6 | 6 |
| 7 | 7 |
| 8 | 8 |

If Moe increases the number of hours worked from 3 hours per day to 6 hours per day, the quantity of lawns mowed will increase from 3 to 6. This is a movement along the curve from point A to point B, as illustrated on the graph on the next page:

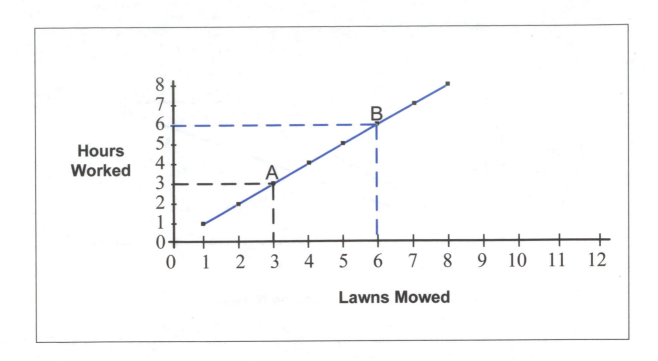

If a variable other than one of the variables illustrated on the graph changes, the relationship between the variables illustrated on the graph may change. This shifts the curve illustrating the relationship between the variables.

**Example 12B:** Moe purchases a new, larger lawn mower. The new mower increases Moe's productivity. The table below shows the new relationship between the number of hours Moe works each day and the number of lawns he can mow with the new mower.

| Hours Worked | Lawns Mowed |
|:---:|:---:|
| 1 | 1.5 |
| 2 | 3.0 |
| 3 | 4.5 |
| 4 | 6.0 |
| 5 | 7.5 |
| 6 | 9.0 |
| 7 | 10.5 |
| 8 | 12.0 |

The graph on the next page illustrates the shift in the curve that results from Moe changing from the old mower (Curve A) to the new mower (Curve B).

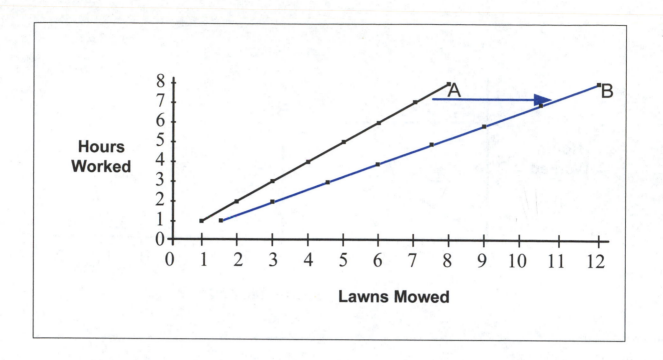

## Appendix: Think Like an Economist – Economic Systems and Individual Freedom

In his 1962 book, "Capitalism and Freedom", Milton Friedman asserts that capitalism is a necessary condition for individual freedom. Capitalism removes the organization of economic activities from the control of government. According to Friedman, socialism and individual freedom are incompatible.

Consider the following scenario: Professor Ima Dissident, a famous author, writes a book entitled, "Why the Current System Should Be Overthrown". The book is likely to appeal to a large number of readers.

If the current system is capitalism, is it likely that Professor Dissident's book will be published? Why or why not?

If the current system is socialism, is it likely that Professor Dissident's book will be published? Why or why not?

## Questions for Chapter 2

### Fill-in-the-blanks:

1. _____ surplus is the difference between the highest price a buyer is willing to pay and the price actually paid.

2. _____ surplus is the difference between the lowest price a seller is willing to accept and the price actually received.

3. An _____ is a benefit or a cost of an activity that affects third parties.

4. A _____ _____ frontier represents the maximum combinations of two goods that an economy can produce.

5. The law of _____ _____ cost says that as production of a good increases, the opportunity cost of producing that good increases.

6. Economic _____ is an increase in the productive capacity of an economy.

7. Technological advance is the ability to produce more _____ per _____.


**Multiple Choice:**

_____ 1. When two parties voluntarily engage in a trade:
    a. the buyer gains, but the seller loses
    b. the seller gains, but the buyer loses
    c. both parties expect to benefit from the trade
    d. both parties will lose

_____ 2. Producing according to comparative advantage:
    a. means producing where one has a lower opportunity cost than other producers
    b. leads to a more productive use of resources
    c. leads to a higher standard of living
    d. All of the above

_____ 3. Millhouse is willing to pay $100 for the first issue of "Radioactive Man". If Millhouse buys a copy from Muntz for $60, he receives consumer's surplus of:
    a. $100
    b. $60
    c. $40
    d. $0

_____ 4. Kenneth is having a garage sale. If Kenneth is willing to sell his old table saw for $50 and manages to get $80 for it, he receives producer's surplus of:
    a. $0
    b. $30
    c. $50
    d. $80

_____ 5. Xavier hires Yolanda to construct a rock garden in front of Xavier's house. The rock garden increases the value of Xavier's house, and also increases the value of Xavier's neighbor Zelda's house. This is an example of:
    a. producer's surplus
    b. consumer's surplus
    c. external benefit
    d. external cost

_____ 6. As production of a good increases:
    a. the opportunity cost of producing the good will decrease
    b. resources that are less well suited for producing the good will have to be used
    c. Both of the above
    d. Neither of the above

_____ 7. When an economy is operating efficiently:
    a. it is operating inside its PPF
    b. it is producing the maximum output with the available resources and technology
    c. it can produce more of one good without producing less of another
    d. All of the above

_____ 8. The production possibilities frontier is:
    a. a boundary that cannot be crossed
    b. bowed outward because of the law of increasing opportunity cost
    c. Both of the above
    d. Neither of the above

_____ 9. Economic growth:
    a. shifts the PPF inward
    b. can only be caused by an increase in the quantity of resources
    c. means that the law of increasing opportunity cost no longer applies
    d. None of the above

_____ 10. The capitalist vision sees private property as desirable because:
    a. private property leads to the efficient use of resources
    b. private property allows the rich to dominate politically and economically
    c. Both of the above
    d. Neither of the above

_____ 11. The capitalist vision sees market prices as:
    a. often manipulated by powerful businesses
    b. contributing to economic efficiency
    c. providing information, incentives, and rationing
    d. Both b. and c. above

_____ 12. The socialist vision sees government ownership of resources:
    a. as beneficial to the general public
    b. as harmful to economic efficiency
    c. as harmful to individual freedom
    d. All of the above

_____ 13. The socialist vision sees market prices as:
    a. providing information, incentives, and rationing
    b. often manipulated by powerful businesses
    c. Both of the above
    d. Neither of the above

_____ 14. The capitalist vision:
   a. favors private ownership of resources
   b. favors market determination of prices
   c. favors limited government
   d. All of the above

_____ 15. The socialist vision:
   a. favors government ownership of resources
   b. favors price controls to ensure fair prices
   c. favors a large and strong government
   d. All of the above

_____ 16. In a market economy, the question of "what to produce" is determined by:
   a. the President's Council of Economic Advisors
   b. the Federal Bureau of Efficient Production
   c. consumer demand
   d. majority vote

_____ 17. In a market economy, the question of "how to produce" is determined by:
   a. consumer demand
   b. the least cost method of production
   c. the distribution of income
   d. All of the above

_____ 18. Determining the "for whom to produce" question by the distribution of income means that:
   a. resource owners have the incentive to develop their resources so that they will produce maximum consumer satisfaction
   b. resource owners may have very unequal shares of income
   c. resource owners have the incentive to direct their resources to their most valuable use
   d. All of the above

_____ 19. According to the book "Capitalism and Freedom",
   a. Capitalism is a necessary condition for individual freedom
   b. In a capitalist system, economic activities are coordinated through the coercive power of the capitalists
   c. A capitalist system maximizes the government's control of economic activities
   d. All of the above

_____ 20. According to the book "Capitalism and Freedom",
   a. Capitalism enables the government to control economic activities through central planning
   b. Capitalism provides for the coordination of the economic activities of millions of people through the voluntary cooperation of individuals
   c. Both of the above
   d. Neither of the above

_____ 21. According to Milton Friedman, the proper functions of government include:
     a. Controlling a nation's international trade
     b. Establishing a minimum wage law
     c. Establishing and enforcing property rights and contract rights
     d. All of the above

Use the graph below to answer questions 22. and 23.:

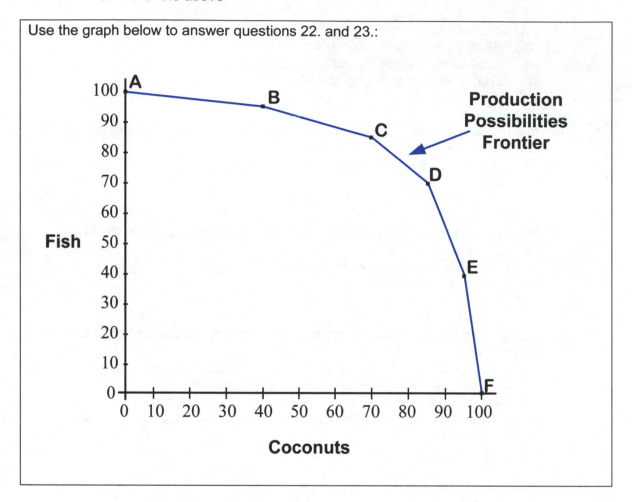

_____ 22. If the number of coconuts produced in this economy is increased from 40 to 70, this will cause:
     a. a shift in the Production Possibilities Frontier
     b. a movement along the Production Possibilities Frontier
     c. Both of the above
     d. Neither of the above

_____ 23. If an increase in the quantity of resources permits this economy to produce more of both coconuts and fish, this will cause:
     a. a shift in the Production Possibilities Frontier
     b. a movement along the Production Possibilities Frontier
     c. Both of the above
     d. Neither of the above

**Problems:**

1.  What are the two general sources of economic growth?

2.  Explain the capitalist vision on the following topic:  government.

3.  Explain the socialist vision on the following topic:  market prices.

4.  Explain how the question of "for whom to produce" is determined in a market economy.

## Answers for Chapter 2

**Fill-in-the-blanks:**
1. Consumer's
2. Producer's
3. externality
4. production possibilities
5. increasing opportunity
6. growth
7. output, resource

**Multiple Choice:**

| | | |
|---|---|---|
| 1. c. | 9. d. | 17. b. |
| 2. d. | 10. a. | 18. d. |
| 3. c. | 11. d. | 19. a. |
| 4. b. | 12. a. | 20. b. |
| 5. c. | 13. b. | 21. c. |
| 6. b. | 14. d. | 22. b. |
| 7. b. | 15. d. | 23. a. |
| 8. c. | 16. c. | |

## Problems:

1. a. An increase in the quantity of resources.
   b. An advance in technology.

2. Government is inherently inefficient and should be limited. Government cannot possess as much information as the millions of individual decision makers in the private market. Nor is the government motivated to secure the self-interest of the millions of individual decision makers. Government may be more responsive to special-interest groups than to concerns about the general welfare. Since the outcome reached in the market is generally efficient, any government intervention is likely to reduce economic efficiency.

3. Market prices are often manipulated by powerful businesses. Big businesses often face few competitors and may cooperate with their competitors to manipulate prices and consumer demand. The government should be willing to use price controls to ensure that prices are fair for all.

4. The "for whom to produce" question is determined by the distribution of income. The distribution of income is determined by the markets for resources.

## Answers to Think Like an Economist:

If the current system is capitalism, it is likely that Professor Dissident's book will be published. The publishing companies will be owned by private individuals, with a goal of profit-maximization. Even if a publishing company disagrees with Professor Dissident's opinion, it will want to publish any book that is likely to appeal to a large number of readers, in order to maximize profits.

If the current system is socialism, it is not likely that Professor Dissident's book will be published. Though the publishing companies will be owned by "the people", they will be controlled by the government. It is not in the best interest of the government to publish Professor Dissident's book.

# Chapter 3  Demand, Supply, and Equilibrium

The basic economic problem is scarcity.  Human wants are unlimited.  Resources are limited.  Because resources are limited, only a limited amount of products can be produced.  In the U.S., the problem of scarcity is dealt with mainly through markets.  This chapter looks at how product markets determine the price and quantity of goods produced.

A product market has two sides.  The buying side is called demand.  The selling side is called supply.  We will look at demand first.

**Demand** - the willingness and ability of buyers to buy different quantities of a good at different prices.

We are interested in the relationship between the various possible prices of a good and the quantities (amounts) of the good that buyers are willing and able to buy.  The relationship between price and quantity demanded is expressed in the law of demand.

**Law of demand** – the price and the quantity demanded of a good are inversely related.

Remember from Chapter 1 that an inverse relationship means that as the value of one variable increases, the value of the other variable decreases.  Thus, the law of demand indicates that as the price of a good increases, the quantity demanded of the good decreases.  And as the price of a good decreases, the quantity demanded of the good increases.

## Substitution Effect

The primary reason for the inverse relationship between price and quantity demanded is the substitution effect.  The substitution effect is caused by the basic economic problem of scarcity.  Because of scarcity, a consumer will have only limited income.

A consumer will try to obtain as much consumer satisfaction as possible from that limited income.  Thus, other things equal, a consumer will substitute lower-priced goods for higher-priced goods.  This is the substitution effect.

> **Example 1A:**  Darla's Delectable Donuts lowers the price of its donuts by 10 percent.  Darla finds that she sells a greater quantity of donuts than before.  Darla's donuts are now relatively lower-priced compared to the donuts of competing donut shops and compared to alternative products, e.g. bagels.  Thus, consumers buy a greater quantity of Darla's donuts.

## Income Effect

The secondary reason for the inverse relationship between price and quantity demanded is the income effect.  The income effect is also caused by scarcity.  Because of scarcity, a consumer will have only limited income.

When the price of a good decreases, a consumer's income has greater buying power, allowing the consumer to buy a greater quantity of the good. When the price of a good increases, a consumer's income has less buying power, allowing the consumer to buy only a lesser quantity of the good. This is the income effect.

**Example 1B:** Darla's Delectable Donuts lowers the price of its donuts by 10 percent. Darla's customers now find that their income has greater buying power. Thus, the lower price allows Darla's customers to buy a greater quantity of donuts.

### Demand Schedule and Demand Curve

The inverse relationship between price and quantity demanded can be illustrated with a demand schedule or with a demand curve. A demand schedule is a table showing the different combinations of price and quantity demanded for a good.

The demand schedule for Good X is shown in Example 2A below:

**Example 2A:**

Market for Good X
Demand Schedule

| Price | Quantity Demanded |
|-------|-------------------|
| $7    | 0                 |
| 6     | 5                 |
| 5     | 10                |
| 4     | 15                |
| 3     | 20                |
| 2     | 25                |
| 1     | 30                |

The same information can be placed on a graph by plotting the points (coordinates) that represent each combination of price and quantity demanded. The demand curve for Good X is then created by connecting the points. The demand curve for Good X is shown in Example 2B on the next page.

Notice that the demand curve in Example 2B on the next page slopes downward from left to right. Demand curves have a negative slope because of the inverse (negative) relationship between price and quantity demanded.

If the price of Good X changes, there is a movement along the demand curve from one combination of price and quantity demanded to another combination of price and quantity demanded. In Example 2B, at a price of $4, the quantity demanded is 15 units. If the price decreases to $3, the quantity demanded increases to 20 units.

**Example 2B:**

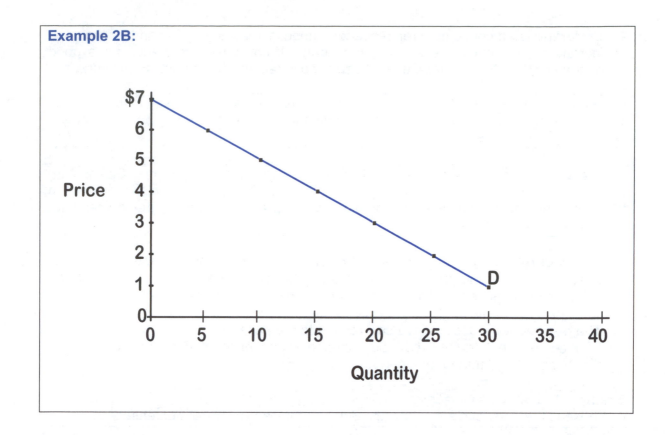

But what would cause the quantity demanded to increase or decrease at every price? In other words, what factors would cause the demand curve to shift to the right (increase) or to the left (decrease)? The factors that shift the demand curve are the determinants of demand.

**Determinants of demand:**

**1. Income;**

    a. **For normal goods, income and demand are directly related.** An increase in income will cause an increase in demand (demand curve shifts to the right). A decrease in income will cause a decrease in demand. Most goods are normal goods.

    b. **For inferior goods, income and demand are inversely related.** An increase in income will cause a decrease in demand (demand curve shifts to the left). A decrease in income will cause an increase in demand. Used clothing is an example of an inferior good.

**Example 3:** The workers at the widget factory across the street from Darla's Delectable Donuts receive a pay increase. This is good news for Darla. The increase in consumer income will increase the demand for her donuts. But the pay increase is bad news for Sarita, who owns Second-Foot Shoes, next door to Darla's Delectable Donuts. The increase in consumer income will decrease the demand for used shoes, an inferior good.

2. **Preferences.** If consumer preference for a good increases, the demand for the good increases (demand curve shifts to the right). If consumer preference for a good decreases, the demand for the good decreases (demand curve shifts to the left).

> **Example 4A:** A new diet book introduces "the donut diet" as a tasty way to lose weight. The popularity of the donut diet increases consumer preference for donuts. As a result, the demand for Darla's donuts increases.

> **Example 4B:** A popular horror movie features a gruesome villain (Homer Slashsome) who munches on donuts while dispatching his victims. The stomach-twisting scenes in the movie decrease consumer preference for donuts. As a result, the demand for Darla's donuts decreases.

3. **Prices of related goods (substitutes or complements).** The demand for a good is directly related to the price of a substitute. If Good Y is a substitute for Good X, an increase in the price Good Y will cause an increase in the demand for Good X.

   The demand for a good is inversely related to the price of a complement. If Good Y is a complement for Good X, an increase in the price of Good Y will cause a decrease in the demand for Good X.

> **Example 5A:** Cindy's Cinnamon Rolls lowers its price by 30 percent. As a result of this decrease in the price of a substitute, the demand for Darla's donuts decreases.

> **Example 5B:** Wholesale coffee prices increase. Darla is forced to increase her price for a cup of coffee by 75 percent. As a result of this increase in the price of a complement, the demand for Darla's donuts decreases.

4. **Number of buyers.** An increase in the number of buyers for a good will increase the demand for the good. A decrease in the number of buyers will decrease the demand.

> **Example 6:** The widget factory across the street from Darla's Delectable Donuts increases its workforce by 50 workers. As a result of this increase in the number of buyers, the demand for Darla's donuts increases.

5. **Expectations of future price.** If buyers expect the price of a good to rise in the future, the demand for the good now will increase. If buyers expect the price to fall in the future, the demand for the good now will decrease.

> **Example 7A:** Darla's hometown announces that a 25% excise tax will be imposed on unhealthy foods (like donuts) beginning June 1. As a result of the expectation of a higher future price, the demand for Darla's donuts increases in the last few days of May.

> **Example 7B:** The state of Oklahoma increased the state tax on a package of cigarettes by 55¢, effective January 1, 2005. There were record cigarette sales across the state on December 31, 2004.

## Change in Demand versus Change in Quantity Demanded

A change in demand refers to a shift in the demand curve. A change in demand is caused by a change in one of the determinants of demand. A shift to the right is an increase in demand. A shift to the left is a decrease in demand.

A change in quantity demanded refers to a movement along the demand curve. A change in quantity demanded is caused by a change in price. An increase in price will cause a decrease in quantity demanded (a movement upward along the demand curve). A decrease in price will cause an increase in quantity demanded (a movement downward along the demand curve).

For a detailed explanation of the difference between a movement along a curve versus a shift in a curve, see the appendix at the end of Chapter 2.

Now we will look at the selling side of a product market.

**Supply** - the willingness and ability of sellers to sell different quantities of a good at different prices.

We are interested in the relationship between the various possible prices of a good and the quantities (amounts) of the good that sellers are willing and able to sell. The relationship between price and quantity supplied is expressed in the law of supply.

**Law of supply** – the price and the quantity supplied of a good are directly related.

Remember from Chapter 1 that a direct relationship means that as the value of one variable increases, the value of the other variable also increases. Thus, the law of supply indicates that as the price of a good increases, the quantity supplied of the good also increases. And as the price of a good decreases, the quantity supplied of the good also decreases.

The reason for the direct relationship between price and quantity supplied is the seller's goal of profit-maximization. For the seller to make a profit, the selling price must be sufficient to cover the seller's cost of production. An increase in the selling price will make it easier for sellers to cover their cost of production. An increase in the selling price will cause existing producers to increase their production and will attract new producers into the market. Thus, an increase in the selling price will cause an increase in the quantity supplied.

---

**Example 8:** Fifty college students are given an opportunity to earn income by participating in a four-hour product testing on Friday afternoon. If the pay offered is low (say $20), few of the students will want to supply their labor to this market. At low pay, few of the students will feel that this is a profitable use of their time. The low pay does <u>not</u> cover the cost of supplying their labor to the market, i.e. their opportunity cost. If the pay offered were higher (say $100), a greater number of the college students would want to supply their labor to this market.

---

The direct relationship between price and quantity supplied can be illustrated with a supply schedule or a supply curve. A supply schedule is a table showing the different combinations of price and quantity supplied for a good. The supply schedule for Good X is shown in Example 9A below:

**Example 9A:**

Market for Good X
Supply Schedule

| Price | Quantity Supplied |
|-------|-------------------|
| $1    | 0                 |
| 2     | 5                 |
| 3     | 10                |
| 4     | 15                |
| 5     | 20                |
| 6     | 25                |
| 7     | 30                |

The same information can be placed on a graph by plotting the points (coordinates) that represent each combination of price and quantity supplied. The supply curve for Good X is then created by connecting the points. The supply curve for Good X is shown in Example 9B below:

**Example 9B:**

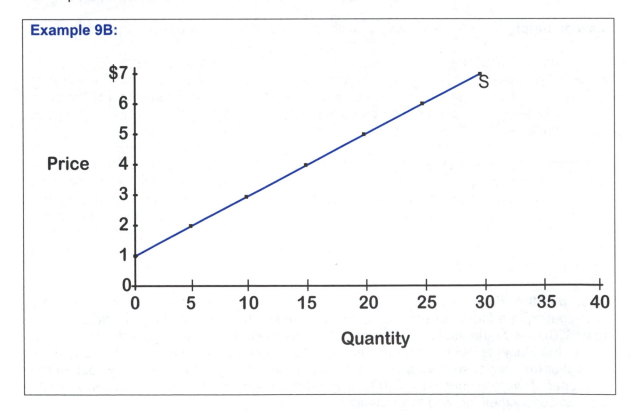

Notice that the supply curve slopes upward from left to right. Supply curves have a positive slope because of the direct (positive) relationship between price and quantity supplied.

If the price of Good X changes, there is a movement along the supply curve from one combination of price and quantity supplied to another. In Example 9B, at a price of $3, the quantity supplied is 10 units. If the price increases to $4, the quantity supplied increases to 15 units.

But what would cause the quantity supplied to increase or decrease at every price? In other words, what factor would cause the supply curve to shift to the right (increase) or to the left (decrease)? The factor that shifts the supply curve is the determinant of supply.

## The determinant of supply is the cost of production.

An increase in the cost of production will cause a decrease in supply (supply curve shifts to the left). A decrease in the cost of production will cause an increase in supply (supply curve shifts to the right).

> **Example 10:** Referring back to Example 8, what if the fifty persons offered a chance to earn income by participating in a four-hour product testing were not college students, but were heart surgeons. Would any of the heart surgeons be willing to supply their labor to this market, even if the pay offered is $100? Probably not. Heart surgeons would have a higher cost of production (opportunity cost) for their time.

The cost of producing a good can be changed by a number of common factors, including:

1. **The prices of labor and other inputs.** An increase in wage rates or in the prices of other inputs (e.g. rent, interest rates, etc.) would increase the cost of production, and would thus decrease supply.

2. **Technology.** **Technological advance** is the ability to produce more output per resource. A technological advance would decrease the cost of production, and would thus increase supply.

3. **Taxes.** A tax imposed on producers would increase the cost of production, and would thus decrease supply.

### Change in Supply versus Change in Quantity Supplied

A change in supply refers to a shift in the supply curve. A change in supply is caused by a change in the cost of production. A shift to the right is an increase in supply. A shift to the left is a decrease in supply.

A change in quantity supplied refers to a movement along the supply curve. A change in quantity supplied is caused by a change in price. An increase in price will cause an increase in quantity supplied. A decrease in price will cause a decrease in quantity supplied.

For a detailed explanation of the difference between a movement along a curve versus a shift in a curve, see the appendix at the end of Chapter 2.

### Equilibrium: Putting Demand and Supply Together

What will the actual price of a good be and what quantity of the good will be produced and consumed? These questions are determined in a market by the interaction of demand and supply (or buyers and sellers).

We begin by assuming a free market. A **free market** is a market in which price is free to adjust up or down in response to demand and supply. Most markets are free markets. When a market is not a free market, it is usually because the government has imposed a price control in the market. Price controls (ceilings and floors) will be discussed later in the chapter.

In a free market, the market price will be the equilibrium price. The **equilibrium price** is the price where quantity demanded equals quantity supplied. The market quantity will be the equilibrium quantity.

The equilibrium price and quantity for a good can be easily determined by placing the demand curve and the supply curve for the good on a graph. The demand curve and the supply curve for Good X (from earlier in the chapter) are shown on the graph in Example 11 below:

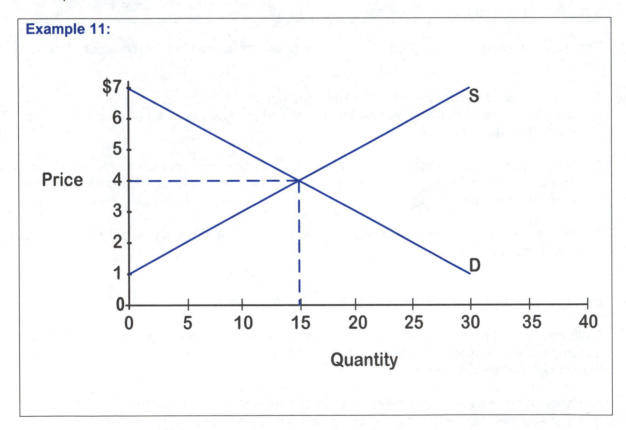

**Example 11:**

Equilibrium price and quantity occur where the two curves intersect. On the graph in Example 11 above, the equilibrium price is $4 and the equilibrium quantity is 15 units.

## Moving From Disequilibrium to Equilibrium

Initially, the market price may be above or below the equilibrium price. If the market price is above the equilibrium price, the quantity supplied will exceed the quantity demanded. This is a **surplus**. In Example 11, if the price were $5, the quantity supplied (20 units) would exceed the quantity demanded (10 units). Competition among the sellers to rid themselves of this surplus would drive the price down until the surplus is eliminated. This occurs at the equilibrium price ($4).

If the market price is below the equilibrium price, the quantity demanded will exceed the quantity supplied. This is a **shortage**. In Example 11, if the price were $3, the quantity demanded (20 units) would exceed the quantity supplied (10 units). Competition among the buyers would drive the price up until the shortage is eliminated. This occurs at the equilibrium price ($4).

## Free Markets and Economic Efficiency I

In a free market, the market price will adjust to the equilibrium price, eliminating any surplus or shortage. Not only does a free market result in an equilibrium with no surplus or shortage, it also generally results in the most efficient quantity of output. We saw in Chapter 1 that any activity should be continued as long as the marginal benefit of the activity exceeds the marginal cost. The optimal (ideal, most efficient) level of the activity occurs where the marginal benefit and the marginal cost are equal.

In a competitive product market, the marginal benefit of the product is indicated by the price that the marginal consumer is willing to pay. The price that the marginal consumer is willing to pay is indicated by the demand curve. The marginal cost of producing the product is indicated by the supply curve. Where the demand curve and the supply curve intersect (equilibrium) is the quantity where the marginal benefit of the product equals the marginal cost of the product. Thus, a free market generally produces the optimal (ideal, most efficient) quantity of output.

## Free Markets and Economic Efficiency II

We saw in Chapter 2 that the net benefit to society of having a market available for trading is the sum of the consumer's surplus and the producer's surplus received by all the buyers and sellers in the market. Consumer's surplus is the difference between the highest price a buyer is willing to pay and the price actually paid. For all the buyers in a market, consumer's surplus is indicated by the area below the demand curve and above the market price.

Producer's surplus is the difference between the lowest price a seller is willing to accept and the price actually received. For all the sellers in a market, producer's surplus is indicated by the area above the supply curve and below the market price.

In a free market, the quantity produced (equilibrium quantity) is the quantity that maximizes the net benefit to society of having the market available for trading (i.e. maximizes the sum of the consumer's surplus and the producer's surplus received by all the buyers and sellers in the market).

**Example 12:** The graph below indicates the consumer's surplus and the producer's surplus in the market for Good X (from Example 11).

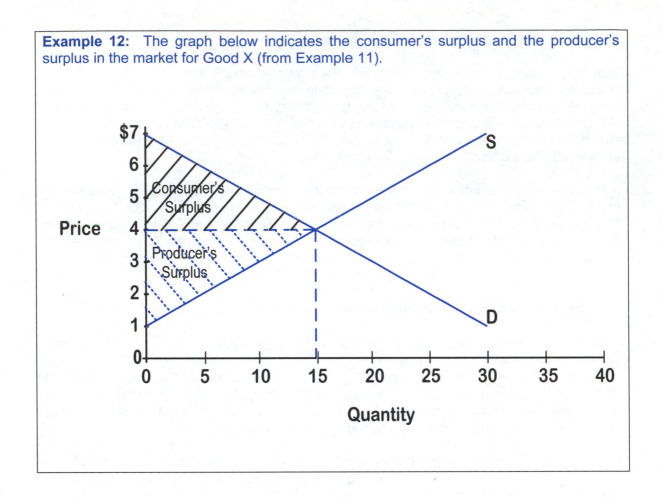

## A Change in Equilibrium Price and Quantity

Equilibrium price and quantity are determined by demand and supply. A change in demand or supply will result in a new equilibrium price and quantity. The table below shows the four possible changes in demand and supply and the effect of each change on equilibrium price and quantity.

| Change | Price | Quantity |
|--------|-------|----------|
| Demand increases | Increases | Increases |
| Demand decreases | Decreases | Decreases |
| Supply increases | Decreases | Increases |
| Supply decreases | Increases | Decreases |

**Example 13:** The table and the graph on the next page illustrate an increase in demand (D$_2$) and a decrease in demand (D$_3$).

### Market for Good X

| Price | Quantity Supplied | Original Quantity Demanded (D₁) | Increased Quantity Demanded (D₂) | Decreased Quantity Demanded (D₃) |
|---|---|---|---|---|
| $7 | 30 | 0 | 10 | 0 |
| 6 | 25 | 5 | 15 | 0 |
| 5 | 20 | 10 | 20 | 0 |
| 4 | 15 | 15 | 25 | 5 |
| 3 | 10 | 20 | 30 | 10 |
| 2 | 5 | 25 | 35 | 15 |
| 1 | 0 | 30 | 40 | 20 |

**Example 14:**  The table below and the graph on the next page illustrate an increase in supply (S₂) and a decrease in supply (S₃).

### Market for Good X

| Price | Quantity Demanded | Original Quantity Supplied (S₁) | Increased Quantity Supplied (S₂) | Decreased Quantity Supplied (S₃) |
|---|---|---|---|---|
| $1 | 30 | 0 | 10 | 0 |
| 2 | 25 | 5 | 15 | 0 |
| 3 | 20 | 10 | 20 | 0 |
| 4 | 15 | 15 | 25 | 5 |
| 5 | 10 | 20 | 30 | 10 |
| 6 | 5 | 25 | 35 | 15 |
| 7 | 0 | 30 | 40 | 20 |

Demand, Supply, and Equilibrium

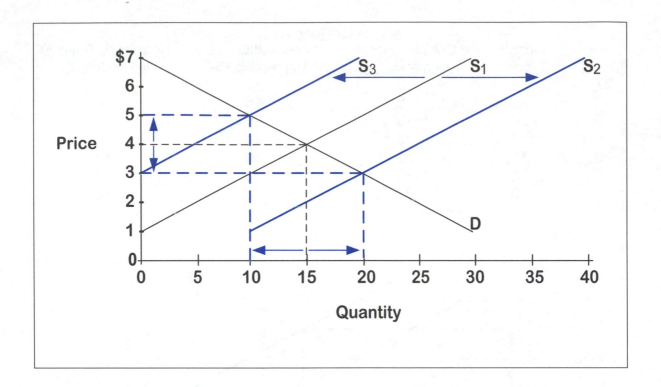

## Price Controls

Dissatisfaction with market-determined prices has often led the government to impose price controls. One type of price control is a price ceiling. A **price ceiling** is a maximum legal price.

As illustrated on the graph in Example 15 on the next page, a price ceiling leads to a shortage. In Example 15, the equilibrium price for Good X is $4. When a price ceiling of $3 is set, a shortage is created. Price ceilings also lead to:

1. **Fewer exchanges than at equilibrium.** In Example 15, 15 units are exchanged at equilibrium, only 10 units are exchanged at the ceiling price.

2. **The use of nonprice rationing devices.** Price is not allowed to adjust and ration goods. Non-price rationing devices, such as government allocation, waiting in line, or favoritism will have to be used. Nonprice rationing devices are less efficient than using market price as the rationing device. Market price rations the goods produced to the consumers who are willing and able to pay the most for them. Nonprice rationing devices will <u>not</u> ration the goods produced to the consumers who are willing and able to pay the most.

3. **Illegal transactions at prices above the ceiling.** Buyers and sellers can benefit from exchanges at prices above the ceiling. Some buyers and sellers will break the law to engage in these mutually beneficial transactions. In terms of economic efficiency, it is better if <u>all</u> buyers and sellers ignore the price ceiling, break the law, and engage in all mutually beneficial transactions.

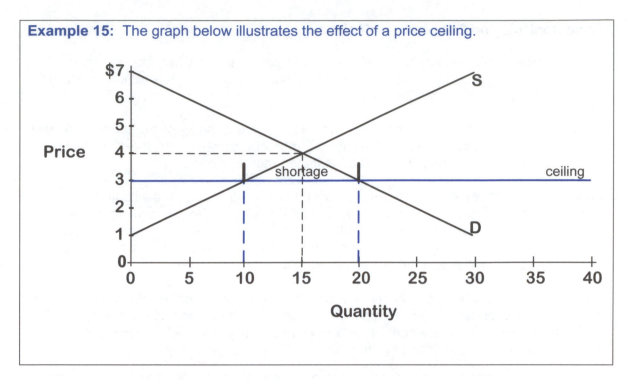

The other type of price control is a price floor. A **price floor** is a minimum legal price. As illustrated on the graph in Example 16 below, a price floor leads to a surplus. In Example 16, the equilibrium price for Good X is $4. When a price floor of $5 is set, a surplus is created. Price floors lead to fewer exchanges than at equilibrium. In Example 16, 15 units are exchanged at equilibrium, only 10 units are exchanged at the floor price. To maintain the artificially high price mandated by a price floor, the government may step in and purchase the surplus goods. The government commonly uses this policy in agricultural markets. (See Chapter 30.)

**Example 16:** The graph below illustrates the effect of a price floor.

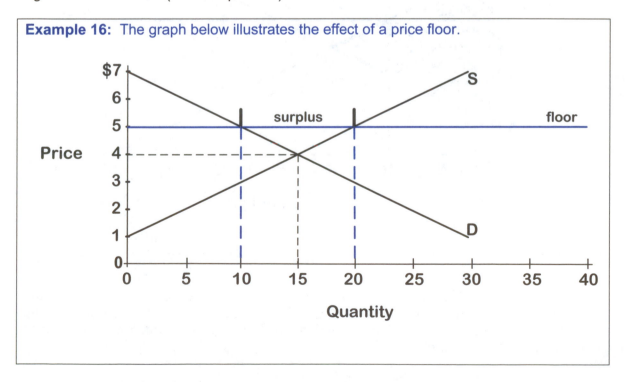

## Price Controls and Economic Inefficiency

Price controls are economically inefficient. We saw earlier in this chapter that a free market generally produces the most efficient quantity of output (where the marginal benefit of the product equals the marginal cost).

A price control, whether a ceiling or a floor, reduces the quantity of exchanges. A price control eliminates exchanges that would be mutually beneficial to the buyer and the seller (would generate more marginal benefit than marginal cost).

Price controls reduce the net benefit to society of having a market available for trading. The net benefit of having a market available is the sum of the consumer's surplus and the producer's surplus received by all the buyers and sellers in the market. We saw earlier in this chapter that the quantity produced in a free market maximizes the sum of the consumer's surplus and the producer's surplus.

A price control reduces the quantity of exchanges. A price control eliminates exchanges that would generate additional consumer's surplus and producer's surplus. The inefficiency caused by price controls is a type of "deadweight loss". (Other examples of deadweight loss are discussed in Chapters 13, 17, 22, 23, and 29.)

**Example 17:** The graph below illustrates the deadweight loss caused by a price control. The graph illustrates the amount of consumer's surplus and producer's surplus that is eliminated when a price floor is imposed (as in Example 16 on the previous page).

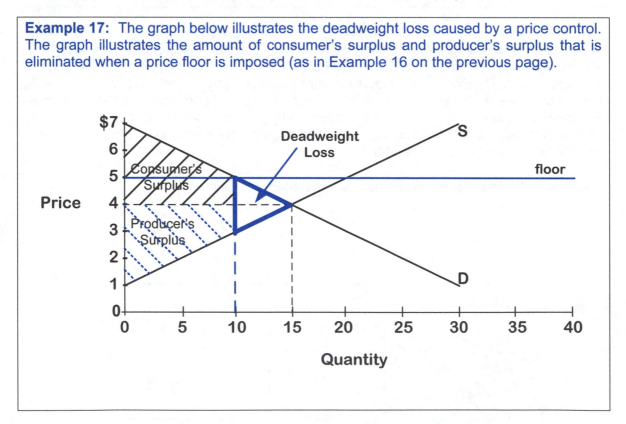

The consumer's surplus and producer's surplus that is eliminated by the price floor is the deadweight loss caused by the price floor. The greater the difference between the market equilibrium price and the controlled price, the greater the deadweight loss caused by the price control.

**Fill-in-the-blanks:**

1. _____ is the willingness and ability of buyers to buy different quantities of a good at different prices.

2. According to the law of demand, the price and the quantity demanded of a good are _____ related.

3. For _____ goods, income and demand are directly related.

4. For _____ goods, income and demand are inversely related.

5. _____ is the willingness and ability of sellers to sell different quantities of a good at different prices.

6. According to the law of supply, the price and the quantity supplied of a good are _____ related.

7. The determinant of supply is the _____ of _____.

8. An increase in the cost of production will cause a(n) _____ in supply.

9. _____ advance is the ability to produce more output per resource.

10. A _____ _____ is a market in which price is free to adjust up or down in response to demand and supply.

11. _____ price is the price where quantity demanded equals quantity supplied.

12. A _____ is when quantity supplied exceeds quantity demanded.

13. A _____ is when quantity demanded exceeds quantity supplied.

14. A price _____ is a maximum legal price.

15. A price _____ is a minimum legal price.

**Multiple Choice:**

_____ 1. Chris is given a dollar each day to buy his breakfast. He normally buys two donuts (for 45¢ apiece) at the Quahog Bakery. Today, the bakery lowers its donut price to 30¢ and Chris is able to buy three donuts with his dollar. This is:
   a. the substitution effect
   b. the income effect
   c. Both of the above

_____ 2. An increase in the demand for donuts could be caused by:
   a. an increase in the number of buyers
   b. a decrease in the cost of producing donuts
   c. a decrease in the price of donuts
   d. All of the above

_____ 3. A good for which an increase in income causes an increase in demand is:
   a. a complement
   b. a substitute
   c. a normal good
   d. an inferior good

_____ 4. If an increase in the price of Good Y causes a decrease in the demand for Good Z, Goods Y and Z must be:
   a. normal goods
   b. complements
   c. substitutes
   d. inferior goods

_____ 5. Which of the following will cause a change in demand for Good A?
   a. a decrease in the cost of producing Good A
   b. a decrease in the price of Good A
   c. a decrease in the number of buyers for Good A
   d. All of the above

_____ 6. A movement along the demand curve caused by a change in price is:
   a. a change in supply
   b. a change in quantity supplied
   c. a change in demand
   d. a change in quantity demanded

_____ 7. An increase in the price of donuts will cause:
   a. a decrease in the demand for donuts
   b. a decrease in the quantity demanded of donuts
   c. a decrease in the demand for bagels
   d. All of the above

_____ 8. If the price of gasoline doubles, what is likely to happen to the demand for public transportation?
   a. decreases
   b. increases
   c. stays the same
   d. None of the above

_____ 9. If the demand for public transportation increases, resulting in a higher market price, this will cause:
   a. an increase in the supply of public transportation
   b. a rightward shift in the supply curve for public transportation
   c. an increase in the quantity supplied of public transportation
   d. None of the above

_____ 10. An increase in the supply of diet books could be caused by:
   a.  an increase in the number of people wanting to lose weight
   b.  an increase in the equilibrium price of diet books
   c.  a decrease in the cost of producing diet books
   d.  All of the above

_____ 11. Free market equilibrium will generally occur:
   a.  where there is no surplus or shortage
   b.  where marginal benefit equals marginal cost
   c.  where the sum of consumer's surplus and producer's surplus is maximized
   d.  All of the above

_____ 12. If demand decreases and supply increases, what happens to price?
   a.  increases
   b.  decreases
   c.  stays the same
   d.  Cannot be determined

_____ 13. Assuming a market originally in equilibrium, an increase in supply would lead to:
   a.  price increase, quantity increase
   b.  price increase, quantity decrease
   c.  price decrease, quantity increase
   d.  price decrease, quantity decrease

_____ 14. A surplus is an indication that the market price is:
   a.  below equilibrium
   b.  above equilibrium
   c.  at equilibrium
   d.  None of the above

_____ 15. Assuming a market originally in equilibrium, a decrease in the number of buyers would lead to:
   a.  price increase, quantity increase
   b.  price increase, quantity decrease
   c.  price decrease, quantity increase
   d.  price decrease, quantity decrease

_____ 16. If there is an increase in enrollment in economics classes, what will happen in the market for economics textbooks?
   a.  price increase, quantity increase
   b.  price increase, quantity decrease
   c.  price decrease, quantity increase
   d.  price decrease, quantity decrease

_____ 17. If the government imposes a price ceiling in a market, this will tend to create:
   a.  a surplus
   b.  a shortage
   c.  more exchanges
   d.  All of the above

Demand, Supply, and Equilibrium

_____ 18. When a price control is imposed:
   a.   the number of exchanges will increase
   b.   the sum of producer's surplus and consumer's surplus is reduced
   c.   the market operates more efficiently
   d.   Both a. and c. above

## Problems:

1.  Explain the reason for the direct relationship between price and quantity supplied.

2.  What is a price ceiling?  List four results that a price ceiling will lead to.

3.  From the information below:
    a.  Graph the demand curve.
    b.  Graph supply curve #1.
    c.  What is equilibrium price and quantity #1?
    d.  Graph supply curve #2.
    e.  What is equilibrium price and quantity #2?

| Price | Quantity Demanded | Quantity Supplied #1 | Quantity Supplied #2 |
|-------|-------------------|----------------------|----------------------|
| $2 | 10 | 0 | 1 |
| $3 | 9 | 0 | 3 |
| $4 | 8 | 2 | 5 |
| $5 | 7 | 4 | 7 |
| $6 | 6 | 6 | 9 |
| $7 | 5 | 8 | 11 |
| $8 | 4 | 10 | 13 |

Price

$8
7
6
5
4
3
2
1
0
0  1  2  3  4  5  6  7  8  9  10  11  12  13

Quantity

## Answers to Chapter 3

**Fill-in-the-blanks:**
1. Demand
2. inversely
3. normal
4. inferior
5. Supply
6. directly
7. cost, production
8. decrease
9. Technological
10. free market
11. Equilibrium
12. surplus
13. shortage
14. ceiling
15. floor

Demand, Supply, and Equilibrium

**Multiple Choice:**

| | | |
|---|---|---|
| 1. b. | 7. b. | 13. c. |
| 2. a. | 8. b. | 14. b. |
| 3. c. | 9. c. | 15. d. |
| 4. b. | 10. c. | 16. a. |
| 5. c. | 11. d. | 17. b. |
| 6. d. | 12. b. | 18. b. |

**Problems:**

1. The reason for the direct relationship between price and quantity supplied is the seller's goal of profit-maximization. For the seller to make a profit, the selling price must be sufficient to cover the seller's cost of production. An increase in the selling price will make it easier for sellers to cover their cost of production. An increase in the selling price will cause existing producers to increase their production and will attract new producers into the market. Thus, an increase in the selling price will cause an increase in the quantity supplied.

2. A price ceiling is a maximum legal price. A price ceiling will lead to:
   a. A shortage.
   b. Fewer exchanges than at equilibrium.
   c. The use of non-price rationing devices.
   d. Illegal transactions at prices above the ceiling.

3.

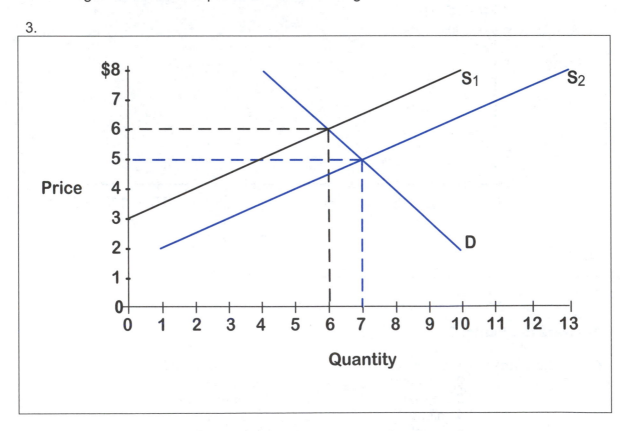

   c. Equilibrium price and quantity #1 is $6 and 6 units
   e. Equilibrium price and quantity #2 is $5 and 7 units

# Chapter 4  Inflation and Unemployment

The basic economic problem is scarcity.  Human wants are unlimited.  Resources are limited.  The basic goal in dealing with the problem of scarcity is to produce as much consumer satisfaction as possible with the limited resources available.

## Three Macroeconomic Goals

Macroeconomics is the branch of economics that focuses on overall economic behavior.  Any society will have certain overall (macroeconomic) goals as it deals with the basic economic problem of scarcity.  Three macroeconomic goals that societies wish to achieve are:

1.  **Price level stability**
2.  **Full employment**
3.  **Economic growth**

Achieving each of these three goals will contribute to the basic goal of producing as much consumer satisfaction as possible with the limited resources available.  These three goals, and how they are measured, are the primary topics in this chapter and the next.

Recent U.S. history in achieving the three macroeconomic goals is covered in an appendix at the end of the chapter.

## Inflation

In pursuing the goal of price level stability, the primary concern generally is to avoid inflation (or at least to keep the inflation rate low).

**Inflation** – an increase in the price level.

The price level does <u>not</u> refer to the price of only one good or service.  If the price of donuts increases, that doesn't mean that the price level will increase.  The price level refers to the weighted average of the prices of all goods and services.

> **Example 1:**  A late frost in Florida may cause an increase in the price of oranges.  This is not inflation, but simply a price adjustment for one good.  If the prices of goods and services in general are rising, this is inflation.

## The Price Level, Money, and Production

The price level in an economy depends on the relationship between the quantity of money spent and the quantity of products purchased in the economy.  If the quantity of money spent increases relative to the quantity of products purchased, the price level will increase.  If the quantity of money spent decreases relative to the quantity of products purchased, the price level will decrease.

**Example 2:** On Gilligan's Island, the castaways produce what they can each day, and then the day's production is auctioned to the high bidders. Each of the seven castaways is allowed to spend 10 units of money (Gills) on Days 1 through 4. On Days 5 through 7, each castaway is allowed to spend 20 units of money.

The table below shows, for each day, the quantity of money spent, the quantity of products purchased, and the price level. The price level is determined by dividing the quantity of products purchased by the quantity of money spent. If 70 Gills will buy 7 products, the price level is 10.

| Day | Money Spent | Products Purchased | Price Level |
|-----|-------------|--------------------|-------------|
| 1 | 70 Gills | 7 | 10 |
| 2 | 70 Gills | 10 | 7 |
| 3 | 70 Gills | 14 | 5 |
| 4 | 70 Gills | 10 | 7 |
| 5 | 140 Gills | 10 | 14 |
| 6 | 140 Gills | 14 | 10 |
| 7 | 140 Gills | 7 | 20 |

Notice that the price level changes each day depending on the relationship between the quantity of money spent and the quantity of products purchased. For instance, when the quantity of money spent doubles on Day 5, and the quantity of products purchased remains the same as on Day 4, the price level doubles.

Also notice that the daily standard of living depends solely on the quantity of production. The castaways have the highest standard of living on Days 3 and 6, because more is produced (14 units) on those days than on the other days. Doubling the money supply for Days 5, 6, and 7 affects the price level, but _not_ the standard of living.

## Consumer Price Index

The price level in the economy is measured by constructing a price index. The most widely reported price index is the consumer price index (CPI). The consumer price index is based on the price of a market basket of goods and services. The market basket consists of a wide variety of goods and services purchased by typical households.

Broken down into categories, the market basket consisted (as of 12/07) of housing (42%), transportation (18%), food and beverages (15%), medical care (6%), education and communication (6%), recreation (6%), apparel (4%), and other (3%). The Bureau of Labor Statistics gathers information on the price of the market basket to calculate the consumer price index.

The CPI for the years 1913 through 2007 is detailed in a table on the next page.

## Consumer Price Index Table

| Year | CPI | Year | CPI | Year | CPI | Year | CPI | Year | CPI |
|------|-----|------|-----|------|-----|------|-----|------|-----|
| 1913 | 9.9 | 1932 | 13.7 | 1951 | 26.0 | 1970 | 38.8 | 1989 | 124.0 |
| 1914 | 10.0 | 1933 | 13.0 | 1952 | 26.5 | 1971 | 40.5 | 1990 | 130.7 |
| 1915 | 10.1 | 1934 | 13.4 | 1953 | 26.7 | 1972 | 41.8 | 1991 | 136.2 |
| 1916 | 10.9 | 1935 | 13.7 | 1954 | 26.9 | 1973 | 44.4 | 1992 | 140.3 |
| 1917 | 12.8 | 1936 | 13.9 | 1955 | 26.8 | 1974 | 49.3 | 1993 | 144.5 |
| 1918 | 15.1 | 1937 | 14.4 | 1956 | 27.2 | 1975 | 53.8 | 1994 | 148.2 |
| 1919 | 17.3 | 1938 | 14.1 | 1957 | 28.1 | 1976 | 56.9 | 1995 | 152.4 |
| 1920 | 20.0 | 1939 | 13.9 | 1958 | 28.9 | 1977 | 60.6 | 1996 | 156.9 |
| 1921 | 17.9 | 1940 | 14.0 | 1959 | 29.1 | 1978 | 65.2 | 1997 | 160.5 |
| 1922 | 16.8 | 1941 | 14.7 | 1960 | 29.6 | 1979 | 72.6 | 1998 | 163.0 |
| 1923 | 17.1 | 1942 | 16.3 | 1961 | 29.9 | 1980 | 82.4 | 1999 | 166.6 |
| 1924 | 17.1 | 1943 | 17.3 | 1962 | 30.2 | 1981 | 90.9 | 2000 | 172.2 |
| 1925 | 17.5 | 1944 | 17.6 | 1963 | 30.6 | 1982 | 96.5 | 2001 | 177.1 |
| 1926 | 17.7 | 1945 | 18.0 | 1964 | 31.0 | 1983 | 99.6 | 2002 | 179.9 |
| 1927 | 17.4 | 1946 | 19.5 | 1965 | 31.5 | 1984 | 103.9 | 2003 | 184.0 |
| 1928 | 17.1 | 1947 | 22.3 | 1966 | 32.4 | 1985 | 107.6 | 2004 | 188.9 |
| 1929 | 17.1 | 1948 | 24.1 | 1967 | 33.4 | 1986 | 109.6 | 2005 | 195.3 |
| 1930 | 16.6 | 1949 | 23.8 | 1968 | 34.8 | 1987 | 113.6 | 2006 | 201.6 |
| 1931 | 15.2 | 1950 | 24.1 | 1969 | 36.7 | 1988 | 118.3 | 2007 | 207.3 |

## Computing the Rate of Inflation

The consumer price index can be used to compute the rate of inflation. The rate of inflation is the percentage annual increase in the index. The percentage annual increase in the index is calculated by dividing the annual change in the index (current year CPI minus previous year CPI) by the previous year's index. The following examples illustrate:

**Example 3A:** The CPI for 1945 was 18.0 and the CPI for 1946 was 19.5. What was the rate of inflation for 1946?

Inflation Rate (1946) = (CPI for 1946 – CPI for 1945) ÷ CPI for 1945 = (19.5 – 18.0) ÷ 18.0 = 1.5 ÷ 18.0 = .083 or 8.3%

**Example 3B:** The CPI for 1964 was 31.0 and the CPI for 1965 was 31.5. What was the rate of inflation for 1965?

Inflation Rate (1965) = (CPI for 1965 – CPI for 1964) ÷ CPI for 1964 = (31.5 – 31.0) ÷ 31.0 = 0.5 ÷ 31.0 = .016 or 1.6%

**Example 3C:** The CPI for 1989 was 124.0 and the CPI for 1990 was 130.7. What was the rate of inflation for 1990?

Inflation Rate (1990) = (CPI for 1990 – CPI for 1989) ÷ CPI for 1989 = (130.7 – 124.0) ÷ 124.0 = 6.7 ÷ 124.0 = .054 or 5.4%

**Example 3D:** The CPI for 2005 was 195.3 and the CPI for 2006 was 201.6. What was the rate of inflation for 2006?

Inflation Rate (2006) = (CPI for 2006 - CPI for 2005) ÷ CPI for 2005 = (201.6 - 195.3) ÷ 195.3 = 6.3 ÷ 195.3 = .032 or 3.2%

## Adjusting Nominal Values to Real Values

One of the functions of money is to serve as a measure of value (see Chapter 10). The basic economic measurement unit in the U.S. is the dollar. But the value of the dollar in terms of buying power changes from year to year because of changes in the price level.

During periods of inflation, the value of the dollar decreases over time. Thus, if nominal (unadjusted) dollar amounts from different years are compared to each other, the comparison is misleading.

If dollar amounts from different years are to be fairly compared, the nominal dollar amounts must be adjusted to real (inflation-adjusted) dollar amounts. The consumer price index can be used to adjust nominal values to real values.

To adjust a nominal value to a real value, the nominal value is divided by the nominal price index (the price index of the year of the nominal value) divided by the price index adjusted to.

**Real value = Nominal Value ÷ (Nominal Price Index ÷ Price Index Adjusted to)**

**Example 4A:** In 1982, the average Oklahoma teacher salary was $16,781. The average Oklahoma teacher salary was $35,061 in 2004. What was real average Oklahoma teacher salary in 2004, adjusted to the 1982 price level?

Real salary (2004) = Nominal salary for 2004 ÷ (CPI for 2004 ÷ CPI for 1982) = $35,061 ÷ (188.9 ÷ 96.5) = $35,061 ÷ 1.9575 = $17,911

**Example 4B:** Based on the facts in Example 4A, what was real average Oklahoma teacher salary in 1982, adjusted to the 2004 price level?

Real salary (1982) = Nominal salary for 1982 ÷ (CPI for 1982 ÷ CPI for 2004) = $16,781 ÷ (96.5 ÷ 188.9) = $16,781 ÷ .5109 = $32,846

Examples 4A and 4B illustrate that real average Oklahoma teacher salaries increased slightly (about 6.7%) between 1982 and 2004. This information is summarized on the table below:

| Stated At: | Oklahoma Teacher Salaries 1982 | 2004 | Percentage Change |
|---|---|---|---|
| 1982 Price Level | $16,781 | $17,911 | + 6.7% |
| 2004 Price Level | $32,846 | $35,061 | + 6.7% |

> **Example 4C:** In 1922, the average Oklahoma teacher salary was $994 and the CPI was 16.8. What was real average Oklahoma teacher salary in 1922, adjusted to the 2004 price level?
>
> Real salary (1922) = $994 ÷ (16.8 ÷ 188.9) = $994 ÷ .0889 = $11,181

Example 4C illustrates that real average Oklahoma teacher salaries increased a great deal (more than tripled) between 1922 and 2004.

## Unemployment

The basic economic problem is scarcity. The basic goal in dealing with the problem of scarcity is to produce as much consumer satisfaction as possible with the limited resources available. The total production that society can achieve will be reduced if some of the limited resources are not employed. Society especially worries about unemployed labor, and not only because unemployed labor reduces total production. Wage income is the primary source of income for most households.

> **Example 5:** Compensation of employees typically makes up about 65% of national income.

A period of unemployment can be financially devastating for the household affected. Most periods of unemployment are relatively short term (less than 6 months). However, about 20% of persons who experience unemployment will be unemployed for longer than 6 months. Thus, unemployment of labor is a major problem both for the overall economy and for the specific households suffering from unemployment.

## Full Employment

Though unemployment of labor is a major problem, the goal for the unemployment rate is not to achieve an unemployment rate of zero. An unemployment rate of zero is not a practical possibility in a market economy. (We will see why later in the chapter when we look at the types of unemployment.)

The goal for the unemployment rate is to achieve full employment (or the natural unemployment rate). The natural unemployment rate is the lowest unemployment rate that can be sustained without causing increasing inflation. When the unemployment rate is at the natural unemployment rate, this is considered to be "full employment".

## Measuring Unemployment

Each month the Bureau of Labor Statistics gathers information to determine the size of the labor force, the number of unemployed workers, and the unemployment rate. In determining these statistics, only persons 16 years old and older are included. Thus, a 15-year-old movie star earning millions of dollars is not counted as employed. A 15-year-old who loses her job delivering newspapers is not counted as unemployed. Those under age 16 can be neither employed nor unemployed.

Those 16 years old or older are classified into one of three categories:

1. **Employed** – those with paying jobs. The job does <u>not</u> have to be full-time. A musician laid-off from the local orchestra and working part-time as a janitor is counted as employed.

2. **Unemployed** – those without paying jobs who are actively seeking employment. A person without a paying job who has become discouraged and quit seeking a job is <u>not</u> counted as unemployed.

3. **Not in the labor force.** Everyone who does not fall into category 1. or category 2. is <u>not</u> in the labor force and has no effect on the unemployment statistics.

The **labor force** is the sum of the number of people employed plus the number unemployed.

---

**Example 6A:** Assume that last month there were 230 million persons aged 16 and older. Of these, 146 million had paying jobs, 9 million did <u>not</u> have paying jobs, but were actively seeking employment, 3 million wanted to work but had given up on seeking employment, and the other 71 million were retired or were otherwise <u>not</u> interested in employment. What was the size of the labor force last month? Answer; 155 million, as computed below. Only those who are employed (146 million) or unemployed (9 million) are included in the labor force. Discouraged workers who are <u>not</u> actively seeking employment are <u>not</u> included in the labor force.

**Labor force = Employed + Unemployed** = 146 million + 9 million = 155 million

---

The unemployment rate is the percentage of the labor force that is unemployed. It is calculated by dividing the number of people unemployed by the number of people in the labor force.

---

**Example 6B:** Based on the information in Example 6A, what is the unemployment rate?

**Unemployment Rate = Unemployed ÷ Labor Force** = 9 million ÷ 155 million = .058 or 5.8%

---

## Types of Unemployment

The basic economic problem is scarcity. In an ideal world, the unemployment rate would be zero. All available members of the labor force would be employed. But an unemployment rate of zero is <u>not</u> a practical possibility in a market economy. Even in the best economic conditions (what economists call "full employment"), the unemployment rate will <u>not</u> be zero. We see why this is true as we look at the types of unemployment.

Types of unemployment:

1. **Frictional unemployment** – due to the time required to match workers with jobs. In frictional unemployment, workers are available and jobs are available. The workers

have the skills required in the available jobs. But it takes time to match the available workers with the available jobs. During that time, the workers are frictionally unemployed.

The U.S. labor force is very mobile, with workers moving into and out of the labor force, relocating, and switching jobs. This mobility often leads to periods of frictional unemployment.

The mobility of the labor force is economically beneficial. It facilitates the continual re-allocation of labor necessary to direct the labor force to its most valuable uses. Labor force mobility also reflects individual freedom. American workers are free to leave the labor force, re-enter the labor force, quit one job to look for another, or relocate to a different part of the country.

Frictional unemployment tends to be a short term situation. But due to the mobile nature of the labor force, there will always be a certain percentage of the labor force that is frictionally unemployed.

> **Example 7A:** Assume that in May, 2009, 4.3 million workers are frictionally unemployed. By August, 2009, most of these workers will have found jobs. But the number of frictionally unemployed workers is still likely to be about 4.3 million, as other workers have become frictionally unemployed.

2. **Structural unemployment** – workers do <u>not</u> have the skills required in the available jobs. In structural unemployment, workers are available and jobs are available. But the skills that the workers have do <u>not</u> match the skills required in the available jobs. It takes time for the workers to acquire the skills in demand in the labor market. During that time, the workers are structurally unemployed.

Structural unemployment is a hardship for the unemployed workers, but is necessary for economic growth. As technological advance occurs, old jobs are destroyed and new jobs are created. The connection between economic growth and job destruction is discussed later in this chapter.

Structural unemployment tends to be a long term situation. Due to the changing nature of labor demand in a growing market economy, there will always be a certain percentage of the labor force that is structurally unemployed.

> **Example 7B:** Assume that in May, 2009, 3.6 million workers are structurally unemployed. In August, 2009, many of these workers may still be unemployed. By May, 2011, most of the workers will have found jobs. But the number of structurally unemployed workers is still likely to be about 3.6 million, as other workers have become structurally unemployed.

The sum of frictional and structural unemployment is called the natural unemployment rate. The **natural unemployment rate** is the lowest unemployment rate that can be sustained without causing increasing inflation. When the economy is at full employment, the unemployment rate will be at the natural unemployment rate.

> **Example 8:** Assume that last month the frictional unemployment rate was 2.8% and the structural unemployment rate was 2.3%. What was the natural unemployment rate?
>
> **Natural unemployment rate** = Frictional unemployment rate + Structural unemployment rate = 2.8% + 2.3% = 5.1%

3. **Cyclical unemployment** – due to downturns in the business cycle. The economy does <u>not</u> always operate at full employment. When there is a downturn in the business cycle, output falls below the level produced at full employment.

   If the economy is not producing enough output to achieve full employment, the actual unemployment rate will be higher than the natural rate. The difference between the actual unemployment rate and the natural unemployment rate is the cyclical unemployment rate.

> **Example 9:** If the actual unemployment rate is 5.8% and the natural unemployment rate is 5.1%, the cyclical unemployment rate is .7%.

### Economic Growth and Job Destruction

One of the three macroeconomic goals is full employment. Another goal is economic growth. In the short run, these two goals may be in conflict. The technological advances that cause economic growth may result in the destruction of jobs and the displacement of workers.

We saw in Chapter 2 that economic growth can be achieved either by an increase in the quantity of resources or by an advance in technology. Technological advance is the ability to produce more output per resource.

> **Example 10:** Between 1992 and 1999, employment in the U.S. steel industry decreased from about 240,000 workers to about 150,000 workers. But steel production in the U.S. increased from 92.9 million tons to 107.4 million tons. Thus, labor productivity increased by 85 percent (from 387 tons annually per worker to 716 tons annually per worker).

Technological advance destroys jobs. Consider the agricultural industry. Two hundred years ago, about 80 percent of the American labor force was employed in agriculture. Over the last two hundred years, labor productivity in agriculture has greatly increased due to technological advances (more and better capital equipment, improved seeds, improved fertilizers, improved farming techniques, etc.) Today, about 2 percent of the American labor force is employed in agriculture. Technological advance has destroyed tens of millions of jobs in agriculture.

Technological advance has also destroyed millions of other jobs. There aren't many scriveners today. Scriveners made hand-written copies of important documents. Copy machines have destroyed the demand for scriveners. ATMs have eliminated many jobs for bank tellers. Far more long distance phone calls are made today than were made eighty years ago. And with far fewer telephone operators.

Job destruction is good. Job destruction frees up labor for new types of production. The destruction of jobs allows the newly unemployed labor to be re-allocated to more valuable production.

But won't technological advance lead to increasing unemployment? Temporarily, it might. The development of a weed-resistant, self-fertilizing lawn grass would throw a lot of lawn service employees out of work. But remember that human wants are unlimited.

We want food and copies and bank services and long distance phone calls and beautiful lawns. And we want an unlimited amount of other goods and services. And we would like to produce these goods and services with as few resources (including labor) as possible.

Individually, we want jobs to enable us to earn income. But as a society, we want to destroy jobs, to free up labor to produce more goods and services. Job destruction makes economic growth possible.


## Appendix: Female Labor Force Participation

One of the major economic (and social) changes of the second half of the twentieth century was the increase in female labor force participation. According to the Bureau of Labor Statistics, the labor force participation rate for females 16 years old and older increased from 33% in 1948 to 59% in 2007. This increase was due in part to cultural changes. Female labor force participation became more socially accepted (and even expected) during this time period.

But the biggest factor causing the increase in female labor force participation was probably the increase in real wage rates for females during this time period. Real wage rates for females increased dramatically during this time period due to general economic growth and due to improved labor market opportunities for females (as more women became doctors, lawyers, accountants, etc.). The rising real wage rates increased the opportunity cost of not being in the labor force.

> **Example 11A:** In 1950, 3% of law school students were female. In 2007, 47% of law school students were female. In 1950, 5% of doctors were female. In 2006, 49% of medical school students were female. In 1970, 11% of females in the labor force were college graduates. In 2004, 33% of females in the labor force were college graduates.

> **Example 11B:** For full-time, year-round workers, women's earnings were 61% of men's earnings in 1961. In 2007, women's earnings were 78% of men's earnings. (Information is from the Census Bureau.)

It seems likely that women's earnings will continue to catch up to men's earnings in the future. Since the early 1980s, the percentage of women enrolled in college has exceeded the percentage of men enrolled in college.

Inflation and Unemployment

**Example 12:** For full-time, year-round workers age 55-64, 40% of men had at least a bachelor's degree, while only 33% of women had at least a bachelor's degree. Women's earnings were 64% of men's earnings for this age group. For full-time, year-round workers ages 25-34, 32% of men had at least a bachelor's degree, while 44% of women had at least a bachelor's degree. Women's earnings were 86% of men's earnings for this age group. (Information is from the Census Bureau and is for 2007.)

## Appendix: Recent U.S. History in Achieving the Three Macroeconomic Goals

The three macroeconomic goals are price level stability, full employment, and economic growth. Achieving each of these three goals will contribute to the basic goal of producing as much consumer satisfaction as possible with the limited resources available. Failing to achieve each of these three goals leads to economic hardship.

During the Great Depression, the U.S. economy failed to achieve any of the three macroeconomic goals.

**Example 13:** Between 1929 and 1933, the price level decreased by 24%. Deflation tends to have a devastating effect on investment spending and is even more harmful economically than inflation. Between 1929 and 1933, the unemployment rate increased from 3.2% to 24.9%. The unemployment rate remained high for the entire decade of the 1930s (averaging 18% for the decade) and did not fall below 14% until 1941, when it was still 9.9%. Between 1929 and 1933, Real GDP decreased by nearly 27%. By 1938, Real GDP was only about 2% greater than it had been in 1929.

Since the Great Depression, the U.S. has had much more success in achieving the three macroeconomic goals. This was especially true from 1983 through 2007.

After some significant post-war inflation (inflation rate of 14.4% in 1946 and 8.1% in 1947), the rate of inflation was generally mild until the late 1960s. From 1968 to 1982, the inflation rate averaged 7.4%, with a peak of 13.5% in 1980. From 1983 through 2007, the inflation rate averaged 3.1%, with a peak of 5.4% in 1990.

The unemployment rate was generally low from 1947 through 1969, with an average unemployment rate of 4.6%. The unemployment rate was higher in recessionary years (1949 – 5.9%, 1954 – 5.5%, 1958 – 6.8%, 1961 – 6.7%). From 1970 through 1982, the unemployment rate averaged 6.9%, with a peak in 1982 of 9.7%, during the most severe recession since the Great Depression. From 1983 through 2007, the unemployment rate averaged 5.7%, with a peak of 7.5% in 1992.

Since the post-war adjustment of 1945-47, the economy has experienced ten recessions. The most severe of these was in 1982, when Real GDP dropped by 1.9%. From 1947 through 1982, Real GDP increased by an average of 3.4% annually, with eight recessions. From 1983 through 2007, Real GDP increased by an average of 3.2% annually, with only two recessions. (Note: The National Bureau of Economic Research announced on December 1, 2008 that a recession began in December, 2007.)

## Appendix: High Unemployment in France

In recent years, France has had an unemployment rate about twice as high as the unemployment rate in the U.S.

> **Example 14:** From 1995 to 2005, the U.S. had an average unemployment rate of 5.1%. During this same time period, France had an average unemployment rate of 10.4%.

The unemployment rate in France is higher than in the U.S. <u>not</u> because French workers are more likely to lose their jobs than American workers, but rather because unemployment lasts longer in France than in the U.S.

> **Example 15:** The majority of workers who become unemployed in the U.S. are unemployed for less than 8 weeks. The percentage of unemployed workers who are unemployed for one year or more is about four times as great in France as in the U.S.

The higher rate of unemployment in France compared to the U.S. is often blamed on structural differences in the French labor market compared to the U.S. labor market, including:

1. It is more difficult and costly to fire workers in France than in the U.S. This makes French employers more hesitant to hire new workers.

> **Example 16:** In France, the administrative procedures required for a large company to fire a worker take an average of over three months to complete. In the U.S., most workers are "at-will" and can be dismissed immediately for any (or no) reason.

2. Payroll taxes in France are about four times as high as payroll taxes in the U.S.

3. Unemployment compensation benefits in France are more generous than in the U.S. and can last as long as three years. In the U.S., unemployment compensation benefits typically last no longer than six months.

4. The minimum wage has been much higher in France than in the U.S.

> **Example 17:** In 2007, France's minimum wage was more than double the minimum wage in the U.S.

In 2003, Forbes magazine published a Free Labor Indicator, ranking selected countries by labor-market freedom. The U.S. ranked first on the list, with a Free Labor Score of 4.55 on a scale of 4 (most free) to 40 (most restrictive). France ranked fifteenth out of the seventeen countries ranked, with a score of 32.25.

In early 2006, the French government enacted a youth employment law creating a "first employment contract". The first employment contract would allow employers to fire any worker under the age of 26 for any (or no) reason during a two-year trial period. The first employment contract was intended to encourage employers to hire more young workers by making it easier for employers to eliminate young workers in the event that a worker proved to be unproductive or if there were a downturn in business.

It was hoped that the first employment contract would reduce the unemployment rate for young workers, which was over 20% (around 50% for young immigrant workers).

The law creating the first employment contract proved very controversial and triggered widespread protests. Opinion polls indicated that about two-thirds of the French people disapproved of the first employment contract. The law was withdrawn by the French government on April 10, 2006.

In May, 2007, France elected Nicolas Sarkozy as its new President. Sarkozy promised to invigorate the sluggish French economy. His campaign slogan was "work more to earn more".

### Appendix: Think Like an Economist – Unemployment Policies

In the U.S., most workers are "at-will" and can be dismissed immediately for any (or no) reason. U.S. policymakers determine that young workers (under the age of 25) are more likely to be fired than older workers. To change this pattern, the U.S. government passes a law making it more difficult and costly for employers to fire workers under the age of 25.

Thinking like an economist, will this law reduce unemployment among young workers? Why or why not?

### Questions for Chapter 4

### Fill-in-the-blanks:

1. _____ is an increase in the price level.

2. The price level in the economy depends on the relationship between the quantity of _____ spent and the quantity of _____ purchased.

3. The _____ _____ is the sum of the number of people employed plus the number unemployed.

4. _____ unemployment is due to the time required to match workers with jobs.

5. _____ unemployment is where workers do not have the skills required in the available jobs.

6. _____ unemployment is due to downturns in the business cycle.

**Multiple Choice:**

_____ 1. Which of the following is <u>not</u> one of the macroeconomic goals?
    a. full employment
    b. money supply growth
    c. economic growth
    d. price level stability

_____ 2. If the quantity of money spent decreases relative to the quantity of products purchased:
    a. the price level will increase
    b. the price level will decrease
    c. the price level will stay the same
    d. All of the above are possible

_____ 3. The largest category in the market basket of goods and services purchased by typical households is:
    a. medical care
    b. transportation
    c. housing
    d. food and beverages

_____ 4. If the CPI was 113.6 in 1987 and was 118.3 in 1988, what was the rate of inflation for 1988?
    a. 4.1%
    b. 4.7%
    c. 16.1%
    d. 18.3%

_____ 5. The CPI in 1954 was:
    a. 19.5
    b. 26.7
    c. 26.9
    d. 30.6

_____ 6. If a gallon of gasoline cost $.25 in 1954, when the CPI was 26.9, and cost $1.75 in 2004, when the CPI was 188.9, what was the 2004 price of a gallon of gasoline, adjusted to the 1954 price level?
    a. $.25
    b. $.50
    c. $.75
    d. $1.50

_____ 7. The average engineer's salary was $74,920 in 2001. The average engineer's salary was $10,248 in 1962. What was the real average engineer's salary in 2001, adjusted to the 1962 price level?
    a. $12,487
    b. $12,776
    c. $24,807
    d. $27,804

Inflation and Unemployment

Answer questions 8. and 9. based on the following information: The average teacher salary was $9,705 in 1972 and was $46,726 in 2004.

_____ 8. What was the real average teacher salary in 1972, adjusted to the 2004 price level?
  a. $23,217
  b. $27,804
  c. $43,858
  d. $48,525

_____ 9. Between 1972 and 2004, real average teacher salaries:
  a. decreased by 6.5%
  b. increased by 6.5%
  c. increased by 68%
  d. increased by 101%

_____ 10. A period of unemployment typically lasts:
  a. less than 6 months
  b. from 6 months to one year
  c. from one year to two years
  d. more than two years

_____ 11. Anyone 16 and older who does <u>not</u> have a paying job and is actively seeking employment is:
  a. employed
  b. unemployed
  c. not in the labor force
  d. All of the above are possible

_____ 12. Out of 227 million persons 16 and older, 149 million had paying jobs, 8 million did not have paying jobs but were actively seeking employment, 4 million wanted to work but had given up seeking employment and 66 million were retired or were otherwise not interested in employment. What is the size of the labor force?
  a. 149 million
  b. 157 million
  c. 161 million
  d. 227 million

_____ 13. Based on the information in question 12., what is the unemployment rate?
  a. 4.9%
  b. 5.1%
  c. 5.4%
  d. 7.6%

_____ 14. When the economy is at "full employment":
  a. the unemployment rate will be zero
  b. there will still be some unemployment
  c. the unemployment rate will be at the natural unemployment rate
  d. Both b. and c. above

15. Cheryl graduates with an accounting degree in May. After searching for two months, she lands a job as an accountant in July. While Cheryl was looking for work, she was:
    a. frictionally unemployed
    b. structurally unemployed
    c. cyclically unemployed
    d. Not in the labor force

16. Cheryl is laid off from her job as an accountant due to a recession. She searches for a job for six months and then is rehired by her old employer when the economy begins to recover. While Cheryl was looking for work, she was:
    a. frictionally unemployed
    b. structurally unemployed
    c. cyclically unemployed
    d. Not in the labor force

17. If the natural unemployment rate is 5.1% and the structural unemployment rate is 2.4%, what is the frictional unemployment rate?
    a. 2.7%
    b. 5.1%
    c. 7.5%
    d. Cannot be determined

18. The natural unemployment rate is:
    a. the sum of frictional and structural unemployment
    b. the lowest unemployment rate that can be sustained without causing increasing inflation
    c. the rate associated with full employment
    d. All of the above

19. Technological advance:
    a. is the ability to produce more output per resource
    b. destroys jobs
    c. Both of the above
    d. Neither of the above

20. Job destruction caused by technological advance:
    a. is an economic disaster that must be prevented by job preservation legislation
    b. allows the newly unemployed labor to be re-allocated to more valuable production
    c. makes economic growth possible
    d. Both b. and c. above

21. The female labor force participation rate increased between 1948 and 2007 as real wage rates:
    a. were stagnant
    b. increased
    c. decreased

_____ 22. The gap between men's earnings and women's earnings:
        a. has widened in recent decades
        b. is likely to narrow in the future due to the higher college enrollment for women compared to men
        c. Both of the above
        d. Neither of the above

_____ 23. During the Great Depression, the U.S. economy:
        a. failed to achieve any of the three macroeconomic goals
        b. suffered from unemployment rates which averaged almost 10% for the 1930s
        c. suffered from high inflation from 1929 to 1933
        d. All of the above

_____ 24. From 1983 through 2007:
        a. the inflation rate was generally higher than it was in the 1970s
        b. the economy suffered from frequent recessions
        c. Both of the above
        d. Neither of the above

_____ 25. Compared to the U.S., France has had:
        a. higher rates of unemployment
        b. a higher percentage of workers who are unemployed for over one year
        c. more generous unemployment compensation benefits
        d. All of the above

_____ 26. Compared to France, the U.S. has had:
        a. a higher minimum wage
        b. higher payroll taxes
        c. lower rates of unemployment
        d. All of the above

_____ 27. The law creating the first employment contract in France:
        a. was intended to reduce the unemployment rate for young workers
        b. would have made it more difficult for employers to fire young workers
        c. Both of the above
        d. Neither of the above

## Problems:

1. The CPI was 14.7 in 1941 and was 16.3 in 1942. Compute the rate of inflation for 1942.

2. Explain why it is necessary to adjust nominal values to real values.

3. Cheryl had income of $20,000 in 1984, when the CPI was 103.9. Cheryl had income of $40,000 in 2004, when the CPI was 188.9. What was Cheryl's real income in 2004, adjusted to the 1984 price level?

4. Out of 226 million persons aged 16 and older, 143.5 million had paying jobs, 8.5 million were without jobs but were actively seeking employment, and 2.5 million wanted jobs but had given up looking for employment.
   a. Calculate the size of the labor force
   b. Calculate the unemployment rate

## Answers for Chapter 4

**Fill-in-the-blanks:**

| | |
|---|---|
| 1. Inflation | 4. Frictional |
| 2. money, products | 5. Structural |
| 3. labor force | 6. Cyclical |

**Multiple Choice:**

| | | |
|---|---|---|
| 1. b. | 10. a. | 19. c. |
| 2. b. | 11. b. | 20. d. |
| 3. c. | 12. b. | 21. b. |
| 4. a. | 13. b. | 22. b. |
| 5. c. | 14. d. | 23. a. |
| 6. a. | 15. a. | 24. d. |
| 7. b. | 16. c. | 25. d. |
| 8. c. | 17. a. | 26. c. |
| 9. b. | 18. d. | 27. a. |

### Problems:

1. Inflation (1942) = (16.3 - 14.7) ÷ 14.7 = 1.6 ÷ 14.7 = .1088 or 10.9%

2. The basic economic measurement unit is the dollar. But the value of the dollar in terms of buying power changes from year to year because of changes in the price level. If dollar amounts from different years are to be fairly compared, the nominal dollar amounts must be adjusted to real (inflation-adjusted) dollar amounts.

3. Real Income (2004) = $40,000 ÷ (188.9 ÷ 103.9) = $40,000 ÷ 1.8181 = $22,001

4. a. Labor Force = Employed + Unemployed = 143.5 million + 8.5 million = 152 million
   b. Unemployment Rate = Unemployed ÷ Labor Force = 8.5 million ÷ 152 million = .056 or 5.6%

### Answer to Think Like an Economist:

The new law is likely to <u>increase</u> unemployment among young workers. While making it more difficult and costly to fire young workers may cause some young workers to keep their jobs who would otherwise be fired, employers will be more hesitant to hire young workers in the first place.

# Chapter 5  Measuring Total Output:  GDP

Three macroeconomic goals that societies wish to achieve are price level stability, full employment, and economic growth.  We looked at inflation and unemployment in the last chapter.  Economic growth refers to an increase in total output for the economy.  Measuring total output is the topic of this chapter.

## Gross Domestic Product

To determine whether total output is increasing from year to year, and by how much, we need a measurement of total output.  The basic measurement of total output is called gross domestic product (GDP).

**Gross domestic product** – the market value of all final goods and services produced annually.

The market value of goods and services means the price that purchasers actually paid for the goods and services.  The price actually paid would include any sales or excise tax paid.

> **Example 1:**  Cindy's Cinnamon Rolls produced and sold 100,000 cinnamon rolls in 2007 and had sales revenue (including sales tax) of $200,000.  Cindy's production had a market value of $200,000 and thus added $200,000 to GDP in 2007.  In 2008, Cindy's produced and sold 110,000 cinnamon rolls and had sales revenue (including sales tax) of $231,000.  Thus, Cindy's production added $231,000 to GDP in 2008.

Notice in Example 1 that Cindy's produced 10 percent more cinnamon rolls in 2008 than in 2007 (110,000 cinnamon rolls versus 100,000 cinnamon rolls).  However, Cindy's contribution to GDP increased by 15.5% percent ($231,000 versus $200,000).  Some of the increase in Cindy's contribution to GDP from 2007 to 2008 is due to higher prices for the cinnamon rolls rather than to increased production.

Nominal GDP numbers will change from year to year for two different reasons.  Nominal GDP numbers change from year to year due to changes in production.  An increase in production will contribute towards an increase in nominal GDP.  Nominal GDP numbers will also change if there is a change in the price level.  This complicates the comparison of GDP numbers from different years.

If GDP numbers from different years are to be fairly compared, an adjustment must be made for the change in the price level in the different years.  We will look at the calculations to adjust nominal GDP to Real GDP later in the chapter.

## What is Excluded in Computing Gross Domestic Product

The primary purpose of computing GDP is to compare total output from year to year.  Thus, GDP needs to be calculated as objectively and as consistently as possible.  For this reason, certain types of production that are difficult to measure objectively are excluded in calculating GDP.  Also, factors that affect the quality of life, but that do <u>not</u>

affect production are excluded from GDP.  And financial transactions that do not result directly in production are excluded from GDP.

Exclusions from GDP are discussed more specifically in the next two pages.

**GDP excludes:**

1. **Intermediate goods.**  An **intermediate good** has not yet reached its final user, but rather is an input in the production of another good.

> **Example 2:**  Darla buys a 5 pound bag of flour at the grocery store for $2.80 (including tax) for use at her home.  The bag of flour is a final good and its market value ($2.80) is included in GDP.  Darla buys 500 pounds of flour from a bulk wholesaler for $240 for use in her donut shop.  This flour is an intermediate good.  It will be used in the production of a final good (donuts).  Since this flour is an intermediate good, the value of the 500 pounds of flour is excluded from GDP.

Darla's donuts (which include the flour as an ingredient) are final goods and their value is included in GDP.  If intermediate goods were included in GDP, this would overstate GDP by double counting.  The flour purchased by the donut shop would be counted once as flour and a second time as an ingredient in the donuts.

2. **Nonproduction transactions.**  The market value of goods and services produced is measured by the price paid in market transactions.  But some transactions do <u>not</u> directly result in production, and are thus excluded from GDP.  These nonproduction transactions include;

    **a. Used goods.**  Used goods were included in GDP when they were first produced.  They are <u>not</u> included in GDP when they are exchanged as used goods, because no new production takes place.

> **Example 3:**  Marshall buys a new Cadillac Escalade for $60,000.  The $60,000 will be included in GDP.  Two years later, Marshall sells the Escalade to his bodyguard for $40,000.  The $40,000 will be <u>excluded</u> from GDP.  No new production takes place as the result of the exchange of a used good.

    **b. Financial transactions.**  Money gifts, loans, and purchases of stocks and bonds are examples of financial transactions where money changes hands but no new production takes place.  Since no new production takes place, the transactions are excluded from GDP.

> **Example 4:**  Darla borrows $20,000 from 1st Bank.  She spends $10,000 on Krispy Kreme common stock, spends $8,000 on a used delivery van for her donut shop, spends $1,800 on a new sign for her donut shop, and sends $200 to her sister Carla as a birthday gift.  Of these various transactions, only the $1,800 spent on the new sign is included in GDP.  The loan, the purchase of common stock, and the birthday gift are all financial transactions where no new production takes place.  The delivery van is excluded from GDP because it is a used good.

**c. Transfer payments.** **Transfer payments** are transfers of income from the government to households or businesses, not in exchange for goods, services, or resources. Since no new production takes place, transfer payments are excluded from GDP.

> **Example 5:** Transfer payments include social security benefits, Temporary Assistance for Needy Families, unemployment compensation, etc.

3. **Nonmarket production.** In nonmarket production, new production is taking place. But there is no market transaction to reveal an objective market value for the production. So the value of nonmarket production is excluded from GDP. Do-it-yourself production is an example of nonmarket production.

> **Example 6:** Dewey's house needs to be painted. Dewey contacts Jasper, a professional housepainter. Jasper quotes Dewey a price of $3,300. Dewey decides to paint the house himself. Dewey spends $350 on paint and brushes. Then he spends four weekends painting his house. Only the $350 worth of paint and brushes will be included in GDP. Dewey's labor is nonmarket production and is excluded from GDP.

4. **Underground production.** This is unreported production. Production may be unreported because it is illegal (e.g. the output of a meth lab) or because the producer is evading taxation (e.g. unreported cash income).

> **Example 7:** Dewey's house needs to be painted. Dewey contacts Jasper, a professional housepainter. Jasper quotes Dewey a price of $3,300, or $2,800 if Dewey pays in cash. Dewey hires Jasper, who paints the house and collects $2,800 in cash from Dewey. Jasper does not report this cash income. So this underground production is excluded from GDP.

5. **Leisure.** Leisure time is by definition nonproduction time. An increase or a decrease in leisure time affects the quality of life, but does not directly affect production. No adjustment is made to GDP for an increase or a decrease in leisure time.

> **Example 8:** In 1900, the average work week in America was about 60 hours. In 2000, the average work week was about 40 hours. This increase in leisure time improved the quality of life, but did not directly affect GDP.

6. **Economic bads.** No adjustment is made to GDP for undesired byproducts of production (pollution) or for unwanted destruction of property (e.g. by earthquake, hurricane, fire, flood, terrorist attack, etc.).

> **Example 9:** In 2005, Hurricane Katrina caused damage roughly estimated at $80 billion. This loss was not deducted from GDP for 2005.

An economic bad could actually increase GDP. The damage done by an oil spill or a hurricane would not be deducted from GDP, but the market value of the production necessary to repair and replace damaged property would add to GDP. This does not mean that economic bads are actually good and add to the standard of living. Flaws in

GDP as a measure of standard of living are discussed in an appendix at the end of the chapter.

## Two Measures of Total Output; GDP and National Income

Total output can be measured by adding up the Total Expenditures on final goods and services. Or total output can be measured by adding up the payments to the resource owners who provided the resources to produce the final goods and services. The two measures of total output can be illustrated on a simple circular flow diagram. A simple circular flow diagram is discussed in an appendix at the end of this chapter.

When total output is measured as the sum of Total Expenditures, the result is gross domestic product. Total Expenditures consists of four types of spending:

1. **Consumption.** Household consumption of goods and services is the largest component of GDP. In 2007, consumption made up 70% of GDP.

2. **Investment.** **Investment** is the acquisition of new physical capital. Investment consists of;
   a. new capital goods
   b. changes in business inventories
   c. new residential housing

**Example 10:** Investment for GDP purposes is different than the common use of the word. A person who purchases common stock, real estate, or a used dump truck would consider each of these purchases an investment. But none of these purchases would be considered investment spending for GDP purposes.

3. **Government purchases.** This includes spending by federal, state, and local governments on goods and services, but does <u>not</u> include transfer payments.

**Example 11:** Government purchases would include, for example, federal spending on the military or the Environmental Protection Agency, state spending on public education or highways, and local spending on police and fire protection or street maintenance.

The market value of government purchases is usually determined by the amount of the government's expenditure, since government production is usually not sold in the marketplace. If the city of Rome, Georgia spent $7,605,494 on public safety in 2006, this is the amount that would be included in GDP.

4. **Net Exports.** Net exports equals exports minus imports.

**Exports** – total foreign purchases of domestic goods.

**Imports** – total domestic purchases of foreign goods.

Exports need to be added to GDP since they will <u>not</u> be included as part of domestic consumption, investment, or government purchases.

**Example 12:** A Ford Focus manufactured in Michigan and purchased by a consumer in Canada will <u>not</u> be included in U.S. consumption (since it was not purchased by a consumer in the U.S.) But the value of the Focus needs to be included in U.S. GDP, since it was produced in the U.S.

Imports need to be subtracted from GDP since they <u>will</u> be included as part of domestic consumption, investment, or government purchases.

**Example 13:** A MINI Cooper manufactured in England and purchased by a consumer in Spearfish, South Dakota will be included in U.S. consumption (since it was purchased by a consumer in the U.S.) But the value of the MINI Cooper needs to be excluded from U.S. GDP, since it was <u>not</u> produced in the U.S.

Below is a summary of gross domestic product and Total Expenditures for 2007:

| Total Expenditures: | |
|---|---|
| Consumption | $9,710 billion |
| Investment | 2,130 billion |
| Government Purchases | 2,675 billion |
| Net Exports | <u>-708 billion</u> |
| Gross Domestic Product | $13,807 billion |

When total output is measured as the sum of all payments to resource owners, the result is national income. National income consists of five types of payments;

1. Employee compensation
2. Proprietors' income
3. Corporate profits
4. Rental income
5. Net interest income

Typically employee compensation makes up about 65% of national income.

## Per Capita Output

When comparing different economies, per capita output numbers may be more informative than total output numbers. (Per capita means "per person".) Per capita GDP comparisons for selected countries are included in Chapter 15.

**Example 14:** India has a much larger economy than Switzerland. In 2007, India's GDP was $2,989 billion, while Switzerland's GDP was only $300 billion. But Switzerland had a much higher per capita GDP, $41,100 versus $2,700.

As mentioned earlier in this chapter, there are flaws in GDP as a measure of standard of living. Thus, there are flaws in per capita GDP as a measure of standard of living. When comparing different economies in terms of standard of living, these flaws must be kept in mind. Flaws in GDP as a measure of standard of living are discussed in an appendix at the end of the chapter.

The U.S. is a high per capita GDP country. But there is significant variation in the standard of living in the different states. In 2007, the per capita personal income in Connecticut was 88% higher than the per capita personal income in Mississippi. The table in Example 15 below shows per capita personal income for the fifty states and Washington D.C. for 2007. The information is from the Bureau of Economic Analysis.

---

**Example 15:**

## Per Capita Personal Income - 2007

| | | | |
|---|---|---|---|
| Washington D.C. | $61,092 | 25. Wisconsin | $36,047 |
| 1. Connecticut | $54,117 | 26. Michigan | $35,086 |
| 2. New Jersey | $49,194 | 27. Iowa | $35,023 |
| 3. Massachusetts | $49,082 | 28. Ohio | $34,874 |
| 4. New York | $47,385 | 29. North Dakota | $34,846 |
| 5. Maryland | $46,021 | 30. Oregon | $34,784 |
| 6. Wyoming | $43,226 | 31. Louisiana | $34,756 |
| 7. California | $41,571 | 32. Missouri | $34,389 |
| 8. New Hampshire | $41,512 | 33. Oklahoma | $34,153 |
| 9. Virginia | $41,347 | 34. South Dakota | $33,905 |
| 10. Colorado | $41,042 | 35. Maine | $33,722 |
| 11. Minnesota | $41,034 | 36. North Carolina | $33,636 |
| 12. Delaware | $40,608 | 37. Indiana | $33,616 |
| 13. Nevada | $40,480 | 38. Georgia | $33,457 |
| 14. Washington | $40,414 | 39. Tennessee | $33,280 |
| 15. Alaska | $40,352 | 40. Arizona | $33,029 |
| 16. Illinois | $40,322 | 41. Montana | $32,458 |
| 17. Rhode Island | $39,463 | 42. Alabama | $32,404 |
| 18. Hawaii | $39,239 | 43. New Mexico | $31,474 |
| 19. Pennsylvania | $38,788 | 44. Idaho | $31,197 |
| **U.S. Average** | **$38,611** | 45. Utah | $31,189 |
| 20. Florida | $38,444 | 46. Kentucky | $31,111 |
| 21. Texas | $37,187 | 47. South Carolina | $31,013 |
| 22. Kansas | $36,768 | 48. Arkansas | $30,060 |
| 23. Vermont | $36,670 | 49. West Virginia | $29,537 |
| 24. Nebraska | $36,471 | 50. Mississippi | $28,845 |

---

### Real GDP

As noted earlier in the chapter, nominal GDP numbers may change from one year to the next either because production has changed, or because of a change in the price level. If GDP numbers from different years are to be fairly compared, an adjustment must be made for changes in the price level. Nominal GDP must be adjusted to Real GDP.

**Real GDP** – GDP adjusted for changes in the price level.

> **Example 16A:** GDP in 1990 was $5,803 billion. GDP in 1991 was $5,996 billion. What was Real GDP in 1991, adjusted to the 1990 price level? CPI in 1990 was 130.7. CPI in 1991 was 136.2.
>
> Real GDP (1991) = Nominal GDP for 1991 ÷ (CPI for 1991 ÷ CPI for 1990) = $5,996B ÷ (136.2 ÷ 130.7) = $5,996B ÷ 1.0421 = $5,754B

Notice that even though nominal GDP increased from 1990 to 1991, Real GDP did not. Real GDP decreased from 1990 to 1991. The increase in nominal GDP was due solely to the increase in the price level (inflation).

> **Example 16B:** GDP in 1991 was $5,996 billion. GDP in 1992 was $6,338 billion. What was Real GDP in 1992, adjusted to the 1991 price level? CPI in 1991 was 136.2. CPI in 1992 was 140.3.
>
> Real GDP (1992) = $6,338B ÷ (140.3 ÷ 136.2) = $6,338B ÷ 1.0301 = $6,153B

In this case, the increase in nominal GDP was caused by both an increase in Real GDP and an increase in the price level.

> **Example 16C:** GDP in 1973 was $1,383 billion. GDP in 1974 was $1,500 billion. What was Real GDP in 1974, adjusted to the 1973 price level? The CPI in 1973 was 44.4. The CPI in 1974 was 49.3.
>
> Real GDP (1974) = $1,500B ÷ (49.3 ÷ 44.4) = $1,500B ÷ 1.1104 = $1,351B

In this case, even though nominal GDP increased from 1973 to 1974, Real GDP did not. Real GDP decreased from 1973 to 1974. The increase in nominal GDP was due solely to the increase in the price level (inflation).

As illustrated in the examples above, an increase in nominal GDP from one year to the next does not necessarily mean that production has increased. To determine if production has increased, we compute Real GDP.

**Absolute economic growth** refers to an increase in Real GDP. (In Chapter 14, we will distinguish between absolute economic growth and per capita economic growth.)

## The Business Cycle

Real GDP tends to behave in a cyclical manner, called the business cycle. The four phases of the business cycle are called:
1. **Expansion** - when Real GDP is increasing.
2. **Peak** - the highest phase of the business cycle.
3. **Contraction** - when Real GDP is decreasing.
4. **Trough** - the lowest phase of the business cycle.

The upturns and downturns in the business cycle are unpredictable in terms of when they will occur, how long they will last, and how severe they will be.

## Appendix: Historical Data on Nominal and Real GDP

The table below shows U.S. nominal GDP and U.S. Real GDP for the years from 1968 through 2007. Notice that nominal GDP increased by more than 15-fold over this forty year period. Real GDP increased by more than 3-fold. Information is from the Bureau of Economic Analysis.

| Year | Nominal GDP | Real GDP (2000 Base) |
|------|-------------|----------------------|
| 1968 | $910 billion | $3,653 billion |
| 1969 | 985 billion | 3,765 billion |
| 1970 | 1,039 billion | 3,772 billion |
| 1971 | 1,127 billion | 3,899 billion |
| 1972 | 1,238 billion | 4,105 billion |
| 1973 | 1,383 billion | 4,342 billion |
| 1974 | 1,500 billion | 4,320 billion |
| 1975 | 1,638 billion | 4,311 billion |
| 1976 | 1,825 billion | 4,541 billion |
| 1977 | 2,031 billion | 4,751 billion |
| 1978 | 2,295 billion | 5,015 billion |
| 1979 | 2,563 billion | 5,173 billion |
| 1980 | 2,790 billion | 5,162 billion |
| 1981 | 3,128 billion | 5,292 billion |
| 1982 | 3,255 billion | 5,189 billion |
| 1983 | 3,537 billion | 5,424 billion |
| 1984 | 3,933 billion | 5,814 billion |
| 1985 | 4,220 billion | 6,054 billion |
| 1986 | 4,463 billion | 6,264 billion |
| 1987 | 4,740 billion | 6,475 billion |
| 1988 | 5,104 billion | 6,743 billion |
| 1989 | 5,484 billion | 6,981 billion |
| 1990 | 5,803 billion | 7,113 billion |
| 1991 | 5,996 billion | 7,101 billion |
| 1992 | 6,338 billion | 7,337 billion |
| 1993 | 6,657 billion | 7,533 billion |
| 1994 | 7,072 billion | 7,836 billion |
| 1995 | 7,398 billion | 8,032 billion |
| 1996 | 7,817 billion | 8,329 billion |
| 1997 | 8,304 billion | 8,704 billion |
| 1998 | 8,747 billion | 9,067 billion |
| 1999 | 9,268 billion | 9,470 billion |
| 2000 | 9,817 billion | 9,817 billion |
| 2001 | 10,128 billion | 9,891 billion |
| 2002 | 10,470 billion | 10,049 billion |
| 2003 | 10,961 billion | 10,301 billion |
| 2004 | 11,686 billion | 10,676 billion |
| 2005 | 12,422 billion | 10,990 billion |
| 2006 | 13,178 billion | 11,295 billion |
| 2007 | 13,807 billion | 11,524 billion |

## Appendix: The Three Macroeconomic Goals and the U.S. Economy

Three macroeconomic goals that societies wish to achieve are price level stability, full employment, and economic growth. A nation's success in achieving these three goals is measured by the nation's inflation rate, unemployment rate, and Real GDP growth rate. The table below indicates these three rates for the U.S. economy for selected years.

| Year | Inflation Rate | Unemployment Rate | Real GDP Growth Rate |
|------|----------------|-------------------|----------------------|
| 1929 | 0% | 3.2% | 6.5% |
| 1930 | -2.3 | 8.7 | -8.6 |
| 1931 | -9.0 | 15.9 | -6.4 |
| 1932 | -9.9 | 23.6 | -13.0 |
| 1933 | -5.1 | 24.9 | -1.4 |
| 1941 | 5.0 | 9.9 | 17.1 |
| 1942 | 10.9 | 4.7 | 18.4 |
| 1943 | 6.1 | 1.9 | 16.5 |
| 1944 | 1.7 | 1.2 | 8.1 |
| 1945 | 2.3 | 1.9 | -1.1 |
| 1946 | 8.3 | 3.9 | -11.0 |
| 1947 | 14.4 | 3.9 | -0.9 |
| 1965 | 1.3 | 5.2 | 6.4 |
| 1966 | 1.6 | 4.5 | 6.6 |
| 1967 | 2.9 | 3.8 | 2.5 |
| 1973 | 6.2 | 4.9 | 5.8 |
| 1974 | 11.0 | 5.6 | -0.6 |
| 1975 | 9.1 | 8.5 | -0.4 |
| 1980 | 13.5 | 7.1 | -0.2 |
| 1981 | 10.3 | 7.6 | 2.5 |
| 1982 | 6.2 | 9.7 | -2.0 |
| 1983 | 3.2 | 9.6 | 4.3 |
| 1984 | 4.3 | 7.5 | 7.3 |
| 1990 | 5.4 | 5.6 | 1.8 |
| 1991 | 4.7 | 6.8 | -0.5 |
| 1992 | 3.0 | 7.5 | 3.0 |
| 2001 | 2.8 | 4.8 | 0.3 |
| 2002 | 1.6 | 5.8 | 2.0 |
| 2003 | 2.3 | 6.0 | 3.5 |
| 2004 | 2.7 | 5.5 | 4.4 |
| 2005 | 3.4 | 5.1 | 3.5 |
| 2006 | 3.2 | 4.6 | 2.6 |
| 2007 | 2.8 | 4.6 | 2.2 |

## Appendix: Circular Flow Diagram

Total output produced in the economy can be measured by adding up the Total Expenditures on final goods and services, or by adding up the payments to the resource owners who provided the resources to produce the final goods and services. A simple circular flow diagram illustrates the flow of goods and services through product markets and the flow of resources through resource markets.

Measuring Total Output:  GDP

The simple circular flow diagram below illustrates the interactions between households and firms through product markets and resource markets. The outer flow on the diagram depicts the physical flow of resources and products. The inner flow on the diagram depicts the payments flow.

Examining the physical flow first, households provide resources (labor, land, capital, and entrepreneurship) to firms through resource markets. The firms use the resources to produce goods and services, which they provide to the households through product markets.

Moving in the opposite direction of the physical flow is the payments flow. Firms pay for the resources purchased through resource markets by making resource payments (wages, rent, interest, and profits). The resource payments are household income to the households. The households use their income to consume goods and services. The consumption spending is revenue for the firms. The firms use their revenue to purchase more resources. And the circular flow continues.

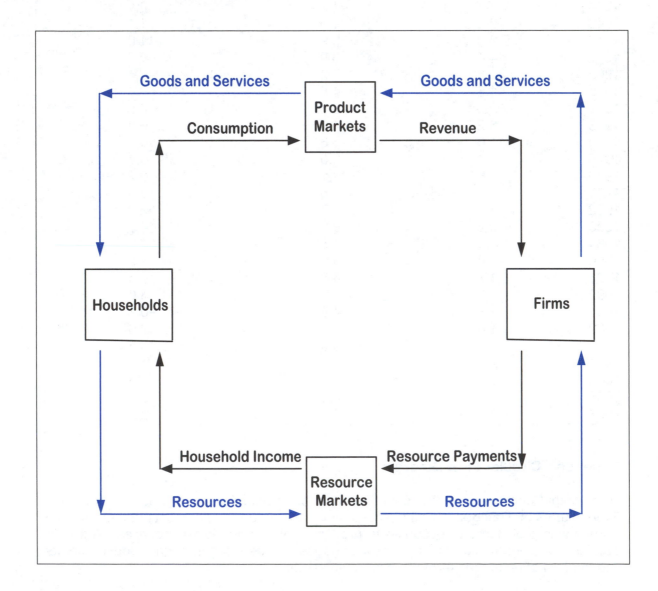

## Appendix:  Flaws in GDP as a Measure of Standard of Living

Gross domestic product (GDP) measures the market value of all final goods and services produced annually.  As such, GDP, particularly when stated on a per capita basis, is considered a measure of a nation's standard of living.  (See the table on page 15-4 for a listing of selected countries in order of per capita GDP.)

As a measure of standard of living, GDP contains a number of flaws, including:

**1.  GDP does not include nonmarket production.**  Nonmarket production (e.g. do-it-yourself) can be very valuable and has a strong impact on a nation's standard of living.  But nonmarket production is not included in GDP.  GDP comparisons between a nation that has a relatively large amount of nonmarket production and a nation that has relatively little nonmarket production will be misleading.

Nonmarket production is typically a larger share of total output in less developed countries than in developed countries.  Comparisons of GDP between developed countries and less developed countries will thus tend to overstate the difference in standard of living.

**2.  GDP does not include underground (unreported) production.**  Production that is unreported for tax evasion purposes is nonetheless valuable production that increases a nation's standard of living.  And production that is unreported because it is illegal also has a market value and arguably increases a nation's standard of living.

Underground production is typically a larger share of total output in less developed countries than in developed countries.  Comparisons of GDP between developed countries and less developed countries will thus tend to overstate the difference in standard of living.

> **Example 17:**  In "An International Comparison of Underground Economic Activity", Friedrich Schneider and Christopher Bajada estimated that the underground economy for the generally developed countries of the Organisation for Economic Co-operation and Development averaged 16.3% of GDP in 2002/2003.  For the generally less developed countries of Central America and South America, the underground economy averaged 43.4% of GDP.  For the generally less developed countries of Africa, the underground economy averaged 43.2% of GDP.

**3.  GDP does not include differences in leisure time.**  Leisure time affects a nation's standard of living.  But leisure time is not included in GDP.

Leisure time is typically greater in less developed countries than in developed countries.  Comparisons of GDP between developed countries and less developed countries will thus tend to overstate the difference in standard of living.

**4.  GDP does not adjust for economic bads.**  An economic bad could actually increase GDP.  The damage done by an industrial accident or a flood would not be deducted from GDP, but the market value of the production necessary to repair and replace damaged property would add to GDP.  Economic bads detract from a nation's standard of living.

## Questions for Chapter 5

### Fill-in-the-blanks:

1.  Gross _____ _____ is the market value of all
    final goods and services produced annually.

2.  A(n) _____ good is an input in the production of another good.

3.  _____ _____ are transfers of income from the
    government to households or businesses, not in exchange for goods, services, or
    resources.

4.  _____ is the acquisition of new physical capital.

5.  _____ is total foreign purchases of domestic goods.

6.  _____ is total domestic purchases of foreign goods.

7.  _____ GDP is GDP adjusted for changes in the price level.

8.  Absolute _____ _____ refers to an increase
    in Real GDP.


### Multiple Choice:

_____ 1. Which of the following would directly affect GDP?
   - a. A refinery buys crude oil
   - b. A refinery takes out a large loan from a bank
   - c. A refinery emits pollution into the air
   - d. None of the above

_____ 2. For GDP purposes, which of the following would be investment spending?
   - a. Warren buys 100 shares of common stock for $6,000
   - b. Charlie buys a used lawn mower for his lawn service business
   - c. Lynda buys a new display case for her jewelry store
   - d. All of the above

_____ 3. Which of the following would directly affect GDP?
   - a. Aunt Lucille receives her Social Security check
   - b. Aunt Lucille spends all day Saturday cleaning her house
   - c. Aunt Lucille's house is destroyed by a tornado
   - d. None of the above

_____ 4. Which of the following statements is false?
   - a. Investment does not include new residential housing
   - b. Consumption is the largest component of GDP
   - c. Government purchases does not include transfer payments
   - d. Net exports equals exports minus imports

_____ 5. When total output is measured as the sum of all payments to resource owners, the result is:
   a. Gross Domestic Product
   b. National Income
   c. Gross National Product
   d. Gross Resource Product

_____ 6. Of Arizona, Colorado, Minnesota, and North Carolina, the state with the highest per capita personal income in 2007 was:
   a. Arizona
   b. Colorado
   c. Minnesota
   d. North Carolina

_____ 7. Of Georgia, Oklahoma, South Dakota, and Virginia, the state with the lowest per capita personal income in 2007 was:
   a. Georgia
   b. Oklahoma
   c. South Dakota
   d. Virginia

_____ 8. Nominal GDP may increase:
   a. if there is an increase in the price level
   b. if there is an increase in production
   c. even if Real GDP decreases
   d. All of the above

_____ 9. In 1950, GDP was $294B and the CPI was 24.1. In 1951, GDP was $340B and the CPI was 26.0. Real GDP for 1951, adjusted to the 1950 price level, would be.
   a. $294B
   b. $315B
   c. $340B
   d. $367B

_____ 10. Using the same information as question 9., what was Real GDP for 1950, adjusted to the 1951 price level?
   a. $272B
   b. $294B
   c. $317B
   d. $367B

_____ 11. Referring to the table on page 5-8, between 1990 and 2000:
   a. Nominal GDP in the U.S. increased by 56%
   b. Real GDP in the U.S. increased by 38%
   c  Both of the above
   d. Neither of the above

_____ 12. The phase of the business cycle when Real GDP is increasing is called:
  a. Trough
  b. Peak
  c. Expansion
  d. Contraction

_____ 13. In which of the following years was the inflation rate the highest?
  a. 1933
  b. 1975
  c. 1980
  d. 1990

_____ 14. In which of the following years was the unemployment rate the lowest?
  a. 1930
  b. 1965
  c. 1973
  d. 2006

_____ 15. In which of the following years was the Real GDP growth rate the highest?
  a. 1966
  b. 1973
  c. 1984
  d. 2004

_____ 16. On a simple circular flow diagram:
  a. firms provide resources
  b. firms pay for resources by making resource payments
  c. Both of the above
  d. Neither of the above

## Problems:

1. Explain what an intermediate good is and why intermediate goods are excluded from GDP.

2. Explain what nonproduction transactions are and list three examples.

3. List the four types of spending making up Total Expenditures.

4. Explain why it is necessary to compute Real GDP in order to get a fair comparison of GDP numbers from different years.

5. In 1931, GDP was $77B and the CPI was 15.2. In 1932, GDP was $59B and the CPI was 13.7. What was Real GDP for 1932, adjusted to the 1931 price level?

6. List four flaws in GDP as a measure of standard of living.

## Answers for Chapter 5

**Fill-in-the-blanks:**
1. domestic product
2. intermediate
3. Transfer payments
4. Investment
5. Exports
6. Imports
7. Real
8. economic growth

**Multiple Choice:**
1. d.
2. c.
3. d.
4. a.
5. b.
6. b.
7. a.
8. d.
9. b.
10. c.
11. b.
12. c.
13. c.
14. d.
15. c.
16. b.

## Problems:

1. An intermediate good has not yet reached its final user, but rather is an input in the production of another good. If intermediate goods were included in GDP, they would overstate GDP by double counting.

2. Nonproduction transactions are transactions that do <u>not</u> directly result in production. Examples include:
   (1) Used goods
   (2) Financial transactions
   (3) Transfer payments

3. Total Expenditures consists of four types of spending:
   (1) Consumption
   (2) Investment
   (3) Government purchases
   (4) Net exports

4. Nominal GDP numbers may change from one year to the next either because production has changed, or because of a change in the price level. If GDP numbers from different years are to be fairly compared, an adjustment must be made for changes in the price level. Nominal GDP must be adjusted to Real GDP.

5. Real GDP (1932) = $59 billion ÷ (13.7 ÷ 15.2) = $59 billion ÷ .9013 = $65 billion

6. As a measure of standard of living, GDP contains a number of flaws, including:
   (1) GDP does not include nonmarket production.
   (2) GDP does not include underground (unreported) production.
   (3) GDP does not include differences in leisure time.
   (4) GDP does not adjust for economic bads.

# Chapter 6 The Aggregate Market

Three macroeconomic goals that societies wish to achieve are price level stability, full employment, and economic growth. The macroeconomic measurements of these goals are price level, unemployment rate, and Real GDP. Price level, unemployment rate, and Real GDP are determined by the interaction of total spending and total production in the overall economy (aggregate market).

In Chapter 3, we saw that the equilibrium price and the equilibrium quantity for an individual good (like donuts) are determined by demand and supply in the market for that good. In the overall economy, the equilibrium price level and the equilibrium quantity of Real GDP are determined by aggregate demand and aggregate supply in the aggregate market.

## Aggregate Demand

In the aggregate (overall) market, the demand side of the market is called aggregate demand.

**Aggregate demand** – the quantity demanded of all goods and services at different price levels.

The aggregate demand curve (AD) indicates an inverse relationship between the price level and the quantity demanded of Real GDP. This inverse relationship results in a downward sloping AD curve, as illustrated on the aggregate market graph below. (For an explanation of why the AD curve is downward sloping, see the appendix at the end of the chapter.)

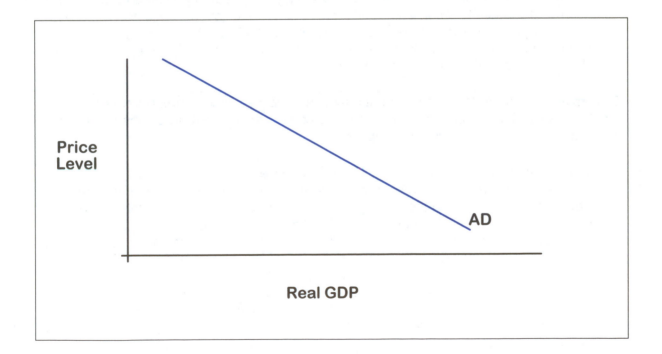

## Shifts in the Aggregate Demand Curve

The aggregate demand curve shifts in response to a change in Total Expenditures. An increase in Total Expenditures will cause an increase in aggregate demand (the AD curve shifts to the right). A decrease in Total Expenditures will cause a decrease in aggregate demand (the AD curve shifts to the left).

As first explained in Chapter 5, Total Expenditures consists of four types of spending; consumption, investment, government purchases, and net exports. The factors that affect each of these four types of spending are discussed below:

1. **Consumption.** Consumption spending is affected by;

   **a. Wealth.** An increase in household wealth will lead to an increase in consumption. A decrease in household wealth will lead to a decrease in consumption.

   **Example 1A:** An increase in stock market prices would increase household wealth, which would increase consumption. A decrease in stock market prices would decrease household wealth, which would decrease consumption.

   **b. Interest rates.** If interest rates decrease, consumption will increase, particularly consumption of durable goods (like automobiles). If interest rates increase, consumption will decrease.

   **Example 1B:** The Federal Reserve Board of Governors (see Chapter 11) decides to increase the money supply in order to decrease interest rates. The lower interest rates cause an increase in consumption.

   **c. Taxes.** We will see in Chapter 8 that consumption is directly related to disposable income. Disposable income is household income after taxes. A decrease in taxes leaves households with more disposable income, which leads to an increase in consumption. An increase in taxes leaves households with less disposable income, which leads to a decrease in consumption.

   **Example 1C:** The federal government enacts a temporary income tax rebate (during an election year). The decrease in income taxes causes an increase in disposable income which leads to an increase in consumption.

   Consumption spending will also be affected by a change in national income. A change in national income will <u>not</u> cause a shift in the aggregate demand curve, but rather a movement along the aggregate demand curve. A change in national income would also mean a change in Real GDP. An increase or a decrease in Real GDP would cause a movement along the aggregate demand curve, not a shift in the curve.

2. **Investment.** Businesses invest in new physical capital in order to increase profits. The investment decision requires a comparison of two percentage rates. One is the expected rate of return on the investment. The other is the interest rate paid to finance the investment.

If the expected rate of return exceeds the interest rate, the investment will add to profits and thus should be made. If the expected rate of return is less than the interest rate, the investment will decrease profits and should <u>not</u> be made.

The expected rate of return on investment is calculated as the additional annual profits expected from the investment divided by the cost of the investment.

---

**Example 2A:** Wenona's Widgets, Inc. can invest in new equipment which costs $12,000,000 and is expected to generate additional annual profits of $900,000. The interest rate to finance the investment is 6%. Should Wenona's make the investment?

**Rate of return = Additional Annual Profits ÷ Cost of the Investment** = $900,000 ÷ $12,000,000 = .075 or 7.5%

Since the expected rate of return (7.5%) exceeds the interest rate (6%), yes, Wenona's should make the investment.

---

**Example 2B:** Assume the same facts as Example 2A, except that Wenona's has become less optimistic about future returns. Now only $600,000 in additional annual profits is expected from the investment in new equipment. Should Wenona's make the investment?

Rate of return = $600,000 ÷ $12,000,000 = .05 or 5%

Since the expected rate of return (5%) is less than the interest rate (6%), no, Wenona's should <u>not</u> make the investment.

---

**Example 2C:** Assume the same facts as Example 2A, except that Wenona's now has to pay an interest rate of 9% to finance the investment. Should Wenona's make the investment?

Rate of return = $900,000 ÷ $12,000,000 = .075 or 7.5%

Since the expected rate of return (7.5%) is less than the interest rate (9%), no, Wenona's should <u>not</u> make the investment.

---

As seen in the examples above, the two factors that affect investment spending are:

a. **Expectations about future returns.** If businesses become more optimistic about future returns, investment spending will increase. If businesses become more pessimistic about future returns, investment spending will decrease.

b. **Interest rates.** If interest rates decrease, investment spending will increase. If interest rates increase, investment spending will decrease.

3. **Government purchases.** The amount of government purchases is determined through the political process.

> **Example 3:** If the federal government decides to increase military spending, or if state governments decide to provide more funding for education, or if local governments decide to increase funding for police and fire protection, government purchases will increase.

4. **Net exports.** Net exports (exports minus imports) will change if there is a change in foreign Real GDP or if there is a change in the exchange rate for a nation's currency. More specifically;

   **a. A change in foreign Real GDP.** Net exports will increase if there is an increase in foreign Real GDP. If U.S. trading partners experience economic growth, they will consume more U.S. exports. Conversely, net exports will decrease if there is a decrease in foreign Real GDP. If U.S. trading partners experience economic recession, they will consume less U.S. exports.

> **Example 4A:** The largest trading partner for the U.S. is Canada. If the Canadian economy is growing rapidly, Canadian demand for U.S. exports will increase. If the Canadian economy falls into recession, Canadian demand for U.S. exports will decrease.

   **b. A change in the exchange rate for a nation's currency.** The exchange rate is the value of one nation's currency in terms of another nation's currency. For example, on December 2, 2008, one U.S. dollar would exchange for 1.2436 Canadian dollars.

   If the exchange rate for the U.S. dollar depreciates (decreases relative to other currencies), U.S. exports will be cheaper and imports to the U.S. will be more expensive. Thus, net exports will increase if the exchange rate for the dollar depreciates.

   If the exchange rate for the U.S. dollar appreciates (increases relative to other currencies), U.S. exports will be more expensive and imports to the U.S. will be cheaper. Thus, net exports will decrease if the exchange rate for the dollar appreciates.

> **Example 4B:** If the U.S. dollar depreciates versus the Canadian dollar, U.S. exports to Canada would increase and U.S. imports from Canada would decrease. If the U.S. dollar appreciates versus the Canadian dollar, U.S. exports to Canada would decrease and U.S. imports from Canada would increase.

Another factor that can affect aggregate demand is the money supply. In the long run, aggregate demand tends to be closely related to the money supply. The money supply will be discussed in later chapters.

## Aggregate Supply

In the aggregate market, the supply side of the market is called aggregate supply.

**Aggregate supply** – the quantity supplied of all goods and services at different price levels.

In looking at aggregate supply, we make a distinction between short-run aggregate supply and long-run aggregate supply. For now, we focus on short-run aggregate supply.

The short-run aggregate supply curve (SRAS) indicates a direct relationship between the price level and the quantity supplied of Real GDP. This direct relationship results in an upward sloping SRAS curve as illustrated on the graph below. (For an explanation of why the SRAS curve is upward sloping, see the appendix at the end of the chapter.)

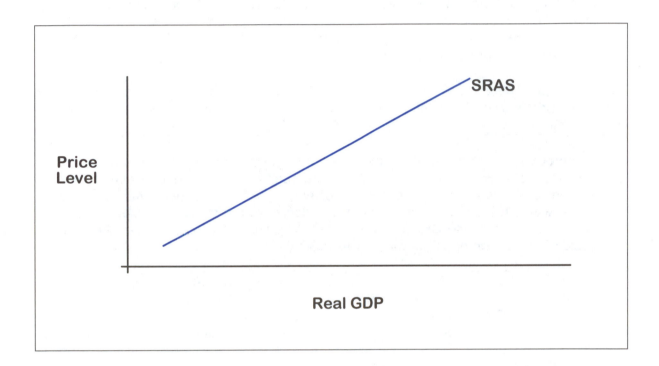

### Shifts in the SRAS Curve

Remember from Chapter 3 that the determinant of supply for a good is the cost of production. A change in the cost of producing a good causes a shift in the supply curve for that good.

Likewise, the determinant of short-run aggregate supply is the <u>overall</u> costs of production. The short-run aggregate supply curve shifts in response to changes in the overall costs of production in the economy.

An increase in the overall costs of production will cause a decrease in short-run aggregate supply (the SRAS curve will shift to the left). A decrease in the overall costs of production will cause an increase in short-run aggregate supply (the SRAS curve will shift to the right).

The overall costs of production will change due to the following factors. Thus, these four factors cause the SRAS curve to shift:

1. **Wage rates.** Labor costs are usually the largest single cost of production. An increase in wage rates in the economy will increase the overall costs of production and thus will decrease SRAS. A decrease in wage rates will increase SRAS.

**Example 5A:** The economy falls into a severe recession with high unemployment. Workers find that they must accept lower wage rates to find employment. The decreasing wage rates cause the SRAS curve to shift to the right.

2. **Prices of nonlabor inputs.** Nonlabor inputs are all inputs to production other than labor. An increase in the prices of nonlabor inputs (e.g. rent, utilities, insurance, fuel, etc.) will increase the overall costs of production and thus will decrease SRAS. A decrease in the prices of nonlabor inputs will increase SRAS.

**Example 5B:** The price of crude oil increases by 40%. The increase in the price of this important nonlabor input will cause an increase in the overall costs of production and a decrease in SRAS.

3. **Productivity.** **Productivity** is measured by the output produced per unit of input. An increase in productivity means that more output can be produced with the same amount of input, or the same amount of output can be produced with less input. Either way, an increase in productivity will decrease the overall costs of production and thus will increase SRAS. A decrease in productivity will increase the overall costs of production and thus will decrease SRAS.

**Example 5C:** According to the Bureau of Labor Statistics, between 1987 and 2005, U.S. labor productivity increased in 85 out of the 86 detailed manufacturing industries studied by the BLS. The most rapid productivity growth (an average of 24.6 percent per year) occurred in computer and peripheral equipment. Unit labor costs in computer and peripheral equipment fell by an average of 18.2 percent per year. Productivity increased by an average of 19.0 percent per year in semiconductors and electronic components and unit labor costs in that industry fell by an average of 13.1 percent per year. For computer and electronic products in general, labor productivity increased by an average of 13.1 percent per year and unit labor costs fell by an average of 8.7 percent per year.

4. **Supply shocks.** Unusual events that affect the overall costs of production are called supply shocks. An adverse supply shock (e.g. unusually bad weather) will increase the overall costs of production and thus will decrease SRAS. A beneficial supply shock (e.g. unusually good weather) will decrease the overall costs of production and thus will increase SRAS.

**Example 5D:** Unusually poor weather for growing corn caused U.S. corn yields per acre to decrease by 29% in 1988 compared to 1987. As a result, corn prices increased by 31%. Unusually favorable weather caused corn yields per acre to increase by 13% in 2004 compared to 2003. As a result, corn prices decreased by 15%.

### Short-Run Equilibrium: Putting AD and SRAS Together

The interaction of aggregate demand and short-run aggregate supply determines short-run equilibrium in the economy.  Short-run equilibrium will determine the price level and Real GDP for the economy, as illustrated on the aggregate market graph in Example 6.

**Example 6:**

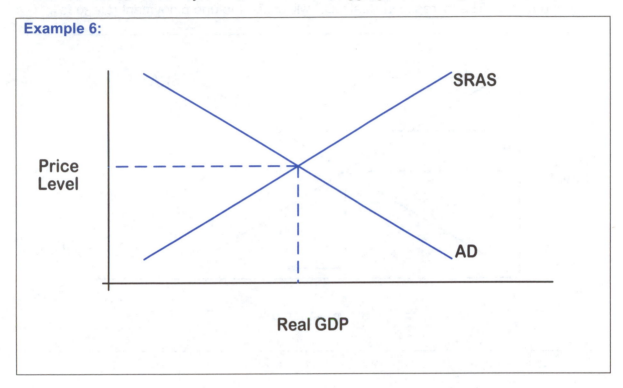

The graph in Example 6 above does <u>not</u> show the unemployment rate.  But we can make assumptions about changes in the unemployment rate based on changes in Real GDP.  If Real GDP increases, we would expect the unemployment rate to fall.  More output would require more workers.  If Real GDP decreases, we would expect the unemployment rate to rise.  Less output would require fewer workers.

### Changes in AD and SRAS

Changes in aggregate demand and short-run aggregate supply will result in a new equilibrium.  The price level, Real GDP, and the unemployment rate will change.  The table below shows the four possible changes in AD and SRAS, and the effect of each change on the price level, Real GDP, and the unemployment rate.  Then each of the four possible changes is discussed and illustrated on graphs.

| Change | Price Level | Real GDP | Unemployment Rate |
|---|---|---|---|
| AD increases | increases | increases | decreases |
| AD decreases | decreases | decreases | increases |
| SRAS increases | decreases | increases | decreases |
| SRAS decreases | increases | decreases | increases |

1.  **Increase in AD.**  An increase in AD is caused by an increase in Total Expenditures (consumption, investment, government purchases, and net exports).  The factors that cause a change in Total Expenditures were discussed earlier in the chapter.  If AD increases, the economy will reach a new short-run equilibrium at a higher price level and a greater quantity of Real GDP.  This is illustrated on the aggregate market graph below.  The increase in Real GDP will cause the unemployment rate to fall.

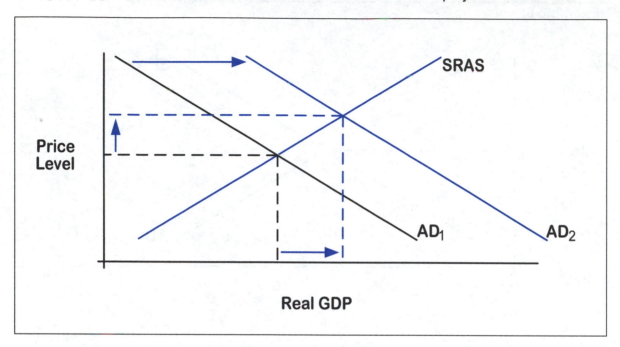

2.  **Decrease in AD.**  A decrease in AD is caused by a decrease in Total Expenditures.  If AD decreases, the economy will reach a new short-run equilibrium at a lower price level and a lesser quantity of Real GDP.  This is illustrated on the aggregate market graph below.  The decrease in Real GDP will cause the unemployment rate to rise.

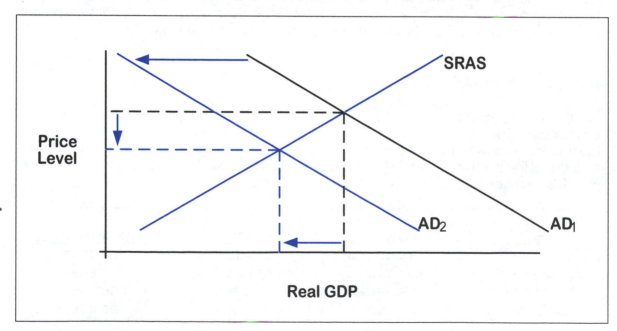

3. **Increase in SRAS.** An increase in SRAS is caused by a decrease in the overall costs of production. The factors that cause a change in the overall costs of production were discussed earlier in the chapter. If SRAS increases, the economy will reach a new short-run equilibrium at a lower price level and a greater quantity of Real GDP. This is illustrated on the aggregate market graph below. The increase in Real GDP will cause the unemployment rate to fall.

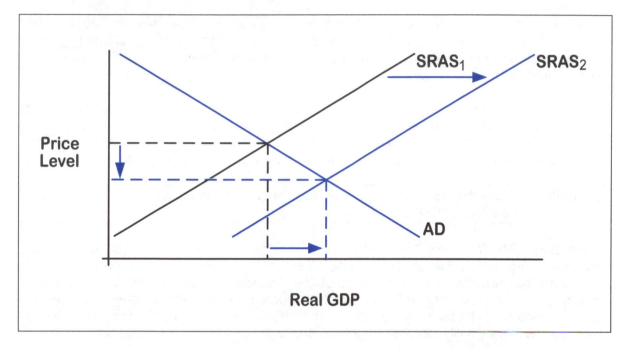

4. **Decrease in SRAS.** A decrease in SRAS is caused by an increase in the overall costs of production. If SRAS decreases, the economy will reach a new short-run equilibrium at a higher price level and a lesser quantity of Real GDP. This is illustrated on the aggregate market graph below. The decrease in Real GDP will cause the unemployment rate to rise.

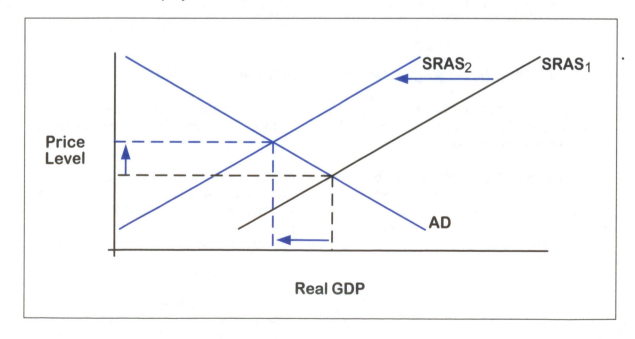

The Aggregate Market

## Appendix: Why Increasing SRAS Has <u>Not</u> Led to a Lower Price Level

Labor productivity in the U.S. economy has generally been increasing. (For instance, see Example 5C earlier in this Chapter.) As labor productivity increases, the overall costs of production decrease and the SRAS curve shifts to the right. This should lead to an increase in Real GDP and to a decrease in the price level.

Real GDP has been increasing. The table on page 5-8 indicates that Real GDP increased by more than 3-fold between 1968 and 2007. But the price level has <u>not</u> been decreasing. Between 1968 and 2007, the Consumer Price Index increased by almost 6-fold. (See the table on page 4-3.)

Why hasn't increasing SRAS led to a lower price level? The price level depends on both SRAS and AD. While the SRAS curve has been shifting to the right, the AD curve has been shifting to the right even faster, causing the price level to rise. The AD curve has been shifting rapidly to the right because the money supply has been increasing.

> **Example 7:** According to the Federal Reserve Board, the money supply (M1) increased by over 7-fold between 1968 and 2007.

Increasing SRAS may not have led to a lower price level, but it has caused goods to become more affordable to the average American household. The percentage of American households that own automobiles, televisions, air conditioners, washing machines, etc. is much higher than it was forty years ago. And even though the nominal price of food and shelter may be much higher than it was years ago, food and shelter have grown increasingly more affordable for the average American household.

> **Example 8:** The percentage of disposable income the average American household spends on food fell from about 25% at the end of World War II to less than 10% today. The percentage of Americans who own their own homes is higher today than it was forty years ago. And the average home today is significantly larger and better equipped than the average home of forty years ago.

## Appendix: Why the Aggregate Demand Curve Slopes Downward

The aggregate demand curve indicates an inverse relationship between the price level and the quantity demanded of Real GDP. Economists have identified three causes of this inverse relationship:

**1. The wealth (real balance) effect.** This is similar to the income effect discussed in Chapter 3. When the price level decreases, consumers are wealthier (their money holdings have more buying power). This means that consumers can afford to buy a greater quantity of goods and services as the price level decreases. This increase in consumption as the price level decreases will cause the aggregate demand curve to be downward sloping.

**2. The interest rate effect.** When the price level decreases, the demand for money will decrease (as households need less money to make their normal purchases). The decrease in the demand for money will cause interest rates to decrease. As discussed earlier in this chapter, lower interest rates will cause increased consumption (particularly of durable goods) and will cause increased investment. The increases in consumption and investment as the price level decreases will cause the aggregate demand curve to be downward sloping.

**3. The exchange rate effect.** As discussed above, when the price level decreases, interest rates will decrease. Lower interest rates in the U.S. will cause depreciation in the exchange rate for the dollar (see Chapter 16). As discussed earlier in this chapter, if the exchange rate for the dollar depreciates, net exports will increase. The increase in net exports as the price level decreases will cause the aggregate demand curve to be downward sloping.

## Appendix: Why the Short-Run Aggregate Supply Curve Slopes Upward

The short-run aggregate supply curve indicates a direct relationship between the price level and the quantity supplied of Real GDP. Economists have identified three causes of this direct relationship.

**1. Sticky-wage effect.** Wages in a market economy can be slow to adjust (especially downward). This stickiness is due to such factors as long-term labor contracts, labor unions, and general employee resistance to wage cuts.

If the price level decreases and nominal wages do <u>not</u> decrease, real wage rates will be higher. The increase in real wage rates will cause employers to employ less labor and produce less output. The decrease in output due to sticky wages as the price level decreases will cause the short-run aggregate supply curve to be upward sloping.

**2. Sticky-price effect.** Prices in a market economy can be slow to adjust (especially downward). This stickiness is due to such factors as menu costs (the costs to producers of changing the prices on their menus, catalogs, etc.) and producer concern about consumer reaction to rising prices in the future.

If the price level decreases and nominal prices do <u>not</u> decrease, real prices will be higher. The increase in real prices will cause a decrease in sales. As sales decline, producers will produce less output. The decrease in output as the price level decreases will cause the short-run aggregate supply curve to be upward sloping.

**3. Misperception effect.** If the price level changes, both workers and producers may misperceive the effect of the change in the price level.

If the price level decreases, workers may perceive a decrease in their nominal wages as a decrease in real wages. Thus, workers may decrease the amount of labor supplied. If the price level decreases, producers may perceive a decrease in their nominal prices as a decrease in real prices and thus reduce the amount of output produced. The decrease in output as the price level decreases due to the misperceptions of workers and producers will cause the short-run aggregate supply curve to be upward sloping.

## Questions for Chapter 6

### Fill-in-the-blanks:

1. _____ demand is the quantity demanded of all goods and services at different price levels.

2. _____ supply is the quantity supplied of all goods and services at different price levels.

3. _____ is measured by the output produced per unit of input.

### Multiple Choice:

_____ 1. Consumption will increase if:
    a. household wealth increases
    b. interest rates decrease
    c. taxes are decreased
    d. All of the above

_____ 2. An investment will be made:
    a. if the expected rate of return equals the interest rate
    b. if the expected rate of return is less than the interest rate
    c. if the expected rate of return is greater than the interest rate

_____ 3. DEF Company can invest in new machinery which costs $500,000 and will generate additional annual profits of $40,000. The rate of return is:
    a. $40,000
    b. 12.5%
    c. 8%
    d. 4%

_____ 4. Investment spending will increase if:
    a. businesses become more optimistic about future returns
    b. interest rates increase
    c. Both of the above
    d. Neither of the above

_____ 5. If the federal government increases its spending on the interstate highway system:
    a. Total Expenditures will decrease
    b. Total Expenditures will increase
    c. Aggregate demand will increase
    d. Both b. and c. above

_____ 6. Net exports will increase if:
    a. there is an increase in foreign Real GDP
    b. the exchange rate for the dollar depreciates
    c. Both of the above
    d. Neither of the above

_____ 7. Which of the following will cause net exports to increase?
   a. the U.S. dollar appreciates versus the Canadian dollar
   b. the economy of Canada grows rapidly
   c. Both of the above
   d. Neither of the above

_____ 8. A decrease in aggregate demand could be caused by:
   a. an increase in tax rates that decreases disposable income
   b. an increase in interest rates that decreases investment
   c. an appreciation in the exchange rate for the dollar that decreases net exports
   d. All of the above

_____ 9. The short-run aggregate supply curve shifts in response to a change in:
   a. wage rates
   b. consumption
   c. net exports
   d. All of the above

_____ 10. A decrease in short-run aggregate supply could be caused by:
   a. an increase in wage rates
   b. a decrease in the prices of nonlabor inputs
   c. an increase in productivity
   d. All of the above

_____ 11. An adverse supply shock would cause:
   a. AD to increase, leading to a higher price level
   b. AD to decrease, leading to a lower price level
   c. SRAS to decrease, leading to a higher price level
   d. SRAS to increase, leading to a lower price level

_____ 12. Decreases in AD tend to cause:
   a. the price level to increase
   b. Real GDP to decrease
   c. the unemployment rate to decrease
   d. Both b. and c. above

_____ 13. Increases in SRAS tend to cause:
   a. the price level to increase
   b. Real GDP to increase
   c. the unemployment rate to increase
   d. Both b. and c. above

_____ 14. As labor productivity in the U.S. has increased over the last forty years:
   a. the price level has decreased
   b. goods have become more affordable to the average American
   c. Both of the above
   d. Neither of the above

_____ 15. When the price level decreases, consumers find that their money holdings have more buying power. This is the:
   a. exchange rate effect
   b. wealth effect
   c. interest rate effect
   d. misperception effect

_____ 16. As the price level decreases:
   a. the demand for money will decrease
   b. interest rates will decrease
   c. consumption and investment will increase
   d. All of the above

_____ 17. When the price level decreases,
   a. wages will always adjust quickly downward to maintain full employment
   b. nominal wages may not adjust downward causing real wage rates to increase
   c. producers will always realize that their real prices have not fallen, and thus they will continue to produce the same amount of output
   d. All of the above

**Problems:**

1. RST Company has an opportunity to invest in new equipment which costs $800,000 and will generate additional annual profits of $76,000. The market interest rate is 8%.
   a. What is the expected rate of return on this investment?
   b. Should RST Company invest in this new equipment?

2. List and explain the two factors that will cause net exports to increase.

3. On the graph below, illustrate the effect of a decrease in government purchases on the Price Level and on the quantity of Real GDP.

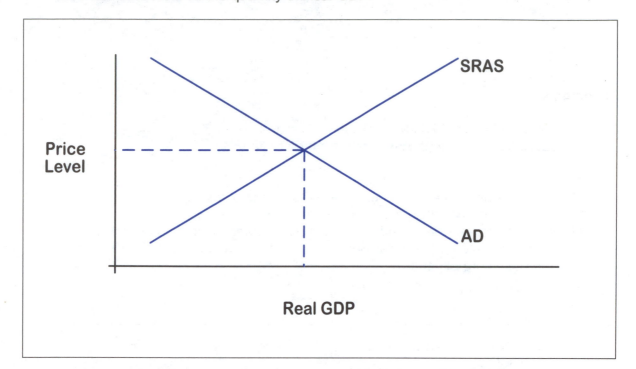

4. Explain the misperception effect.

**Multiple Choice:**

| | | |
|---|---|---|
| 1. d. | 7. b. | 13. b. |
| 2. c. | 8. d. | 14. b. |
| 3. c. | 9. a. | 15. b. |
| 4. a. | 10. a. | 16. d. |
| 5. d. | 11. c. | 17. b. |
| 6. c. | 12. b. | |

**Problems:**

1.  a. Rate of Return = $76,000 ÷ $800,000 = .095 or 9.5%
    b. Yes, Rate of Return (9.5%) exceeds interest rate (8%)

2.  Net exports will increase:
    (1) If there is an increase in foreign Real GDP. If U.S. trading partners experience economic growth, they will consume more U.S. exports.
    (2) If the exchange rate for the U.S. dollar depreciates. Depreciation in the exchange rate for the dollar would make U.S. exports cheaper and imports to the U.S. more expensive.

3.

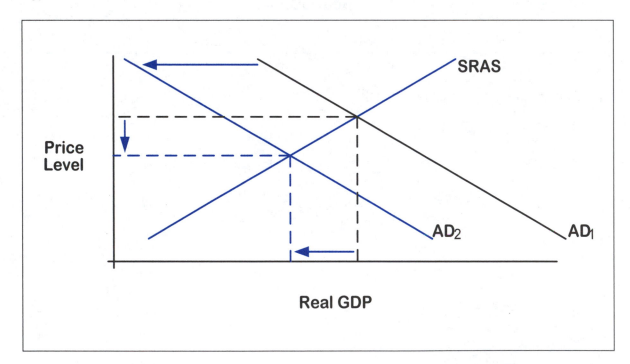

4.  If the price level changes, both workers and producers may misperceive the effect of the change in the price level. If the price level decreases, workers may perceive a decrease in their nominal wages as a decrease in real wages, and decrease the amount of labor supplied, and producers may perceive a decrease in their nominal prices as a decrease in real prices and reduce the amount of output produced. The decrease in output due to the misperceptions of workers and producers will cause the short-run aggregate supply curve to be upward sloping.

# Chapter 7  Classical Economic Theory

The basic economic problem is scarcity.  Human wants are unlimited.  Resources are limited.  The basic goal in dealing with the problem of scarcity is to produce as much consumer satisfaction as possible with the limited resources available.  Producing the ideal quantity of total output will contribute toward reaching this basic goal.  According to classical economic theory, a market economy is self-regulating and will automatically adjust to the ideal quantity of total output.

Classical economic theory refers to the theory introduced by Scottish economist Adam Smith in the latter half of the 18th century.  Smith's most famous work is the book "An Inquiry into the Nature and Causes of the Wealth of Nations" published in 1776.  (This book is commonly referred to as "The Wealth of Nations".)

Other economists (David Ricardo, Jean-Baptiste Say, John Stuart Mill, etc.) contributed to the development of classical economic theory.  Classical economic theory was the predominant theory in industrialized nations from the time of Adam Smith until the Great Depression of the 1930s.

## The Ideal Quantity of Total Output

The ideal quantity of total output is the quantity that will yield full employment of labor.  Remember from Chapter 4 that full employment does <u>not</u> mean an unemployment rate of zero.  Full employment means an unemployment rate equal to the natural unemployment rate.

The natural unemployment rate is the lowest unemployment rate that can be sustained without causing increasing inflation.  The quantity of total output that results in the natural unemployment rate is called Natural Real GDP.  Thus, Natural Real GDP is the ideal quantity of total output.

## The Self-Regulating Economy

We saw in Chapter 5 that Real GDP tends to behave in a cyclical manner, called the business cycle.  As the economy moves through the phases of the business cycle, Real GDP may deviate from Natural Real GDP.  During the trough phase of the business cycle, the unemployment rate may be higher than the natural unemployment rate.  Real GDP will be less than Natural Real GDP.  This is called a recessionary gap.

During the peak phase of the business cycle, the unemployment rate may be lower than the natural unemployment rate.  Real GDP will be greater than Natural Real GDP.  This is called an inflationary gap.

One of the major ideas of classical economic theory is that these deviations from full employment are temporary and self-correcting.  According to classical economic theory, a market economy is self-regulating and will automatically adjust to Natural Real GDP.  Example 1 on the next page provides an example of a self-regulating system.

> **Example 1:** On a calm summer day, Maynard is sitting in the shade of an oak tree next to his pond. Maynard is serenely admiring the smooth surface of the pond, when an acorn drops into the water. Maynard is distressed by the ripples on the surface of the pond. He begins tossing pebbles in the pond, attempting to flatten out the waves. The surface of the pond becomes even more disturbed. Eventually, Maynard tires of throwing pebbles at the waves and gives up. Soon, the surface of the pond is smooth again.

## Marx's Criticism of Classical Theory

The extended economic downturn of the 1930s caused many economists to question classical theory. (Most notably, John Maynard Keynes. See Chapter 8.) But classical theory had its critics long before the Great Depression.

The most famous 19<sup>th</sup> century critic of classical theory and market economies (capitalism) was Karl Marx. Marx argued that market economies do not automatically adjust to Natural Real GDP. Marx said that market economies would be unstable, because of inadequate demand.

According to Marx, workers in a market economy would be exploited. Capitalists would pay their workers less than the value of the workers' output. Marx referred to this difference as surplus labor value. Surplus labor value was the source of profit for the capitalist.

The exploitation of labor would mean that income would be distributed very unequally in a market economy. The unequal distribution of income would mean that workers would not have enough income to consume all that they produced. Inadequate demand would lead to increasingly severe downturns in the business cycle. Eventually, a market economy would collapse.

## Say's Law

Classical theory argues that inadequate demand cannot be a problem in a market economy. There will always be sufficient demand to purchase as much total output as is supplied. This is due to Say's Law.

**Say's Law** – supply creates its own demand.

According to Say's Law, supply creates its own demand. The act of production leads to equivalent income to resource owners.

> **Example 2:** Old MacDonald has a farm. He produces $10,000 worth of corn. Old MacDonald will receive $10,000 of income in exchange for the corn. Old MacDonald has income (buying power) equal to the value of his production. Likewise, other resource owners will receive income equal to the value of their production. Total income in the economy will be equal to the value of total production. Supply creates its own demand.

### Say's Law, Savings, and Flexible Interest Rates

But what if Old MacDonald chooses to <u>not</u> consume the entire $10,000 of income? Old MacDonald may choose to save a portion of the $10,000. Likewise, other resource owners may choose to save a portion of their income. Will this savings cause demand to be less than supply? No, says classical theory.

Flexible interest rates in the credit market cause any consumer savings to be exactly offset by business investment. This assumes that the quantity of both savings and investment is determined by the interest rate. The graph in Example 3 below illustrates equilibrium in the credit market.

**Example 3:**

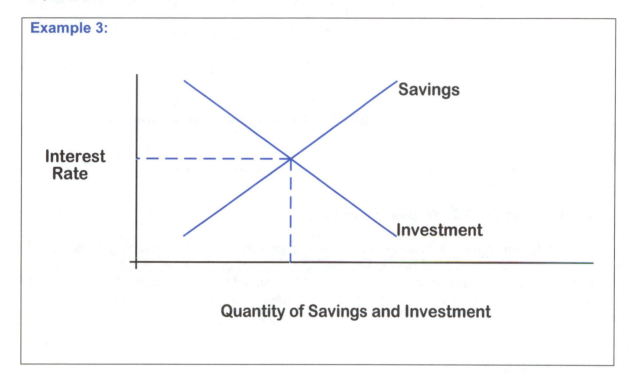

**Quantity of Savings and Investment**

Notice that the investment demand curve is downward sloping. Businesses will borrow and invest a greater quantity as the interest rate decreases. (See Chapter 6.) The savings supply curve is upward sloping. Households will save a greater quantity as the interest rate increases. (See Chapter 26.) The actual interest rate will be the equilibrium rate (where quantity of savings and quantity of investment are equal).

What if household desire to save increases (savings supply curve shifts right)? Will this cause a surplus of savings and a decrease in aggregate demand? Classical theory says no. The increase in savings will cause the interest rate to fall and equilibrium will be restored with the quantity of savings equal to the quantity of investment.

Flexible interest rates assure that any consumer savings will be exactly offset by business investment. The graph in Example 4 on the next page illustrates the increase in savings and the new equilibrium.

**Example 4:**

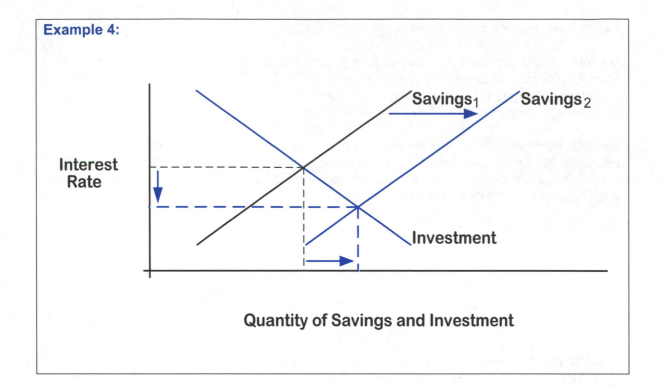

**Quantity of Savings and Investment**

## Say's Law and Flexible Wages and Prices

Just as interest rates are flexible, wages and prices are flexible, according to classical theory. Any surpluses or shortages in the labor market or the market for goods will be eliminated by wage and price adjustments. These adjustments occur automatically, and will cause the economy to be self-regulating. These adjustments are discussed later in the chapter.

## Natural Real GDP

Remember from earlier in the chapter that the ideal quantity of total output is the quantity that will result in the natural unemployment rate (full employment). The quantity of total output that results in the natural unemployment rate is called Natural Real GDP. Thus, Natural Real GDP is the ideal quantity of total output. According to classical economic theory, a market economy will automatically adjust to Natural Real GDP. But it is possible for the economy to be temporarily in a recessionary gap or an inflationary gap.

## A Recessionary Gap

If Real GDP is less than Natural Real GDP, the economy is in a **recessionary gap**.

**Example 5A:** Assume that Natural Real GDP is $15,500 billion. Equilibrium Real GDP (where AD and SRAS intersect) is only $15,000 billion. The economy is in a recessionary gap. The unemployment rate will be higher than the natural unemployment rate. The graph on the next page illustrates this recessionary gap situation.

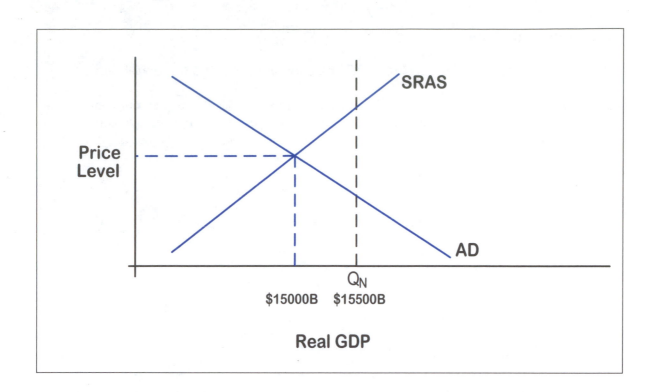

## An Inflationary Gap

If Real GDP is greater than Natural Real GDP, the economy is in an **inflationary gap**.

**Example 5B:** Assume that Natural Real GDP is $15,500 billion. Equilibrium Real GDP is $16,000 billion. The economy is in an inflationary gap. The unemployment rate will be lower than the natural unemployment rate. The graph below illustrates this situation.

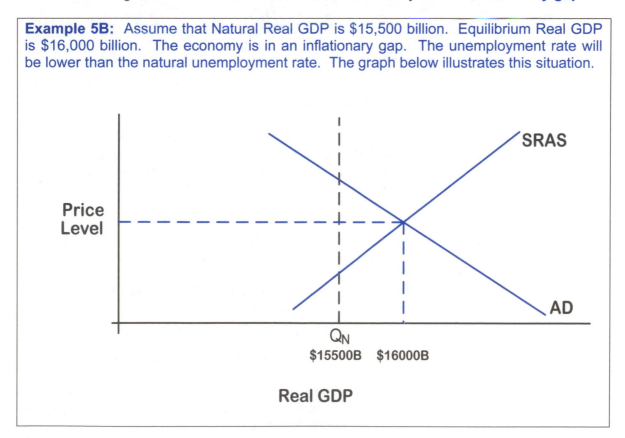

Classical Economic Theory

## Long-Run Equilibrium

If Real GDP is equal to Natural Real GDP, the economy is in long-run equilibrium.

**Example 5C:**  Assume that Natural Real GDP is $15,500 billion.  Equilibrium Real GDP is $15,500 billion.  The economy is in long-run equilibrium.  The unemployment rate will be the natural unemployment rate.  The graph below illustrates long–run equilibrium.

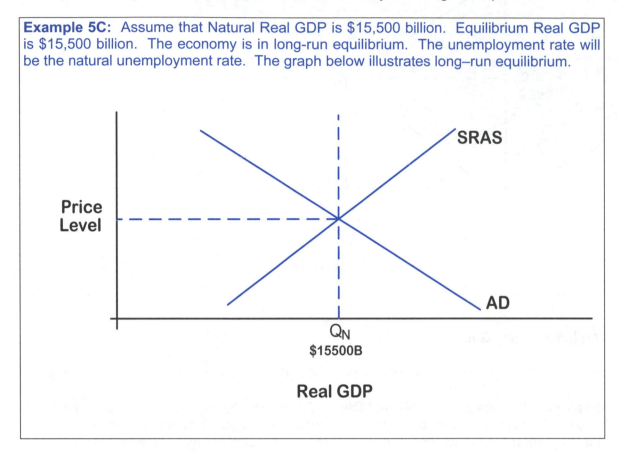

## Automatically Closing a Recessionary Gap

If the economy is in a recessionary gap, as in Example 5A on pages 7-4 and 7-5, Real GDP is less than Natural Real GDP.  Because the quantity of total output is less than the quantity that results in the natural unemployment rate, the unemployment rate will be higher than the natural unemployment rate.  There is a surplus of labor in the labor market.  The surplus of labor will cause wage rates in the economy to fall.

In Chapter 6, we saw that the determinant of short-run aggregate supply is the overall costs of production.  A decrease in wage rates will reduce the overall costs of production, shifting the SRAS curve to the right.  As the SRAS curve shifts to the right, equilibrium Real GDP will increase, and the unemployment rate will fall.  As long as the unemployment rate is greater than the natural unemployment rate, wage rates will continue to fall and the SRAS curve will continue to shift to the right.

When Real GDP equals Natural Real GDP, the unemployment rate will be equal to the natural unemployment rate, and the economy will be in long-run equilibrium.  According to classical economic theory, this adjustment from a recessionary gap to Natural Real GDP is automatic and requires no government intervention.  The graph in Example 6A on the next page illustrates closing a recessionary gap.

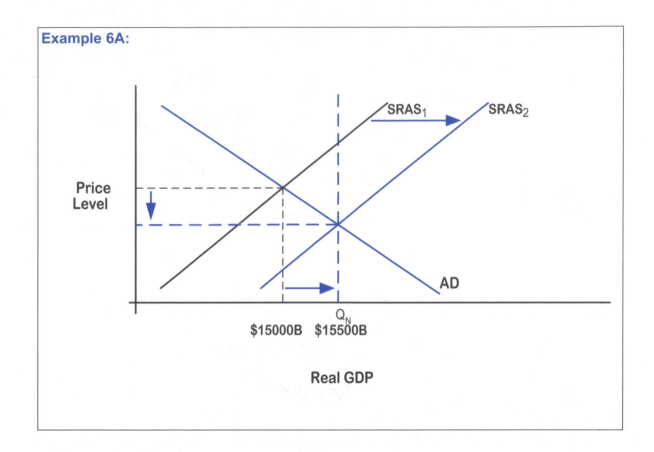

Notice on the graph in Example 6A above that the adjustment from a recessionary gap to Natural Real GDP results in a decrease in the price level.

## Automatically Closing an Inflationary Gap

If the economy is in an inflationary gap, as in Example 5B on page 7-5, Real GDP is greater than Natural Real GDP. Because the quantity of total output is greater than the quantity that results in the natural unemployment rate, the unemployment rate will be lower than the natural unemployment rate. There is a shortage of labor in the labor market. The shortage of labor will cause wage rates in the economy to rise.

The determinant of short-run aggregate supply is the overall costs of production. An increase in wage rates will increase the overall costs of production, shifting the SRAS curve to the left. As the SRAS curve shifts to the left, equilibrium Real GDP will decrease, and the unemployment rate will rise. As long as the unemployment rate is less than the natural unemployment rate, wage rates will continue to rise and the SRAS curve will continue to shift to the left.

When Real GDP equals Natural Real GDP, the unemployment rate will be equal to the natural unemployment rate, and the economy will be in long-run equilibrium. According to classical economic theory, this adjustment from an inflationary gap to Natural Real GDP is automatic and requires no government intervention. The graph in Example 6B on the next page illustrates closing an inflationary gap.

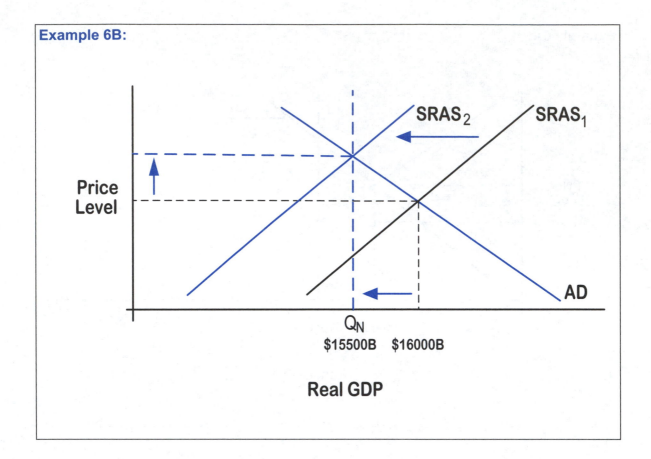

**Example 6B:**

Notice on the graph in Example 6B above that the adjustment from an inflationary gap to Natural Real GDP results in an increase in the price level.

## Long-Run Aggregate Supply

The concept of aggregate supply was introduced in Chapter 6, where we focused on the short-run aggregate supply curve. Now we need to look at the long-run aggregate supply curve.

The short-run aggregate supply curve indicates a direct relationship between the price level and the quantity supplied of Real GDP. As a result, changes in aggregate demand will affect both the price level and Real GDP. This is illustrated on the graph in Example 7 on the next page.

But what does the long-run aggregate supply curve (LRAS) look like? If the economy is self-regulating, Real GDP will always tend to adjust back to Natural Real GDP. Thus, the long-run aggregate supply curve will be vertical at Natural Real GDP.

If the LRAS curve is vertical at Natural Real GDP, then changes in AD have no effect on total output in the long run, but affect only the price level. This is illustrated on the graph in Example 8 on the next page.

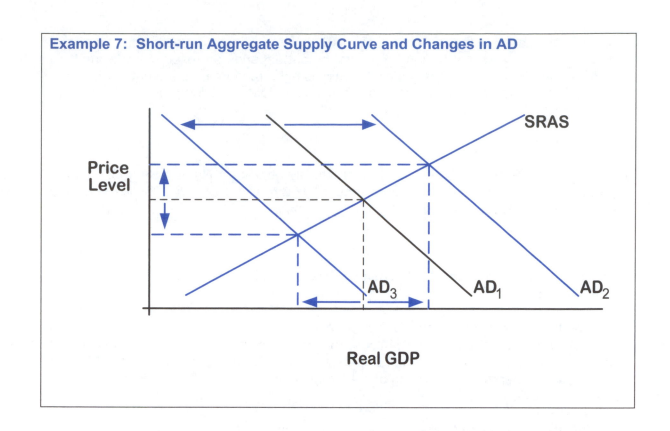

**Example 7: Short-run Aggregate Supply Curve and Changes in AD**

Price Level

SRAS

AD₃   AD₁   AD₂

Real GDP

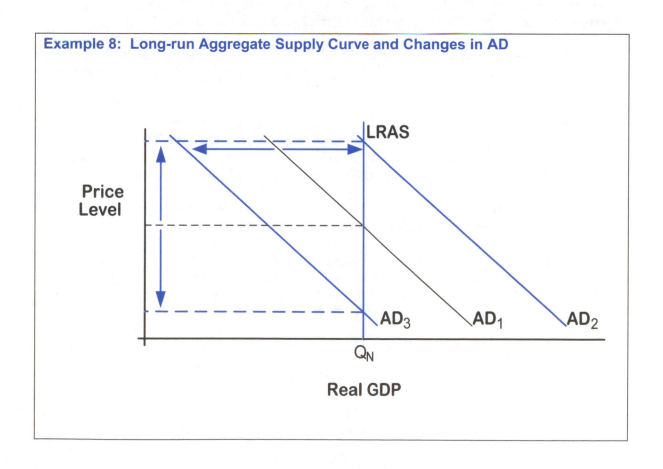

**Example 8: Long-run Aggregate Supply Curve and Changes in AD**

Price Level

LRAS

AD₃   AD₁   AD₂

Q_N

Real GDP

Classical Economic Theory

According to classical theory, changes in AD logically should have no effect on total output in the long run. In the long run, total output depends on resources. In the long run, AD depends on the money supply. Money is not a resource. The amount of money (or spending) in the economy should not affect total output in the long run.

## Laissez-faire

If the economy is self-regulating and automatically adjusts to Natural Real GDP, what macroeconomic policy should the government follow? The answer is "laissez-faire", do nothing, leave it alone, do not interfere with the economy.

## Appendix: The Stock Market Crash of 1929, the Smoot-Hawley Tariff, and the Great Depression

Classical theory, with its laissez-faire approach to economic policy, was the dominant economic theory in industrialized nations from the time of Adam Smith until the Great Depression of the 1930s. The Great Depression officially started in August of 1929. But popular culture marks the beginning of the Great Depression with the stock market crash of October, 1929.

In reality, the stock market did not crash in 1929. It is true that the Dow Jones Industrial Average (DJIA) decreased dramatically in late 1929, with some historically large daily decreases in October. But the real crash in stock prices occurred after 1929.

The DJIA peaked at 381 on September 3, 1929. This was the culmination of a massive run-up in stock prices that began in 1924. The peak DJIA of 381 was almost four times as high as the DJIA had been in January of 1924.

From this peak, the DJIA dropped over the next couple of months to 199 on November 12. Especially large losses occurred on October 24 ("Black Thursday") and October 29 ("Black Tuesday"). However, the DJIA of 199 on November 12, 1929, though a decrease of almost 50% from the peak, was still double the DJIA as of January, 1924.

The stock market rallied through the rest of 1929 and into 1930, ending May of 1930 at around 270. The unemployment rate had risen to around 6%.

On June 17, 1930, President Herbert Hoover signed into law the Smoot-Hawley Tariff. This law increased the average tariff rate on dutiable goods to almost 60 percent. Other nations responded with retaliatory tariff increases. U.S. exports and imports both decreased by over 60 percent between 1929 and 1933.

With the passage of the Smoot-Hawley Tariff, stock prices began to fall again. The DJIA fell from around 270 at the end of May, 1930 to a low of 41 on July 8, 1932. The DJIA would not reach the peak of 381 again until November of 1954.

With the passage of the Smoot-Hawley Tariff, the unemployment rate began a rapid rise. The unemployment rate, which was around 6% in May of 1930, reached 25 percent in 1933.

## Questions for Chapter 7

### Fill-in-the-blanks:

1. According to _____ Law, supply creates its own demand.

2. If Real GDP is less than Natural Real GDP, the economy is in a(n) _____ gap.

3. If Real GDP is greater than Natural Real GDP, the economy is in a(n) _____ gap.

4. If Real GDP is _____ _____ Natural Real GDP, the economy is in long-run equilibrium.

### Multiple Choice:

_____ 1. Classical economic theory began with the book:
- a. "Das Kapital" by Karl Marx
- b. "An Inquiry into the Nature and Causes of the Wealth of Nations" by Adam Smith
- c. "The General Theory of Employment, Interest, and Money" by John Maynard Keynes
- d. "Market Economies Are Like, You Know, Classical" by Jeff Holt

_____ 2. The ideal quantity of total output:
- a. yields an unemployment rate of zero
- b. yields full employment of labor
- c. Both of the above
- d. Neither of the above

_____ 3. According to classical economic theory:
- a. Real GDP never deviates from Natural Real GDP
- b. a market economy is self-regulating
- c. with proper government policy, full employment can be maintained at all times
- d. All of the above

_____ 4. According to Marxist theory, a market economy:
- a. is self-regulating
- b. would be unstable, because of inadequate demand
- c. would become increasingly stable
- d. All of the above

_____ 5. According to Say's Law:
- a. supply creates its own demand
- b. demand creates its own supply
- c. the act of production leads to equivalent income to resource owners
- d. Both a. and c. above

Classical Economic Theory

_____ 6. According to classical economic theory:
   a. a market economy will automatically adjust to Natural Real GDP
   b. supply creates its own demand
   c. flexible interest rates assure that any consumer savings will be exactly offset by business investment
   d. All of the above

_____ 7. According to classical economic theory:
   a. government intervention is necessary to maintain adequate demand
   b. interest rates, wages, and prices are inflexible
   c. the proper economic policy is laissez-faire
   d. All of the above

_____ 8. According to classical economic theory, savings and investment will be equal because:
   a. demand creates its own supply
   b. interest rates are flexible
   c. wages rise in a recessionary gap
   d. All of the above

_____ 9. According to classical economic theory, if the desire to save increases:
   a. the interest rate will fall
   b. the savings supply curve will shift right
   c. the quantity of savings and investment will be equal
   d. All of the above

_____ 10. The ideal quantity of total output in the economy:
   a. is called Natural Real GDP
   b. is the one that will result in zero unemployment
   c. can be reached only with government intervention, according to classical theory
   d. All of the above

_____ 11. If Real GDP is less than Natural Real GDP:
   a. the economy is in a recessionary gap
   b. the unemployment rate will be lower than the natural unemployment rate
   c. the shortage of labor will cause wage rates to rise
   d. All of the above

_____ 12. If Real GDP is greater than Natural Real GDP:
   a. the economy is in an inflationary gap
   b. the unemployment rate will be higher than the natural unemployment rate
   c. the shortage of labor will cause wage rates to rise
   d. Both a. and c. above

_____ 13. According to classical economic theory, a market economy will automatically close an inflationary gap by:
   a. the shortage of labor will cause wage rates to rise
   b. the increase in wage rates will shift the SRAS curve to the left
   c. the SRAS curve will shift to the left until Real GDP equals Natural Real GDP
   d. All of the above

_____ 14. According to classical economic theory:
   a. the LRAS curve is vertical at Natural Real GDP
   b. changes in AD affect only the output level in the long run
   c. since the economy is self-regulating, the proper economic policy is laissez-faire
   d. Both a. and c. above

_____ 15. After the stock market crash of 1929, the Dow Jones Industrial Average:
   a. had decreased almost 50% from its peak
   b. was lower than it had been since 1921
   c. Both of the above
   d. Neither of the above

_____ 16. When the Smoot-Hawley Tariff was enacted in 1930:
   a. the Dow Jones Industrial Average had already dropped below its level of 1924
   b. the unemployment rate had already risen to over 20%
   c. Both of the above
   d. Neither of the above

_____ 17. The Smoot-Hawley Tariff:
   a. increased the average tariff rate on dutiable goods to almost 60 percent
   b. boosted U.S. exports and put the economy on the road to recovery
   c. marked the beginning of the recovery of stock prices
   d. All of the above

## Problems:

1. Explain the effect of an increase in household desire to save, according to classical economic theory.

Classical Economic Theory

2. On the graph below, draw an aggregate demand curve that would result in an inflationary gap, and indicate the equilibrium price level and Real GDP.

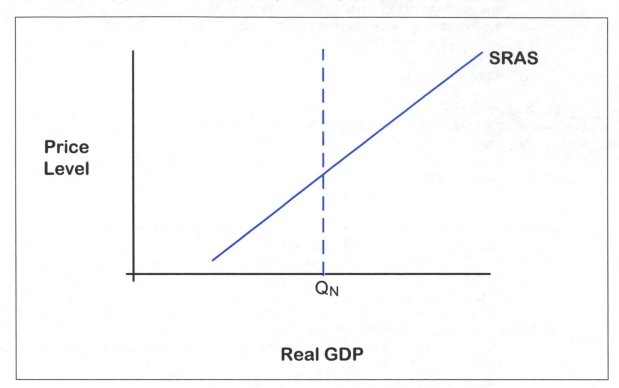

3. Explain and illustrate on the graph below how a market economy will close a recessionary gap, according to classical economic theory.

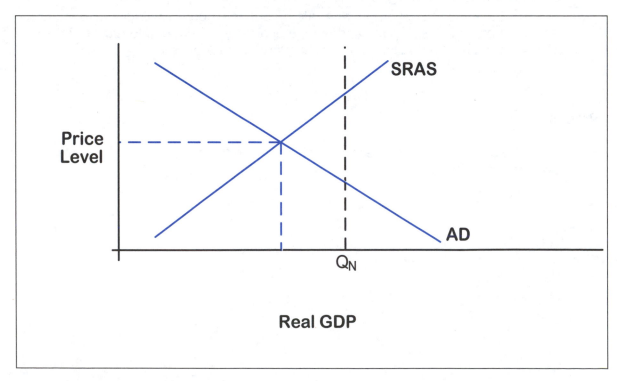

4. What assumptions make laissez-faire the proper macroeconomic policy?

## Answers for Chapter 7

**Fill-in-the-blanks:**
1. Say's
2. recessionary
3. inflationary
4. equal to

**Multiple Choice:**

| | | |
|---|---|---|
| 1. b. | 7. c. | 13. d. |
| 2. b. | 8. b. | 14. d. |
| 3. b. | 9. d. | 15. a. |
| 4. b. | 10. a. | 16. d. |
| 5. d. | 11. a. | 17. a. |
| 6. d. | 12. d. | |

## Problems:

1. An increase in household desire to save will cause savings to increase. The increase in savings will cause the interest rate to fall and equilibrium will be restored with the quantity of savings equal to the quantity of investment.

2.

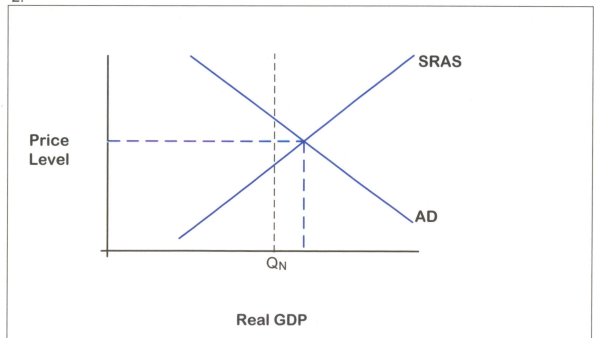

3. Explanation: In a recessionary gap, the unemployment rate will be higher than the natural unemployment rate. The surplus of labor will cause wage rates to fall. As wage rates fall, the SRAS curve will shift to the right until Real GDP equals Natural Real GDP.

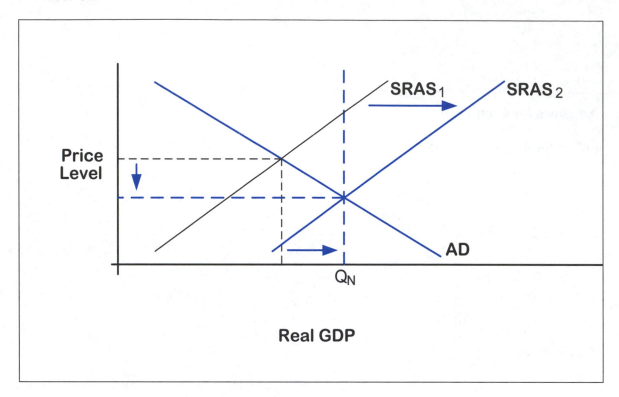

4. If the economy is self-regulating and automatically adjusts to Natural Real GDP, then laissez-faire is the proper economic policy.

# Chapter 8  Keynesian Economic Theory

Classical economic theory was the predominant theory in industrialized nations from the time of Adam Smith until the Great Depression of the 1930s. During the Great Depression, market economies were <u>not</u> automatically adjusting to Natural Real GDP.

In 1936, economist John Maynard Keynes (Cānes) published "The General Theory of Employment, Interest, and Money". This book established Keynesian theory as a major alternative to classical theory.

For a review of this book, see the appendix at the end of the chapter.

## Keynesian Theory and Say's Law

According to classical theory (Say's Law), "supply creates its own demand". The act of production leads to equivalent income to the resource owners. And if the resource owners choose to save a part of their income, this consumer savings will <u>not</u> reduce demand. Any consumer savings will be exactly offset by business investment. This will be true, according to classical theory, since the quantity of both savings and investment is determined by the interest rate.

Keynesian theory rejects Say's Law. Keynesian theory holds that factors other than the interest rate would affect savings and investment. Expectations of future returns would affect business investment. If investors become pessimistic about future rates of return, they may <u>not</u> invest more in response to lower interest rates.

So an increase in savings may <u>not</u> be offset by an equal increase in investment. If savings is greater than investment, supply will be greater than demand. Thus, excessive savings could lead to inadequate Total Expenditures.

## Keynesian Theory and Closing a Recessionary Gap

Classical theory argues that wages and prices are flexible and cause the economy to be self-regulating. A recessionary gap would automatically be closed. The surplus of labor would cause wage rates to fall, shifting SRAS to the right until Natural Real GDP is reached. The price level would be lower.

But Keynesian theory argues that wages and prices are <u>not</u> flexible downward. Factors such as long-term labor contracts, labor unions, and general employee resistance to wage cuts may make wage rates inflexible downward. And if wage rates do <u>not</u> fall, SRAS does <u>not</u> shift to the right, and the economy can get stuck in a recessionary gap for an extended period of time.

How can the economy get out of a recessionary gap? If SRAS does not shift right, then AD must shift right to move the economy back to Natural Real GDP. According to Keynesian theory, the solution to a recessionary gap would be an increase in Total Expenditures to shift the AD curve right. This is illustrated on the graph in Example 1 on the next page:

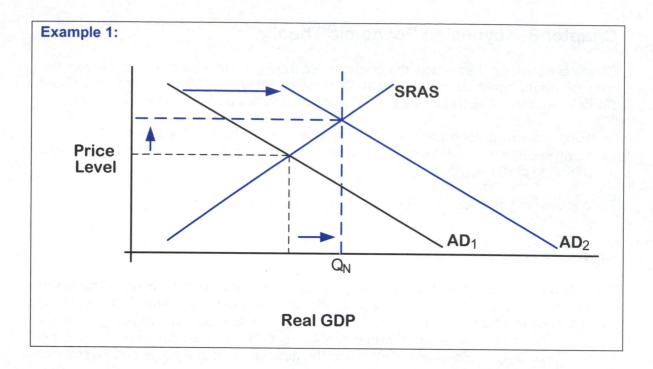

**Example 1:**

Price Level — Real GDP graph showing SRAS, AD₁, AD₂, and Q_N.

Classical theory emphasizes supply, and takes demand for granted. After all, "supply creates its own demand". Keynesian theory emphasizes spending as the driving force in the economy. According to Keynesian theory, the level of Total Expenditures determines the level of total output. Next, we look at the components of Total Expenditures (consumption, investment, government purchases, and net exports) and how they are related to total output (Real GDP).

## Consumption

Consumption is the largest of the four types of spending making up Total Expenditures. Consumption is determined primarily by disposable income.

**Example 2A:** Assume that the table below shows the relationship between disposable income and consumption for different levels of disposable income:

| Disposable Income | Consumption |
|---|---|
| $3,000 | $6,600 |
| 6,000 | 8,400 |
| 9,000 | 10,200 |
| 12,000 | 12,000 |
| 15,000 | 13,800 |
| 18,000 | 15,600 |
| 21,000 | 17,400 |

Notice from the table above that consumption increases as disposable income increases. Each time disposable income increases by $3,000, consumption increases by $1,800.

When disposable income is less than $12,000, consumption is greater than disposable income. The households are dissaving. When disposable income is greater than $12,000, consumption is less than disposable income. The households are saving. At $12,000 of disposable income, consumption equals disposable income.

**Example 2B:** The graph below illustrates the relationship between disposable income and consumption.

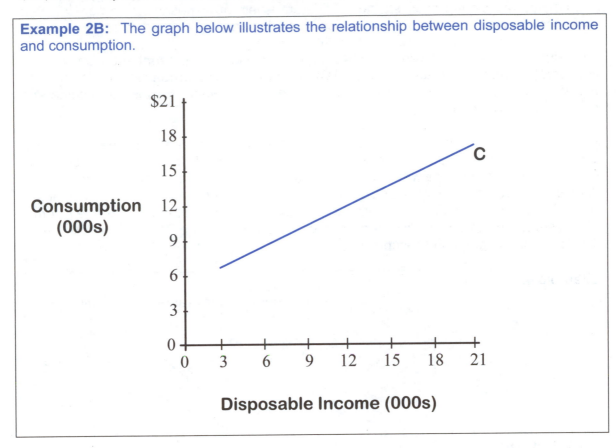

## Marginal Propensity to Consume

The curve showing the relationship between disposable income and consumption (labeled C) is called the consumption function.

The slope of the consumption function is the **marginal propensity to consume** (MPC). Marginal propensity to consume is a very important number in Keynesian theory. MPC is calculated as the change in consumption divided by the change in income.

**MPC = change in consumption ÷ change in income**

**Example 3:** For Example 2A, the MPC is .60, calculated as;

MPC = change in consumption ÷ change in income = $1,800 ÷ $3,000 = .60

The MPC of .60 means that for every additional dollar of income received, households will consume an additional 60 cents.

## The 45° Angle Line

The graph on the previous page shows the relationship between consumption and disposable income. It is <u>not</u> immediately obvious from looking at the graph whether households are saving or dissaving at different levels of disposable income. We can make the saving or dissaving easier to see by adding another line to the graph.

If we draw a line from the vertex at a 45° angle, this line will represent equal amounts of consumption and disposable income. Where the consumption function intersects with the 45° angle line is the one level of disposable income where disposable income and consumption are equal.

At disposable income levels less than the intersection amount, the consumption function lies above the 45° angle line, indicating that consumption is greater than disposable income. The distance between the two lines represents the amount of dissaving. At disposable income levels greater than the intersection amount, the consumption function lies below the 45° angle line, indicating that consumption is less than disposable income. The distance between the two lines is the amount of saving. The 45° angle line is illustrated on the graph in Example 4 below:

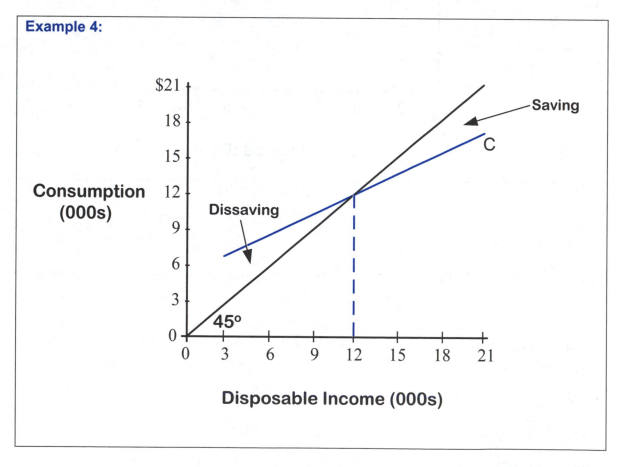

**Example 4:**

Notice on the graph above that consumption and disposable income are equal at $12,000.

## The Total Expenditures Curve

According to Keynesian theory, spending drives the economy. The level of Total Expenditures determines the level of total output (Real GDP). An increase in Total Expenditures will cause an increase in Real GDP. A decrease in Total Expenditures will cause a decrease in Real GDP.

A Total Expenditures curve (TE) shows the relationship between Total Expenditures and Real GDP. Total Expenditures consists of four types of spending; consumption, investment, government purchases, and net exports.

In deriving a Total Expenditures curve, the following assumptions are made:

1. Consumption is directly related to Real GDP. As Real GDP increases, consumption will increase. The rate of increase in consumption is the marginal propensity to consume.

2. The levels of investment, government purchases, and net exports are all unrelated to the current level of Real GDP. Other factors cause these types of spending to increase or decrease (as discussed in Chapter 6). A change in the current level of Real GDP will not change the level of investment, government purchases, or net exports.

---

**Example 5:** Assume that the table below shows the amount of consumption, investment, government purchases, and net exports at different levels of Real GDP. Notice that consumption is directly related to Real GDP and increases with the level of Real GDP. The MPC is .60.

The levels of investment, government purchases, and net exports are all unrelated to the current level of Real GDP. Thus, investment, government purchases and net exports are unchanged by changes in current Real GDP. Total Expenditures (TE) is the sum of consumption, investment, government purchases, and net exports. All dollar amounts on the table are in billions.

| Real GDP | Consumption | Investment | Gov't Purchases | Net Exports | TE |
|----------|-------------|------------|-----------------|-------------|----------|
| $15,000  | $10,500     | $2,500     | $3,000          | $-800       | $15,200  |
| 15,100   | 10,560      | 2,500      | 3,000           | -800        | 15,260   |
| 15,200   | 10,620      | 2,500      | 3,000           | -800        | 15,320   |
| 15,300   | 10,680      | 2,500      | 3,000           | -800        | 15,380   |
| 15,400   | 10,740      | 2,500      | 3,000           | -800        | 15,440   |
| 15,500   | 10,800      | 2,500      | 3,000           | -800        | 15,500   |
| 15,600   | 10,860      | 2,500      | 3,000           | -800        | 15,560   |
| 15,700   | 10,920      | 2,500      | 3,000           | -800        | 15,620   |
| 15,800   | 10,980      | 2,500      | 3,000           | -800        | 15,680   |
| 15,900   | 11,040      | 2,500      | 3,000           | -800        | 15,740   |
| 16,000   | 11,100      | 2,500      | 3,000           | -800        | 15,800   |

---

Keynesian Economic Theory

The graph below illustrates the relationship between Real GDP and Total Expenditures (TE) in Example 5.

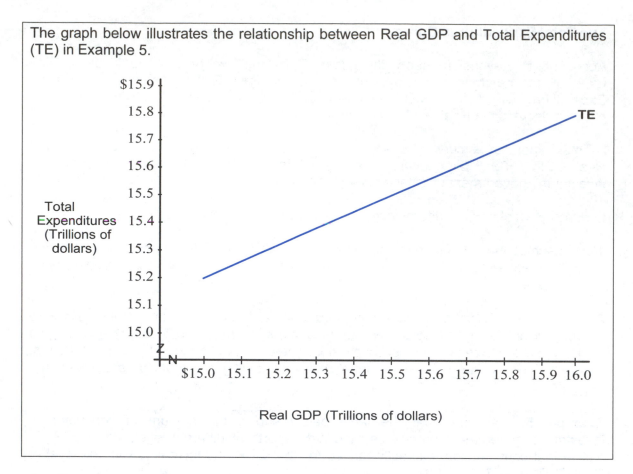

## Equilibrium Real GDP

In Example 5, what is the actual (equilibrium) Real GDP? In Keynesian theory, equilibrium Real GDP occurs where Total Expenditures equals Real GDP (total production). On the table in Example 5, equilibrium occurs at $15,500 billion. But why does equilibrium Real GDP occur where Total Expenditures and Real GDP are equal?

If Total Expenditures were greater than Real GDP, producers would be selling more than they were producing. Thus, inventories would decrease. This would signal producers to increase production. Production (Real GDP) would increase until it was equal to TE.

If TE were less than Real GDP, producers would be producing more than they were selling. Thus, inventories would increase. This would signal producers to decrease production. Production (Real GDP) would decrease until it was equal to TE.

## Equilibrium Real GDP and the 45° Angle Line

Remember the 45° angle line we used earlier in the chapter to help locate the equilibrium between consumption and disposable income? We can use the same approach to identify equilibrium Real GDP. If we add a 45° angle line to the Total Expenditures graph, the Total Expenditures curve will intersect the 45° angle line at the level of Real GDP where Total Expenditures and Real GDP are equal. See Example 6 on the next page:

**Example 6:**

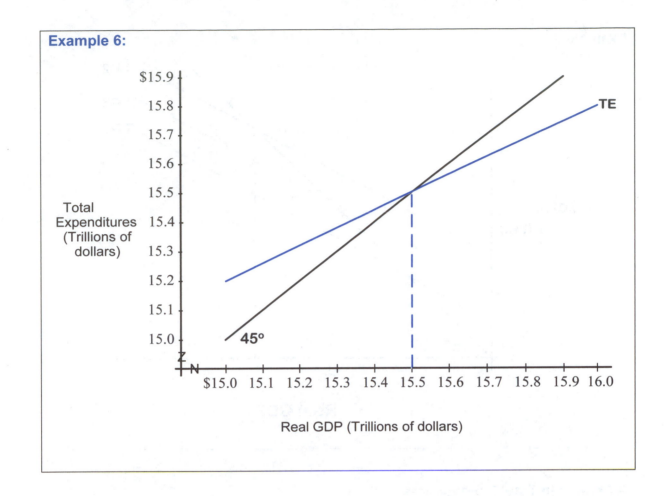

Notice on the graph above that the Total Expenditures curve intersects the 45° angle line at $15,500 billion. This is equilibrium Real GDP.

## Ideal Total Expenditures

Ideally, equilibrium Real GDP will occur at Natural Real GDP. If Natural Real GDP is $15,500 billion and equilibrium Real GDP is $15,500 billion, then the economy is in long-run equilibrium. There is no recessionary gap or inflationary gap. The economy is at full employment.

But is there any guarantee that there will be exactly the right amount of Total Expenditures in the economy to achieve Natural Real GDP? According to Keynesian theory, there is no guarantee. The level of Total Expenditures may <u>not</u> be the level that will cause the economy to achieve Natural Real GDP.

The graph in Example 7 on the next page shows three possible levels of Total Expenditures. $TE_1$ is less than the ideal level of Total Expenditures and would result in a recessionary gap. (Real GDP is less than Natural Real GDP.) $TE_2$ is more than the ideal level of Total Expenditures and would result in an inflationary gap. (Real GDP is greater than Natural Real GDP.) $TE_3$ is the ideal level of Total Expenditures and results in Natural Real GDP.

**Example 7:**

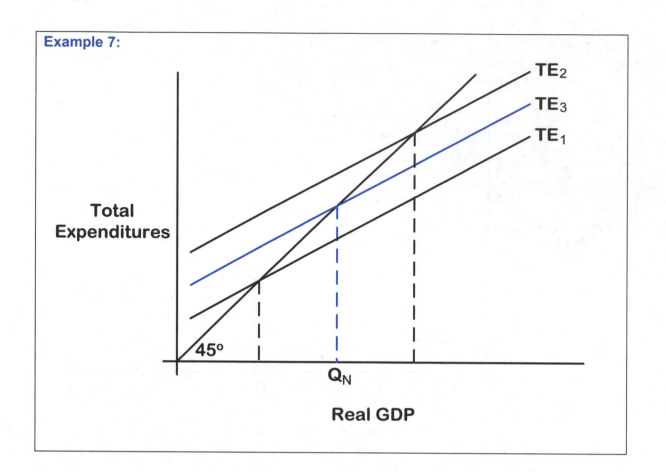

## A Change in Total Expenditures

In Example 5 earlier in the chapter, equilibrium Real GDP was $15,500 billion. What if one of the components of Total Expenditures changes? What will happen to Real GDP?

**Example 8:** Assume the same facts as in Example 5, except that investors become more optimistic about future returns and investment spending increases by $120 billion (from $2,500 billion to $2,620 billion). The table below shows the amount of consumption, investment, government purchases, net exports, and Total Expenditures at different levels of Real GDP. All dollar amounts on the table are in billions.

| Real GDP | Consumption | Investment | Gov't Purchases | Net Exports | TE |
|----------|-------------|------------|-----------------|-------------|------|
| $15,000 | $10,500 | $2,620 | $3,000 | $-800 | $15,320 |
| 15,100 | 10,560 | 2,620 | 3,000 | -800 | 15,380 |
| 15,200 | 10,620 | 2,620 | 3,000 | -800 | 15,440 |
| 15,300 | 10,680 | 2,620 | 3,000 | -800 | 15,500 |
| 15,400 | 10,740 | 2,620 | 3,000 | -800 | 15,560 |
| 15,500 | 10,800 | 2,620 | 3,000 | -800 | 15,620 |
| 15,600 | 10,860 | 2,620 | 3,000 | -800 | 15,680 |
| 15,700 | 10,920 | 2,620 | 3,000 | -800 | 15,740 |
| 15,800 | 10,980 | 2,620 | 3,000 | -800 | 15,800 |
| 15,900 | 11,040 | 2,620 | 3,000 | -800 | 15,860 |
| 16,000 | 11,100 | 2,620 | 3,000 | -800 | 15,920 |

The graph below shows the relationships between Real GDP and Total Expenditures. TE$_5$ represents Total Expenditures from Example 5. TE$_8$ represents Total Expenditures from Example 8.

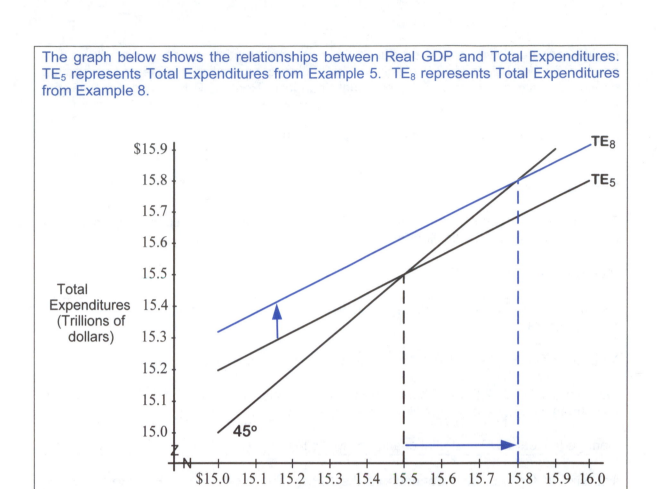

Real GDP (Trillions of dollars)

Notice from the graph above and the table on the previous page that equilibrium Real GDP in Example 8 is $15,800 billion, a $300 billion increase over equilibrium Real GDP in Example 5. The increase in investment ($120 billion) has led to a <u>multiplied</u> increase in Real GDP ($300 billion). This is the multiplier effect.

According to Keynesian theory, a change in one of the components of Total Expenditures will lead to a multiplied change in Real GDP. The multiplier effect occurs because the initial change in Total Expenditures triggers a chain reaction.

In Example 8, investment spending increases by $120 billion. This new production generates $120 billion in new income for the resource owners who produced the new physical capital. What will the recipients of this income do with $120 billion in new income?

With an MPC of .60, consumption will increase by $72 billion ($120 billion x .60). This new production generates $72 billion in new income for the resource owners who produced the new consumption goods. This will lead to another $43.2 billion ($72 billion x .60) in new consumption. This new production generates $43.2 billion in new income for the resource owners who produced the new consumption goods. This will lead to another $25.92 billion ($43.2 billion x .60) in new consumption. The chain reaction continues. We can compute the eventual change in Real GDP by using the following formula:

**Change in Real GDP = Initial change x Multiplier**

### The Multiplier

The size of the multiplier effect depends on a factor called the multiplier. The multiplier is computed using the following formula:

**Multiplier = 1 ÷ (1 – MPC)**

---

**Example 9:** In Example 8 above, the MPC was .60. Thus, the multiplier would be 2.5, as computed below:

Multiplier = 1 ÷ (1 – MPC) = 1 ÷ (1 – .60) = 1 ÷ .40 = 2.5

With a multiplier of 2.5, the Change in Real GDP resulting from a $120 billion increase in investment would be a $300 billion increase, as computed below:

Change in Real GDP = Initial change x Multiplier = $120 billion x 2.5 = $300 billion

---

The size of the multiplier depends on the MPC. The greater the MPC, the larger the multiplier. The larger the multiplier, the larger the eventual change in Real GDP.

---

**Example 10:** Assume the same facts as Example 8, except that the MPC is .75. When investment spending increases by $120 billion, what is the change in Real GDP?

Multiplier = 1 ÷ (1 – MPC) = 1 ÷ (1 - .75) = 1 ÷ .25 = 4

Change in Real GDP = Initial change x Multiplier = $120 billion x 4 = $480 billion

---

In Examples 9 and 10, the initial change was an increase in Total Expenditures. What if the initial change is a decrease in Total Expenditures?

According to Keynesian theory, the multiplier effect works the same for an initial decrease in Total Expenditures. The initial decrease in Total Expenditures would lead to a multiplied decrease in Real GDP.

---

**Example 11:** If investment spending decreases by $100 billion when the MPC is .80, what is the change in Real GDP?

Multiplier = 1 ÷ (1 – MPC) = 1 ÷ (1 - .80) = 1 ÷ .20 = 5

Change in Real GDP = Initial change x Multiplier = $100 billion decrease x 5 = $500 billion decrease

---

## Appendix: Book Review – "The General Theory of Employment, Interest, and Money"

In January of 1935, Maynard Keynes wrote a letter to the playwright George Bernard Shaw in which he stated, "…I believe myself to be writing a book on economic theory which will largely revolutionize – not, I suppose, at once but in the course of the next ten years – the way the world thinks about economic problems". That book, published in 1936, was "The General Theory of Employment, Interest, and Money". Whether for good or for ill, Keynes's book has had the kind of revolutionary impact that he anticipated.

"The General Theory" was controversial when published, and remains so to this day. Keynes's prescription for ending the Great Depression – government deficit spending – was not immediately put into practice. The consensus at the time was that government deficit spending was dangerous and irresponsible behavior. The only legitimate excuse for deficit spending was to finance a military effort. In peacetime, budget surpluses were to be accomplished in order to pay down previous war debt. War debt needed to be paid down because, well, there would always be another war that would need to be financed. President Franklin Roosevelt signed a tax increase in 1936, hoping to balance the federal budget.

And then came World War II. The nations involved in the war engaged in deficit spending on an unprecedented scale. And the Great Depression, which had lingered for over a decade, abruptly came to an end. The Keynesian prescription for ending the Great Depression appeared to have been proven correct. After the war, the U.S. federal government enacted the Employment Act of 1946, which established the federal government's responsibility to "promote maximum employment, production, and purchasing power".

Keynesian theory, as expressed in "The General Theory" and as developed in the writings of such economists as John Hicks, Alvin Hansen, and Paul Samuelson, dominated economic theory and practice through the 1960s.

Even one of the harshest critics of "The General Theory", Henry Hazlitt, wrote in 1959, "The most famous economist of the twentieth century is John Maynard Keynes; and the most influential economic book of the present era, both on theory and on economic policy, is his "General Theory of Employment, Interest, and Money…".

The December 31, 1965 issue of "Time" magazine featured a cover story entitled, "We Are All Keynesians Now". The article stated, "Today, some 20 years after his (Keynes) death, his theories are a prime influence on the world's free economies, especially on America's, the richest and most expansionist. In Washington the men who formulate the nation's economic policies have used Keynesian principles not only to avoid the violent cycles of prewar days but to produce a phenomenal economic growth and to achieve remarkably stable prices."

In the 1970s, the U.S. economy suffered from a combination of high unemployment and high inflation, dubbed "stagflation". According to Keynesian theory, high unemployment is caused by inadequate aggregate demand and high inflation is caused by excessive aggregate demand. Keynesian theory provides no explanation for stagflation.

"The General Theory" is a tough read. Keynesian economist Paul Samuelson wrote, "It is a badly written book, poorly organized…It is not well suited for classroom use. It is arrogant, bad-tempered, polemical, and not overly generous in its acknowledgements. It abounds in mares' nests and confusion…"

---

The most influential assertions of "The General Theory" can be summarized as follows:

1. Say's Law (supply creates its own demand) is incorrect. Equilibrium total output is determined by Total Expenditures, and will <u>not</u> necessarily correspond to full employment.

2. A decrease in investment caused by a decrease in expected rates of return is the most likely cause of a recession.

3. If investors are very pessimistic about future rates of return, they may <u>not</u> invest more in response to lower interest rates (thus monetary policy may be ineffective to restore full employment).

4. Expansionary fiscal policy (government deficit spending) is the most effective way to restore full employment.

5. Any change in government spending or taxation will have a multiplied effect on total output.

---

"The General Theory" also includes a number of assertions that have <u>not</u> proven influential.

1. Keynes found an "element of scientific truth in mercantilist doctrine". Mercantilist doctrine, which calls for trade restrictions to maintain a "favorable" balance of trade, has been generally rejected by broadly accepted economic theory.

2. Keynes proposed that usury laws to maintain low interest rates might be good policy. Price controls have been generally rejected by broadly accepted economic theory.

3. Keynes proposed a type of tax to be imposed on money holders as a way to discourage the holding of money and thus achieve lower interest rates.

4. Keynes proposed that "a somewhat comprehensive socialisation of investment will prove the only means of securing an approximation to full employment…If the State is able to determine the aggregate amount of resources devoted to augmenting the instruments and the basic rate of reward to those who own them, it will have accomplished all that is necessary".

5. Keynes asserted that the adoption of his theory, by providing full employment, would reduce the competitive struggle for international markets and would thus be favorable to maintaining peace. However, earlier in the book Keynes had spoken favorably of mercantilist doctrine which calls for trade restrictions to maintain a "favorable" balance of trade. Free international trade is generally believed to be more favorable to maintaining peace than is a policy of trade restrictions.

## Questions for Chapter 8

### Fill-in-the-blanks:

1. The slope of the consumption function is the _____
   _____ to consume.

2. Total Expenditures consists of consumption, _____ , government
   purchases, and net exports.

### Multiple Choice:

_____ 1. According to Keynesian theory:
    a. expectations of future returns affect business investment
    b. if investors are pessimistic about future rates of return, they may <u>not</u>
        invest more as interest rates decrease
    c. Both of the above
    d. Neither of the above

_____ 2. According to Keynesian theory:
    a. excessive savings could lead to inadequate Total Expenditures
    b. wages and prices are <u>not</u> flexible downward
    c. the economy can get stuck in a recessionary gap for an extended period
        of time
    d. All of the above

_____ 3. According to Keynesian theory:
    a. the economy is self-regulating
    b. spending is the driving force in the economy
    c. supply creates its own demand
    d. All of the above

_____ 4. Consumption:
    a. is the largest component of Total Expenditures
    b. is determined primarily by disposable income
    c. is unrelated to the current level of Real GDP
    d. Both a. and b. above

_____ 5. If disposable income increases from $16,000 to $20,000, and consumption
increases from $14,000 to $17,400, the marginal propensity to consume is:
    a. .75
    b. .85
    c. 1.18
    d. 3400

_____ 6. The marginal propensity to consume is:
    a. the slope of the consumption function
    b. the change in consumption divided by the change in income
    c. the slope of the Total Expenditures curve
    d. All of the above

_____ 7. If the consumption function lies below the 45° angle line:
      a. consumption is greater than disposable income
      b. saving is occurring at this level of disposable income
      c. Both of the above
      d. Neither of the above

_____ 8. According to Keynesian theory:
      a. the level of Total Expenditures determines the level of Real GDP
      b. as Real GDP increases, investment will increase
      c. as Real GDP increases, consumption will stay the same
      d. All of the above

_____ 9. According to Keynesian theory:
      a. as Real GDP increases, government purchases will increase
      b. a change in the current level of Real GDP will <u>not</u> change the level of net exports
      c. Both of the above
      d. Neither of the above

_____ 10. According to Keynesian theory, equilibrium Real GDP occurs where:
      a. Total Expenditures equals Real GDP
      b. the Total Expenditures curve intersects the 45° angle line
      c. Both of the above
      d. Neither of the above

_____ 11. According to Keynesian theory, if Total Expenditures is greater than Real GDP:
      a. the economy is in an inflationary gap
      b. inventories will increase
      c. production will increase
      d. All of the above

_____ 12. According to Keynesian theory, the multiplier effect occurs because:
      a. the initial change in Total Expenditures triggers a chain reaction
      b. any change in production causes a change in consumption
      c. Both of the above
      d. Neither of the above

_____ 13. If the MPC is .775, what is the Multiplier?
      a. 2.25
      b. 3.75
      c. 4.25
      d. 4.44

_____ 14. If the MPC is .667, and investment decreases by $60 billion, what is the resulting change in Real GDP?
      a.   $60 billion increase
      b.   $60 billion decrease
      c. $180 billion decrease
      d. $180 billion increase

_____ 15. If the MPC is .90, and investment spending increases by $25 billion, how much will Real GDP increase?
- a. $500 billion
- b. $250 billion
- c. $125 billion
- d. $25 billion

_____ 16. If an increase in investment of $75 billion leads to an increase in Real GDP of $300 billion, the MPC must be:
- a. .75
- b. .80
- c. 2.00
- d. 4.00

_____ 17. "The General Theory of Employment, Interest, and Money":
- a. proposed deficit spending as the cure for the Great Depression
- b. immediately caused a revolution in U.S. economic policy
- c. provided the explanation for the stagflation of the 1970s
- d. All of the above

_____ 18. "The General Theory" asserted:
- a. a decrease in investment caused by a decrease in expected rates of return is the most likely cause of recession
- b. government control of investment will prove necessary to achieve full employment
- c. Both of the above
- d. Neither of the above

## Problems:

1. When disposable income increases from $14,500 to $18,700, consumption increases from $12,300 to $15,240. Compute the marginal propensity to consume.

2. Explain the relationship between Total Expenditures and Real GDP, according to Keynesian theory.

3. Using the graph below:
   a. Indicate the equilibrium Price Level and Real GDP
   b. Show the effect of an increase in investment on the Total Expenditures curve and on Real GDP

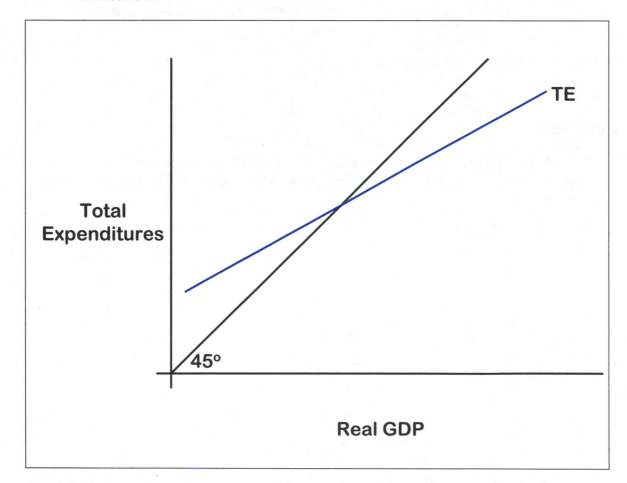

4. If the MPC is .667, and investment decreases by $45 billion, what is the resulting change in Real GDP?

## Answers for Chapter 8

**Fill-in-the-blanks:**  1. marginal propensity
2. investment

**Multiple Choice:**

| | | |
|---|---|---|
| 1. c. | 7. b. | 13. d. |
| 2. d. | 8. a. | 14. c. |
| 3. b. | 9. b. | 15. b. |
| 4. d. | 10. c. | 16. a. |
| 5. b. | 11. c. | 17. a. |
| 6. d. | 12. c. | 18. c. |

## Problems:

1. MPC = Change in consumption ÷ Change in income = $2,940 ÷ $4,200 = .70

2. According to Keynesian theory, the level of Total Expenditures determines the level of Real GDP. An increase in Total Expenditures will cause an increase in Real GDP. A decrease in Total Expenditures will cause a decrease in Real GDP.

3.

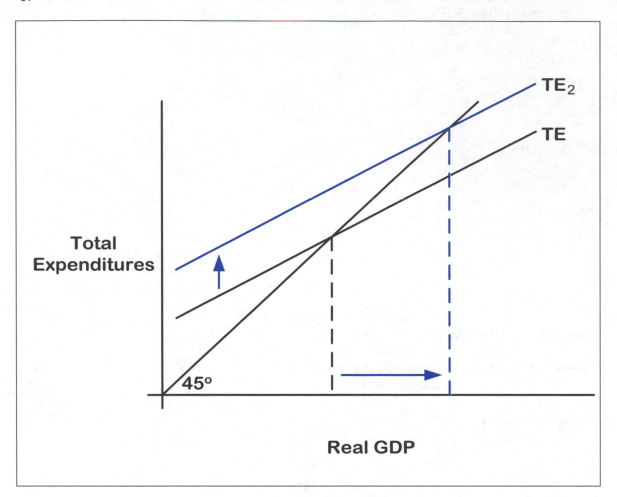

4. Multiplier = 1 ÷ (1 – MPC) = 1 ÷ (1 - .667) = 1 ÷ .333 = 3
   Change in Real GDP = Initial change x Multiplier = $45 billion decrease x 3 =
   $135 billion decrease

# Chapter 9  Fiscal Policy

The basic economic problem is scarcity. Human wants are unlimited. Resources are limited. The basic goal in dealing with the problem of scarcity is to produce as much consumer satisfaction as possible with the limited resources available. Achieving each of the three macroeconomic goals (price level stability, full employment, and economic growth) will contribute toward reaching this basic goal.

We saw in earlier chapters that the ideal quantity of total output is called Natural Real GDP. Natural Real GDP is the quantity of total output that results in the natural unemployment rate (full employment).

The economy may produce at Natural Real GDP in the short run, or may suffer from a recessionary gap or an inflationary gap.

Whether or not the economy produces at Natural Real GDP in the short run may be affected by the government's fiscal policy. Fiscal policy may also affect the level of economic growth in the long run (according to supply-side theory, discussed later in this chapter).

**Fiscal policy** – changes in government expenditures and taxation to achieve macroeconomic goals.

Changes in fiscal policy affect the federal government's budget. The federal government's budget could be balanced, with tax revenues equal to government expenditures. Typically, the government's budget will be in deficit or surplus.

**Budget deficit** – when government expenditures are greater than tax revenues.

**Budget surplus** – when tax revenues are greater than government expenditures.

A history of the federal government's budget, detailing annual tax revenues, expenditures, and budget surpluses (or deficits) is provided in an appendix to this chapter. The history covers the fiscal years from 1929 through 2008.

## Keynesian Fiscal Policy Theory

According to Keynesian theory, the level of Real GDP is determined by the level of Total Expenditures (see Chapter 8). An increase in Total Expenditures will cause an increase in Real GDP. A decrease in Total Expenditures will cause a decrease in Real GDP.

The level of Total Expenditures may not be the level that will cause the economy to achieve Natural Real GDP. If Total Expenditures is less than the ideal, the result will be a recessionary gap. If Total Expenditures is greater than the ideal, the result will be an inflationary gap.

The government may be able to move the level of Total Expenditures toward the ideal level (and move Real GDP toward Natural Real GDP) by using fiscal policy.

## Keynesian Fiscal Policy Theory and a Recessionary Gap

According to Keynesian theory, fiscal policy can be used to move the economy toward Natural Real GDP. If the economy is in a recessionary gap, Real GDP is less than Natural Real GDP. To close a recessionary gap, Total Expenditures needs to increase.

An increase in Total Expenditures can be caused by expansionary fiscal policy (an increase in government expenditures and/or a decrease in taxation). To close a recessionary gap, Keynesian theory calls for the use of expansionary fiscal policy.

Expansionary fiscal policy will alter the government's budget situation. Assuming that the budget is initially balanced, expansionary fiscal policy will create a budget deficit. Thus, Keynesian theory calls for the use of deficit spending to close a recessionary gap.

> **Example 1:** If Real GDP is $15,000 billion and Natural Real GDP is $15,500 billion, the economy is in a recessionary gap. Keynesian theory calls for expansionary fiscal policy to close this recessionary gap. If the MPC is .80, the multiplier will be 5 (1 ÷ [1 – MPC]). With a multiplier of 5, an increase in government purchases of $100 billion would cause an eventual increase in Real GDP of $500 billion (Change in Real GDP = Initial Change x Multiplier). If Real GDP increases by $500 billion, the recessionary gap is closed and Real GDP equals Natural Real GDP.

The graphs below and on the next page illustrate the recessionary gap and the return to Natural Real GDP triggered by the increase in government purchases.

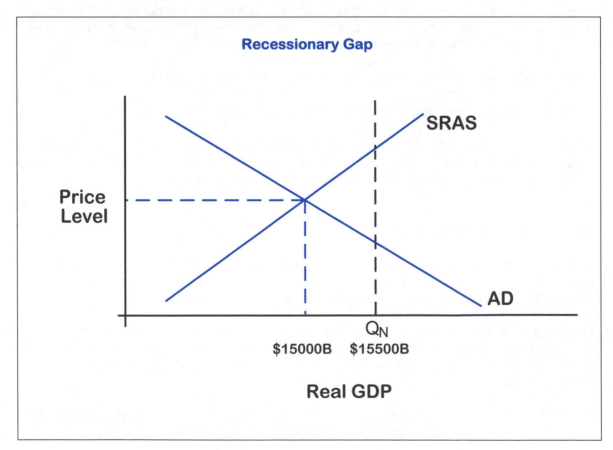

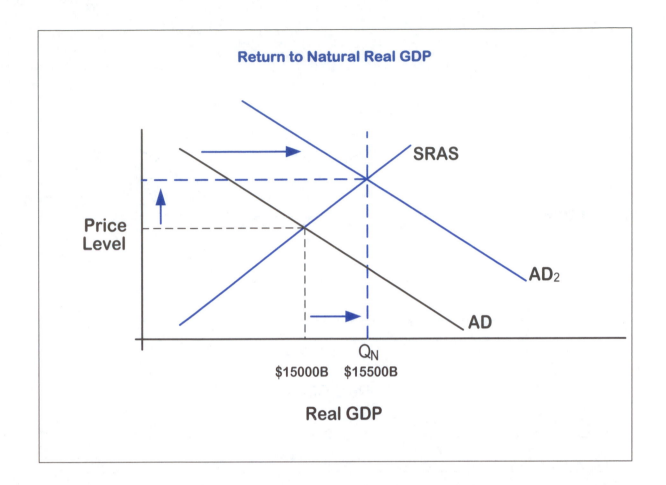

**Return to Natural Real GDP**

## Keynesian Fiscal Policy Theory and an Inflationary Gap

If the economy is in an inflationary gap, Real GDP is greater than Natural Real GDP. To close an inflationary gap, Total Expenditures needs to decrease.

A decrease in Total Expenditures can be caused by contractionary fiscal policy (a decrease in government expenditures and/or an increase in taxation). To close an inflationary gap, Keynesian theory calls for the use of contractionary fiscal policy.

Contractionary fiscal policy will alter the government's budget situation. Assuming that the budget is initially balanced, contractionary fiscal policy will create a budget surplus. Thus, Keynesian theory calls for the use of budget surpluses to close an inflationary gap.

**Example 2:** If Real GDP is $16,000 billion and Natural Real GDP is $15,500 billion, the economy is in an inflationary gap. Keynesian theory calls for contractionary fiscal policy to close this inflationary gap. If the MPC is .80, the multiplier will be 5 $(1 \div [1 - MPC])$. With a multiplier of 5, a decrease in government purchases of $100 billion would cause an eventual decrease in Real GDP of $500 billion (Change in Real GDP = Initial Change x Multiplier). If Real GDP decreases by $500 billion, the inflationary gap is closed and Real GDP equals Natural Real GDP.

The graphs on the next page illustrate the inflationary gap and the return to Natural Real GDP triggered by the decrease in government purchases.

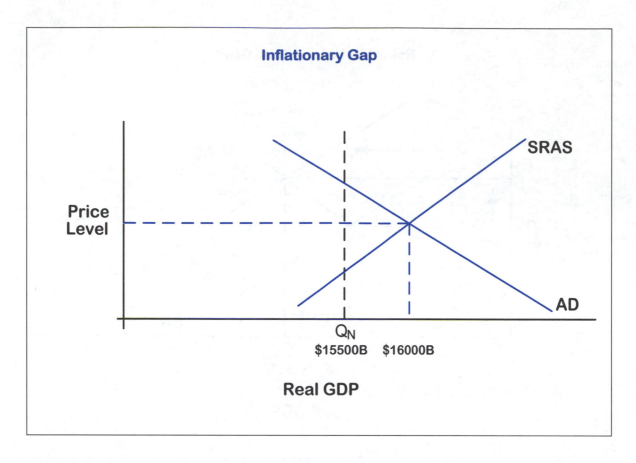

Inflationary Gap

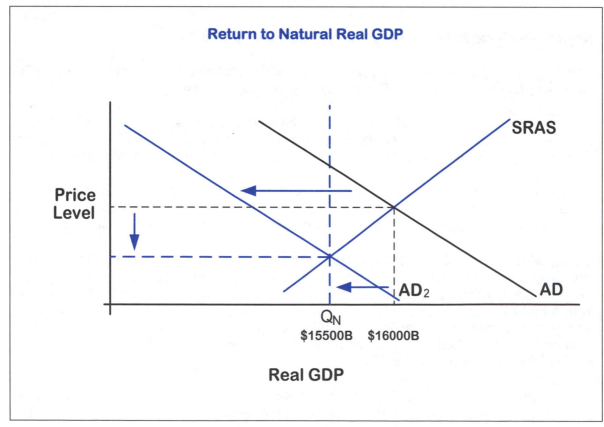

Return to Natural Real GDP

## Automatic Stabilizers

Keynesian fiscal policy theory calls for deficit spending to close a recessionary gap and for budget surpluses to close an inflationary gap. Certain aspects of the federal government's budget will tend to automatically increase the budget deficit (or reduce the surplus) during a recessionary gap and will tend to automatically increase the budget surplus (or reduce the deficit) during an inflationary gap.

These aspects of the budget are called automatic stabilizers. They are automatic in that they do not require any legislative change in fiscal policy. They are stabilizers in that they will tend to move equilibrium Real GDP toward Natural Real GDP.

**Automatic stabilizers** – taxes and transfer payments that automatically tend to move equilibrium Real GDP toward Natural Real GDP.

The automatic stabilizers are taxes and transfer payments. Certain transfer payments will automatically increase during a recessionary gap and will automatically decrease during an inflationary gap. For example, during a recessionary gap, the number of people qualifying for unemployment compensation will increase.

Certain taxes will automatically decrease during a recessionary gap and will automatically increase during an inflationary gap. For example, during an inflationary gap, the income tax paid by individuals and corporations will increase.

---

**Example 3:** The unemployment rate increased from 4% in 2000 to 6% in 2003. Unemployment compensation increased from $23 billion in 2000 to $57 billion in 2003. Corporate income taxes decreased from $207 billion in 2000 to $132 billion in 2003.

---

## Potential Problems with Fiscal Policy

According to Keynesian theory, fiscal policy can and should be used to move the economy toward Natural Real GDP. But there are four potential problems with attempting to use fiscal policy to stabilize the economy:

1. **There may be a political bias toward expansionary fiscal policy at all times.** Keynesian theory calls for expansionary fiscal policy to close recessionary gaps, and contractionary fiscal policy to close inflationary gaps. But contractionary fiscal policy (raising taxes and/or reducing government spending) may be unpopular with the voters. Elected officials may prefer expansionary fiscal policy (lowering taxes and/or increasing government spending) at all times.

---

**Example 4:** Since the U.S. Constitution took effect in 1789, the federal government has had annual budget surpluses in more years than it has had annual budget deficits. However, since Keynesian theory was introduced in 1936, the federal government has had budget deficits in all but 12 years.

---

2. **Crowding out may occur. Crowding out** occurs when increases in government spending lead to decreases in private spending. The basic economic problem is scarcity. When government spending increases, the government is using more of

the limited resources. Fewer resources are available for the private sector (consumption and investment). Which type of private spending will be crowded out depends on how the increased government spending is financed;

a. If increased government spending is paid for with increased taxes, this will mainly reduce consumption. Tax increases reduce disposable income. A decrease in disposable income will cause a decrease in both consumption and investment, but will primarily reduce consumption.

**Example 5A:** The federal government decides to increase its spending on the interstate highway system. To pay for the increase in government spending, the federal gasoline excise tax is doubled. Millions of American households are left with less disposable income. Consumption decreases.

b. If increased government spending is paid for with deficit spending, this will mainly reduce investment. Deficit spending means a greater government demand for loanable funds, which will increase interest rates. Higher interest rates will cause a decrease in both consumption and investment, but will primarily reduce investment.

**Example 5B:** The federal government decides to increase its spending on the interstate highway system. To pay for the increase in government spending, federal government borrowing is increased. As a result, interest rates increase. Investment decreases.

3. **Fiscal policy may be mistimed because of lags;**

a. **The information lag.** Government policymakers have access to information about upturns or downturns in the business cycle only after some time has passed.

**Example 6A:** An economic downturn begins in February. Will government policymakers know in February that a downturn has begun and that it is time to enact expansionary fiscal policy? No. Accurate total output numbers for the economy will not be available until some time after the fact. For instance, the Bureau of Economic Analysis released "preliminary" GDP estimates for the third quarter of 2008 (July through September) on November 25, 2008.

b. **The policy lag.** Enacting a change in fiscal policy (a tax cut, a new spending program) takes time. Given the nature of the political process, bargaining over the details of a change in fiscal policy may take many months, or even years.

**Example 6B:** An economic downturn begins in February. By May, government policymakers decide that expansionary fiscal policy should be used. They decide to increase federal government spending on the interstate highway system. They begin to negotiate over how the spending will be divided among different congressional districts. This bargaining process takes time. For instance, President Kennedy proposed a major tax cut on April 20, 1961. The tax cut was finally enacted on February 26, 1964.

c. **The impact lag.** Once a change in fiscal policy is enacted, it takes time before the new policy has its full effect on Real GDP.

> **Example 6C:** An economic downturn begins in February. In October, legislation is enacted to increase federal government spending on the interstate highway system. Will this legislation immediately boost Total Expenditures? No. It will take time for the competitive bidding process, the gathering of resources, and the "steps" in the multiplier process. By the time that Total Expenditures begins to significantly increase, the downturn that began in February may be over. Since World War II, recessions have lasted on average a little more than ten months.

4. **Fiscal policy may be miscalculated.** In theory, the government determines what Real GDP is, what Natural Real GDP is, what the multiplier is, and then implements the appropriate fiscal policy to close an inflationary gap or a recessionary gap. (See Examples 1 and 2 from earlier in this chapter.) Unfortunately, the government doesn't really know how large the multiplier will be, what Natural Real GDP is, or even what the current level of Real GDP is.

Given these potential problems with fiscal policy, government attempts to stabilize the economy with fiscal policy may do more harm than good.

## Supply-side Economics

Supply-side economics is a branch of economics based on classical theory. Supply-side economics arose in the 1970s as an alternative to the dominant Keynesian economic theory.

Supply-side economics emphasizes long run economic growth rather than short run economic stability. Supply-side economics argues that long run economic growth can be best achieved by maximizing the incentives that producers have to increase production. In other words, by encouraging the supply side of the economy.

## Supply-side Fiscal Policy versus Keynesian Fiscal Policy

Keynesian fiscal policy theory emphasizes using fiscal policy to manipulate aggregate demand in order to achieve economic stability (full employment) in the short run. But supply-side economists assert that fiscal policy will also affect the supply side of the economy, both in the short run and in the long run. Supply-side economists argue that Keynesian fiscal policy has had a harmful effect on the supply side of the economy.

Keynesian theory has made deficit spending politically acceptable. Since Keynesian theory was introduced, deficit spending has become the norm for fiscal policy. As mentioned earlier in the chapter, the federal government has had budgets deficits in all but 12 years since Keynesian theory was introduced.

Deficit spending has led to a growing federal government. It is politically easier to increase government spending if taxes are not increased at the same time that the government spending is increased. Deficit spending makes this possible.

> **Example 7A:** In 1929 (before Keynesian theory made deficit spending politically acceptable), federal government expenditures were equal to about 2.5% of GDP. Currently, federal government expenditures are typically equal to about 20% of GDP.

> **Example 7B:** In 1929, federal government expenditures were $3.1 billion. In 2008, federal government expenditures were $2,979 billion. After adjusting for inflation, federal government expenditures increased by about 77-fold.

The growing federal government has led to higher marginal tax rates in order to finance (most) of the government spending. According to supply-side theory, high marginal tax rates have a harmful effect on the supply side of the economy, both in the short run and in the long run.

High marginal tax rates reduce the incentive to earn higher income in the short run. Thus, high marginal tax rates will tend to reduce SRAS. High marginal tax rates also reduce the incentive to increase the productive capacity of one's resources in the long run. Thus, high marginal tax rates will tend to reduce LRAS.

High marginal tax rates will likely affect LRAS more than SRAS, as illustrated in Example 8 below.

> **Example 8:** If the top marginal income tax rate were increased from 35% (where it is in 2008) to 70% (where it was before the tax cuts of the 1980s), not very many surgeons, research scientists, software designers, etc. would give up their high income careers for something less demanding. But how many young people would decide that the sacrifice and cost of training to become a surgeon, research scientist, software designer, etc. was no longer worth the effort?

The importance of incentives is discussed in an appendix at the end of this chapter.

Supply-side economists support lowering marginal tax rates. Lower marginal tax rates will increase incentives to earn higher income in the short run and to increase the productive capacity of one's resources in the long run. Thus, lower marginal tax rates will increase production in both the short run and the long run.

### The Laffer Curve

What will happen to the government's tax revenues if tax rates are reduced? The obvious answer would seem to be that lower tax rates will result in less tax revenue. But supply-side economists believe that the opposite may be true.

Lower tax rates increase incentives and production. According to supply-side economist Arthur Laffer, the increase in production may increase the tax base (income) enough to more than offset the decrease in tax rates. Thus, lower tax rates may generate more tax revenue.

The relationship between tax rates and tax revenue is illustrated on a Laffer curve. The **Laffer curve** indicates that lowering tax rates may increase tax revenue.

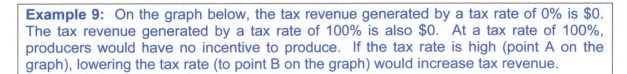

**Example 9:** On the graph below, the tax revenue generated by a tax rate of 0% is $0. The tax revenue generated by a tax rate of 100% is also $0. At a tax rate of 100%, producers would have no incentive to produce. If the tax rate is high (point A on the graph), lowering the tax rate (to point B on the graph) would increase tax revenue.

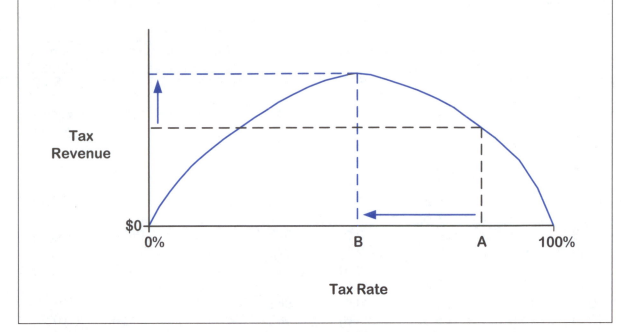

## Supply-side Tax Cuts

Ronald Reagan became President in 1981. That same year, Congress enacted a supply-side tax cut, which lowered the top marginal tax rate from 70% to 50%. In 1986, the top marginal tax rate was lowered to 28%.

Did these tax cuts reduce taxes paid by high income taxpayers? On the contrary, the taxes paid by the highest income taxpayers increased, while the taxes paid by most taxpayers stayed essentially the same. Overall, tax revenue increased after the tax cuts.

**Example 10A:** In 1990, the top 1% of income earners paid 51% more federal income taxes (in real dollars) than they had paid in 1980. Likewise, the top 5% of income earners paid 36% more and the top 10% paid 28% more. The bottom 90% of income earners paid essentially the same in 1990 as they had in 1980.

**Example 10B:** The percentage of income tax paid by the top 1% of income earners increased from 17.6% of federal personal income taxes in 1981 to 27.5% in 1988. The percentage paid by the top 10% of income earners increased from 48.0% in 1981 to 57.2% in 1988, and the percentage paid by the bottom 50% of income earners decreased from 7.5% in 1981 to 5.7% in 1988.

The focus of supply-side theory is <u>not</u> on setting tax rates so as to maximize tax revenues. Most supply-side economists are more concerned with maximizing economic growth. Supply-siders support a smaller government and much lower tax rates in order to provide more incentives and to achieve more economic growth.

Fiscal Policy

## Appendix: History of the Federal Government's Budget

The table below shows the federal government's tax revenues, expenditures, and budget surplus (or deficit) for the years from 1929 to 2008. The amounts are in billions of dollars.

| Year | Tax Revenues | Government Expenditures | Surplus (Deficit) | Year | Tax Revenues | Government Expenditures | Surplus (Deficit) |
|---|---|---|---|---|---|---|---|
| 1929 | $3.8 | $3.1 | $0.7 | 1969 | $186.9 | $183.7 | $3.2 |
| 1930 | 4.0 | 3.3 | 0.7 | 1970 | 192.8 | 195.6 | (2.8) |
| 1931 | 3.1 | 3.6 | (0.5) | 1971 | 187.1 | 210.2 | (23.0) |
| 1932 | 1.9 | 4.6 | (2.7) | 1972 | 207.3 | 230.7 | (23.4) |
| 1933 | 2.0 | 4.6 | (2.6) | 1973 | 230.8 | 245.7 | (14.9) |
| 1934 | 2.9 | 6.5 | (3.6) | 1974 | 263.2 | 269.3 | (6.1) |
| 1935 | 3.6 | 6.4 | (2.8) | 1975 | 279.1 | 332.3 | (53.2) |
| 1936 | 3.9 | 8.2 | (4.3) | 1976 | 298.1 | 371.8 | (73.7) |
| 1937 | 5.4 | 7.6 | (2.2) | 1977 | 355.5 | 409.2 | (53.7) |
| 1938 | 6.7 | 6.8 | (0.9) | 1978 | 399.6 | 458.8 | (59.2) |
| 1939 | 6.3 | 9.1 | (2.8) | 1979 | 463.3 | 504.0 | (40.7) |
| 1940 | 6.6 | 9.5 | (2.9) | 1980 | 517.1 | 590.9 | (73.8) |
| 1941 | 8.7 | 13.6 | (4.9) | 1981 | 599.3 | 678.3 | (79.0) |
| 1942 | 14.6 | 35.1 | (20.5) | 1982 | 617.8 | 745.8 | (128.0) |
| 1943 | 24.0 | 78.6 | (54.6) | 1983 | 600.6 | 808.4 | (207.8) |
| 1944 | 43.7 | 91.3 | (47.6) | 1984 | 666.5 | 851.9 | (185.4) |
| 1945 | 45.2 | 92.7 | (47.6) | 1985 | 734.1 | 946.4 | (212.3) |
| 1946 | 39.3 | 55.2 | (15.9) | 1986 | 769.2 | 990.4 | (221.2) |
| 1947 | 38.5 | 34.5 | 4.0 | 1987 | 854.3 | 1004.1 | (149.8) |
| 1948 | 41.6 | 29.8 | 11.8 | 1988 | 909.3 | 1064.5 | (155.2) |
| 1949 | 39.4 | 38.8 | 0.6 | 1989 | 991.2 | 1143.7 | (152.5) |
| 1950 | 39.4 | 42.5 | (3.1) | 1990 | 1032.1 | 1253.1 | (221.0) |
| 1951 | 51.6 | 45.5 | 6.1 | 1991 | 1055.1 | 1324.3 | (269.2) |
| 1952 | 66.2 | 67.7 | (1.5) | 1992 | 1091.3 | 1381.6 | (290.3) |
| 1953 | 69.6 | 76.1 | (6.5) | 1993 | 1154.5 | 1409.5 | (255.0) |
| 1954 | 69.7 | 70.9 | (1.2) | 1994 | 1258.7 | 1461.9 | (203.2) |
| 1955 | 65.4 | 68.4 | (3.0) | 1995 | 1351.9 | 1515.9 | (164.0) |
| 1956 | 74.6 | 70.7 | 3.9 | 1996 | 1453.2 | 1560.6 | (107.4) |
| 1957 | 80.0 | 76.6 | 3.4 | 1997 | 1579.4 | 1601.3 | (21.9) |
| 1958 | 79.6 | 82.4 | (2.8) | 1998 | 1722.0 | 1652.7 | 69.3 |
| 1959 | 79.3 | 92.1 | (12.8) | 1999 | 1827.6 | 1702.0 | 125.6 |
| 1960 | 92.5 | 92.2 | 0.3 | 2000 | 2025.5 | 1789.2 | 236.2 |
| 1961 | 94.4 | 97.7 | (3.3) | 2001 | 1991.4 | 1863.2 | 128.2 |
| 1962 | 99.7 | 106.8 | (7.1) | 2002 | 1853.4 | 2011.2 | (157.8) |
| 1963 | 106.5 | 111.3 | (4.8) | 2003 | 1782.5 | 2160.1 | (377.6) |
| 1964 | 112.6 | 118.5 | (5.9) | 2004 | 1880.3 | 2293.0 | (412.7) |
| 1965 | 116.8 | 118.2 | (1.4) | 2005 | 2153.9 | 2472.2 | (318.3) |
| 1966 | 130.8 | 134.5 | (3.7) | 2006 | 2407.3 | 2655.4 | (248.1) |
| 1967 | 148.8 | 157.4 | (8.6) | 2007 | 2568.2 | 2730.2 | (162.0) |
| 1968 | 153.0 | 178.2 | (25.2) | 2008 | 2524.0 | 2979.0 | (455.0) |

## Appendix: The Importance of Incentives

A fundamental assumption of economic reasoning is that people are rational and thus respond to incentives. Steven Landsburg began his 1993 book, "The Armchair Economist", by stating, "Most of economics can be summarized in four words: 'People respond to incentives.' The rest is commentary."

The following story (inspired by the classic television series "The Many Loves of Dobie Gillis"), illustrates the importance of incentives.

On the first day of school, the principal of Central High announces that an emphasis will be placed on physical fitness in the upcoming school year. A number of students are selected at random to participate in a push-up competition. One of the students selected for the competition is Maynard, a gangly beatnik (who bears a striking resemblance to Gilligan).

Maynard manages only seven push-ups before giving up. When the principal encourages Maynard to "try harder", Maynard replies, "Push-ups ain't my scene, daddy-o". If Maynard's push-up ability were re-tested a week later or at the end of the school year, it seems unlikely that his performance would improve.

But the plot thickens. A local millionaire, Mr. Armitage, learns of Maynard's paltry push-up performance from his son Milton (who looks a lot like Clyde). Mr. Armitage is outraged at Maynard's poor performance and offers Maynard a $100 payment for every push-up that he can perform in a re-test one week after the initial competition. Maynard is still a gangly beatnik, but now he has more incentive, and manages thirteen push-ups before collapsing in exhaustion.

Mr. Armitage is pleased with Maynard's improved performance and announces that Maynard will be re-tested again at the end of the school year and will be paid $1,000 for every push-up that he can perform. How will Maynard spend the upcoming school year? Hanging out with his buddy, Dobie, and playing the bongo drums? Or hanging out in the gym, lifting weights? Incentives are important. People respond to incentives.

## Questions for Chapter 9

### Fill-in-the-blanks:

1. _____ policy is changes in government expenditures and taxation to achieve macroeconomic goals.

2. A budget _____ occurs when government expenditures are greater than tax revenues.

3. A budget _____ occurs when tax revenues are greater than government expenditures.

4. _____ _____ are taxes and transfer payments that automatically tend to move equilibrium Real GDP toward Natural Real GDP.

5. _____ _____ occurs when increases in government spending lead to decreases in private spending.

6. The _____ curve indicates that lowering tax rates might actually increase tax revenue.

**Multiple Choice:**

_____ 1. According to Keynesian theory:
    a. fiscal policy can be used to move the economy toward Natural Real GDP
    b. to close a recessionary gap, contractionary fiscal policy should be used
    c. to close an inflationary gap, expansionary fiscal policy should be used
    d. All of the above

_____ 2. Which of the following would be expansionary fiscal policy?
    a. an increase in taxation
    b. an increase in government expenditures
    c. an increase in the money supply
    d. All of the above

_____ 3. According to Keynesian theory, during a recessionary gap the government's budget:
    a. should be balanced
    b. should be in deficit
    c. should be in surplus

_____ 4. A decrease in government expenditures:
    a. would tend to cause a budget deficit
    b. would be expansionary fiscal policy
    c. would be proper fiscal policy during an inflationary gap, according to Keynesian theory
    d. All of the above

_____ 5. If Real GDP is $15,950 billion and Natural Real GDP is $15,500 billion, and the MPC is .667, how large a change in government purchases would be necessary to close the inflationary gap?
    a. $450 billion decrease
    b. $225 billion decrease
    c. $150 billion decrease
    d. $150 billion increase

_____ 6. Automatic stabilizers:
    a. require legislative changes in fiscal policy
    b. will tend to move equilibrium Real GDP toward Natural Real GDP
    c. Both of the above
    d. Neither of the above

_____ 7. During a recessionary gap:
   a. unemployment compensation payments will increase, acting as an automatic stabilizer
   b. corporate income tax payments will increase, acting as an automatic stabilizer
   c. Both of the above
   d. Neither of the above

_____ 8. Crowding out:
   a. occurs when increases in government spending lead to decreases in private spending
   b. can be caused by a decrease in the money supply
   c. does not occur when the government deficit spends
   d. All of the above

_____ 9. Fiscal policy may be mistimed because of:
   a. the jet lag
   b. the putting lag
   c. the impact lag
   d. All of the above

_____ 10. Since World War II:
   a. recessions have been eliminated by proper use of Keynesian fiscal policy
   b. recessions have occurred predictably every five years
   c. recessions have lasted on average a little more than ten months
   d. None of the above

_____ 11. Which of the following is a potential problem with fiscal policy?
   a. crowding out may cause an increase in private spending
   b. there may a political bias toward contractionary fiscal policy
   c. fiscal policy may be miscalculated
   d. All of the above

_____ 12. Since Keynesian theory was introduced in 1936, the federal government:
   a. has had budget deficits in most years
   b. has grown relative to the size of the economy
   c. Both of the above
   d. Neither of the above

_____ 13. Supply-side economists argue that Keynesian fiscal policy:
   a. has had a beneficial effect on the supply side of the economy
   b. has made deficit spending politically acceptable
   c. has led to a shrinking federal government
   d. All of the above

_____ 14. According to supply-side fiscal policy, a decrease in marginal tax rates:
   a. will always result in more tax revenues
   b. will increase incentives
   c. will increase production in the short run, but not in the long run
   d. All of the above

Fiscal Policy

_____ 15. The supply-side tax cuts of 1981 and 1986:
  a. resulted in less tax revenue
  b. increased the taxes paid by lower income taxpayers
  c. increased the taxes paid by the highest income taxpayers
  d. Both a. and b. above

_____ 16. Supply-side economists:
  a. believe Keynesian fiscal policy harms the economy
  b. favor lower marginal tax rates
  c. favor a smaller government
  d. All of the above

_____ 17. Between 1961 and 1997, the federal government's nominal expenditures increased by:
  a. more than 5-fold
  b. more than 9-fold
  c. more than 13-fold
  d. more than 16-fold

_____ 18. Between 1961 and 1997, the federal government's budget was in surplus:
  a. one year
  b. three years
  c. seven years
  d. nine years

_____ 19. According to Steven Landsburg, most of economics can be summarized in these four words:
  a. "Demand and supply equal"
  b. "People respond to incentives"
  c. "The rich get richer"
  d. "According to Adam Smith"

## Problems:

1. Explain the proper fiscal policy for closing a recessionary gap, according to Keynesian theory.

2. Explain what automatic stabilizers are and give two examples of automatic stabilizers.

3. List the four potential problems with attempting to use fiscal policy to stabilize the economy.

4. How has Keynesian fiscal policy had a harmful effect on the supply side of the economy, according to supply-side economists?

## Answers for Chapter 9

**Fill-in-the-blanks:**
1. Fiscal
2. deficit
3. surplus
4. Automatic stabilizers
5. Crowding out
6. Laffer

**Multiple Choice:**

| | | |
|---|---|---|
| 1. a. | 8. a. | 15. c. |
| 2. b. | 9. c. | 16. d. |
| 3. b. | 10. c. | 17. d. |
| 4. c. | 11. c. | 18. a. |
| 5. c. | 12. c. | 19. b. |
| 6. b. | 13. b. | |
| 7. a. | 14. b. | |

## Problems:

1. To close a recessionary gap, Keynesian theory calls for the use of expansionary fiscal policy (an increase in government expenditures or a decrease in taxation). Thus, Keynesian theory calls for the use of deficit spending to close a recessionary gap.

2. Automatic stabilizers are taxes and transfer payments that automatically tend to move equilibrium Real GDP toward Natural Real GDP. Automatic stabilizers will tend to automatically increase a budget deficit during a recessionary gap and automatically increase a budget surplus during an inflationary gap. For example, during a recessionary gap, the number of people qualifying for unemployment compensation will increase. During an inflationary gap, the income tax paid by individuals and corporations will increase.

3. There are four potential problems with attempting to use fiscal policy to stabilize the economy:
   (1) There may be a political bias toward expansionary fiscal policy at all times
   (2) Crowding out may occur
   (3) Fiscal policy may be mistimed because of lags
   (4) Fiscal policy may be miscalculated

4. Supply-side economists argue that Keynesian fiscal policy has had a harmful effect on the supply side of the economy by:
   (1) Keynesian theory has made deficit spending politically acceptable.
   (2) Deficit spending has led to a growing federal government.
   (3) The growing federal government has led to higher marginal tax rates in order to finance (most) of the government spending.
   (4) High marginal tax rates have a harmful effect on the supply side of the economy by reducing incentives.

# Chapter 10  Money and Money Creation

The basic economic problem is scarcity.  Human wants are unlimited.  Resources are limited.  In the U.S., the problem of scarcity is dealt with mainly through markets.  Market exchanges can be made by barter, but most market exchanges are made through the use of money.

## Money

What is money?  We often use the word "money" when we really mean something else, such as income ("Pro athletes earn a lot of money") or wealth ("Bill Gates has a lot of money") or resources ("There isn't enough money to provide quality health care for everyone").  In the next three chapters, we need to use the word "money" more precisely.

**Money** – whatever is generally accepted as a medium of exchange.

Money is whatever is generally accepted as a medium of exchange.  Historically, various commodities have been used as money (e.g. gold, silver, salt, rice, cattle, tobacco, corn, etc.). Almost anything can be used as money, as long as people are willing to accept it as a medium of exchange.

> **Example 1:**  The castaways on Gilligan's Island decide to use Monopoly money as their medium of exchange.  As long as they are willing to accept Monopoly money in trade, it will be money for them.

The money we use today is not a commodity.  It is fiat money.  **Fiat money** is money by government decree or fiat (because the government says that it is money).  Fiat money has no intrinsic value.  But fiat money is valuable as long as it is generally accepted as a medium of exchange.  More about this later.

If the money we use has no intrinsic value, then why do we want money?  We want money in order to make trades for goods and services or resources.

Money is <u>not</u> a good or a service.  We don't want money to consume.  We want money to trade for goods and services that we can consume.

Money is <u>not</u> a resource.  We cannot produce anything with money (except maybe a fire).  We don't want money to use as a factor of production.  We want money to trade for resources that we can use as factors of production.

Though money is not useful for consumption or production, money is very useful in a market economy.  If we didn't have money (a medium of exchange), we would have to make exchanges by barter.

**Barter** – the direct exchange of goods.

Barter as a means of exchange seems simple. You just trade stuff for stuff. But there is a problem. To make a trade by barter requires a double coincidence of wants. You must find someone who has what you want and who wants what you have. This is much more difficult than making a trade through the use of money.

> **Example 2:** Donita, a dressmaker in a barter economy, wants a new pair of shoes. She offers to trade a dress to Carl the Cobbler for a pair of shoes. Unfortunately, Carl doesn't want a dress. Carl is willing to trade the shoes for a bag of hobnails. Donita offers to trade a dress to Blake the Blacksmith for a bag of hobnails. Unfortunately, Blake doesn't want a dress. Blake is willing to trade the hobnails for a new cooking pot. Donita offers to trade a dress to Tim the Tinker for a new cooking pot. Unfortunately, Tim doesn't want a dress. Tim is willing to trade the cooking pot for a new hat. Donita offers to trade a dress to Millicent the Milliner for a new hat. Unfortunately, Millicent doesn't want a dress. Millicent is willing to trade the hat for flowers. Donita offers to trade a dress to Fatima the Florist for flowers. Fortunately, Fatima wants a dress. So, Donita trades a dress to Fatima for flowers, trades the flowers to Millicent for a hat, trades the hat to Tim for a new cooking pot, trades the cooking pot to Blake for the hobnails, and trades the hobnails to Carl for the shoes. Whew.

With money as the medium of exchange, a double coincidence of wants is not required. You find someone who wants what you have and sell it to him or her for money. Then you take the money and buy what you want from someone who has what you want.

Using money to make the exchange eliminates the need for a double coincidence of wants. Thus, money reduces the transaction costs of making exchanges. This allows for a greater degree of specialization and trade, which leads to a higher standard of living.

The primary function of money is to serve as a medium of exchange.


## Functions of Money

1.  **Medium of exchange.** As discussed above, money serves as a medium of exchange, a way to make trades more easily. Using money as a medium of exchange reduces the transaction costs of making exchanges. This enables people to make more exchanges and to specialize in producing according to comparative advantage. This is the most important function of money.

2.  **Measure of value.** Money is used to measure value. The value of goods, services, and resources is expressed in terms of the monetary unit. When we compare the prices of different goods, services, or resources, we are using money as a measure of value. Having a measure of value makes it easier to discover mutually beneficial exchanges.

3.  **Store of value.** When we receive money, we don't have to spend it immediately. We can store up the buying power for later use by holding onto the money. This allows us to use our buying power when it is most valuable to us. Money is not a perfect store of value. Money can be lost or stolen. Another problem with using money as a store of value is that inflation can reduce money's value (buying power).

> **Example 3:**  Cathey goes to the dress store.  She compares the prices of the dresses available.  The red dress is $180.  The blue dress is $120.  Cathey likes the red dress better, but the blue dress is cheaper.  Cathey is using money as a measure of value.  Cathey decides to buy the blue dress.  She hands the clerk the necessary money ($120 plus tax) to pay for the dress.  Cathey is using money as a medium of exchange.  Then Cathey changes her mind.  She decides to keep her money and wait for the red dress to go on sale.  She is using money as a store of value.

## Why Money Is Valuable

Money is valuable.  Practically everyone would agree with that statement.  But why is money valuable?  Is money valuable because it is backed by gold?  No.  The U.S. went off the gold standard years ago.  And even when our currency was backed by gold, the gold was not the source of the money's value.

Money has value because it is generally accepted as a medium of exchange.  Money is not valuable in itself.  We do not want money to keep.  We want money to trade for what we really want.

Since we use money as a measure of value, we tend to think that money makes goods valuable.  But it's the other way around.  The goods and services we produce make our money valuable.  Because we can trade the money for the goods and services.

> **Example 4:**  The castaways on Gilligan's Island are using Monopoly money as their medium of exchange.  One day a crate floats up to the island.  When Gilligan opens the crate, he discovers that it contains a dozen Monopoly games.  Gilligan is ecstatic.  "We're rich!" he shouts.  But the castaways are no better off than before.  With the increase in the money supply, the price of coconuts will increase.  But the money does not make the coconuts valuable.  The coconuts make the money valuable.

## Measuring the Money Supply

Money is whatever is generally accepted as a medium of exchange.  There are different measures of the money supply:

1.  **Currency.**  Currency is the most basic measure of the money supply.  Currency consists of the coins and paper money issued by the federal government.

2.  **M1.**  M1 consists of currency in circulation (held outside banks) plus checkable deposits.  **Checkable deposits** are deposits in banks or other financial institutions on which checks can be written.  M1 is sometimes called "transactions money".

3.  **M2.**  M2 consists of M1 plus small-denomination time deposits, savings deposits, and money market accounts.

The measure of the money supply we will use is M1.  As of November, 2008, the money supply (M1) was approximately $1,520 billion.

## Checks and Credit Cards

A large percentage of transactions are made through the use of checks and credit cards. Are checks and credit cards money? Checks are <u>not</u> money. Checks are a way to transfer the money held in a checkable deposit. The checkable deposit is money, but the check is not.

> **Example 5:** Professor D. Imwit writes a check for $1500 to purchase a new plasma television. Has Professor Imwit spent money? If the balance in Professor Imwit's checking account is sufficient to cover the amount of the check, Professor Imwit has spent money. The check allows Professor Imwit to use some of his money (checkable deposit) to pay for the TV. If the balance of Professor Imwit's checking account is not sufficient to cover the check, Professor has <u>not</u> spent money. He has committed fraud.

Are credit cards money? Credit cards are <u>not</u> money. When a purchase is made through the use of a credit card, the purchaser is not spending money to make the purchase, he or she is taking out a loan.

> **Example 6:** Professor Imwit purchases a new plasma television for $1500 using his credit card. Professor Imwit has not spent money to buy the television. He has taken out a loan. When he writes a check to make a payment on his credit card balance, he is spending money (assuming that the balance in his checking account is sufficient to cover the amount of the check).

## Money Creation

Our banking system is a fractional reserve system. In a fractional reserve system, banks are able to create money.

**Money creation** – increases in checkable deposits made possible by fractional reserve banking.

In a fractional reserve system, banks hold reserves equal to only a fraction of their deposits. Fractional reserve banking makes it possible for banks to serve as financial intermediaries.

**Financial intermediation** – the process by which banks make depositors' savings available to borrowers.

Financial intermediation is discussed in more detail in the appendix at the end of this chapter.

The fraction of deposits that a bank must hold in reserve is determined by the required-reserve ratio. The required-reserve ratio is set by the Federal Reserve System.

As of January 9, 2009, the actual reserve ratio on checkable deposits was 10% on checkable deposit balances in excess of $44.4 million, was 3% on checkable deposit balances of $10.3 million to $44.4 million, and was 0% for checkable deposit balances of less than $10.3 million.

For simplicity, we will generally assume that all checkable deposit balances are subject to the 10% reserve ratio. There is no reserve requirement for savings deposits and time deposits.

> **Example 7:** 1$^{st}$ Bank receives a checkable deposit of $5,000. 1$^{st}$ Bank is legally required to keep a portion of the deposits it receives in reserve. If the reserve ratio is 10%, 1$^{st}$ Bank must keep $500 (10%) of the new deposit in reserve, and may loan out the other $4,500.

The required-reserve ratio is multiplied by a bank's total checkable deposits to determine the bank's required reserves.

**Required reserves** – the minimum amount of reserves that a bank is legally required to hold against its deposits.

> **Example 8A:** 1$^{st}$ Bank has total checkable deposits of $75,000,000. If the reserve ratio is 10%, the required reserves for 1$^{st}$ Bank equal $7,500,000 ($75,000,000 x .10).

What assets may a bank hold to meet its reserve requirement? Only two types of assets are counted as reserves; vault cash and bank deposits with the Fed.

**Reserves** – vault cash plus bank deposits with the Fed.

Most banks maintain a deposit account with the Fed (Federal Reserve System). All banks hold vault cash to meet the needs of their customers. A bank could hold sufficient vault cash to meet its reserve requirement. But most banks hold only as much vault cash as necessary to meet depositors' needs (typically less than 1% of checkable deposits) and hold the rest of their required reserves as a deposit with the Fed.

A bank earns no revenue from vault cash. As of October 1, 2008, the Federal Reserve began paying interest on bank deposits with the Fed. The interest rate paid by the Fed is quite low (.1% below the federal funds rate). Thus, a bank will usually try to hold only enough reserves to meet its reserve requirement. If it has reserves in excess of those required, these are called excess reserves. Excess reserves may be loaned out.

**Excess reserves** – the excess of reserves over required reserves.

> **Example 8B:** 1$^{st}$ Bank has received total checkable deposits of $75,000,000. The reserve ratio is 10%. If 1$^{st}$ Bank has vault cash of $750,000 and a deposit with the Fed of $6,900,000, 1$^{st}$ Bank has reserves of $7,650,000 and excess reserves of $150,000 (Reserves of $7,650,000 minus required reserves of $7,500,000 equal excess reserves of $150,000). 1$^{st}$ Bank would be able to loan out $150,000.

## A Simplified Bank Balance Sheet

Since a bank earns little revenue from its reserves, a bank will usually try to hold only enough reserves to meet its reserve requirement. Assume that the balance sheet on the next page represents a simplified balance sheet for Bank X. We are still assuming that the reserve ratio is 10%.

Looking at the balance sheet below, we see that Bank X has total checkable deposits of $50,000,000. With a 10% reserve ratio, the required reserves for Bank X total $5,000,000. Bank X currently has reserves of $5,000,000. Thus, Bank X has no excess reserves. Loans outstanding for Bank X total $45,000,000. Of particular importance for us is the $1,000,000 of U.S. government securities that Bank X is holding.

Bank X – Balance Sheet

Liabilities:
  Checkable Deposits $50,000,000

Assets:
 Reserves;
  Vault Cash  $500,000
  Deposit with the Fed $4,500,000
 Loans Outstanding;
  Mortgage Loans $20,000,000
  Business Loans 13,000,000
  Personal Loans 11,000,000
  U.S. Government Securities 1,000,000
   Total Loans Outstanding $45,000,000
   Total Assets $50,000,000

## U.S. Government Securities

U.S. government securities are debt instruments issued by the federal government. When someone buys a newly issued U.S. government security, that person is making a loan to the federal government.

**Example 9:** On November 17, 2008, Marcella buys a $10,000, 10-year Treasury Note, with a 3.75% interest rate. She is loaning $10,000 to the federal government. If Marcella holds the Note to maturity, she will receive her $10,000 investment back on November 15, 2018. She will also have received interest payments of $375 each year.

The federal government issues a tremendous amount of debt securities in order to finance deficit spending. U.S. government securities are classified as Treasury Bills, (maturities of up to one year), Treasury Notes (maturities between one year and ten years) and Treasury Bonds (maturities of more than 10 years). Banks often invest in U.S. government securities.

U.S. government securities are an attractive asset for a bank to hold for three reasons:

1. **U.S. government securities pay interest.** The interest rate paid by U.S. government securities is typically low, but a bank earns little or no interest on excess reserves. Purchasing U.S. government securities is a way for a bank to temporarily invest excess reserves until an opportunity to make a more attractive loan comes available.

2. **U.S. government securities are risk free.**  The federal government always pays its debts as they come due, often by issuing new U.S. government securities to new lenders.

3. **U.S. government securities are highly liquid.**  A **liquid asset** is an asset that can be converted quickly into cash at a low transaction cost.  Because they are risk free and are traded in huge volumes, U.S. government securities can be converted quickly into cash at a low transaction cost.  There is an established market for U.S. government securities similar to the markets for corporate stocks and bonds.  The Securities Industry and Financial Markets Association website states that U.S. government securities "represent the most liquid capital investment in the world".

   The liquid nature of U.S. government securities is very important to a bank.  If Bank X discovers a more attractive loan opportunity, Bank X can sell some of its U.S. government securities.   This will create excess reserves for Bank X.  Then Bank X will be able to make the new loan.

We are now ready to look at an example of money creation.  We are still assuming a 10% reserve ratio.

---

**Example 10:**  Arlene receives a $5,000 cash gift from her great-uncle Wilbur for her college graduation.  She deposits the $5,000 into her checking account in Bank X.  (Arlene's deposit does <u>not</u> change the money supply.  Arlene previously had $5,000 of currency in circulation, which is included in M1.  After the deposit is made, Arlene has a $5,000 checkable deposit, which is included in M1.  The $5,000 of currency is no longer in circulation since it is held by a bank.  Thus the $5,000 of currency is no longer included in M1.)  Bank X now has excess reserves and loans out $4,500 (.90 x $5,000), which is spent and eventually ends up in a checking account in Bank Y.  (Now the money supply has increased.  Arlene has a $5,000 checkable deposit in Bank X.  Someone else has a $4,500 checkable deposit in Bank Y.)  Bank Y now has excess reserves and loans out $4,050 (.90 x $4,500), which is spent and eventually ends up in a checking account in Bank Z.  (The money supply has increased again, by the $4,050 checkable deposit in Bank Z.)  Bank Z now has excess reserves, etc.

---

Arlene's initial deposit sets off a chain of lending and depositing, which leads to a multiplied increase in checkable deposits.

The actual size of the increase in the money supply cannot be predicted accurately.  It will depend on such factors as how much excess reserves banks choose to hold and how much of the money loaned out ends up in another checking account.  We can calculate the maximum possible change in the money supply by using the potential deposit multiplier.

**Potential deposit multiplier  =  1  ÷  reserve ratio**

---

**Example 11:**  In Example 10 above, the reserve ratio was 10%.  This would result in a potential deposit multiplier of 10, as computed below:

Potential deposit multiplier  =  1  ÷  reserve ratio  =  1  ÷  .10  =  10

---

With a potential deposit multiplier of 10, the maximum possible change in the money supply caused by Arlene's initial deposit of $5,000 would be $50,000 (10 x $5,000).

The money creation process also works in reverse. If Arlene withdraws the $5,000 from her checking account and hides it under a mattress, money destruction (a multiplied decrease in the money supply) occurs.

## Appendix: Financial Intermediation

The earliest banks simply provided a safe storage place for money. Banks continue to provide a safe place to store money, but the primary function of banks today is financial intermediation.

Intermediate means "in between". A bank stands in between savers, who supply funds to the bank by making deposits, and borrowers, who borrow those funds from the bank.

Savers can provide funds directly to borrowers, e.g. by purchasing corporate or government bonds. But savers often prefer to deposit their savings in a bank and let the bank select the ultimate borrowers. And borrowers often prefer to borrow from banks rather than seek loans directly from savers. Financial intermediation has a number of advantages for savers and borrowers, including:

1. Savers reduce their risk of loss.

> **Example 12A:** Saver invests $10,000 in a bond issued by XYZ Corporation. If XYZ Corporation fails, Saver may lose some or all of the $10,000.

> **Example 12B:** Saver deposits $10,000 into 1st Bank. 1st Bank may make loans to XYZ Corporation. But if XYZ Corporation fails, 1st Bank will probably not fail since it has a diversified portfolio of loans (doesn't have all its financial eggs in one basket). And even if 1st Bank fails, Saver's deposit is protected by federal deposit insurance.

2. Savers do not have to evaluate the ability of borrowers to repay a loan.

> **Example 13A:** Saver has $10,000 available to lend. Saver places an advertisement in the newspaper notifying prospective borrowers of Saver's willingness to make a loan. A large number of prospective borrowers apply for the loan. Saver would need to evaluate the ability of each prospective borrower to repay the loan. Saver's transaction cost of making the loan would be very high.

> **Example 13B:** Saver deposits $10,000 into 1st Bank. 1st Bank has expertise in evaluating the ability of prospective borrowers to repay a loan and can make much larger loans than a typical saver could. Thus, 1st Bank can loan Saver's money at a much lower transaction cost.

3. Borrowers do not have to seek out numerous savers in order to borrow a large sum.

> **Example 14A:**  Borrower wishes to borrow $13,000,000 for business expansion.  If Borrower attempts to borrow the money directly from savers, Borrower might have to enter into loan agreements with hundreds of individual savers in order to borrow such a large amount.  The transaction cost of the many loan agreements would be very high.

> **Example 14B:**  Borrower borrows the $13,000,000 from 1st Bank.  Borrower will enter into only one loan agreement.  The bank will have received deposits from thousands of savers, and can bring the savers and Borrower together at a much lower transaction cost.

### Appendix:  Article Review – "The Economic Organization of a P.O.W. Camp"

British economist R.A. Radford was a prisoner of war (P.O.W.) in Germany during World War II.  After the war, he wrote an article, "The Economic Organization of a P.O.W. Camp", which was published in "Economica" in November, 1945.

A P.O.W. camp is very different than normal society.  Nonetheless, Radford felt that the economic organization of a P.O.W. camp was instructive in considering the economic organization of normal society.  Quoting from the article, "…a P.O.W. camp provides a living example of a simple economy…*But the essential interest lies in the universality and the spontaneity of this economic life; it came into existence not by conscious imitation but as a response to the immediate needs and circumstances*."

There was little production in a P.O.W. camp.  Therefore economic activities were not as important in a P.O.W. camp as they were in normal society.  Nevertheless, quoting from the article, "it would be wrong to underestimate the importance of economic activity. Everyone receives a roughly equal share of essentials; it is by trade that individual preferences are given expression and comfort increased. All at some time, and most people regularly, make exchanges of one sort or another".

Though the prisoners were not dependent on their own production for meeting their needs, they could enhance their standard of living by trade.   The articles traded consisted mainly of the contents of Red Cross parcels – canned beef, canned milk, cheese, biscuits, butter, jam, chocolate, sugar, cigarettes, etc.   Bread rations were issued by the camp twice a week.  Private parcels of clothing, toiletries, and cigarettes were also received occasionally.

The prisoners quickly realized the potential for gain by trade.  For example, a nonsmoker might barter his ration of cigarettes for a smoker's chocolate ration.  As trade became more common and better organized, cigarettes were quickly established (not by any authority, but by common practice) as the medium of exchange (money).  And market prices were established (measured in cigarettes) by demand and supply.

Initially, trades were arrived at by prisoners wandering around calling out offers of trades.  This system was soon replaced by a notice board listing items offered and wanted, and proposed terms.  The public nature of the transactions led to the market prices (in cigarettes) of the various commodities being known throughout the camp. Eventually, a camp shop was organized where commodities could be bought and sold for pre-determined prices in cigarettes.

Cigarettes made reasonably good money. They were accepted as the medium of exchange by smokers and nonsmokers alike. They were relatively homogeneous, fairly durable, and could be traded in small or large quantities. The use of cigarettes as money facilitated trade and led to established market prices. They could be spent as money, consumed as a commodity (smoked) or retained as a store of value and then spent when their value in trade was at its greatest.

Cigarettes also had some disadvantages as money. They were subject to Gresham's Law ("bad money drives good money out of circulation"). Low-quality brands were used as money and high-quality brands were smoked. When hand-rolled cigarettes were introduced, they drove machine-made cigarettes out of circulation. Hand-rolled cigarettes were often debased (rolled with a substandard quantity of tobacco).

The biggest problem with cigarettes as money was price level instability. Cigarettes are a commodity with a use (smoking) outside of its use as a medium of exchange. Thus, over time the supply of cigarettes would decrease (as they were smoked) and the price level would fall. The decline in the money supply would inhibit trade and force a return to barter. When a large shipment of cigarettes would arrive at the camp, prices would soar. And then the gradual deflation would begin again as the money supply was smoked.

Not only would the general price level change with changes in the supply of cigarettes and other commodities, specific prices fluctuated as well, due to changes in supply and demand. When the supply of oatmeal increased, its price fell. In hot weather the price of cocoa would fall and the price of soap would rise.

In August, 1944, the supplies of all commodities, including cigarettes, were cut in half. Since the ratio of cigarettes to other commodities was unchanged, it was anticipated that the price level would be unaffected. But that was not the case. The demand for cigarettes to smoke was less elastic than the demand for other commodities (smokers continued to smoke about as much as before), so the supply of cigarettes decreased more quickly than the supply of other commodities, and the price level fell.

The decrease in the standard of living due to the cut in rations also affected relative prices. The prices of luxuries like chocolate and sugar fell. The prices of necessities like bread rose.

As is often seen in normal society, the prisoners had a general contempt for "middlemen" and "speculators". They also had a sense that there was a "just price" at which commodities should sell and would grow angry when market prices deviated significantly from the "just price".

The leadership among the prisoners decided to establish price controls. As long as the authorized prices were close to the market prices, the controls were successful. But when rations were cut in August, 1944, the price level fell and relative prices changed. Market prices deviated more and more from the authorized prices causing shortages and surpluses. Trades at unauthorized prices (black market activity) increased. Eventually the leadership among the prisoners gave up the price controls and allowed prices to adjust to changes in demand and supply.

## Appendix: Think Like an Economist – Price Changes in a P.O.W. Camp

In R.A. Radford's P.O.W. camp, the price level fluctuated as did the prices of specific commodities. Let's say that in August, 1944, the supplies of all commodities, including cigarettes, were doubled:

1. What would happen to the price level, and why?
2. What would happen to the prices of luxuries, and why?
3. What would happen to the prices of necessities, and why?

## Questions for Chapter 10

### Fill-in-the-blanks:

1. _____ is whatever is generally accepted as a medium of exchange.

2. _____ money is money by government decree.

3. _____ is the direct exchange of goods.

4. M1 consists of currency in circulation plus _____ deposits.

5. Money _____ is increases in checkable deposits made possible by fractional reserve banking.

6. Financial _____ is the process by which banks make depositors' savings available to borrowers.

7. _____ reserves is the minimum amount of reserves that a bank is legally required to hold against its deposits.

8. Reserves consists of vault cash plus bank _____ with the _____ .

9. _____ reserves is the excess of reserves over required reserves.

10. A _____ asset is an asset that can be converted quickly into cash at a low transaction cost.

### Multiple Choice:

_____ 1. Money is:
   a. a valuable good
   b. a valuable resource
   c. valuable because it can be used for making exchanges
   d. All of the above

_____ 2. The direct exchange of goods:
   a. is barter
   b. requires a double coincidence of wants
   c. is harder than making a trade through the use of money
   d. All of the above

_____ 3. Compared to barter, money:
   a. increases transaction costs
   b. requires a double coincidence of wants
   c. increases specialization
   d. All of the above

_____ 4. The most important function of money is:
   a. measure of value
   b. medium of exchange
   c. store of value
   d. makes goods valuable

_____ 5. When we hold onto money instead of spending it immediately:
   a. we are using money as a store of value
   b. we can use our buying power when it is most valuable to us
   c. we may lose buying power if there is inflation
   d. All of the above

_____ 6. Money has value because:
   a. it is backed by gold
   b. it is backed by the full faith and credit of the U.S. government
   c. it is generally accepted as a medium of exchange
   d. All of the above

_____ 7. M1 consists of:
   a. currency in circulation
   b. checkable deposits
   c. savings deposits
   d. Both a. and b. above

_____ 8. Which of the following is money?
   a. a check
   b. a credit card
   c. Both of the above
   d. Neither of the above

_____ 9. In our fractional reserve banking system:
   a. banks hold reserves equal to only a fraction of their deposits
   b. the fraction of deposits that must be held is determined by the required-reserve ratio
   c. the required-reserve ratio is set by the Federal Reserve System
   d. All of the above

_____ 10. If checkable deposits in 1$^{st}$ Bank total $500 million and the required-reserve ratio is 10%, then required reserves for 1$^{st}$ Bank equal:
   a.    $5 million
   b.    $10 million
   c.    $50 million
   d.    $450 million

_____ 11. To meet its reserve requirement, a bank may count which of the following assets?
   a.    Business loans
   b.    U.S. government securities
   c.    Deposit with the Fed
   d.    All of the above

_____ 12. If the required-reserve ratio is 12%, and a bank receives a deposit of $1,000, how much may the bank loan out?
   a.    $120
   b.    $760
   c.    $880
   d.    $1,000

_____ 13. Excess reserves:
   a.    is the excess of reserves over required reserves
   b.    may be loaned out
   c.    earn little or no revenue for the bank
   d.    All of the above

_____ 14. U.S. government securities:
   a.    are debt instruments issued by the federal government
   b.    pay a high rate of interest since they are high risk
   c.    must be held by the original buyer until maturity
   d.    All of the above

_____ 15. U.S. government securities are an attractive investment for a bank because they:
   a.    pay interest
   b.    are highly liquid
   c.    are risk free
   d.    All of the above

_____ 16. If the required-reserve ratio is 10%, the potential deposit multiplier is:
   a.    10
   b.    8
   c.    5
   d.    4

_____ 17. According to "The Economic Organization of a P.O.W. Camp", economic activity in the camp:
a. was organized by the Germans to keep the prisoners occupied
b. was organized by the leadership among the prisoners to improve discipline
c. arose spontaneously as prisoners attempted to enhance their standard of living
d. None of the above

_____ 18. In the P.O.W. camp, cigarettes had the following flaws when used as money:
a. they were not accepted as money by nonsmokers
b. their quantity fluctuated causing price level instability
c. Both of the above
d. Neither of the above

## Problems:

1. What is barter? What is the problem with barter as a means of exchange?

2. List the three functions of money.

3. List three reasons that U.S. government securities are an attractive asset for a bank to hold.

4. Referring to the balance sheet for Bank X below, answer the following questions:
   a. Assuming a 9% reserve ratio, what is the amount of required reserves for Bank X?
   b. What dollar amount of excess reserves does Bank X have?
   c. If Bank X receives a checkable deposit of $60,000, how much would Bank X be able to loan out as a result of receiving the deposit?

---

### Bank X – Balance Sheet

| | | Liabilities: | |
| --- | --- | --- | --- |
| | | Checkable Deposits | $80,000,000 |
| **Assets:** | | | |
| Reserves; | | | |
| Vault Cash | | $800,000 | |
| Deposit with the Fed | | $6,600,000 | |
| Loans Outstanding; | | | |
| Mortgage Loans | $28,600,000 | | |
| Business Loans | 23,000,000 | | |
| Personal Loans | 19,000,000 | | |
| U.S. Government Securities | 2,000,000 | | |
| Total Loans Outstanding | | $72,600,000 | |
| Total Assets | | $80,000,000 | |

---

5. List three advantages of financial intermediation for savers and borrowers.

## Answers for Chapter 10

**Fill-in-the-blanks:**

1. Money
2. Fiat
3. Barter
4. checkable
5. creation

6. intermediation
7. Required
8. deposits, Fed
9. Excess
10. liquid

**Multiple Choice:**

| | | |
|---|---|---|
| 1. c. | 7. d. | 13. d. |
| 2. d. | 8. d. | 14. a. |
| 3. c. | 9. d. | 15. d. |
| 4. b. | 10. c. | 16. a. |
| 5. d. | 11. c. | 17. c. |
| 6. c. | 12. c. | 18. b. |

## Problems:

1.  Barter is the direct exchange of goods. The problem with barter as a means of exchange is that to make a trade by barter requires a double coincidence of wants. You must find someone who has what you want <u>and</u> who wants what you have.

2.  The three functions of money are:
    (1) Medium of exchange
    (2) Measure of value
    (3) Store of value

3.  U.S. government securities are an attractive asset for a bank to hold because:
    (1) U.S. government securities pay interest
    (2) U.S. government securities are risk free
    (3) U.S. government securities are highly liquid

4.  a. $7,200,000   b. $200,000   c. $54,600

5.  Financial intermediation has a number of advantages for savers and borrowers, including:
    (1) Savers reduce their risk of loss.
    (2) Savers do <u>not</u> have to evaluate the ability of borrowers to repay a loan.
    (3) Borrowers do <u>not</u> have to seek out numerous savers in order to borrow a large sum.

## Answers to Think Like an Economist:

1. The price level would rise. The demand for cigarettes to smoke is less elastic than the demand for other commodities (smokers would continue to smoke about the same amount as before the increase in the standard of living), so the supply of cigarettes would decrease more slowly than the supply of other commodities, and the price level would rise.

2. The prices of luxuries would rise. The increase in the standard of living would increase the demand for luxuries more than the demand for necessities, causing the prices of luxuries to rise.

3. The prices of necessities would fall. The increase in the standard of living would increase the demand for necessities less than the demand for luxuries, causing the prices of necessities to fall.

# Chapter 11  The Federal Reserve System and Inflation

The basic economic problem is scarcity.  Human wants are unlimited.  Resources are limited.  The basic goal in dealing with the problem of scarcity is to produce as much consumer satisfaction as possible with the limited resources available.  Achieving each of the three macroeconomic goals (price level stability, full employment, and economic growth) will contribute toward reaching this basic goal.

Proper control of a nation's money supply is essential to achieving the macroeconomic goals.  A nation's money supply is controlled by its central bank.

Most nations have a central bank.  Some examples are; the Reserve Bank of Australia, the Bank of Canada, the Bank of England, the Reserve Bank of India, the Bank of Japan, the Banco de Mexico and the Central Bank of the Russian Federation.  The central bank of the European Union is called the European Central Bank.

The Federal Reserve System (commonly called the Fed) is the U.S. central bank.  The Federal Reserve System was created by the Federal Reserve Act in 1913.  There are twelve Federal Reserve District Banks in the Federal Reserve System.

The governing body of the Fed is the Federal Reserve Board of Governors.  The seven members of the Board are appointed by the President with the consent of the Senate.  The Board is headed by the Chairman of the Federal Reserve Board of Governors (Ben Bernanke, since February 1, 2006).  The Chairman of the Federal Reserve Board is the key person in establishing monetary policy in the U.S.

## Functions of the Federal Reserve System

The Federal Reserve System serves a number of important functions in the U.S. economy.  Among the functions of the Fed are:

1. **Control the money supply.**  This is the most important function of the Fed, and will be discussed in more detail later in this chapter.

2. **Supervise and regulate banking institutions.**  Regulations, such as the required-reserve ratio, are established by the Board of Governors.  Supervision, such as audits of bank lending policies, is carried out by the Federal Reserve District Banks.

3. **Serve as the lender of last resort.**  A bank in need of reserves can borrow reserves from other banks or from the Fed.  A bank in need of reserves will usually borrow reserves from other banks through the federal funds market.  In a fractional reserve banking system, it is possible for widespread financial panic to occur.  The creation of the Federal Reserve System was largely motivated by the Panic of 1907.  In a financial panic, many banks would need reserves.  The Fed acts as the lender of last resort.

4. **Hold banks' reserves.**  Banks are required to hold reserves (vault cash plus the bank's deposit with the Fed) to back up their checkable deposits.  Most banks maintain a deposit with the Fed as part of their reserves.

5. **Supply the economy with currency.** The Fed does not produce currency. Paper money (Federal Reserve Notes) is printed by the Bureau of Engraving and Printing. Coins are minted by the U.S. Mint. The currency is put into circulation through depository institutions by the twelve Federal Reserve District Banks.

6. **Provide check-clearing services.** When Arlene writes a check on her account at Bank X to pay her auto insurance, the money in her account has to move to the auto insurance company's account in Bank Y. The Fed is a large provider of check-clearing services in the U.S. economy. In 2006, the Fed handled about 14 billion checks.

## Monetary Base and the Money Supply

The primary function of the Fed is controlling the money supply. But the Fed does not directly control the money supply. The Fed influences the money supply by changing the monetary base.

**Monetary base** – currency in circulation plus bank reserves (vault cash plus bank deposits with the Fed).

When the Fed makes a purchase or a sale, the monetary base changes. (What the Fed primarily buys and sells is U.S. government securities.) When the Fed makes a purchase, the monetary base increases.

> **Example 1A:** The Fed buys $250,000 of U.S. government securities in the open market. The seller is Bank Y. The Fed pays Bank Y for the securities by increasing Bank Y's deposit account balance with the Fed by $250,000. Bank Y now has $250,000 in new reserves. Thus, there is a $250,000 increase in monetary base.

When the Fed makes a sale, the monetary base decreases.

> **Example 1B:** The Fed sells $100,000 of its holdings in U.S. government securities. The buyer is Bank Z. Bank Z pays for the securities by using some of its excess reserves. Bank Z now has $100,000 less in reserves. Thus, there is a $100,000 decrease in monetary base.

## The Actual Money Multiplier

When the monetary base changes, money creation or money destruction is triggered, and the money supply changes by a multiplied amount. The actual money multiplier measures the change in the money supply for a given dollar change in monetary base.

**Actual money multiplier = Change in Money Supply ÷ Change in Monetary Base**

> **Example 2:** The Fed increases the monetary base by $150 million. The money supply increases by $375 million. The actual money multiplier is 2.5 ($375 million ÷ $150 million = 2.5).

## Tools for Controlling the Money Supply

The Fed has three major monetary policy tools available for controlling the money supply. The most important monetary policy tool is open market operations. Open market operations refers to the Fed buying and selling U.S. government securities in the open market.

The Federal Open Market Committee (FOMC) determines the policy for open market operations. The voting members of the FOMC are the seven Federal Reserve Board Governors, the president of the Federal Reserve Bank of New York, and four of the other eleven Federal Reserve District Bank presidents, who serve on a rotating basis. The Chairman of the Board of Governors also serves as the Chairman of the FOMC. Open market operations, along with the other two monetary policy tools, are discussed below:

1. **Open market operations.** As discussed earlier in the chapter, when the Fed makes a purchase or a sale, the monetary base changes. When the monetary base changes, the money supply changes by a multiplied amount. What the Fed primarily buys and sells is U.S. government securities. U.S. government securities are an attractive asset for the Fed to hold for the same reasons (discussed in Chapter 10) that U.S. government securities are an attractive asset for banks to hold.

   If the Fed buys securities in the open market, bank reserves increase. When bank reserves increase, banks have excess reserves, which they can loan out triggering the money creation process. The money creation process leads to a multiplied expansion of the money supply.

---

**Example 3:** The Fed buys $300,000 of U.S. government securities in the open market. The seller is Bank X. The Fed pays Bank X for the securities by increasing Bank X's deposit account balance with the Fed by $300,000. Below is the updated balance sheet for Bank X from page 10-6. After Bank X sells the $300,000 of U.S. government securities to the Fed, Bank X's holdings of U.S. government securities decrease by $300,000 and its reserves increase by $300,000. Bank X now has $300,000 in excess reserves, which it may loan out, triggering the money creation process.

<u>Bank X – Balance Sheet</u>

|  |  |  |  |
|---|---|---|---|
|  |  | Liabilities: |  |
|  |  | Checkable Deposits | <u>$50,000,000</u> |
| Assets: |  |  |  |
| Reserves; |  |  |  |
| Vault Cash |  | $500,000 |  |
| Deposit with the Fed |  | $4,800,000 (+$300,000) |  |
| Loans Outstanding; |  |  |  |
| Mortgage Loans | $20,000,000 |  |  |
| Business Loans | 13,000,000 |  |  |
| Personal Loans | 11,000,000 |  |  |
| U.S. Government Securities | <u>700,000</u> | (-$300,000) |  |
| Total Loans Outstanding |  | $44,700,000 |  |
| Total Assets |  | $50,000,000 |  |

---

If the Fed wanted to reduce the money supply, it would sell U.S. government securities in the open market. If the Fed sells securities in the open market, bank reserves decrease. When bank reserves decrease, this leads to a multiplied contraction of the money supply. Open market operations is the Fed's most important tool for controlling the money supply.

2. **Changing the reserve requirement.** The Fed sets the required-reserve ratio. Lowering the reserve ratio would give banks excess reserves. The excess reserves would allow the banks to make new loans, which would trigger the money creation process. Thus, lowering the reserve ratio will cause the money supply to increase. If the Fed raises the reserve ratio, the money supply will decrease.

---

**Example 4:** Refer to the balance sheet for Bank X in Example 3. Initially the reserve ratio is 10%. Bank X has deposits of $50,000,000, and is required to hold $5,000,000 in reserves. If the Fed lowers the reserve ratio to 9%, Bank X would be required to hold only $4,500,000 in reserves. Bank X would now have $500,000 of new excess reserves, which it could loan out, triggering the money creation process.

---

3. **Changing the discount rate.** A bank in need of reserves can borrow reserves from other banks or from the Fed. A bank can borrow reserves from other banks in the federal funds market. The interest rate charged in the federal funds market is the federal funds rate.

**Federal funds rate** – the interest rate one bank charges another bank to borrow reserves.

A bank also can borrow reserves from their Federal Reserve District Bank. When a bank borrows reserves from the Fed, the interest rate charged is the discount rate.

**Discount rate** – the interest rate the Fed charges banks that borrow reserves from it.

If a bank borrows reserves from other banks, the money supply is not changed. The borrowing bank has more reserves, but the lending bank has fewer reserves. There is no change in overall bank reserves. Thus, the money supply is <u>not</u> changed.

If a bank borrows reserves from the Fed, the Fed is injecting new reserves into the financial system and the money supply increases. To encourage borrowing from the Fed, the Fed would lower the discount rate. Thus, lowering the discount rate will increase the money supply. To discourage borrowing from the Fed, the Fed would raise the discount rate. Thus, raising the discount rate will decrease the money supply.

## Inflation

One of the Fed's goals as it controls the money supply is to achieve price level stability. If the Fed increases the money supply too rapidly, this will cause inflation. This section of the chapter looks at the causes and effects of inflation.

Inflation is an increase in the price level. We can distinguish between a one-time increase in the price level versus continued increases in the price level.

**One-shot inflation** is a one-time increase in the price level. One-shot inflation can come from the demand side of the economy, or from the supply side. One-shot inflation can be caused by an increase in AD or a by decrease in SRAS.

## Demand-side One-shot Inflation

**Example 5A:** In Year 1, the government passes legislation to reduce taxes. This reduction in taxes increases disposable income. The increase in disposable income causes an increase in consumption. The increase in consumption shifts the AD curve to the right.

The graph below illustrates the change. Notice that both the price level and Real GDP increase. This is demand-side inflation. There is no tax cut in Year 2, so this is one-shot inflation.

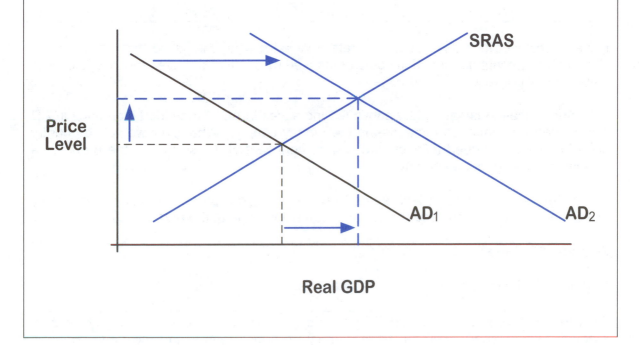

## Supply-side One-shot Inflation

**Example 5B:** In Year 1, an adverse supply shock (really bad weather) occurs. The adverse supply shock increases the overall costs of production. The increase in the overall costs of production shifts the SRAS curve to the left.

The graph on the next page illustrates the change. Notice that the price level increases and Real GDP decreases. This is supply-side inflation. The weather is normal in Year 2, so this is one-shot inflation.

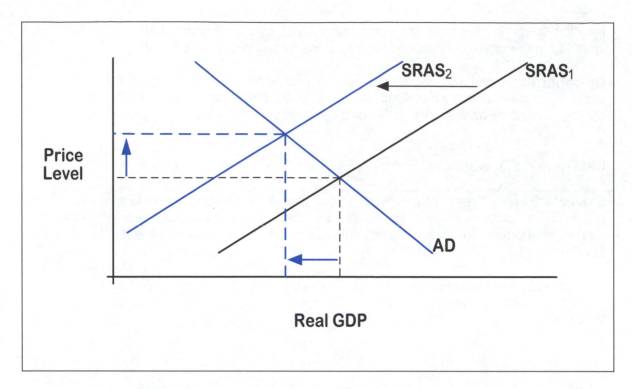

If the price level increases at a high rate year after year, this is **continued inflation**. Theoretically, continued inflation could be caused by continued decreases in SRAS. But this is highly unlikely.

Continued inflation is caused by continued increases in AD. Continued increases in AD are caused by continued increases in the money supply. Whenever we see a country suffering from continued inflation, we can be confident of the source of the problem; a rapidly increasing money supply.

For a discussion of why a less developed country might pursue a policy of a rapidly increasing money supply, see the appendix on seignorage at the end of the chapter.

### Effects of Inflation

Potentially, inflation could have no practical effect.

> **Example 6:** The castaways on Gilligan's Island are using Monopoly money as their medium of exchange. Gilligan finds another Monopoly game and the new money is issued to everyone in proportion to their current money holdings. As a result of this doubling of the money supply, prices will double. But everyone will have twice as much money to spend. No one is better off or worse off because of the inflation.

Realistically, inflation usually does have effects. Some will gain from inflation and others will lose. The overall economy may be affected. Among the effects of inflation are:

1. **Inflation decreases the buying power of people who hold money.** This effect is minor as long as the rate of inflation is low and people don't hold money for very long. But if a person holds money for an extended period of time or when the inflation rate is high, that person will lose significant buying power.

> **Example 7:** Karen receives $5,000 as a graduation present. One month later, she spends the money. If the annual rate of inflation is 3%, Karen will have lost .25% of her buying power ($12.50 in this case) because of the inflation. What if Karen had received the $5,000 in 1987 (when the CPI was 113.6), and then held the money until 2007 (when the CPI was 207.3)? In 2007, Karen spends the money. She will have lost 45% of her buying power ($2,260 in this case) because of the inflation.

2. **Inflation reduces the real interest rate earned on savings.** The real interest rate is equal to the nominal interest rate minus the rate of inflation.

> **Example 8A:** In Year 1, Arlene invests $10,000 in a one-year corporate bond which pays a 5% interest rate. At the end of one year, Arlene receives $10,500 ($10,000 principal plus $500 interest). The rate of inflation for the year is 3%. Arlene's real interest rate is 2%, as computed below;
>
> **Real interest rate = Nominal interest rate - Inflation rate** = 5% - 3% = 2%

3. **Increasing inflation benefits borrowers and hurts lenders.** The interest rate agreed to between a borrower and a lender will reflect their expectations of the future rate of inflation. If the rate of inflation increases, the borrower will benefit because the real rate of interest that the borrower is paying will be lower than expected. Likewise, the lender will suffer because the increase in inflation will lower the real interest rate the lender is earning on the loan.

> **Example 8B:** In Year 2, Arlene lends $10,000 to Professor at an interest rate of 10%. Arlene is expecting the rate of inflation to be 3%, giving her a real interest rate of 7%. The rate of inflation increases to 9%. Arlene's real interest rate on the loan is only 1%. Arlene (the lender) has suffered because of the unexpected increase in inflation. Professor's real interest rate paid is also 1%, rather than the 7% real rate Professor expected to pay. Professor (the borrower) has benefited because of the unexpected increase in inflation.

4. **Inflation increases uncertainty and can thus discourage investment.** Changes in the rate of inflation change the real interest rate. The higher the rate of inflation, the more unpredictable the inflation rate tends to be.

> **Example 9A:** For the ten years from 1972 to 1981, the average rate of inflation in the U.S. was 8.5%. The average change in the inflation rate from year to year was 2.4%. For the ten years from 1996 to 2005, the average rate of inflation was 2.5%. The average change in the inflation rate from year to year was .7%.

Thus, higher inflation increases the uncertainty faced by both savers and investors about what the real interest rate will be. The increasing uncertainty discourages investment. A lower level of investment means a lower rate of long run economic growth.

> **Example 9B:** For the ten years from 1972 to 1981, real gross private domestic investment increased by 32%. For the ten years from 1996 to 2005, real gross private domestic investment increased by 52%. (Information is from the Bureau of Economic Analysis.)

## Appendix: Seignorage and Counterfeiting

**Seignorage** (seen′ yer ij) is the profit derived by the issuer of money by issuing new money. Historically, money was usually in the form of metal coins. When money was in the form of metal coins, seignorage was the difference between the face value of coins minted and placed in circulation and the cost of minting the coins.

---

**Example 10:** The government of the Land of Oz mints and puts into circulation gold-plated coins with a face value of 20 ozdollars. The cost of minting each coin is only 1 ozdollar, so the government earns a 19 ozdollar profit on each coin. This is seignorage.

---

When the Federal Reserve System puts new currency (Federal Reserve Notes) into circulation, it would appear that it is earning an enormous seignorage profit. A new $100 bill costs only about 4¢ to print. However, Federal Reserve Notes are liabilities of the Federal Reserve System. Potentially, the Fed could have to redeem the Notes at face value in the future. So the issuing of currency is <u>not</u> considered as creating a seignorage profit for the Fed.

However, while the Federal Reserve Notes are outstanding, the holders of the Notes are essentially making an interest-free loan to the Fed for the convenience of having the currency in hand. The Fed uses the proceeds from the issuance of the currency to invest in U.S. government securities. The interest earned on these U.S. government securities is a kind of seignorage profit for the Fed.

The Fed uses the interest earnings from its holdings of U.S. government securities to cover its operating costs, and to pay dividends to member banks. Any excess earnings are transferred to the U.S. Treasury. Thus, the seignorage profits of the Fed end up benefiting the general public.

But what about counterfeiting? The profit of a counterfeiter is seignorage. If a counterfeiter can produce a passable fake bill for less than the face value of the bill, the counterfeiter's profit is seignorage.

---

**Example 11A:** Jacob sets up a counterfeiting operation, producing passable $20 bills at a cost of $2 each to produce. For each bill that Jacob puts into circulation (by spending it), Jacob receives $20 worth of value at a cost of only $2. Jacob receives a seignorage profit of $18 on each bill.

---

The counterfeiter gains from counterfeiting. But who loses? If the counterfeit bill is eventually discovered to be counterfeit, the person holding it at the time suffers the loss.

---

**Example 11B:** Jacob spends a counterfeit $20 bill at Gaurika's Grocery Store. When Gaurika attempts to deposit the store receipts at her bank, the counterfeit $20 bill is discovered. Gaurika suffers a loss of $20.

---

If the counterfeit bill is so skillfully printed that it is never discovered to be counterfeit, does that mean that no one suffers a loss because of the counterfeiting? No. By putting counterfeit currency into circulation, the counterfeiter decreases the buying power of the currency already in circulation. In essence, the counterfeiter is stealing a little bit of buying power from everyone who holds currency.

## Appendix: Seignorage and Inflation

We saw earlier in the chapter that continued inflation is linked to continued increases in the money supply. Many countries (particularly less developed countries) suffer from continued inflation. Why do the governments of these countries excessively increase their money supply? The inflation resulting from excessive money supply growth is an obstacle to economic growth (see Chapter 15).

Governments of less developed countries may increase the money supply in order to receive seignorage profits. Let's say that the Land of Oz is a less developed country. Dorothy Gale has just been elected as Supreme Ruler, having gained popularity by killing the Wicked Witch of the West and sending the incompetent former Supreme Ruler packing in a hot air balloon. Dorothy sees that the Land of Oz has major infrastructure needs; new highways, harbors, airports, schools, hospitals, etc.

To pay for these improvements, Dorothy considers a large increase in taxes. But collecting taxes in the Land of Oz may be very difficult. Much production is either do-it-yourself or is exchanged by barter. If higher taxes are imposed on the market activity that exists, much of that market activity may go underground. Another consideration is that a large tax increase will be very politically unpopular.

So Dorothy decides to pay for the infrastructure improvements by minting new money. Hundreds of millions of newly minted ozdollars are used to pay for new highways, harbors, airports, schools, hospitals, etc. Since the cost of minting the new ozdollars is much less than the value of what they will buy, the government of Oz earns a large seignorage profit. And all the improvements are paid for without any increase in taxes. Right? Not exactly.

The increase in the money supply will mean inflation. The buying power of the Ozians who hold money will decrease. So the increase in the money supply is basically an indirect form of taxation.

Is this taxation by inflation beneficial to the Land of Oz? It may be. If the infrastructure improvements lead to economic growth, the cost to the public in lost buying power may be more than made up for in the long run by economic growth. A government may pay for the use of resources by directly collecting taxes from the private sector, or it may pay for the use of resources by indirectly taking buying power from the private sector by inflation. If the government's use of the resources is more valuable than the use of the resources by the private sector, then the country benefits from the transfer of the resources from the private sector to the public sector.

But what if Dorothy is not especially wise? She may choose to spend the newly minted money on fancy palaces that improve her quality of life but don't contribute to economic growth. She may invest heavily in the military (to secure her regime from overthrow by foreign enemies) and in a domestic secret police force (to secure her regime from overthrow by domestic enemies). She may spend to expand the civil service in order to provide cushy jobs for her political supporters (to reward them for their support and to guarantee their continuing support). Whether Dorothy spends wisely or unwisely, she may choose to pay for the spending by increasing the money supply rather than by increasing taxes.

## Appendix:  The Independence of the Federal Reserve System

The Federal Reserve System is intended to be an independent central bank.  Some nations have created central banks that are relatively independent of political influence (like the Fed).  Other nations have central banks that are more influenced by elected officials.  History indicates that the more independent central banks are more successful at avoiding inflationary policies.

The Fed is independent in that its decisions do not have to be approved by the President or by Congress.  The Board of Governors is only required to submit a bi-annual report to Congress on the state of the economy and the conduct of monetary policy.  The independence of the Fed is intended to allow the Fed to make policy decisions relatively free of political influence.

The Fed's political independence is enhanced by its financial independence.  The Fed is not dependent on Congress for its funding.  In fact, the Fed is a unique government agency in that it earns a profit every year.  As of December 31, 2007, the Fed's assets totaled almost $919 billion.  The Fed's holdings of U.S. government securities made up about 80% of the Fed's total assets.

The Fed had income in 2007 of about $40 billion.  About 95% of the Fed's income came from interest on its holdings of U.S. government securities.  After paying operating expenses and paying out dividends to member banks, the Fed transferred over $34 billion to the U.S. Treasury.


## Appendix:  Recent Fed Monetary Policy

The Fed's primary tool for conducting monetary policy is open market operations.  The Fed uses open market operations to increase or decrease the money supply.  In the 1980s, the Fed shifted its focus from achieving a certain quantity for the money supply to achieving a specific rate for the federal funds rate.  The Fed attempts to achieve the target for the federal funds rate by increasing or decreasing the money supply.

In an attempt to stimulate the economy, the Fed lowered the target for the federal funds rate from 8.00% on 7/13/90 to 3.00% on 9/4/92.

In 1994, the Fed became concerned that the economy was overheating and raised the target for the federal funds rate from 3.25% on 2/4/94 to 6.00% on 2/1/95.

In 2000, the Fed began lowering the target for the federal funds rate, eventually reducing the target from 6.50% on 5/16/00 to 1.00% on 6/25/03.

In 2007, the Fed became concerned about the possibility of a recession and began lowering the target for the federal funds rate, dropping the rate from 5.25% to 2.00% over the course of eight months.  The most recent change (before the publication of this book) was a decrease in the target to 1.00% on 10/29/08.

The table on the next page indicates selected target levels for the federal funds rate that the Fed has pursued since 1990.

| Date | Target for the Federal funds rate |
|---|---|
| 7/13/90 | 8.00% |
| 2/1/91 | 6.25% |
| 12/2091 | 4.00% |
| 9/4/92 | 3.00% |
| 2/4/94 | 3.25% |
| 11/17/98 | 4.75% |
| 11/16/99 | 5.50% |
| 5/16/00 | 6.50% |
| 3/20/01 | 5.00% |
| 5/15/01 | 4.00% |
| 9/17/01 | 3.00% |
| 11/6/01 | 2.00% |
| 6/25/03 | 1.00% |
| 6/30/04 | 1.25% |
| 9/21/04 | 1.75% |
| 3/22/05 | 2.75% |
| 8/9/05 | 3.50% |
| 11/1/05 | 4.00% |
| 1/31/06 | 4.50% |
| 5/10/06 | 5.00% |
| 6/29/06 | 5.25% |
| 9/18/07 | 4.75% |
| 12/11/07 | 4.25% |
| 1/22/08 | 3.50% |
| 1/30/08 | 3.00% |
| 3/18/08 | 2.25% |
| 4/30/08 | 2.00% |
| 10/08/08 | 1.50% |
| 10/29/08 | 1.00% |

## Appendix:  The Federal Reserve and the Financial Crisis of 2007/2008

During the financial crisis of 2007/2008, the Federal Reserve took unprecedented steps to attempt to prevent a liquidity crisis in the financial system.

The financial crisis of 2007/2008 was sparked by a reversal in house prices.  House prices in the U.S. (measured by the Case-Shiller Home Price Index) increased by 124 percent between 1997 and 2006.  House prices reached a peak in the 2nd Quarter of 2006 and dropped by almost 27 percent by the 3rd Quarter of 2008.

A number of factors contributed to the rapid increase in house prices, including an increase in the number of subprime mortgages.  Subprime mortgages are home loans given to persons who are considered a poor credit risk.  Subprime mortgages charge a higher interest rate than conventional mortgages to offset the greater risk of default.  Subprime mortgages increased from 5% of new home loans in 1994 to 20% in 2006.

When house prices began to fall in 2006, many subprime borrowers, particularly those who had taken out adjustable rate mortgages, found themselves unable to make their monthly house payments. And they were unable to refinance their loans, because the drop in house prices meant that they owed more than their homes were worth. Mortgage foreclosures greatly increased.

**Example 12A:** According to ReatlyTrac, the number of foreclosure filings increased by 75% in 2007 compared to 2006.

**Example 12B:** According to a Mortgage Bankers Association survey, almost 10% of all mortgage loans were either delinquent or in foreclosure at the end of September, 2008.

The increase in foreclosures added to the inventory of houses available for sale. This further decreased house prices, putting more home owners into a negative equity position. The increase in foreclosures also decreased the value of mortgage-backed securities. Mortgage-backed securities were widely held throughout the financial system, including by the two largest government-sponsored enterprises (GSEs), Fannie Mae and Freddie Mac. As a result, these institutions faced increasing liquidity problems.

In September of 2007, the Federal Reserve began to take steps to attempt to prevent a liquidity crisis in the financial system. On September 18, 2007, the Fed lowered the target for the federal funds rate from 5.25% to 4.75%. The Fed also began to lend billions of dollars directly to financial institutions (through such programs as the Term Auction Facility) to enhance the Fed's ability to provide liquidity to the financial system.

On January 22, 2008, the Fed lowered the federal funds rate from 4.25% to 3.50%. Eight days later, the Fed lowered the rate to 3.00%. On March 18, 2008, the Fed lowered the rate to 2.25%. Also in March, the Fed provided a $29 billion loan to facilitate the purchase of Bear Stearns, an investment bank on the brink of bankruptcy, by JPMorgan Chase.

In September, 2008, the Fed provided an $85 billion loan to AIG, the largest insurance company in the world, to prevent its bankruptcy. The Fed received an 80% equity stake in the company.

Also in September, the Fed supported the Federal Housing Finance Agency's decision to place Fannie Mae and Freddie Mac into conservatorship and supported the Treasury Department's decision to provide up to $200 billion to keep Fannie Mae and Freddie Mac solvent.

The Fed supported the Treasury Department's proposed $700 billion bailout of the financial system. The bailout was enacted into law on October 3, 2008 as the Emergency Economic Stabilization Act of 2008.

In October, 2008, the Fed announced that it would buy up commercial paper issued by companies outside the financial sector, in order to improve liquidity among business firms. Also in October, the Fed lowered the federal funds rate, in two steps, from 2.00% to 1.00%.

On November 25, 2008, the Fed announced a program to provide up to $200 billion to support the issuance of asset-backed securities backed by newly and recently originated consumer and small business loans. That same day the Fed announced another program to purchase up to $100 billion in the direct obligations of Fannie Mae and Freddie Mac and to purchase up to $500 billion in mortgage-backed securities backed by Fannie Mae and Freddie Mac.

## Questions for Chapter 11

### Fill-in-the-blanks:

1.  The Federal Reserve System is the U.S. _____ bank.

2.  The most important function of the Fed is controlling the _____
    _____ .

3.  The _____ _____ rate is the interest rate one
    bank charges another bank to borrow reserves.

4.  The _____ rate is the interest rate the Fed charges banks that
    borrow reserves from it.

5.  _____ inflation is a one-time increase in the price level.

6.  _____ is the profit derived by the issuer of money by issuing new
    money.

### Multiple Choice:

_____ 1. The functions of the Fed include:
- a.  holding banks' reserves
- b.  supplying the economy with currency
- c.  controlling the money supply
- d.  All of the above

_____ 2. A bank in need of reserves:
- a.  will usually borrow reserves from other banks
- b.  as a last resort, may borrow from the Fed
- c.  Both of the above
- d.  Neither of the above

_____ 3. Monetary base consists of:
- a.  currency in circulation
- b.  bank reserves
- c.  checkable deposits
- d.  Both a. and b. above

_____ 4. When the Fed makes a sale:
   a. the monetary base increases
   b. the monetary base decreases
   c. the monetary base doesn't change
   d. All of the above are possible

_____ 5. If the monetary base increases by $200 million and the money supply increases by $550 million, the actual money multiplier is:
   a.  .36
   b.  2.50
   c.  2.75
   d.  5.5

_____ 6. Open market operations:
   a. refers to the Fed acting as lender of last resort for banks
   b. refers to the Fed changing the required-reserve ratio
   c. refers to the Fed buying and selling U.S. government securities in the open market
   d. None of the above

_____ 7. If the Fed buys U.S. government securities in the open market:
   a. bank reserves will increase
   b. monetary base will increase
   c. the money supply will increase by a multiplied amount
   d. All of the above

_____ 8. If the Fed lowers the reserve ratio:
   a. banks will be short on reserves
   b. the money supply will decrease
   c. Both of the above
   d. Neither of the above

_____ 9. When a bank borrows from the Fed:
   a. the interest rate paid is the discount rate
   b. the Fed is injecting new reserves into the financial system
   c. the money supply increases
   d. All of the above

_____ 10. The Fed can decrease the money supply by:
   a. lowering the required-reserve ratio
   b. selling U.S. government securities in the open market
   c. lowering the discount rate
   d. All of the above

_____ 11. The Fed's most important tool for controlling the money supply is:
   a. printing more currency
   b. changing the discount rate
   c. open market operations
   d. changing the required-reserve ratio

_____ 12. One-shot inflation can be caused by:
- a. an increase in AD
- b. an increase in SRAS
- c. continued increases in AD
- d. Both a. and b. above

_____ 13. If the price level increases at a high rate year after year:
- a. this is continued inflation
- b. this is caused by continued increases in AD
- c. the money supply must be increasing rapidly
- d. All of the above

_____ 14. An increase in the rate of inflation:
- a. increases the buying power of people who hold money
- b. increases the real interest rate earned on savings
- c. benefits lenders and hurts borrowers
- d. None of the above

_____ 15. If Karen earns a 6% interest rate on her savings when the inflation rate is 4%, her real interest rate is:
- a. -2%
- b. 2%
- c. 4%
- d. 10%

_____ 16. A successful counterfeiter:
- a. earns profit by seignorage
- b. gains at no expense to the rest of society
- c. Both of the above
- d. Neither of the above

_____ 17. When a government pays for government spending by issuing new currency:
- a. the increase in the money supply will cause inflation
- b. this is an indirect tax on the holders of money
- c. Both of the above
- d. Neither of the above

_____ 18. When the Fed wants to make a change in monetary policy:
- a. it must first obtain the approval of the President
- b. the proposed change must be approved by a majority of the Senate
- c. Both of the above
- d. Neither of the above

_____ 19. The primary source of income for the Fed is:
- a. funding provided by Congress
- b. interest that it earns on loans that it makes to banks
- c. interest on its holdings of U.S. government securities
- d. fines imposed on banks that violate its regulations

_____ 20. Between 5/16/00 and 6/25/03, the Fed changed the target for the federal funds rate:
   a. from 4.75% to 6.00%
   b. from 3.25% to 6.00%
   c. from 6.50% to 1.00%
   d. from 5.25% to 2.75%

_____ 21. Subprime mortgages:
   a. are home loans given to persons who are considered a poor credit risk
   b. were a factor contributing to the rapid increase in house prices between 1997 and 2006
   c. made up an increasing percentage of new home loans between 1997 and 2006
   d. All of the above

_____ 22. During the financial crisis of 2007/2008:
   a. the Fed took a "hands-off" approach consistent with free market theory
   b. the Fed took steps to control the inflationary pressure created by the continuing rise in house prices
   c. Both of the above
   d. Neither of the above

_____ 23. Among the steps taken by the Fed during the financial crisis of 2007/2008 were:
   a. lowering the federal funds rate from 5.25% to 1.00%
   b. providing hundreds of billions of dollars in loans to private companies
   c. supporting the Treasury Department's effort to keep Fannie Mae and Freddie Mac solvent
   d. All of the above

**Problems:**

1. When the Fed increases the monetary base by $35 million, the money supply increases by $84 million. What is the actual money multiplier?

2. Explain how the Fed buying U.S. government securities in the open market will increase the money supply.

3. On the graph below, illustrate how a decrease in interest rates could cause one-shot inflation.

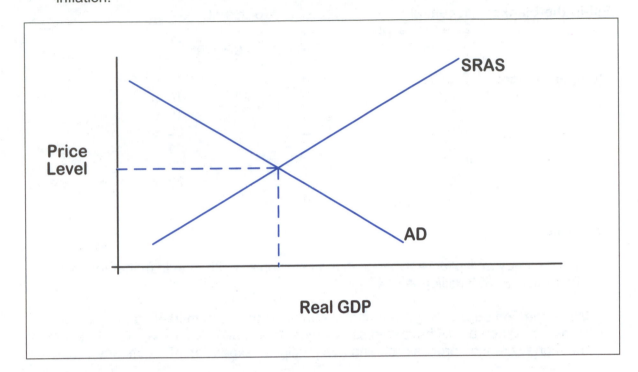

4. List the effects of inflation.

5. Explain why the Fed is intended to be an independent central bank.

## Answers for Chapter 11

**Fill-in-the-blanks:**
1. central
2. money supply
3. federal funds
4. discount
5. One-shot
6. Seignorage

**Multiple Choice:**

| | | |
|---|---|---|
| 1. d. | 9. d. | 17. c. |
| 2. c. | 10. b. | 18. d. |
| 3. d. | 11. c. | 19. c. |
| 4. b. | 12. a. | 20. c. |
| 5. c. | 13. d. | 21. d. |
| 6. c. | 14. d. | 22. d. |
| 7. d. | 15. b. | 23. d. |
| 8. d. | 16. a. | |

### Problems:

1. Actual money multiplier = Change in money supply ÷ Change in monetary base = $84 million ÷ $35 million = 2.4

2. When the Fed buys U.S. government securities in the open market, bank reserves increase. When banks have excess reserves, they make new loans. This triggers the money creation process, leading to a multiplied expansion of the money supply.

3.

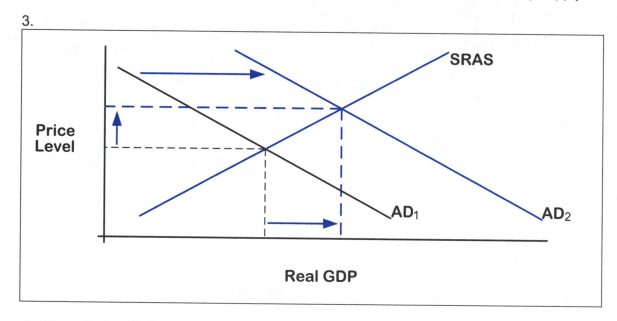

4. The effects of inflation:
   (1) Inflation decreases the buying power of people who hold money.
   (2) Inflation reduces the real interest rate earned on savings.
   (3) Increasing inflation benefits borrowers and hurts lenders.
   (4) Inflation increases uncertainty and can thus discourage investment.

5. The Fed is intended to be an independent central bank because history indicates that the more independent central banks are more successful at avoiding inflationary policies.

# Chapter 12  Monetary Policy

The basic economic problem is scarcity.  Human wants are unlimited.  Resources are limited.  The basic goal in dealing with the problem of scarcity is to produce as much consumer satisfaction as possible with the limited resources available.  Achieving each of the three macroeconomic goals (price level stability, full employment, and economic growth) will contribute toward reaching this basic goal.

We saw in earlier chapters that the ideal quantity of total output is called Natural Real GDP.  Natural Real GDP is the quantity of total output that results in the natural unemployment rate (full employment).  The economy may produce at Natural Real GDP, or may suffer from a recessionary gap or an inflationary gap.

One of the major tools that the federal government can use to try to move the economy out of a recessionary gap or an inflationary gap and toward Natural Real GDP is fiscal policy.  Fiscal policy (see Chapter 9) is changes in government expenditures and taxation to achieve macroeconomic goals.

The other major tool that the federal government can use to try to move the economy toward Natural Real GDP is monetary policy.

**Monetary policy** – changes in the money supply to achieve macroeconomic goals.

We saw in Chapter 11 that the most important function of the Federal Reserve System is to control the money supply.  The Fed conducts monetary policy.  The Fed increases (or decreases) the money supply primarily through the use of open market operations.

Open market operations involves buying (or selling) U.S. government securities in the open market.  When the Fed buys U.S. government securities in the open market, the money supply increases.  When the Fed sells U.S. government securities in the open market, the money supply decreases.

When the Fed changes the money supply, the overall economy (price level, Real GDP, and unemployment rate) is affected.  There are different theories about how changes in the money supply affect the economy.  In this chapter, we will examine classical monetary theory, monetarism, and Keynesian monetary theory.

## Classical Monetary Theory

Classical economists see a direct relationship between the money supply and the price level.  According to classical monetary theory, if the money supply increases by 10% in a short period of time, the price level will increase by 10%.  If the money supply decreases by 10% in a short period of time, the price level will decrease by 10%.

To understand why this direct relationship between the money supply and the price level exists, according to classical monetary theory, we must understand a measure called the velocity of money.

**Velocity of money (V)** – the average number of times that a dollar is spent annually.

Velocity of money is calculated by dividing the dollar value of market transactions (nominal GDP) by the money supply.

**V = Nominal GDP ÷ M**   (M is the money supply)

---

**Example 1:**  In Year 1, nominal GDP was $14,000 billion and the average money supply was $1,400 billion.  The velocity of money was 10 ($14,000 billion ÷ $1,400 billion).

---

We can adjust the velocity formula to focus on the relationship between the money supply and the price level.  We multiply both sides of the equation by M.  This restates the equation as:

$$M \times V = \text{Nominal GDP}$$

Then we break nominal GDP into price level (P) and Real GDP (Q).  This gives us an equation known as the equation of exchange:

$$M \times V = P \times Q$$

Classical monetary theory assumes that the velocity of money is constant.  The only reason that people want to hold money is for spending.  The relationship between the quantity of money that people want to hold and the quantity that they want to spend will be constant.  Thus, if nominal GDP increases by 5%, M will also increase by 5% and V will remain constant.

Q (Real GDP) is also assumed to be constant in the short run.  Since (according to classical theory) the economy is self-regulating and automatically adjusts towards Natural Real GDP, it will tend to be close to Natural Real GDP at all times.  Real GDP will not change significantly in a short period of time.

If V is constant and Q is constant, then there must be a directly proportional relationship between M (money supply) and P (price level).  This is illustrated in the example below:

---

**Example 2A:**  Assume that the equation of exchange numbers are originally; M = $1,400 billion, V = 10, P = 1.00, Q = $14,000 billion.  Then the money supply increases by 10%.  The price level also increases by 10%, as illustrated below:

$$M \times V = P \times Q$$

$$\$1,400B \times 10 = 1.00 \times \$14,000B$$

$$+10\% \quad +0\% \quad +10\% \quad +0\%$$

$$\$1,540B \times 10 = 1.10 \times \$14,000B$$

$$\$15,400B \quad = \quad \$15,400B$$

---

Classical monetary theory sees a directly proportional relationship between the money supply and the price level. Is this what we see in the actual economy? No. In the actual economy, velocity has not been constant. Velocity generally rose from the late 1980s through the late 1990s, and has followed a downward trend since.

If velocity is not constant, then there will not be a directly proportional relationship between the money supply and the price level.

---

**Example 2B:** Assume the same original equation of exchange numbers as in example 2A. Then the money supply increases by 10% and velocity decreases by 5%. What happens to the price level? The price level increases by 4.5%, as illustrated below:

$$M \times V = P \times Q$$

$$\$1,400B \times 10 = 1.00 \times \$14,000B$$

$$+10\% \quad -5\% \quad +4.5\% \quad +0\%$$

$$\$1,540B \times 9.5 = 1.045 \times \$14,000B$$

$$\$14,630B \quad = \quad \$14,630B$$

---

In the long run, increases in the money supply do tend to cause increases (but not directly proportional increases) in the price level. The inaccuracy of classical monetary theory (especially in the short run) led to the development of the theory called monetarism.

## Monetarism

Monetarism is an economic theory based on classical theory, but with some differences from classical monetary theory. Monetarism holds that:

1. Velocity is not constant, but changes in predictable ways. Changes in certain variables will cause velocity to change. The variables include the interest rate and the expected rate of inflation. Monetarists see velocity as relatively stable in the long run. (Classical monetary theory holds that velocity is constant.)

2. Changes in the money supply and/or in velocity can change AD. An increase in the money supply and/or in velocity would increase AD. A decrease in the money supply and/or in velocity would decrease AD. (Classical monetary theory holds that only changes in the money supply affect AD, since the velocity of money is constant.)

3. Changes in AD will change both the price level and Real GDP in the short run. Monetarists see the SRAS curve as upward sloping. An increase in AD will cause an increase in both the price level and Real GDP. A decrease in AD will cause a decrease in both the price level and Real GDP. (Classical monetary theory sees the aggregate supply curve as vertical in both the short run and the long run. Thus,

classical monetary theory holds that changes in AD affect only the price level, both in the short run and in the long run.)

**Example 3A:** The graph below illustrates the effect of an increase or a decrease in AD, assuming that the SRAS curve is upward sloping. Both the price level and Real GDP are changed by a change in AD. This represents the monetarist view.

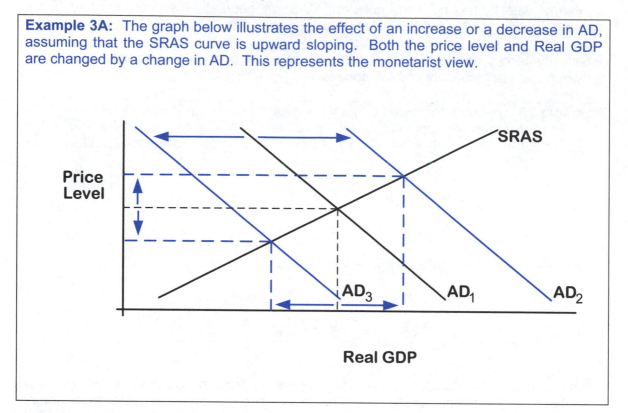

**Example 3B:** The graph below illustrates the effect of an increase or a decrease in AD, assuming that the SRAS curve is vertical. A change in AD affects only the price level. This represents the classical view.

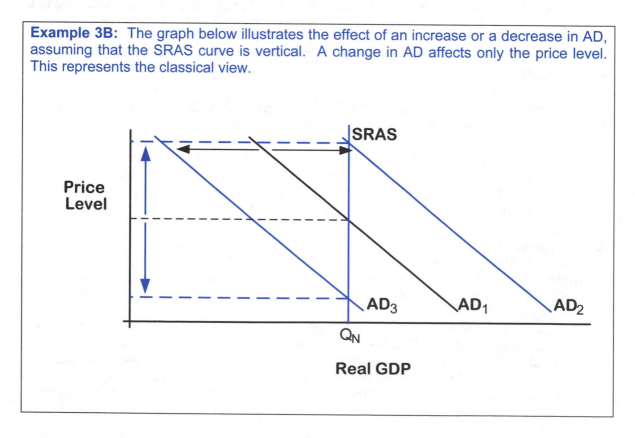

Since monetarism is based on classical theory, it assumes that the economy is self-regulating and automatically adjusts back to Natural Real GDP. The increases and decreases in Real GDP caused by changes in AD will not last in the long run. Thus, like classical theory, monetarism holds that, in the long run, AD affects only the price level.

## Keynesian Monetary Theory

According to Keynesian theory, monetary policy can be used to increase or decrease Total Expenditures, in order to increase or decrease Real GDP. Keynesian theory holds that changes in the money supply affect Real GDP indirectly, through a series of steps called the Keynesian monetary transmission mechanism. If the Fed wants to trigger an increase in Real GDP, the Fed would increase the money supply. The steps in the Keynesian monetary transmission mechanism would be:

1. **An increase in the money supply leads to**
2. **a decrease in interest rates, which leads to**
3. **an increase in investment, which leads to**
4. **an increase in Total Expenditures, which leads to**
5. **an increase in Real GDP.**

The Fed conducts monetary policy. If the Fed wants to trigger an increase in Real GDP, the Fed would buy U.S. government securities in the open market. This would cause an increase in the money supply, beginning the steps in the Keynesian monetary transmission mechanism.

If the Fed wants to trigger a decrease in Real GDP, the Fed would sell U.S. government securities in the open market. This would cause a decrease in the money supply, leading to an increase in interest rates, a decrease in investment, a decrease in Total Expenditures, and a decrease in Real GDP.

## Failure of the Keynesian Monetary Transmission Mechanism

The Keynesian monetary transmission mechanism is indirect, with the money supply affecting Real GDP through a series of steps. A failure may occur in this series of steps to break the link between the change in the money supply and an eventual change in Real GDP. There are two reasons why the Keynesian monetary transmission mechanism may fail:

1. **Investment may be interest-insensitive.** A decrease in interest rates will generally lead to an increase in investment. But if investors are extremely pessimistic about the future returns available from investment, they may be insensitive to a decrease in interest rates. And if a decrease in interest rates does <u>not</u> increase investment, the change in the money supply has no effect on Real GDP.

> **Example 4:** In a severe recession, investors may be so pessimistic about future returns that an interest rate near zero would still <u>not</u> induce them to borrow and invest.

2. **The liquidity trap.** The liquidity trap means that an increase in the money supply does <u>not</u> cause a decrease in interest rates. Interest rates will only fall so low. Once they have fallen as low as they will fall, an increase in the money supply has no effect on interest rates. And if an increase in the money supply does <u>not</u> decrease interest rates, the change in the money supply has no effect on Real GDP.

> **Example 5:** In a severe recession, interest rates may fall to near zero percent. Once interest rates have fallen to near zero percent, they cannot fall any lower. Savers are not going to be willing to lend at an interest rate of zero percent, and they certainly are not going to be willing to lend at a negative interest rate.

## Monetarist Transmission Mechanism

Compared to the Keynesian monetary transmission mechanism, the monetarist transmission mechanism is more direct: an increase in the money supply means increased Total Expenditures and Real GDP. A decrease in the money supply means decreased Total Expenditures and Real GDP.

## Monetary Policy and Closing Gaps

In Chapter 9, we looked at how fiscal policy might be used to attempt to close a recessionary gap or an inflationary gap. Similarly, monetary policy can be used to attempt to close a recessionary gap or an inflationary gap.

When the economy is in a recessionary gap, Real GDP is less than Natural Real GDP. To close a recessionary gap, the money supply would be increased. This is expansionary monetary policy. The increase in the money supply would cause an increase in Real GDP, either through a series of steps (Keynesian theory) or more directly (monetarist theory).

When the economy is in an inflationary gap, Real GDP is greater than Natural Real GDP. To close an inflationary gap, the money supply would be decreased. This is contractionary monetary policy. The decrease in the money supply would cause a decrease in Real GDP.

## Keynesian Theory and the Proper Policies

As discussed in Chapter 9, Keynesians call for the use of expansionary fiscal policy to close recessionary gaps, and contractionary fiscal policy to close inflationary gaps. Similarly, Keynesians call for expansionary monetary policy to close recessionary gaps, and contractionary monetary policy to close inflationary gaps.

Though Keynesians support the use of both fiscal and monetary policy to move the economy toward Natural Real GDP, Keynesians put more confidence in fiscal policy. As discussed earlier in this chapter, the Keynesian monetary transmission mechanism may fail. Keynesians see fiscal policy as more reliable than monetary policy.

## Monetarist Theory and the Proper Policies

Monetarism is based on classical economic theory. Monetarists believe that a market economy is self-regulating and will automatically adjust to Natural Real GDP. Thus, monetarists are generally opposed to activist fiscal and monetary policies. As discussed in Chapter 9, activist fiscal policy may encounter problems with political bias, crowding out, lags, and miscalculation.

Similarly, monetarists believe that activist monetary policy may be biased toward expansionary monetary policy. The Fed may be biased toward expansionary monetary policy as the Fed attempts to maintain low interest rates in hopes of maintaining rapid economic growth. Expansionary monetary policy will eventually lead to continued inflation. As a result, activist fiscal and monetary policies may have a destabilizing effect on the economy rather than a stabilizing effect.

Most monetarists favor an annually balanced budget as the rule for fiscal policy. Likewise, most monetarists favor a monetary rule for monetary policy. A monetary rule would link money supply growth to Real GDP growth to achieve a stable price level.

---

**Example 6:** Assume that the average annual growth rate for Real GDP is 3%, and that the average annual change in velocity is 0%. What annual change in the money supply would result in price level stability (a 0% average annual change in the price level)? Answer; 3%, as indicated by the equation of exchange.

$$M \times V = P \times Q$$

$$+3\% \quad +0\% \quad +0\% \quad +3\%$$

---

## Appendix: The Great Depression

Classical economic theory was the predominant theory in industrialized nations from the time of Adam Smith until the Great Depression of the 1930s. The free market, laissez-faire policies followed by the industrialized world during this time corresponded with a period of unprecedented economic growth. Then along came the Great Depression.

Economic downturns, some quite severe, had occurred periodically in the U.S. between 1776 and 1929. But no downturn was as severe or as long-lasting as the Great Depression of the 1930s.

---

**Example 7:** Between 1929 and 1933, Real GDP decreased by nearly 27%. Investment spending collapsed. The consumer price index fell by 24%. The **deflation** (decrease in the price level) caused the real prime lending rate to rise from 6% in 1929 to 14% in 1931. The unemployment rate increased from 3.2% in 1929 to 24.9% in 1933.

---

After the economy bottomed out in 1933, a weak recovery began. But Real GDP was only slightly greater in 1938 than it had been in 1929. Investment spending did not reach the 1929 level until 1941. The unemployment rate did not fall below 14% until 1941, when it was still 9.9%.

According to classical economic theory, a market economy is self-regulating and will automatically adjust to Natural Real GDP. During the Great Depression, the U.S. economy did not automatically adjust to Natural Real GDP.

The table in Example 8 below illustrates the severity and the length of the Great Depression.

**Example 8:**

| Year | Real GDP (2000 Base) | Inflation Rate | Unemployment Rate |
|------|----------------------|----------------|-------------------|
| 1929 | $865.2 billion       | 0.0%           | 3.2%              |
| 1930 | 790.7 billion        | -2.3%          | 8.7%              |
| 1931 | 739.9 billion        | -9.0%          | 15.9%             |
| 1932 | 643.7 billion        | -9.9%          | 23.6%             |
| 1933 | 635.5 billion        | -5.1%          | 24.9%             |
| 1934 | 704.2 billion        | 3.1%           | 21.7%             |
| 1935 | 766.9 billion        | 2.2%           | 20.1%             |
| 1936 | 866.6 billion        | 1.5%           | 16.9%             |
| 1937 | 911.1 billion        | 3.6%           | 14.4%             |
| 1938 | 879.7 billion        | -2.1%          | 19.0%             |
| 1939 | 950.7 billion        | -1.4%          | 17.2%             |
| 1940 | 1034.1 billion       | 0.7%           | 14.6%             |
| 1941 | 1211.1 billion       | 5.0%           | 9.9%              |

## Keynesian Theory of the Great Depression

What caused the Great Depression? Keynesian economists blame the Great Depression on the inherent instability of a market economy. The stock market crash of 1929 caused investors to become extremely pessimistic. The extreme pessimism of investors caused a collapse in investment spending. The decrease in investment spending led to a multiplied decrease in Real GDP.

The federal government might have triggered a rapid recovery with proper fiscal and monetary policy. But the federal government's fiscal policy was not truly expansionary until the military buildup corresponding with World War II.

The Fed's monetary policy was not intentionally contractionary from 1929 to 1933. But the large number of bank failures caused the money supply to decrease by 25% from 1929 to 1933. Nearly 10,000 banks failed from 1929 to 1933. The bank failures directly decreased checkable deposits and motivated large amounts of withdrawals from banks that did not fail.

With the coming of World War II, the government's fiscal and monetary policy became strongly expansionary.

> **Example 9:** Federal government expenditures increased from $15.1 billion in 1940 to $105.5 billion in 1944. The money supply (M1) increased from $41.9 billion in 1940 to $90.7 billion in 1944. The expansionary fiscal and monetary policy finally restored full employment. The unemployment rate dropped from 14.6% in 1940 to 1.2% in 1944.

The recovery of the economy corresponding to the expansionary fiscal and monetary policy associated with World War II supports the Keynesian belief that proper fiscal and monetary policy can stabilize the economy.

## Classical Theory of the Great Depression

Classical economists disagree with the Keynesian interpretation of the Great Depression. Classical economists lay the blame for the severity and length of the Great Depression on government policy. What began as a normal downturn in the business cycle was turned into an economic collapse by two government policy mistakes.

The Federal Reserve System failed in its roles as lender of last resort and controller of the money supply. Nearly 10,000 banks failed causing a 25% decrease in the money supply. The decrease in the money supply caused significant deflation. (See the table on the previous page.)

Significant deflation can have a catastrophic affect on financial markets. A deflation rate of 9% (as occurred in 1931) means that if the equilibrium real interest rate (the rate that equalizes savings and investment) is 4%, the nominal interest rate would have to be negative 5%. A negative nominal interest rate is impossible. Lenders will <u>not</u> be willing to pay borrowers to borrow their money. Deflation in essence causes a price floor on interest rates, leading to a surplus of savings (or a shortage of investment).

The deflation of the early 1930s caused real interest rates to skyrocket. (The real prime lending rate rose to 14% in 1931.) The high real interest rates caused investment spending to collapse.

> **Example 10:** Investment spending decreased by over 90% between 1929 and 1933.

The second government policy mistake was the Smoot-Hawley Tariff, enacted in 1930. This protectionist tariff led to retaliatory tariff increases by U.S. trading partners, leading to a collapse in international trade. (For a more detailed discussion of the relationship between the stock market crash of 1929, the Smoot-Hawley Tariff, and the Great Depression, see the appendix at the end of Chapter 7.)

When the monetary situation was finally stabilized in 1933, the economic recovery was hobbled by the excessive (and inconsistent) government intervention of President Franklin Roosevelt's New Deal.

## Appendix: Book Review – "The Age of Turbulence: Adventures in a New World"

In 2007, Alan Greenspan published "The Age of Turbulence: Adventures in a New World". The first half of the book is an autobiography of the man who was Chairman of the Federal Reserve Board of Governors for over 18 years. The second half of the book is Greenspan's attempt to "try to convey my understanding of the forces that bind together the world economy and drive its evolution, as well as the forces that threaten to pull it apart."

Alan Greenspan was Chairman of the Federal Reserve Board of Governors from August, 1987 through January, 2006. Greenspan's tenure as Chairman was marked by a number of historic events, including:

1.  The October 19, 1987 plunge in stock market prices. The Dow Jones Industrial Average (DJIA) dropped by 22.6%, the largest one-day decrease in history. The largest one-day decrease previously had been the 13% decline on October 28, 1929.

2.  The fall of the Berlin Wall in 1989 and German reunification in 1990.

3.  The dot-com boom and bust. The DJIA first closed above 5,000 on November 21, 1995 and reached 11,722 on January 14, 2000. By October, 2002, the DJIA was back down to around 7,300. The technology heavy NASDAQ composite index first closed above 1,000 on July 17, 1995 and reached 5,046 on March 10, 2000. By October, 2002, the NASDAQ composite index was back down to around 1,100.

4.  The September 11, 2001 terrorist attacks on the World Trade Center and the Pentagon.

During Greenspan's tenure as Fed Chairman, the economy enjoyed a remarkable run of economic stability, with only two mild recessions (in 1991 and 2001). The annual rate of inflation averaged only 3.1% from 1988 through 2005, after having averaged 6.5% from 1970 through 1987. Greenspan's apparent skill at conducting the American economy led Bob Woodward to title his biography of Greenspan "Maestro: Greenspan's Fed and the American Boom".

Among the observations that Greenspan puts forth in the second half of "The Age of Turbulence" are:

1.  The three keys to a country's economic growth are;
    a.  The quality of the country's institutions, especially private property rights.
    b.  The extent of the country's competition domestically and its openness to international trade.
    c.  The success of the country's policymakers in achieving macroeconomic stability.

2.  China, despite its recent economic success, faces a difficult future choice; continue on the path to a more market-oriented economy and accept the inevitable loss in political power this will mean for the Communist Party or "revert to an orthodox regime of central planning and authoritarianism, which would almost surely undermine the prosperity on which the leadership depends for legitimacy".

3. Globalization, despite the intense criticism from those who see only the destructive side of creative destruction, is beneficial both economically and politically. Free trade not only promotes economic growth but also promotes democracy.

4. The increasing income inequality in the U.S. economy can best be dealt with by improvement in elementary and secondary education to increase the supply of skilled workers and by allowing open immigration of skilled workers from other countries to the U.S.

5. After assuming that, in 2030, the rule of law will still prevail, protectionism will be in check, global warming will <u>not</u> have had a significant economic impact, and terrorist attacks will have been kept at bay, Greenspan puts forth the following forecasts;
    a. Real GDP will be 75 percent larger in 2030 than in 2006.
    b. Intellectual property will be increasingly important and intellectual property rights will be a source of increasing legislation and litigation.
    c. The Federal Reserve System will face more inflationary pressures and more challenges from populist politics than in recent years.
    d. Countries will continue to face a trade-off; "…the greater the freedom to compete and the stronger the rule of law, the greater the material wealth produced. But…the greater the degree of competition…the greater the degree of stress and anxiety experienced by market participants."

## Questions for Chapter 12

### Fill-in-the-blanks:

1. _____ policy is changes in the money supply to achieve macroeconomic goals.

2. The _____ of money is the average number of times that a dollar is spent annually.

3. _____ is a decrease in the price level.

### Multiple Choice:

_____ 1. If nominal GDP is $13,175 billion and the money supply is $1,550 billion, the velocity of money is:
    a.    .118
    b.    .85
    c.    8.5
    d.    11.8

_____ 2. The velocity of money is equal to:
    a.  the CPI divided by the money supply
    b.  nominal GDP divided by the money supply
    c.  Real GDP divided by the CPI
    d.  the money supply times the CPI

_____ 3. According to classical monetary theory:
     a. the velocity of money is constant
     b. there is no relationship between the money supply and the price level
     c. Both of the above
     d. Neither of the above

_____ 4. If the money supply increases by 10%, Real GDP is constant, and velocity is constant, the price level must:
     a. remain constant
     b. increase by 10%
     c. decrease by 4%
     d. increase by about 3%

_____ 5. If the money supply increases by 10%, Real GDP increases by 3%, and velocity decreases by 4%, the price level must:
     a. remain constant
     b. increase by 10%
     c. decrease by 4%
     d. increase by about 3%

_____ 6. A difference between monetarism and classical theory is:
     a. monetarism holds that velocity is constant
     b. monetarism holds that AD affects Real GDP in the long run
     c. monetarism holds that AD affects Real GDP in the short run
     d. All of the above

_____ 7. According to the Keynesian monetary transmission mechanism:
     a. an increase in the money supply leads to an increase in interest rates
     b. an increase in interest rates leads to an increase in investment
     c. an increase in investment leads to an increase in Total Expenditures
     d. All of the above

_____ 8. The Keynesian monetary transmission mechanism:
     a. is indirect
     b. may fail because investment may be interest-insensitive
     c. may fail because of the liquidity trap
     d. All of the above

_____ 9. If investors are insensitive to a decrease in interest rates:
     a. an increase in the money supply may have no effect on investment.
     b. an increase in the money supply may have no effect on Real GDP.
     c. Both of the above
     d. Neither of the above

_____ 10. The liquidity trap:
     a. may cause interest rates to fall below zero
     b. means that interest rates will only fall so low
     c. may cause an increase in the money supply to have no effect on interest rates
     d. Both b. and c. above

_____ 11. Expansionary monetary policy:
   a. means an increase in the money supply
   b. according to Keynesian theory, would cause interest rates to decrease
   c. would be used to close an inflationary gap
   d. Both a. and b. above

_____ 12. Contractionary monetary policy:
   a. means an increase in the money supply
   b. according to Keynesian theory, would cause interest rates to decrease
   c. would be used to close an inflationary gap
   d. Both a. and b. above

_____ 13. Which of the following is true?
   a. Keynesians put more confidence in monetary policy than in fiscal policy
   b. Monetarists are generally opposed to activist policies
   c. Monetarists favor rapid growth in the money supply to maximize economic growth
   d. All of the above

_____ 14. A monetary rule:
   a. would return the economy to the gold standard
   b. would link money supply growth to Real GDP growth
   c. would require rapid growth in the money supply to keep interest rates low
   d. would require rapid growth in the money supply to maximize economic growth

_____ 15. Between 1929 and 1933, investment spending:
   a. increased by only 5%
   b. decreased by 25%
   c. decreased by 50%
   d. decreased by 90%

_____ 16. The high unemployment associated with the Great Depression lasted for:
   a. twelve years
   b. eight years
   c. five years
   d. three years

_____ 17. The New Deal policies beginning in 1933:
   a. included strongly expansionary fiscal and monetary policies
   b. quickly restored the economy to full employment
   c. according to classical economists, hobbled the economic recovery
   d. Both a. and b. above

_____ 18. Alan Greenspan's tenure as Chairman of the Federal Reserve Board was marked by:
   a. the severe recession triggered by the stock market crash of October 19, 1987
   b. the severe recession triggered by the terrorist attacks of September 11, 2001
   c. a remarkable run of economic stability and low inflation
   d. All of the above

_____ 19. According to Alan Greenspan:
   a. the increasing income inequality in the U.S. economy can best be dealt with by doubling the minimum wage
   b. China's movement toward a more market-oriented economy will inevitably strengthen the power of the Communist Party
   c. free trade promotes both economic growth and democracy
   d. None of the above

_____ 20. Alan Greenspan forecasts that, by 2030, U.S. Real GDP will be:
   a. 150 percent larger than in 2006
   b. 75 percent larger than in 2006
   c. 30 percent larger than in 2006
   d. essentially the same as in 2006

## Problems:

1. If the Fed wants to trigger a decrease in Real GDP, the Fed would decrease the money supply. List the four steps in the Keynesian monetary transmission mechanism that would follow the decrease in the money supply.

2. Explain two reasons why the Keynesian monetary transmission mechanism may fail.

3. Explain what caused the Great Depression, according to Keynesian economists.

4. Explain what caused the Great Depression, according to Classical economists.

5. According to Alan Greenspan, what are the three keys to a country's economic growth?

## Answers for Chapter 12

**Fill-in-the-blanks:**   1. Monetary
2. velocity
3. Deflation

**Multiple Choice:**

| | | |
|---|---|---|
| 1. c. | 8. d. | 15. d. |
| 2. b. | 9. c. | 16. a. |
| 3. a. | 10. d. | 17. c. |
| 4. b. | 11. d. | 18. c. |
| 5. d. | 12. c. | 19. c. |
| 6. c. | 13. b. | 20. b. |
| 7. c. | 14. b. | |

**Problems:**

1.  (1)  an increase in interest rates, which leads to
    (2)  a decrease in investment, which leads to
    (3)  a decrease in Total Expenditures, which leads to
    (4)  a decrease in Real GDP

2.  The Keynesian monetary transmission mechanism may fail because:
    a.  Investment may be interest-insensitive.  If investors are extremely pessimistic, a decrease in interest rates may not increase investment.
    b.  The liquidity trap.  The liquidity trap means that an increase in the money supply does not cause a decrease in interest rates.

3.  Keynesian economists blame the Great Depression on the inherent instability of a market economy.  The stock market crash of 1929 caused investors to become extremely pessimistic.  The extreme pessimism of investors caused a collapse in investment spending.  The decrease in investment spending led to a multiplied decrease in Real GDP.

4.  Classical economists lay the blame for the severity and the length of the Great Depression on government policy.  What began as a normal downturn in the business cycle was turned into an economic collapse by two government policy mistakes:
    (1)  The Federal Reserve System failed in its roles as lender of last resort and controller of the money supply.  Deflation caused real interest rates to skyrocket and investment spending to collapse.
    (2)  The Smoot-Hawley Tariff of 1930 led to retaliatory tariff increases by U.S. trading partners, leading to a collapse in international trade.

5.  According to Alan Greenspan, the three keys to a country's economic growth are;
    a.  The quality of the country's institutions, especially private property rights.
    b.  The extent of the country's competition domestically and its openness to international trade.
    c.  The success of the country's policymakers in achieving macroeconomic stability.

# Chapter 13  Taxes, Deficits, and the National Debt

The basic economic problem is scarcity.  Human wants are unlimited.  Resources are limited.  Taxation transfers limited resources from the private sector (households and business firms) to the public sector (government).

## Classifications of Taxes

Taxes can be classified as proportional, progressive, or regressive.  A **proportional tax** imposes the same tax rate on all levels of income.  A **progressive tax** imposes higher tax rates on higher levels of income.  A **regressive tax** imposes higher tax rates on lower levels of income.  Each of these classifications of taxes is illustrated in the examples below:

---

**Example 1A:**  Max has before-tax income of $200,000.  Minnie has before-tax income of $10,000.  A proportional tax is imposed.  The rate for both taxpayers is 20%.  The table below shows the effect of the tax.

|  | Max | Minnie |
|---|---|---|
| Before-tax Income | $200,000 | $10,000 |
| Tax Rate | 20% | 20% |
| Taxes Paid | $40,000 | $2,000 |
| After-tax Income | $160,000 | $8,000 |

---

Notice that the proportional tax does <u>not</u> change the distribution of income.  Max has 20 times as much income as Minnie before the tax.  After the tax, Max still has 20 times as much income as Minnie.

---

**Example 1B:**    Same facts as Example 1A, except that a progressive tax is imposed.  Minnie's income is taxed at 10%.  Max's income is taxed at 30%.  The table below shows the effect of the tax.

|  | Max | Minnie |
|---|---|---|
| Before-tax Income | $200,000 | $10,000 |
| Tax Rate | 30% | 10% |
| Taxes Paid | $60,000 | $1,000 |
| After-tax Income | $140,000 | $9,000 |

---

Notice that the progressive tax changes the distribution of income by making it more equal.  Max has 20 times as much income as Minnie before the tax.  After the tax, Max has 15.6 times as much income as Minnie.

Notice that the regressive tax changes the distribution of income by making it more unequal. Max has 20 times as much income as Minnie before the tax. After the tax, Max has 25.7 times as much income as Minnie.

## Most Taxes Are Regressive

Most taxes imposed in the U.S. are regressive. Two of the three largest taxes imposed by the federal government are regressive. As will be discussed in the next section, the social security tax and the federal corporate income tax are both regressive taxes.

At the state and local level, sales taxes are very important. Sales taxes (with the exception of sales taxes imposed on luxury goods) are regressive. Lower income households spend a higher percentage of their incomes on purchases subject to sales tax compared to higher income households. Thus, lower income households pay a higher percentage of their incomes in sales tax.

Property taxes are a major source of local government funding. Since lower income households consume a higher percentage of their incomes compared to higher income households, any tax that increases the prices of non-luxury goods will be regressive. Thus, property taxes are regressive.

Among the most regressive taxes are cigarette taxes and state-run lotteries. Research indicates that cigarettes and lottery tickets have an income elasticity of demand (see Chapter 17) of around zero. Thus, consumer spending on cigarettes and lottery tickets does not increase as household income increases. (Some research indicates that consumer spending on cigarettes and lottery tickets may decrease as household income increases.)

> **Example 3:** Max and Minnie both live in a state where the combined federal and state cigarette tax is $1.50 per pack. If Minnie smokes 100 packs of cigarettes per year, she will pay $150 in cigarette tax, which is 1.5% of her income. In order for Max to pay 1.5% of his income on cigarette tax, he would have to smoke 2000 packs per year. If Max smokes 100 packs per year (the same amount as Minnie), he will pay $150 in cigarette tax, which is .075% of his income.

## Major Federal Taxes

Over 90 percent of the federal government's tax revenues come from the three largest federal taxes:

1.  **Personal income tax.** In 2008, the federal personal income tax generated about 45% of all federal tax revenues. The personal income tax is a progressive tax, meaning that it makes the distribution of income more equal. However, the progressive structure of the tax may hurt productivity. The federal personal income tax is discussed in more detail later in the chapter.

2.  **Social security tax.** In 2008, the social security tax generated about 36% of all federal tax revenues. The social security tax (which initially had a tax rate of 2% of earned income) has become a very large tax (the rate for most taxpayers is now 15.3% of earned income). For most taxpayers, the social security tax is a larger tax than the federal personal income tax.

    The social security tax is a regressive tax. The social security tax rate is the same (15.3%) for earned income up to a certain income level ($106,800 in 2009). Above this income level, the rate drops to 2.9%. The higher a person's income beyond this threshold, the lower the percentage of income paid in social security tax. As a regressive tax, the social security tax falls more heavily on lower income taxpayers, as illustrated in Example 4.

> **Example 4:** In 2009, Taxpayer A had $40,000 of earned income, Taxpayer B had $400,000 of earned income, and Taxpayer C had $4,000,000 of earned income. Taxpayer A paid $6,120 in social security tax ($40,000 x .153). Taxpayer B paid $24,843 in social security tax ([$106,800 x .153] + [$293,200 x .029]). Taxpayer C paid $129,243 in social security tax ([$106,800 x .153] + [$3,893,200 x .029]). The table below summarizes the percentage of income each taxpayer paid in social security tax.
>
> | | Taxpayer A | Taxpayer B | Taxpayer C |
> |---|---|---|---|
> | Earned Income | $40,000 | $400,000 | $4,000,000 |
> | Social security tax paid | $6,120 | $24,843 | $129,243 |
> | Social security tax as a percentage of Income | 15.3% | 6.2% | 3.2% |

Other characteristics of the social security tax and the social security system include:

a. The social security tax is collected in such a way that it is partially hidden from the taxpayers. The employee's share of the social security tax is withheld from the employee's paycheck. The employer's share is collected directly from the employer. Most employees are probably unaware of the total amount of social security tax that they pay. Self-employed persons are much more aware of the social security tax burden than are employees.

b. The social security system encourages retirement by taxing earned income, and by providing a subsidy to retirement. This is counterproductive to achieving the basic goal in dealing with the problem of scarcity: Produce as much consumer satisfaction as possible with the limited resources available.

c. The social security system rewards long life. The longer a recipient of social security benefits lives, the more benefits the person will receive. This causes a redistribution of income from groups with a shorter average life expectancy (males, smokers, certain minority groups) to groups with a longer average life expectancy.

3. **Corporate income tax.** In 2008, the corporate income tax generated about 12% of all federal tax revenues. The corporate income tax is probably regressive in the long run, as the tax increases corporate costs of production and drives up consumer prices. Higher consumer prices are a larger burden for lower income taxpayers, who consume a relatively high percentage of their incomes.

## Characteristics of a Good Tax

The essential purpose of taxation is to fund government operations. Taxation transfers resources (by transferring purchasing power) from the private sector (households and business firms) to the public sector (government). Taxation imposes a burden on the taxpayers, while providing funding for the government.

Ideally, the burden imposed by a tax would be no greater than the funding provided to the government. Quoting from "The Wealth of Nations" by Adam Smith, "Every tax ought to be so contrived as both to take out and to keep out of the pockets of the people as little as possible, over and above what it brings into the treasury of the state…"

Realistically, a tax will impose a burden on the taxpayers larger than the funding provided to the government. This is called excess burden.

**Excess burden** – the amount that the burden imposed by a tax exceeds the funding provided by the tax.

**Example 5:** The government wants to provide $100 million to fund a new government program. If a tax is imposed which provides the government with $100 million for the new program and imposes a burden on the taxpayers of only $100 million, there will be no excess burden.

Any tax is likely to impose excess burden. Some taxes will impose a very large excess burden. A good (economically efficient) tax is one which imposes as little excess burden as possible.

The sources of excess burden include:

1. **The cost for the government to collect the tax.** The government will incur costs to administer and enforce a tax. To minimize the collection cost of a tax, the tax should be as simple as possible.

> **Example 6:** The government wants to provide $100 million to fund a new government program. If it costs the government $5 million to collect the tax, it will be necessary to collect $105 million from the taxpayers in order to fund the program. Thus, there is an excess burden of $5 million.

2. **The cost for the taxpayers to comply with the tax.** Taxpayers will have to keep certain records, fill out forms, etc. to comply with a tax. To minimize the compliance cost of a tax, the tax should be as simple as possible.

> **Example 7:** The government wants to provide $100 million to fund a new government program. If the taxpayers spend thousands of hours keeping the necessary records and filling out the necessary forms to comply with the tax (or if the taxpayers pay experts to keep the records and fill out the forms), there will be a compliance cost imposed on the taxpayers. This adds to the tax burden without adding to the government's funding, and is thus an excess burden.

3. **The deadweight loss of the tax.** We saw in Chapter 3 that private market equilibrium is generally efficient, equalizing marginal benefit and marginal cost, and maximizing the net benefit of having the market available (the sum of consumer's surplus and producer's surplus).

   A tax may distort the decisions made in the private market. When a tax distorts the decisions made in the private market, the tax eliminates mutually beneficial transactions and thus reduces the net benefit of having the market available. This reduction is the deadweight loss of the tax.

> **Example 8:** The graphs on the next page represent the market for Good X from Example 12 in Chapter 3. The first graph shows the amount of consumer's surplus and producer's surplus before a tax is imposed. The sum of consumer's surplus and producer's surplus is the net benefit of having the market available. The market equilibrium is a price of $4 and a quantity of 15 units.
>
> The second graph shows the effect of a $2 per unit tax imposed on the sellers of Good X. The supply curve shifts vertically by the amount of the tax. The after-tax equilibrium is a price of $5 and a quantity of 10 units. The mutually beneficial exchange of 5 units has been eliminated by the tax. The consumer's and producer's surplus lost due to the exchanges eliminated by the tax is the deadweight loss of the tax, as indicated on the second graph.

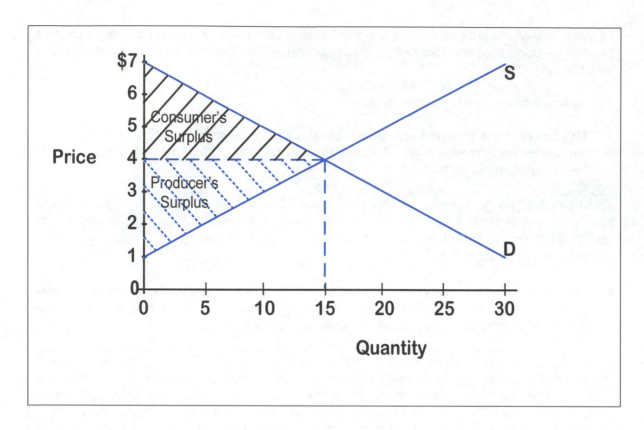

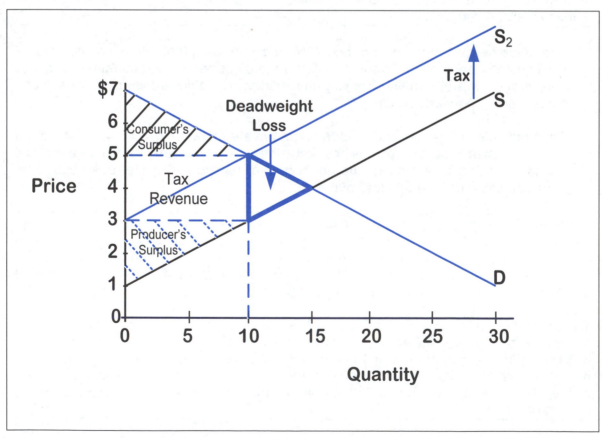

To minimize the deadweight loss, a tax should;

a. **Be broad-based.** A broad-based tax has little effect on relative prices, and thus has little effect on the decisions made in the private market.

> **Example 9:** If a 1% sales tax is imposed on all consumer goods and services, consumption will fall. But since the relative prices of goods and services will be unchanged, the mix of goods and services consumed will be unchanged. The market equilibrium, after the tax, will still reflect private decisions about costs and benefits.

If a narrowly-based tax is imposed (e.g. a 50% sales tax on dairy products), the decisions in the private market will be distorted (people buy fewer dairy products, not based on costs and benefits, but based on the tax). For an extreme example; a 5000% tax is imposed on ice cream. At this tax rate, no ice cream is produced or consumed. Many mutually beneficial transactions are eliminated. And the government collects zero tax revenue from the tax. The only effect of the tax is to impose excess burden.

b. **Have low rates.** Low tax rates help to minimize the effect on the decisions made in the private market.

> **Example 10A:** A tax rate of 1% on income would have very little effect on the production decisions of households. Probably no one will withdraw from the labor market due to the disincentive caused by a 1% income tax. A tax rate of 50% on income would have a larger effect on the production decisions of households. Many persons may withdraw from the labor market due to the disincentive caused by a 50% income tax or may be less motivated to improve the productivity of their labor. What if a 100% tax is imposed on income? At this rate, no income will be produced. The economy loses out on trillions of dollars worth of production. And the government collects zero tax revenue from the tax. The only effect of the tax is to impose excess burden.

> **Example 10B:** We will see in Chapter 17 that one of the factors that determines the size of the deadweight loss of a tax is the tax rate. A lower tax rate will mean a smaller deadweight loss. A higher tax rate will mean a larger deadweight loss. Refer to Examples 14 and 16 in Chapter 17 to see how an increase in the tax rate increases the deadweight loss of a tax.

c. **Be imposed on inelastic goods.** The price elasticity of demand and supply for a good determines how responsive buyers and sellers are to a change in the price of the good. For inelastic goods, buyers and sellers are not very responsive to a change in price. Thus a tax imposed on an inelastic good will have a relatively small effect on the market outcome.

> **Example 11:** We will see in Chapter 17 that one of the factors that determines the size of the deadweight loss of a tax is the price elasticity of demand and supply. The more elastic the demand curve, the greater the deadweight loss of the tax. The less elastic the demand curve, the smaller the deadweight loss of the tax. Likewise, the more elastic the supply curve, the greater the deadweight loss of the tax. And the less elastic the supply curve, the smaller the deadweight loss of the tax. Refer to Examples 14 and 15 in Chapter 17 to see how an increase in the price elasticity of demand for a good increases the deadweight loss of a tax imposed on the good.

## Is the Federal Personal Income Tax a Good Tax?

The largest source of revenue for the federal government is the federal personal income tax. Having just considered the characteristics of a good tax, we can evaluate whether the personal income tax is a good (economically efficient) tax. Unfortunately, it is not. The federal personal income tax imposes a large excess burden.

The personal income tax is extremely complicated. The federal income tax code and regulations contain about 7 million words. (That's about 9 times as many words as are in the Bible.) This complexity causes the collection cost of the tax to be high. In 2007, the IRS had about 100,000 full-time employees and a budget of about $11 billion.

The complexity of the tax law also causes the compliance cost of the tax to be high. According to the IRS, taxpayers spend over 6 billion hours annually keeping records and filling out forms required to comply with the tax law. They pay billions of dollars for professional tax help. For the year 2005, the Tax Foundation estimated the compliance cost of the federal personal income tax and the corporate income tax at $265 billion.

The federal personal income tax also imposes a large deadweight loss. The tax appears to be broad-based, with its general rules that all income is subject to tax and that no expense is deductible. However, the tax base is made narrower by the presence of numerous loopholes.

**Loopholes** - exclusions and exemptions from income, deductible expenses, and tax credits.

The presence of loopholes distorts the decisions made in private markets. Taxpayers will alter their behavior to generate income and expenses that receive favorable tax treatment and to avoid income and expenses that receive unfavorable tax treatment.

Many of the loopholes are large. The table in Example 12 below lists some of the larger loopholes for the tax year 2008, and the estimated amount of taxes avoided by each loophole. The information is from the Office of Management and Budget.

---

**Example 12:**

| Loophole | Taxes Avoided |
|---|---|
| Exclusion of employer provided medical insurance | $152 billion |
| Exclusion of pension contributions and earnings | 119 billion |
| Deduction of home mortgage interest | 95 billion |
| Deduction of state and local income and property taxes | 49 billion |
| Deduction of charitable contributions | 43 billion |
| Child tax credit | 30 billion |

---

Collectively, the loopholes reduce the tax base (personal income) by around 50 percent. This means that higher tax rates must be imposed to collect the same amount of tax revenue that could be collected with lower tax rates and a broader tax base. The loopholes are also a big factor in making the tax complicated.

## What Would Make the Federal Personal Income Tax a Better Tax?

A good (economically efficient) tax is one which imposes as little excess burden as possible. The federal personal income tax imposes a large excess burden. To make the federal personal income tax a better tax, the excess burden it imposes would need to be reduced. How can that be done?

Make the federal personal income tax simpler. Eliminate most (or all) of the loopholes. This would reduce the collection cost and the compliance cost dramatically. IRS agents and tax accountants could be retrained to do something productive. Taxpayers could spend minutes on their tax returns instead of hours.

Eliminating the loopholes would stop the distortion of private market decisions currently caused by the loopholes. Eliminating the loopholes would also broaden the tax base, allowing the same amount of tax revenue to be collected with lower tax rates.

What about the rate structure? Would the federal personal income tax be a better tax if it were more progressive or less progressive? This question involves a trade-off. Making the tax more progressive would help in achieving the goal of equalizing the distribution of income. Increasing income equality might increase the consumer satisfaction produced from the limited resources (see Chapter 31). Making the tax less progressive would help in achieving the goal of minimizing the deadweight loss. The best choice for the rate structure depends on the relative value assigned to each goal.

## The Burden of the Federal Personal Income Tax

The federal personal income tax is a progressive tax. As a result, the burden of the tax falls more heavily on higher income taxpayers. According to the Internal Revenue Service, in 2006 the average income tax rate was 12.6%. The top 1% of income earners paid an average rate of 22.8%.

Because the top income earners pay a higher tax rate and have a higher share of total income, the bulk of the federal personal income tax is paid by a relatively small percentage of top income earners. In 2006, the top 1% of income earners had 22.1% of total adjusted gross income and paid 39.9% of total income taxes paid.

Other information on average tax rates, average income tax paid, shares of total income by income group, and shares of income taxes paid by income group is detailed below:

| Income Group | Average Federal Income Tax Rate | Average Federal Income Tax Paid | Group's Share of Total AGI | Group's Share of Total Income Taxes |
|---|---|---|---|---|
| Top 1% | 22.8% | $300,893 | 22.1% | 39.9% |
| Top 5% | 20.7% | 90,729 | 36.7% | 60.1% |
| Top 10% | 18.9% | 53,400 | 47.3% | 70.8% |
| Top 25% | 16.0% | 26,029 | 68.2% | 86.3% |
| Top 50% | 14.0% | 14,636 | 87.5% | 97.0% |
| Bottom 50% | 3.0% | 452 | 12.5% | 3.0% |
| All Taxpayers | 12.6% | 7,543 | 100% | 100% |

## Major Federal Spending Programs

Most federal government expenditures are on a handful of major federal spending programs. These are listed below, with the amount of spending for fiscal year 2007. (From the Office of Management and Budget.)

| | |
|---|---|
| Social security | $586 billion |
| National defense | $553 billion |
| Medicare | $375 billion |
| Income security | $366 billion |
| Health (including Medicaid) | $266 billion |
| Interest on the National Debt | $237 billion |

An appendix at the end of the chapter explains why spending on two of the major federal spending programs (social security and Medicare) is likely to increase rapidly in coming years.

## Deficits and the National Debt

In most of the last seventy-five years, the federal government has had annual budget deficits. A **budget deficit** occurs when government expenditures are greater than tax revenues. For fiscal year 2008, the federal government had tax revenues of $2,524 billion and expenditures of $2,979 billion, for a budget deficit of $455 billion. Years of budget deficits have led to a huge national debt (about $10.5 trillion as of November, 2008).

**National debt** – the total amount the federal government owes its creditors.

## The Burden of Deficit Spending

When the federal government pays for current expenditures by deficit spending (by borrowing), who bears the burden of this deficit spending? Is the current generation receiving the benefit of the current government spending and passing the burden on to future generations? To an extent, deficit spending does create a burden on future generations. But the burden of deficit spending also falls on the current generation.

## The Burden on the Current Generation

The current generation bears the burden of deficit spending to the extent that private consumption is crowded out by increased government use of resources. The basic economic problem is scarcity. Deficit spending allows the government to use a larger share of the limited resources. This leaves fewer resources for the private sector (consumption and investment). Deficit spending increases the government's demand for loanable funds, driving up interest rates. The higher interest rates will reduce consumption. To the extent that consumption is crowded out, the current generation bears the burden of deficit spending.

## The Burden on Future Generations

The burden of deficit spending also falls on future generations, in two ways. As mentioned above, deficit spending drives up interest rates. The higher interest rates will reduce investment. The reduction in investment in the present will lead to slower economic growth in the future. Thus, future generations will experience a lower standard of living because deficit spending reduces current investment.

Any government spending tends to crowd out private spending (consumption and investment). But deficit spending crowds out investment more than would occur with a balanced budget. If the government has a balanced budget, tax revenues must equal government expenditures. Taxation tends to crowd out consumption more severely than it does investment. When the government deficit spends, the increase in interest rates tends to crowd out investment more severely than it does consumption. Thus, deficit spending creates a burden on future generations to the extent that deficit spending favors current consumption rather than investment.

The second way that deficit spending creates a burden on future generations is if the deficit spending is financed by foreign creditors. The budget deficit is financed primarily by internal borrowing (about 73% of the national debt is financed by borrowing from American creditors). This internal borrowing does not increase total resources available. It shifts resources from the private sector to the public sector.

But the budget deficit is also financed by external borrowing (about 27% of the national debt is financed by borrowing from foreign creditors). This external borrowing amounts to borrowing resources from other economies. When the external borrowing is repaid, fewer resources will be available to the domestic economy. Thus, deficit spending creates a burden on future generations to the extent that the deficit spending is financed by foreign creditors. (The data on external debt is from the U.S. Treasury Department, as of 08/08.)

## Appendix: Future Social Security and Medicare Spending

Social security and Medicare are two of the largest federal government spending programs. Spending on social security and Medicare has increased tremendously in recent decades.

> **Example 13:** Since 1970, Medicare spending has increased by about 45-fold. Social Security benefits have increased by about 17-fold in that same time.

Spending on social security and Medicare is likely to continue to increase rapidly in coming years for three reasons:

1. **Increase in life expectancy.** Life expectancy in the U.S. was about 61 years in 1935 (when the social security system was created). Today it is about 78 years. A 65-year-old American today has a remaining life expectancy of about 19 years. An increase in life expectancy means that a growing percentage of the population will be eligible for social security and Medicare.

> **Example 14:** Since 1950, the U.S. population has slightly more than doubled. But the number of Americans 65 and older has more than tripled.

2. **Aging of the baby boom generation.** The baby boom generation consists of Americans born between 1946 and 1964, when the birth rate in the U.S. was unusually high. As this large cohort moves into the retirement years, the number of Americans eligible for social security and Medicare will increase.

> **Example 15:** Between 2011 and 2029, the baby boom generation will be entering into the post-65 years. The number of Americans 65 and older is expected to increase from about 40 million in 2010 to over 70 million in 2030.

3. **For spending on Medicare, the increase in the amount of medical care available.** Health care spending in the U.S. has generally been increasing. Health care spending as a percentage of GDP has increased from 5% in 1950 to over 15% today. Part of this is due to health care costs rising faster than the rate of inflation. Another part is due to the increased demand for health care caused by the rising standard of living. And another part is due to the increase in the amount of medical care available.

> **Example 16A:** In 1949, Grandpa visits his doctor complaining of shortness of breath, a persistent cough, swollen feet, and a general fatigue. After a number of tests, Grandpa is diagnosed with an advanced case of heart disease. The doctor's advice to Grandpa is, "Make a will."

> **Example 16B:** In 2009, Grandpa visits his doctor complaining of shortness of breath, a persistent cough, swollen feet, and a general fatigue. After a number of tests, Grandpa is diagnosed with an advanced case of heart disease. The doctor goes over Grandpa's treatment options. These include a variety of medications to prevent blood clots, lower bad cholesterol, control heartbeat force and rhythm, relax and dilate blood vessels, control blood pressure, and thin the blood. There are also a number of surgical options, such as angioplasty, coronary stent placement, coronary bypass surgery, and possibly even heart transplant.

It is likely that the amount of medical care available will continue to increase in the future. New prescription medicines will be discovered and new surgical techniques will be developed. And health care spending as a percentage of GDP will continue to increase.

## Appendix: History of the Federal Personal Income Tax

The Sixteenth Amendment to the U.S. Constitution, ratified in 1913, gave the federal government the authority to impose a personal income tax. The initial personal income tax was a very minor burden. Most individuals did not earn enough annual income to have any personal income tax liability. Individuals with annual income of less than $3,000 (about $63,000 in current dollars) paid no income tax.

The tax rate was 1% on incomes from $3,000 up to $20,000 (about $420,000 in current dollars.) Thus, most individuals who did have a tax liability were taxed at a rate of 1%.

The top marginal tax rate was 7% and was imposed on annual incomes over $500,000 (about $10,500,000 in current dollars).

The tax rates imposed by the federal personal income tax were soon increased. By 1918, the top tax rate had risen to 77% (on incomes of over $1,000,000) and the minimum tax rate had risen to 6% (on incomes of up to $4,000). After the First World War, tax rates were gradually lowered, so that the top tax rate was 25% from 1925 to 1931. Tax rates were increased in 1932, 1936, and 1941, so that the U.S. entered the Second World War with a top tax rate of 81% (on incomes of over $5,000,000). The top rate hit a peak of 94% (on incomes of over $200,000) in 1944. The top tax rate was 91% from 1946 through 1963.

The top rate was lowered to 70% by the Kennedy tax cut of 1964. The top rate was lowered to 50% in 1982 and to 28% in 1988. The top rate was increased to 31% in 1991, and to 39.6% in 1993. The top rate was lowered to 35% in 2003.

The table below indicates the tax rates for single taxpayers for the year 2009.

| Taxable Income | Tax Rate |
|---|---|
| $0 – $8,350 | 10% |
| 8,350 – 33,950 | 15% |
| 33,950 – 82,250 | 25% |
| 82,250 – 171,550 | 28% |
| 171,550 – 372,950 | 33% |
| over 372,950 | 35% |

## Questions for Chapter 13

### Fill-in-the-blanks:

1. A _____ tax imposes the same tax rate on all levels of income.

2. A _____ tax imposes higher tax rates on higher levels of income.

3. A _____ tax imposes higher tax rates on lower levels of income.

4. _____ _____ is the amount that the burden imposed by a tax exceeds the funding provided by the tax.

5. _____ are exclusions and exemptions from income, deductible expenses, and tax credits.

6. A budget _____ occurs when government expenditures are greater than tax revenues.

7. The _____ debt is the total amount the federal government owes its creditors.

## Multiple Choice:

_____ 1. Which type of tax causes the distribution of income to be unchanged?
    a. proportional
    b. progressive
    c. regressive

_____ 2. Which of the following taxes is regressive?
    a. sales tax
    b. property tax
    c. lottery tax
    d. All of the above

_____ 3. The federal personal income tax:
    a. is the largest source of federal tax revenue
    b. is a progressive tax
    c. may hurt productivity
    d. All of the above

_____ 4. The social security tax:
    a. is the largest source of federal tax revenue
    b. is a progressive tax
    c. is partially hidden from taxpayers
    d. All of the above

_____ 5. The social security system:
    a. encourages retirement
    b. redistributes income from groups with a shorter average life expectancy to groups with a longer average life expectancy
    c. Both of the above
    d. Neither of the above

_____ 6. The corporate income tax:
    a. is the largest source of federal tax revenue
    b. is a progressive tax
    c. has no effect on consumers
    d. None of the above

_____ 7. Excess burden:
    a. is the amount that the burden imposed by a tax exceeds the funding provided by the tax
    b. occurs with all taxes
    c. is minimized if a tax is simple, broad-based, has low rates, and is imposed on inelastic goods
    d. All of the above

_____ 8. The sources of excess burden include:
    a. the cost for the taxpayers to comply with the tax
    b. the deadweight loss of the tax
    c. the cost for the government to collect the tax
    d. All of the above

_____ 9. To minimize the deadweight loss, a tax should:
   a. be narrowly-based, so as to affect only a few goods
   b. have low rates, so as to minimize the effect on decisions made in the private market
   c. Both of the above
   d. Neither of the above

_____ 10. The federal personal income tax:
   a. is extremely complicated
   b. imposes a large deadweight loss
   c. has little effect on decisions made in private markets
   d. Both a. and b. above

_____ 11. Loopholes:
   a. are exclusions and exemptions from income, deductible expenses, and tax credits
   b. reduce the tax base by nearly a billion dollars
   c. distort the decisions made in private markets
   d. Both a. and c. above

_____ 12. Making the federal personal income tax less progressive:
   a. would increase the size of the deadweight loss
   b. would help in achieving the goal of equalizing the distribution of income
   c. Both of the above
   d. Neither of the above

_____ 13. The average federal income tax rate for the bottom 50% of income earners was ___% in 2006.
   a. 2.1%
   b. 3.0%
   c. 12.6%
   d. 22.8%

_____ 14. The top 25% of income earners received ___ % of total AGI in 2006.
   a. 86.3%
   b. 68.2%
   c. 47.3%
   d. 36.7%

_____ 15. The top 5% of income earners paid ___% of total federal income taxes in 2006.
   a. 22.1%
   b. 39.9%
   c. 60.1%
   d. 70.8%

_____ 16. Of the following, which is the largest federal spending program?
   a. Interest on the National Debt
   b. National Defense
   c. Social Security
   d. Medicare

_____ 17. The burden of deficit spending falls on the current generation:
   a. not at all
   b. to the extent that deficit spending favors current consumption rather than investment
   c. to the extent that private consumption is crowded out by increased government use of resources
   d. entirely

_____ 18. The burden of deficit spending falls on future generations:
   a. to the extent that deficit spending favors current consumption rather than investment
   b. because the deficit is financed entirely by foreign creditors
   c. entirely
   d. Both b. and c. above

_____ 19. The baby boom generation:
   a. will be entering the post-65 years between 2030 and 2050
   b. will cause the number of Americans eligible for social security and Medicare to greatly increase
   c. Both of the above
   d. Neither of the above

_____ 20. The federal personal income tax:
   a. was authorized in 1863 by the Thirteenth Amendment
   b. initially had a top marginal tax rate of 20%
   c. has much higher tax rates today than it initially had
   d. All of the above

## Problems:

1. What is a progressive tax and how does a progressive tax affect the distribution of income?

2. List the sources of excess burden.

3. How would eliminating the loopholes affect the federal personal income tax?

4. List two ways that the burden of deficit spending falls on future generations.

5. List and explain the three reasons that spending on social security and Medicare is likely to increase rapidly in coming years.

**Multiple Choice:**

| | | |
|---|---|---|
| 1. a. | 8. d. | 15. c. |
| 2. d. | 9. b. | 16. c. |
| 3. d. | 10. d. | 17. c. |
| 4. c. | 11. d. | 18. a. |
| 5. c. | 12. d. | 19. b. |
| 6. d. | 13. b. | 20. c. |
| 7. d. | 14. b. | |

**Problems:**

1. A progressive tax imposes higher tax rates on higher levels of income. A progressive tax changes the distribution of income by making it more equal.

2. The sources of excess burden include:
   (1) The cost for the government to collect the tax.
   (2) The cost for the taxpayers to comply with the tax.
   (3) The deadweight loss of the tax.

3. Eliminating the loopholes would simplify the tax, reducing the collection cost and the compliance cost. Eliminating the loopholes would stop the distortion of private market decisions currently caused by the loopholes. Eliminating the loopholes would broaden the tax base, allowing the same amount of tax revenue to be collected with lower tax rates.

4. The burden of deficit spending falls on future generations in two ways:
   (1) Deficit spending creates a burden of future generations to the extent that deficit spending favors current consumption rather than investment.
   (2) Deficit spending creates a burden on future generations to the extent that the deficit spending is financed by foreign creditors.

5. The three reasons that spending on social security and Medicare is likely to increase rapidly in coming years are:
   (1) Increase in life expectancy. An increase in life expectancy means that a growing percentage of the population will be eligible for social security and Medicare.
   (2) Aging of the baby boom generation. As the baby boom generation moves into the retirement years, the number of Americans eligible for social and Medicare will increase.
   (3) For spending on Medicare, the increase in the amount of medical care available. The increase in health care spending in the U.S. is partially due to the increase in the amount of medical care available.

## Chapter 14  Economic Growth

The basic economic problem is scarcity.  Human wants are unlimited.  Resources are limited.  The basic goal in dealing with the problem of scarcity is to produce as much consumer satisfaction as possible with the limited resources available.

Economic growth is one of the three macroeconomic goals.  In the long run, a nation's success in dealing with the basic economic problem of scarcity depends on its success in achieving economic growth.  Economic growth will not allow a nation to satisfy all human wants.  But economic growth will help a nation to produce as much consumer satisfaction as possible with the limited resources available.

Chapter 5 defined absolute economic growth as an increase in Real GDP.  This chapter distinguishes between absolute economic growth and per capita economic growth.

**Absolute economic growth** – an increase in Real GDP.

If a nation increases its Real GDP over time, then it has achieved absolute economic growth.

---

**Example 1A:**  The table below shows Real GDP for Country X in 1978 and 2008. Country X has achieved absolute economic growth.  It has increased its Real GDP by 80%, from $100 billion to $180 billion.

| Country X | 1978 | 2008 |
|---|---|---|
| Real GDP | $100,000,000,000 | $180,000,000,000 |

---

But has Country X achieved per capita economic growth?   Per capita means "per person", so per capita economic growth means an increase in Real GDP per person (an increase in the standard of living).

**Per capita economic growth** – an increase in per capita Real GDP.

---

**Example 1B:**  The table below shows Real GDP for Country X in 1978 and 2008.  The table also shows the population of Country X in the two years and the per capita Real GDP (Real GDP ÷ population) for each year.   Though Country X achieved absolute economic growth, it did not achieve per capita economic growth.  Per capita Real GDP decreased by 10%.  Output did not grow as fast as population, and the standard of living in Country X declined.

| Country X | 1978 | 2008 |
|---|---|---|
| Real GDP | $100,000,000,000 | $180,000,000,000 |
| Population | 25,000,000 | 50,000,000 |
| Per capita Real GDP | $4,000 | $3,600 |

---

## Economic Growth in the World

Most countries in the world have been achieving both absolute economic growth and per capita economic growth in recent decades. According to the Penn World Tables, 84% of the countries for which data was available achieved per capita economic growth between 1970 and 2000.

The six most populous countries in the world (containing about 51% of the world's total population) all achieved per capita economic growth between 1970 and 2000. The countries, and their percentage increases in per capita Real GDP between 1970 and 2000, are listed on the table below:

| Country | Percentage increase in per capita Real GDP from 1970 to 2000 |
|---|---|
| China | 700% |
| India | 129% |
| U.S. | 89% |
| Indonesia | 195% |
| Brazil | 81% |
| Pakistan | 100% |

Other nations that achieved large increases in per capita Real GDP between 1970 and 2000 included Botswana (513%), Hong Kong (290%), Ireland (222%), Macao (246%), Malaysia (343%), Malta (525%), Singapore (330%), South Korea (499%), Swaziland (208%), Taiwan (568%), Thailand (270%), and the United Arab Emirates (230%).

The economic growth between 1970 and 2000 led to decreasing world poverty. According to research by economist Xavier Sala-i-Martin, the percentage of the world's population living in extreme poverty (income of less than $1 per day, 1985 base) fell from 15.4% in 1970 to 5.7% in 2000.

## Economic Growth in the U.S.

The table below illustrates that the U.S. achieved both absolute economic growth and per capita economic growth over the period from 1930 to 2007. The information is from the Bureau of Economic Analysis.

| Year | Real GDP (Base Year 2000) | Population (Rounded) | Per Capita Real GDP |
|---|---|---|---|
| 1930 | $791 billion | 123 million | $6,418 |
| 1940 | 1,034 billion | 132 million | 7,827 |
| 1950 | 1,777 billion | 152 million | 11,717 |
| 1960 | 2,502 billion | 181 million | 13,840 |
| 1970 | 3,772 billion | 205 million | 18,391 |
| 1980 | 5,162 billion | 228 million | 22,666 |
| 1990 | 7,113 billion | 250 million | 28,429 |
| 2000 | 9,817 billion | 282 million | 34,759 |
| 2007 | 11,524 billion | 302 million | 38,148 |

## Determinants of Economic Growth

Absolute economic growth is defined as an increase in Real GDP. A country may be able to increase its Real GDP in the short run by moving from a point <u>inside</u> its production possibilities frontier to a point <u>on</u> its production possibilities frontier. But, in the long run, a country must shift its production possibilities frontier outward (increase its productive capacity) in order to achieve absolute economic growth.

What factors determine a country's ability to increase its productive capacity? These are the determinants of economic growth:

1. **Natural resources.** Having abundant natural resources is probably helpful to achieving economic growth. U.S. economic growth has almost certainly been enhanced by the abundance of fertile farmland, temperate weather, fossil fuels, minerals, etc. But some countries with abundant natural resources (e.g. Russia) have achieved relatively little economic growth. And some countries with few natural resources (e.g. Singapore) have achieved a great deal of economic growth.

   Some economists argue that abundant natural resources may be a hindrance to economic growth. See an appendix at the end of the chapter for a discussion of "the resource curse".

2. **Labor.** Labor can contribute to economic growth in two ways;

   a. An increase in the quantity of labor will increase Real GDP. A larger labor force can produce more than a smaller labor force. But if an increase in the quantity of labor is not accompanied by an increase in capital and/or an improvement in technology, labor productivity will tend to decrease (due to the law of diminishing marginal returns, discussed later in this chapter). If labor productivity decreases, per capita Real GDP will tend to decrease.

   > **Example 2:** If the population on Gilligan's Island doubles, but there is no increase in capital and no improvement in technology, labor productivity will likely decrease and so will the standard of living.

   b. An increase in labor productivity (output per unit of labor) will increase both Real GDP <u>and</u> per capita Real GDP. Labor productivity can be increased by;

      (1) An increase in human capital. Human capital is developed ability that increases a person's productivity. Human capital is developed primarily through education and training and through work experience. To increase human capital requires saving and investing, just as increasing physical capital requires saving and investing.

   > **Example 3:** According to the American Medical Student Association, the annual cost of educating a medical student in the U.S. in 2002 ranged from $128,000 to $156,000.

      (2) An increase in physical capital. Physical capital is increased by investment in physical capital (see point 3. below). If each worker has more physical capital to work with, labor productivity will increase.

> **Example 4:** India is the largest milk producer in the world. The U.S. is second. India has about three times as many dairy cows as the U.S., but only produces about 15 percent more milk. The vast majority of Indian dairy farms consist of herds of from 2 to 8 cows. In the U.S., the average dairy farm has 88 cows. U.S. dairy farmers have far more capital equipment than Indian dairy farmers. Labor productivity on U.S. dairy farms is about 100 times greater than labor productivity on Indian dairy farms.

For a more detailed discussion of the importance of labor productivity, see the appendix at the end of Chapter 15 on "The Power of Productivity".

3. **Capital.** Increases in capital lead to increases in labor productivity and in per capita Real GDP. Increases in capital are made possible by saving (delaying consumption). Resources must be used to produce capital goods instead of consumer goods. Thus, increases in capital require a sacrifice in the form of a lower current standard of living. Nations with higher savings rates (and thus higher investment rates) tend to achieve more rapid economic growth, particularly when investment decisions are determined in competitive markets.

4. **Technology.** **Technological advance** is the ability to produce more output per resource. Technological advance can result from;

   a. Improved capital. A typist using a word processor will be much more productive than the same typist using a manual typewriter.

   b. Increased human capital. As the work force becomes better educated and trained and gains more work experience, labor productivity improves. When Gilligan first becomes stranded on his island, he won't be very proficient at catching fish. With experience, his fish-catching productivity should increase.

   c. Improved production techniques. As improvements are made in both physical and human capital, better production techniques can be developed and implemented.

   d. Free international trade. Free trade causes resources to be allocated to their most productive uses. This allows for more production from the same amount of resources. Chapter 16 provides more detail on how free international trade increases productivity.

A nation's success in achieving economic growth depends on the quantity and quality of its resources, and the development of its technology. But the quantity and quality of resources and the development of technology depend greatly on the governmental policies within the nation.

## Governmental Policies and Economic Growth

Historical evidence indicates that certain governmental policies are conducive to economic growth. Nations that have followed these policies have been more successful in achieving economic growth than nations that have not followed these policies. The growth-inducing policies include:

1. **Strong private property rights.** The strength of private property rights determines the amount of incentive that resource owners will have in the development and directing of their resources. The stronger the private property rights of resource owners, the more incentive they will have to develop and to direct their resources to their most valuable uses.

   Governmental policies that strengthen private property rights include:

   a. **Enforcement of private property rights by both criminal and civil law.** Resource owners need to be confident that their property rights are secure against foreign invasion, theft, fraud, and government expropriation. Private contracts, freely entered into, must be legally enforceable. The court system needs to be reasonably efficient and free from corruption.

   b. **Relatively low tax rates.** The essential purpose of taxation is to provide funds for government operations. But taxes weaken private property rights. Lower tax rates on income increase the incentive to be highly productive now and to develop one's resources to be more productive in the long run.

      Lower tax rates on earnings from savings will encourage increased saving, which makes more investment possible. More investment now means more economic growth in the future. To maintain low tax rates, the tax base needs to be broad (see Chapter 13) and the government needs to be relatively small.

   c. **A minimum of government regulation.** Government regulation may be necessary to control externalities or other sources of market failure. But government regulation weakens private property rights, and should be limited. Government regulation is discussed in more detail in Chapter 29.

   d. **A minimum of government corruption.** Government corruption weakens private property rights in a number of ways. Government corruption creates a sense of insecurity and uncertainty for resource owners. Corrupt governments often impose extensive regulations on economic activity. The extensive regulations can provide opportunities for corrupt government officials to solicit bribes (e.g. to cut through government red tape) and illegal campaign contributions (e.g. for favorable regulations). Government corruption leads to extensive rent seeking (see Chapter 22), which is a socially wasteful use of limited resources.

      Countries with a minimum of government corruption typically achieve a high standard of living. Countries with a high degree of government corruption typically suffer from a low standard of living. A table in an appendix at the end of Chapter 15 illustrates the relationship between corruption and standard of living for selected countries.

2. **Free and competitive markets.** Free and competitive markets lead to economic efficiency in the allocation of resources and goods (see Chapter 3). Governments may restrict free and competitive markets by restricting entry into markets (e.g. licensing requirements), by restricting international trade (e.g. tariffs and quotas), and by imposing price controls (e.g. ceilings and floors).

Governments can encourage free and competitive markets by permitting free entry into markets, free international trade, free market prices, and by prohibiting anticompetitive behavior (e.g. cartels).

3.  **Free international trade.** Even governments that generally promote free and competitive markets often restrict international trade. In Chapter 16, we will see that nations benefit from specialization and trade according to comparative advantage. Free international trade is a type of technological advance, in that it allows for more production from the same amount of resources. Governments can encourage free international trade by resisting the political temptation to restrict trade for the benefit of special-interest groups and by maintaining flexible exchange rates.

4.  **A stable price level.** In the long run, price level stability depends on proper monetary policy. A government must avoid excessive money supply growth in order to avoid excessive inflation. Excessive money supply contraction must also be avoided, to avoid deflation. Either inflation or deflation can have a damaging effect on the level of investment. Lack of investment hinders economic growth.

5.  **A small government.** The basic economic problem is scarcity. The private sector tends to use resources more efficiently than the public sector. There are necessary functions of government, which justify the transfer of limited resources from the private sector to the public sector. Among these are the protection of private property rights (e.g. through national defense, police, the court system, etc.), provision of public goods (e.g. national defense, highways, infrastructure, etc.), control of externalities (e.g. pollution), promoting competition (e.g. through antitrust laws), and some degree of income redistribution.

    But as the government grows larger, more resources are being transferred from the generally efficient private sector to the generally less efficient public sector. A larger government also necessitates higher tax rates. High tax rates weaken private property rights and increase the amount of deadweight loss from taxation (see Chapter 13). A larger government also increases the opportunity for socially wasteful rent seeking.

## Industrial Policy

The governmental policies that have proven to be conducive to economic growth generally call for a passive role for the government. The government protects but does not interfere with private property rights, for example. Some economists (and many politicians) favor a more active role for the government.

The government can provide aid to those industries that have (in the government's opinion) the greatest potential for future growth. This aid might come in the form of tax breaks, government subsidies, government loans at low interest rates, or protection from foreign competition. This strategy for promoting economic growth is called industrial policy.

**Industrial policy** – government aid to those industries that have the greatest potential for future growth.

If the government tries to implement industrial policy, certain problems are likely to be encountered:

1. **Aid may be determined by politics, <u>not</u> economics.** Aid may go to the industries with the most political influence, rather than those with the greatest potential for growth.

2. **The government cannot predict the future.** Private investors cannot predict the future either. But private investors, putting their own money at risk, are highly motivated to predict the future accurately. A government agency, putting the taxpayers' money at risk, is less motivated to predict the future accurately.

3. **Industrial policy might include trade restrictions.** Nations that have implemented industrial policy have typically included trade restrictions in their government aid package. As we will see in Chapter 16, trade restrictions cause a misallocation of resources and a reduction in productivity. Free trade promotes economic growth. Trade restrictions hinder economic growth.

**Example 5:** The government of Japan has been very active in pursuing industrial policy. The industries that have received the most government aid (e.g. aircraft manufacturing and chemicals) have fallen behind in the world marketplace. The Japanese industries that have received less government aid (e.g. automobiles, video games, cameras, and video cameras) have been more successful in the world marketplace.

## Theories of Economic Growth

In the long run, a nation's success in dealing with the basic economic problem of scarcity depends on its success in achieving economic growth. Some nations have achieved a great deal of economic growth while other nations have lagged behind. Different theories have been developed to explain the causes of economic growth.

### Classical Growth Theory

Classical growth theory is most closely associated with Thomas Robert Malthus and his "Essay on Population" (1798). According to classical growth theory, absolute economic growth is possible but per capita economic growth can <u>not</u> be sustained.

Classical growth theory emphasizes land, labor, and capital. The quantity of land is assumed to be fixed. If the population (and the labor force) grows, total output will grow, but per capita output will fall, due to the law of diminishing marginal returns.

**Law of diminishing marginal returns** - as larger amounts of a variable input are combined with fixed inputs, eventually the marginal physical product of the variable input declines.

**Example 6:** Ten laborers combined with ten acres of land can produce a certain amount of output. Twenty laborers combined with ten acres of land can produce more output than ten laborers, but not twice as much. Thus, output per worker will fall.

An improvement in technology (e.g. a better plow) would lead to investment in more capital. The increased capital would increase per capita output, temporarily achieving per capita economic growth (a higher standard of living). But the higher standard of living would lead to more rapid population growth. As the population grew, the law of diminishing marginal returns would cause per capita output to decrease until the standard of living fell to a subsistence level.

## Neoclassical Growth Theory

Neoclassical growth theory is most closely associated with Robert Solow. According to neoclassical growth theory, a high standard of living can be achieved, but an ever-increasing standard of living will be difficult to sustain due to the law of diminishing marginal returns.

Neoclassical growth theory emphasizes capital and technology. An improvement in technology would lead to investment in more capital. An increase in the amount of capital per unit of labor will lead to greater per capita output (a higher standard of living). But as more capital is accumulated, the return from new capital will decrease due to the law of diminishing marginal returns.

The diminishing marginal returns to capital can be overcome only by continued technological advance. Neoclassical growth theory treats technological advance as essentially random (a matter of luck). There is no guarantee that technological advance will continue at a sufficient rate to allow for an ever-increasing standard of living.

Neoclassical growth theory does not see population growth as dooming society to a subsistence standard of living. As the standard of living increases, population growth rates tend to decrease. Thus, a high standard of living can be achieved and maintained.

## New Growth Theory

New growth theory is most closely associated with Paul Romer. According to new growth theory, an ever-increasing standard of living can be achieved because the technological advance made possible by new ideas is virtually unlimited.

Physical resources (land, labor, and capital) are scarce and are subject to the law of diminishing marginal returns. New ideas (e.g. new ways to combine land, labor, and capital) are virtually unlimited. And once a new idea is developed, it is not subject to the law of diminishing marginal returns because the new idea can be used by everyone.

> **Example 7:** A medical researcher discovers a better treatment for a common disease. This new idea can be used not only by the researcher who discovered it, but by doctors all over the world.

New growth theory assumes that technological advance is not random. Any particular new idea that leads to a technological advance may involve a good degree of luck. But if a large number of people are diligently searching for the next new idea, the discovery of that new idea becomes much more likely and is not just a matter of chance.

Will large numbers of people be motivated to diligently search for new ideas? New growth theory assumes that they will, if the proper governmental policies are in place. The governmental policies that are conducive to economic growth (e.g. strong private property rights, free and competitive markets, etc.) are also conducive to the diligent search for new ideas.

People will be motivated to diligently search for new ideas because the new ideas can result in economic profit for the discoverer (assuming strong private property rights). But the economic profit will be only temporary (assuming free and competitive markets). Thus the search for new ideas (and technological advance) will continue. And an ever-increasing standard of living can be achieved.

New growth theory takes the emphasis away from physical resources (land, labor, and capital) as the sources of economic growth and shifts the attention to new ideas and technological advance. Nations that are best able to discover (or adopt) new ideas and technological advances will be the most successful in achieving economic growth. Nations that have governmental policies that encourage the discovery of new ideas and reward successful research and development should achieve the most economic growth.

## Appendix: New Ideas and Central Planning

Economies that have relied heavily on central planning have <u>not</u> been very successful at achieving economic growth. The problem is <u>not</u> a lack of investment. Centrally planned economies (e.g. the former Soviet Union) can achieve a high level of capital investment. But central planning is at a disadvantage in developing the new ideas that are so essential according to new growth theory.

**Example 8A:** Imagine that a centrally planned economy is designing a donut shop: A team of donut industry experts is put together, meetings are held, a consensus is reached on the optimal design. And then every donut shop in the economy is built to this optimal design. One idea is put into practice. Maybe it will be a good idea. Maybe not.

**Example 8B:** Imagine a free market economy with thousands of entrepreneurs operating donut shops. Each shop owner has an incentive to develop new ideas that improve their shop's productivity. Most of the new ideas will probably not work, and will quickly be abandoned. But the new ideas that work (that increase profits) will spread. They will spread because the successful shop owners will expand their businesses (open more donut shops or buy up failing shops). The shop owners who did not develop successful new ideas will either imitate the successful shop owners, or will go out of business.

So a free market economy generates a lot more new ideas than a centrally planned economy. In a free market economy, the bad ideas are quickly abandoned. In a centrally planned economy, bad ideas may linger (because of the lack of competition). In a free market economy, good ideas will spread and there will be a continuous search for successful new ideas.

## Appendix: "The Resource Curse"

The negative correlation between economic growth and abundant natural resources has been called "the resource curse". Research by economist Thorvaldur Gylfason indicates that as the value of a country's natural resources as a share of its national wealth increases, per capita Real GDP growth decreases. The resource curse has also been indicated in research by Richard Auty, as well as research by Jeffrey Sachs and Andrew Warner.

The resource curse may be caused by a number of factors. Abundant natural resources:

1. May lead to counterproductive governmental policies;
   a. Reduced democracy, since the government can secure funding through the sale of natural resources instead of through taxation. The government is not answerable to taxpayers.
   b. Increased corruption and rent seeking, since the revenues from the sale of natural resources create a strong temptation for theft by government officials and/or rent seeking by special-interest groups.
   c. A growing government, since the revenues from the sale of natural resources may fund a growing government and/or may enable more government borrowing.

2. May hinder the development of other sectors of the economy, since the sale of natural resources may be more profitable in the short run.

3. May lead to an underinvestment in human capital, since the sale of natural resources may be more profitable in the short run than investment in human capital.

4. May lead to civil wars, as different groups strive for control of the natural resources.

The table below shows the economic growth rates (as measured by the change in per capita Real GDP from 1970 to 2000) for the 10 largest oil exporting countries of 2006. The table indicates that six of the ten largest oil exporting countries had very little or negative change in per capita Real GDP over this time period. Conversely, the ten largest oil importing countries in 2006 (U.S., Japan, China, Germany, South Korea, France, India, Italy, Spain, and Taiwan) had increases in per capita Real GDP over this time frame of from 85% (Germany) to 700% (China). (Information is from the Penn World Tables and International Petroleum Monthly.)

| Country | Change in per capita Real GDP 1970-2000 |
|---|---|
| Saudi Arabia | 6% |
| Russia (from 1990 to 2000) | -25% |
| Norway | 150% |
| Iran | 4% |
| United Arab Emirates | 230% |
| Venezuela | -6% |
| Kuwait | -61% |
| Nigeria | 4% |
| Algeria | 34% |
| Mexico | 58% |

## Appendix: Future Economic Growth – Doom or Boom?

As discussed earlier in this chapter, most countries in the world have been achieving both absolute economic growth and per capita economic growth in recent decades. But will this trend continue? Can economic growth be sustained in the future?

One viewpoint is that economic growth cannot be sustained in the future. This opinion is typically based on a number of related ideas:

1. **The world's population is growing faster than its capacity to produce food.** This viewpoint can be traced back to Thomas Robert Malthus and his "Essay on Population", discussed earlier in this chapter. The Malthusian predictions have <u>not</u> come to pass. Nonetheless, there is still strong support for the belief that they will eventually come to pass.

   In 1968, Paul R. Ehrlich published, "The Population Bomb". This book argued that population growth was outstripping the world's capacity to produce food. Ehrlich wrote, "The battle to feed all of humanity is over…In the 1970s and 1980s hundreds of millions of people will starve to death in spite of any crash programs embarked upon now." This prediction obviously did not come true. In fact, the number of deaths from famine in the last decades of the 20$^{th}$ century was much less than the number of deaths from famine in the last decades of the 19$^{th}$ century.

   In later writings, Ehrlich predicted rising food prices and a falling life expectancy. In reality, food is cheaper and more abundant than at any time in human history and life expectancies have generally been rising, particularly in developing countries.

> **Example 9:** In developing countries, wheat production per acre increased by over 5-fold between 1950 and 2000. Life expectancy in developing countries has increased by more than 20 years since 1950.

2. **Economic growth combined with population growth will hasten the depletion of nonrenewable resources.** This viewpoint assumes that the more rapidly economic output increases, the more rapidly nonrenewable resources (e.g. fossil fuels, metals, minerals, etc.) will be depleted.

   It seems logical that increased economic output would increase depletion of nonrenewable resources. But it hasn't happened yet. As economic output has increased, the real prices of nonrenewable resources have generally been falling and the known reserves have generally been rising.

3. **Economic growth combined with population growth will hasten environmental degradation.** This viewpoint assumes that the more rapidly economic output increases, the more environmental degradation will occur.

   It seems logical that increased production would also lead to an increase in undesirable byproducts of production (pollution). However, the quality of both air and water in developed countries has been improving. The most severe pollution problems occur in less developed countries.

An alternative to the doomster viewpoint is the boomster viewpoint that economic growth can be sustained in the future. The boomster viewpoint disputes the ideas of the doomsters:

1. **A growing population is <u>not</u> a hindrance to economic growth.** According to Julian Simon's 1981 book "The Ultimate Resource", human beings, with their intelligence and imagination, are the ultimate resource. As the population grows, the stock of human intelligence and imagination grows.

2. **Depletion of nonrenewable resources is <u>not</u> a hindrance to future economic growth.** As economic growth has occurred in the past, the prices of nonrenewable resources have generally fallen. If the price of a nonrenewable resource increases, this provides incentives for the discovery of additional sources of the resource or for alternative sources of the service provided by the resource.

> **Example 10:** Kerosene replaced whale oil for lighting in the 19th century. Fiber optics began replacing copper wiring for communications in the late 1970s.

3. **Economic growth leads to environmental improvement rather than degradation.** There is a strong correlation between a nation's standard of living and its environmental quality. High-income countries can afford better environmental quality than low-income countries. The most dangerous environmental problems (e.g. air-borne and water-borne diseases) are much more common in low-income countries than in high-income countries.

> **Example 11:** The environmental problems in London were much worse in the 1800s than they are today. Poor sanitation in London contributed to cholera epidemics in 1832 and 1849, in which thousands of people died. Many sewers were little more than open ditches. The combination of open sewers and streets crowded with horses caused a prevailing stench. The odor became so bad in 1858 that the House of Commons considered relocating. 1858 became known as the year of The Great Stink.

## Questions for Chapter 14

**Fill-in-the-blanks:**

1. _____ economic growth is an increase in Real GDP.

2. _____ _____ economic growth is an increase in per capita Real GDP.

3. _____ advance is the ability to produce more output per resource.

4. _____ policy is government aid to those industries that have the greatest potential for future growth.

**Multiple Choice:**

_____ 1. An increase in Real GDP:
   a. is absolute economic growth
   b. may or may not result in a higher standard of living
   c. Both of the above
   d. Neither of the above

| Answer questions 2. through 4. by referring to the table below for Country Z | | |
|---|---|---|
| | **1988** | **2008** |
| Real GDP | $3,000,000,000 | $5,600,000,000 |
| Population | 1,000,000 | 2,000,000 |

_____ 2. In 2008, Country Z had per capita Real GDP of:
   a. $5,600,000,000
   b. $5,600,000
   c. $5,600
   d. $2,800

_____ 3. Between 1988 and 2008, Country Z:
   a. did <u>not</u> achieve absolute economic growth since per capita Real GDP decreased
   b. did achieve absolute economic growth
   c. improved its standard of living
   d. Both b. and c. above

_____ 4. Between 1988 and 2008, Country Z:
   a. did <u>not</u> achieve per capita economic growth
   b. did achieve per capita economic growth
   c. improved its standard of living
   d. Both b. and c. above

_____ 5. Between 1970 and 2000:
   a. most countries in the world suffered a decrease in per capita Real GDP
   b. the percentage of the world's population living in extreme poverty increased
   c. Both of the above
   d. Neither of the above

_____ 6. The six most populous countries in the world:
   a. contain almost one-third of the world's total population
   b. achieved increases in per capita Real GDP between 1970 and 2000 ranging from 81% to 700%
   c. Both of the above
   d. Neither of the above

_____ 7. The standard of living (per capita Real GDP) in the U.S.:
  a. increased in every decade from 1930 to 2000
  b. increased by more than five-fold between 1930 and 2000
  c. Both of the above
  d. Neither of the above

_____ 8. Which of the following is correct?
  a. Only countries with abundant natural resources have achieved a great deal of economic growth
  b. All countries with abundant natural resources have achieved a great deal of economic growth
  c. Some economists argue that abundant natural resources may be a hindrance to economic growth
  d. Both a. and b. above

_____ 9. If the quantity of labor increases, but there is no increase in capital and no improvement in technology:
  a. Real GDP will likely decrease
  b. per capita Real GDP will likely decrease
  c. per capita Real GDP will likely increase
  d. None of the above

_____ 10. Labor productivity can be increased by:
  a. an increase in human capital
  b. an increase in physical capital
  c. an increase in the quantity of labor
  d. Both a. and b. above

_____ 11. Increases in capital:
  a. are made possible by saving
  b. require an initial reduction in consumption
  c. lead to per capita economic growth
  d. All of the above

_____ 12. Technological advance:
  a. is the ability to produce more output per resource
  b. can result from improved capital
  c. can result from free international trade
  d. All of the above

_____ 13. Technological advance:
  a. can result only from new technology
  b. can result from improved production techniques
  c. is unaffected by international trade
  d. Both a. and c. above

_____ 14. Strong private property rights:
   a.   provide more incentive for resource owners to develop and direct their resources to their most valuable uses
   b.   help a nation's efforts to achieve economic growth
   c.   Both of the above
   d.   Neither of the above

_____ 15. Private property rights can be strengthened:
   a.   by decreasing government corruption
   b.   by increasing government regulation
   c.   by decreasing taxes
   d.   Both a. and c. above

_____ 16. Governments can encourage free and competitive markets by:
   a.   imposing licensing requirements
   b.   imposing tariffs and quotas
   c.   imposing price controls
   d.   None of the above

_____ 17. Among the necessary functions of government are:
   a.   provision of public goods
   b.   control of externalities
   c.   protection of private property rights
   d.   All of the above

_____ 18. A large government hinders economic growth because:
   a.   a large government necessitates high tax rates
   b.   high tax rates reduce private property rights
   c.   a large government increases the opportunity for rent seeking
   d.   All of the above

_____ 19. Governmental policies that are growth-inducing include:
   a.   a stable price level
   b.   tight control over international trade
   c.   strong private property rights
   d.   Both a. and c. above

_____ 20. Industrial policy:
   a.   ensures that aid will go to the industries with the greatest potential for growth
   b.   might include trade restrictions
   c.   has proven very successful in Japan
   d.   All of the above

_____ 21. Classical growth theory:
   a.   is most closely associated with Thomas Robert Malthus
   b.   holds that per capita economic growth can not be sustained
   c.   holds that an increase in the standard of living would lead to population growth.
   d.   All of the above

Economic Growth

_____ 22. Neoclassical growth theory:
      a.  is most closely associated with Paul Romer
      b.  emphasizes capital and technology
      c.  holds that technological advance will allow for ever-increasing standards of living
      d.  All of the above

_____ 23. New growth theory:
      a.  is most closely associated with Paul Romer
      b.  emphasizes new ideas and technological advance
      c.  holds that technological advance will allow for ever-increasing standards of living
      d.  All of the above

_____ 24. In a centrally planned economy:
      a.  fewer new ideas will be developed than in free market economy
      b.  bad ideas will quickly be abandoned because of the competitive pressure
      c.  Both of the above
      d.  Neither of the above

_____ 25. Between 1970 and 2000, economic growth rates:
      a.  were generally higher for oil importing countries than for oil exporting countries
      b.  were generally higher for oil exporting countries than for oil importing countries
      c.  were about the same for oil importing countries and for oil exporting countries

_____ 26. The opinion that economic growth cannot be sustained in the future is based on which of the following ideas?
      a.  the world's population is growing faster than its capacity to produce food
      b.  economic growth combined with population growth will hasten the depletion of nonrenewable resources
      c.  economic growth combined with population growth will hasten environmental degradation
      d.  All of the above

_____ 27. In the past, as economic growth occurred:
      a.  the real prices of nonrenewable resources generally rose
      b.  environmental quality generally degraded
      c.  Both of the above
      d.  Neither of the above

**Problems:**

1.  List the four determinants of economic growth.

2.  Explain the relationship between saving and increases in capital.

3.  List four governmental policies that strengthen private property rights.

4.  Why is it possible to achieve an ever-increasing standard of living, according to new growth theory?

## Answers for Chapter 14

**Fill-in-the-blanks:**   1. Absolute
2. Per capita
3. Technological
4. Industrial

**Multiple Choice:**

| | | |
|---|---|---|
| 1. c. | 10. d. | 19. d. |
| 2. d. | 11. d. | 20. b. |
| 3. b. | 12. d. | 21. d. |
| 4. a. | 13. b. | 22. b. |
| 5. d. | 14. c. | 23. d. |
| 6. b. | 15. d. | 24. a. |
| 7. c. | 16. d. | 25. a. |
| 8. c | 17. d. | 26. d. |
| 9. b | 18. d. | 27. d. |

## Problems:

1.  The four determinants of economic growth are:
    (1) Natural resources
    (2) Labor
    (3) Capital
    (4) Technology

2.  Increases in capital are made possible by saving. Resources must be used to produce capital goods instead of consumer goods.

3.  Governmental policies that strengthen private property rights include:
    (1) Enforcement of private property rights by both criminal and civil law.
    (2) Relatively low tax rates.
    (3) A minimum of government regulation.
    (4) A minimum of government corruption.

4.  According to new growth theory, an ever-increasing standard of living can be achieved because the technological advance made possible by new ideas is virtually unlimited. New ideas are virtually unlimited. And once a new idea is developed, it is not subject to the law of diminishing marginal returns because the new idea can be used by everyone.

# Chapter 15 Less Developed Countries

Countries differ widely in their level of economic development. Some countries have achieved a high per capita GDP. Others have a much lower per capita GDP. This is the difference between developed countries and less developed countries (LDCs).

**Developed country** – has a relatively high per capita GDP.

**Less developed country (LDC)** – has a relatively low per capita GDP.

There are large differences in per capita GDP between developed countries and LDCs. Per capita GDP in developed countries (e.g. the U.S., Canada, Germany, Japan, etc.) may be over thirty times higher than per capita GDP in less developed countries (e.g. North Korea, Ethiopia, Afghanistan, etc.)

The differences in per capita GDP for selected countries can be seen in a table on page 15-4.

## Common Hardships for LDCs

Less developed countries have a relatively low per capita GDP (low standard of living). Because of the low standard of living, LDCs tend to suffer from common hardships:

1. **High infant mortality rates.** The infant mortality rate is the number of infants who die before reaching one year of age out of every 1,000 live births. Infant mortality rates are typically much higher in LDCs than in developed countries.

**Example 1:** The ten lowest per capita GDP nations in the table on page 15-4 have an average infant mortality rate 19 times higher than the ten highest per capita GDP nations.

2. **Inadequate diets.** Obesity is a growing health problem in developed countries. In LDCs, malnutrition is a much more common problem.

**Example 2:** The Food and Agricultural Organization of the United Nations reported that the number of undernourished people worldwide was over 850 million in 2007. 820 million of the undernourished were in LDCs.

At its most severe, malnutrition can lead to starvation. Less severe malnutrition contributes to general health problems. Malnutrition hinders physical and mental growth in children.

**Example 3A:** In the lowest income LDCs, nearly half of young children are abnormally short due to malnutrition.

**Example 3B:** In nineteenth century England, the average working class adult male was 5 inches shorter than the average upper class adult male.

Malnutrition increases susceptibility to illness, causes normally minor medical problems (e.g. diarrhea) to be life threatening, and reduces a person's capacity to recover from illness. Malnutrition is an important factor contributing to high infant mortality rates.

3. **Unsafe drinking water and inadequate sanitation.** Persons in developed countries can usually take for granted that they will have access to safe drinking water and adequate sanitation. In LDCs, often many people do not have access to safe drinking water and adequate sanitation.

> **Example 4:** According to a report by the World Health Organization and the United Nations Children's Fund, in 2002 over 1 billion people did not have access to improved drinking water sources and over 2 billion did not have access to adequate sanitation. Most of these people were in less developed countries.

Unsafe drinking water and inadequate sanitation contribute to health problems and to the spread of disease.

4. **Inadequate medical services.** Training medical doctors is extremely expensive. As a result, LDCs tend to have far fewer doctors relative to population than developed countries.

> **Example 5:** The ratio of doctors to population in the U.S. is about 1 doctor for every 400 persons. In Uganda, a less developed country, the ratio is about 1 doctor for every 25,000 persons.

In LDCs, many people have limited or no access to medical services. Illnesses and injuries that would be minor in developed countries may prove to be fatal or permanently disabling in LDCs because of the lack of medical treatment.

> **Example 6:** According to the World Health Organization, about 1.8 million people die each year from diarrheal diseases. Ninety percent of the fatalities are children under 5 years of age. Millions of children in LDCs suffer from ailments (e.g. polio, tetanus, measles, bacterial pneumonia, Vitamin A deficiency, and intestinal parasites) which can be either prevented or cured with relatively inexpensive medical care. But such care is often unavailable in LDCs.

## Economic Growth and the Rule of 70

In order to escape the hardships just discussed, less developed countries need to achieve rapid economic growth. The Rule of 70 can be used to calculate how many years it will take a country to double its per capita GDP.

The Rule of 70 is a rule of thumb for calculating the approximate time required for any variable to double at a given growth rate. Using the Rule of 70, the time required for a variable to double is calculated by dividing 70 by the percentage annual growth rate.

**Rule of 70:** **Time to double = 70 ÷ Annual Growth Rate**

**Example 7A:** Country A achieves an annual growth in per capita GDP of 1%. How many years will it take Country A to double its per capita GDP? 70 years (70 ÷ 1)

**Example 7B:** Country B achieves an annual growth in per capita GDP of 2%. How many years will it take Country B to double its per capita GDP? 35 years (70 ÷ 2)

**Example 7C:** Country C achieves an annual growth in per capita GDP of 5%. How many years will it take Country C to double its per capita GDP? 14 years (70 ÷ 5)

## The Importance of Economic Growth Rates

Economic growth rates are very important. The importance of economic growth rates can be seen in the table in Example 8 below.

**Example 8:** Countries A, B, and C from Examples 7A, 7B, and 7C above are assumed to be equal in per capita GDP in 2008. With their different annual growth rates, per capita GDP for each country is very different by 2078.

| Country | A | B | C |
|---|---|---|---|
| Per capita GDP growth rate | 1% | 2% | 5% |
| | | | |
| Per capita GDP (2008) | $5,000 | $5,000 | $5,000 |
| Per capita GDP (2022) | X | X | $10,000 |
| Per capita GDP (2036) | X | X | $20,000 |
| Per capita GDP (2043) | X | $10,000 | X |
| Per capita GDP (2050) | X | X | $40,000 |
| Per capita GDP (2064) | X | X | $80,000 |
| Per capita GDP (2078) | $10,000 | $20,000 | $160,000 |

**Example 9:** In 1960, Argentina's per capita GDP was about 2.7 times higher than Singapore's. From 1960 to 1999, Argentina's economy grew about 1 percent per year, and Singapore's economy grew about 6.2 percent per year. By 1999, Singapore's per capita GDP was about 2.6 times higher than Argentina's.

Even a small difference in economic growth rates can make a large difference in standard of living over a long period of time. This is true due to the power of compounding (discussed in Chapter 31).

**Example 10:** In 2000, U.S. per capita GDP was $34,759. A table in an appendix at the end of this chapter indicates what U.S. per capita Real GDP (Base 2000) will be over the course of the 21$^{st}$ century assuming different annual growth rates in per capita Real GDP. At an annual growth rate of 1%, U.S. per capita Real GDP will increase by 2.7 times over the 21$^{st}$ century. At an annual growth rate of 2.5%, U.S. per capita Real GDP will increase by over 12 times.

## Per Capita GDP for Selected Countries

The table below provides information for selected countries, listed in order of per capita GDP. The information is for 2007, and is from the "CIA World Factbook".

| Nation | per capita GDP | Infant Mortality/1000 | % Population Growth Rate | % of Population Age 0-14 | Population per sq. km |
|---|---|---|---|---|---|
| U.S. | $45,800 | 6 | .9 | 20 | 31 |
| Hong Kong | 42,000 | 3 | .6 | 13 | 6392 |
| Netherlands | 38,500 | 5 | .5 | 18 | 399 |
| Canada | 38,400 | 5 | .9 | 17 | 3 |
| Australia | 36,300 | 5 | .8 | 19 | 3 |
| United Kingdom | 35,100 | 5 | .3 | 17 | 248 |
| Germany | 34,200 | 4 | 0 | 14 | 231 |
| Japan | 33,600 | 3 | 0 | 14 | 337 |
| France | 33,200 | 3 | .6 | 19 | 101 |
| Italy | 30,400 | 6 | 0 | 14 | 193 |
| Spain | 30,100 | 4 | .1 | 14 | 80 |
| Taiwan | 30,100 | 6 | .3 | 18 | 635 |
| Israel | 25,800 | 7 | 1.2 | 26 | 309 |
| South Korea | 24,800 | 6 | .4 | 18 | 498 |
| Saudi Arabia | 23,200 | 12 | 2.1 | 38 | 13 |
| Poland | 16,300 | 7 | 0 | 16 | 123 |
| Russia | 14,700 | 11 | -.5 | 15 | 8 |
| Argentina | 13,300 | 14 | .9 | 25 | 15 |
| Malaysia | 13,300 | 17 | 1.8 | 32 | 75 |
| Turkey | 12,900 | 38 | 1.0 | 25 | 91 |
| Mexico | 12,800 | 20 | 1.2 | 30 | 55 |
| Venezuela | 12,200 | 23 | 1.5 | 32 | 29 |
| Iran | 10,600 | 38 | .7 | 23 | 40 |
| **World** | **10,000** | **44** | **1.2** | **27** | **44** |
| South Africa | 9,800 | 59 | -.5 | 29 | 36 |
| Brazil | 9,700 | 28 | 1.0 | 25 | 22 |
| Thailand | 7,900 | 19 | .7 | 22 | 127 |
| Ukraine | 6,900 | 10 | -.7 | 14 | 77 |
| Colombia | 6,700 | 20 | 1.4 | 30 | 39 |
| Egypt | 5,500 | 30 | 1.7 | 32 | 80 |
| China | 5,300 | 21 | .6 | 20 | 138 |
| Cuba | 4,500 | 6 | .3 | 19 | 103 |
| Indonesia | 3,700 | 32 | 1.2 | 27 | 122 |
| Iraq | 3,600 | 47 | 2.6 | 39 | 63 |
| Philippines | 3,400 | 22 | 1.8 | 35 | 304 |
| India | 2,700 | 35 | 1.6 | 32 | 344 |
| Pakistan | 2,600 | 69 | 1.8 | 37 | 205 |
| Vietnam | 2,600 | 24 | 1.0 | 26 | 259 |
| Sudan | 2,200 | 92 | 2.1 | 42 | 16 |
| Nigeria | 2,000 | 96 | 2.4 | 42 | 146 |
| Burma | 1,900 | 51 | .8 | 26 | 70 |
| North Korea | 1,900 | 23 | .8 | 23 | 193 |
| Bangladesh | 1,300 | 59 | 2.1 | 33 | 1045 |
| Tanzania | 1,300 | 72 | 2.1 | 44 | 42 |
| Haiti | 1,300 | 64 | 2.5 | 42 | 314 |
| Afghanistan | 1,000 | 157 | 2.6 | 45 | 49 |
| Ethiopia | 800 | 92 | 2.3 | 43 | 68 |
| Somalia | 600 | 113 | 2.8 | 44 | 14 |

## Economic Freedom and Economic Growth

Most economists believe that economic freedom is important to economic growth. Economic freedom is measured by such factors as property rights, relative size of government, level of taxation, degree of government regulation of economic activity, international trade policy, etc.

> **Example 11:** According to the "Economic Freedom of the World, 2007 Annual Report", the twenty-five percent of nations with the freest economies experienced an average annual increase in per capita Real GDP of 2.3% from 1990 to 2005. The twenty-five percent of nations with the least free economies experienced an average annual increase in per capita Real GDP of .4% from 1990 to 2005.

## Obstacles to Economic Development for LDCs

Given the hardships associated with low standards of living, LDCs usually desire to achieve economic development. But LDCs often face one or more of the following obstacles to economic development:

1. **Rapid population growth.** Population growth rates tend to be higher in LDCs than in developed countries.

> **Example 12:** The ten highest per capita GDP nations in the table on page 15-4 have an average population growth rate of .5%. The ten lowest per capita GDP nations in the table have an average population growth rate of 2.1%.

The problem created by a rapid population growth rate is <u>not</u> overpopulation. Generally, developed countries are more densely populated (more population per square kilometer) than LDCs.

> **Example 13:** Taiwan is over four times more densely populated than China. South Korea is over twice as densely populated as North Korea. The Netherlands is more densely populated than India. Germany and the United Kingdom are both more densely populated than Pakistan.

The problem created by a rapid population growth rate is a high dependency ratio. A high dependency ratio means that a large percentage of the population consists of children and the elderly.

> **Example 14:** For the ten highest per capita GDP nations in the table on page 15-4, 17% of their populations are age 0-14. For the ten lowest per capita GDP nations in the table, 38% of their populations are age 0-14.

A high dependency ratio makes it difficult for the working-age population to support themselves and the large number of dependents, and also make investments toward economic development.

Some economists (e.g. Peter Bauer) have argued that rapid population growth is <u>not</u> an obstacle to economic development. Bauer pointed out that most developed countries had high population growth rates in their earlier stages of economic development, which did not hinder their economic development.

> **Example 15:** The U.S. had a population growth rate of about 3% per year from 1790 to 1860. The eight-fold increase in the population during this seventy year period accompanied significant economic growth.

2. **Low savings rate.** Standards of living are very low in LDCs. These low standards of living make it difficult to save (delay consumption). But saving is necessary if investments in physical capital and human capital are to be made. This situation, where LDCs have low standards of living because they don't save and invest, and don't save and invest because they have low standards of living is called the "vicious circle of poverty".

   An LDC might be able to escape the vicious circle of poverty by attracting foreign investment. Foreign investment in physical capital will increase labor productivity and the standard of living. The higher standard of living will make it easier to save, leading to more investment.

   To attract foreign investment, an LDC needs to avoid the counterproductive governmental policies discussed later in this chapter.

   Some economists (e.g. Peter Bauer) have argued that no "vicious circle of poverty" exists. Bauer pointed out that every developed country was at one time less developed, and obviously managed to save and invest and escape from low development.

3. **Cultural norms that hinder economic development.** Different cultures have different cultural norms, or standards of behavior and thought. In the U.S., individual economic success is generally seen in a positive light. Most people desire and strive for a higher standard of living. This economic striving is conducive to economic development.

   LDCs often have cultural norms that are hostile to or hinder economic development. Some cultures are very traditional. The emphasis on maintaining traditional ways hinders the introduction of new technology. A traditional social structure may limit economic activity and mobility among certain groups in the population (e.g. females).

   Some LDCs have cultures that are very fatalistic. Fatalism is the belief that the course of a person's life is predetermined. Fatalism has a negative effect on work effort, educational attainment, investment choices, etc.

4. **Counterproductive governmental policies.** Historical evidence indicates that certain governmental policies are a hindrance to economic development. Nations that have followed these policies have been less successful in achieving economic development than nations that have avoided these policies. Governments in LDCs often follow some or all of these counterproductive policies. The counterproductive policies include:

a.  **Weak private property rights.** The importance of strong private property rights to economic growth was detailed in Chapter 14. Weak private property rights not only discourage the development of resources by the domestic economy, they also discourage foreign investment in the domestic economy. Governments of LDCs often weaken private property rights by;

    (1)  **Failing to enforce private property rights through criminal and civil law.** High rates of crime, corrupt and inefficient courts systems, failure to enforce private contracts, and even government expropriation of private property are common problems in LDCs.

         In LDCs, much of the land and capital may lack clear ownership. In India, for example, about 90 percent of land titles are subject to dispute.

    (2)  **Imposing high tax rates.** Many LDCs have marginal tax rates of over 50% on relatively low levels of income. Such high tax rates decrease the incentive resource owners have for developing and directing their resources to their most valuable uses.

         High tax rates also increase the amount of deadweight loss from taxation (see Chapter 13). Research by economist Alvin Rabushka indicates that LDCs with lower marginal tax rates achieve higher economic growth rates than LDCs with higher marginal tax rates.

    (3)  **Imposing excessive government regulations.** In many LDCs, the regulatory requirements to simply begin a new business can take many months to comply with, involve a large expenditure of money, and may necessitate the payment of bribes to numerous government officials.

    (4)  **Permitting excessive government corruption.** Governments in LDCs are often <u>not</u> subject to regular, free elections. This makes excessive government corruption more likely. Research indicates that excessive government corruption is associated with low or negative economic growth. Counterproductive economic policies (like excessive government regulations) may be pursued to increase the opportunities for government graft.

         A table in an appendix at the end of the chapter illustrates the relationship between corruption and standard of living for selected countries.

b.  **Restrictions on competitive markets.** In LDCs, large industries are often directly controlled by the state, or a favored producer is granted a monopoly position. Excessive regulations may hinder the entry of new firms into markets. Price controls are often imposed.

    For more on the importance of competitive markets, see the Appendix on "The Power of Productivity" at the end of this chapter.

c.  **Restrictions on international trade.** Governments in LDCs often impose severe barriers (tariffs and quotas) to international trade. Research indicates that high trade barriers are associated with low or negative economic growth.

Governments in LDCs also often maintain a fixed exchange rate that overvalues the domestic currency. This has the effect of acting as a tax on exporters. Research indicates that a fixed exchange rate that significantly overvalues the domestic currency is associated with low or negative growth rates.

d. **Excessive inflation.** Governments in LDCs often pursue rapid money supply growth (in an attempt to keep interest rates low, or to pay for a large budget deficit, or to impose an "inflation tax") which leads to high inflation. Research indicates that periods of high inflation are associated with low or negative economic growth. (For a more detailed discussion of why governments in LDCs may pursue rapid money supply growth, see the appendix at the end of Chapter 11 on seignorage and inflation.)

During periods of high inflation, governments in LDCs often place price ceilings on nominal interest rates. Price ceilings on nominal interest rates during periods of high inflation can cause real interest rates that are negative. Negative real interest rates have a devastating effect on financial markets. Research indicates that periods of negative real interest rates are associated with low or negative economic growth.

e. **A large government.** LDCs often have governments that are large relative to the size of the nation's economy. The large government may be caused by a large military (and/or secret police force), or by an excessively large civil service, with positions granted for political patronage purposes.

The large government often leads to large budget deficits. Research indicates that large budget deficits are associated with low or negative economic growth. The large government also necessitates high tax rates (discussed earlier).

f. **Poor provision of public services.** Governments in LDCs often provide poor public roads, unreliable electricity delivery, unreliable water delivery, unreliable phone service, and inadequate public health services. The poor provision of public services hinders economic growth.

### Appendix: U.S. per capita Real GDP (Base 2000) at Different Growth Rates

| Year | 1.0% | 1.5% | 2.0% | 2.5% |
|------|------|------|------|------|
| 2000 | $34,759 | $34,759 | $34,759 | $34,759 |
| 2010 | 38,396 | 40,339 | 43,218 | 45,607 |
| 2020 | 42,413 | 46,815 | 52,683 | 58,381 |
| 2030 | 46,850 | 54,332 | 64,220 | 74,732 |
| 2040 | 51,751 | 63,053 | 78,285 | 95,663 |
| 2050 | 57,166 | 73,176 | 95,428 | 122,188 |
| 2060 | 63,147 | 84,924 | 116,326 | 156,756 |
| 2070 | 69,753 | 98,557 | 141,801 | 200,660 |
| 2080 | 77,051 | 114,390 | 172,854 | 256,862 |
| 2090 | 85,112 | 132,743 | 210,709 | 328,806 |
| 2100 | 94,017 | 154,053 | 256,853 | 420,899 |

**Appendix: Book Review – "The Power of Productivity"**

In 2004, William W. Lewis, Founding Director of the McKinsey Global Institute, published "The Power of Productivity". The book is based on studies by the McKinsey Global Institute of the economies of thirteen countries. The studies were motivated largely by the belief that "the disparity between rich and poor is the most serious and the most intractable problem facing the world today."

> **Example 16:** About 13% of the world's population live in high-income countries, with a per capita GDP at least 70% of U.S. per capita GDP. About 5% of the world's population live in middle-income countries, with a per capita GDP of between 25% and 70% of U.S. per capita GDP. Over 80% of the world's population live in low-income countries, with per capita GDP less than 25% of U.S. per capita GDP.

The book draws conclusions about the crucial question: Why do some countries achieve economic growth and grow rich, while other countries fail to achieve economic growth and remain poor?

> Among the conclusions reached in the book are:
>
> 1. A country's standard of living (per capita GDP) depends almost exclusively on the productivity of its labor.
>
> 2. A poorly educated labor force and a low level of savings are not huge barriers to increasing the productivity of labor.
>
> 3. Sound macroeconomic policies make high productivity possible, but do not guarantee high productivity.
>
> 4. A large government is a hindrance to productivity growth, especially for low-income countries
>
> 5. Free and competitive product markets are vitally important for achieving high productivity.
>
> 6. A focus on consumer interests rather than on producer interests is necessary to achieve free and competitive product markets.

**Productivity**

A country's standard of living (per capita GDP) depends almost exclusively on the productivity of its labor. The productivity of labor varies widely from country to country.

> **Example 17:** In 2007, the average American worker produced about $92,000 worth of output and about one-half of the population was in the labor force. This yields a per capita GDP of about $46,000. In 2007, the average French worker produced about $66,000 worth of output and about one-half of the population was in the labor force. This yields a per capita GDP of about $33,000.

Less Developed Countries

Many countries place a strong emphasis on manufacturing productivity. But developed economies tend to be service-oriented, with a larger service sector than manufacturing sector. The average productivity of labor for the entire economy will be more strongly influenced by large sectors of the economy than by small sectors of the economy.

**Example 18:** Japanese workers are more productive than American workers in the production of steel, automotive parts, metalworking, automobiles, and consumer electronics. These industries employ about 1.5 million workers in Japan.

In the retail sector, Japanese workers are only about one-half as productive as American workers. The retail sector employs about 7.5 million workers in Japan. The low productivity of the 7.5 million retail workers is much more important to determining per capita GDP in Japan than the high productivity of the 1.5 million manufacturing workers in steel, automotive parts, metalworking, automobiles, and consumer electronics. Per capita GDP in Japan is about 75% as high as in the U.S.

**Example 19:** South Korea has achieved higher productivity than the U.S. in steel production. However, the steel industry employs less than .5% of the South Korean labor force.

In the retail sector, South Korea is only about one-third as productive as the U.S. The retail sector employs about 8% of the South Korean labor force. Per capita GDP in South Korea is about 54% as high as in the U.S.

**Example 20:** India is the largest producer of milk in the world and the second largest producer of wheat (behind China). But the productivity of dairy and wheat farmers in India is only about 1% of the productivity of dairy and wheat farmers in America. India's low standard of living (per capita GDP only about 6% as high as for the U.S.) is strongly influenced by the extremely low productivity of its huge agricultural sector.

## Education and Capital

A poorly educated labor force and a low level of savings are <u>not</u> huge barriers to increasing the productivity of labor. A low education level does not necessarily mean that a worker lacks high capability. The primary means through which workers attain the skills to perform at high productivity is through on-the-job training.

**Example 21:** At a housing project in Houston, Texas, many of the construction workers were illiterate and did not speak English, yet they achieved high productivity working at a productively organized construction site.

If a country achieves high productivity with the capital that it has, additional financing will flow to the country from foreign investors seeking high returns.

**Example 22:** According to Alan Greenspan in "The Age of Turbulence", foreign direct investment into China increased from $57 million in 1980, to $4 billion in 1991, to $70 billion in 2006.

## Macroeconomic Policies

Sound macroeconomic policies make high productivity possible. Sound macroeconomic policies include low inflation, flexible exchange rates, and government solvency. Sound macroeconomic policies do not guarantee high productivity.

> **Example 23:** Japan has sound macroeconomic policies. However, throughout the 1990s the Japanese economy was stagnant.

Without sound macroeconomic policies, countries are unable to achieve high productivity and will remain poor. Even with sound macroeconomic policies, countries need free and competitive product markets in order to achieve high productivity.

## Government Size

Most low-income countries, like most high-income countries, have a relatively large government.

> **Example 24:** In Brazil, total government spending is about 39% of GDP. In the U.S., total government spending is about 37% of GDP. However, when the U.S. was at the same stage of development that Brazil is at today, total government spending in the U.S. was only about 8% of GDP.

A large government means relatively high tax rates. This is particularly a problem for low-income countries, because much of their economic activity takes place in the informal economy.

> **Example 25:** In Brazil, about half the labor force is employed in the informal economy.

The informal economy consists of unregulated and untaxed business activities, such as street vendors, at-home manufacturing, self-employed service providers, etc. Since the informal economy generally avoids taxation, the formal economy must be taxed heavily to support the large government.

The heavy taxation of the formal economy takes away much of the productivity advantage that formal companies have over informal companies and makes it difficult for the more productive formal companies to drive the less productive informal companies out of business. To increase productivity, the more productive companies need to expand and the less productive companies need to shrink or disappear.

## Free and Competitive Product Markets

Free and competitive product markets are vitally important for achieving high productivity. In a competitive product market, a firm can increase its profits by increasing its productivity. This increase in productivity may arise from developing a more valuable product or a more efficient method of production. The more productive firm gains market share from less productive firms. The less productive firms must either increase their productivity or go out of business.

**Example 26:** In 1987, Wal-Mart had 9% of the general merchandise market in the U.S. and had a 44% productivity advantage over the rest of this market. Wal-Mart's productivity advantage allowed it to gain market share. By 1995, Wal-Mart had 27% of the general merchandise market and a slightly larger productivity advantage than in 1987. By 1999, Wal-Mart had 30% of the general merchandise market and had increased its productivity by 5.1% per year from 1995 to 1999. However, its chief competitors had increased productivity even faster, by 6.4% per year, and were catching up with Wal-Mart in productivity.

## Focus on Consumer Interests

A focus on consumer interests rather than on producer interests is necessary to achieve free and competitive product markets. Governments often restrict competition in product markets to benefit special-interest groups.

**Example 27:** Small shopkeepers are a powerful special-interest group in Japan. For many years, Japan restricted the size of retail stores. This protected traditional small shops from competition against larger (and more productive) stores. As a result, traditional small shops make up a large percentage of retail stores in Japan. The traditional small shops are much less productive than larger modern stores. Moreover, the large number of traditional small shops hinders productivity in the wholesale sector. (It is much more efficient to deliver goods to one Wal-Mart than to deliver goods to 100 mom-and-pop stores.)

**Example 28:** In India, the tariff on imported cars is 44%. Also in India, the Small-scale Reservation law limits production of over 800 products to small-scale firms.

## Increasing Labor Productivity

To increase labor productivity, countries need to increase competition in product markets.

This can be accomplished by:
1. Reducing trade restrictions on imports. This will force domestic producers to compete with the most productive firms from around the world.

2. Permitting foreign direct investment in the domestic economy. LDCs do not have to "discover" the best methods of production. Foreign companies allowed to make direct investments will bring the best methods of production to the LDCs.

3. Loosening restrictions on store size, hours of operation, etc. This increases consumer choice and allows competition to determine the most efficient store size, most profitable hours of operation, etc.

4. Reducing the size of government. A large government means high tax rates. Larger (and more productive) firms usually pay taxes. Smaller (and less productive) firms often don't pay taxes in LDCs. Thus, the high taxes distort competition between larger and smaller firms.

## Appendix:  Corruption and Standard of Living

The table below contains information for selected countries from the Corruption Perceptions Index for 2007, released by Transparency International.  The lower the Corruption Perceptions Index number, the greater the perceived corruption in a country.  The table also contains information on per capita GDP for 2007 from the CIA World Factbook.  The Top Ten (least corrupt) countries on the table have an average per capita GDP of $38,050.  The Bottom Ten (most corrupt) countries on the table have an average per capita GDP of $3,660.

| Nation | Corruption Perceptions Index | per capita GDP |
|---|---|---|
| Denmark | 9.4 | $37,400 |
| Finland | 9.4 | 35,300 |
| Singapore | 9.3 | 49,700 |
| Netherlands | 9.0 | 38,500 |
| Canada | 8.7 | 38,400 |
| Australia | 8.6 | 36,300 |
| United Kingdom | 8.4 | 35,100 |
| Hong Kong | 8.3 | 42,000 |
| Germany | 7.8 | 34,200 |
| Japan | 7.5 | 33,600 |
| Ireland | 7.5 | 43,100 |
| France | 7.3 | 33,200 |
| United States | 7.2 | 45,800 |
| Chile | 7.0 | 14,400 |
| Spain | 6.7 | 30,100 |
| Israel | 6.1 | 25,800 |
| Taiwan | 5.7 | 30,100 |
| United Arab Emirates | 5.7 | 37,300 |
| Botswana | 5.4 | 16,400 |
| Malaysia | 5.1 | 13,300 |
| South Africa | 5.1 | 9,800 |
| Jordan | 4.7 | 4,900 |
| Turkey | 4.1 | 12,900 |
| Colombia | 3.8 | 6,700 |
| Brazil | 3.5 | 9,700 |
| China | 3.5 | 5,300 |
| India | 3.5 | 2,700 |
| Mexico | 3.5 | 12,800 |
| Argentina | 2.9 | 13,300 |
| Egypt | 2.9 | 5,500 |
| Vietnam | 2.6 | 2,600 |
| Philippines | 2.5 | 3,400 |
| Pakistan | 2.4 | 2,600 |
| Indonesia | 2.3 | 3,700 |
| Russia | 2.3 | 14,700 |
| Nigeria | 2.2 | 2,000 |
| Zimbabwe | 2.1 | 200 |
| Bangladesh | 2.0 | 1,300 |
| Somalia | 1.4 | 600 |

Less Developed Countries

## Appendix: Foreign Aid Curse

Developed countries have been providing foreign aid to less developed countries for over 50 years. The basic goal of this aid has been to enhance economic growth for the recipient countries. However, research by various economists has found no significant correlation between the amount of aid received and the economic growth rates of the recipient countries.

Research also indicates that foreign aid may have the same kind of detrimental effect on economic growth as abundant natural resources. (See an appendix at the end of Chapter 14 for a discussion of "the resource curse".) Foreign aid may hinder economic growth in the same way and for the same reasons that abundant resources may hinder economic growth.

Economist Peter Bauer argued decades ago that foreign aid was actually government-to-government aid, and often amounted to subsidizing and strengthening bad governments. Research by William Easterly finds no evidence that foreign aid increases economic growth, even in countries with good economic policies.

## Appendix: "Sweatshops" in LDCs

American multinational corporations are often criticized for operating "sweatshops" in less developed countries. In these American-owned or American-controlled factories, wages are extremely low by American standards. Some American politicians (e.g. Rep. Dick Gephardt) have called for "global minimum wage laws" to protect workers employed by American multinational companies in less developed countries.

Economists respond by pointing out that less developed countries have low labor productivity. Their only industrial comparative advantage over more developed countries may be their extremely low wages. When workers in LDCs voluntarily choose jobs in "sweatshops", it is because these are the most attractive jobs available.

If a global minimum wage were imposed, it would take away the comparative advantage of extremely low wages and cause the "sweatshops" to relocate to markets with higher labor productivity. How can a global minimum wage improve conditions for workers in LDCs if it deprives those workers of their best alternative and compels them to accept an inferior choice?

## Appendix: Think Like an Economist – Working in a "Sweatshop"

You live in a less developed country. You recently quit your job on a farm and got hired at an American-owned "sweatshop", where you are paid $2 for a 12-hour working day. You've just heard a rumor that the U.S. government is going to impose on American-owned companies a global minimum wage of $5 per day, with a limit of an 8-hour working day.

Do you hope that this global minimum wage is imposed? Why or why not?

## Questions for Chapter 15

### Fill-in-the-blanks:

1. A _____ country has a relatively high per capita GDP.

2. A _____ _____ country has a relatively low
per capita GDP.

### Multiple Choice:

_____ 1. LDCs tend to have:
   - a. inadequate medical services
   - b. unsafe drinking water and inadequate sanitation
   - c. inadequate diets
   - d. All of the above

_____ 2. Malnutrition:
   - a. affects over 850 million people worldwide
   - b. increases susceptibility to illness
   - c. is an important factor contributing to high infant mortality rates
   - d. All of the above

_____ 3. At a growth rate of 5% a year, a nation will double its per capita GDP in ___
years.
   - a. 5
   - b. 12
   - c. 14
   - d. 70

_____ 4. Which of the following countries would be classified as a less developed
country?
   - a. Italy
   - b. Hong Kong
   - c. Cuba
   - d. South Korea

_____ 5. Economic growth and economic freedom tend to be:
   - a. inversely related
   - b. unrelated
   - c. directly related
   - d. second cousins

_____ 6. Among the obstacles to economic development faced by LDCs is:
   - a. high savings rate
   - b. overpopulation
   - c. counterproductive governmental policies
   - d. All of the above

Less Developed Countries

_____ 7. A rapid population growth rate is an obstacle to economic development for LDCs because it means:
    a. overpopulation
    b. excessive population density
    c. a high dependency ratio
    d. All of the above

_____ 8. An LDC may be trapped in a vicious circle of poverty because:
    a. its standard of living is very low
    b. increasing its standard of living requires saving and investment
    c. its low standard of living makes saving and investment difficult
    d. All of the above

_____ 9. A cultural norm that may hinder economic development is:
    a. fatalism
    b. traditionalism
    c. Both of the above
    d. Neither of the above

_____ 10. Weak private property rights:
    a. discourage the development of resources by the domestic economy
    b. encourage foreign investment in the domestic economy
    c. Both of the above
    d. Neither of the above

_____ 11. Governments of LDCs may weaken private property rights by:
    a. failing to enforce private contracts
    b. imposing high tax rates
    c. permitting excessive government corruption
    d. All of the above

_____ 12. Among the counterproductive policies often followed by governments in LDCs are:
    a. poor provision of public services
    b. a large government
    c. excessive inflation
    d. All of the above

_____ 13. Among the counterproductive policies often followed by governments in LDCs are:
    a. free international trade
    b. lack of restrictions on competitive markets
    c. weak private property rights
    d. All of the above

_____ 14. Compared to developed countries, LDCs:
    a. tend to have less competitive markets
    b. tend to impose severe restrictions on international trade
    c. tend to have more governmental corruption
    d. All of the above

_____ 15. Governments in LDCs:
   a.  tend to be small compared to the size of the economy
   b.  tend to grant a lot of positions for political patronage purposes
   c.  Both of the above
   d.  Neither of the above

_____ 16. If the U.S. achieves an annual per capita Real GDP growth of 1.5% during the 21$^{st}$ century, by 2100 per capita Real GDP will be about _____ times as high as in 2000.
   a.  2.7
   b.  4.4
   c.  5.2
   d.  7.4

_____ 17. If the U.S. achieves an annual per capita Real GDP growth of 2.5% during the 21$^{st}$ century, by 2100 per capita Real GDP will be about _____ times as high as in 2000.
   a.  2.5
   b.  5.2
   c.  12.1
   d.  20.6

_____ 18. According to "The Power of Productivity":
   a.  countries with sound macroeconomic policies are certain to achieve economic growth
   b.  a country's standard of living depends almost exclusively on the productivity of its labor
   c.  trade restrictions are the best way to achieve high labor productivity
   d.  All of the above

_____ 19. According to "The Power of Productivity":
   a.  the majority of the world's population lives in middle-income countries
   b.  a country must develop a highly educated labor force before it can hope to significantly improve labor productivity
   c.  Both of the above
   d.  Neither of the above

_____ 20. Which of the following is correct?
   a.  Japanese workers are more productive than American workers in most types of manufacturing
   b.  the manufacturing sector of the economy is much more important than the retail sector for determining standard of living
   c.  Japan's high manufacturing productivity explains why the standard of living is higher in Japan than in the U.S.
   d.  All of the above

_____ 21. According to the Corruption Perceptions Index:
   a.  greater corruption is associated with a higher standard of living
   b.  greater corruption is associated with a lower standard of living
   c.  there is no relationship between corruption and standard of living

Less Developed Countries

____ 22. Foreign aid:
   a. is intended to enhance economic growth for the aid recipients
   b. does not have a good record of enhancing economic growth
   c. may amount to subsidizing and strengthening bad governments
   d. All of the above

**Problems:**

1. If Country A has a per capita GDP of $12,000 in 2005 and has a growth rate of 4% over the next 35 years, what will per capita GDP be for Country A in 2040?

2. List the four obstacles to economic development often faced by LDCs.

3. Explain why a high population growth rate is an obstacle to economic development for LDCs.

4. List four ways that governments in LDCs often weaken private property rights.

5. List four ways that countries can increase competition in product markets, according to "The Power of Productivity".

**Answers for Chapter 15**

**Fill-in-the-blanks:**   1. developed
                          2. less developed

**Multiple Choice:**

| | | |
|---|---|---|
| 1. d. | 9. c. | 17. c. |
| 2. d. | 10. a. | 18. b. |
| 3. c. | 11. d. | 19. d. |
| 4. c. | 12. d. | 20. a. |
| 5. c. | 13. c. | 21. b. |
| 6. c. | 14. d. | 22. d. |
| 7. c. | 15. b. | |
| 8. d. | 16. b. | |

## Problems:

1.  At a growth rate of 4%, per capita GDP will double in 17.5 years.  Thus, by 2040, Country A will have per capita GDP of $48,000.

2.  LDCs often face one or more of the following obstacles to economic development:
    (1)  Rapid population growth
    (2)  Low savings rate
    (3)  Cultural norms that hinder economic development
    (4)  Counterproductive governmental policies

3.  A high population growth rate means a high dependency ratio.  A high dependency ratio means a high percentage of the population consists of children and the elderly.  A high dependency ratio makes it difficult for the working-age population to support themselves and their dependents, and to make investments toward economic development.

4.  Governments in LDCs often weaken private property rights by:
    (1)  Failing to enforce private property rights through criminal and civil law
    (2)  Imposing relatively high tax rates
    (3)  Imposing excessive government regulations
    (4)  Permitting excessive government corruption

5.  Countries can increase competition in product markets by:
    (1)  Reducing trade restrictions on imports
    (2)  Permitting foreign direct investment in the domestic economy
    (3)  Loosening restrictions on store size, hours of operations, etc.
    (4)  Reducing the size of government

## Answer to Think Like an Economist:

You do not want the global minimum wage law to be imposed.  If it is, the "sweatshop" where you are employed will probably close.  The American owner will relocate the factory to a country with higher labor productivity since it will be forced to pay higher wages.  And you will be back to working on the farm.

# Chapter 16 International Trade

The basic economic problem is scarcity. Human wants are unlimited. Resources are limited. International trade can help a nation to achieve the basic goal of producing as much consumer satisfaction as possible with the limited resources available.

## Some International Trade Facts

International trade is an important part of the U.S. economy and the U.S. economy is an important part of international trade. The U.S. is the largest international trader in the world. The U.S. is the world's largest importer and one of the world's largest exporters.

In recent years, the U.S. has had large trade deficits. A **trade deficit** occurs when a nation's imports exceed its exports.

> **Example 1:** In 2007, the U.S. had exports of $1,662 billion and imports of $2,370 billion, for a trade deficit of $708 billion. (Information is from the Bureau of Economic Analysis.)

## Why Nations Trade

Why do nations engage in international trade? People in different nations trade with each other for the same reason that people within the same nation trade with each other: To benefit themselves. People do not willingly engage in trade unless they expect to benefit from the exchange.

If the U.S. has a trade deficit, does that mean that the U.S. economy suffers a loss from international trade? No. When two nations voluntarily engage in international trade, both nations benefit from the exchange.

> **Example 2A:** In 2008, Professor D. Imwit spent $3,000 on services provided by Dr. Pena, an orthodontist. Dr. Pena did not enroll in any of Professor Imwit's classes. Professor Imwit had a $3,000 trade deficit with Dr. Pena. Nonetheless, both Dr. Pena and Professor Imwit benefited from their trade.

> **Example 2B:** In 2007, the U.S. had a trade deficit with Saudi Arabia of almost $24 billion. Would the U.S. have been better off refusing to import oil from Saudi Arabia? Would Saudi Arabia have been better off refusing to export oil to the U.S.? Both nations benefited from the trade.

How do nations know what international trade to engage in? The law of comparative advantage guides them. The law of comparative advantage states that trade between nations is beneficial to both if there is a difference in opportunity costs.

A nation should specialize in producing where it has a comparative advantage (can produce at a lower opportunity cost). A nation should trade for goods where it has a comparative disadvantage (must incur a higher opportunity cost to produce).

## Comparative Advantage Example

To illustrate the benefit of trading according to comparative advantage, we will look at a simplified example. To make the example as simple as possible, we will assume that there are only two countries involved; Country X and Country Y. And we will assume that each country can produce only two goods; wheat and bananas. We assume that each country's crucial limited resource is land, and that each country has 1,000 hectares of land available.

The table below shows the productivity and opportunity cost for Country X and for Country Y.

| <u>Country X</u> | <u>Opportunity Cost per Ton</u> |
|---|---|
| Wheat -- 4 tons per hectare | 1 ton of bananas |
| Bananas -- 4 tons per hectare | 1 ton of wheat |
| | |
| <u>Country Y</u> | <u>Opportunity Cost per Ton</u> |
| Wheat -- 2 tons per hectare | 30 tons of bananas |
| Bananas -- 60 tons per hectare | 1/30 ton of wheat |

**Example 3A:** Assume that Country X and Country Y do <u>not</u> trade with each other. Rather, each country produces both wheat and bananas. Each country uses half of its land (500 hectares) to produce wheat and half (500 hectares) to produce bananas. Country X will be able to produce 2,000 tons of wheat (500 hectares x 4 tons per hectare) and 2,000 tons of bananas (500 hectares x 4 tons per hectare). Country Y will be able to produce 1,000 tons of wheat (500 acres x 2 tons per hectare) and 30,000 tons of bananas (500 hectares x 60 tons per hectare). Total production for the two countries combined is 3,000 tons of wheat and 32,000 tons of bananas.

**Example 3B:** Assume that Country X and Country Y produce and trade according to comparative advantage. Country X uses all 1,000 hectares of land to produce wheat, producing 4,000 tons of wheat (1,000 hectares x 4 tons per hectare). Country Y uses all 1,000 hectares to produce bananas, producing 60,000 tons of bananas (1,000 hectares x 60 tons per hectare). By producing according to comparative advantage, the output produced by the two countries combined has been increased.

The examples above show that both countries can benefit from specialization and trade according to comparative advantage. The specialization according to comparative advantage causes resources to be allocated to their most productive uses. This allows for more production from the same amount of resources, and is a type of technological advance.

But how do countries determine where their comparative advantage lies? Do the governments of Country X and Country Y need to carefully study opportunity cost and direct production accordingly? No. In a free market, profit-seeking will lead to production and trade according to comparative advantage.

Profit-seeking producers in Country X will discover that producing wheat is profitable (they can produce at a lower opportunity cost than producers in Country Y) and that producing bananas is unprofitable. Thus, they will specialize in wheat production.

Profit-seeking producers in Country Y will discover that producing bananas is profitable and that producing wheat is unprofitable. Thus, they will specialize in banana production.

And what role will the governments of Country X and Country Y need to play to ensure that trade follows comparative advantage? Simply allow free trade. Don't interfere with the competitive markets. In other words, do nothing.

## Other Benefits of Free International Trade

Along with the gain that arises from producing and trading according to comparative advantage, free international trade results in other benefits, including:

1. Free international trade extends markets, which allows nations to take more advantage of economies of scale and increases the potential returns to innovation.

2. Free international trade increases competition which compels domestic firms to increase their efficiency and to improve the quality of their products.

3. Free international trade speeds the flow of technological advances as firms are exposed to the improved production techniques of their foreign competitors and are motivated to adopt (or surpass) these improved production techniques.

4. Free international trade gives consumers access to a greater variety of goods.

5. Free international trade improves international relations. Nations that are engaged in mutually beneficial trade have a strong incentive to avoid war (and lesser conflicts) that would disrupt the mutually beneficial trade.

## Trade Restrictions

When nations engage in free international trade according to comparative advantage, the nations benefit overall. But not everyone within the nations may benefit personally (especially in the short run) from free international trade.

Domestic producers who face increased competition from imports may suffer losses. Thus, domestic producers may seek governmentally imposed restrictions on trade (especially restrictions on imports). The two most commonly imposed trade restrictions are tariffs and quotas.

**Tariff** – a tax on an imported good.

**Quota** – a legal limit on the quantity of a good that may be imported.

Both tariffs and quotas will reduce the supply of imports. This will allow domestic producers to sell a greater quantity at a higher price. Domestic producers will thus receive more producer's surplus than before the trade restriction. This is the gain to domestic producers from trade restrictions.

**Producer's surplus** – the difference between the lowest price a seller is willing to accept and the price actually received.

But while domestic producers gain from trade restrictions, domestic consumers lose. The domestic consumers will buy a lesser quantity at a higher price. Domestic consumers will thus receive less consumer's surplus than before the trade restriction. This is the loss to domestic consumers from trade restrictions.

**Consumer's surplus** – the difference between the highest price a buyer is willing to pay and the price actually paid.

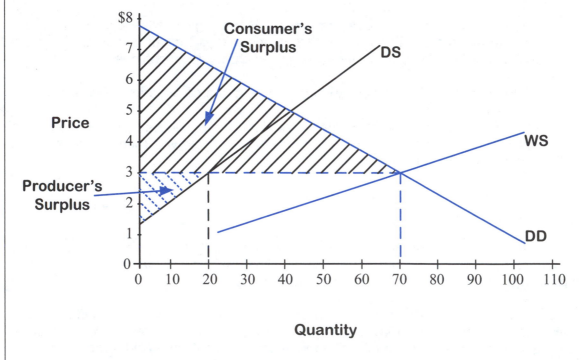

**Example 4:** The graph below illustrates producer's surplus for domestic producers and consumer's surplus for domestic consumers under free trade. The curve labeled DD represents Domestic Demand. The curve labeled WS represents World Supply. The curve labeled DS represents Domestic Supply.

On the graph on the previous page, the market price is $3 (where the Domestic Demand curve intersects the World Supply curve). Domestic consumer's surplus is the area below the Domestic Demand curve and above the market price of $3. Domestic producer's surplus is the area above the Domestic Supply curve and below the market price of $3.

The market quantity is 70 units (where the Domestic Demand curve intersects the World Supply curve). Domestic production is 20 units (where the $3 market price intersects the Domestic Supply curve). The quantity of imports is 50 units (the 70 unit market quantity minus the 20 units of domestic production).

## The Effects of a Quota of Zero

What happens to domestic producers and consumers if a trade restriction is imposed? The ideal situation for domestic producers would be a tariff high enough to eliminate imports, or a quota on imports of zero. In either case, the supply available would no longer be indicated by the World Supply curve, but by the Domestic Supply curve.

**Example 5:** The graph below illustrates producer's surplus for domestic producers, consumer's surplus for domestic consumers, and the net loss after a quota of zero is imposed on imports.

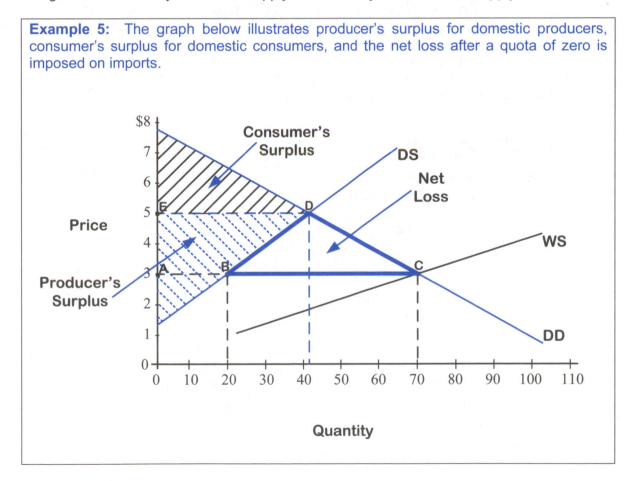

The market price after imposing a quota of zero is $5 (where the Domestic Demand curve intersects the Domestic Supply curve). The market quantity after imposing a quota of zero is about 42 units. The entire market quantity is produced by domestic producers.

On the graph on the previous page, domestic consumer's surplus is the area below the Domestic Demand curve and above the market price of $5. The quota of zero has caused domestic consumer's surplus to decrease by the area identified by the points A, C, D, and E.

Domestic producer's surplus is the area above the Domestic Supply curve and below the market price of $5. The quota of zero has caused domestic producer's surplus to increase by the area identified by the points A, B, D, and E.

The loss to domestic consumers caused by the quota of zero exceeds the gain to domestic producers caused by the quota of zero. The net loss is the area identified by the points B, C, and D.

Thus, a trade restriction (e.g. a quota of zero) causes a net economic loss to the nation imposing the restriction. Trade restrictions are an economically inefficient way to redistribute income from domestic consumers to domestic producers.

A trade restriction (e.g. a quota of zero) will also impose a loss on foreign producers. Some (or all) of the producer's surplus received by foreign producers under free trade will be eliminated by the trade restriction.

Should a nation considering imposing a trade restriction care about the loss imposed on foreign producers by the restriction? Yes, if only because the nation of the injured foreign producers may retaliate with trade restrictions of its own.

## The Politics of Trade Restrictions

Trade restrictions are economically inefficient. Then why are they imposed? There is a political reason that trade restrictions are imposed:

Though the consumer loss caused by trade restrictions exceeds the producer gain caused by trade restrictions, the benefits of trade restrictions are concentrated on a few producers, while the costs of trade restrictions are dispersed over many consumers.

We will see in Chapter 28 that elected officials will tend to favor policies that yield concentrated benefits and impose dispersed costs.

---

**Example 6:** If the gain to domestic producers from a trade restriction is $100 million, and there are five domestic producers, the average producer gain is $20 million. The domestic producers will be motivated to lobby the government, to make campaign contributions, and to engage in public relations efforts in order to gain the trade restriction.

The loss to domestic consumers will be larger than the gain to domestic producers. If the loss to domestic consumers is $200 million, and there are 10 million domestic consumers, the average consumer loss is $20. The consumers will be much less motivated to work to eliminate the trade restriction. In fact, the average consumer will probably be unaware of (rationally ignorant of) the loss imposed by the trade restriction.

---

## Arguments for Trade Restrictions

Trade restrictions are imposed to redistribute income from the many (often uninformed) consumers to the few (politically active) producers. (This is an example of rent seeking. See Chapter 22.) It would be bad public relations (and bad politics) to defend trade restrictions as a highly inefficient welfare plan, so arguments have been developed to justify trade restrictions.

1. **National defense argument.** This argument says that national defense concerns may require certain trade restrictions. The economic cost of the trade restrictions is trumped by the national defense concerns. The U.S. would not be wise to export weapons to nations that might use those weapons against the U.S.

> **Example 7:** A U.S. defense contractor has an opportunity to make a profitable sale of advanced weapons to North Korea. The U.S. government would not permit this export sale to take place, because of the potential harm to national security.

But the national defense argument has been used to justify restrictions on a wide variety of imports in order to maintain domestic production for "defense purposes". Often the goods are not really crucial to defense (e.g. shoes). Where goods are crucial to defense, it is usually more economically efficient to stockpile imports during peacetime, rather than to maintain a high-cost domestic industry.

2. **Infant industry argument.** This argument can be traced back to the first U.S. Secretary of the Treasury, Alexander Hamilton. Hamilton argued that new or "infant" industries need temporary protection from foreign competition so that they can mature and become competitive.

   However, if an "infant" domestic industry has the potential to become competitive, it doesn't really need temporary protection from foreign competition. Investors are willing to suffer short run losses in hopes of long run profits. And, if "temporary" protection is granted to an industry, the domestic producers may never become competitive with foreign producers since they are being shielded from competition with the foreign producers. Thus, it may never be politically feasible to remove the "temporary" protection.

3. **Unfair foreign competition argument.** Domestic producers may suffer in the face of foreign competitive practices that put the domestic producers at an unfair disadvantage.

   a. Dumping is the practice of selling exports at a price below the price charged in the home market. If foreign companies dump goods in the U.S. market, this puts U.S. producers at a competitive disadvantage. But dumping will mean lower prices for U.S. consumers and a net gain to the U.S. economy. The U.S. will be obtaining the goods at a lower cost than the cost of producing the goods in the U.S.

   b. Foreign governments sometimes subsidize exports, allowing the exports to be sold at a lower price. This puts U.S. producers at a competitive disadvantage.

But, as with dumping, foreign subsidies for exports will mean lower prices for U.S. consumers and a net gain to the U.S. economy.

4. **Low foreign wages argument.** This argument says that American producers cannot compete with foreign producers because American wages are high and foreign wages are low. If domestic producers are not protected from imports, American wages will be driven down to low levels.

**Example 8:** If textile manufacturers in North Carolina have to compete with textile manufacturers in Bangladesh, textile workers in North Carolina will see their wages fall.

It is true that wages for workers who are in direct competition with imports may be driven down by the competition. But high wages overall are made possible by high productivity. Restricting trade reduces a nation's overall productivity. Free international trade increases a nation's productivity and makes high wages overall possible.

5. **Saving domestic jobs argument.** Restricting imports can save specific domestic jobs. But protecting noncompetitive jobs interferes with the allocation of labor to its most productive use. And the cost to save the jobs will be greater than what the jobs are worth.

**Example 9:** Restrictions on imported sugar cost consumers about $1 billion per year and save about 2,000 U.S. jobs, for an annual cost per job saved of about $500,000. (Information from the International Trade Commission)

Also remember from the appendix to Chapter 4 that technological advance destroys jobs. International trade is a type of technological advance and thus destroys jobs. But job destruction is good. Job destruction frees up labor for new types of production. The destruction of jobs allows the newly unemployed labor to be re-allocated to more valuable production.

**Example 10:** In the last forty years, imports have nearly quadrupled as a portion of the U.S. economy. Yet the unemployment rate in the U.S. today is similar to what it was forty years ago.

## The Movement toward Freer Trade

Nations that practice relatively free international trade generally experience more economic growth than nations that restrict trade.

**Example 11:** According to the "Economic Freedom of the World, 2007 Annual Report", the twenty-five percent of nations with the most free economies had a per capita Real GDP about 8 times as high as the twenty-five percent of nations with the least free economies.

In recent years, there has been a movement toward freer international trade. Most nations have been reducing tariff rates and easing quotas on imports. As a result, international trade has been a growing part of the world economy.

> **Example 12:** According to the "Economic Freedom of the World, 2004 Annual Report", the mean tariff rate worldwide was decreased from 26.1 percent in 1980 to 10.4 percent in 2002. Between 1980 and 2002, exports plus imports as a share of worldwide GDP increased by 25.2 percent.

The U.S. has dramatically reduced trade barriers since the Great Depression. In 1932, (after the enactment of the Smoot-Hawley Tariff in 1930) the average tariff rate on dutiable imports was almost 60%. Today the average tariff rate on dutiable imports is less than 4%. The resulting increase in international trade, especially after World War II, has greatly benefited the U.S. economy.

> **Example 13:** According to research by Bradford, Grieco, and Hufbauer, the reduction of trade barriers since World War II has added between $800 billion and $1,400 billion annually to the U.S. economy. Removal of remaining U.S. trade barriers would add between $400 billion and $1,300 billion annually to the U.S. economy.

Still, there will always be domestic producers who would like to see increased restrictions on imports. And there will always be elected officials willing to sacrifice economic efficiency for political gain.

### Appendix: "Petition of the Candlemakers"

In 1845, French economist Frédéric Bastiat published "Economic Sophisms". Included in Chapter 7 of the First Series was a satirical attack on trade restrictions in the form of a fictitious petition of the candlemakers for protection from unfair competition. The petition, abridged, is below:

> "A Petition from the Manufacturers of Candles, Tapers, Lanterns, Candlesticks, Street Lamps,...and Generally of Everything Connected with Lighting

> To the Honorable Members of the Chamber of Deputies.

> Gentlemen:

> You are on the right track. You reject abstract theories and have little regard for abundance and low prices. You concern yourselves mainly with the fate of the producer. You wish to free him from foreign competition, that is, to reserve the domestic market for the domestic industry.

> We are suffering from the ruinous competition of a rival who apparently works under conditions so far superior to our own for the production of light that he is flooding the domestic market with it at an incredibly low price; for the moment he appears, our sales cease, all the consumers turn to him, and a branch of French industry...is all at once reduced to complete stagnation. This rival...is none other than the sun...

> We ask you to be so good as to pass a law requiring the closing of all windows, dormers, skylights, inside and outside shutters, curtains...in short, all openings, holes, chinks, and fissures through which the light of the sun is wont to enter houses..."

## Appendix: Comparative Advantage versus Absolute Advantage

In the comparative advantage example on page 16-2, Country X has a comparative advantage in producing wheat (can produce wheat at a lower opportunity cost than Country Y). Country X also has an absolute advantage (greater productivity than Country Y) in producing wheat.

Country Y has a comparative advantage in producing bananas (can produce bananas at a lower opportunity cost than Country X). Country Y also has an absolute advantage (greater productivity than Country X) in producing bananas.

Is it necessary for a country to have an absolute advantage in producing a good in order to have a comparative advantage? No. A country can be at an absolute disadvantage (less productivity) in producing all goods and still have a comparative advantage in producing some goods.

Let's alter the comparative advantage example from page 16-2 to put Country X at an absolute disadvantage in producing <u>both</u> wheat and bananas. We will do this by assuming that Country X is only 25% as productive as before in producing both wheat and bananas. The table below shows the productivity and the opportunity cost for Country X and for Country Y, after making the alteration:

| Country X | Opportunity Cost per Ton |
|---|---|
| Wheat -- 1 ton per hectare | 1 ton of bananas |
| Bananas -- 1 ton per hectare | 1 ton of wheat |
| | |
| Country Y | Opportunity Cost per Ton |
| Wheat -- 2 tons per hectare | 30 tons of bananas |
| Bananas -- 60 tons per hectare | 1/30 ton of wheat |

Notice on the table above that the opportunity cost numbers are the same as on the table on page 16-2. Country X is at an absolute disadvantage in producing wheat (less productivity per hectare than Country Y), but has a comparative advantage in producing wheat (can produce wheat at a lower opportunity cost than Country Y).

Since Country X has a comparative advantage in producing wheat and Country Y has a comparative advantage in producing bananas, both nations can benefit by specializing and trading according to comparative advantage.

## Appendix: Exchange Rates

The **exchange rate** is the value of one nation's currency in terms of another nation's currency.

> **Example 14:** On December 2, 2008, one U.S. dollar would exchange for 1.2436 Canadian dollars.

We saw in Chapter 6 that if the exchange rate for the U.S. dollar depreciates, U.S. net exports will increase. If the exchange rate for the U.S. dollar appreciates, U.S. net exports will decrease.

The exchange rate for a nation's currency will appreciate (increase) or depreciate (decrease) relative to other nations' currencies due to certain factors that affect the demand for and the supply of the currencies. The determinants of exchange rates include:

1. **Differences in inflation rates.** If one nation has a higher rate of inflation than another nation, this will change the exchange rate for the two nations' currencies. The currency of the higher-inflation nation will depreciate versus the currency of the lower-inflation nation.

> **Example 15:** If the inflation rate in the U.S. is 8%, and the rate of inflation in Canada is 2%, the exchange rate of the U.S. dollar will depreciate relative to the Canadian dollar.

2. **Differences in economic growth rates.** If one nation has a higher rate of economic growth than another nation, this will change the exchange rate for the two nations' currencies. The currency of the higher-growth nation will depreciate versus the currency of the lower-growth nation.

> **Example 16:** If the economic growth rate for the U.S. is 4%, and the economic growth rate for Canada is 1%, the exchange rate of the U.S. dollar will depreciate relative to the Canadian dollar.

3. **Changes in real interest rates.** If one nation's real interest rates increase relative to another nation's real interest rates, this will change the exchange rate for the two nations' currencies. The currency of the increasing-real interest rates nation will appreciate versus the currency of the decreasing-real interest rates nation.

> **Example 17:** If real interest rates in the U.S. increase relative to real interest rates in Canada, the exchange rate of the U.S. dollar will appreciate relative to the Canadian dollar.

4. **Changes in foreign investment attractiveness.** If one nation's attractiveness to foreign investors increases relative to another nation's attractiveness to foreign investors, this will change the exchange rate for the two nations' currencies. The currency of the increasing-attractiveness nation will appreciate versus the currency of the decreasing-attractiveness nation.

### Appendix: Book Review – "The Wealth of Nations, Book 4"

In Book 4 of his 1776 book "An Inquiry into the Nature and Causes of the Wealth of Nations", Adam Smith addresses international trade. In Chapter 2 of Book 4, Smith discusses restraints on imports. Smith asserts that restraints on imports divert resources from one direction to another. But it seems unlikely that this diversion will be advantageous to society.

According to Smith, every individual attempts to employ his resources to produce the greatest possible value. By doing this, the best interest of society is also promoted. Quoting Smith:

"…every individual, therefore, endeavours as much as he can…to direct that industry that its produce may be of the greatest value…He generally, indeed, neither intends to promote the public interest, nor knows how much he is promoting it…he intends only his own gain, and he is in this, as in many other cases, led by an invisible hand to promote an end which is no part of his intention…By pursuing his own interest he frequently promotes that of the society more effectually than when he really intends to promote it."

Smith was skeptical of government attempts to divert resources from the course of employment chosen by individual resource owners. Quoting Smith:

"…which produce is likely to be of the greatest value, every individual, it is evident, can, in his local situation, judge much better than any statesman or lawgiver can do for him. The statesman, who should attempt to direct private people in what manner they ought to employ their capitals, would not only load himself with a most unnecessary attention, but assume an authority which could safely be trusted, not only to no single person, but to no council or senate whatever, and which would nowhere be so dangerous as in the hands of a man who had folly and presumption enough to fancy himself fit to exercise it."

Instead of restraining trade, nations should behave like prudent householders. Quoting Smith:

"It is the maxim of every prudent master of a family, never to attempt to make at home what it will cost him more to make than to buy…What is prudence in the conduct of every private family, can scarce be folly in that of a great kingdom. If a foreign country can supply us with a commodity cheaper than we ourselves can make it, better buy it of them with some part of the produce of our own industry, employed in a way in which we have some advantage."

In Chapter 8 of Book 4, as Smith was concluding his discussion of the mercantile system, he wrote of the interests of the consumers versus the interests of the producers. Quoting Smith:

"Consumption is the sole end and purpose of all production; and the interest of the producer ought to be attended to, only so far as it may be necessary for promoting that of the consumer."

## Questions for Chapter 16

### Fill-in-the-blanks:

1. A trade deficit occurs when a nation's _____ exceed its _____ .

2. A _____ is a tax on an imported good.

3. A _____ is a legal limit on the quantity of a good that may be imported.

4. _____ _____ is the difference between the lowest price a seller is willing to accept and the price actually received.

5. _____ _____ is the difference between the highest price a buyer is willing to pay and the price actually paid.

6. The _____ rate is the value of one nation's currency in terms of another nation's currency.

### Multiple Choice:

_____ 1. The largest international trader in the world is:
   a. U.S.
   b. China
   c. Japan
   d. Germany

_____ 2. In recent years, the U.S. has had:
   a. large trade surpluses
   b. small trade surpluses
   c. large trade deficits
   d. small trade deficits

_____ 3. When nations engage in international trade according to comparative advantage:
   a. the selling nation gains from trade and the buying nation loses
   b. a nation gains from trade only if it has a trade surplus
   c. both nations gain from trade
   d. the buying nation gains from trade and the selling nation loses

Answer questions 4. through 7. based on the following information:

One acre of land in Country X can produce 50 bushels of rice or 20 bushels of corn

One acre of land in Country Y can produce 5 bushels of rice or 20 bushels of corn

_____ 4. For Country X, what is the opportunity cost of producing one bushel of corn?
  a. 1 bushel of rice
  b. 2/5 bushel of rice
  c. 2½ bushels of rice

_____ 5. For Country Y, what is the opportunity cost of producing one bushel of rice?
  a. 1 bushel of corn
  b. 4 bushels of corn
  c. ¼ bushel of corn

_____ 6. Country Y has a comparative advantage in producing:
  a. corn
  b. rice
  c. Both corn and rice
  d. Neither corn nor rice

_____ 7. Country X has a comparative advantage in producing:
  a. corn
  b. rice
  c. Both corn and rice
  d. Neither corn nor rice

_____ 8. In order for a nation to trade according to comparative advantage:
  a. its government must restrict imports in order to maintain its producers' comparative advantage
  b. its government must direct producers to their comparative advantage
  c. its government must allow free trade
  d. Both a. and b. above

_____ 9. The effect of a quota on imported shoes would include:
  a. higher wages for U.S. shoe industry workers
  b. higher profits for U.S. shoemakers
  c. higher prices for U.S. shoe consumers
  d. All of the above

_____ 10. When a trade restriction is imposed:
  a. domestic consumers lose
  b. domestic producers gain
  c. consumer loss exceeds producer gain
  d. All of the above

Answer questions 11. through 14. by referring to the graph below:

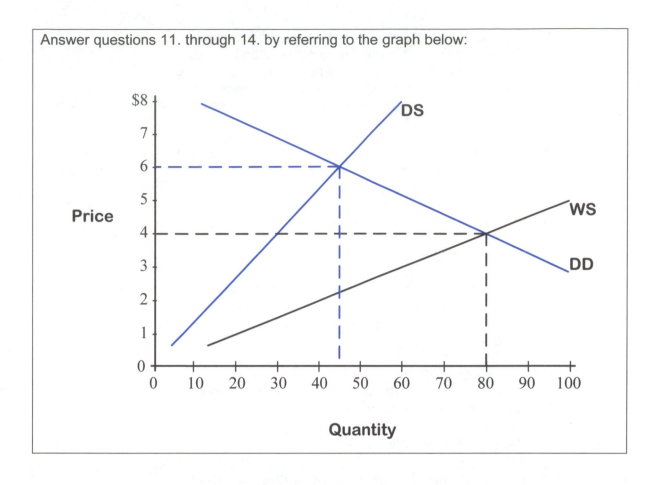

_____ 11. The equilibrium quantity under free trade is:
    a.  30 units
    b.  50 units
    c.  80 units
    d.  100 units

_____ 12. The quantity of domestic production under free trade is:
    a.  0 units
    b.  30 units
    c.  50 units
    d.  80 units

_____ 13. The quantity of imports under free trade is:
    a.  0 units
    b.  30 units
    c.  50 units
    d.  80 units

_____ 14. The market price, after imposing a quota of zero, is:
    a.  $4
    b.  $5
    c.  $6
    d.  $7

_____ 15. The political reason that trade restrictions are imposed is:
      a. trade restrictions benefit the domestic economy
      b. trade restrictions improve a nation's standard of living
      c. the benefits of trade restrictions are concentrated on a few producers, while the costs of trade restrictions are dispersed over many consumers
      d. Both a. and b. above

_____ 16. Which of the following is <u>not</u> an argument for trade restrictions?
      a. Infant industry argument
      b. Consumer choice argument
      c. Unfair foreign competition argument
      d. Saving domestic jobs argument

_____ 17. Over the last couple of decades:
      a. Average tariff rates have been falling
      b. International trade has grown in importance
      c. Nations with more open economies have experienced more growth than nations with more closed economies
      d. All of the above

_____ 18. Frédéric Bastiat's "Petition of the Candlemakers":
      a. is an argument for the wisdom of trade restrictions
      b. is a satirical attack on trade restrictions
      c. Both of the above
      d. Neither of the above

---

Answer questions 19. through 22. based on the following information:

One acre of land in Country X can produce 50 bushels of rice or 20 bushels of corn

One acre of land in Country Y can produce 3 bushels of rice or 12 bushels of corn

---

_____ 19. For Country Y, what is the opportunity cost of producing one bushel of rice?
      a. 1 bushel of corn
      b. 4 bushels of corn
      c. ¼ bushel of corn

_____ 20. Country X has a comparative advantage in producing:
      a. corn
      b. rice
      c. Both corn and rice
      d. Neither corn nor rice

_____ 21. Country Y has an absolute advantage in producing:
      a. corn
      b. rice
      c. Both corn and rice
      d. Neither corn nor rice

_____ 22. Country Y has a comparative advantage in producing:
   a. corn
   b. rice
   c. Both corn and rice
   d. Neither corn nor rice

_____ 23. If Nation A's attractiveness to foreign investors increases relative to Nation B's:
   a. the exchange rate for Nation A's currency will appreciate relative to Nation B's currency
   b. Nation A's net exports will increase
   c. Both of the above
   d. Neither of the above

_____ 24. The exchange rate for Nation A's currency will appreciate versus that of Nation B if:
   a. Nation A has a higher inflation rate than Nation B
   b. Nation A has a higher economic growth rate than Nation B
   c. Nation A's real interest rates increase relative to Nation B's real interest rates
   d. All of the above

_____ 25. According to Adam Smith:
   a. as individuals attempt to employ their resources to produce the greatest possible value, the best interest of society is also promoted
   b. if a foreign country can supply us with a commodity cheaper than we can make it, our domestic producers should be protected by trade restrictions
   c. the interests of consumers must give way to the interests of producers
   d. All of the above

## Problems:

1. Explain why nations engage in international trade.

2. List five other benefits of free international trade.

3. On the graph below:

   (1) What is the free trade price?
   (2) What is the free trade quantity?
   (3) What is the quantity of imports under free trade?
   (4) What is the price after imposing a quota of zero?

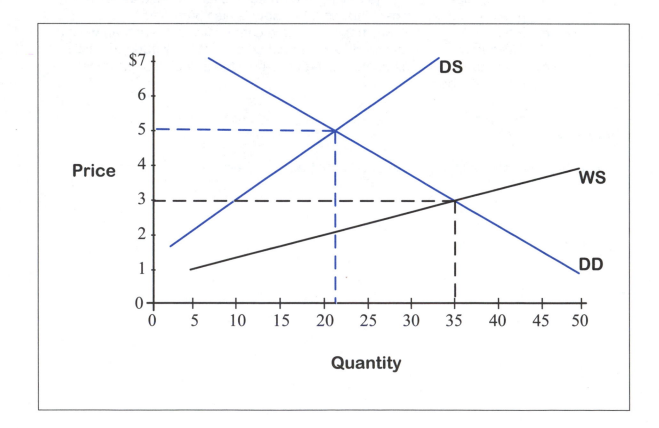

4. Explain the political reason that trade restrictions are imposed.

5. List four determinants of exchange rates.

## Answers for Chapter 16

**Fill-in-the-blanks:**   1. imports, exports          4. Producer's surplus
                          2. tariff                    5. Consumer's surplus
                          3. quota                     6. exchange

**Multiple Choice:**   1. a.          10. d.          19. b.
                       2. c.          11. c.          20. b.
                       3. c.          12. b.          21. d.
                       4. c.          13. c.          22. a.
                       5. b.          14. c.          23. a.
                       6. a.          15. c.          24. c.
                       7. b.          16. b.          25. a.
                       8. c.          17. d.
                       9. d.          18. b.

**Problems:**

1.  People in different nations trade with each other for the same reason that people within the same nation trade with each other:  To benefit themselves.  By specializing and trading according to comparative advantage, a nation will enjoy a higher standard of living.

2.  The five other benefits of free international trade are:
    (1)  Free international trade extends markets, which allows nations to take more advantage of economies of scale and increases the potential returns to innovation.
    (2)  Free international trade increases competition which compels domestic firms to increase their efficiency and to improve the quality of their products.
    (3)  Free international trade speeds the flow of technological advances as firms are exposed to the improved production techniques of their foreign competitors and are motivated to adopt (or surpass) these improved production techniques.
    (4)  Free international trade gives consumers access to a greater variety of goods.
    (5)  Free international trade improves international relations.  Nations that are engaged in mutually beneficial trade have a strong incentive to avoid war (and lesser conflicts) that would disrupt the mutually beneficial trade.

3.  (1)  $3   (2)  35 units   (3)  25 units   (4)  $5

4.  Though the consumer loss caused by trade restrictions exceeds the producer gain caused by trade restrictions, the benefits of trade restrictions are concentrated on a few producers, while the costs of trade restrictions are dispersed over many consumers.  Elected officials will tend to favor policies that yield concentrated benefits and impose dispersed costs.

5.  The determinants of exchange rates include:
    (1)  Differences in inflation rates
    (2)  Differences in economic growth rates
    (3)  Changes in real interest rates
    (4)  Changes in foreign investment attractiveness

# Chapter 17  Elasticity

We are often interested in how a change in one variable will affect another variable.  For example, the law of demand (see Chapter 3) indicates that a change in price will lead to an inverse change in quantity demanded.  But how large will the change in quantity demanded be relative to the change in price?  The question of how responsive one variable is to changes in another variable is answered by measuring elasticity.

**Elasticity** – a measure of the responsiveness of one variable to changes in another variable.

> **Example 1:**  Stephanie Student earned a 2.7 grade point average last semester.  She would like to do better this semester, so she determines to increase her study time by 50 percent.  But how responsive will her grades be to a change in her study time?  Perhaps a 50 percent increase in study time will increase her grade point average to 4.0.  Or perhaps a 50 percent increase in study time will only increase her grade point average to 2.8.  Elasticity measures the responsiveness of one variable to changes in another variable.

## Price Elasticity of Demand ($E_D$)

The first measure of elasticity examined in this chapter is price elasticity of demand.  The law of demand indicates that a change in price will lead to an inverse change in quantity demanded.  Price elasticity of demand measures the relative sizes of the changes in quantity demanded and price.  The formula for price elasticity of demand is:

**$E_D$ = Percentage Change in Quantity Demanded ÷ Percentage Change in Price**

> **Example 2:**  When Darla increases the price of her donuts by 10%, the quantity demanded decreases by 25%.  The price elasticity of demand for this change in the price of Darla's donuts is 2.5 (25% ÷ 10%).

Notice in Example 2 that a positive answer was reached even though the percentage change in price was positive and the percentage change in quantity demanded was negative.  In computing price elasticity of demand, the common practice is to treat changes as absolute values and arrive at a positive answer.

## Two Extreme Examples

Before looking at the calculation of price elasticity of demand in more detail, we look at two extreme examples.

The first extreme example is perfectly inelastic demand.  When demand is perfectly inelastic, the quantity demanded is unchanged by a change in price.  The price elasticity of demand is zero.  A good that is essential to the buyer (e.g. insulin to a person with Type 1 diabetes) might have a perfectly inelastic demand curve.

**Example 3A:** The graph below illustrates a perfectly inelastic demand curve.

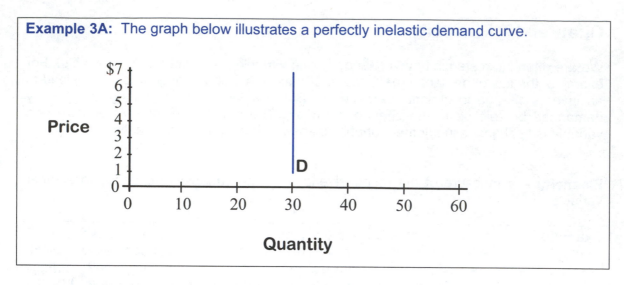

The second extreme example is perfectly elastic demand. When demand is perfectly elastic, the demand curve is horizontal. This indicates that a seller has no ability to change the selling price. We will see in Chapter 21 that a perfectly competitive firm faces a perfectly elastic demand curve for its product.

**Example 3B:** The graph below illustrates a perfectly elastic demand curve.

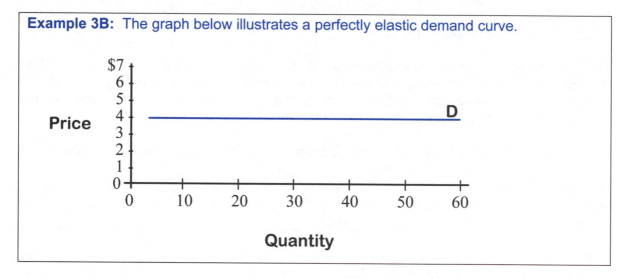

## Computing Price Elasticity of Demand

In computing price elasticity of demand, the percentage change in quantity demanded is calculated by dividing the change in quantity demanded by the average quantity demanded. The percentage change in price is calculated by dividing the change in price by the average price. The formula is expressed below:

$$E_D = \dfrac{\dfrac{\text{Change in Quantity Demanded}}{\text{Average Quantity Demanded}}}{\dfrac{\text{Change in Price}}{\text{Average Price}}} = \dfrac{\dfrac{Q_2 - Q_1}{(Q_2 + Q_1)/2}}{\dfrac{P_2 - P_1}{(P_2 + P_1)/2}}$$

To illustrate this formula, we will use the following demand schedule and demand curve:

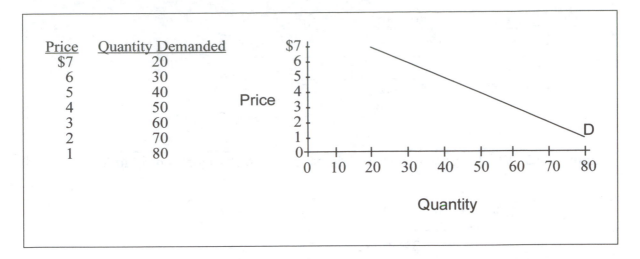

| Price | Quantity Demanded |
|-------|-------------------|
| $7 | 20 |
| 6 | 30 |
| 5 | 40 |
| 4 | 50 |
| 3 | 60 |
| 2 | 70 |
| 1 | 80 |

**Example 4A:** What is price elasticity of demand if price changes from $7 to $6?

The percentage change in quantity demanded is calculated as the change in quantity demanded (30 − 20 = 10) divided by the average quantity demanded ([30 + 20]/2 = 25) or 10 ÷ 25 = .4000.

The percentage change in price is calculated as the change in price (6 − 7 = 1) divided by the average price ([6 + 7]/2 = 6.5) or 1 ÷ 6.5 = .1538.

Thus, the price elasticity of demand for a change in price from $7 to $6 is .4000 ÷ .1538 = 2.60.

The above calculations can be expressed using the formula, as shown below:

$$E_D = \dfrac{\dfrac{Q_2 - Q_1}{(Q_2 + Q_1)/2}}{\dfrac{P_2 - P_1}{(P_2 + P_1)/2}} = \dfrac{\dfrac{30 - 20}{(30 + 20)/2}}{\dfrac{6 - 7}{(6 + 7)/2}} = \dfrac{\dfrac{10}{25}}{\dfrac{1}{6.5}} = \dfrac{.4000}{.1538} = 2.60$$

**Example 4B:** What is price elasticity of demand if price changes from $6 to $5?

$$E_D = \dfrac{\dfrac{Q_2 - Q_1}{(Q_2 + Q_1)/2}}{\dfrac{P_2 - P_1}{(P_2 + P_1)/2}} = \dfrac{\dfrac{40 - 30}{(40 + 30)/2}}{\dfrac{5 - 6}{(5 + 6)/2}} = \dfrac{\dfrac{10}{35}}{\dfrac{1}{5.5}} = \dfrac{.2857}{.1818} = 1.57$$

**Example 4C:** What is price elasticity of demand if price changes from $5 to $4?

$$E_D = \dfrac{\dfrac{Q_2 - Q_1}{(Q_2 + Q_1)/2}}{\dfrac{P_2 - P_1}{(P_2 + P_1)/2}} = \dfrac{\dfrac{50 - 40}{(50 + 40)/2}}{\dfrac{4 - 5}{(4 + 5)/2}} = \dfrac{\dfrac{10}{45}}{\dfrac{1}{4.5}} = \dfrac{.2222}{.2222} = 1.00$$

**Example 4D:** What is price elasticity of demand if price changes from $4 to $3?

$$E_D = \dfrac{\dfrac{Q_2 - Q_1}{(Q_2 + Q_1)/2}}{\dfrac{P_2 - P_1}{(P_2 + P_1)/2}} = \dfrac{\dfrac{60 - 50}{(60 + 50)/2}}{\dfrac{3 - 4}{(3 + 4)/2}} = \dfrac{\dfrac{10}{55}}{\dfrac{1}{3.5}} = \dfrac{.1818}{.2857} = .64$$

**Example 4E:** What is price elasticity of demand if price changes from $3 to $2?

$$E_D = \dfrac{\dfrac{Q_2 - Q_1}{(Q_2 + Q_1)/2}}{\dfrac{P_2 - P_1}{(P_2 + P_1)/2}} = \dfrac{\dfrac{70 - 60}{(70 + 60)/2}}{\dfrac{2 - 3}{(2 + 3)/2}} = \dfrac{\dfrac{10}{65}}{\dfrac{1}{2.5}} = \dfrac{.1538}{.4000} = .38$$

**Example 4F:** What is price elasticity of demand if price changes from $2 to $1?

$$E_D = \dfrac{\dfrac{Q_2 - Q_1}{(Q_2 + Q_1)/2}}{\dfrac{P_2 - P_1}{(P_2 + P_1)/2}} = \dfrac{\dfrac{80 - 70}{(80 + 70)/2}}{\dfrac{1 - 2}{(1 + 2)/2}} = \dfrac{\dfrac{10}{75}}{\dfrac{1}{1.5}} = \dfrac{.1333}{.6667} = .20$$

## Price Elasticity of Demand Classifications

If $E_D$ is greater than one, demand is elastic.

If $E_D$ is less than one, demand is inelastic.

If $E_D$ equals one, demand is unitary elastic.

## Price Elasticity of Demand and Total Revenue

One of the uses of price elasticity of demand information is to predict how a change in price will affect total revenue.

## Total Revenue = Price x Quantity

If demand is elastic ($E_D > 1$), price and total revenue are inversely related.

If demand is inelastic ($E_D < 1$), price and total revenue are directly related.

If demand is unitary elastic ($E_D = 1$), a change in price does not change total revenue.

The table below, based on Examples 4A – 4F, illustrates these relationships:

| Price | Quantity | Total Revenue | Change in Total Revenue | $E_D$ from previous price |
|---|---|---|---|---|
| $7 | 20 | $140 | X | X |
| 6 | 30 | 180 | $40 | 2.60 |
| 5 | 40 | 200 | 20 | 1.57 |
| 4 | 50 | 200 | 0 | 1.00 |
| 3 | 60 | 180 | -20 | .64 |
| 2 | 70 | 140 | -40 | .38 |
| 1 | 80 | 80 | -60 | .20 |

## Determinants of Price Elasticity of Demand

The determinants of price elasticity of demand are the factors that determine whether the demand for a good is elastic or inelastic. The four determinants of price elasticity of demand are:

1.  **The number of substitutes for the good.**  The more substitutes for a good, the more elastic the demand for the good.  The fewer substitutes for a good, the less elastic the demand for the good.

**Example 5A:**  Gertie's Gas and Go increases the price of its gasoline by 10¢ per gallon. No other gas outlets in town raise their prices.  Gertie's sells much less gasoline than before the price increase.  Since there are many substitutes for Gertie's gasoline, the demand for Gertie's gasoline is very elastic.

**Example 5B:**  Gertie's Gas and Go increases the price of its gasoline by 10¢ per gallon. All other gas outlets in town raise their prices by 10¢.  Gertie's and the other gas outlets sell nearly as much gasoline as before the price increase.  Since there is no close substitute for gasoline, the demand for gasoline is very inelastic.

2.  **The percentage of a person's budget spent on the good.**  The greater the percentage of a person's budget spent on a good, the more elastic the demand for the good.  The smaller the percentage of a person's budget spent on a good, the less elastic the demand for the good.

> **Example 6:** When the price of a loaf of bread increases by 20%, Tammy does <u>not</u> decrease her consumption of bread. When Tammy's rent increases by 20%, she begins looking for a new apartment.

3. **Nature of the good; luxury versus necessity.** For luxury goods, demand tends to be elastic. For necessities, demand tends to be inelastic.

> **Example 7:** When the price of Ahmad's heart medicine increases by 30%, he continues to purchase the same quantity of heart medicine. When the prices at Ahmad's favorite restaurant increase by 30%, he cuts back dramatically on his trips to the restaurant.

4. **Time consumers have to respond.** The more time consumers have to respond to a price change for a good, the more elastic the demand for the good. The less time consumers have to respond to a price change for a good, the less elastic the demand for the good.

> **Example 8:** If the price of gasoline increases by 75%, the quantity demanded in the next week would decrease by a small amount. If the price of gasoline stays high for a year, the quantity demanded will decrease more, as consumers trade for more fuel-efficient cars, form car pool arrangements, switch to public transportation, etc.

### Income Elasticity of Demand ($E_Y$)

One of the determinants of demand (factors that shift the demand curve) discussed in Chapter 3 is consumer income. A change in consumer income will cause a change in demand in the same direction (for normal goods) or in the opposite direction (for inferior goods). Income elasticity of demand measures the responsiveness of demand to a change in income. The formula for income elasticity of demand is:

**$E_Y$ = Percentage Change in Quantity Demanded ÷ Percentage Change in Income**

In computing income elasticity of demand, the percentage changes are calculated in the same manner used in computing price elasticity of demand. However, we will no longer be treating the changes as absolute values. For income elasticity of demand and for cross elasticity of demand (discussed on the next page), whether the answer is positive or negative is significant. Income elasticity is positive for normal goods and negative for inferior goods. The formula for income elasticity of demand is:

$$E_Y = \frac{\dfrac{\text{Change in Quantity Demanded}}{\text{Average Quantity Demanded}}}{\dfrac{\text{Change in Income}}{\text{Average Income}}} = \frac{\dfrac{Q_2 - Q_1}{(Q_2 + Q_1)/2}}{\dfrac{Y_2 - Y_1}{(Y_2 + Y_1)/2}}$$

To illustrate the formula, we will use the following examples:

**Example 9A:** When income increases from $1800 to $2200 per month, quantity demanded of Good X increases from 150 units to 170 units per month. The income elasticity of demand for Good X is computed as:

$$E_Y = \cfrac{\cfrac{170-150}{(170+150)/2}}{\cfrac{2200-1800}{(2200+1800)/2}} = \cfrac{\cfrac{20}{160}}{\cfrac{400}{2000}} = \cfrac{.1250}{.2000} = .63$$

Since income elasticity of demand for Good X is a positive number, Good X is a normal good.

**Example 9B:** When income increases from $2200 to $2600 per month, quantity demanded of Good Y decreases from 205 units to 195 units per month. The income elasticity of demand for Good Y is computed as:

$$E_Y = \cfrac{\cfrac{195-205}{(195+205)/2}}{\cfrac{2600-2200}{(2600+2200)/2}} = \cfrac{\cfrac{-10}{200}}{\cfrac{400}{2400}} = \cfrac{-.0500}{.1667} = -.30$$

Since income elasticity of demand for Good Y is a negative number, Good Y is an inferior good.

## Cross Elasticity of Demand ($E_C$)

One of the determinants of demand discussed in Chapter 3 is prices of related goods (substitutes or complements). If Good Y is a substitute for Good X, a change in the price of Good Y will cause a change in the demand for Good X in the same direction. If Good Y is a complement for Good X, a change in the price of Good Y will cause a change in the demand for Good X in the opposite direction.

Cross elasticity of demand measures the responsiveness of demand for one good to a change in price for another good. Cross elasticity is positive for substitutes and negative for complements. The formula for cross elasticity of demand is:

**$E_C$ = % Change in Quantity Demanded Good X ÷ % Change in Price Good Y**

In computing cross elasticity of demand, the percentage changes are calculated in the same manner used in computing price elasticity of demand. Thus, the formula on the next page:

Elasticity

$$E_C = \cfrac{\dfrac{\text{Change in Quantity Demanded Good X}}{\text{Average Quantity Demanded Good X}}}{\dfrac{\text{Change in Price Good Y}}{\text{Average Price Good Y}}} = \cfrac{\dfrac{Q_2 - Q_1}{(Q_2 + Q_1)/2}}{\dfrac{P_2 - P_1}{(P_2 + P_1)/2}}$$

To illustrate the formula, we will use the following examples:

**Example 10A:** When the price of Good Y increases from $40 to $60, the quantity demanded of Good X increases from 38 units to 42 units. The cross elasticity of demand for Goods X and Y is computed as:

$$E_C = \cfrac{\dfrac{42 - 38}{(42 + 38)/2}}{\dfrac{60 - 40}{(60 + 40)/2}} = \cfrac{\dfrac{4}{40}}{\dfrac{20}{50}} = \cfrac{.1000}{.4000} = .25$$

Since cross elasticity of demand for Goods X and Y is a positive number, Goods X and Y are substitutes for each other.

**Example 10B:** When the price of Good B increases from $300 to $340, the quantity demanded of Good A decreases from 162 units to 158 units. The cross elasticity of demand for Goods A and B is computed as:

$$E_C = \cfrac{\dfrac{158 - 162}{(158 + 162)/2}}{\dfrac{340 - 300}{(340 + 300)/2}} = \cfrac{\dfrac{-4}{160}}{\dfrac{40}{320}} = \cfrac{-.0250}{.1250} = -.20$$

Since cross elasticity of demand for Goods A and B is a negative number, Goods A and B are complements for each other.

**Example 10C:** When the price of Good D decreases from $12 to $8, the quantity demanded of Good C remains unchanged at 45 units. The cross elasticity of demand for Goods C and D is computed as:

$$E_C = \cfrac{\dfrac{45 - 45}{(45 + 45)/2}}{\dfrac{8 - 12}{(8 + 12)/2}} = \cfrac{\dfrac{0}{45}}{\dfrac{-4}{10}} = \cfrac{.0000}{-.4000} = 0.00$$

Since cross elasticity of demand for Goods C and D is zero, Goods C and D are unrelated to each other.

## Price Elasticity of Supply (E$_S$)

The law of supply indicates that there is a direct relationship between price and quantity supplied. Price elasticity of supply measures the relative sizes of the changes in quantity supplied and price. The formula for price elasticity of supply is:

### E$_S$ = Percentage Change in Quantity Supplied ÷ Percentage Change in Price

In computing price elasticity of supply, the percentage changes are calculated in the same manner used in computing price elasticity of demand. Thus, the formula below:

$$E_S = \frac{\dfrac{\text{Change in Quantity Supplied}}{\text{Average Quantity Supplied}}}{\dfrac{\text{Change in Price}}{\text{Average Price}}} = \frac{\dfrac{Q_2 - Q_1}{(Q_2 + Q_1)/2}}{\dfrac{P_2 - P_1}{(P_2 + P_1)/2}}$$

**Example 11:** When the price of Good Z increases from \$27 to \$33, the quantity supplied of Good Z increases from 2100 units to 2300 units. The price elasticity of supply for Good Z is computed as:

$$E_S = \frac{\dfrac{2300 - 2100}{(2300 + 2100)/2}}{\dfrac{33 - 27}{(33 + 27)/2}} = \frac{\dfrac{200}{2200}}{\dfrac{6}{30}} = \frac{.091}{.200} = .46$$

The biggest factor affecting price elasticity of supply is time. The more time producers have to respond to a price change for a good, the more elastic the supply for the good.

**Example 12:** If the price of crude oil increases by 75%, the quantity supplied monthly from the state of Texas would increase by a small amount in the first month after the price increase. New oil wells cannot be drilled in one month. If the price remains high for a year, the quantity supplied each month would increase much more.

## The Burden of a Tax and Price Elasticity

The burden of a tax refers to who actually feels the impact of a tax. If a tax is imposed on (collected from) the sellers of a good, the burden of the tax will probably fall on both the sellers and the buyers of the good.

If a tax is imposed on (collected from) the buyers of a good, the burden of the tax will probably fall on both the buyers and the sellers of the good.

The relative burden of a tax depends on the price elasticity of demand and supply. Buyers bear a greater burden of a tax if supply is more elastic than demand. Sellers bear a greater burden of a tax if demand is more elastic than supply. The burden of the tax is the same whether the tax is collected from the buyer or from the seller.

---

**Example 13A:** On the graph below, the demand and supply curves are similar in elasticity. The initial equilibrium price and quantity are $8 and 50 units. Then a tax of $6 per unit is imposed on the sellers. This shifts the supply curve vertically by the amount of the tax.

After the tax, the new equilibrium is at a price of $11 and a quantity of 40 units. Thus, the buyers bear half the burden of the tax (paying $3 more than before the tax was imposed) and the sellers bear half the burden (receiving $3 less after-tax).

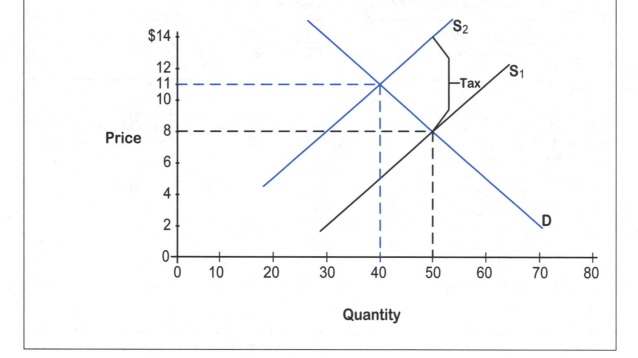

---

**Example 13B:** On the graph on the next page, supply is more elastic than demand. The demand curve is perfectly inelastic. Otherwise the graph is exactly like the graph in Example 13A above, with an initial equilibrium price and quantity at $8 and 50 units. Once again a $6 per unit tax is imposed on the sellers. After the tax, the new equilibrium is at a price of $14 and a quantity of 50 units. Thus, the buyers bear the entire burden of the tax.

---

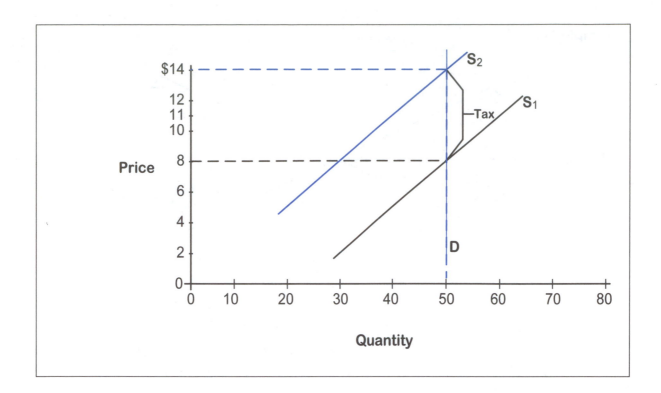

## Appendix: The Deadweight Loss of a Tax

In Chapter 13, we introduced the concept of the excess burden of a tax. The excess burden of a tax is the amount that the burden imposed by a tax exceeds the funding provided by the tax. One of the sources of excess burden is the deadweight loss of the tax.

We saw in Chapter 3 that private market equilibrium is generally efficient, maximizing the net benefit of having the market available (the sum of consumer's surplus and producer's surplus). When a tax is imposed, a wedge is created between the price paid by the buyers and the price received by the sellers. This tax wedge decreases the number of mutually beneficial transactions that take place and reduces the amount of consumer's surplus and producer's surplus generated in the market. The lost consumer's and producer's surplus due to the reduction in the number of transactions is the deadweight loss of the tax.

One of the factors that determines the size of the deadweight loss of a tax is the price elasticity of demand and supply. The more elastic the demand curve, the greater the deadweight loss of the tax. The less elastic the demand curve, the smaller the deadweight loss of the tax. Likewise, the more elastic the supply curve, the greater the deadweight loss of the tax. And the less elastic the supply curve, the smaller the deadweight loss of the tax.

The graph in Example 14 on the next page illustrates the pre-tax consumer's surplus and producer's surplus. The sum of the consumer's surplus and producer's surplus is the net benefit of having the market available. Equilibrium occurs at $4 and 15 units.

**Example 14:**

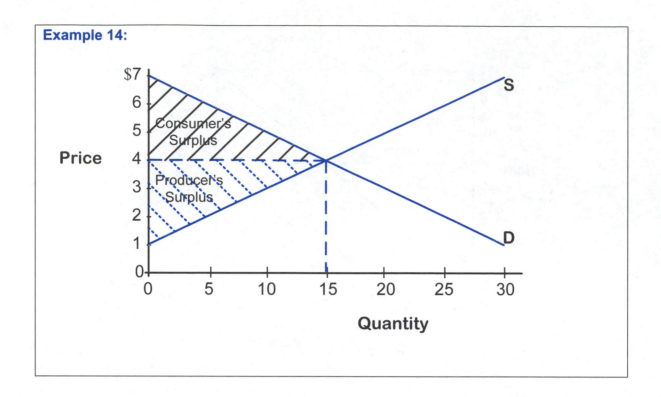

**Example 15:** Assume that a tax of $2 per unit is imposed on the sellers of the good. (Remember from earlier in this chapter that it doesn't matter whether the tax is imposed on the buyers or on the sellers, the burden of the tax will be the same either way.) The $2 per unit tax shifts the supply curve upward by $2, resulting in a new after-tax equilibrium of $5 and 10 units. See the graph below.

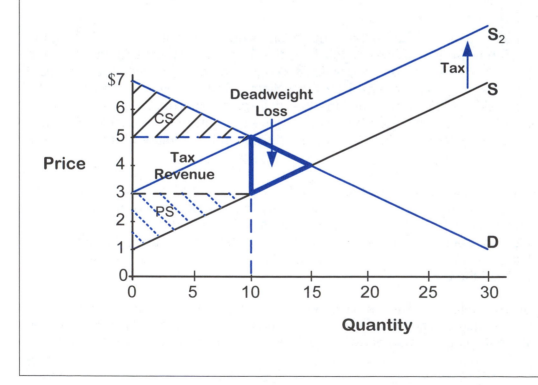

On the graph in Example 15, CS is Consumer's Surplus and PS is Producer's Surplus. Notice that the sum of Consumer's Surplus and Producer's Surplus has been reduced. This is the burden of the tax on the buyers and sellers. The tax revenue amounts to $20 ($2 tax multiplied by 10 units exchanged). The deadweight loss is the excess burden of the tax.

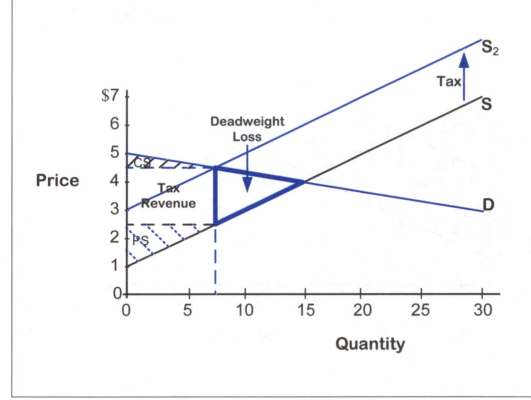

**Example 16:** Assume that everything is the same as in Example 15, except that the demand curve is more elastic. The increased elasticity of demand will mean an increase in the deadweight loss of the tax. This is illustrated on the graph below.

Because the demand curve is more elastic, the number of units exchanged has been reduced more than before. In the graph in Example 15, the number of units exchanged was reduced from 15 to 10 by the $2 tax. In the graph in Example 16, the number of units exchanged is reduced from 15 to 7 by the $2 tax. Thus, the deadweight loss of the tax is greater because the demand curve is more elastic.

Likewise, if the supply curve were more elastic, the deadweight loss of the tax would be greater. If the demand curve or the supply curve were less elastic, the deadweight loss of the tax would be less.

Another factor that affects the size of the deadweight loss of a tax is the tax rate. As was explained in Chapter 13, low tax rates help to minimize the effect of the tax on the decisions made in the private market. Thus, a lower tax rate will mean a smaller deadweight loss. A higher tax rate will mean a larger deadweight loss.

**Example 17:** The graph below is the same as the graph in Example 15, except that the tax rate is higher. A tax of $3 per unit is imposed instead of a tax of only $2 per unit.

The graph illustrates that the higher tax rate has a larger effect on the decisions made in the private market. The number of units exchanged is reduced from 15 to 7 by the $3 per unit tax. The $2 per unit tax of Example 15 only decreased the number of units exchanged from 15 to 10. The deadweight loss imposed by the $3 per unit tax is larger than the deadweight loss imposed by the $2 per unit tax of Example 15.

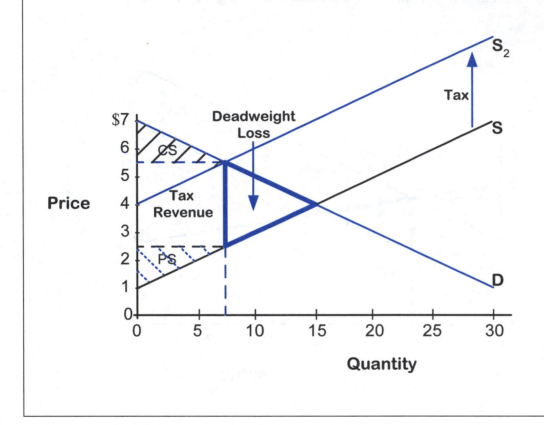

## Appendix: Think Like an Economist – An Increase in the Gasoline Tax

The federal government imposes a tax on gasoline of 18.4 cents per gallon. The fifty states also impose gasoline taxes which range from 8 cents per gallon in Alaska to over 30 cents per gallon in a number of states.

Let's say that the federal government decides to increase the federal gasoline tax by 50 cents per gallon. In the short run, would this increased tax likely create a relatively large deadweight loss or a relatively small deadweight loss? Why?

In the long run, would the deadweight loss caused by the increased gasoline tax grow larger or smaller? Why?

If the federal government decides to increase the gasoline tax by $2 per gallon, will this cause a larger or smaller deadweight loss than a 50 cent per gallon increase? Why?

## Questions for Chapter 17

### Fill-in-the-blanks:

1. _____ is a measure of the responsiveness of one variable to changes in another variable.

2. When demand is perfectly _____ , quantity demanded is unchanged by a change in price.

3. _____ elasticity of demand measures the responsiveness of demand to a change in income.

4. _____ elasticity of demand measures the responsiveness of demand for one good to a change in price for another good.


### Multiple Choice:

_____ 1. If the demand curve for a good is vertical, the demand for the good is:
a. perfectly inelastic
b. unitary elastic
c. perfectly elastic
d. All of the above are possible

_____ 2. If the demand curve is horizontal:
a. a seller has no ability to change the selling price
b. demand is perfectly elastic
c. Both of the above
d. Neither of the above

_____ 3. Assume that when the price of a good decreases from $32 to $24, the quantity demanded of the good increases from 80 to 100. What is the price elasticity of demand?
a. .22
b. .29
c. .78
d. 1.29

_____ 4. Assume that when the price of a good increases from $45 to $55, the quantity demanded of the good decreases from 275 to 225. What is the price elasticity of demand?
a. .20
b. .50
c. 1.00
d. 1.50

_____ 5. When the price elasticity of demand is greater than one, price and total revenue:
    a.  are directly related
    b.  are inversely related
    c.  are unrelated
    d.  All of the above are possible

_____ 6. When the price of Good A increases, the total revenue from Good A is unchanged. From this we know that the demand for Good A is:
    a.  elastic
    b.  inelastic
    c.  unitary elastic
    d.  All of the above are possible

_____ 7. The factors that determine whether demand for a good is elastic or inelastic are called the:
    a.  determinants of price elasticity of demand
    b.  determinants of demand
    c.  determinants of supply
    d.  The Determinators

_____ 8. The larger the percentage of their budgets that consumers spend on Good B:
    a.  the more inelastic the supply of Good B
    b.  the more elastic the supply of Good B
    c.  the more inelastic the demand for Good B
    d.  the more elastic the demand for Good B

_____ 9. The demand for a good is likely to be inelastic if:
    a.  there are few substitutes for the good
    b.  the good is a luxury item
    c.  the consumers have a lot of time to respond to a price change
    d.  All of the above

_____ 10. When the average income of consumers of Good B increased from $2300 to $2500, the quantity demanded of Good B decreased from 82 units to 78 units. The income elasticity of demand for Good B is:
    a.  -.60
    b.  -1.67
    c.  1.67
    d.  .60

_____ 11. Good C has an income elasticity of demand of -.27. Good C is:
    a.  a normal good
    b.  an abnormal good
    c.  an inferior good
    d.  a superior good

_____ 12. When the price of Good Q decreased from $1.00 to $.80, the quantity demanded of Good P increased from 95 to 105. The cross elasticity of demand for Goods P and Q is:
   a.  2.22
   b.  .45
   c.  -.45
   d.  -2.22

_____ 13. The cross elasticity of demand for Goods D and E is .71. Goods D and E are:
   a.  normal goods
   b.  unrelated to each other
   c.  complements
   d.  substitutes

_____ 14. When the price of Good R decreases from $18 to $12, the quantity supplied of Good R decreases from 125 to 75. The price elasticity of supply for Good R is:
   a.  -1.25
   b.  -.80
   c.  .80
   d.  1.25

_____ 15. A tax is placed on the sellers of Good F. The burden of the tax on Good F will fall mainly on the buyers if:
   a.  the demand for Good F is more elastic than the supply of Good F
   b.  the supply of Good F is more elastic than the demand for Good F
   c.  the demand for Good F is perfectly inelastic
   d.  Both b. and c. above

_____ 16. When a tax is imposed on the buyers or the sellers of a good:
   a.  a wedge is created between the price paid by the buyers and the price received by the sellers
   b.  the number of mutually beneficial transactions that take place is reduced
   c.  a deadweight loss is created
   d.  All of the above

_____ 17. The deadweight loss of a tax will be greater:
   a.  the more elastic demand and supply are
   b.  the higher the tax rate is
   c.  Both of the above
   d.  Neither of the above

## Problems:

1.  List the four determinants of price elasticity of demand.

Use the following demand schedule to answer questions 2. and 3.

| Price | Quantity Demanded |
|---|---|
| $16 | 30 |
| 14 | 40 |
| 12 | 50 |
| 10 | 60 |
| 8 | 70 |
| 6 | 80 |
| 4 | 90 |

2. Based on the demand schedule above, compute the price elasticity of demand for a change in price from:
   a. $16 to $14
   b. $14 to $12
   c. $12 to $10
   d. $10 to $8
   e. $8 to $6
   f. $6 to $4

3. a. Which price (or prices) from the demand schedule results in the maximum total revenue?
   b. How much total revenue is generated at that price (or prices)?

4. When the average income of the consumers of Good A decreased from $3,000 to $2,400, the quantity demanded of Good A decreased from 160 units to 140:
   a. What is the income elasticity of demand for Good A?
   b. Is Good A a normal good or an inferior good?

5. When the price of Good Y decreased from $23 to $17, the quantity demanded of Good X increased from 450 to 550:
   a. What is the cross elasticity of demand for Goods X and Y?
   b. Are Goods X and Y substitutes or complements?

## Answers for Chapter 17

**Fill-in-the-blanks:**
1. Elasticity
2. inelastic
3. Income
4. Cross

**Multiple Choice:**

| | | |
|---|---|---|
| 1. a. | 7. a. | 13. d. |
| 2. c. | 8. d. | 14. d. |
| 3. c. | 9. a. | 15. d. |
| 4. c. | 10. a. | 16. d. |
| 5. b. | 11. c. | 17. c. |
| 6. c. | 12. c. | |

Elasticity

## Problems:

1. The determinants of price elasticity of demand are:
   (1) The number of substitutes for the good
   (2) The percentage of a person's budget spent on the good
   (3) Nature of the good; luxury versus necessity
   (4) Time consumers have to respond

2. a. $(10 \div 35) \div (2 \div 15) = .2857 \div .1333 = 2.14$

   b. $(10 \div 45) \div (2 \div 13) = .2222 \div .1538 = 1.44$

   c. $(10 \div 55) \div (2 \div 11) = .1818 \div .1818 = 1.00$

   d. $(10 \div 65) \div (2 \div 9) = .1538 \div .2222 = .69$

   e. $(10 \div 75) \div (2 \div 7) = .1333 \div .2857 = .47$

   f. $(10 \div 85) \div (2 \div 5) = .1176 \div .4000 = .29$

3. a. $12 or $10    b. $600

4. a. $(-20 \div 150) \div (-\$600 \div \$2700) = -.1333 \div -.2222 = +.60$    b. normal

5. a. $(100 \div 500) \div (-6 \div 20) = .2000 \div -.3000 = -.667$    b. complements

## Answers to Think Like an Economist:

In the short run, a 50 cent increase in the federal gasoline tax would likely create a relatively small deadweight loss. Both the demand for gasoline and the supply of gasoline tend to be price inelastic in the short run.

In the long run, a 50 cent increase in the federal gasoline tax would create a larger deadweight loss. An increase in the length of time will increase the price elasticity of both the demand for and the supply of gasoline.

A $2 increase in the federal gasoline tax would cause a larger deadweight loss than a 50 cent increase. A higher tax rate will increase the effect of the tax on decisions made in the private market.

# Chapter 18  Utility

The basic economic problem is scarcity.  Human wants are unlimited.  Resources are limited.  The basic goal in dealing with the problem of scarcity is to produce as much consumer satisfaction as possible with the limited resources available.

At the individual level, the problem of scarcity means that a consumer will have only limited income to spend in trying to satisfy his or her unlimited wants.  How will a consumer spend that limited income?  A consumer's goal will be to receive as much satisfaction as possible from his or her limited income.

Consumer satisfaction is measured by utility.  So consumers will attempt to maximize the total utility that they receive from their limited income.

**Utility** – a measure of the satisfaction received from the consumption of a good.

Utility is an unusual type of measurement.  Most measurements have a standard, unchanging meaning.  For instance, one pound, one gallon, and one meter are all standard, unchanging measurements.  Weight, volume, and length can be measured objectively.  But utility cannot be measured objectively.

> **Example 1:**  If Cathey and Ellen each order 4 ounces of gourmet chocolate candy from the candy store, they will each receive the same amount (4 ounces) of chocolate candy.  But will Cathey and Ellen each receive the same amount (utility) of satisfaction from eating their chocolate candy?  We can't know.  Satisfaction cannot be measured in an objective sense like weight can.

The best measure of the satisfaction (utility) that a person receives from consuming a good is the price that the person is willing to pay for the good.

> **Example 2A:**  If Bertram is willing to pay $4 for a chili dog, then Bertram is anticipating at least $4 worth of utility from consuming the chili dog.  If Jeeves is unwilling to pay $4 for a chili dog, then Jeeves is anticipating less than $4 worth of utility from consuming a chili dog.

But the price that a person is willing to pay for a good is a subjective decision, varying from person to person.  And the price that different persons are willing to pay for a good varies not only because of differences in anticipated utility, but also because of differences in income.

> **Example 2B:**  During halftime of the football game, Bertram and Jeeves go to the concession stand.  Bertram buys a chili dog for $4.  Jeeves considers buying a chili dog, decides that $4 is too expensive, and does not buy a chili dog.  Does this prove that Bertram receives more utility from a chili dog than Jeeves does?  Not necessarily.  Jeeves may anticipate a great deal of utility from consuming a chili dog.  But if Jeeves has little income, he may decide that he cannot afford to spend $4 on a chili dog.  Bertram may anticipate only a little utility from consuming a chili dog.  But if Bertram has high income, he may decide that he can afford to spend $4 on a chili dog, even if the chili dog gives him only a little utility.

Utility is a measure of satisfaction. This means that utility is impossible to measure in an objective sense. Thus, there is no standardized measure of utility. If Jan eats a slice of pizza, we might say that she received 1 util of satisfaction, or 50 utils, or 1,000 utils. We can create our own standard.

If we decide that Jan received 50 utils of satisfaction from eating the slice of pizza, we have established a subjective standard for this situation. If Jan eats a second slice of pizza and finds it to be 80 percent as satisfying as the first slice, then the second slice yields 40 utils of satisfaction.

We saw in Chapter 1 that economic decisions are made by comparing the marginal benefits of a choice with the marginal costs. The marginal benefit of consuming an additional unit of a good is measured by marginal utility.

**Marginal utility** – the additional utility received from consuming an additional unit of a good.

---

**Example 3:** To illustrate marginal utility, let's say that Jan eats one slice of pizza and receives 50 utils of satisfaction. Then Jan eats additional slices, and experiences the following results:

| Slices of Pizza | Total Utility | Marginal Utility |
|:---:|:---:|:---:|
| 0 | 0 utils | X |
| 1 | 50 utils | 50 utils |
| 2 | 90 utils | 40 utils |
| 3 | 120 utils | 30 utils |
| 4 | 135 utils | 15 utils |
| 5 | 140 utils | 5 utils |

---

As Jan eats additional slices of pizza, each additional slice adds less to her total utility. Thus the marginal utility of each additional slice decreases (diminishes). Jan is experiencing the law of diminishing marginal utility.

**Law of diminishing marginal utility** – the marginal utility from consuming additional units of a good eventually declines.

This law assumes that consumption takes place over a relatively short period of time. If the second slice of pizza is eaten a week after the first slice, the second slice may be just as satisfying as the first slice.

## Diminishing Marginal Utility and Income Distribution

Because of the basic economic problem of scarcity, it is not possible to satisfy all human wants. The basic goal in dealing with the problem of scarcity is to produce as much consumer satisfaction as possible with the limited resources available. Or stated another way, the basic goal is to produce as much total utility for society as possible.

A market economy contributes toward achieving the goal of producing as much total utility for society as possible by giving resource owners the incentive to produce the output that generates the most satisfaction for the consumers. The output that generates the most satisfaction for the consumers will also generate the most income for the resource owners. However, a market economy also results in an unequal distribution of income.

The distribution of income in the U.S. economy is quite unequal. (We will see how unequal in Chapter 31.) Those with much income can consume much. They can afford goods that give them a great deal of marginal utility. They can also afford goods that give them little marginal utility. Those with little income can consume little. They may be unable to afford goods that would give them a great deal of marginal utility. Remember Bertram and Jeeves from Example 2B earlier in this chapter.

Does the unequal distribution of income mean less total utility for society? Or, stated another way, would redistributing income from those with more income to those with less income increase total utility for society? The law of diminishing marginal utility seems to indicate that it would.

---

**Example 4:** Imagine that there are only two persons in society. Max has annual income of $200,000. Minnie has annual income of $10,000. Which person would gain more marginal utility from an extra $100 of income? The law of diminishing marginal utility seems to indicate that Minnie would.

---

But the law of diminishing marginal utility does <u>not</u> actually indicate which person would receive greater marginal utility from additional income. Utility cannot be measured objectively. There is no objective way to measure or to compare the marginal utility that Max and Minnie would receive from an extra $100 of income. Thus, marginal utility cannot be scientifically compared for different persons.

Nonetheless, society generally assumes that extra income <u>would</u> yield more utility to a low-income person than to a high-income person. And billions of dollars in income are redistributed each year, generally from persons with more income to persons with less income, with the goal of increasing total utility for society. (We will look more closely at income distribution and redistribution in Chapter 31.)

## Diamond-Water Paradox

Is the price of a good related to the utility received from consuming the good? Logically, we would expect the price of a good to be related to the good's utility. If Bertram is willing to pay $4 for a chili dog, Bertram must be anticipating at least $4 worth of utility from consuming the chili dog. But what about the diamond-water paradox?

**Diamond-water paradox** – the observation that essential goods are often lower priced than non-essential goods.

Some goods that are essential to life (like water) have a very low price. Other goods that are non-essential (like diamonds) have a very high price. This seems paradoxical. Shouldn't a good's price be related to its utility? Actually, it is.

The price of a good is equal to the marginal utility of the last unit of the good consumed. This is the explanation of the diamond-water paradox.

Water has a very high total utility. A person would be willing to pay a very high price to have sufficient water for drinking purposes.

> **Example 5:** If the only source of drinking water had a price of $20 per gallon, a person would willingly pay the high price, rather than perish from thirst.

But a person consumes many units of water, for a variety of uses. The first units of water purchased have very valuable uses, such as drinking. As more units of water are consumed, less valuable uses are made of water, such as bathing, washing clothes, washing cars, watering flowers, etc.

The last units of water consumed have a very low marginal utility, and are consumed only because of the very low price of water. If water had a price of $20 per gallon, a person would not buy water for its less valuable uses. (Good luck, flowers, you are on your own.)

A person consumes few diamonds. The last diamond consumed has a very high price, and is consumed only because the buyer expects a very high marginal utility. If diamonds were more abundant and had a lower price, they would be consumed for less valuable purposes. If diamonds were as abundant as gravel, they would be used to pave driveways.

So which is more valuable, water or diamonds? Water is more valuable than diamonds in terms of total utility, but diamonds have a higher marginal utility, and thus a higher price.

> **Example 6:** Pat buys a diamond engagement ring in March, paying $2500. Pat's water bill in March is $15 for 1,500 gallons of water, or an average price of 1¢ per gallon. The diamond ring provides Pat with more <u>marginal</u> utility than the fifteen hundredth gallon of water (which dripped out of a leaky faucet). But the water that Pat consumed in March provided Pat with more <u>total</u> utility than the diamond ring.

## Utility Maximization

Consumers will attempt to maximize the utility (satisfaction) that they receive from their limited incomes. To determine the utility-maximizing combination of goods to consume requires consumers to consider how much marginal utility different goods yield, and also the prices of the different goods.

To illustrate this, assume that Consumer A is trying to choose the combination of Good X and Good Y that will maximize Consumer A's utility. Good X and Good Y yield the amounts of total and marginal utility to Consumer A indicated on the table on the next page:

| Units of X | Good X Total Utility | Marginal Utility | Units of Y | Good Y Total Utility | Marginal Utility |
|---|---|---|---|---|---|
| 0 | 0 | X | 0 | 0 | X |
| 1 | 40 | 40 | 1 | 30 | 30 |
| 2 | 75 | 35 | 2 | 55 | 25 |
| 3 | 105 | 30 | 3 | 75 | 20 |
| 4 | 130 | 25 | 4 | 90 | 15 |
| 5 | 150 | 20 | 5 | 100 | 10 |
| 6 | 165 | 15 | 6 | 105 | 5 |
| 7 | 175 | 10 | 7 | 109 | 4 |
| 8 | 180 | 5 | 8 | 112 | 3 |
| 9 | 183 | 3 | 9 | 114 | 2 |
| 10 | 184 | 1 | 10 | 115 | 1 |

**Example 7A:** Assume that Consumer A has $1 of income, and that Goods X and Y each cost $1 per unit. What would Consumer A buy? Answer; one unit of Good X. Because the first unit of Good X yields 40 marginal utils of satisfaction and the first unit of Good Y yields only 30 marginal utils of satisfaction, and they both cost $1.

**Utility Maximization Rule No. 1** – Always choose the marginal unit of the good that yields the most marginal utility per price.

**Example 7B:** Assume the same facts as Example 7A, but this time Consumer A has $2 of income. What would Consumer A buy? Answer; two units of Good X. This choice follows Utility Maximization Rule No. 1

**Example 7C:** Assume the same facts as Example 7A, but this time Consumer A has $10 of income. What would Consumer A buy? Answer; six units of Good X and four units of Good Y. This combination yields 255 total utils of satisfaction. No other combination of Goods X and Y yields as much total utility for $10. With this combination of Goods X and Y, the ratio of marginal utility per price is equalized for Goods X and Y. The sixth unit of Good X and the fourth unit of Good Y both yield 15 marginal utils for $1.

**Utility Maximization Rule No. 2** – Always choose the combination of goods that equalizes the ratio of marginal utility per price for all goods.

**Example 7D:** Assume the same facts as Example 7C but this time Good Y costs $3. What would Consumer A buy? Answer; seven units of Good X and one unit of Good Y. This combination yields 205 total utils of satisfaction. No other combination of Goods X and Y yields as much total utility for $10. Also, the ratio of marginal utility per price is equalized for Goods X and Y. The seventh unit of Good X yields 10 marginal utils for $1, the first unit of Good Y yields 30 marginal utils for $3.

> **Example 7E** Assume the same facts as Example 7C but this time Good Y costs $2, and Consumer A has $13 of income. What would Consumer A buy? Answer; seven units of Good X and three units of Good Y. This combination yields 250 total utils of satisfaction. No other combination of Goods X and Y yields as much total utility for $13. Also the ratio of marginal utility per price is equalized for Goods X and Y. The seventh unit of Good X yields 10 marginal utils for $1, the third unit of Good Y yields 20 marginal utils for $2.

## Providing Essential Goods Free of Charge

As mentioned earlier in this chapter, the distribution of income in the U.S. economy is quite unequal. Persons with very low income may be unable to afford essential goods, such as food, shelter, and medical care.

Should essential goods be distributed through markets like other goods? Should low-income persons be forced to do without essential goods because they cannot afford the market price? Maybe the government should provide essential goods to everyone (or at least to those with low income) free of charge. Then no one would have to do without essential goods.

> **Example 8:** Capital City operates a grocery store where low-income persons can pick up basic food items (bread, milk, cereal, etc.) free of charge. As a result, no one in Capital City need go hungry.

Unfortunately, government provision of essential goods free of charge would be very economically inefficient. If the government provided essential goods free of charge, consumers would overconsume these goods. Consumers would consume the "free" goods up to the quantity where the marginal utility of the goods would be zero. (Remember from earlier in the chapter that the price of a good is equal to the marginal utility of the last unit of the good consumed.)

Consuming a good to the point of zero marginal utility would be an inefficiently large quantity of consumption, because the marginal cost of producing the goods would be greater than zero. Given the basic economic problem of scarcity, society does <u>not</u> want to use resources to produce goods that cost more to produce than they yield in utility.

> **Example 9A:** Cyrus, a senior citizen, suffers from frequent bouts of heartburn. The only medicine that provides Cyrus with relief is a prescription medicine which Cyrus would be willing to pay $20 per month for. Unfortunately, the medicine costs $200 per month. At this high price, Cyrus chooses to live with the heartburn. Then a government program is created which provides free prescription medicines to senior citizens. Cyrus can now have his heartburn medicine for free. But the cost to produce the medicine may be far greater than the benefit to Cyrus ($20 per month).

If society wishes to provide essential goods to low-income persons, providing the goods free of charge is a very inefficient approach. It would be more efficient to provide income to the low-income persons. Then the low-income persons could spend the income as they choose, depending on the marginal utility that they anticipate from different goods and the marginal cost of production.

### Efficiency: Equating Marginal Benefit and Marginal Cost

The consumption of goods yields marginal utility. The production of goods incurs marginal cost. What is the optimal (ideal, most efficient) quantity of a good to produce and consume?

If the marginal unit of a good will result in more marginal utility than marginal cost, then society will receive a net benefit from producing the marginal unit. It is an efficient use of limited resources to continue producing more units of the good as long as the marginal utility exceeds the marginal cost.

If the marginal unit of a good will result in more marginal cost than marginal utility, then society will suffer a net loss from producing the marginal unit. It is an inefficient use of limited resources to continue producing more units of the good when the marginal cost exceeds the marginal utility.

As more units of a good are produced and consumed, the marginal utility of additional units will decrease (due to the law of diminishing marginal utility, discussed earlier in this chapter) and the marginal cost of additional units will increase (due to the law of diminishing marginal returns, discussed in Chapter 20).

When the marginal utility and the marginal cost are equal, this is the optimal (ideal, most efficient) quantity of the good to produce.

Speaking more generally, any activity results in marginal benefits and marginal costs. Economic decisions are made by comparing the marginal benefits of a choice with the marginal costs of the choice.

**Example 10A:** If the marginal benefit of another half hour of study exceeds the marginal cost of the lost sleep, a person studies for another half hour. If the marginal cost of the lost sleep exceeds the marginal benefit of another half hour of study, a person does not continue to study.

Any activity should be continued as long as the marginal benefit of the activity exceeds the marginal cost. The optimal (ideal, most efficient) level of the activity occurs where marginal benefit and marginal cost are equal.

**Example 10B:** The table on the next page applies to some activity (maybe studying for a test). As more units of the activity are produced, the marginal benefit of the activity decreases and the marginal cost of the activity increases. As long as the marginal benefit exceeds the marginal cost, the activity yields a positive marginal net benefit (marginal benefit minus marginal cost) and an increase in the total net benefit.

The optimal level of the activity (where total net benefit is maximized) occurs where the marginal benefit of the activity and the marginal cost of the activity are equal (7 units). If the marginal cost of another unit of the activity exceeds the marginal benefit (units 8 through 10), the total net benefit is reduced by continuing the activity.

| Units of Activity | Marginal Benefit | Marginal Cost | Marginal Net Benefit | Total Net Benefit |
|---|---|---|---|---|
| 1 | 65 | 5 | 60 | 60 |
| 2 | 60 | 10 | 50 | 110 |
| 3 | 55 | 15 | 40 | 150 |
| 4 | 50 | 20 | 30 | 180 |
| 5 | 45 | 25 | 20 | 200 |
| 6 | 40 | 30 | 10 | 210 |
| 7 | 35 | 35 | 0 | 210 |
| 8 | 30 | 40 | -10 | 200 |
| 9 | 25 | 45 | -20 | 180 |
| 10 | 20 | 50 | -30 | 150 |

## Appendix: Consumer Behavior, Indifference Curves, and Budget Constraints

In this chapter, we have examined consumer behavior using utility theory. Consumer behavior can also be examined using indifference curves and budget constraints.

**Indifference curve** – a curve showing different combinations of two goods that provide equal total utility to a consumer.

The graph on the next page illustrates indifference curves for Consumer A. The graph is based on the table on page 18-5. Some of the curves are extended for illustrative purposes. For each of the indifference curves the number of total utils provided by each combination of goods on the curve is indicated.

The indifference curves represent larger amounts of total utility the farther they are to the right. This reflects that consumers receive greater utility from consuming more units rather than less.

The indifference curves will have a convex slope. This reflects the law of diminishing marginal utility. As more units of a good are consumed, the marginal utility of the good will diminish. Thus, a consumer will be willing to sacrifice a decreasing amount of one good (Good Y) in order to consume an increasing amount of another good (Good X). The slope of an indifference curve is called the marginal rate of substitution.

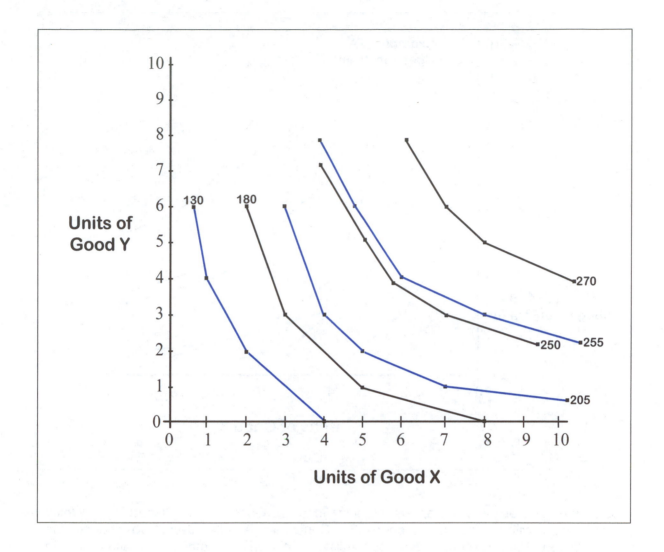

**Marginal rate of substitution** – the quantity of one good that a consumer is willing to sacrifice in order to obtain a unit of another good.

A consumer will attempt to maximize the total utility that they receive from their limited income. We used utility theory to examine utility maximization in Examples 7A-7E earlier in the chapter. Now we will use indifference curves and budget constraints.

**Budget constraint** – a curve showing the different combinations of two goods that a consumer can purchase with a certain amount of income.

A consumer's budget constraint depends on the consumer's income and the prices of the two goods under consideration.

**Example 11A:** Refer back to Example 7C. Consumer A has $10 of income and Good X and Good Y each cost $1 each. The graph on the next page illustrates the budget constraint for Consumer A.

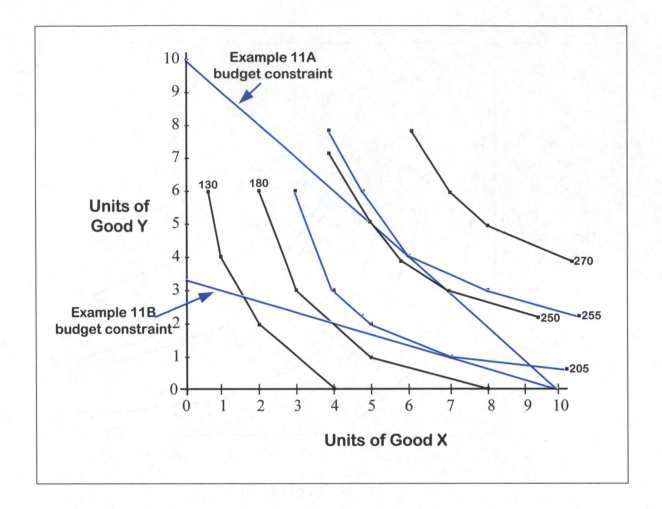

Consumer A can afford various combinations of Good X and Good Y. Which combination will Consumer A choose? Consumer A will attempt to choose the combination that maximizes A's total utility. This will be the combination on the indifference curve that is tangent to (has the same slope as) the budget constraint. For the utility-maximizing combination of units, the marginal rate of substitution will be the same as the slope of the budget constraint.

In this case (as in Example 7C), the utility-maximizing combination is six units of Good X and 4 units of Good Y. The marginal utility of the sixth unit of Good X is 15 utils. The marginal utility of the fourth unit of Good Y is also 15 utils. So the marginal rate of substitution will be 1 unit of Good X for 1 unit of Good Y. This is also the slope of the budget constraint (since the price of both Good X and Good Y is $1).

**Example 11B:** Refer back to Example 7D. The price of Good Y increases to $3. The graph above illustrates the new budget constraint for Consumer A.

In this case (as in Example 7D), the utility-maximizing combination is seven units of Good X and 1 unit of Good Y. The marginal utility of the seventh unit of Good X is 10 utils. The marginal utility of the first unit of Good Y is 30 utils. So the marginal rate of substitution will be 3 units of Good X for 1 unit of Good Y. This is also the slope of the budget constraint (since the price of Good Y is 3 times the price of Good X).

With the increase in the price of Good Y from $1 to $3, the quantity demanded of Good Y decreases from 4 units to 1 unit. So we can derive a demand curve for Good Y. See the graph below:

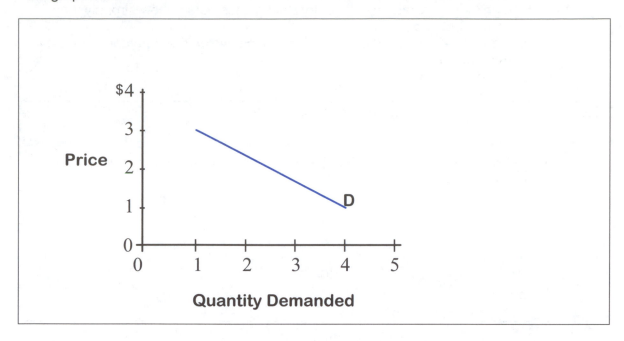

## Questions for Chapter 18

### Fill-in-the-blanks:

1. _____ is a measure of the satisfaction received from the consumption of a good.

2. _____ _____ is the additional utility received from consuming an additional unit of a good.

3. The diamond-water _____ is the observation that essential goods are often lower priced than non-essential goods.

4. A(n) _____ curve is a curve showing different combinations of two goods that provide equal total utility to a consumer.

5. A(n) _____ _____ is a curve showing the different combinations of two goods that a consumer can purchase with a certain amount of income.

### Multiple Choice:

_____ 1. Utility:
   a.  is a measure of the satisfaction received from the consumption of a good
   b.  has a standardized meaning
   c.  can be compared objectively between different persons
   d.  All of the above

_____ 2. The utility received by two different persons from consuming a good:
   a. can be compared objectively by looking at the price each is willing to pay for the good
   b. can be compared objectively by asking each person how strongly they desire the good
   c. cannot be compared objectively since the two different persons may have unequal income
   d. Both a. and b. above

Complete the following table to answer questions 3. and 4.:

| Units of Good X | Total Utility | Marginal Utility |
|---|---|---|
| 0 | 0 | X |
| 1 | 30 | 30 |
| 2 | 54 | — |
| 3 | 72 | — |
| 4 | 84 | — |
| 5 | 90 | — |
| 6 | 92 | — |

_____ 3. What is the marginal utility of the 3$^{rd}$ unit of Good X?
   a. 72
   b. 24
   c. 18
   d. 12

_____ 4. What is the marginal utility of the 5$^{th}$ unit of Good X?
   a. 0
   b. 6
   c. 18
   d. 90

_____ 5. A market economy:
   a. gives resource owners the incentive to produce the output that generates the most satisfaction for the consumers
   b. results in an equal distribution of income
   c. Both of the above
   d. Neither of the above

_____ 6. Max has annual income of $20 million. Minnie has annual income of $20,000. If each received an additional $1,000 of income:
   a. this clearly would provide Max with more marginal utility, since he obviously likes money more than Minnie.
   b. this clearly would provide Minnie with more marginal utility due to the law of diminishing marginal utility
   c. it is impossible to objectively determine who would receive more marginal utility

_____ 7. Diamonds have a higher price than water because:
    a.  diamonds provide greater total utility than water
    b.  the water that a person drinks has very little utility
    c.  the price of a good is equal to the marginal utility of the last unit consumed
    d.  All of the above

_____ 8. Diamonds are more valuable than water:
    a.  in terms of marginal utility
    b.  in terms of total utility
    c.  Both of the above
    d.  Neither of the above

Complete the table below to answer questions 9. through 13.:

| Units of Y | Good Y Total Utility | Marginal Utility | | Units of Z | Good Z Total Utility | Marginal Utility |
| --- | --- | --- | --- | --- | --- | --- |
| 0 | 0 | X | | 0 | 0 | X |
| 1 | 20 | 20 | | 1 | 10 | 10 |
| 2 | 36 | _ | | 2 | 18 | _ |
| 3 | 48 | _ | | 3 | 24 | _ |
| 4 | 56 | _ | | 4 | 28 | _ |
| 5 | 60 | _ | | 5 | 30 | _ |
| 6 | 62 | _ | | 6 | 31 | _ |

_____ 9. What is the marginal utility of the 3$^{rd}$ unit of Good Y?
    a.  20
    b.  16
    c.  12
    d.  8

_____ 10. What is the marginal utility of the 4$^{th}$ unit of Good Z?
    a.  4
    b.  6
    c.  8
    d.  10

_____ 11. Assuming that the price of both goods is $5 per unit and that Consumer has $15 to spend, what is the utility-maximizing combination of Goods Y and Z?
    a.  3-Y, 0-Z
    b.  2-Y, 1-Z
    c.  1-Y, 2-Z
    d.  0-Y, 3-Z

_____ 12. Assuming that the price of both Goods is $5 per unit and that Consumer has $30 to spend, what is the utility-maximizing combination of Goods Y and Z?
  a. 5 – Y, 1 – Z
  b. 4 – Y, 2 – Z
  c. 3 – Y, 3 – Z
  d. 2 – Y, 4 – Z

_____ 13. Assuming that the price of Good Y increases to $10 per unit and that Consumer still has $30 to spend, what is the utility-maximizing combination of Goods Y and Z?
  a. 3 – Y, 0 – Z
  b. 2 – Y, 2 – Z
  c. 1 – Y, 4 – Z
  d. 0 – Y, 6 – Z

_____ 14. If the government provides an essential good (like bread) free of charge:
  a. this will be efficient because no one is deprived of bread
  b. this will be efficient because everyone can eat as much bread as they like
  c. this will be inefficient because bread will be overconsumed
  d. Both a. and b. above

_____ 15. At the optimal level of any activity:
  a. marginal benefit will be greater than marginal cost
  b. marginal benefit will be less than marginal cost
  c. marginal benefit will be equal to marginal cost
  d. Any of the above are possible

_____ 16. Indifference curves:
  a. show different combinations of two goods that provide equal total utility to a consumer
  b. will slope upward since consumers prefer consuming more units rather than less
  c. will be straight lines since marginal utility from each additional unit consumed is the same
  d. All of the above

_____ 17. For the utility-maximizing combination of units:
  a. the marginal rate of substitution will be the same as the slope of the budget constraint
  b. the combination will be on the indifference curve that is tangent to the budget constraint
  c. Both of the above
  d. Neither of the above

**Problems:**

1.  Explain the law of diminishing marginal utility.

2.  What is the diamond-water paradox and what is its explanation?

3.  Explain the problem with the government providing essential goods free of charge.

4. The graph below shows indifference curves for Goods X and Y for Consumer A.

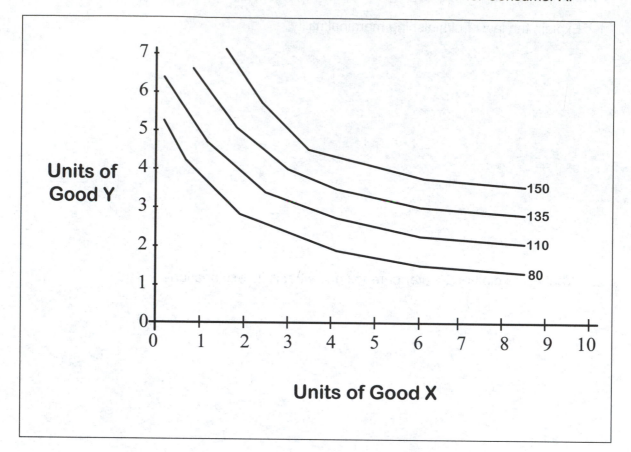

**Units of Good Y**

**Units of Good X**

If Consumer A has income of $18 and the price of Good X is $2 and the price of Good Y is $3:
    a. On the graph above, draw the budget constraint.
    b. What is the utility-maximizing combination of Goods X and Y?
    c. How much total utility does Consumer A receive?
    d. If the marginal utility of the third unit of Good X is 10 utils, what is the marginal utility of the fourth unit of Good Y?

## Answers for Chapter 18

**Fill-in-the-blanks:**
| | |
|---|---|
| 1. Utility | 4. indifference |
| 2. Marginal utility | 5. budget constraint |
| 3. paradox | |

**Multiple Choice:**
| | | |
|---|---|---|
| 1. a. | 7. c. | 13. b. |
| 2. c. | 8. a. | 14. c. |
| 3. c. | 9. c. | 15. c. |
| 4. b. | 10. a. | 16. a. |
| 5. a. | 11. a. | 17. c. |
| 6. c. | 12. b. | |

**Problems:**

1. The law of diminishing marginal utility states that the marginal utility from consuming additional units of a good eventually declines. For example, if a person eats a number of slices of pizza, eventually the marginal utility from each additional slice will decrease.

2. The diamond-water paradox is the observation that essential goods are often lower-priced than non-essential goods. The explanation of the paradox is that the price of a good is equal to the marginal utility of the last unit consumed.

3. If the government provided essential goods free of charge, consumers would overconsume these goods. Consumers would consume these "free" goods up to the quantity where the marginal utility of the goods would be zero. This would be an inefficiently large quantity of consumption, because the marginal cost of producing the goods would be greater than zero.

4. a. See the graph below
   b. 3 units of Good X and 4 units of Good Y
   c. 135 utils
   d. The marginal utility of the fourth unit of Good Y is 15 utils

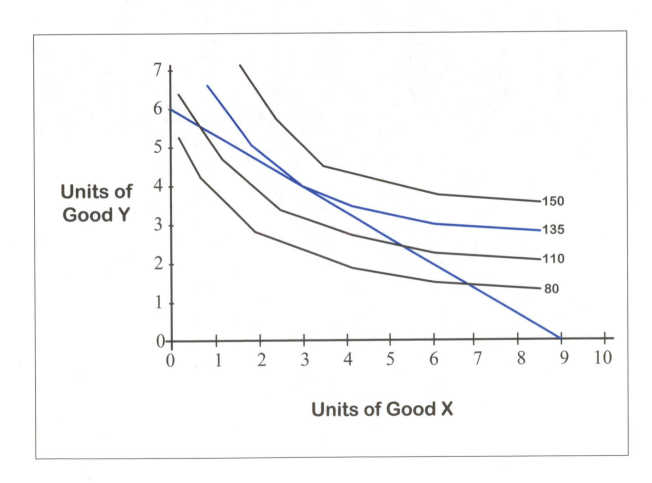

Table for Multiple Choice Questions 3. and 4.:

| Units of Good X | Total Utility | Marginal Utility |
|---|---|---|
| 0 | 0 | X |
| 1 | 30 | 30 |
| 2 | 54 | 24 |
| 3 | 72 | 18 |
| 4 | 84 | 12 |
| 5 | 90 | 6 |
| 6 | 92 | 2 |

Table for Multiple Choice Questions 9. through 13.:

| Units of Y | Good Y Total Utility | Marginal Utility | Units of Z | Good Z Total Utility | Marginal Utility |
|---|---|---|---|---|---|
| 0 | 0 | X | 0 | 0 | X |
| 1 | 20 | 20 | 1 | 10 | 10 |
| 2 | 36 | 16 | 2 | 18 | 8 |
| 3 | 48 | 12 | 3 | 24 | 6 |
| 4 | 56 | 8 | 4 | 28 | 4 |
| 5 | 60 | 4 | 5 | 30 | 2 |
| 6 | 62 | 2 | 6 | 31 | 1 |

# Chapter 19  The Firm

The basic economic problem is scarcity.  Human wants are unlimited.  Resources are limited.  The basic goal in dealing with the problem of scarcity is to produce as much consumer satisfaction as possible with the limited resources available.  To produce as much consumer satisfaction as possible with the limited resources available, society must use its limited resources as efficiently as possible.

Whatever is produced must be produced with as few resources as possible (at the lowest opportunity cost).  Most production in a developed economy takes place through firms; either business firms or nonprofit firms.

**Firm** – an entity that employs resources to produce goods and services.

Most resources (labor, land, capital, entrepreneurship) are owned by households.  For instance, each person owns his or her own labor.  Potentially, all production could take place at the household level.

A great deal of production does take place at the household level; e.g. child care, food preparation, clothes washing, etc.  But most production takes place through firms.  Why does most production take place through firms?


## Firms and Efficiency

Firms are often the best way to organize the limited resources for production.  For many types of production, firms can produce more efficiently (at lower cost) than households.

> **Example 1:**  Juanita produces some of the goods and services that she consumes using her own resources.  She cooks her own meals, cleans her own house, washes her own hair, etc.  But Juanita also purchases goods and services from firms.  She pays a stylist to cut her hair rather than cutting it herself.  She buys food (e.g. fruits and vegetables) at the supermarket rather than growing her own garden.  She buys numerous manufactured goods (e.g. a new refrigerator) rather than making them herself.  Most of the goods and services that she consumes are produced by firms, because she finds it cheaper to buy the goods than to produce them herself.


## Firms and Reduced Transaction Costs

The efficiency advantage that firms have over household production may occur because firms can reduce transaction costs.

**Transaction costs** – the costs of bringing buyers and sellers together for exchanges.

When two parties voluntarily engage in a trade, both parties expect to benefit from the trade.  But if the transaction costs of carrying out the trade are large, the transaction costs may outweigh the benefit of the trade.  A firm may be able to reduce transaction costs, creating more opportunities for mutually beneficial exchanges.

> **Example 2A:** Juanita, living in Tulsa, Oklahoma, wants three pounds of bananas and is willing to pay 80¢ per pound. Lucio, a banana farmer living in Ecuador, is willing to sell bananas for 20¢ per pound. But the transaction costs of carrying out the exchange directly between Juanita and Lucio would outweigh the benefit of the trade. Firms, such as wholesale distributors and supermarkets, can reduce transaction costs and make it possible for Juanita to purchase bananas grown by Lucio.

> **Example 2B:** The transaction costs of buying groceries would be very high if the consumer tried to buy directly from each producer. This might involve a drive to the nearest dairy farm to purchase milk, a drive to the nearest bakery to purchase bread, a drive to the nearest orchard to purchase apples, a flight to Ecuador to purchase bananas, etc. Instead, supermarkets make a variety of groceries available at low transaction costs.

Wal-Mart Corporation, the largest retailer in the world, exists primarily because it is able to reduce transaction costs. Wal-Mart uses its efficient distribution system to make products from all over the world conveniently (and inexpensively) available to the local consumer.

### Firms and Team Production

The efficiency advantage that firms have over household production may occur because team production is more productive than individual production. **Productivity** is measured by output per unit of input.

> **Example 3:** One worker can produce 3 widgets in an hour. The productivity of the one worker is 3 widgets per labor/hour. A team of 10 workers can produce 100 widgets in an hour. The productivity of the team is 10 widgets per labor/hour. In this example, team production is more productive than individual production.

Team production allows for two advantages over individual production:

1. **Specialization of labor.** In individual production, the individual must attempt to master every step in the production process. In team production, each worker may be able to specialize in a specific task. Each worker may become very skilled and productive at his or her specific task.

> **Example 4:** Jeff is hired to work in a refrigerator assembly plant. Jeff's job on the assembly line is installing the back wheels on each refrigerator. Jeff doesn't have to learn how to assemble an entire refrigerator, and can quickly learn to do his specific task very efficiently.

Adam Smith discussed the importance of specialization (division) of labor in Book 1 of "The Wealth of Nations". See the appendix at the end of this chapter.

2. **Extensive use of capital.** Team production may allow for the use of large amounts of highly specialized and highly productive capital. A large assembly plant may include hundreds of millions of dollars worth of capital, making the team of workers employed at the plant highly productive.

> **Example 5:** Juanita is planning a formal dinner party for 40 people. Though Juanita normally does her own cooking, she decides that her kitchen is not equipped for the preparation of such a large and elaborate meal. So Juanita hires a catering firm to prepare the meal. The catering firm has a very large, well-equipped kitchen.

## Shirking in Team Production

In individual production, if an individual is less productive than he or she could be, that individual suffers the consequences. Thus, the individual producer is motivated to be as productive as possible. But individuals employed as part of a team don't always have this motivation. Individuals employed as part of a team may be motivated to avoid their obligations as part of the team.

> **Example 6:** Meg is assigned an individual research report for her Economics class. She works diligently on the report (an analysis of the causes of high textbook prices) and earns a grade of A. Meg is also assigned to a team to prepare a group research project in her Sociology class. Meg calculates that the rest of the team will prepare an adequate report, even if she doesn't participate in preparing the report. Meg devotes her time to her other classes. The team (including Meg) receives a grade of B for the report. Meg has engaged in shirking.

**Shirking** – avoiding the performance of an obligation.

An employee who engages in shirking may still benefit from the other team members' production. The shirking employee may be motivated to engage in activities beneficial to themselves rather than contributing to team production.

Shirking activities might include arriving late for work, taking long breaks, leaving work early, making personal phone calls, surfing the internet, etc. Most of the harm of this shirking may fall on the other members of the team.

Firms often employ managers to oversee teams of employees. One of a manager's duties is to limit shirking behavior and to promote productive behavior. But what is to keep a manager from shirking his or her own duties?

One way to encourage a manager to be diligent to limit the shirking behavior of employees is to make the manager a residual claimant (e.g. with a profit-sharing plan or a bonus based on firm profitability or team productivity). Residual claimants of a firm receive a share of the firm's profits. Some firms take the additional step of making all employees residual claimants.

## The Principal-Agent Problem

The problem of shirking by employees is a specific example of a common problem called the principal-agent problem. An agent is a person who agrees to act for the benefit of another, the principal. In an employment situation, the employee is an agent of the firm. The employee agrees to work for the benefit of the firm.

But humans are by nature self-interested. Any agent who finds a conflict between his or her self-interest and the principal's interest will tend to pursue self-interest. This is the principal-agent problem. Thus, managers try to compel employees to pursue the firm's interest. And business firms sometimes make employees residual claimants so that the employees will have a self-interest in pursuing the firm's goal of profit-maximization.

## Business Firms

Firms are either business firms or nonprofit firms. Business firms are owned by individuals; proprietors, partners, or stockholders. These owners are the residual claimants of the business firm. Business firms come in different legal types, and vary widely in size. The most common legal type of business firm is the proprietorship, but in terms of total sales, corporations are the most important type of business firm.

> **Example 7A:** According to the "Statistical Abstract of the United States: 2008", proprietorships make up 72% of business firms, and have 4% of total sales, partnerships make up 9% of business firms, and have 12% of total sales, and corporations make up 19% of business firms and have 84% of total sales.

Most corporations are small businesses. But the small percentage of corporations that are large provide the majority of total corporate sales.

> **Example 7B:** According to the "Statistical Abstract of the United States: 2008", over 80% of corporations have annual sales of under $1 million. The .5% of corporations with annual sales of over $50 million have 74% of total corporate sales.

## The Chief Goal of Business Firms

All types of business firms are assumed to pursue profit-maximization as their chief goal. It is in the best interest of the residual claimants of a business firm for the firm to achieve maximum profits.

But what about the best interest of the rest of society? Is it in the best interest of society that business firms seek to maximize profits? Generally, yes. In a competitive market, the goal of profit-maximization will compel a business firm to do two things that serve the best interest of society:

1. **The firm will use its resources to produce in response to consumer demand.** Competition forces a profit-seeking firm to be responsive to consumer demand. In a competitive market, a firm that is <u>not</u> responsive to consumer demand will lose customers to its competitors. Producing in response to consumer demand contributes to the goal (in dealing with the basic economic problem of scarcity) of producing as much consumer satisfaction as possible with the limited resources available.

> **Example 8A:** Darla opens a donut shop featuring tofu-based donuts. But consumers find the donuts unappealing. If Darla wants to stay in business and have a chance to earn a profit, she will have to change her donuts in response to consumer demand.

2.  **The firm will use its resources as efficiently as possible.**  The firm must use its resources efficiently in order to minimize production costs and thus maximize profits. Using resources efficiently also contributes to the goal of producing as much consumer satisfaction as possible with the limited resources available.

---

**Example 8B:**  Darla employs a large number of her relatives as employees at her donut shop.  She has the employees place the sprinkles on the donuts one sprinkle at a time. This production technique justifies her large number of employees.  Unfortunately, this inefficient use of labor causes the donuts to be so costly that they are <u>not</u> competitive.  If Darla wants to stay in business and have a chance to earn a profit, she will have to use her resources more efficiently.

---

## Legal Types of Business Firms

One of the key characteristics of a business firm is its legal type.  Most business firms are proprietorships, partnerships, or corporations.  Each of these legal types of business firm is discussed over the next few pages:

**Proprietorship** – a firm owned and operated by one individual.

Proprietorships are the most common type of business firm.  As mentioned previously, proprietorships make up over 70 percent of business firms.  One reason proprietorships are so common is that they are easy to form and to dissolve.

In many cases, all that is required to form a proprietorship is for the proprietor to bring the necessary resources together and begin conducting business.  Certain regulatory requirements may have to be met as well.  To dissolve a proprietorship, the proprietor fulfills any remaining obligations of the firm and then stops conducting business.

---

**Example 9:**  A huge snowstorm hits Springfield.  Homer sees an opportunity to make a profit.  He invests $10,000 in a used snowplow and starts a driveway clearing business. Homer can form his proprietorship by simply bringing the necessary resources together and offering his services to the public.  If Homer decides to dissolve his proprietorship, he will simply fulfill any remaining obligations and then stop offering his services to the public.

---

Another advantage of the proprietorship is the direct connection between ownership and control.  The owner controls the business and can quickly make decisions in pursuit of self-interest without the need to consult others.

A major disadvantage of the proprietorship is that the proprietor has unlimited liability. Unlimited liability means that the proprietor is personally liable for the debts of the proprietorship.  The proprietor's personal assets are subject to the business debts. Thus, a person who invests $10,000 to start a proprietorship is putting at risk the $10,000 invested in the business <u>and</u> all the proprietor's other assets.

> **Example 10:** Homer invests $10,000 in a used snowplow to start a driveway clearing business. Unfortunately, Homer carelessly plows into a parked Rolls Royce. Homer offers the car's owner (a Mr. Burns) the snowplow as compensation for the destroyed car. Mr. Burns sues Homer's business and wins a $150,000 judgment. Homer will have to pay the business debt out of his personal assets.

Other disadvantages of the proprietorship include:

1. **Difficulty in raising large amounts of financial capital.** Proprietorships rely mainly on self-financing and borrowing from financial institutions for their financial capital. A proprietor's ability to self-finance is limited to his or her personal wealth. And financial institutions may be hesitant to make large loans to proprietorships. Most proprietorships are small businesses and may have difficulty expanding.

2. **Proprietorships end with the death of the proprietor.** Thus, a proprietorship lacks the permanent nature of a corporation.

**Partnership** – a firm owned and operated by two or more co-owners.

An advantage of partnerships over proprietorships is the possibility of specialization. One partner may be better at one aspect of the business (e.g. production), while another partner may be better at another aspect (e.g. sales). Each partner can specialize in his or her area of expertise.

> **Example 11:** Homer enters into a partnership with his best friend, Barney. The partnership operates a small winery. Homer, with his delightful personality, specializes in sales. Barney, who has expertise in all things alcoholic, specializes in production.

Like proprietorships, partnerships are fairly easy to form. The partners will need to enter into a partnership agreement detailing each partner's contributions to the partnership, responsibilities, and share of profits and losses. This agreement should be in writing.

The major disadvantage of the partnership is that the partners have unlimited liability. This is an even bigger problem for partners than for proprietors. A partner is liable for <u>all</u> debts incurred by the partnership, including debts arising from the actions of the other partners.

A partner can face financial ruin due to the incompetence, dishonesty, or bad luck of the other partners. A person who enters into a partnership is entrusting his or her life savings to the other partners. Thus, most partnerships have only two partners.

> **Example 12:** Homer invests $10,000 in a partnership that operates a small winery. Homer's partner is his best friend, Barney. Unfortunately, due to Barney's incompetence, the partnership produces a batch of tainted wine. The persons injured by the tainted wine file a lawsuit against the partnership and win a judgment for $300,000. Barney has no assets, so Homer will have to pay the entire business debt out of his personal assets.

**Corporation** – an organization owned by stockholders that is considered a legal person, separate from its owners.

To "incorporate" means "to give a body to". When a state grants a firm a corporate charter it is creating a new legal person; the corporation. As a separate legal person, a corporation can own property, enter into contracts, commit crimes, and be personally liable for its own debts.

Because the corporation is a separate legal person, the stockholders (owners) of the corporation have limited liability. Limited liability means that the stockholders are not personally liable for the debts of the corporation. Thus, a person who invests $10,000 in corporate stock is putting at risk only the $10,000 invested in the business.

> **Example 13:** Homer invests $10,000 in a corporation that produces nuclear power. Unfortunately, due to the incompetence of an unidentified employee in Sector 7G of the plant, a nuclear accident occurs. The corporation is sued and loses a judgment for $3,000,000,000. The corporation files for bankruptcy. Homer's stock becomes worthless. But, Homer is not liable for the debts of the corporation.

Other advantages of the corporation include:

1. **Relative ease in raising large amounts of financial capital.** Limited liability encourages investment in corporate stock. Some corporations have hundreds of thousands of stockholders.

> **Example 14:** In 2008, the Visa, Inc. initial public offering raised $17.9 billion.

2. **Corporations do not end with the death of a stockholder.** Since a corporation is a separate legal person, it can continue to exist as stockholders die or sell their stock to other investors.

Despite the advantages of corporations, most small businesses are not incorporated. Compared to proprietorships or partnerships, corporations have a number of disadvantages:

1. **Corporations are relatively complex and expensive to organize, to operate, and to dissolve.**

> **Example 15:** Homer decides to incorporate his driveway clearing business. He hires an attorney (Lionel Hutz) to prepare articles of incorporation. The articles of incorporation must be filed with the Secretary of State in the state of incorporation. Attorney Hutz also assists Homer in preparing corporate bylaws. The corporation has to pay an initial incorporation fee and pay annual filing fees. The corporation will be required to hold periodic shareholder meetings and meetings of the board of directors, and to record minutes of these meetings.

2. **Corporations are subject to double taxation.** The net income of a corporation is subject to corporate income tax. Any after-tax income that is distributed to the stockholders as dividends will be taxable as personal income to the stockholders.

> **Example 16:** Homer forms a driveway clearing business as a proprietorship. During its first year in operation, the proprietorship has a profit of $30,000. The profit will be taxable income for Homer, reported on his personal income tax return. After paying the tax, Homer may use the after-tax profit as he wishes. In the next year, Homer incorporates the business. The corporation has a profit of $30,000. The corporation will pay corporate income tax on its profit. If the after-tax profit is distributed to Homer as a dividend, Homer will pay personal income tax on the dividend. Thus, the income is taxed twice; once at the corporate level, and a second time at the stockholder level.

3. **Corporations are subject to problems caused by separation of ownership and control.** The owners of a corporation are its stockholders. Control of corporate activities is in the hands of the corporate managers. This is an example of the principal-agent problem discussed earlier in this chapter. Corporate managers are agents of the stockholders, and should pursue the goals of the stockholders. But the managers may pursue their own goals (e.g. high salaries, luxurious offices, job security, etc.), rather than the goals of the stockholders (e.g. profit-maximization).

> **Example 17A:** Bernard Ebbers, former CEO of WorldCom, was convicted in March, 2005 of fraud, conspiracy, and other charges. WorldCom went into bankruptcy in 2002, in the largest bankruptcy case in U.S. history.

> **Example 17B:** Dennis Kozlowski, former CEO of Tyco International, was convicted in June, 2005 of grand larceny, falsifying business records, securities fraud, and other charges. Kozlowski and a co-defendant unjustly enriched themselves by nearly $600 million.

## Financing Business Activity

Business firms often need to raise financial capital, especially when starting or expanding the firm. Proprietorships and partnerships rely mainly on two types of financing:

1. **Self-financing.** The owners contribute personal assets to the firm.

2. **Borrowing from financial institutions.** The owners take out loans from banks, credit unions, etc.

Corporations also use self-financing. The initial stockholders contribute money or other assets in exchange for stock. The corporation may re-invest yearly profits in the business. Corporations also borrow from financial institutions.

Corporations have two additional sources of financial capital:

1. **Corporations can issue additional shares of stock.** The new stockholders receive an ownership interest in the corporation.

> **Example 18A:** The AT&T Wireless Group initial public offering raised $10.6 billion in 2000, as 360 million new shares of stock were issued.

2. **Corporations can sell bonds.** A bond is a debt obligation. The person who buys the bond is making a loan to the corporation, which the corporation promises to repay in the future, with interest.

> **Example 18B:** In September, 2007, Kohl's Corporation issued $650 million in 10-year bonds and $350 million in 30-year bonds.

These additional sources of financing make it possible for corporations to become extremely large.

> **Example 19:** For 2007, Wal-Mart Corporation (the largest in the world) had sales revenue of $379 billion. This was similar to the amount of GDP for the nations of Belgium ($376 billion), Malaysia ($357 billion) and Venezuela ($335 billion).

## The Balance Sheet of a Business Firm

The balance sheet of a business firm shows the assets, liabilities, and net worth of the firm. The **net worth** of a firm is equal to the firm's assets minus its liabilities. Thus, a firm with assets of $150 million and liabilities of $130 million would have a net worth of $20 million.

> **Example 20:** In 2007, Wal-Mart Corporation had assets of $163,514 million and liabilities of $98,906 million, for a net worth of $64,608 million.

## Nonprofit Firms

Not all production at the firm level is done by profit-seeking business firms. Much production takes place through nonprofit firms such as government agencies, schools, churches, and charitable organizations.

Nonprofit firms have no residual claimants. There are no "owners" of a nonprofit firm to seek a share of profits. If a nonprofit firm has excess funds at the end of its budget year, those funds carry over to the budget for the next year.

The absence of residual claimants in nonprofit firms is likely to lead to:

1. **Employees engaging in more shirking in nonprofit firms than in profit-seeking firms.** Managers in nonprofit firms may be less diligent to limit shirking behavior than managers in business firms. Nonprofit managers are not residual claimants, nor are their actions being overseen by residual claimants.

2. **Top administrators spending any excess funds within the firm to benefit themselves.** The administrators of a nonprofit firm are agents of the firm and are supposed to pursue the objectives of the firm. But the actions of top administrators are not overseen by residual claimants. The top administrators may pursue their own objectives by using any excess funds to; inflate their own salaries, enlarge their staffs, upgrade their office space, embark on unnecessary travel, etc.

> **Example 21:** William Aramony headed the United Way for 22 years before resigning in 1992. He was convicted of fraud and conspiracy charges in 1995. Prosecutors alleged that Aramony spent hundreds of thousands of dollars of United Way money to finance his womanizing lifestyle and to pay for trips to such destinations as Las Vegas, Paris, and London.

Nonprofit firms can be classified as either private or public. A private nonprofit firm is financed by the voluntary actions of private individuals (customers and contributors). A public nonprofit firm is financed by involuntary contributions (taxes).

Since a private nonprofit firm relies on the voluntary actions of customers and contributors, a private nonprofit firm will be very responsive to their desires. A public nonprofit firm does not have to be as responsive to the desires of taxpayers, since their support is involuntary.

> **Example 22:** Vladimir and Estragon organize a nonprofit community theater. In its first year, the theater is a private nonprofit firm. It is financed by ticket sales and by private donations from supporters of the theater. To keep its customers and donors happy, the theater performs popular plays. In its second year, the theater receives a government grant to cover its operating costs. The theater is now a public nonprofit firm and is free to perform more "experimental" plays, with less concern about appealing to the public tastes.

### Appendix: Book Review – "The Wealth of Nations, Book 1"

In the introduction to his 1776 book "An Inquiry into the Nature and Causes of the Wealth of Nations", Adam Smith explains that the standard of living in a nation depends on the productivity of its labor. (This is the same conclusion reached in 2004 by "The Power of Productivity". See the appendix at the end of Chapter 15.) Smith asserts that the greatest improvement in the productivity of labor is caused by the division (specialization) of labor.

Chapter 1 of Book 1 of "The Wealth of Nations" is entitled, "Of the Division of Labor". Smith begins the chapter with an example of the division of labor that has become famous, the pin factory:

> "...the way in which this business is now carried on,...it is divided into a number of branches...One man draws out the wire, another straights it, a third cuts it, a fourth points it, a fifth grinds it at the top for receiving the head; to make the head requires two or three distinct operations; to put it on, is a peculiar business, to whiten the pins is another; it is even a trade by itself to put them into the paper; and the important business of making a pin is, in this manner, divided into about eighteen distinct operations..."

Smith went on to state that a factory of ten workers, taking advantage of division of labor, could produce about forty-eight thousand pins in a day. Working separately, each worker could not have produced more than twenty pins in a day, and maybe not even one.

Smith asserts that the division of labor increases labor productivity for three reasons:

1. **"The increase of dexterity in every particular workman."** The division of labor reduces each worker's business to one simple operation and makes that operation the sole employment of the worker's life. Naturally, this greatly increases the dexterity of the worker.

> **Example 23:** A blacksmith who produces a wide variety of products (e.g. nails, horseshoes, knives, gates, swords, farm implements, etc.) is not likely to be highly productive in any particular type of production. A blacksmith who specializes in making nails is likely to become very expert and productive in nail production.

2. **"The saving of the time which is commonly lost in passing from one species of work to another."**

> **Example 24:** A blacksmith who produces a wide variety of products will lose some time in each change of production. Each transition from producing nails to producing horseshoes to producing farm implements, etc. will result in lost time.

3. **"The invention of a great number of machines which facilitate and abridge labour, and enable one man to do the work of many."** A worker concentrating on one type of production is more likely to discover superior methods of production than a worker whose efforts are spread over many types of production.

> **Example 25:** A blacksmith who produces only nails is more likely to discover a better method of producing nails or to invent machinery that enhances nail production than a blacksmith who produces a wide variety of products.

Smith further observes that the division of labor means that even the poorer members of society benefit from the industry of a great number of people.

> **Example 26:** A day-laborer in Adam Smith's Scotland purchases a pair of boots. How many people have contributed to the production of the boots? The cobbler – who manufactures the boots, the blacksmith – who produces the hobnails, the tanner – who tans the leather, the rancher – who raises the cattle (source of the leather), the collier – who mines the coal to fuel the blacksmith's forge, the miner – who mines the iron ore that the blacksmith turns into hobnails, etc.

In Chapter 2 of Book 1, Smith explains that the division of labor is a consequence of the human propensity to trade. This propensity to trade arises from the unique neediness of human beings:

> "In almost every other race of animals each individual, when it is grown up to maturity, is entirely independent, and in its natural state has occasion for the assistance of no other living creature. But man has almost constant occasion for the help of his brethren,…Whoever offers to another a bargain of any kind, proposes to do this. Give me that which I want, and you shall have this which you want,…it is in this manner that we obtain from one another the far greater part of those good offices which we stand in need of."

In Chapter 3 of Book 1, Smith explains that the extent of the division of labor is limited by the extent of the market. In a small market, a worker will not be able to specialize in only one type of production because the market demand for that type of production will not be large enough to consume all that the worker could produce.

**Example 27:** A blacksmith employed in a small village would not be able to specialize in producing only nails, because the village demand for nails would be less than the amount the blacksmith could produce. Instead, the blacksmith will produce a variety of products in accordance with the market demand.

Access to low-cost transportation can extend a market and allow for division of labor. Smith explains that this is the reason why economic development has occurred first along seacoasts and navigable rivers. The low cost of water-carriage compared to land-carriage creates a more extensive market and allows for more division of labor. In Smith's words:

> "As by means of water-carriage a more extensive market is opened to every sort of industry than what land-carriage alone can afford it, so it is upon the sea-coast, and along the banks of navigable rivers, that industry of every kind naturally begins to subdivide and improve itself…"

Even in a modern economy, large markets can benefit more from the division of labor than small markets and are thus likely to enjoy a higher standard of living. Population density is a factor determining the size of a market. Greater population density increases the size of a market, and is associated with a higher standard of living.

**Example 28:** The five states with the highest per capita income in 2007 (see Chapter 5 of this book) had an average population density of about 720 people per square mile. The five states with the lowest per capita income had an average population density of about 85 people per square mile.

## Appendix: Think Like an Economist – Hiring an Attorney

You live in a small town and you need an attorney. Aunt Marcella has died and you are the executor of her rather complicated estate. You need an attorney who is an expert at probate work to help you with probating the will.

You could hire one of the two attorneys in your small town, or you could hire one of the hundreds of attorneys from the big city down the highway. Thinking like an economist, will you want to hire a small town attorney or a big city attorney to help you with this complicated estate, and why?

## Questions for Chapter 19

### Fill-in-the-blanks:

1. A _____ is an entity that employs resources to produce goods and services.

2. _____ costs are the costs of bringing buyers and sellers together for exchanges.

3. _____ is measured as output per unit of input.

4. _____ is avoiding the performance of an obligation.

5. A _____ is a firm owned and operated by one individual.

6. A _____ is a firm owned and operated by two or more co-owners.

7. A _____ is an organization owned by stockholders that is considered a legal person, separate from its owners.

8. The _____ _____ of a firm is equal to the firm's assets minus its liabilities.

### Multiple Choice:

_____ 1. Firms may be able to produce more efficiently than households because:
    a. firms can increase transaction costs
    b. team production may be more productive than individual production
    c. firms own most resources
    d. All of the above

_____ 2. Team production may be more productive than individual production because:
    a. team production allows for specialization of labor
    b. team production allows for extensive use of capital
    c. team members are less likely to engage in shirking
    d. Both a. and b. above

_____ 3. A manager who is a residual claimant:
    a. is more likely to shirk than a manager who is <u>not</u> a residual claimant
    b. is entitled to receive a share of the firm's profits
    c. is more likely to be diligent to monitor shirking
    d. Both b. and c. above

_____ 4. An agent:
    a. is a person who agrees to act for the benefit of another
    b. may pursue self-interest against the interest of the principal
    c. Both of the above
    d. Neither of the above

_____ 5. Corporations have --% of total sales:
   a. 95%
   b. 84%
   c. 72%
   d. 58%

_____ 6. The chief goal of all business firms is assumed to be:
   a. sales maximization
   b. market share maximization
   c. profit-maximization
   d. maximum cost efficiency

_____ 7. In a competitive market, the goal of profit-maximization will compel a business firm to:
   a. disregard consumer demand
   b. use its resources as efficiently as possible
   c. go against the best interest of society
   d. All of the above

_____ 8. The most common legal type of business firm is the:
   a. proprietorship
   b. partnership
   c. corporation
   d. nonprofit firm

_____ 9. Unlimited liability means that a proprietor:
   a. is personally liable for the debts of the proprietorship
   b. is putting at risk only the amount invested in the business
   c. is not liable for the debts of the proprietorship
   d. Both b. and c. above

_____ 10. Among the disadvantages of a proprietorship are:
   a. proprietorships end with the death of the proprietor
   b. ease of raising large amounts of financial capital
   c. limited liability
   d. All of the above

_____ 11. An advantage of a partnership compared to a proprietorship is:
   a. limited liability
   b. the possibility of specialization
   c. Both of the above
   d. Neither of the above

_____ 12. A corporation:
   a. has the advantage of limited liability
   b. has difficulty in raising large amounts of financial capital
   c. ends with the death of the owners
   d. All of the above

_____ 13. Corporations:
   a.  are complex to form, to operate, and to dissolve
   b.  are subject to double taxation
   c.  are subject to problems caused by separation of ownership and control
   d.  All of the above

_____ 14. Corporate managers:
   a.  are agents of the stockholders
   b.  will always pursue the stockholders' goal of profit-maximization
   c.  Both of the above
   d.  Neither of the above

_____ 15. A corporate bond:
   a.  is the same as a share of stock
   b.  is an ownership interest in the corporation
   c.  is a debt obligation of the corporation
   d.  Both a. and b. above

_____ 16. If Firm Y has assets of $350 million and liabilities of $310 million, its net worth is:
   a.  $-40 million
   b.  $40 million
   c.  $350 million
   d.  $660 million

_____ 17. A difference between private nonprofit firms and public nonprofit firms is:
   a.  private nonprofit firms have residual claimants
   b.  private nonprofit firms are financed by taxes
   c.  private nonprofit firms are more responsive to the desires of their customers and contributors
   d.  All of the above

_____ 18. According to "The Wealth of Nations", a nation's standard of living depends on:
   a.  the fruitfulness of its land
   b.  the abundance of its mineral resources
   c.  the productivity of its labor
   d.  All of the above

_____ 19. According to Adam Smith, the human propensity to trade arises:
   a.  from the unique neediness of human beings
   b.  due to natural self-sufficiency of human beings
   c.  because of the natural human instinct to defraud one another
   d.  All of the above

_____ 20. According to Adam Smith, the extent of the division of labor will be increased:
   a.  by an increase in the size of the market
   b.  by a decrease in transportation costs
   c.  Both of the above
   d.  Neither of the above

_____ 21. Per capita income in U.S. states:
   a. tends to be directly related to population density
   b. tends to be inversely related to population density
   c. tends to be unaffected by population density

**Problems:**

1.  List the two advantages that team production allows over individual production.

2.  In a competitive market, the goal of profit-maximization will compel a business firm to do what two things that serve the best interest of society?

3.  Explain why unlimited liability is such a big problem for partners.

4.  Explain what limited liability means to the stockholders of a corporation.

5. List two things that the absence of residual claimants in nonprofit firms is likely to lead to.

6. List the three reasons that division of labor increases labor productivity, according to Adam Smith.

## Answers for Chapter 19

**Fill-in-the-blanks:**

| | |
|---|---|
| 1. firm | 5. proprietorship |
| 2. Transaction | 6. partnership |
| 3. Productivity | 7. corporation |
| 4. Shirking | 8. net worth |

**Multiple Choice:**

| | | |
|---|---|---|
| 1. b. | 8. a. | 15. c. |
| 2. d. | 9. a. | 16. b. |
| 3. d. | 10. a. | 17. c. |
| 4. c. | 11. b. | 18. c. |
| 5. b. | 12. a. | 19. a. |
| 6. c. | 13. d. | 20. c. |
| 7. b. | 14. a. | 21. a. |

The Firm

**Problems:**

1. Two advantages of team production over individual production are:
   (1) Specialization of labor
   (2) Extensive use of capital

2. In a competitive market, the goal of profit-maximization will compel business firms to do two things that serve the best interest of society:
   (1) The firm will use its resources to produce in response to consumer demand
   (2) The firm will use its resources as efficiently as possible

3. A partner in a partnership has unlimited liability and is liable for <u>all</u> debts incurred by the partnership, including debts arising from the actions of the other partners. A partner can face financial ruin due to the incompetence, dishonesty, or bad luck of the other partners. A person who enters into a partnership is trusting his or her life savings to the other partners.

4. Because a corporation is a separate legal person, the stockholders (owners) of a corporation have limited liability. Limited liability means that the stockholders are <u>not</u> personally liable for the debts of the corporation. Thus, a person who invests money in corporate stock is putting at risk only the amount of money invested in the business.

5. The absence of residual claimants in nonprofit firms is likely to lead to :
   (1) Employees engaging in more shirking in nonprofit firms than in profit-seeking firms.
   (2) Top administrators spending any excess funds within the firm to benefit themselves.

6. According to Adam Smith, the division of labor increases labor productivity for three reasons:
   (1) "The increase of dexterity in every particular workman."
   (2) "The saving of the time which is commonly lost in passing from one species of work to another."
   (3) "The invention of a great number of machines which facilitate and abridge labour, and enable one man to do the work of many."

**Answer to Think Like an Economist:**

You will want to hire an attorney from the big city. Neither of the small town attorneys is likely to specialize in probate work. Because of the small market, each small town attorney is likely to do a wide variety of legal work. Division of labor is limited by the extent of the market. You are more likely to find an attorney in the big city who specializes in (and is thus an expert in) probate work.

# Chapter 20  Production and Costs

The basic economic problem is scarcity.  Human wants are unlimited.  Resources are limited.  The basic goal in dealing with the problem of scarcity is to produce as much consumer satisfaction as possible with the limited resources available.  To achieve this goal, society must use its limited resources as efficiently as possible.  Whatever is produced must be produced with as few resources as possible (at the lowest opportunity cost).  This chapter examines production and the costs of production.

## Explicit Costs versus Implicit Costs

Remember from Chapter 1 that **opportunity cost** is the value of the best alternative surrendered when a choice is made.  Sometimes opportunity cost involves an actual expenditure of money.  This is an explicit cost.  Wage expense, utilities expense, rent expense, and tax expense are examples of explicit costs.

But opportunity cost can also be incurred without an expenditure of money.  This is an implicit cost.  The value of a business owner's labor devoted to the business is an example of an implicit cost.

> **Example 1:**  Professor D. Imwit buys his son's collection of old video games for $300.  The next Saturday, Professor Imwit sets up shop in a parking lot, selling the video games out of the trunk of his car.  Eight hours later, Professor Imwit has sold every video game for a grand total of $320.  Professor Imwit's explicit costs are the $300 that he paid for the video games and the gasoline he burned driving to and from the parking lot.  His implicit cost is the value of eight hours of his labor.

## Accounting Profit versus Economic Profit

Accounting profit is the difference between total revenue and explicit costs.  Thus, the formula:

### Accounting Profit = Total Revenue – Explicit Costs

Economic profit is the difference between total revenue and total opportunity costs, including both explicit and implicit costs.  Thus, the formula:

### Economic Profit = Total Revenue – Total Opportunity Costs (explicit and implicit)

> **Example 2A:**  Cheryl works as a chef, earning an annual salary of $45,000.  She decides to quit her job and open her own restaurant.  In her first year as a proprietor, her total revenue is $325,000 and her explicit costs are $275,000, leaving her with an accounting profit of $50,000.  But after subtracting her implicit costs (the $45,000 she could earn in her best alternative), her economic profit is only $5,000.

Is Cheryl's small economic profit in Example 2A an indication that she made a bad choice in quitting her job? On the contrary, even a small economic profit is very good.  It means that she is doing better than her best alternative.  If she were only doing as well as her best alternative, she would have zero economic profit. Zero economic profit does not mean zero accounting profit. Zero economic profit is considered a normal profit.

> **Example 2B:** Assume that Cheryl, from Example 2A, does not do quite as well as a restaurant owner. She earns an accounting profit of only $42,000. This would leave her with an economic loss of $3,000. She is not doing as well as her best alternative. If Cheryl's only goal is profit-maximization, then she was better off as an employee than she is as a proprietor.

An economic loss does not necessarily indicate that a person is headed for bankruptcy. But it does indicate that a better alternative exists. A profit-maximizing producer will tend to move to the best alternative available and leave a market that yields economic loss.


## Sunk Cost

In making economic decisions, the benefits and costs associated with the decision are considered. But what if a cost has already been incurred and cannot be changed by the current decision? Should such a cost influence the current decision? No. Such a cost is a sunk cost.

**Sunk cost** – a past cost that cannot be changed by current decisions.

> **Example 3:** Poppy's Paper Products, Inc. has spent $20,000 to produce personalized stationary for EFG Co. EFG has now filed for bankruptcy and will not be using or paying for the stationary. Poppy's can spend $3,000 altering the stationary and then can sell it to FGH Co. for $5,000. Or Poppy's can throw the stationary away. As Poppy's decides what to do with the stationary, how important is the $20,000 cost already incurred? Not at all important. The $20,000 is a sunk cost. Poppy's should alter the stationary and sell it to FGH Co. The revenue from this choice ($5,000) exceeds the cost incurred because of this choice ($3,000).

A sunk cost is a past cost that cannot be changed by current decisions. Thus, a sunk cost should not influence current decisions. But we humans have a hard time forgetting about sunk costs.

> **Example 4:** Bernard endures the first half of a terribly boring play. At the intermission, he is considering going home. Will Bernard's decision be affected by whether he paid $2 for his ticket or $100? Should his decision be affected by the ticket price?

If a person allows a sunk cost to influence a current decision, he or she is more likely to make a bad current decision, as illustrated in the dialogue below:

Julia: How did you like that new French restaurant?
Emeril: Not much.
Julia: Really? What happened?
Emeril: I ordered some dish that was terrible. I don't know what it was, but it tasted
      awful. I wouldn't want it again if it were free.
Julia: Maybe it's an acquired taste. How many bites did you try?
Emeril: Oh, I choked down the whole dish. I had to -- I paid fifty bucks for it!

## Short Run Production versus Long Run Production

Production of goods and services requires resources (inputs). In a limited amount of time, some of these inputs will be fixed in amount. This is the short run.

**Short run** - a period in which at least one input is fixed.

> **Example 5A:** Robin Birdwell starts a business building birdhouses. Birdwell rents a small shop in an industrial park. The rental on the shop is $1,200 per month under a six month lease. For the next six months, the shop is a fixed input. Birdwell's short run lasts six months.

After a sufficient amount of time has passed, all inputs can be varied. This is the long run.

**Long run** - a period in which all inputs can be varied.

In Example 5A, at the end of six months, Birdwell will have a long run decision to make. The rental of the original shop can be continued, a new shop can be rented, or Birdwell can get out of the birdhouse building business altogether. Long run decisions are very important, but most production decisions are made in the short run. This chapter focuses on short run production.

> **Example 5B:** Robin Birdwell begins production of birdhouses. The most important variable input is labor. Experiments with different numbers of workers give the following results:
>
> | Workers | Total Product | Marginal Physical Product |
> |---------|---------------|---------------------------|
> | 0 | 0 | X |
> | 1 | 12 | 12 |
> | 2 | 26 | 14 |
> | 3 | 36 | 10 |
> | 4 | 42 | 6 |
> | 5 | 44 | 2 |

Birdwell finds that one worker can produce 12 birdhouses per day. Two workers can produce 26 birdhouses, more than twice as many birdhouses as only one worker. It turns out that there are efficiency advantages of having two workers instead of only one.

Greater efficiency often occurs as workers are initially added to production. The increased number of workers allows for more specialization of labor. Thus, the marginal physical product of the second worker (14) is greater than the marginal physical product of the first worker (12).

**Marginal physical product (MPP)** – the change in output with one additional unit of input.

From the third worker on, the MPP of each additional worker declines. This is because Birdwell is adding additional workers to a fixed amount of shop, and is confronting the law of diminishing marginal returns.

**Law of diminishing marginal returns** – as larger amounts of a variable input are combined with fixed inputs, eventually the marginal physical product of the variable input declines.

Birdwell runs into the law of diminishing marginal returns with the third worker. If Birdwell's shop were larger, the law of diminishing marginal returns would <u>not</u> have been encountered at such a small amount of labor. But, since the shop is a fixed input, eventually diminishing marginal returns would have occurred as additional workers were added.

### Diminishing Marginal Returns and Marginal Cost

To produce additional units of output, additional units of the variable input must be added to production. This causes an increase in variable cost and total cost. The change in total cost (and variable cost) that results from producing an additional unit of output is the marginal cost of production.

**Marginal cost** – the change in total cost that results from producing an additional unit of output.

When production reaches the point of diminishing marginal returns, the marginal cost of production will begin to rise. With diminishing marginal returns, the marginal physical product of the variable input decreases. Thus, larger amounts of the variable input must be added to production in order to produce the additional output.

The relationship between diminishing marginal returns and increasing marginal cost is illustrated in the example below:

**Example 5C:** Birdwell hires workers to build birdhouses at a daily wage of $100 per worker. The table below shows the marginal physical product of each worker and the marginal cost of the additional birdhouses produced (calculated as the $100 cost of each additional worker divided by the MPP of each additional worker). As the MPP decreases, the marginal cost increases.

| Workers | Wage | MPP | Marginal Cost |
|---------|------|-----|---------------|
| 0 | $100 | X | X |
| 1 | 100 | 12 | $8.33 |
| 2 | 100 | 14 | 7.14 |
| 3 | 100 | 10 | 10.00 |
| 4 | 100 | 6 | 16.67 |
| 5 | 100 | 2 | 50.00 |

## Fixed Costs versus Variable Costs

In short run production, at least one input is fixed in amount. The costs associated with a fixed input do <u>not</u> change as output is changed, and are called fixed costs.

**Fixed costs** – costs that do <u>not</u> vary with output.

In Example 5A, the $1200 per month rent on Robin Birdwell's shop is a fixed cost. Whether Birdwell produces zero birdhouses each day, or forty-four, the $1200 monthly rent does <u>not</u> change.

As short run production is increased, the amount of variable inputs used in production must be increased. Thus, the costs associated with variable inputs (variable costs) increase with output.

**Variable costs** – costs that vary with output.

In Example 5B, the labor cost incurred by Robin Birdwell is a variable cost. The more birdhouses that are produced each day, the more workers that will be required, and the greater the labor costs.

For simplicity, we will assume that all costs are either fixed or variable. Thus, the sum of fixed costs and variable costs equals total cost.

**Total cost** – the sum of fixed and variable costs.


## Average Costs of Production

Average production costs are calculated by dividing the specific type of production cost by the quantity of output produced. Thus the following formulas:

**Average total cost (ATC) = total cost ÷ quantity of output**

**Average fixed cost (AFC) = fixed costs ÷ quantity of output**

**Average variable cost (AVC) = variable costs ÷ quantity of output**

Just as the sum of fixed costs and variable costs equals total cost, the sum of average fixed cost and average variable cost equals average total cost.

**Average fixed cost + Average variable cost = Average total cost**

> **Example 6:** Robin Birdwell starts a new business building luxury birdhouses. The fixed cost (rental on a shop) is $120 per day. The primary variable input is labor. The maximum number of luxury birdhouses that can be produced in the shop each day is eight. Birdwell incurs the following production costs:

| Birdhouse Quantity | Total Cost | Fixed Cost | Variable Cost | Marginal Cost | AFC | AVC | ATC |
|---|---|---|---|---|---|---|---|
| 0 | $120 | $120 | $0 | X | X | X | X |
| 1 | 160 | 120 | 40 | $40 | $120 | $40 | $160 |
| 2 | 190 | 120 | 70 | 30 | 60 | 35 | 95 |
| 3 | 230 | 120 | 110 | 40 | 40 | 37 | 77 |
| 4 | 285 | 120 | 165 | 55 | 30 | 41 | 71 |
| 5 | 360 | 120 | 240 | 75 | 24 | 48 | 72 |
| 6 | 460 | 120 | 340 | 100 | 20 | 57 | 77 |
| 7 | 590 | 120 | 470 | 130 | 17 | 67 | 84 |
| 8 | 755 | 120 | 635 | 165 | 15 | 79 | 94 |

Notice that marginal cost initially decreases, indicating an efficiency advantage from producing two birdhouses instead of only one. As mentioned earlier in this chapter, greater efficiency often occurs as workers are initially added to production. The increased number of workers allows for more specialization of labor. But with the third birdhouse, the law of diminishing marginal returns sets in, and the marginal cost begins to increase.

The average fixed cost decreases as additional units of output are produced. This will always be the case, as fixed costs are being spread over an increasing amount of output.

The average variable cost initially decreases, for the same reason that marginal cost initially decreases. But from the third birdhouse onward, the average variable cost increases due to the law of diminishing marginal returns.

The average total cost is the sum of the average fixed cost and the average variable cost. The average total cost initially decreases, mainly due to the rapid decrease in average fixed cost. Eventually, the effect of diminishing marginal returns causes average variable cost to increase more rapidly than average fixed cost is decreasing. This causes average total cost to increase.

The marginal cost, average fixed cost, average variable cost, and average total cost curves are illustrated on the graph on the next page. Notice from the graph that the marginal cost curve eventually slopes upward (from unit two onward). This is because, as discussed earlier, diminishing marginal returns causes increasing marginal cost.

Also, notice that the marginal cost curve intersects the ATC curve and the AVC curve at their minimum points. This will always be the case. Marginal cost is the change in total cost (and variable cost) that results from producing an additional unit of output. If the marginal cost of the additional output is less than the ATC (or the AVC), the ATC (or the AVC) will decrease. If the marginal cost is greater than the ATC (or the AVC), the ATC (or the AVC) will increase.

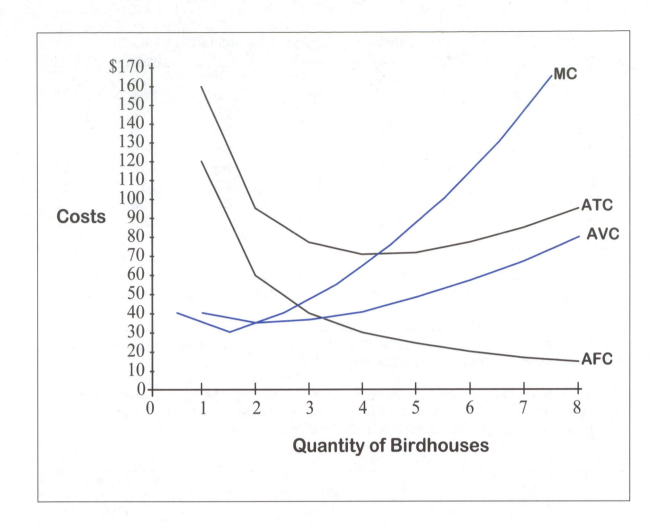

## Appendix: Total Revenue, Total Cost, and Break-Even

This chapter has focused on production and costs of production. Emphasis has been placed on the marginal cost of production and the average costs of production. These costs will be emphasized in Chapter 21 as we look at the profit-maximization rule.

Our understanding of fixed costs, variable costs, and total cost can be enhanced by examining these cost curves on a graph. We will also include a total revenue curve and a marginal revenue curve. We will identify the break-even quantity (where total revenue and total cost are equal) and the profit-maximizing quantity (where marginal revenue and marginal cost are equal).

Total revenue is equal to the selling price of the output multiplied by the quantity sold. Marginal revenue is the change in total revenue from selling an additional unit of output.

**Example 7:** Refer back to Example 6. Assume that Robin Birdwell can sell the luxury birdhouses for $85 each. The table on the next page shows the costs of production, total revenue, marginal revenue (explained in Chapter 21) and profit.

Production and Costs

| Birdhouse Quantity | Total Cost | Fixed Cost | Variable Cost | Marginal Cost | Marginal Revenue | Total Revenue | Profit |
|---|---|---|---|---|---|---|---|
| 0 | $120 | $120 | $0 | X | X | $0 | $-120 |
| 1 | 160 | 120 | 40 | $40 | $85 | 85 | -75 |
| 2 | 190 | 120 | 70 | 30 | 85 | 170 | -20 |
| 3 | 230 | 120 | 110 | 40 | 85 | 255 | 25 |
| 4 | 285 | 120 | 165 | 55 | 85 | 340 | 55 |
| 5 | 360 | 120 | 240 | 75 | 85 | 425 | 65 |
| 6 | 460 | 120 | 340 | 100 | 85 | 510 | 50 |
| 7 | 590 | 120 | 470 | 130 | 85 | 595 | 5 |
| 8 | 755 | 120 | 635 | 165 | 85 | 680 | -75 |

The graph below illustrates the fixed cost curve, the variable cost curve, the total cost curve, the marginal cost curve, the total revenue curve, and the marginal revenue curve.

The break-even quantity occurs where total revenue and total cost are equal (where the TR curve and the TC curve intersect). The break-even quantity for Robin Birdwell occurs between two and three birdhouses.

We will see in Chapter 21 that the profit-maximizing quantity occurs where marginal revenue and marginal cost are equal (where the MR curve and the MC curve intersect). The profit-maximizing quantity for Robin Birdwell occurs at five birdhouses.

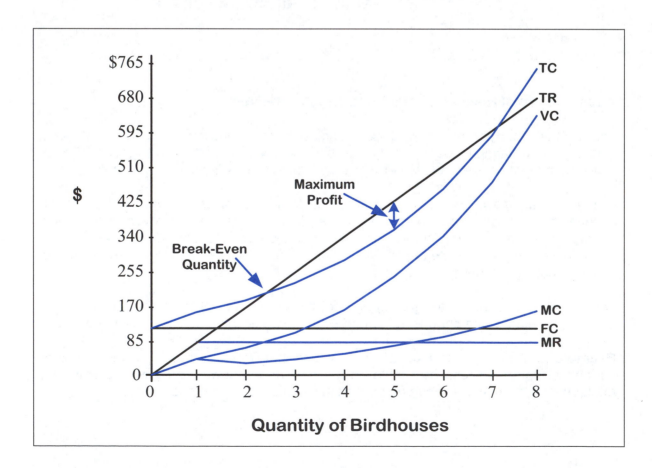

## Appendix: Completing a Cost Table

Two of the problems in the study guide portion of this chapter require the student to complete a cost table. The purpose of such an exercise is to help the student better grasp how the different costs are calculated and how they relate to each other.

The steps to completing a cost table will be illustrated in Example 8 below:

**Example 8:** The cost table below contains partial information. The table can be completed if the student understands how the different costs are calculated and how they relate to each other.

| Quantity | TC | MC | AFC | AVC | ATC |
|---|---|---|---|---|---|
| 0 | 240 | X | X | X | X |
| 1 | ___ | 60 | | | |
| 2 | ___ | ___ | 120 | ___ | 190 |
| 3 | 480 | ___ | | ___ | |
| 4 | ___ | | ___ | 90 | ___ |
| 5 | ___ | 140 | ___ | ___ | |
| 6 | ___ | ___ | ___ | ___ | 150 |

The first step to completing a cost table is to determine the fixed cost. For the cost table above, the fixed cost can be determined in one of two ways:

1. The total cost at a quantity of zero is the fixed cost. Any cost incurred at zero output must be fixed cost, since variable costs can be avoided by not producing. Thus, the fixed cost on this table is 240.

2. The AFC for two units is given as 120. The formula for computing AFC (AFC = FC ÷ Q) can be adjusted to solve for FC. The formula would now be FC = AFC x Q. Thus, FC = 120 x 2 = 240.

Once the fixed cost is determined, the average fixed cost for the different quantities can be calculated using the formula AFC = FC ÷ Q. Thus, AFC for a quantity of one is 240 ÷ 1 = 240. AFC for a quantity of two is 240 ÷ 2 = 120. AFC for a quantity of three is 240 ÷ 3 = 80, etc.

The table below is updated for the newly calculated AFC numbers.

| Quantity | TC | MC | AFC | AVC | ATC |
|---|---|---|---|---|---|
| 0 | 240 | X | X | X | X |
| 1 | ___ | 60 | **240** | ___ | ___ |
| 2 | ___ | ___ | 120 | ___ | 190 |
| 3 | 480 | ___ | **80** | ___ | ___ |
| 4 | ___ | ___ | **60** | 90 | ___ |
| 5 | ___ | 140 | **48** | ___ | ___ |
| 6 | ___ | ___ | **40** | ___ | 150 |

Once AFC has been calculated, the table is completed row by row. At a quantity of one, the marginal cost is 60. Marginal cost is the increase in total cost incurred by producing one additional unit. So the TC at a quantity of one is the 240 TC at a quantity of zero plus the 60 MC of the first unit equals 300. Once the TC at a quantity one is computed, the ATC at a quantity of one can be calculated. ATC = TC ÷ Q or ATC = 300 ÷ 1 = 300. Once the ATC is calculated, AVC can be calculated. AFC + AVC = ATC. If two of the three averages are known, the third average can be solved. In this case AFC = 240 and ATC = 300, therefore, AVC must equal 60.

The table below is updated for the newly calculated costs at a quantity of one.

| Quantity | TC | MC | AFC | AVC | ATC |
|---|---|---|---|---|---|
| 0 | 240 | X | X | X | X |
| 1 | **300** | 60 | 240 | **60** | **300** |
| 2 | ___ | ___ | 120 | ___ | 190 |
| 3 | 480 | ___ | 80 | ___ | ___ |
| 4 | ___ | ___ | 60 | 90 | ___ |
| 5 | ___ | 140 | 48 | ___ | ___ |
| 6 | ___ | ___ | 40 | ___ | 150 |

At a quantity of two, the ATC is 190. The formula for computing ATC (ATC = TC ÷ Q) can be adjusted to solve for TC. The formula would now be TC = ATC x Q. Thus, TC at a quantity of two is 190 x 2 = 380. MC is the increase in TC. So if the TC of two units is 380 and the TC of one unit is 300, the MC of unit two must be 80. AVC can be calculated as before: If AFC = 120 and ATC = 190, AVC must equal 70.

The table below is updated for the newly calculated costs at a quantity of two.

| Quantity | TC | MC | AFC | AVC | ATC |
|---|---|---|---|---|---|
| 0 | 240 | X | X | X | X |
| 1 | 300 | 60 | 240 | 60 | 300 |
| 2 | **380** | **80** | 120 | **70** | 190 |
| 3 | 480 | ___ | 80 | ___ | ___ |
| 4 | ___ | ___ | 60 | 90 | ___ |
| 5 | ___ | 140 | 48 | ___ | ___ |
| 6 | ___ | ___ | 40 | ___ | 150 |

At a quantity of three, the TC is 480. MC is the increase in TC. So if the TC of three units is 480 and the TC of two units is 380, the MC of unit three must be 100. ATC = TC ÷ Q. If TC is 480 and Q is 3, ATC is 160. AVC can be calculated as before: If AFC = 80 and ATC = 160, AVC must be 80.

The table on the next page is updated for the newly calculated costs at a quantity of three.

| Quantity | TC | MC | AFC | AVC | ATC |
|---|---|---|---|---|---|
| 0 | 240 | X | X | X | X |
| 1 | 300 | 60 | 240 | 60 | 300 |
| 2 | 380 | 80 | 120 | 70 | 190 |
| 3 | 480 | **100** | 80 | **80** | **160** |
| 4 | ___ | ___ | 60 | 90 | ___ |
| 5 | ___ | 140 | 48 | ___ | ___ |
| 6 | ___ | ___ | 40 | ___ | 150 |

At a quantity of four, AFC = 60 and AVC = 90, thus ATC must be 150. If ATC = 150, TC (calculated as ATC x Q) must be 600. If the TC of four units is 600 and the TC of three units is 480, the MC of unit four must be 120.

The table below is updated for the newly calculated costs at a quantity of four.

| Quantity | TC | MC | AFC | AVC | ATC |
|---|---|---|---|---|---|
| 0 | 240 | X | X | X | X |
| 1 | 300 | 60 | 240 | 60 | 300 |
| 2 | 380 | 80 | 120 | 70 | 190 |
| 3 | 480 | 100 | 80 | 80 | 160 |
| 4 | **600** | **120** | 60 | 90 | **150** |
| 5 | ___ | 140 | 48 | ___ | ___ |
| 6 | ___ | ___ | 40 | ___ | 150 |

At a quantity of five, the MC is 140. So the TC of five units must be the 600 TC of four units plus the 140 MC of unit five. Thus, the TC of five units is 740. ATC = TC ÷ Q. If TC is 740 and Q is 5, ATC is 148. AVC can be calculated as before: If AFC = 48 and ATC = 148, AVC must be 100.

The table below is updated for the newly calculated costs at a quantity of five.

| Quantity | TC | MC | AFC | AVC | ATC |
|---|---|---|---|---|---|
| 0 | 240 | X | X | X | X |
| 1 | 300 | 60 | 240 | 60 | 300 |
| 2 | 380 | 80 | 120 | 70 | 190 |
| 3 | 480 | 100 | 80 | 80 | 160 |
| 4 | 600 | 120 | 60 | 90 | 150 |
| 5 | **740** | 140 | 48 | **100** | **148** |
| 6 | ___ | ___ | 40 | ___ | 150 |

At a quantity of six, the ATC is 150. The formula for computing ATC (ATC = TC ÷ Q) can be adjusted to solve for TC. The formula would now be TC = ATC x Q. Thus, TC at a quantity of six is 150 x 6 = 900. MC is the increase in TC. So if the TC of five units is 740 and the TC of six units is 900, the MC of unit six must be 160. AVC can be calculated as before: If AFC = 40 and ATC = 150, AVC must be 110.

The table below is updated for the newly calculated costs at a quantity of six.

| Quantity | TC | MC | AFC | AVC | ATC |
|---|---|---|---|---|---|
| 0 | 240 | X | X | X | X |
| 1 | 300 | 60 | 240 | 60 | 300 |
| 2 | 380 | 80 | 120 | 70 | 190 |
| 3 | 480 | 100 | 80 | 80 | 160 |
| 4 | 600 | 120 | 60 | 90 | 150 |
| 5 | 740 | 140 | 48 | 100 | 148 |
| 6 | **900** | **160** | 40 | **110** | 150 |

## Questions for Chapter 20

### Fill-in-the-blanks:

1. _____ cost is the value of the best alternative surrendered when a choice is made.

2. _____ economic profit is considered to be a normal profit.

3. A _____ cost is a past cost that cannot be changed by current decisions.

4. The _____ run is a period in which at least one input is fixed.

5. The _____ run is a period in which all inputs can be varied.

6. Marginal _____ _____ is the change in output with one additional unit of input.

7. _____ cost is the change in total cost from producing an additional unit of output.

8. _____ costs are costs that do <u>not</u> vary with output.

9. _____ costs are costs that vary with output.

### Multiple Choice:

_____ 1. Which of the following is an example of an implicit cost?
   a. value of the owner's labor devoted to the business
   b. utilities expense
   c. rent expense
   d. All of the above

_____ 2. Zero economic profit:
     a. means that accounting profit is negative
     b. is considered to be a normal profit
     c. is the same thing as zero accounting profit
     d. None of the above

_____ 3. Sunk costs are:
     a. past costs that cannot be changed by current decisions
     b. irrelevant to current decisions
     c. crucial to making current decisions
     d. Both a. and b. above

_____ 4. If nine workers can produce 780 units of output and ten workers can produce 820 units of output, the marginal physical product of the tenth worker is:
     a. 820 units
     b. 780 units
     c. 82 units
     d. 40 units

_____ 5. Marginal physical product:
     a. is the change in total revenue from selling one additional unit of output
     b. is the change in total cost that results from producing an additional unit of output
     c. will eventually decrease due to the law of diminishing marginal returns
     d. Both a. and c. above

_____ 6. The law of diminishing marginal returns:
     a. applies eventually when larger amounts of a variable input are combined with fixed inputs
     b. causes a decrease in the marginal cost of production
     c. always applies from the first unit onward
     d. All of the above

_____ 7. Marginal cost:
     a. is the change in total cost that results from adding an additional unit of input
     b. will begin to decrease when production reaches the point of diminishing marginal returns
     c. Both of the above
     d. Neither of the above

_____ 8. When production reaches the point of diminishing marginal returns:
     a. average fixed cost will begin to increase
     b. marginal cost will begin to increase
     c. Both of the above
     d. Neither of the above

Complete the table below to answer questions 9. and 10.:

| Workers | Wage | MPP | Marginal Cost |
|---------|------|-----|---------------|
| 0 | $180 | X | X |
| 1 | 180 | 36 | $5 |
| 2 | 180 | 45 | 4 |
| 3 | 180 | 30 | ___ |
| 4 | 180 | 20 | ___ |
| 5 | 180 | 10 | ___ |
| 6 | 180 | 5 | ___ |

_____ 9. What is the marginal cost of the output produced by the 4$^{th}$ worker?
    a.   $6
    b.   $9
    c.  $12
    d.  $18

_____ 10. What is the marginal cost of the output produced by the 6$^{th}$ worker?
    a.  $48
    b.  $42
    c.  $36
    d.  $30

_____ 11. Concerning the cost curves:
    a.  the AFC curve always slopes upward
    b.  the AVC and ATC curves eventually slope downward due to diminishing marginal returns
    c.  the MC curve always intersects the ATC curve and the AVC curve at their lowest points
    d.  All of the above

_____ 12. If marginal cost is less than ATC:
    a.  ATC must be increasing
    b.  ATC must be decreasing
    c.  ATC must be at it lowest point
    d.  All of the above are possible

_____ 13. If the total cost of six units is $380, and the total cost of seven units is $490, the marginal cost of the seventh unit is:
    a.   $70
    b.  $110
    c.  $380
    d.  $490

_____ 14. If the ATC of eight units is $75, the total cost of eight units is:
    a.   $9.38
    b.   $75
    c.  $600
    d.  $750

_____ 15. If the ATC of ten units is $73.50, and the AFC of ten units is $35.00, the AVC
of ten units is:
   a.   $38.50
   b.   $73.50
   c.   $108.50
   d.   $385

_____ 16. Regarding the cost curves:
   a.   the fixed cost curve will be horizontal
   b.   the total cost curve will run parallel to the variable cost curve, and will be
        higher by the amount of fixed costs
   c.   Both of the above
   d.   Neither of the above

_____ 17. The break-even quantity of output:
   a.   occurs where profits are maximized
   b.   occurs where total revenue and total cost are equal
   c.   Both of the above
   d.   Neither of the above

## Problems:

1.   Explain the difference between an explicit cost and an implicit cost.

2.   Explain the meaning of zero economic profit.

3. Complete the following table:

| Workers | Total Product | Marginal Physical Product |
|---|---|---|
| 0 | 0 | X |
| 1 | 50 | 50 |
| 2 | 110 | ___ |
| 3 | 160 | ___ |
| 4 | 200 | ___ |
| 5 | 230 | ___ |
| 6 | 250 | ___ |
| 7 | 260 | ___ |

4. Complete the following cost table:

| Quantity | TC | MC | AFC | AVC | ATC |
|---|---|---|---|---|---|
| 0 | 420 | X | X | X | X |
| 1 | ___ | 30 | 420 | ___ | ___ |
| 2 | ___ | ___ | ___ | ___ | 250 |
| 3 | ___ | ___ | ___ | 50 | ___ |
| 4 | 660 | ___ | ___ | ___ | ___ |
| 5 | ___ | 110 | ___ | ___ | ___ |
| 6 | ___ | ___ | ___ | 80 | ___ |
| 7 | ___ | ___ | ___ | ___ | 150 |
| 8 | ___ | 170 | 52.5 | ___ | ___ |
| 9 | 1410 | ___ | ___ | ___ | ___ |

5. Complete the following cost table:

| Quantity | TC | MC | AFC | AVC | ATC |
|---|---|---|---|---|---|
| 0 | ___ | X | X | X | X |
| 1 | ___ | ___ | ___ | 40 | ___ |
| 2 | ___ | 50 | 270 | ___ | ___ |
| 3 | ___ | ___ | ___ | ___ | 233 |
| 4 | ___ | ___ | ___ | 65 | ___ |
| 5 | 940 | ___ | ___ | ___ | ___ |
| 6 | ___ | 190 | ___ | ___ | ___ |
| 7 | ___ | ___ | ___ | ___ | 197 |
| 8 | ___ | ___ | 67.5 | 145 | ___ |
| 9 | ___ | 400 | ___ | ___ | ___ |

## Answers for Chapter 20

**Fill-in-the-blanks:**
1. Opportunity
2. Zero
3. sunk
4. short
5. long

6. physical product
7. Marginal
8. Fixed
9. Variable

**Multiple Choice:**

| | | |
|---|---|---|
| 1. a. | 7. d. | 13. b. |
| 2. b. | 8. b. | 14. c. |
| 3. d. | 9. b. | 15. a. |
| 4. d. | 10. c. | 16. c. |
| 5. c. | 11. c. | 17. b. |
| 6. a. | 12. b. | |

## Problems:

1. An explicit cost is an opportunity cost that involves an actual expenditure of money. Wage expense, utilities expense, rent expense, and tax expense are examples of explicit costs. An implicit cost is an opportunity cost that does not involve an expenditure of money. The value of the owner's labor devoted to the business is an example of an implicit cost.

2. Zero economic profit does not mean zero accounting profit. Zero economic profit means that a person is doing as well as his or her best alternative. Zero economic profit is considered to be a normal profit.

3. Table:

| Workers | Total Product | Marginal Physical Product |
|---|---|---|
| 0 | 0 | X |
| 1 | 50 | 50 |
| 2 | 110 | 60 |
| 3 | 160 | 50 |
| 4 | 200 | 40 |
| 5 | 230 | 30 |
| 6 | 250 | 20 |
| 7 | 260 | 10 |

4. Cost Table:

| Quantity | TC | MC | AFC | AVC | ATC |
|----------|------|-----|-----|-----|-------|
| 0 | 420 | X | X | X | X |
| 1 | **450** | 30 | 420 | **30** | **450** |
| 2 | **500** | **50** | **210** | **40** | 250 |
| 3 | **570** | **70** | **140** | 50 | **190** |
| 4 | 660 | **90** | **105** | **60** | **165** |
| 5 | **770** | 110 | **84** | **70** | **154** |
| 6 | **900** | **130** | **70** | 80 | **150** |
| 7 | **1050** | **150** | **60** | **90** | 150 |
| 8 | **1220** | 170 | 52.5 | **100** | **152.5** |
| 9 | 1410 | **190** | **46.7** | **110** | **156.7** |

5. Cost Table:

| Quantity | TC | MC | AFC | AVC | ATC |
|----------|------|-----|-----|-----|-------|
| 0 | **540** | X | X | X | X |
| 1 | **580** | **40** | **540** | 40 | **580** |
| 2 | **630** | 50 | 270 | **45** | **315** |
| 3 | **700** | **70** | **180** | **53** | 233 |
| 4 | **800** | **100** | **135** | 65 | **200** |
| 5 | 940 | **140** | **108** | **80** | **188** |
| 6 | **1130** | 190 | **90** | **98** | **188** |
| 7 | **1380** | **250** | **77** | **120** | 197 |
| 8 | **1700** | **320** | 67.5 | 145 | **212.5** |
| 9 | **2100** | 400 | **60** | **173** | **233** |

Table for Multiple Choice Questions 9. and 10.

| Workers | Wage | MPP | Marginal Cost |
|---------|------|-----|---------------|
| 0 | $180 | X | X |
| 1 | 180 | 36 | $5 |
| 2 | 180 | 45 | 4 |
| 3 | 180 | 30 | **6** |
| 4 | 180 | 20 | **9** |
| 5 | 180 | 10 | **18** |
| 6 | 180 | 5 | **36** |

# Chapter 21  Perfect Competition

The basic economic problem is scarcity.  Human wants are unlimited.  Resources are limited.  The basic goal in dealing with the problem of scarcity is to produce as much consumer satisfaction as possible with the limited resources available.  To achieve this goal, society must use its limited resources as efficiently as possible.  How efficiently a particular firm uses its resources will depend on the market structure that the firm operates in.

Economists have identified four different market structures, ranging from perfect competition at one extreme to monopoly at the other extreme.  The four different market structures will be examined in this chapter and the next two chapters.  The four different market structures are characterized by different levels of market power.

**Market power** – the ability of a seller or a buyer to affect market price.

The market structure that a firm operates in will affect the firm's market power.  The degree of market power that a firm has will affect the output and pricing decisions that the firm makes as it attempts to maximize profits.

The degree of market power that a firm has will also affect the firm's economic efficiency (or inefficiency).  The ideal (most efficient) market structure is perfect competition.

**Perfect competition** – many sellers of identical products.

Perfect competition is the ideal market structure.  For reasons detailed later in this chapter, a perfect competitor will generally produce the economically efficient quantity of output.

The key characteristic of perfect competition is a lack of market power.  Each perfect competitor has <u>no</u> ability to affect market price.

The two primary reasons that a perfect competitor has no market power are:

1.  **There are many sellers in a perfectly competitive market.**  Each seller is relatively small compared to the total market.  No single seller produces a significant share of the total market output.  Thus, if a perfect competitor increases or decreases its output, the market price will be unaffected.

> **Example 1:**  In a typical year, about 2 billion bushels of wheat are produced in the U.S. A five-hundred acre wheat farm (about the average size) would produce around 20,000 bushels, or .001% of the nation's total crop.

2.  **All firms in a perfectly competitive market sell an identical product.**  Thus, no buyer would be willing to pay more for one firm's product than for another firm's product. All firms will sell at the same price, the market price.

> **Example 2:**  When was the last time you saw a television commercial featuring a farmer?  Imagine Farmer Vilsack boasting, "Buy my corn.  It's the best corn.  It costs a little more, but it's worth it."

## The Demand Curve for a Perfect Competitor

A perfect competitor has no market power. Since a perfect competitor is unable to affect the market price for its product, a perfect competitor will face a demand curve for its product that is horizontal (perfectly elastic) at the market price.

**Example 3:** Percomp Company is a perfect competitor. Percomp produces about .001% of the total production in its market. The product that Percomp produces has a market price of $10. If Percomp increases or decreases the quantity that it produces, this will not have a significant effect on the supply in the market. The market price will remain at $10. Thus, the demand curve for Percomp is horizontal at the market price of $10, as illustrated by the demand schedule and the demand curve below:

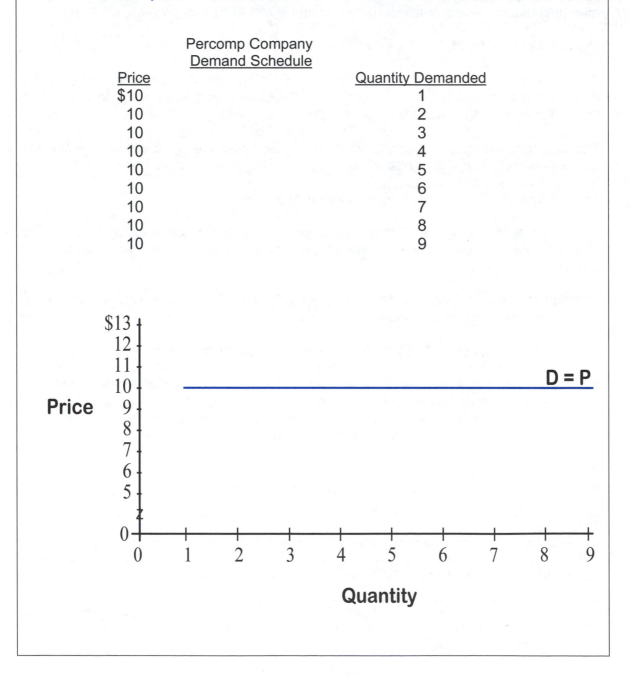

Percomp Company
Demand Schedule

| Price | Quantity Demanded |
|-------|-------------------|
| $10 | 1 |
| 10 | 2 |
| 10 | 3 |
| 10 | 4 |
| 10 | 5 |
| 10 | 6 |
| 10 | 7 |
| 10 | 8 |
| 10 | 9 |

Since a perfect competitor has no market power, a perfect competitor is a price taker. It cannot "make" the market price change, but must simply "take" the market price as it is.

Even though a perfect competitor cannot affect the market price for its product, the market price can change, due to factors beyond the control of any one firm.

**Example 4A:** A single wheat farmer cannot affect the market price of wheat. But changes in the overall demand for wheat (e.g. due to a change in export demand) or changes in the overall supply of wheat (e.g. due to the weather) can affect the market price of wheat.

If the market price changes, a perfect competitor will still face a horizontal demand curve for its product. The demand curve will be horizontal at the new market price.

**Example 4B:** If the market price for Percomp Company from Example 3 decreased to $8, Percomp's demand curve would be horizontal at $8.

## Profit-Maximization

As discussed in Chapter 19, all business firms are assumed to pursue the same chief goal: profit-maximization. A perfect competitor will adjust its production level to try to achieve profit-maximization. It will try to produce according to the profit-maximization rule for producing output.

**Profit-maximization rule** – produce the quantity of output where marginal revenue equals marginal cost.

Marginal cost was defined in Chapter 20 as the change in total cost that results from producing an additional unit of output. When production reaches the point of diminishing marginal returns, the marginal cost of production will begin to increase.

Marginal revenue is the change in total revenue from selling one additional unit of output.

**Marginal revenue** – the change in total revenue from selling one additional unit of output.

Total revenue is equal to the selling price of the output multiplied by the quantity sold.

**Total revenue = Price x Quantity**

**Example 5A:** The table on the next page is for Percomp Company, the perfect competitor from Example 3. The table shows price, quantity demanded, total revenue (Price x Quantity), and marginal revenue for Percomp. Notice that marginal revenue is the same as the selling price. For a perfect competitor, marginal revenue equals market price, and the firm's marginal revenue curve will be the same as its demand curve.

| | Percomp Company | | |
|---|---|---|---|
| Price | Quantity Demanded | Total Revenue | Marginal Revenue |
| $10 | 0 | $0 | X |
| 10 | 1 | 10 | $10 |
| 10 | 2 | 20 | 10 |
| 10 | 3 | 30 | 10 |
| 10 | 4 | 40 | 10 |
| 10 | 5 | 50 | 10 |
| 10 | 6 | 60 | 10 |
| 10 | 7 | 70 | 10 |
| 10 | 8 | 80 | 10 |
| 10 | 9 | 90 | 10 |

**Example 5B:** The table below illustrates the profit-maximization rule (produce the quantity of output where marginal revenue equals marginal cost). Percomp Company, a perfect competitor, produces in a market where the market price is $10. The demand information, marginal revenue, marginal cost, and marginal profit (marginal revenue minus marginal cost) are detailed on the table.

The table shows that producing up to the profit-maximizing quantity (6 units) generates positive marginal profit. Producing more than the profit-maximizing quantity generates negative marginal profit.

| | | Percomp Company | | |
|---|---|---|---|---|
| Price | Quantity | Marginal Revenue | Marginal Cost | Marginal Profit |
| $10 | 0 | X | X | X |
| 10 | 1 | $10 | $5 | $5 |
| 10 | 2 | 10 | 6 | 4 |
| 10 | 3 | 10 | 7 | 3 |
| 10 | 4 | 10 | 8 | 2 |
| 10 | 5 | 10 | 9 | 1 |
| 10 | 6 | 10 | 10 | 0 |
| 10 | 7 | 10 | 11 | -1 |
| 10 | 8 | 10 | 12 | -2 |
| 10 | 9 | 10 | 13 | -3 |

The graph on the next page shows the demand curve and the marginal cost curve, indicates that marginal revenue is the same as price and that the marginal revenue curve is the same as the demand curve, and shows that the profit-maximizing quantity of output (where marginal revenue equals marginal cost) is 6 units of output.

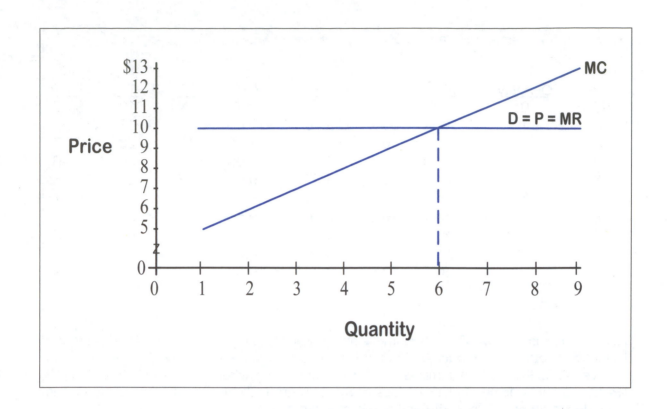

**Example 5C:** This example builds on Example 5B. The table below adds information for Average Total Cost, Average Variable Cost, Total Cost, Total Revenue, and Economic Profit. Profit is equal to Total Revenue minus Total Cost. Fixed cost is assumed to be $12.

| Price | Quantity | MR | MC | AVC | ATC | TR | TC | Profit |
|-------|----------|------|------|-------|--------|----|------|--------|
| $10 | 0 | X | X | X | X | X | $12 | $-12 |
| 10 | 1 | $10 | $5 | $5.00 | $17.00 | 10 | 17 | -7 |
| 10 | 2 | 10 | 6 | 5.50 | 11.50 | 20 | 23 | -3 |
| 10 | 3 | 10 | 7 | 6.00 | 10.00 | 30 | 30 | 0 |
| 10 | 4 | 10 | 8 | 6.50 | 9.50 | 40 | 38 | 2 |
| 10 | 5 | 10 | 9 | 7.00 | 9.40 | 50 | 47 | 3 |
| 10 | 6 | 10 | 10 | 7.50 | 9.50 | 60 | 57 | 3 |
| 10 | 7 | 10 | 11 | 8.00 | 9.71 | 70 | 68 | 2 |
| 10 | 8 | 10 | 12 | 8.50 | 10.00 | 80 | 80 | 0 |
| 10 | 9 | 10 | 13 | 9.00 | 10.33 | 90 | 93 | -3 |

Since price is above ATC, Percomp Company will earn an economic profit. At the profit-maximizing quantity of six units, the price is $10 and the ATC is $9.50. Note that maximum profit ($3) occurs where MR = MC (6 units). Also, note that since fixed cost is $12, the profit at zero output is $-12. A graph illustrating the economic profit is included in an appendix at the end of this chapter.

Perfect Competition

**Example 5D:** Same as Example 5C, but price falls to $8.

| Price | Quantity | MR | MC | AVC | ATC | TR | TC | Profit |
|---|---|---|---|---|---|---|---|---|
| $8 | 0 | X | X | X | X | X | $12 | $-12 |
| 8 | 1 | $8 | $5 | $5.00 | $17.00 | 8 | 17 | -9 |
| 8 | 2 | 8 | 6 | 5.50 | 11.50 | 16 | 23 | -7 |
| 8 | 3 | 8 | 7 | 6.00 | 10.00 | 24 | 30 | -6 |
| 8 | 4 | 8 | 8 | 6.50 | 9.50 | 32 | 38 | -6 |
| 8 | 5 | 8 | 9 | 7.00 | 9.40 | 40 | 47 | -7 |
| 8 | 6 | 8 | 10 | 7.50 | 9.50 | 48 | 57 | -9 |
| 8 | 7 | 8 | 11 | 8.00 | 9.71 | 56 | 68 | -12 |
| 8 | 8 | 8 | 12 | 8.50 | 10.00 | 64 | 80 | -16 |
| 8 | 9 | 8 | 13 | 9.00 | 10.33 | 72 | 93 | -19 |

Since price is below ATC, Percomp Company will incur an economic loss whatever quantity of output it produces. Should Percomp Company shut down? Since price is above AVC, Percomp minimizes its loss by producing where MR = MC (4 units). If Percomp shuts down, it incurs a loss of $-12. A graph illustrating the economic loss is included in an appendix at the end of this chapter.

**Example 5E:** Same as Example 5C, but price falls to $4.

| Price | Quantity | MR | MC | AVC | ATC | TR | TC | Profit |
|---|---|---|---|---|---|---|---|---|
| $4 | 0 | X | X | X | X | X | $12 | $-12 |
| 4 | 1 | $4 | $5 | $5.00 | $17.00 | 4 | 17 | -13 |
| 4 | 2 | 4 | 6 | 5.50 | 11.50 | 8 | 23 | -15 |
| 4 | 3 | 4 | 7 | 6.00 | 10.00 | 12 | 30 | -18 |
| 4 | 4 | 4 | 8 | 6.50 | 9.50 | 16 | 38 | -22 |
| 4 | 5 | 4 | 9 | 7.00 | 9.40 | 20 | 47 | -27 |
| 4 | 6 | 4 | 10 | 7.50 | 9.50 | 24 | 57 | -33 |
| 4 | 7 | 4 | 11 | 8.00 | 9.71 | 28 | 68 | -40 |
| 4 | 8 | 4 | 12 | 8.50 | 10.00 | 32 | 80 | -48 |
| 4 | 9 | 4 | 13 | 9.00 | 10.33 | 36 | 93 | -57 |

Since price is below ATC, Percomp Company will incur an economic loss whatever quantity of output it produces. Should Percomp Company shut down? Since price is also below AVC, Percomp minimizes its loss by producing zero units (shutting down). Thus, the shutdown point occurs if price falls below AVC. By shutting down, the firm limits its loss to its fixed costs. If the firm produces, it will incur a loss greater than its fixed costs.

## The Supply Curve for a Perfect Competitor

A supply curve indicates the quantity supplied at different prices. We have seen in Examples 5C, 5D, and 5E that a perfect competitor will produce the quantity of output where price equals marginal cost, as long as the price is greater than average variable cost. If the price falls below AVC, the perfect competitor will shut down. Thus, the supply curve for a perfect competitor is the portion of the firm's marginal cost curve that lies above the shutdown point.

## Perfect Competition in the Long Run

In a perfectly competitive market, will the price be high enough that firms earn economic profits? Or will the price be so low that firms suffer economic losses? Either of these situations may occur in the short run. But in the long run, either economic profits or losses will be eliminated, and price will equal minimum ATC.

To see how economic profits or losses are eliminated in the long run, we will refer back to previous examples. In Example 5C, the market price was $10 and Percomp Company (along with the other firms in the market) was earning economic profit. If economic profits are available in a perfectly competitive market, new firms will be attracted to the market.

As new firms enter the market, the market supply increases, and the market price decreases. As long as the market price is above ATC, economic profits will be earned, new firms will continue to enter the market, and the market price will continue to decrease.

What if market price is below ATC (as in Example 5D)? If price is below ATC, Percomp Company (along with the other firms in the market) will suffer economic loss. If economic losses are occurring in a perfectly competitive market, existing firms will be motivated to leave the market.

As existing firms exit the market, the market supply decreases, and the market price increases. As long as the market price is below ATC, economic losses will occur, existing firms will continue to exit the market, and the market price will continue to increase.

At what price will there be neither economic profit nor loss? At minimum ATC. In the long run, the price will be equal to minimum ATC, and the firms will be earning zero economic profit (a normal profit). A graph illustrating perfect competition in the long run is included in an appendix at the end of this chapter.

## Perfect Competition and Economic Efficiency

The basic economic problem is scarcity. The basic goal in dealing with the problem of scarcity is to produce as much consumer satisfaction as possible with the limited resources available. To achieve this goal, society must use its limited resources as efficiently as possible.

The concept of the economically efficient level of an activity was introduced in Chapter 1 and was further explained in Chapter 18. In Chapters 1 and 18, we saw that the optimal (ideal, most efficient) level of an activity occurs where the marginal benefit and the marginal cost of the activity are equal. In this chapter, and for the rest of the textbook, we will refer to this economic efficiency rule with slightly altered terminology.

**Economic efficiency rule** – produce the quantity of output where marginal social benefit equals marginal social cost.

Marginal social benefit (MSB) is the value (benefit) to society of the marginal unit of output. If there is an external benefit (see Chapter 27), marginal social benefit will be different than marginal private benefit. Assuming no external benefits, marginal social benefit is the same as marginal private benefit and is measured by market price.

Marginal social cost (MSC) is the cost to society of producing the marginal unit of output. If there is an external cost (see Chapter 27), marginal social cost will be different than marginal private cost. Assuming no external costs, marginal social cost is the same as marginal private cost and is measured by marginal cost.

Thus, if there are no externalities, the ideal (economically efficient) quantity of output occurs where price equals marginal cost.

Perfect competition is the ideal (most efficient) market structure because it results in the quantity of output where price equals marginal cost and thus (assuming no externalities) where marginal social benefit equals marginal social cost. Referring back to Example 5C, at the profit-maximizing quantity of six units, price ($10) equals marginal cost ($10), and thus MSB equals MSC.

## Perfect Competition's Happy Coincidence

A perfect competitor, like any other business firm, has a chief goal of profit-maximization. To achieve this goal, a perfect competitor will produce according to the profit-maximization rule (produce the quantity of output where marginal revenue equals marginal cost). By a happy coincidence, the profit-maximizing quantity of output is also the economically efficient quantity of output (where price equals marginal cost and thus where MSB equals MSC).

So the goal of the firm (profit-maximization) and the goal of society (economic efficiency) are both reached at the same quantity of output. This is why perfect competition is the ideal market structure.

## Perfect Competition and Individual Freedom

Another advantage of perfect competition is that perfect competition contributes to individual freedom. In a perfectly competitive market, production and distribution decisions can be made by individuals, not by central authority, thus maximizing individual freedom. Because the goal of the firm (profit-maximization) and the goal of society (economic efficiency) are both reached at the same quantity of output, society can leave perfect competitors alone, free to pursue their self-interest.

## Appendix: Economic Profit and Economic Loss

In Example 5C, the selling price ($10) was above ATC ($9.50). Percomp Company produced six units of output and earned an economic profit of $3. This is illustrated on the graph below:

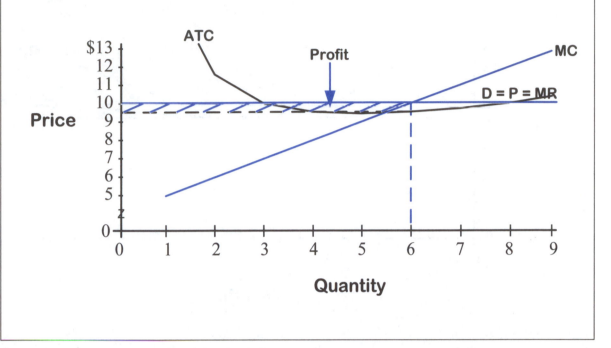

In Example 5D, the selling price ($8) was below ATC ($9.50). Percomp Company produced four units of output and incurred an economic loss of $-6. This is illustrated on the graph below:

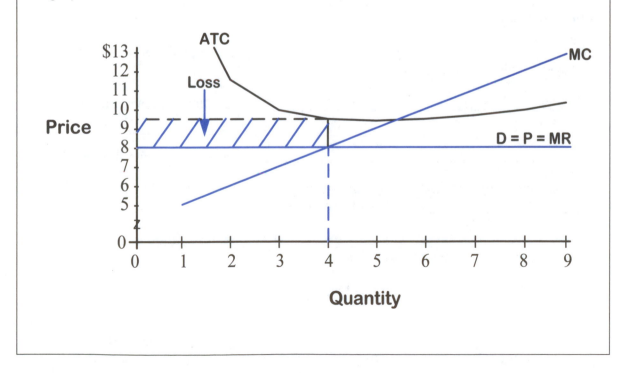

## Appendix: Perfect Competition in the Long Run

In the long run, the selling price for Percomp Company will equal minimum ATC and Percomp will have zero economic profit. This is illustrated on the graph below:

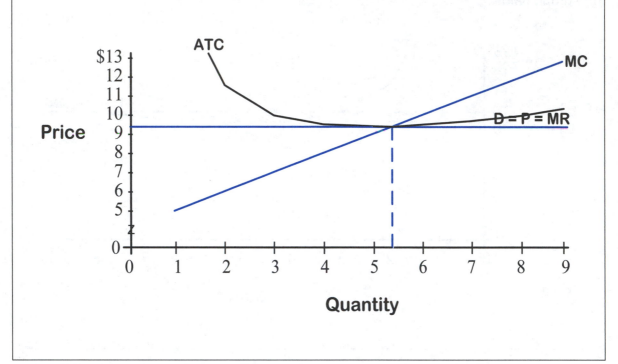

## Questions for Chapter 21

### Fill-in-the-blanks:

1. _____ _____ is the ability of a seller or a buyer to affect market price.

2. _____ _____ is many sellers of identical products.

3. _____ _____ is the ideal market structure.

4. A perfect competitor will face a demand curve for its product that is _____ at the market price.

5. _____ _____ is the change in total revenue from selling one additional unit of output.

6. The shutdown point occurs if price falls below _____ _____ cost.

7. The _____ _____ rule says produce the quantity of output where marginal social benefit equals marginal social cost.

**Multiple Choice:**

_____ 1. A perfect competitor:
    a.  is one of many sellers in a market
    b.  sells a product identical to its competitors' product
    c.  is unable to affect the market price
    d.  All of the above

_____ 2. A perfect competitor:
    a.  has maximum market power
    b.  has only a small amount of market power
    c.  has no market power
    d.  All of the above are possible

_____ 3. If a perfect competitor decreases its output:
    a.  the market price will increase
    b.  the market price will be unaffected
    c.  the market price will decrease
    d.  All of the above are possible

_____ 4. By producing the quantity of output where marginal revenue equals marginal cost, a firm will:
    a.  maximize total revenue
    b.  maximize profits
    c.  minimize costs
    d.  All of the above

_____ 5. For a perfect competitor:
    a.  the demand curve and the marginal revenue curve are the same
    b.  price equals marginal revenue
    c.  Both of the above
    d.  Neither of the above

Complete the table below to answer questions 6. through 8.:

| Price | Quantity | Total Revenue | Marginal Revenue | Total Cost | Marginal Cost | Profit |
|---|---|---|---|---|---|---|
| $10 | 0 | $0 | X | $13 | X | $-13 |
| 10 | 1 | 10 | $10 | 15 | $2 | -5 |
| 10 | 2 | 20 | 10 | 19 | 4 | 1 |
| 10 | 3 | 30 | ___ | 25 | ___ | ___ |
| 10 | 4 | 40 | ___ | 33 | ___ | ___ |
| 10 | 5 | 50 | ___ | 43 | ___ | ___ |
| 10 | 6 | 60 | ___ | 55 | ___ | ___ |
| 10 | 7 | 70 | ___ | 69 | ___ | ___ |

_____ 6. What is the marginal cost of the 4$^{th}$ unit of output?
    a.  $4
    b.  $6
    c.  $8
    d.  $10

_____ 7. What is the profit when six units of output are produced?
  a. $7
  b. $5
  c. $3
  d. $1

_____ 8. What is the profit-maximizing quantity of output?
  a. 6
  b. 5
  c. 3
  d. 2

_____ 9. If a perfect competitor produces the quantity of output where marginal revenue equals marginal cost, when price is greater than ATC, it:
  a. will earn economic profit
  b. incurs a loss less than fixed costs
  c. incurs a loss greater than fixed costs
  d. All of the above are possible

_____ 10. If a perfect competitor produces the quantity of output where marginal revenue equals marginal cost, when price is less than ATC, but greater than AVC, it:
  a. incurs a loss greater than fixed costs
  b. incurs a loss equal to fixed costs
  c. incurs a loss less than fixed costs
  d. All of the above are possible

_____ 11. If a perfect competitor produces the quantity of output where marginal revenue equals marginal cost, when price is less than AVC, it:
  a. incurs a loss greater than fixed costs
  b. incurs a loss equal to fixed costs
  c. incurs a loss less than fixed costs
  d. All of the above are possible

_____ 12. In a perfectly competitive market, in the long run:
  a. firms will tend to earn zero economic profit
  b. price will be equal to minimum ATC
  c. Both of the above
  d. Neither of the above

_____ 13. Perfect competition results in:
  a. the most efficient quantity of output
  b. the quantity of output where price equals marginal cost
  c. the quantity of output where marginal social benefit equals marginal social cost (assuming no externalities)
  d. All of the above

_____ 14. The goal of a perfect competitor:
  a. is to maximize profits
  b. coincides with society's goal of economic efficiency
  c. Both of the above
  d. Neither of the above

_____ 15. Perfect competition:
   a. requires government direction of production to protect the interests of society
   b. maximizes individual freedom
   c. Both of the above
   d. Neither of the above

Answer questions 16. through 20. by referring to the following information. Complete the table to answer the questions below for XYZ Company, a perfect competitor.

| Quantity | TC | MC | Price | TR | MR |
|----------|------|------|-------|-------|------|
| 10 | $475 | X | $40 | $400 | $40 |
| 11 | 490 | $15 | 40 | 440 | 40 |
| 12 | 510 | _____ | 40 | _____ | _____ |
| 13 | 535 | _____ | 40 | _____ | _____ |
| 14 | 565 | _____ | 40 | _____ | _____ |
| 15 | 600 | _____ | 40 | _____ | _____ |
| 16 | 640 | _____ | 40 | _____ | _____ |

_____ 16. What is the marginal cost of the 14$^{th}$ unit of output?
   a. $15
   b. $20
   c. $25
   d. $30

_____ 17. What is the marginal revenue of the 15$^{th}$ unit of output?
   a. $20
   b. $30
   c. $40
   d. $600

_____ 18. What is the total revenue of 16 units of output?
   a. $600
   b. $640
   c. $680
   d. $720

_____ 19. What is the profit-maximizing quantity of output?
   a. 16
   b. 14
   c. 12
   d. 11

_____ 20. What profit is earned at the profit-maximizing quantity of output?
   a. $-5
   b. $0
   c. $5
   d. $10

**Problems:**

1. The graph below illustrates the marginal cost curve for a perfect competitor. Assuming that the market price is $7:
   (1) draw the demand curve
   (2) draw or otherwise indicate the marginal revenue curve
   (3) indicate the profit-maximizing quantity

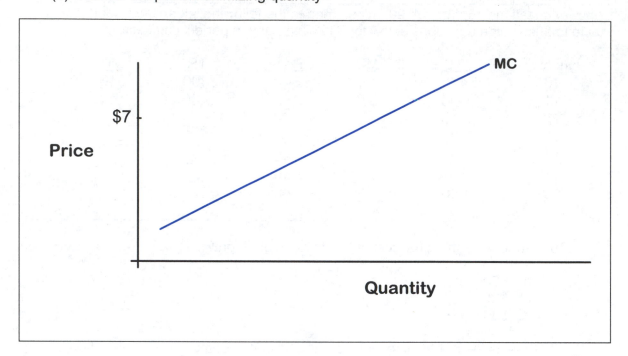

2. What is the shutdown point? Why should a firm shut down if the price falls below the shutdown point?

3. If economic losses are occurring in a perfectly competitive market, what is likely to happen in the long run to:
   (1) the number of firms in the market
   (2) the market price in the market
   (3) the economic loss in the market

## Answers for Chapter 21

**Fill-in-the-blanks:**
1. Market power
2. Perfect competition
3. Perfect competition
4. horizontal
5. Marginal revenue
6. average variable
7. economic efficiency

**Multiple Choice:**
1. d
2. c.
3. b.
4. b.
5. c.
6. c.
7. b.
8. b.
9. a.
10. c.
11. a.
12. c.
13. d.
14. c.
15. b.
16. d.
17. c.
18. b.
19. a.
20. b.

## Problems:

1.

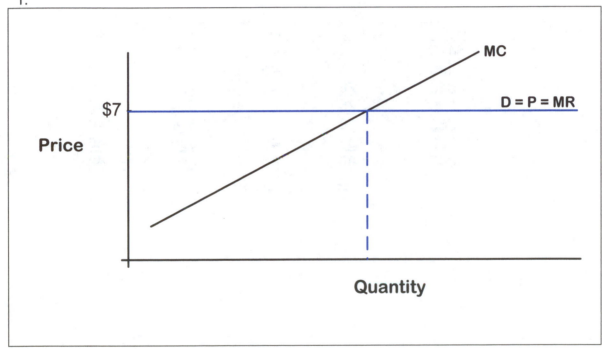

2. The shutdown point occurs if price falls below AVC. By shutting down, a firm limits its loss to its fixed costs. If the firm continued producing, it would incur a loss greater than its fixed costs.

3. If economic losses are occurring in a perfectly competitive market:
   (1) the number of firms will decrease as existing firms leave the market
   (2) the market price will increase as the market supply decreases
   (3) the economic loss will be eliminated

Table for Multiple Choice Questions 6. through 8.:

| Price | Quantity | Total Revenue | Marginal Revenue | Total Cost | Marginal Cost | Profit |
|---|---|---|---|---|---|---|
| $10 | 0 | $0 | X | $13 | X | $-13 |
| 10 | 1 | 10 | $10 | 15 | $2 | -5 |
| 10 | 2 | 20 | 10 | 19 | 4 | 1 |
| 10 | 3 | 30 | **10** | 25 | **6** | **5** |
| 10 | 4 | 40 | **10** | 33 | **8** | **7** |
| 10 | 5 | 50 | **10** | 43 | **10** | **7** |
| 10 | 6 | 60 | **10** | 55 | **12** | **5** |
| 10 | 7 | 70 | **10** | 69 | **14** | **1** |

Table for Multiple Choice Questions 16. through 20.:

| Quantity | TC | MC | Price | TR | MR |
|---|---|---|---|---|---|
| 10 | $475 | X | $40 | $400 | $40 |
| 11 | 490 | $15 | 40 | 440 | 40 |
| 12 | 510 | **20** | 40 | **480** | **40** |
| 13 | 535 | **25** | 40 | **520** | **40** |
| 14 | 565 | **30** | 40 | **560** | **40** |
| 15 | 600 | **35** | 40 | **600** | **40** |
| 16 | 640 | **40** | 40 | **640** | **40** |

# Chapter 22  Monopoly

Of the four market structures, monopoly is at the opposite extreme from perfect competition.  A perfect competitor has no ability to affect market price (no market power).  A monopoly has maximum market power.

**Monopoly** – a firm that is the lone seller of a product with no close substitutes.

---

**Example 1:**  Darla's Delectable Donuts has a unique recipe for donuts that is unlike any of the other 73 donut shops in town.  Does this make Darla's a monopoly?  No.  There are many close substitutes available.  To be a monopoly, a firm must be selling a product with <u>no</u> close substitutes available.

---

## Monopoly and Barriers to Entry

As the lone seller in a market, a monopoly is in a good position to earn economic profit.  If a monopoly earns economic profit, the economic profit would tend to attract new firms into the market.

In order for a monopoly to maintain its position as the lone seller in the market, there will need to be factors blocking the entry of new firms into the market.  These factors, called barriers to entry, can also limit the number of firms in an oligopoly market (see Chapter 23).

**Barriers to Entry** – factors that block the entry of new firms into a market.

Barriers to entry are classified into three general types:

1.  **Legal barriers.**  Legal barriers are created by government action.  Examples include;

    a.  **Public franchise.**  The government grants one firm an exclusive right to provide a good or a service to a market.   In the past, public franchises were sometimes granted to the family, friends, and political cronies of the top government officials as a way to enrich them.  This still occurs today in many countries.  See the appendix at the end of the chapter on corruption and public franchise.

    In the U.S., granting a firm a public franchise is often part of the regulation of a natural monopoly.  In a natural monopoly market, one firm will be granted a public franchise to serve that market, but will then be subject to government regulation. Natural monopoly results from economies of scale and is defined later in the chapter.

    b.  **Patent.**  A **patent** is a government granted monopoly on the production and sale of an invention granted to the inventor.  Most patents are legally effective for 20 years from the date of application.  Developing new inventions is often very costly and uncertain of success.  The monopoly position granted by a patent is a reward for inventive behavior.  Patents are a way to encourage invention.

**Example 2B:** Patents can be very valuable. Eli Lilly and Company held various patents on Prozac beginning in 1974. On August 9, 2000, the Court of Appeals for the Federal Circuit held the last of the Prozac patents to be invalid. On August 10, the value of Eli Lilly and Company stock dropped by nearly one-third. Competition from generics meant that Prozac prescriptions would drop by 90% in the next year.

    c.  **Copyright.** A **copyright** is a government granted monopoly on the production and sale of a creative work granted to the creator. Most copyrights are legally effective for the life of the author plus 70 years. The monopoly position granted by copyright protection is a reward for creative behavior. Copyrights are a way to encourage creativity.

**Example 3:** Copyrights can be very valuable. Each year, Forbes magazine publishes a list of the top-earning dead celebrities. For most of the dead celebrities, the bulk of their earnings is from royalties on copyrighted works. The top-earning dead celebrities for 2007 included Elvis Presley ($49 million), John Lennon ($44 million), "Peanuts" creator Chuck Schulz ($35 million), George Harrison ($22 million), Albert Einstein ($18 million), Dr. Seuss ($13 million), Tupac Shakur ($9 million), and Marilyn Monroe ($7 million).

    d.  **License.** A **license** is a permit issued by the government authorizing a person to conduct a certain type of business. Entry into many occupations and markets requires a government license.

        Licensing requirements may be intended to protect the public safety (e.g. medical licensing), or may be intended to protect existing firms from competition (e.g. restrictions on the number of taxis allowed to operate in a city).

**Example 4:** In New York City, the number of taxis is limited by city licensing laws created during the Great Depression. In order to legally pick up customers, a taxi must have a city issued medallion. The number of medallions is fixed at fewer than 13,000. In May, 2007, two taxi medallions were purchased at auction for $600,000 each.

    e.  **Trade restrictions.** Trade restrictions are government imposed limitations on international trade. Tariffs and quotas are often imposed on imports. This reduces the competition faced by domestic producers. Trade restrictions (see Chapter 16) are an inefficient way to redistribute income from consumers to favored producers.

2.  **Economies of scale.** **Economies of scale** exist when, as the scale of production is increased, average costs of production decrease. Economies of scale usually occur when fixed costs (e.g. a large factory) are very great. Once the fixed costs are incurred, average total cost will decrease over a large range of output.

For a new firm to successfully enter an industry where economies of scale exist, the new firm will have to operate on a large scale. This makes it difficult for a new firm to break into the market.

> **Example 5A:** If the annual market demand for widgets is 100,000 units and the most efficient factory is one large enough to produce 25,000 widgets per year, it will be difficult for a new firm to break into the widget market. To be cost competitive, a new firm would need to capture 25% of the market.

The extreme situation of economies of scale is called natural monopoly. A **natural monopoly** is an industry in which economies of scale are so important that only one firm can survive. Natural monopolies are often granted a public franchise and then are subject to government regulation. The regulation of natural monopoly is examined in Chapter 29.

> **Example 5B:** If the annual market demand for widgets is 100,000 units and the most efficient factory is one large enough to produce 100,000 widgets per year, the widget market is a natural monopoly market. Only one firm will be able to survive in the market.

3. **Exclusive ownership of an essential resource.** If one or a few firms have exclusive ownership of an essential resource, this blocks the entry of new firms into the market.

> **Example 6:** Early in the twentieth century, Alcoa (formerly Aluminum Company of America) owned or controlled most of North America's known supply of bauxite. Bauxite is the chief ore of commercial grade aluminum. Such exclusive ownership is very rare today.

## Demand and Marginal Revenue for a Monopoly

A monopoly is the lone seller of a product with no close substitutes. As the lone seller in a market, a monopoly faces the market demand curve. The market demand curve will be downward sloping. (Remember the law of demand from Chapter 3.) Thus a monopoly faces a downward sloping demand curve.

A monopoly has maximum market power. Market power is the ability to affect market price. A monopoly can sell a greater quantity at a lower price, or a lesser quantity at a higher price.

Since a monopoly must generally lower the price of all units sold in order to sell a greater quantity, the marginal revenue of each additional unit sold will be less than the unit's price. Thus, the marginal revenue curve will <u>not</u> be the same as the demand curve.

> **Example 7A:** Monop Company is a monopoly. The table on the next page shows the demand schedule for Monop. Note that Monop must lower its selling price to sell more units. The table also shows total revenue (Price x Quantity) and marginal revenue (change in total revenue from selling one additional unit of output).

| Price | Quantity | Monop Company Total Revenue | Marginal Revenue |
|-------|----------|----------------------------|------------------|
| $22 | 0 | $0 | X |
| 20 | 1 | 20 | 20 |
| 18 | 2 | 36 | 16 |
| 16 | 3 | 48 | 12 |
| 14 | 4 | 56 | 8 |
| 12 | 5 | 60 | 4 |
| 10 | 6 | 60 | 0 |
| 8 | 7 | 56 | -4 |
| 6 | 8 | 48 | -8 |

The demand curve for Monop Company is downward sloping and has a slope of –2 (for every $2 decrease in price, quantity demanded increases by 1 unit). The marginal revenue curve for Monop is also downward sloping and has a slope of –4 (for every 1 unit increase in quantity, marginal revenue decreases by $4). The demand curve and the marginal revenue curve for Monop are illustrated on the graph below:

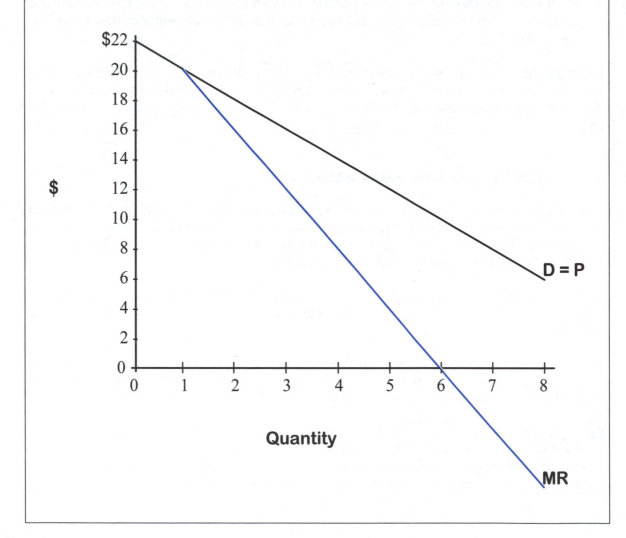

## Demand Curve and MR Curve for a Monopoly

As illustrated in Example 7A on the previous page, the demand curve and the marginal revenue curve for a monopoly are not the same curve. The marginal revenue curve will always slope downward twice as steeply as the demand curve.

In fact, any time a firm faces a downward sloping demand curve, its marginal revenue curve will be twice as steeply downward sloping as its demand curve.

## Profit-Maximization

All business firms are assumed to pursue the same chief goal: profit-maximization. The profit-maximization rule for producing output was introduced in Chapter 21.

**Profit-maximization rule** – produce the quantity of output where marginal revenue equals marginal cost.

A monopoly, like a perfect competitor, will maximize profits by producing the quantity of output where marginal revenue equals marginal cost.

---

**Example 7B:** The table below illustrates profit-maximization for Monop Company. The information for marginal revenue, marginal cost, and marginal profit (marginal revenue minus marginal cost) is detailed on the table. The table indicates that producing up to the profit-maximizing quantity (4 units) creates positive marginal profit. Producing more than the profit-maximizing quantity creates negative marginal profit.

| Price | Quantity | Marginal Revenue | Marginal Cost | Marginal Profit |
|-------|----------|------------------|---------------|-----------------|
| $22 | 0 | X | X | X |
| 20 | 1 | $20 | $5 | $15 |
| 18 | 2 | 16 | 6 | 10 |
| 16 | 3 | 12 | 7 | 5 |
| 14 | 4 | 8 | 8 | 0 |
| 12 | 5 | 4 | 9 | -5 |
| 10 | 6 | 0 | 10 | -10 |
| 8 | 7 | -4 | 11 | -15 |
| 6 | 8 | -8 | 12 | -20 |

---

The graph on the next page shows the demand curve for Monop Company and its marginal revenue and marginal cost curves. The graph indicates that the profit-maximizing quantity is 4 units. This is the quantity where marginal revenue equals marginal cost (MR = MC).

But what price will Monop charge? The price is indicated by the demand curve. If Monop produces 4 units of output, both the table above and the graph on the next page indicate that the price charged will be $14.

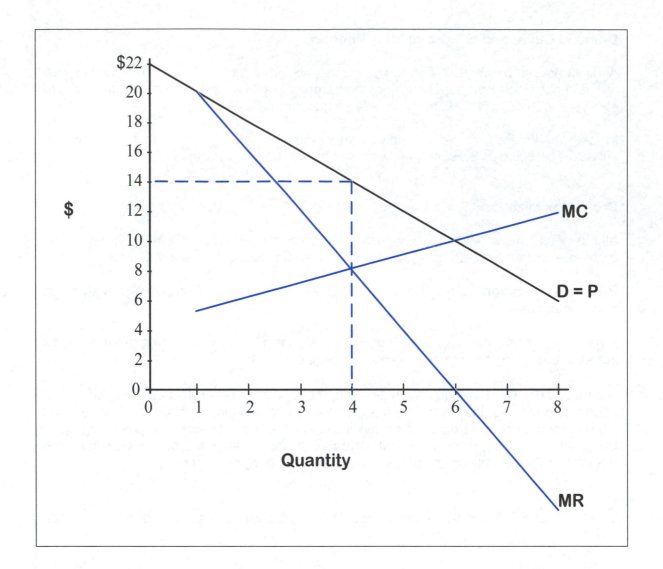

## Comparing Monopoly to Perfect Competition

Monop Company (the monopoly in this chapter) and Percomp Company (the perfect competitor in the Chapter 21; Example 5C) are similar firms. Both firms have the same costs of production. (Their marginal cost curves are identical.) And the demand curve for each firm intersects the marginal cost curve at the same point on the marginal cost curve (at $10 and 6 units of output).

Despite these similarities, the profit-maximization rule leads to different results in terms of quantity and price.

For Percomp, the profit-maximizing quantity is 6 units, and the profit-maximizing price is $10. (See the graph on page 21-5.) For Monop, the profit-maximizing quantity is 4 units, and the profit-maximizing price is $14. (See the graph above.)

The only difference between the two firms is that one (Percomp) is a perfect competitor and the other (Monop) is a monopoly. But Monop Company produces a lesser output (4 units versus 6 units) and charges a higher price ($14 versus $10) than Percomp Company. In comparison to perfect competition, monopoly results in less output at a higher price.

Monopoly and perfect competition also differ in their likelihood of earning economic profit, and in the size of that profit. This comparison is discussed in the appendix at the end of this chapter.

## The Economic Inefficiency of Monopoly

The economic efficiency rule was introduced in Chapter 21. The economic efficiency rule indicates that the ideal quantity of output occurs where marginal social benefit equals marginal social cost.

Perfect competition is the ideal (most efficient) market structure. As we saw in Chapter 21, perfect competition results in the quantity of output where price equals marginal cost and thus (assuming no externalities) where marginal social benefit equals marginal social cost.

Monopoly results in an economically inefficient quantity of output. Monopoly is inefficient because it results in a quantity of output where price exceeds marginal cost, and thus where marginal social benefit exceeds marginal social cost. A monopoly will underproduce compared to the ideal quantity of output.

> **Example 8A:** Percomp Company (the perfect competitor in Chapter 21; Example 5C) maximizes profit by producing 6 units of output. At 6 units of output, the price is $10 and the marginal cost is $10. The profit-maximizing quantity (where marginal revenue equals marginal cost) is also the economically efficient quantity (where marginal social benefit equals marginal social cost).

> **Example 8B:** Monop Company (the monopoly in this chapter) maximizes profit by producing 4 units of output. At 4 units of output, the price is $14 and the marginal cost is $8. The profit-maximizing quantity (where marginal revenue equals marginal cost) is less than the economically efficient quantity (where marginal social benefit equals marginal social cost). Society would benefit from the firm producing additional units of output as long as marginal social benefit exceeds marginal social cost.

A monopoly underproduces compared to the economically efficient quantity. This inefficiency is a type of deadweight loss. The deadweight loss of monopoly is the area between the demand curve and the marginal cost curve for the amount of underproduction.

The deadweight loss for Monop Company is highlighted on the graph on the next page:

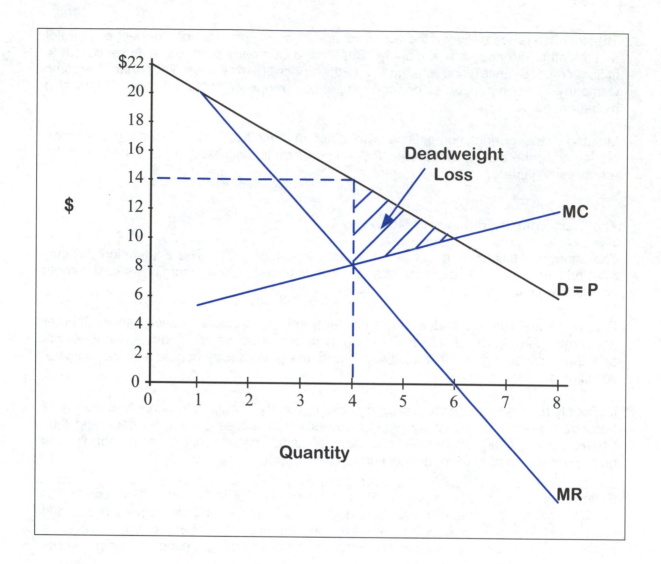

## Rent Seeking

A monopoly is in a better position to earn economic profit than is a competitive firm. If the government takes action that gives a competitive firm a monopoly position (or even some protection from competition), that action will benefit the firm. Will a firm seek such benefits from the government? If so, the firm is engaged in a socially wasteful practice called rent seeking.

**Rent seeking** – when people use resources to manipulate public policy in order to redistribute income to themselves from others.

Rent seeking may take the form of lobbying, campaign contributions, public relations efforts, etc. The rent seeking is socially wasteful because limited resources are being used, <u>not</u> to produce goods and services, but to attempt to redistribute income.

If the rent seeking is successful, the government restraints on competition (licensing requirements, trade restrictions, etc.) are also likely to be economically inefficient.

**Example 9:** Widgetworks Co. is facing greater competition from imported widgets. Widgetworks calculates that a 15% tariff on imported widgets would increase Widgetworks' annual profits by $100 million. Widgetworks will find it beneficial to spend millions of dollars on lobbying efforts, campaign contributions, public relations efforts, etc. if this will result in the government imposing a 15% tariff on imported widgets. Not only is the rent seeking by Widgetworks socially wasteful spending, but if it successfully leads to a tariff, the tariff will also be economically inefficient (see Chapter 16).

## Other Problems with Monopoly

Compared to more competitive firms, monopoly producers also tend to be:

1. **Less responsive to consumer demand.** Society wants producers to be highly responsive to consumer demand. Society wants to produce as much consumer satisfaction as possible with the limited resources available. The individual consumers are usually the best judges of what production will generate maximum consumer satisfaction. Monopoly producers tend to be less responsive to consumer demand because of the lack of competitive pressure.

**Example 10A:** A restaurant operating in a competitive market is likely to serve food that its customers enjoy. Otherwise, the customers will take their business elsewhere, and the restaurant will fail. A grade school cafeteria, facing no competition, may regularly serve the students food that they find unappealing.

2. **Less diligent to minimize costs of production.** Society wants producers to be very diligent to minimize costs of production. The basic economic problem is scarcity. Society wants to produce whatever is produced with as few resources (at as low cost) as possible. Monopoly producers tend to be less diligent to minimize costs of production because of the lack of competitive pressure.

**Example 10B:** The restaurant in Example 10A will need to be diligent to minimize its costs of production in order to successfully compete with other restaurants in the market. The grade school cafeteria, facing no competition, may be less diligent to minimize costs of production.

## Price Discrimination

A monopoly, or any firm with market power (a downward sloping demand curve), has the potential to practice price discrimination.

**Price discrimination** – occurs when a seller charges different prices to different buyers for the same good.

To see why a firm might try to practice price discrimination, we will refer back to Monop Company and Example 7B. Monop maximized profits by producing 4 units of output and charging a price of $14 for all 4 units. But what if Monop could identify which buyers would still be willing to buy if the price were higher?

If Monop raised its price to $18, 2 units would be demanded. If Monop could find a way to charge those two buyers $18 per unit and the other two buyers $14 per unit, it would increase its total revenue from $56 (4 units x $14 price) to $64 (2 units x $18 price plus 2 units x $14 price). Price discrimination allows a firm to increase its profits by gaining some of the consumer's surplus.

A firm may practice price discrimination by:

1. Making coupons and discounts available that more cost-conscious buyers will use, and that buyers willing to pay a higher price will not.

> **Example 11:** Megacorp sells Sugarbites, a popular brand of breakfast cereal. Megacorp has determined that its profit-maximizing quantity of Sugarbites is 100,000 boxes per month. Megacorp can sell 100,000 boxes of Sugarbites per month at a price of $2.75 per box. Megacorp sets the price of a box of Sugarbites at $3.25, and makes a 50¢ coupon readily available. Megacorp reasons that many buyers will be willing to pay the full price, and will not bother with the coupon. Buyers who are more cost-conscious will use the coupon. The coupon allows Megacorp to charge a higher price to less cost-conscious buyers.

2. Negotiating, beginning at a high price and working down to a lower price. Less cost-conscious buyers may stop negotiating at a higher price than the more cost-conscious buyers.

> **Example 12:** Most car dealerships set a high "sticker price" for their cars and are willing to negotiate down to a lower price. A dealership hopes to charge each buyer the highest price that he or she is willing to pay.

## Appendix: Comparing Monopoly to Perfect Competition; Profit

As noted earlier in this chapter, Monop Company (the monopoly in this chapter) and Percomp Company (the perfect competitor in Chapter 21; Example 5C) are similar firms. Both firms have the same costs of production. The demand curve for each firm intersects the marginal cost curve at the same point on the marginal cost curve.

Despite these similarities, the profit outcome for the two firms is quite different. In comparison to perfect competition, monopoly results in greater economic profit.

We saw in Chapter 21 (Example 5C) that Percomp earned an economic profit of $3. This economic profit is illustrated on a graph on page 21-9 and also on the next page.

Monop (Example 7B in this chapter) earned an economic profit of $18. Monop's total revenue was $56 (4 units x $14 selling price) and its total cost was $38 (see the table for Percomp on page 21-5). Monop's economic profit is illustrated on the next page.

In comparison to perfect competition, a monopoly is more likely to be able to sustain economic profit. We saw in Chapter 21 that it is unlikely for a perfect competitor to earn economic profit in the long run. A monopoly, if it is able to maintain its monopoly position, is likely to continue earning economic profit in the long run.

## Perfect Competitor's Economic Profit

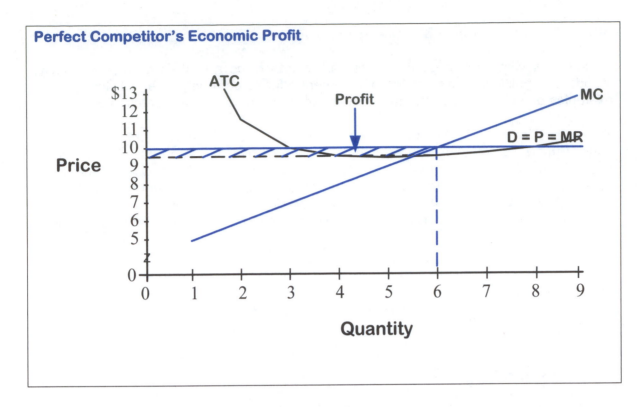

## Monopoly's Economic Profit

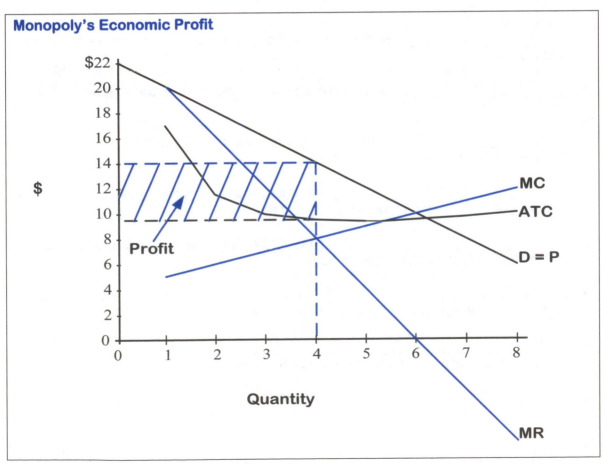

## Appendix: Corruption and Public Franchise

In countries with corrupt governments, public franchises are often granted to family, friends and political cronies of top government officials as a way to enrich them. Two examples of such corruption through the use of public franchises are detailed below.

---

**Example 13A:** Suharto was President of Indonesia from 1967 to 1998. Early in his reign, Suharto granted a political crony a monopoly over the importation, distribution, and milling of wheat and flour. Later, Suharto's daughter, Tutut, was granted the franchise to process drivers' licenses. One of Suharto's daughters-in-law was granted the franchise to produce Indonesia's mandatory identification cards. In 1999, "Time Asia" magazine reported that Suharto's family had accumulated assets worth $15 billion.

---

**Example 13B:** Ferdinand Marcos was President of the Philippines from 1966 to 1986. Marcos granted monopolies to his political cronies in various industries, including tobacco, sugar, and long distance phone service. Transparency International named Marcos the second most corrupt government head ever, after Suharto.

---

## Questions for Chapter 22

### Fill-in-the-blanks:

1. _____ is a firm that is the lone seller of a product with no close substitutes.

2. _____ to entry are factors that block the entry of new firms into a market.

3. A _____ is a government granted monopoly on the production and sale of an invention granted to the inventor.

4. A _____ is a government granted monopoly on the production and sale of a creative work granted to the creator.

5. A _____ is a permit issued by the government authorizing a person to conduct a certain type of business.

6. Economies of _____ exist when, as the scale of production is increased, average costs of production decrease.

7. A(n) _____ _____ is an industry in which economies of scale are so important that only one firm can survive.

8. _____ seeking occurs when people use resources to manipulate public policy in order to redistribute income to themselves from others.

9. _____ _____ occurs when a seller charges different prices to different buyers for the same good.

**Multiple Choice:**

_____ 1. A monopoly:
   a. has the ability to affect market price
   b. faces a downward sloping demand curve
   c. has maximum market power
   d. All of the above

_____ 2. Which of the following is an example of a legal barrier to entry?
   a. trade restrictions
   b. patent
   c. license
   d. All of the above

_____ 3. A natural monopoly is the result of:
   a. extreme economies of scale
   b. legal barriers to entry
   c. a cartel agreement
   d. All of the above

_____ 4. If a monopoly can sell ten units for $15 each or eleven units for $14 each, what is the marginal revenue of the 11$^{th}$ unit?
   a. $154
   b. $150
   c. $14
   d. $4

_____ 5. For a monopoly, the marginal revenue curve:
   a. is the same as the demand curve
   b. is horizontal
   c. is twice as steeply downward sloping as the demand curve
   d. is upward sloping

Complete the table below to answer questions 6. through 9.:

| Price | Quantity | Total Revenue | Marginal Revenue |
|---|---|---|---|
| $40 | 0 | $0 | X |
| 38 | 1 | 38 | $38 |
| 36 | 2 | 72 | 34 |
| 34 | 3 | — | — |
| 32 | 4 | — | — |
| 30 | 5 | — | — |
| 28 | 6 | — | — |

_____ 6. The total revenue when 6 units are produced is:
   a. $156
   b. $168
   c. $180
   d. $240

_____ 7. The marginal revenue of the 5th unit of output is:
   a. $30
   b. $26
   c. $22
   d. $18

_____ 8. The slope of the demand curve is:
   a. 2
   b. 0
   c. −2
   d. −4

_____ 9. The slope of the marginal revenue curve is:
   a. 2
   b. 0
   c. −2
   d. −4

_____ 10. A monopoly finds that at the present quantity of output, marginal revenue equals $7.00 and marginal cost equals $4.00. Which of the following will increase profits?
   a. leave price and output unchanged
   b. increase price and leave output unchanged
   c. increase price and decrease output
   d. decrease price and increase output

_____ 11. In comparison to perfect competition, monopoly results in:
   a. more output, higher price
   b. more output, lower price
   c. less output, higher price
   d. less output, lower price

_____ 12. Monopoly is inefficient because it results in a quantity of output:
   a. where price exceeds marginal cost
   b. where marginal social benefit exceeds marginal social cost
   c. Both of the above
   d. Neither of the above

Answer questions 13. through 16. by referring to the following information. Complete the table to answer the questions below for ZYX Company, a monopoly.

| Quantity | TC | MC | Price | TR | MR |
|---|---|---|---|---|---|
| 10 | $475 | X | $64.50 | $645 | X |
| 11 | 490 | $15 | 60 | 660 | _____ |
| 12 | 510 | _____ | 56 | _____ | _____ |
| 13 | 535 | _____ | 52 | _____ | _____ |
| 14 | 565 | _____ | 48 | _____ | _____ |
| 15 | 600 | _____ | 44 | _____ | _____ |
| 16 | 640 | _____ | 40 | _____ | _____ |

_____ 13. What is the marginal cost of the 15$^{th}$ unit of output?
- a. $40
- b. $35
- c. $30
- d. $25

_____ 14. What is the marginal revenue of the 16$^{th}$ unit of output?
- a. $-20
- b. $-12
- c. $4
- d. $12

_____ 15. What is the profit-maximizing quantity of output?
- a. 16
- b. 14
- c. 12
- d. 11

_____ 16. What profit is earned at the profit-maximizing quantity of output?
- a. $170
- b. $160
- c. $60
- d. $0

_____ 17. Monopoly producers:
- a. may attain their monopoly position through rent seeking
- b. will be very responsive to consumer demand
- c. will be very diligent to minimize costs of production
- d. All of the above

_____ 18. Price discrimination:
- a. may be achieved by making coupons and discounts available
- b. may be achieved by negotiating
- c. may allow a firm to increase its profits by gaining some of the consumer's surplus
- d. All of the above

_____ 19. In comparison to perfect competition, monopoly results in:
- a. greater economic profit
- b. the same economic profit
- c. lesser economic profit

_____ 20. In comparison to perfect competition, a monopoly is:
- a. more likely to be able to sustain economic profit
- b. just as likely to be able to sustain economic profit
- c. less likely to be able to sustain economic profit

## Problems:

1. List the three general types of barriers to entry.

2. On the graph below for a monopoly:
   (1) draw the approximate marginal revenue curve
   (2) indicate the profit-maximizing quantity and price
   (3) indicate the amount of deadweight loss

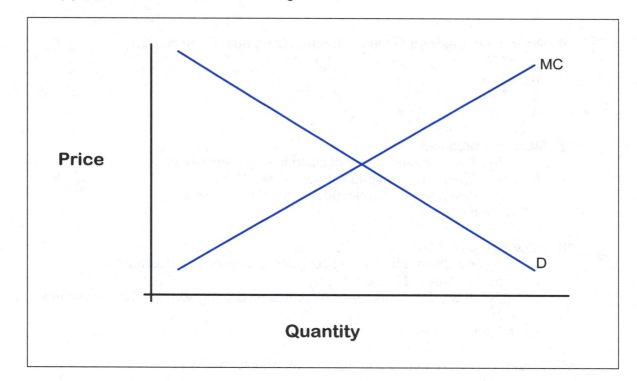

3. List some of the forms that rent seeking might take and explain why rent seeking is socially wasteful.

## Answers for Chapter 22

**Fill-in-the-blanks:**

| | |
|---|---|
| 1. Monopoly | 6. scale |
| 2. Barriers | 7. natural monopoly |
| 3. patent | 8. Rent |
| 4. copyright | 9. Price discrimination |
| 5. license | |

**Multiple Choice:**

| | | |
|---|---|---|
| 1. d. | 8. c. | 15. d. |
| 2. d. | 9. d. | 16. a. |
| 3. a. | 10. d. | 17. a. |
| 4. d. | 11. c. | 18. d. |
| 5. c. | 12. c. | 19. a. |
| 6. b. | 13. b. | 20. a. |
| 7. c. | 14. a. | |

**Problems:**

1. (1) Legal barriers
   (2) Economies of scale
   (3) Exclusive ownership of an essential resource

2.

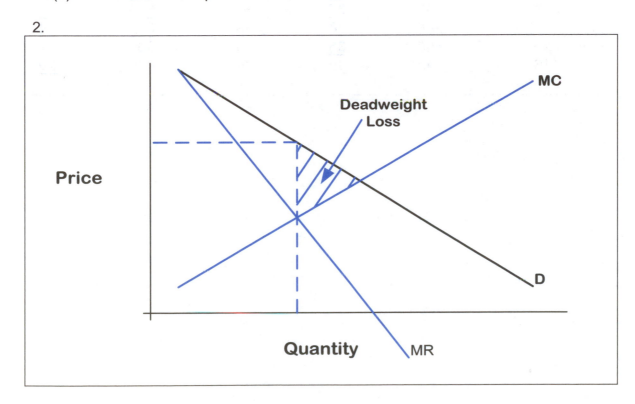

3. Rent seeking may take the form of lobbying, campaign contributions, public relations efforts, etc. Rent seeking is socially wasteful because limited resources are being used, <u>not</u> to produce goods and services, but to attempt to redistribute income. If the rent seeking is successful, the government restraints on competition are also likely to be economically inefficient.

Table for Multiple Choice Questions 6. through 9.:

| Price | Quantity | Total Revenue | Marginal Revenue |
|-------|----------|---------------|------------------|
| $40 | 0 | $0 | X |
| 38 | 1 | 38 | $38 |
| 36 | 2 | 72 | 34 |
| 34 | 3 | **102** | **30** |
| 32 | 4 | **128** | **26** |
| 30 | 5 | **150** | **22** |
| 28 | 6 | **168** | **18** |

Table for Multiple Choice Questions 13. through 16.:

| Quantity | TC | MC | Price | TR | MR |
|----------|------|------|--------|------|------|
| 10 | $475 | X | $64.50 | $645 | X |
| 11 | 490 | $15 | 60 | 660 | **$15** |
| 12 | 510 | **20** | 56 | **672** | **12** |
| 13 | 535 | **25** | 52 | **676** | **4** |
| 14 | 565 | **30** | 48 | **672** | **- 4** |
| 15 | 600 | **35** | 44 | **660** | **- 12** |
| 16 | 640 | **40** | 40 | **640** | **- 20** |

# Chapter 23  Monopolistic Competition and Oligopoly

The basic economic problem is scarcity.  Human wants are unlimited.  Resources are limited.  The basic goal in dealing with the problem of scarcity is to produce as much consumer satisfaction as possible with the limited resources available.  To achieve this goal, society must use its limited resources as efficiently as possible.  How efficiently a particular firm uses its resources will depend on the market structure that the firm operates in.

In Chapter 21, we looked at the market structure called perfect competition.  We saw that perfect competition is the ideal market structure because a perfect competitor will generally produce the economically efficient quantity of output.

In Chapter 22, we looked at the market structure called monopoly.  We saw that monopoly was economically inefficient.  A monopoly underproduces compared to the economically efficient quantity of output.  The deadweight loss of a monopoly producer is illustrated on a graph on page 22-8.

In this chapter, we look at the two market structures that fall between the extremes of perfect competition and monopoly.

## Monopolistic Competition

Falling nearer to the perfect competition end of the spectrum is the market structure called monopolistic competition.  A perfect competitor has no ability to affect market price (no market power).  A monopolistic competitor has some degree of market power.

**Monopolistic competition** – many sellers of similar products.

Like perfect competition, there are many sellers in monopolistic competition.  Unlike perfect competition, each monopolistic competitor sells a product that is similar to (but not identical to) the products of its competitors.  Since a monopolistic competitor sells a product that is different than its competitors, it will have some degree of market power (ability to affect market price).

A monopolistic competitor will be motivated to differentiate its product from its competitors' products as much as possible.

**Product differentiation** – the process of distinguishing a firm's product from similar products.

Product differentiation benefits a monopolistic competitor in two ways:

1. **Product differentiation increases the firm's market power.**  Perfect competitors sell identical products.  As a result, a perfect competitor has no market power and faces a demand curve that is perfectly elastic (horizontal).  By differentiating its product, a monopolistic competitor gains some degree of market power and puts some downward slope in its demand curve.

> **Example 1A:** Gertie's Gas and Go, located in a large city, has very little market power. It faces many competitors selling a very similar product. If Gertie raises her price by 5¢ per gallon, she will lose a lot of sales.

> **Example 1B:** Gomer's Gas and Git, located on a lonely stretch of interstate highway, has more market power. It has a more differentiated product due to its isolated location. If Gomer raises his price by 5¢ per gallon, he will not lose as many sales.

2. **Product differentiation increases the demand for the firm's product.** By differentiating its product ("our donuts are better than their donuts"), a monopolistic competitor shifts its demand curve to the right and can charge a higher price for any particular quantity of output.

> **Example 2:** Darla's Delectable Donuts develops an even more delectable donut. The consumer preference for the improved donut increases. This causes an increase in the demand for Darla's donuts.

## Demand and Marginal Revenue for a Monopolistic Competitor

Since a monopolistic competitor sells a product that is differentiated from its competitors, it will face a downward sloping demand curve. The degree of slope will depend largely on product differentiation. The more successful the monopolistic competitor is at achieving product differentiation, the more steeply its demand curve will slope downward.

> **Example 3A:** Hank's Hamburgers is one of many restaurants in College Town and sells a product very similar to that sold by many of its competitors. Hank's will have little market power.

> **Example 3B:** Elyana's Exotic Cuisine is one of many restaurants in College Town, but features a unique menu. Elyana's will have more market power than Hank's.

Since a monopolistic competitor faces a downward sloping demand curve, its marginal revenue curve will <u>not</u> be the same as its demand curve. As discussed in Chapter 22, any time a firm faces a downward sloping demand curve, its marginal revenue curve will be twice as steeply downward sloping.

## Profit-Maximization for a Monopolistic Competitor

All business firms are assumed to pursue the same chief goal: profit-maximization. A monopolistic competitor will maximize profits by producing the quantity of output where marginal revenue equals marginal cost.

> **Example 4A:** Monocomp Company is a monopolistic competitor. The graph on the next page illustrates profit-maximization for Monocomp:

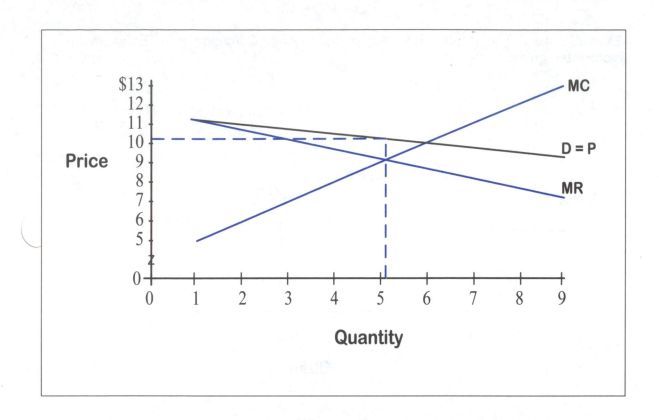

## Comparing Monopolistic Competition to Perfect Competition

Monocomp Company (the monopolistic competitor in Example 4A) and Percomp Company (the perfect competitor in Chapter 21; Example 5C) are very similar firms. Both firms have the same costs of production. (Their marginal cost curves are identical.) And the demand curve for each firm intersects the marginal cost curve at the same point on the marginal cost curve (at $10 and 6 units of output). Despite these similarities, the profit-maximization rule leads to different results in terms of price and quantity.

For Percomp (the perfect competitor in Chapter 21), the profit-maximizing quantity is 6 units, and the profit-maximizing price is $10. For Monocomp (the monopolistic competitor in Example 4A), the profit-maximizing quantity is less than 6 units and the profit-maximizing price is slightly greater than $10. Thus, in comparison to perfect competition, monopolistic competition results in less output at a higher price.

## The Economic Inefficiency of Monopolistic Competition

Monopolistic competition, like monopoly, is economically inefficient. Monopolistic competition is inefficient because it results in a quantity of output where price exceeds marginal cost, and thus where marginal social benefit exceeds marginal social cost.

Monopolistic competition is not as inefficient as monopoly. Monopolistic competition results in a smaller deadweight loss than monopoly. The deadweight loss is the area between the demand curve and the marginal cost curve for the amount of underproduction.

**Example 4B:** The deadweight loss of Monocomp Company from Example 4A is highlighted on the graph below:

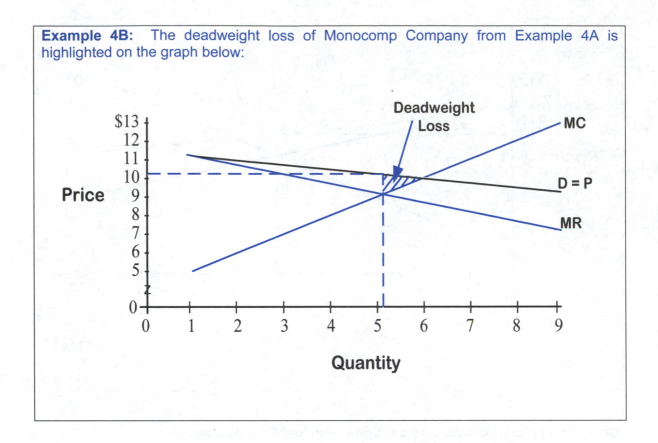

## Monopolistic Competition and Profits in the Long Run

We saw in Chapter 21 that perfect competitors were unlikely to earn economic profit in the long run. If the market price were high enough that firms earned economic profit, new firms would be attracted to the market. As new firms enter the market, market supply increases, and market price decreases. Eventually, the price will reach the point of zero economic profit (a normal profit).

The same type of price adjustment is likely in monopolistic competition. Once again, if the market price is high enough that firms earn economic profit, new firms will be attracted to the market. As new firms enter the market, market supply increases, and market price decreases. Eventually, the price will reach the point of zero economic profit for most firms.

**Example 5:** The market price of donuts in a particular market is 65¢. At this price, the average firm in the market is able to earn economic profit. The economic profit available in this market attracts new firms into the market. The increased supply of donuts drives the market price down to 60¢. At this price, the average firm in the market earns zero economic profit.

A monopolistic competitor will have to achieve a great deal of product differentiation in order to maintain a price high enough to earn economic profit in the long run.

## Oligopoly

Falling nearer to the monopoly end of the market structure spectrum is the market structure called oligopoly. An oligopoly will not have as much market power as a monopoly, unless the firms in the industry conspire to behave like a monopoly.

**Oligopoly** – an industry dominated by a few mutually interdependent firms.

Because there are only a few firms in an oligopolistic industry, each firm produces a significant quantity of output. Thus, each firm's production decision affects market price, and the other firms in the industry. This is mutual interdependence. Each firm's actions affect the other firms.

> **Example 6:** Nguyen's Widgets is one of four firms in the widget market. Nguyen's tries to increase its market share by lowering its price by 10%. Nguyen's action will affect the three other firms in the widget market. If the other firms lower their prices by 20%, Nguyen's may lose market share. Nguyen's is affected by the actions of the other firms. This is mutual interdependence.

Why does an industry end up being dominated by a few firms? Oligopoly usually results from barriers to entry. Remember (from Chapter 22) that barriers to entry are factors that block the entry of new firms into a market. Economies of scale is the barrier that most commonly leads to oligopoly.

## Theories of Oligopoly Behavior

There is not a consensus among economists as to how oligopoly firms behave. We will look at three different theories of oligopoly behavior.

**1. Kinked demand curve theory.** Kinked demand curve theory was developed in the 1930s by Paul Sweezy. This theory assumes that if one of the oligopoly firms lowers its price, the other firms will match the price reduction (in order to maintain market share). But if one of the oligopoly firms raises its price, the other firms will <u>not</u> match the price increase. The other firms can gain market share by simply maintaining their price.

The different response of competitors to an increase in price versus a decrease in price will cause an oligopoly to face a demand curve that is kinked at its current price and quantity. If an oligopoly increases its price, it will see a relatively large decrease in quantity demanded, since its competitors do <u>not</u> match price increases. Thus, an oligopoly faces a relatively elastic demand curve for an increase in price.

If an oligopoly decreases its price, it will see a relatively small increase in quantity demanded, since its competitors do match the price decrease. Thus, an oligopoly faces a relatively inelastic demand curve for a decrease in price. The graph in Example 7A on the next page illustrates the kinked demand curve.

Any time a firm faces a downward sloping demand curve, its marginal revenue curve will be twice as steeply downward sloping. But an oligopoly faces a demand curve that is kinked at the current price and quantity. What will its marginal revenue curve look like?

The graph in Example 7A illustrates that an oligopoly has a marginal revenue curve with two separate portions, corresponding to the two differently sloped portions of its demand curve.

**Example 7A:** The graph below represents the demand curve and the marginal revenue curve for an oligopoly, according to the kinked demand curve theory.

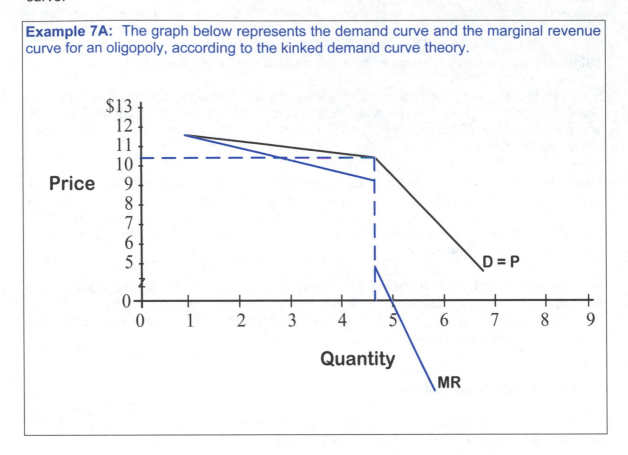

The graph in Example 7A above illustrates that the kink in the demand curve results in a gap in the marginal revenue curve at the current quantity of output.

An oligopoly will attempt to produce the profit-maximizing quantity of output. This occurs where marginal revenue equals marginal cost.

Since there is a gap in an oligopoly's marginal revenue curve, profit-maximization will occur where the marginal cost curve passes through the gap in the marginal revenue curve. This is illustrated in Example 7B below.

**Example 7B:** The graph on the next page represents profit-maximization for an oligopoly, according to the kinked demand curve theory. Profit-maximization occurs where the marginal cost curve passes through the gap in the marginal revenue curve. This occurs at a quantity of slightly less than 5 units, and corresponds to a price of slightly higher than $10.

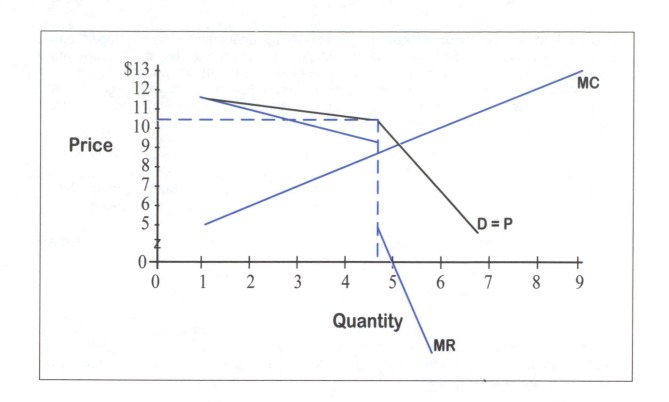

What if there is a change in marginal cost? Notice on the graph in Example 7C below that a shift in the marginal cost curve (from $MC_1$ to $MC_2$) may have <u>no</u> effect on price or quantity. As long as the marginal cost curve passes through the gap in the marginal revenue curve, an oligopoly will continue to produce the same quantity at the same price. Thus, the kinked demand curve theory predicts "sticky" prices for an oligopoly.

**Example 7C:** A change in marginal cost may result in <u>no</u> change in price or quantity.

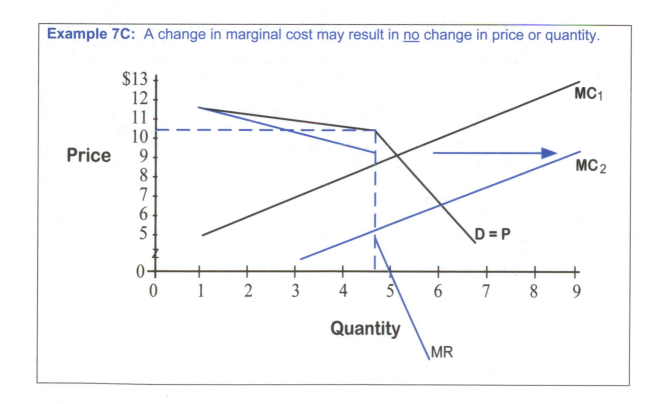

**2. Unkinked demand curve theory.** Research by economist George Stigler cast doubt on the kinked demand curve theory. Stigler's research disputed the fundamental assumption that oligopolists match price decreases but do <u>not</u> match price increases. If this assumption is incorrect, then there is no kink in the demand curve, no gap in the marginal revenue curve, and no "sticky" prices. Thus, according to Stigler, oligopoly is similar to monopolistic competition.

**3. Cartel theory.** A **cartel** is an organization through which members jointly make decisions about prices and production. Competing firms can benefit from forming a cartel. A cartel sets output for the industry, as would a monopoly. Industry output will be reduced by the cartel, price will be increased, and industry profits will be increased.

> **Example 8:** In the 1950s, General Electric, Westinghouse, and other firms maintained a cartel agreement in selling heavy electrical equipment to the government. The cartel members determined the firm to enter the "low" bid based on the phases of the moon. Research estimated the cost of the cartel to consumers as about $175 million per year.

After setting output for the industry, the cartel allocates production to member firms. This may be difficult, as each member of the cartel would like to increase production (in response to the higher cartel price), but industry production must be decreased (to achieve the higher cartel price).

In America, most cartel agreements would be illegal as a violation of antitrust law. Even if the cartel is legal, it will still prove difficult to maintain, for two reasons:

**(1) Noncartel competition**. If the cartel successfully sets a production level for the industry that yields high profits, those high profits will tend to attract new firms to the industry. This noncartel competition will drive the industry price back down.

> **Example 9:** The Organization of the Petroleum Exporting Countries (OPEC) acted as a cartel to increase oil prices from about $3 per barrel in 1973 to about $35 per barrel in 1981. This led to increased production by non-OPEC countries. OPEC's share of the world oil market fell from about 60% in 1973 to under 40% in 1985.

The cartel will need some type of barrier to entry to keep noncartel competition out of the industry. Economies of scale may make it extremely difficult for small firms to enter the industry. Sometimes, the government will create legal barriers that block the entry of new firms. This may be justified as preventing "cutthroat competition".

**(2) The tendency of cartel members to "cheat" on the agreement**. As mentioned before, the cartel can increase the price in the industry by reducing industry production. The members of the cartel must agree to cut production for this to work.

But each member of the cartel can increase its own profits by "cheating" on the cartel agreement and producing more. The cartel will need to come up with some method to identify and punish cheaters, or the cartel agreement is likely to fall apart.

> **Example 10:** Throughout its history, OPEC has had trouble maintaining its production agreements. OPEC members have often cheated on the cartel agreement by producing in excess of their production quotas.

The tendency of cartel members to "cheat" on a cartel agreement is an example of a "prisoners' dilemma". The concept of prisoners' dilemma is explained in the appendix on game theory below.

## The Economic Inefficiency of Oligopoly

In each of the theories of oligopoly behavior, an oligopoly faces a downward sloping demand curve. As a result, oligopoly will be economically inefficient. Oligopoly is inefficient for the same reason that monopoly and monopolistic competition are inefficient. Oligopoly results in a quantity of output where price exceeds marginal cost, and thus where marginal social benefit exceeds marginal social cost.

The deadweight loss of oligopoly will be less than that of monopoly, unless the oligopoly firms form a successful cartel.

## Appendix: Game Theory

There is not a consensus among economists as to how oligopoly firms behave. We looked at three different theories of oligopoly behavior in this chapter. Oligopoly behavior can also be analyzed through the use of game theory.

**Game theory** – a method for analyzing strategic behavior.

Game theory was developed by mathematician John von Neumann. The groundbreaking book, "Theory of Games and Economic Behavior" was published by von Neumann and economist Oskar Morgenstern in 1944. Game theory is a method for analyzing strategic behavior. The mutual interdependence of oligopoly firms forces them to use strategic behavior in their decision making process.

> **Example 11:** Nguyen's Widgets is one of four firms in the widget market. If Nguyen's tries to increase its market share by lowering its price by 10%, Nguyen's action will affect the three other firms in the widget market. If the other firms respond by lowering their prices by 20%, Nguyen's may lose market share. Nguyen's is affected by the actions of the other firms, so Nguyen's will have to think strategically in deciding whether to lower the price of its widgets.

A famous "game" that illustrates the power of game theory in analyzing strategic behavior is called "prisoners' dilemma". The following is an example of the prisoners' dilemma game.

> **Example 12:** Bo and Luke are caught red-handed committing a crime (breaking and entering). The district attorney of Hazzard County suspects that they are also guilty of committing a more serious crime (the manufacture, transportation, and sale of illegal beverages). The D.A. has sufficient evidence to convict Bo and Luke of breaking and entering, but does not have sufficient evidence to convict them of the more serious crime.

If Bo and Luke do not confess that they have committed the more serious crime, they will be convicted of the lesser crime, and each will be sentenced to two years in prison. However, the D.A. believes that Bo and Luke can be persuaded to confess to the more serious crime.

The D.A. places Bo and Luke in separate cells so that they cannot communicate with each other. Then the D.A. speaks to Bo: "If you confess to the more serious crime and Luke does not confess, you will be given probation and Luke will be convicted of the more serious crime (based on your confession) and will be sentenced to ten years in prison. If Luke confesses to the more serious crime and you do not confess, Luke will be given probation and you will be convicted and will be sentenced to ten years in prison. If you both confess, you will each be sentenced to five years in prison."

The D.A. then presents the same alternatives to Luke.

Will Bo and Luke confess that they have committed the more serious crime or will they not confess?

The payoff matrix below illustrates the strategies available to Bo and Luke and the payoff (results) of each pair of strategies:

|  |  | Bo's Strategies | |
| --- | --- | --- | --- |
|  |  | Confess | Not Confess |
| Luke's Strategies | Confess | Bo - 5 years  Luke - 5 years | Bo - 10 years  Luke - probation |
|  | Not Confess | Bo - probation  Luke - 10 years | Bo - 2 years  Luke - 2 years |

Bo will reason as follows: "If Luke confesses, then the best strategy for me is to confess. That way, I will only be sentenced to five years in prison instead of ten years. And if Luke does not confess, then the best strategy for me is to confess. That way, I will receive probation instead of being sentenced to two years in prison." Thus, Bo's dominant strategy is to confess.

**Dominant strategy** – a strategy that always yields the best result regardless of the strategies of the other players.

Luke will reason the same way as Bo. Luke's dominant strategy is also to confess. Thus, the Nash equilibrium will be for Bo and Luke to both confess, and to both receive a five year prison sentence.

**Nash equilibrium** – the outcome when each game player has chosen their best strategy, assuming that all other players have also chosen their best strategies.

Now we see the dilemma in the prisoners' dilemma. The Nash equilibrium is for Bo and Luke to both confess. This is the best strategy for each player. But it does not yield the best result. If both players would not confess, they would each be sentenced to only two years in prison. When they both confess, they are each sentenced to five years in prison.

The prisoners' dilemma game can illustrate why members of a cartel are likely to "cheat" on the cartel agreement. Each member of a cartel will realize that the best result for the group will occur if all cartel members honor the cartel agreement. But the dominant strategy for each member of the cartel is to "cheat" on the cartel agreement.

**Example 13:** OPEC's oil revenues will be maximized if the members of OPEC obey their production quotas. But each member of OPEC can maximize its own revenues by producing more than their quota.

Members of the cartel may resist the temptation to cheat if they are likely to be caught and punished by the cartel, or if they fear that their cheating will cause the cartel to collapse. The more members that are in the cartel, and the more difficult it is for the cartel to detect and punish cheaters, the more likely that cartel members will cheat on the cartel agreement.

## Appendix: The NCAA Cartel

On its website, the National Collegiate Athletic Association (NCAA) describes itself as "a voluntary organization through which the nation's colleges and universities govern their athletic programs". The website does not mention that the NCAA is also a cartel.

Unlike OPEC, the NCAA is not a selling cartel. Each college or university is free to set ticket prices for its athletic events as it sees fit.

**Example 14:** The price for a season ticket to University of Alabama football games was $355 for the 2008 season. The price for a season ticket to University of Alabama at Birmingham football games was $125 for the 2008 season.

The NCAA is a buying cartel. The members of the NCAA have agreed among themselves to a maximum price for the basic resource needed to produce college athletic events – college athletes.

NCAA rules limit financial aid to athletes to the "cost of attendance" (e.g. tuition and fees, room and board, books and supplies). This financial aid package may be worth thousands or even tens of thousands of dollars per year to the athlete. But it does not reflect a free market price.

We will see in Chapter 24 that the demand for a resource (like a college athlete) depends on how much revenue that resource can generate. The big-revenue college sports (football and basketball) can generate tens of millions of dollars in revenue per year for their colleges. Of course, a college's football or basketball program will generate more revenue the more successful the team is.

---

**Example 15:** At the end of the 2006 season, the University of Notre Dame football team played in the Sugar Bowl, and received a payout of $21.5 million. If Notre Dame had played in the Insight Bowl (as it did following the 2004 season) its payout would have been only $1.2 million.

---

A successful football or basketball program requires superior college athletes. A top college football or basketball player may generate millions of dollars in revenue per year for their college. One wonders how much additional revenue the Syracuse University basketball program would have generated if Carmelo Anthony had spent four years at Syracuse instead of only one. One wonders how much a college basketball program would have been willing to pay in a free market for the services of Lebron James for four years. One wonders how much the Ohio State University would have been willing to pay Greg Oden to remain in college for three more years, if NCAA rules permitted such payment.

The effect of the NCAA buying cartel is that NCAA members get their college athletes in the big-revenue sports at below free market prices. As a result, income is redistributed from the athletes in the big-revenue sports to the colleges' athletic departments. This redistribution benefits the employees of the athletic department, especially the coaches, and also benefits athletes in non-revenue sports.

---

**Example 16:** The University of Alabama football program employs ten coaches, headed by Nick Saban, who is paid $4 million per year. The Alabama athletic department fields 19 varsity sports teams, including cross country, golf, swimming & diving, and women's rowing.

---

As a cartel, the NCAA runs into predictable difficulties. The NCAA struggles against noncartel competition. Their top football and basketball players often leave school early for the NFL or the NBA. These players might stay in college longer if the rules allowed the colleges to pay their athletes a competitive salary.

There is a strong tendency for the NCAA members to "cheat" on the cartel agreement by offering payment to athletes in excess of the "cost of attendance". There is a powerful incentive for a college coach to violate the NCAA rules, knowing that an athlete who may generate millions of dollars in revenue for their college (and also boost the coach's career) might be attracted to their college by a relatively small extra payment. There is also a powerful incentive for a college booster to violate the NCAA rules, knowing that an athlete who may generate wins over a hated rival and bring athletic glory to their college might be attracted to their college at the price of a "no-show" job or access to a nice automobile.

---

**Example 17:** In 2008, nineteen NCAA Division I-A athletic programs were on probation for violating NCAA rules.

---

## Questions for Chapter 23

### Fill-in-the-blanks:

1. _____ _____ is many sellers of similar products.

2. _____ _____ is the process of distinguishing a firm's product from similar products.

3. _____ is an industry dominated by a few mutually interdependent firms.

4. A _____ is an organization through which members jointly make decisions about prices and production.

5. _____ _____ is a method for analyzing strategic behavior.

6. _____ _____ is a strategy that always yields the best result regardless of the strategies of the other players.

7. _____ _____ is the outcome when each game player has chosen their best strategy, assuming that all other players have also chosen their best strategies.

### Multiple Choice:

____ 1. Product differentiation benefits a monopolistic competitor by:
   a. increasing the firm's market power
   b. increasing the demand for the firm's product
   c. Both of the above
   d. Neither of the above

____ 2. Like perfect competition, monopolistic competition:
   a. has many sellers
   b. has no market power
   c. Both of the above
   d. Neither of the above

____ 3. For a monopolistic competitor:
   a. the demand curve and the marginal revenue curve are the same
   b. price equals marginal revenue
   c. profit-maximization occurs at the economically efficient quantity
   d. None of the above

_____ 4. In comparison to perfect competition, monopolistic competition results in:
   a. more output, at a lower price
   b. more output, at a higher price
   c. less output, at a higher price
   d. less output, at a lower price

_____ 5. Monopolistic competition is:
   a. economically efficient, like perfect competition
   b. economically inefficient, like monopoly
   c. not as inefficient as monopoly
   d. Both b. and c. Above

_____ 6. Monopolistic competition results in a quantity of output where:
   a. price equals marginal cost
   b. marginal social benefit is less than marginal social cost
   c. Both of the above
   d. Neither of the above

_____ 7. In the long run, a monopolistic competitor is likely to earn:
   a. a small economic loss
   b. zero economic profit
   c. a small economic profit
   d. a large economic profit

_____ 8. The kinked demand curve theory assumes that other firms:
   a. will match price decreases, but not price increases
   b. will match price increases, but not price decreases
   c. will not match either price increases or price decreases
   d. will match both price increases and price decreases

_____ 9. The kinked demand curve theory:
   a. results in a gap in the marginal revenue curve
   b. predicts "sticky" prices for oligopoly
   c. has been criticized by George Stigler
   d. All of the above

_____ 10. If the firms in an oligopolistic industry form a cartel:
   a. industry output will be reduced
   b. price will be increased
   c. industry profits will be increased
   d. All of the above

_____ 11. Which of the following factors can make a cartel difficult to maintain?
   a. noncartel competition
   b. the tendency of cartel members to "cheat" on the agreement
   c. Both of the above
   d. Neither of the above

_____ 12. An oligopoly produces:
   a. the quantity of output where price equals marginal cost
   b. more output than perfect competition
   c. where marginal social benefit equals marginal social cost
   d. None of the above

_____ 13. An oligopoly produces a quantity of output:
   a. greater than the economically efficient quantity
   b. equal to the economically efficient quantity
   c. less than the economically efficient quantity

_____ 14. Game theory:
   a. is a method for analyzing strategic behavior
   b. was developed by Stephen Hawking
   c. Both of the above
   d. Neither of the above

_____ 15. The Nash equilibrium in the prisoners' dilemma game:
   a. is for both prisoners to confess
   b. does not yield the best result for the prisoners
   c. Both of the above
   d. Neither of the above

_____ 16. A cartel is more likely to be successful if:
   a. there are many members in the cartel
   b. members in the cartel who cheat are likely to be caught and punished by
      the cartel
   c. Both of the above
   d. Neither of the above

_____ 17. The NCAA:
   a. limits the financial aid to college athletes to "fifty percent of the revenue
      generated by the athletic program"
   b. limits the maximum ticket prices that colleges can charge for athletic
      events
   c. limits the salaries that colleges can pay their coaches
   d. None of the above

_____ 18. The NCAA rules that limit the financial aid to college athletes:
   a. redistribute income from the football and basketball players to the
      coaches
   b. redistribute income from the football and basketball players to the athletes
      in non-revenue sports
   c. Both of the above
   d. Neither of the above

**Problems:**

1.  Explain the mutual interdependence of oligopoly firms.

2.  On the graph below for a monopolistic competitor:
    (1) Draw the approximate marginal revenue curve.
    (2) Indicate the profit-maximizing quantity and price.

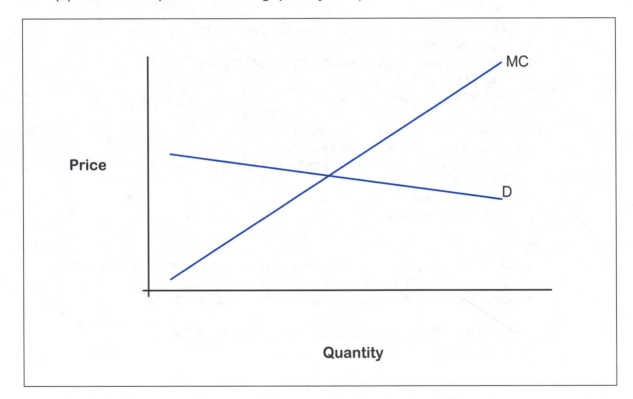

3.  List two reasons that even a legal cartel will prove difficult to maintain.

4. On the graph below, based on the kinked demand curve theory of oligopoly:
   (1) draw the approximate marginal revenue curve and indicate the profit-maximizing price and quantity
   (2) explain what will happen to price and quantity if the marginal cost curve shifts slightly to the right.

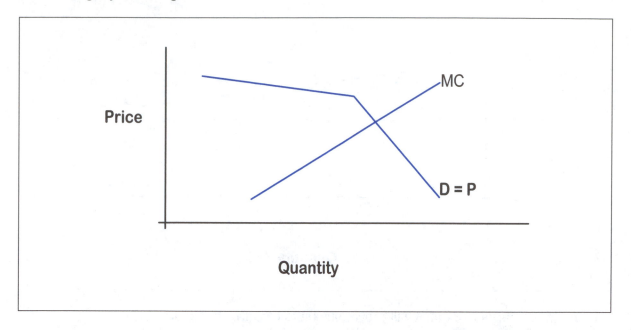

## Answers for Chapter 23

**Fill-in-the-blanks:**   1. Monopolistic competition   5. Game theory
2. Product differentiation   6. Dominant strategy
3. Oligopoly   7. Nash equilibrium
4. cartel

**Multiple Choice:**   1. c.       7. b.       13. c.
2. a.       8. a.       14. a.
3. d.       9. d.       15. c.
4. c.      10. d.       16. b.
5. d.      11. c.       17. d.
6. d.      12. d.       18. c.

## Problems:

1. Because there are only a few firms in an oligopoly market, each firm produces a significant quantity of output. Thus, each firm's production decision affects market price, and the other firms in the industry. This is mutual interdependence. Each firm's actions affect the other firms.

2.

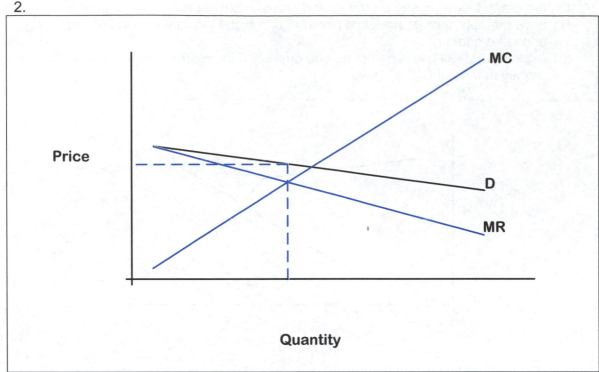

3. Even if a cartel is legal, it will prove difficult to maintain because of:
   (1) Noncartel competition
   (2) The tendency of cartel members to "cheat" on the agreement

4.
   (1)

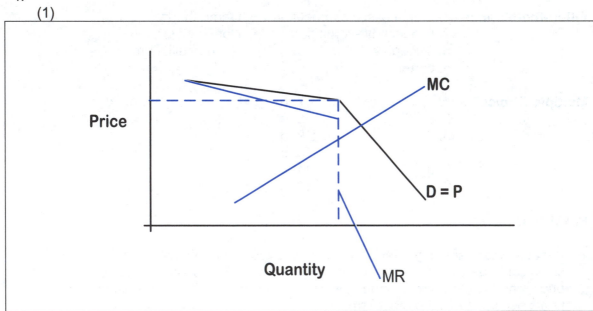

   (2) If the marginal cost curve shifts slightly to the right, but still passes through the gap in the marginal revenue curve, the price and quantity will be unchanged.

# Chapter 24  Factor Markets

The basic economic problem is scarcity. Human wants are unlimited. Resources are limited. This chapter and the next two examine the markets for resources (factors of production). In a product market, equilibrium price and quantity for the product is determined by the demand for and the supply of the product. In a factor (resource) market, equilibrium is determined by the demand for and the supply of the factor.

## Demand for a Factor

The demand for a factor (labor, land, capital, entrepreneurship) is a derived demand. It is derived from (depends on) the demand for the product that the factor produces.

> **Example 1:** In 2007, the 25 highest paid NBA players earned an average salary of $17 million each. All the players in the WNBA earned a total salary of about $10 million. Why are NBA players paid so much more than WNBA players? Because there is a much greater consumer demand for NBA games than for WNBA games.

If the demand for a product changes, the demand for the factors that produce that product will change. If there is an increase in the demand for iPhones, there will be an increase in the demand for the factors (labor, capital, etc.) that produce iPhones.

This chapter focuses on perfectly competitive labor markets. The labor demand for a particular employer depends on the marginal revenue product of labor for that employer.

**Marginal revenue product (MRP)** – the change in total revenue from employing an additional factor unit.

One way to calculate the marginal revenue product of each additional unit of labor is to calculate the total revenue generated with different quantities of labor. The MRP of labor is the change in total revenue for each additional unit of labor.

> **Example 2:** Percomp Company, a perfect competitor, produces Gadgets, which it sells for $10 each. The following table details the results for Percomp Company from employing different numbers of workers.
>
> | Workers | Gadget Output | MPP | Total Revenue (P x Q) | Marginal Revenue Product |
> |---------|---------------|-----|-----------------------|--------------------------|
> | 0 | 0 | X | $0 | X |
> | 1 | 24 | 24 | 240 | $240 |
> | 2 | 44 | 20 | 440 | 200 |
> | 3 | 60 | 16 | 600 | 160 |
> | 4 | 72 | 12 | 720 | 120 |
> | 5 | 80 | 8 | 800 | 80 |
> | 6 | 84 | 4 | 840 | 40 |

Notice on the table in Example 2 that the marginal revenue product of each worker is the change in total revenue from employing that worker. For example, when the fifth worker is added, total revenue increases from $720 to $800. Thus, the MRP of Worker 5 is $80.

A second way to calculate the MRP of each additional unit of labor is to multiply the marginal physical product (MPP) of the labor unit by the marginal revenue of the output.

In Example 2, Percomp Company is a perfect competitor. Thus, the marginal revenue of the output is the same as the selling price ($10 per Gadget). Multiplying this amount by the MPP of each worker gives the MRP of each worker. For example, Worker 4 has an MRP of $120, which is the marginal revenue of $10 per Gadget multiplied by the MPP of 12 units for Worker 4.

For the workers in Example 2, the MPP decreases as additional workers are added. This is due to the law of diminishing marginal returns. (As larger amounts of a variable input are combined with fixed inputs, eventually the MPP of the variable input declines.)

Since the MPP of the workers is decreasing, the MRP of the workers is also decreasing. Thus, the MRP curve will always eventually slope downward due to the law of diminishing marginal returns.

In Example 2, how many workers would Percomp Company employ in order to maximize profits? We can't determine the answer to that question based solely on the marginal revenue product generated by the workers. We also need to know the additional cost incurred by employing each additional worker. This amount is the marginal factor cost (MFC).

**Marginal factor cost (MFC)** – the additional cost from employing an additional factor unit.

A perfectly competitive labor employer is a small employer in a large labor market. A perfectly competitive labor employer will have no market power (no ability to affect the wage rate in the labor market). Thus, a perfectly competitive labor employer can hire additional workers without affecting the wage rate in the market.

> **Example 3:** Percomp Company (from Example 2) is a perfectly competitive employer of labor. If Percomp's cost of hiring its first worker is $80 per day, the cost of hiring each additional worker will be $80 per day, and the marginal factor cost of each worker will be the same as the wage rate ($80).

## Profit-Maximization Rule for Employing Factors

In Chapter 21, we introduced the profit-maximization rule for producing output. The rule: Produce the quantity of output where marginal revenue equals marginal cost.

The profit-maximization rule for employing factors is similar, but the terminology is different. Once again, it is profitable to employ a factor if it generates more marginal revenue than marginal cost.

The marginal revenue generated by employing an additional factor unit is called marginal revenue product. The marginal cost incurred by employing an additional factor unit is called marginal factor cost. Thus, to maximize profits, a producer employs additional factor units up to the quantity where marginal revenue product equals marginal factor cost (MRP = MFC).

**Example 4:** The graph below shows the marginal revenue product (MRP) curve for Percomp Company (from Examples 2 and 3). If the wage is initially $80 per day, then $MFC_1$ is the initial marginal factor cost curve. The profit-maximizing quantity of workers would be indicated by the intersection of MRP and $MFC_1$. Thus, five workers would be employed.

If the wage rate increases to $130 per day, then $MFC_2$ is the new marginal factor cost curve. The profit-maximizing quantity of workers would be indicated by the intersection of MRP and $MFC_2$. Thus, three workers would be employed. Notice that the MRP of Worker 3 ($160) exceeds the MFC ($130). But Worker 4 would <u>not</u> be employed, since the MRP of Worker 4 ($120) is less than the MFC ($130).

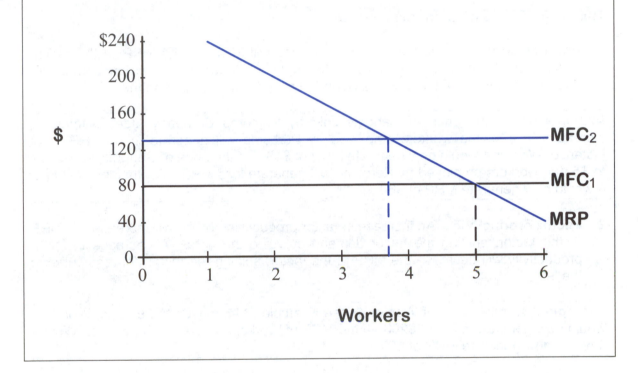

## Demand Curve for a Factor

In Example 4, as the price (wage rate) paid for labor increased, the number of workers employed decreased. We moved upward along the MRP curve to a higher wage rate and a lesser quantity of labor demanded.

The MRP curve tells the employer how many workers to employ at different wage rates. A curve that tells a buyer how many units to buy at different prices is a demand curve. Thus, the demand curve for a factor is that factor's MRP curve.

Understanding that the demand for a factor depends on the MRP of the factor is essential to understanding factor markets. Why does a 2 acre lot in Dallas, Texas have a higher rental price than a 2 acre lot in Bugtussle, Oklahoma? Because the lot in Dallas can generate more MRP. Why is the salary of an NBA player greater than the salary of a WNBA player? Because the NBA player can generate more MRP.

**Example 5:** Dale and Mack are both employees at the University of Texas. Dale has a Ph.D. in economics from the University of California at Berkeley. Mack has a bachelor's degree in education from Florida State University. Which employee would you guess is higher paid? By the way, Dale's last name is Stahl, and he is the Chair of the Economics Department. Mack's last name is Brown, and he is the head football coach.

## Determinants of Factor Demand

The determinants of factor demand cause the MRP of a factor to increase or decrease. Thus, the factor demand curve (MRP curve) shifts to the right (an increase in factor demand) or to the left (a decrease in factor demand).

**The determinants of factor demand are:**

1. **Product price.** An increase in product price will increase the MRP of the factor, shifting the factor demand curve to the right. A decrease in product price will decrease the MRP of the factor, shifting the factor demand curve to the left.

**Example 6A:** If the price of Gadgets sold by Percomp Company (see Example 2) increases to $15, the workers employed by Percomp will generate more MRP. For instance, Worker 4 would now generate MRP of $180. If the price of Gadgets decreases to $5, the workers employed by Percomp will generate less MRP. For instance, Worker 4 would now generate MRP of $60.

2. **Factor productivity.** An increase in factor productivity (MPP) will increase the MRP of the factor, shifting the factor demand curve to the right. A decrease in factor productivity will decrease the MRP of the factor, shifting the factor demand curve to the left.

**Example 6B:** If the MPP of Worker 4 (see Example 2) increases to 20 units, Worker 4 would now generate MRP of $200. If the MPP of Worker 4 decreases to 5 units, Worker 4 would now generate MRP of $50

3. **Prices of related factors.** A change in the price of a factor that is a substitute for or a complement to the factor being examined will shift the demand curve for that factor. The demand curve for a factor will shift in the same direction as the change in price for a substitute factor and in the opposite direction as the change in price for a complementary factor.

**Example 6C:** A decrease in the price of word processors would cause a decrease in the demand for typewriters (a substitute factor). A decrease in the price of computers would cause an increase in the demand for computer programmers (a complementary factor).

## Value of the Marginal Product

The value to society of an additional unit of output is called the marginal social benefit. Marginal social benefit is generally measured by the price of the product. What is the value to society of the output produced by the marginal factor? The value to society of the output produced by the marginal factor is called the value of the marginal product (VMP).

Value of the marginal product is equal to the price of the product times the MPP of the factor. The price of the product indicates how greatly society values the product. The MPP of the factor indicates how many additional units of the product the factor produces.

> **Example 7A:** In Example 2, the price of the Gadgets is $10 and the MPP of Worker 3 is 16 Gadgets. Thus, the VMP of Worker 3 is $160.

Since the price of the output will always be greater than or equal to the marginal revenue of the output, the VMP of a factor is always at least as great as the factor's MRP. Thus, an employee who generates $50,000 of MRP for his or her employer is also generating at least $50,000 of VMP for society.

> **Example 7B:** In Example 2, the MRP of Worker 4 is $120 (MR of $10 times MPP of 12 units). The VMP of Worker 4 is also $120 (Price of $10 times MPP of 12 units).

## Cost-Minimizing Combination of Factors

Producers will attempt to employ the combination of factors that will produce the desired output at the minimum cost of production. To achieve the cost-minimizing combination of factors, producers will consider factor productivity (MPP) for each factor and the price of each factor. At the cost-minimizing combination of factors, the ratio of MPP to factor price will be the same for all factors.

> **Example 8:** Alpha Co. employs two factors, Factor A and Factor B. The MPP of Factor A is 50 units. The MPP of Factor B is 100 units. The price of Factor A is $1. The price of Factor B is $10. Is Alpha employing the cost-minimizing combination of Factors A and B? No. The ratio of MPP to factor price is greater for Factor A (50 units per $1) than for Factor B (100 units per $10). Alpha should employ more units of Factor A and fewer units of Factor B, until the ratio of MPP to factor price is the same for both factors.

Since producers will attempt to equalize the ratio of MPP to factor price for all factors, the price of a factor will depend on the factor's productivity. If Factor B is twice as productive as Factor A, Factor B will have a price twice as high as factor A.

## Elasticity of Demand for Labor

The elasticity of demand for labor measures the responsiveness of employers to a change in the wage rate. The elasticity of demand for labor is the percentage change in the quantity demanded of labor divided by the percentage change in the wage rate.

There are three determinants of the elasticity of demand for labor:

1. **The number of substitute factors.** The more substitute factors for labor, the more elastic the demand for labor. The fewer substitute factors for labor, the less elastic the demand for labor.

> **Example 9A:** The donut makers at Darla's Delectable Donuts ask for a 10% raise. If Darla can readily replace these workers with equally skilled donut makers, she is unlikely to grant the raise. With many substitute factors available, the demand for Darla's donut makers will be elastic.

> **Example 9B:** The rocket scientists at Roger's Rockets, Inc. ask for a 10% raise. If Roger can **not** readily replace these rocket scientists with equally skilled rocket scientists, he is likely to grant the raise. With few substitute factors available, the demand for Roger's rocket scientists will be inelastic.

2. **The price elasticity of demand for the product that the labor produces.** The more elastic the demand for the product, the more elastic the demand for the labor that produces the product. The less elastic the demand for the product, the less elastic the demand for the labor that produces the product.

> **Example 10A:** Darla's Delectable Donuts faces competition from numerous other donut shops. The demand for Darla's donuts is highly elastic. As a result, the demand for Darla's donut makers is highly elastic.

> **Example 10B:** Roger's Rockets, Inc. faces little competition in the rocket market. The demand for Roger's rockets is highly inelastic. As a result, the demand for Roger's rocket scientists is highly inelastic.

3. **The percentage that labor costs make up of total costs.** The higher the percentage that labor costs make up of total costs, the more elastic the demand for labor. The lower the percentage that labor costs make up of total costs, the less elastic the demand for labor.

> **Example 11A:** Labor costs make up 80% of total costs at Farah's Fashionable Hairstyles. A 10% raise for Farah's stylists would mean a large increase in Farah's total costs. As a result, the demand for Farah's stylists is highly elastic.

> **Example 11B:** Labor costs make up 15% of total costs at Roger's Rockets, Inc. A 10% raise for Roger's rocket scientists would mean a small increase in Roger's total costs. As a result, the demand for Roger's rocket scientists is highly inelastic.

## Labor Supply Curve for a Perfectly Competitive Employer

The labor supply curve shows the quantity of labor supplied at different wage rates. A perfectly competitive labor employer is a small employer in a large labor market. A perfectly competitive labor employer has no market power (no ability to affect the market wage rate). For a perfectly competitive labor employer, the labor supply curve will be horizontal (perfectly elastic) at the market wage rate. Wage and marginal factor cost are the same.

> **Example 12:** Khalid's Kwik Shop, located in Fort Worth, employs 90 to 120 hours of convenience store clerk labor each week. The total quantity of this type of labor employed in Fort Worth is about 60,000 hours per week. Khalid's hiring decision will not affect the market wage rate for convenience store clerk labor. Khalid's marginal factor cost will be the same as the market wage rate.

## Labor Supply Curve in a Particular Labor Market

The labor supply curve in a particular labor market will be upward sloping. The quantity of labor supplied in the market will increase as the wage rate increases, and decrease as the wage rate decreases. Changes in the wage rate change the quantity supplied of labor (a movement along the labor supply curve) but do not cause a change in labor supply (a shift of the labor supply curve).

**Example 13:** If convenience stores in Fort Worth want to employ 20 percent more convenience store clerk labor, the wage rate will have to increase in order to attract a greater quantity supplied of this type of labor.

## Determinants of Labor Supply

If the labor supply curve shifts to the right (increase) or to the left (decrease), this is a change in labor supply. Factors that cause the labor supply curve to shift are the determinants of labor supply:

1. **Wage rates in alternative labor markets.** An increase in wage rates in alternative labor markets will cause a decrease in labor supply in the particular labor market being examined. A decrease in wage rates in alternative labor markets will cause an increase in labor supply in the particular labor market being examined.

**Example 14:** If the state of Maine increases salaries for its public school teachers, the supply of public school teachers in New Hampshire will decrease (as some New Hampshire teachers move to the Maine market).

2. **Nonmoney aspects of a job.** Workers prefer pleasant working conditions rather than unpleasant working conditions. If a job becomes more pleasant (e.g. safer, cleaner, less stressful, etc.), the supply of labor in that labor market will increase. If a job becomes more unpleasant (e.g. more dangerous, dirtier, more stressful, etc.), the supply of labor in that labor market will decrease.

**Example 15:** If medical researchers discover that prolonged exposure to chemical cleansers causes janitors to have a high rate of cancer, the supply of persons willing to work as janitors will decrease.

## Differences in Wage Rates

Wage rates in different labor markets differ. The average major league baseball player may earn 70 times more than the average public school teacher. A heart surgeon will earn much more than a tree surgeon. Why are there differences in wage rates?

Five factors cause wage rates in different labor markets to differ:

1. **Differences in workers' MRP.** The more MRP a worker can generate, the greater the demand for that worker's labor.

> **Example 16:** The head football coach at State University may generate millions of dollars in revenue for the university, and will be paid accordingly. The head football coach at Local High School will generate much less revenue, and will be paid accordingly.

2. **Differences in nonmoney aspects of jobs.** Other things being equal, unpleasant jobs will attract a smaller supply of labor than pleasant jobs, and will thus have a higher wage rate.

> **Example 17:** A convenience store will find that it must pay a higher wage rate to attract clerks to the graveyard shift rather than to a more pleasant working schedule.

3. **Rareness of the skills required.** Some jobs require skills that are relatively rare (e.g. not many people can throw a baseball 95 miles per hour). Thus, the supply of labor for these jobs will be relatively small, and wage rates will be relatively high.

4. **Training costs.** Some jobs (e.g. heart surgeon) require extremely high training costs. This reduces the supply of labor, and increases wage rates for these jobs.

5. **Relocation costs.** Relocation costs include the cost of moving possessions as well as the emotional cost of moving away from family, friends, and familiar surroundings.

   If relocation costs were insignificant, labor would relocate from low-wage markets to high-wage markets, moving the wage levels toward equality. But relocation costs are often significant, and thus wage differences in different labor markets persist.

> **Example 18:** According to Salary.com, an auto mechanic I working in Hartford, Connecticut can expect to earn about $36,000. An auto mechanic I working in Forth Smith, Arkansas can expect to earn about $28,000. If there were no costs to relocate, auto mechanics would move from Fort Smith to Hartford, until the average earnings were the same in both cities (except for cost of living differences).

## Screening Devices

Employers seek to hire and promote employees who will be highly productive. Employers do <u>not</u> have perfect information about which employees will be the most productive. So employers often rely on some type of screening device to help them select the most productive workers.

**Screening device** – a characteristic used by employers as the basis for hiring and promoting employees.

Certain characteristics will increase an employee's productivity in almost any job (e.g. being diligent, responsible, cooperative, etc.). Other characteristics may be desirable only for specific jobs (e.g. professional football players need to be big, strong, fast, etc.). Employers try to determine which screening devices will most accurately predict worker productivity.

An employer who discovers screening devices that more accurately predict worker productivity will have a competitive advantage over other employers in the same industry. According to the 2003 book "Moneyball: The Art of Winning an Unfair Game", by Michael Lewis, the Oakland Athletics major league baseball team had done this.

> **Example 19:** The Oakland Athletics are a small-market team with one of the lowest payrolls in the major leagues. Nevertheless, they managed to win an average of 96 games per season from 1999 through 2002. The key to this success, according to the book "Moneyball", was that the Athletics' general manager, Billy Beane, had discovered screening devices that more accurately predicted a player's productivity than the screening devices generally used by other major league baseball teams. For more on the Athletics' screening devices, see the Appendix on the next page.

Some commonly used screening devices are seen as generally legitimate (e.g. work experience, grade point average, education level). But these screening devices may not be legitimate for all jobs.

> **Example 20A:** A major league pitching prospect with an undergraduate degree in economics is no more likely to be a successful major league pitcher than a pitching prospect with only a high school diploma.

And even where these screening devices are legitimate, they will not always predict worker productivity accurately.

> **Example 20B:** The accounting graduate with the highest grade point average will not always make the most productive accountant.

Other screening devices are seen as less legitimate (e.g. physical appearance, clothing). These screening devices may be relevant for certain jobs (e.g. fashion model, television personality). They tend to be used for almost all jobs. Research indicates that persons who are judged to be more attractive earn higher incomes than persons who are judged to be less attractive.

> **Example 21:** According to research by Daniel Hamermesh and Jeff Biddle, attractive people earn about 5% more than average-looking people and unattractive people earn about 7% less than average-looking people. The attractiveness advantage is stronger for men than for women.

> **Example 22:** According to the book "Blink" by Malcolm Gladwell, 14.5% of American males are six feet or taller. Only 3.9% of American males are 6'2" or taller. Among the Fortune 500 companies that Gladwell surveyed, 58% reported that their CEOs were six feet or taller, and 30% reported that their CEOs were 6'2" or taller.

Some screening devices are not only generally illegitimate, but may amount to illegal discrimination (e.g. gender, race, age).

> **Example 23:** In 2005, a jury awarded an 85-year-old doctor $20 million in an age discrimination suit the doctor filed against the California Department of Corrections. The doctor alleged that he was forced to retire in 2001 because of his age.

## Appendix: Book Review – "Moneyball"

The 2003 book, "Moneyball: The Art of Winning an Unfair Game", by Michael Lewis, poses the question, "How did one of the poorest teams in baseball, the Oakland Athletics, win so many games?" The answer, according to the book, was the use of superior screening devices.

The Oakland A's are a small-market baseball team. They have been forced to operate with a smaller budget than most other major league teams.

> **Example 24:** In 2002, the Oakland A's had a payroll of $40 million, while the New York Yankees had a payroll of $126 million. Still, both teams won 103 games that season. How did the A's put together a winning roster of players with such a small payroll?

Oakland's general manager, Billy Beane, believed that the screening devices that most major league teams used to predict the productivity of players were inaccurate. As a result, most major league teams paid too much for players who had characteristics that were not good predictor's of productivity, and paid too little for players who had characteristics that were good predictors of productivity.

Major league teams tended to evaluate position players based on such characteristics as size, speed, body type, defensive skills, etc. Players who were rated as too small, too slow, too fat, too defensively inept, etc. were seen as unfit for the major leagues.

Billy Beane, based on statistical analysis, believed that the most important measure of a position player's value to a team was his on base percentage. Since other teams did not value on base percentage as highly as they did other characteristics, the A's could acquire, at bargain prices, position players who were small, slow, fat, or defensively inept, but had a high on base percentage.

Major league teams tended to evaluate pitchers by the speed of their fastballs. Pitchers who were deemed to have insufficient "heat" were seen as unfit for the major leagues.

Billy Beane, based on statistical analysis, believed that the most important measures of a pitcher's value to a team were his strikeouts, walks, and home runs allowed. Since other teams did not value these characteristics as highly as they did fastball speed, the A's could acquire, at bargain prices, pitchers with poor velocity who were good at accumulating strikeouts while giving up few walks and allowing few home runs.

The A's also disagreed with other major league teams as to the best screening devices to use in evaluating young players for draft purposes. The A's believed that past performance (as measured by objective statistics) was a better way to evaluate the potential of a young player than a scout's subjective opinion. Scouts were too likely to be influenced by a player's size, speed, body type, and even facial structure. (Scouts looked for players with "the good face".)

The A's also believed that the performance of college baseball players (particularly on base percentage for position players and strikeouts, walks, and home runs allowed for pitchers) was a better predictor of future success than the performance of high school players. Thus, the A's generally avoided drafting high school players.

## Appendix: Think Like an Economist – The New CEO

You are a stockholder in XYZ Corporation. For years your investment has done very well. However, the company recently announced the upcoming retirement of the long-time CEO. You eagerly await the introduction of the new CEO.

While channel-surfing this morning, you caught a glimpse of the press conference where the new CEO was introduced. Thinking like an economist, which situation would give you more confidence in the future of XYZ Corporation, and why?

Situation #1: The new CEO is tall, strikingly attractive, and extremely well dressed.

Situation #2: The new CEO is short, somewhat homely, and unfashionably dressed.

## Appendix: Think Like an Economist – How to Treat Employees

You have just been hired to manage a business. You ask a couple of experienced managers for advice on how to treat your employees. Manager A advises, "You want your employees to be as productive as possible, so don't hesitate to treat them harshly. Keep the pressure on and maintain strict discipline. They may not enjoy it, but work is not supposed to be fun."

Manager B advises, "You want your employees to be as productive as possible, so try to keep them happy. Maintain a relaxed atmosphere and be flexible in your rules to meet your employees' needs. Work may not be fun, but try to make it as pleasant as possible."

Assume that either management style will yield about the same level of productivity. Thinking like an economist, which management style, A or B, will likely yield the greater profits, and why?

## Questions for Chapter 24

### Fill-in-the-blanks:

1. Marginal _____ _____ is the change in total revenue from employing an additional factor unit.

2. Marginal _____ _____ is the additional cost from employing an additional factor unit.

3. A _____ _____ is a characteristic used by employers as the basis for hiring and promoting employees.

## Multiple Choice:

_____ 1. If the demand for dog grooming increases, the demand for dog groomers will
_____ and their wage rate will _____ .
   a. increase, increase
   b. decrease, decrease
   c. increase, decrease
   d. decrease, increase

_____ 2. Due to the law of diminishing marginal returns:
   a. marginal revenue product will eventually decline
   b. the marginal revenue product curve will eventually slope downward
   c. Both of the above
   d. Neither of the above

_____ 3. To maximize profits, a producer employs additional factor units up to the quantity where:
   a. marginal factor cost is minimized
   b. marginal revenue product equals marginal factor cost
   c. marginal revenue product is maximized
   d. marginal physical product is maximized

Answer questions 4. through 9. after completing the table below.  Assume an output price of $4.

| Workers | Gadgets | MPP | Total Revenue | MRP | MFC |
|---|---|---|---|---|---|
| 0 | 0 | X | $0 | X | X |
| 1 | 80 | 80 | $320 | $320 | $180 |
| 2 | 150 | 70 | 600 | 280 | 180 |
| 3 | 210 | ___ | ___ | ___ | 180 |
| 4 | 260 | ___ | ___ | ___ | 180 |
| 5 | 300 | ___ | ___ | ___ | 180 |
| 6 | 330 | ___ | ___ | ___ | 180 |
| 7 | 350 | ___ | ___ | ___ | 180 |

_____ 4. What is the marginal physical product of the fifth worker?
   a. 40
   b. 50
   c. 60
   d. 70

_____ 5. What is the total revenue when four workers are employed?
   a. $720
   b. $840
   c. $1040
   d. $1200

_____ 6. What is the marginal revenue product of the sixth worker?
  a.  $40
  b.  $80
  c.  $120
  d.  $160

_____ 7. What is the profit-maximizing number of workers to employ?
  a.  3
  b.  4
  c.  5
  d.  6

_____ 8. If the output price increased to $5, what would the profit-maximizing number of workers be?
  a.  3
  b.  4
  c.  5
  d.  6

_____ 9. If the output price is back to $4, and the MFC increased to $220, what would the profit-maximizing number of workers be?
  a.  3
  b.  4
  c.  5
  d.  6

_____ 10. A decrease in the price of domestic steel, due to an increase in competition from imported steel, would have what effect on the demand curve for domestic steelworkers?
  a.  cause a movement along the curve
  b.  shift it to the right
  c.  shift it to the left
  d.  no effect

_____ 11. An increase in the wage rate for librarians would have what effect on the demand curve for librarians?
  a.  cause a movement along the curve
  b.  shift it to the right
  c.  shift it to the left
  d.  Both a. and b. above

_____ 12. At the cost-minimizing combination of factors:
  a.  the MFC of all factors will be equal
  b.  the MPP of all factors will be equal
  c.  the MRP of all factors will be equal
  d.  the ratio of MPP to factor price will be the same for all factors

_____ 13. Which of the following is a determinant of the elasticity of demand for labor?
   a. the wage rate in alternative labor markets
   b. the number of substitute factors
   c. nonmoney aspects of the job
   d. All of the above

_____ 14. A perfectly competitive labor employer:
   a. faces a horizontal labor supply curve
   b. has no market power
   c. is a small employer in a large labor market
   d. All of the above

_____ 15. A shift in the supply curve for convenience store clerks in Mesa, Arizona will result from which of the following?
   a. an increase in the wage rate for convenience store clerks in Mesa
   b. an increase in the wage rate for convenience store clerks in Phoenix
   c. an increase in the danger of being a convenience store clerk in Mesa
   d. Both b. and c. above

_____ 16. If a job becomes more pleasant:
   a. the supply of labor in that market will increase
   b. the wage rate in that market will increase
   c. Both of the above
   d. Neither of the above

_____ 17. Wage rates in different labor markets differ because:
   a. some jobs are more pleasant than others
   b. training costs differ
   c. there are differences in workers' MRP
   d. All of the above

_____ 18. Screening devices:
   a. are intended to help employers hire employees who will be highly productive
   b. may include such factors as work experience and education level
   c. are not always successful
   d. All of the above

_____ 19. According to the book, "Moneyball", the Oakland A's won a lot of games from 1999 to 2002 because:
   a. they had the highest payroll in the major leagues, other than the Yankees
   b. they had discovered screening devices that more accurately predicted a player's productivity than the screening devices generally used by other major league teams
   c. Both of the above
   d. Neither of the above

_____ 20. If Billy Beane is looking for a new third baseman, he would be most impressed with a prospect:
   a. who is hitting a lot of home runs for his high school team
   b. who is big, fast, and plays great defense
   c. who has had a high on base percentage for four years on his college team

_____ 21. If Billy Beane were running a legal practice, he would hire new attorneys:
   a. who had a proven record of winning a high percentage of their cases
   b. who were attractive, well-dressed, and had recently graduated from a prestigious law school
   c. Both of the above
   d. Neither of the above

## Problems:

1. a. Complete the following table. Assume an output price of $6.

| Workers | Widgets | MPP | Total Revenue | MRP |
|---------|---------|-----|---------------|-----|
| 0 | 0 | X | $0 | X |
| 1 | 50 | 50 | $300 | $300 |
| 2 | 95 | ____ | 570 | ____ |
| 3 | 135 | ____ | ____ | ____ |
| 4 | 170 | ____ | ____ | ____ |
| 5 | 200 | ____ | ____ | ____ |
| 6 | 225 | ____ | ____ | ____ |
| 7 | 245 | ____ | ____ | ____ |

   b. Based on the table above, construct the demand curve for widget workers. How many widget workers are hired if the marginal factor cost for widget workers is $160?

2. List and explain the three determinants of factor demand.

3. List and explain the two determinants of labor supply.

4. Give an example of a screening device and explain why screening devices are used.

## Answers for Chapter 24

**Fill-in-the-blanks:**    1. revenue product
2. factor cost
3. screening device

**Multiple Choice:**    1. a.          8. c.          15. d.
2. c.          9. a.          16. a.
3. b.          10. c.          17. d.
4. a.          11. a.          18. d.
5. c.          12. d.          19. b.
6. c.          13. b.          20. c.
7. b.          14. d.          21. a.

**Problems:**

1. a.

| Workers | Widgets | MPP | Total Revenue | MRP |
|---|---|---|---|---|
| 0 | 0 | X | $0 | X |
| 1 | 50 | 50 | $300 | $300 |
| 2 | 95 | 45 | 570 | 270 |
| 3 | 135 | 40 | 810 | 240 |
| 4 | 170 | 35 | 1020 | 210 |
| 5 | 200 | 30 | 1200 | 180 |
| 6 | 225 | 25 | 1350 | 150 |
| 7 | 245 | 20 | 1470 | 120 |

b.

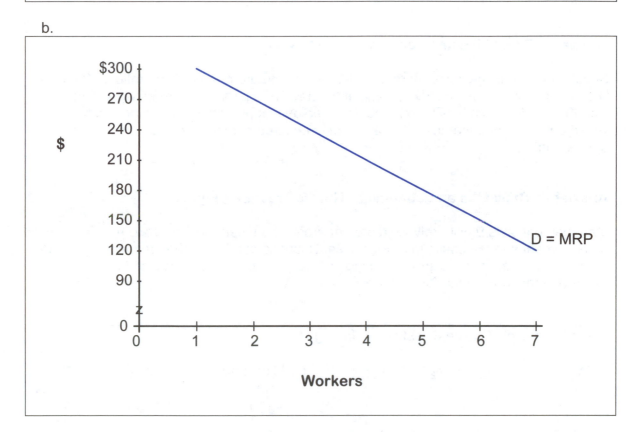

At a marginal factor cost of $160, 5 workers would be employed.

2. The determinants of factor demand are:
   (1) Product price.  An increase in product price will increase the MRP of the factor, shifting the factor demand curve to the right.
   (2) Factor productivity.  An increase in factor productivity (MPP) will increase the MRP of the factor, shifting the factor demand curve to the right.
   (3) Prices of related factors.  The demand curve for a factor will shift in the same direction as the change in price for a substitute factor and in the opposite direction as the change in price for a complementary factor.

Factor Markets

3. The two determinants of labor supply are:
   (1) Wage rates in alternative labor markets. An increase in wage rates in alternative labor markets will cause a decrease in labor supply in the particular labor market being examined. A decrease in wage rates in alternative labor markets will cause an increase in labor supply in the particular labor market being examined.
   (2) Nonmoney aspects of a job. Workers prefer pleasant working conditions rather than unpleasant working conditions. If a job becomes more pleasant, the supply of labor in that labor market will increase. If a job becomes more unpleasant, the supply of labor in that labor market will decrease.

4. An example of a screening device is education level. Employers seek to hire and promote employees who will be highly productive. Employers do not have perfect information about which employees will be the most productive. So employers often rely on some type of screening device.

## Answer to Think Like an Economist – The New CEO:

Situation #2 would give you more confidence in the future of XYZ Corporation. Thinking like an economist, you would reason that the new CEO must be extremely gifted to have won the job despite a less than impressive personal appearance. In Situation #1, you would be concerned that the new CEO had been hired primarily because of personal appearance.

## Answer to Think Like an Economist – How to Treat Employees:

Management style B will likely yield greater profits than management style A. Management style B results in more pleasant working conditions than management style A. This will mean that the supply of labor will be greater and the wage rate lower for management style B than for management style A.

Table for Multiple Choice Questions 4. through 9.:

| Workers | Gadgets | MPP | Total Revenue | MRP | MFC |
|---------|---------|-----|---------------|-----|-----|
| 0 | 0 | X | $0 | X | X |
| 1 | 80 | 80 | $320 | $320 | $180 |
| 2 | 150 | 70 | 600 | 280 | 180 |
| 3 | 210 | 60 | 840 | 240 | 180 |
| 4 | 260 | 50 | 1040 | 200 | 180 |
| 5 | 300 | 40 | 1200 | 160 | 180 |
| 6 | 330 | 30 | 1320 | 120 | 180 |
| 7 | 350 | 20 | 1400 | 80 | 180 |

# Chapter 25  Labor Unions

Labor markets tend to be highly competitive.  Workers find that they are in competition with many other workers for the available jobs.  Individual workers will typically find that they have little bargaining power in negotiating with their employer.  Workers can increase their bargaining power and avoid competing with one another by forming a labor union.

A labor union is an organization of workers.  The union represents all of the eligible workers in negotiating with management over wages and other issues.  This is called collective bargaining.  The union gives the workers a monopoly or cartel position in selling their labor.

## Types of Labor Unions

There are different types of labor unions:

1.  **Craft union.**  This is a union made up of workers who practice the same craft, such as actors, carpenters, electricians, plumbers, airline pilots, etc.

2.  **Industrial union.**  This is a union made up of workers in the same industry, such as autoworkers, teamsters, steelworkers, etc.

3.  **Public employee union.**  This is a union made up of workers employed by the government, such as school teachers, municipal employees, firefighters, etc.

Union membership has been declining in the American workforce.  In the 1950s, around one-third of the labor force was unionized.  According to the Bureau of Labor Statistics, the percentage of wage and salary workers who were union members had fallen to 20% by 1983, and had fallen to 12.1% by 2007.

Unionization rates are much higher for public sector employees than for private sector employees.  In 2007, 35.9% of public sector employees were union members.  Only 7.5% of private sector employees were union members.

## Largest Labor Unions

The table below lists the eight largest labor unions in the U.S. in 2005.

| Union | Membership |
| --- | --- |
| National Education Association | 2.73 million |
| Service Employees International Union | 1.51 million |
| American Federation of State, County & Municipal Employees | 1.46 million |
| International Brotherhood of Teamsters | 1.40 million |
| United Food and Commercial Workers | 1.38 million |
| American Federation of Teachers | .83 million |
| United Steelworkers | .75 million |
| International Brotherhood of Electrical Workers | .70 million |

## Demand Curve for a Union

As a kind of cartel, a labor union has market power (the ability to affect the market wage rate). A union faces a downward sloping demand curve for its labor. Thus, a labor union faces a trade-off between wages and employment. If a union negotiates a higher wage rate, this will generally mean fewer union members employed.

**Example 1A:** Assume that the graph below represents the labor demand curve faced by a labor union. If the union negotiates a wage rate of $12, the quantity of labor employed will be 12,000 hours. If the union negotiates a wage rate of $15, the quantity of labor employed will decrease to 9,000 hours.

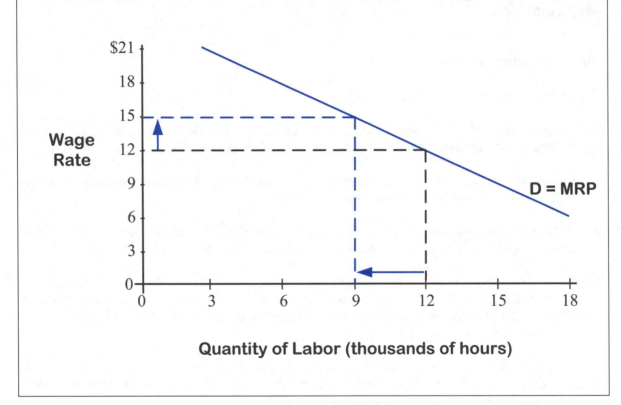

**Quantity of Labor (thousands of hours)**

## Union Goals

Given the trade-off between wages and employment, all unions will tend to have certain predictable goals:

1. **Reduce the elasticity of demand for union labor.** The less elastic the demand for union labor, the more market power the union will have. More market power means that fewer jobs will be lost with any wage increase.

**Example 1B:** Assume that the labor demand curve in Example 1A becomes less elastic. When the wage is increased from $12 to $15, fewer jobs are lost. See the graph on the next page:

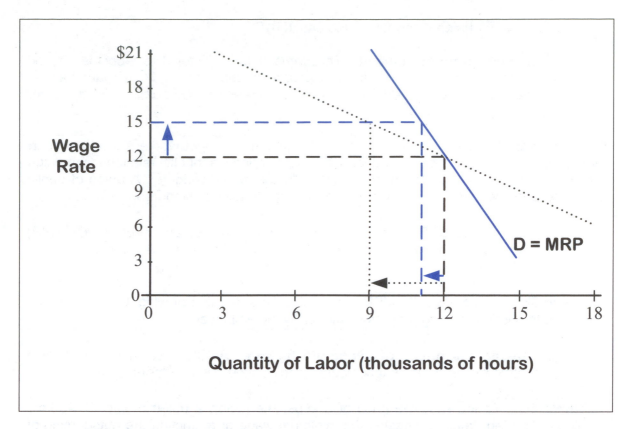

The elasticity of demand for union labor can be reduced by;

    a.  **Reducing the availability of substitute factors.** The number of substitute factors is a determinant of the elasticity of demand for labor (see Chapter 24). The fewer substitute factors for labor, the less elastic the demand for labor.

> **Example 2A:** Unions have often attempted to achieve their goals through the political process. To reduce the availability of substitute factors, unions would support restrictions on immigration and restrictions on the employment of nonunion workers during strikes.

    b.  **Reducing the availability of substitute products.** Another determinant of the elasticity of demand for labor is the price elasticity of demand for the product that the labor produces (see Chapter 24). The less elastic the demand for the product, the less elastic the demand for the labor that produces the product. Reducing the availability of substitute products reduces the elasticity of demand for the product. Reducing the elasticity of demand for the product reduces the elasticity of demand for labor.

> **Example 2B:** To reduce the availability of substitute products, a union of widget workers would support legislation restricting imported widgets. Likewise, a union of public school teachers would oppose legislation providing for school vouchers that could be used to pay tuition at private schools.

2.  **Increase the demand for union labor.** An increase in the demand for union labor will result in more union jobs at every wage rate.

The demand for union labor can be increased by;

a. **Increasing product demand.** The demand for a factor (like labor) is derived from the demand for what the factor produces (see Chapter 24). An increase in the demand for the product will cause an increase in the demand for the labor that produces the product.

> **Example 3A:** To increase product demand, a union of widget workers would support legislation restricting imported widgets, or might launch a public relations campaign urging consumers to buy "American-made" or "union-made" widgets. A union of public school teachers would support a move from half-day to full-day kindergarten.

b. **Increasing the MPP of union workers.** An increase in labor productivity (MPP) will increase the MRP of the labor, shifting the labor demand curve to the right (see Chapter 24).

> **Example 3B:** To increase the MPP of union workers, a union of widget workers might negotiate for worker training programs paid for by the employer.

c. **Increasing the prices of substitute factors.** An increase in the price of a substitute factor for union labor would increase the demand for union labor.

> **Example 3C:** To increase the price of a substitute factor, a union of widget workers would support legislation increasing the minimum wage or restricting the outsourcing of jobs to foreign countries.

3. **Decrease the supply of union labor.** A decrease in labor supply will lead to a higher equilibrium wage rate. The ideal situation to allow a union to control the supply of labor is a closed shop agreement with the employer.

**Closed shop** – requires union membership as a condition for employment.

A closed shop agreement would give a union the ability to restrict the supply of labor available by simply not admitting new members to the union. As discussed below, closed shop agreements are illegal. But most states allow for an alternative called a union shop agreement.

**Union shop** – requires employees to join the union within a specified time.

A union shop agreement ensures that all eligible workers will be union members. This increases the union's bargaining power. A threat of a strike is more convincing when there is 100 percent union membership. As discussed below, union shops are illegal in some states.

The Taft-Hartley Act (1947) prohibited closed shop agreements in all states. The Act also gave the individual states the power to pass right-to-work laws. Right-to-work laws prohibit union shops.

In the twenty-two states that have enacted right-to-work laws, every shop must be an open shop. In open shops, workers may join the union or may choose to <u>not</u> join the union.  Workers who choose to <u>not</u> join the union are still covered by the collective bargaining agreement.  The more workers who choose to <u>not</u> join the union, the weaker is the union's bargaining power.  The most recent state to pass right-to-work was Oklahoma, in 2001.

## Collective Bargaining

**Collective bargaining** is where a union bargains with management on behalf of the workers.  The union, as a type of labor monopoly or cartel, will have more bargaining power than the individual workers would have.  A union has market power and can directly affect the wage rate through collective bargaining.

The most important bargaining tool available to a union is the threat of a strike.  A union might use the threat of a strike to negotiate a wage rate above equilibrium.

**Example 4A:**  Assume that the graph below represents labor market equilibrium without a union.  The equilibrium wage rate is $12 and the equilibrium quantity of labor employed is 12,000 hours.

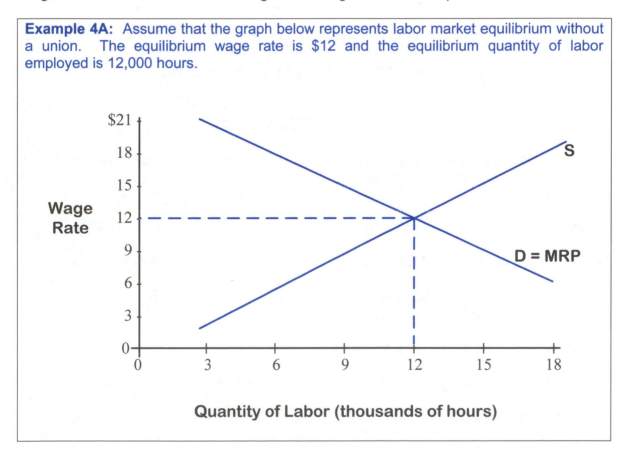

**Example 4B:**  Now assume that the workers in Example 4A above form a union.  The union negotiates on behalf of the workers, and threatens to strike unless the wage rate is increased to $15.  The union wants to convince the management that the workers will strike if offered a wage below $15.  If the union is willing to strike, the quantity of labor supplied will fall to zero if a wage below $15 is offered.  The labor supply curve will be horizontal at $15.  The MFC of labor will be $15 and MRP and MFC will be equal at 9,000 hours of labor.  As illustrated on the graph on the next page, the new wage rate will be $15 and the new quantity of labor employed will be 9,000 hours.

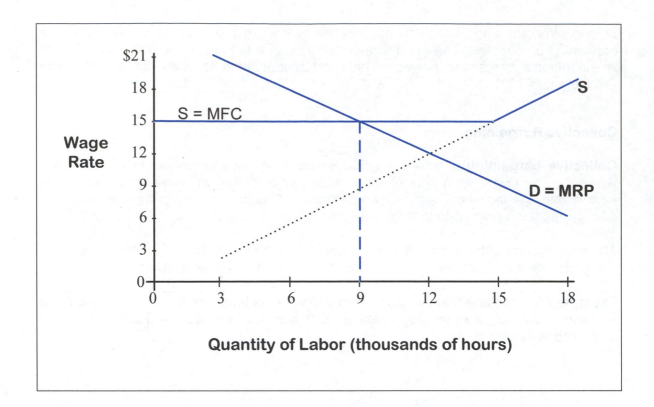

As seen in the Examples 4A and 4B, collective bargaining will generally result in higher wages and fewer workers employed.

## Monopsony

A labor union faces a trade-off between wages and employment. Collective bargaining will generally result in higher wages and fewer workers employed. But collective bargaining may result in higher wages and more jobs, if the union is negotiating with a monopsony employer.

**Monopsony** – a lone buyer in a factor market.

An example of a monopsony employer of labor would be a company that is the only employer in a small town. This type of situation was much more common fifty or one hundred years ago, when a mine, a mill, or a factory might be the only employer in a "company town".

**Example 5:** The town of McIntyre, Pennsylvania was established in 1910 by the Rochester and Pittsburgh Coal and Iron Company. The company operated a company store and owned most of the buildings in the town. When the coal mines in the area became unprofitable, the company sold the town in 1947.

Workers in a company town commonly lived in housing owned by the company. Rent would be deducted from the workers' paychecks. The workers would often be paid in company scrip, which could be spent only at the company store.

As the lone buyer in a factor market, a monopsony has market power and faces an upward sloping labor supply curve. A monopsony's hiring decision will affect the wage rate in the market. A monopsony will have to pay a higher wage to employ more labor.

A monopsony's marginal factor cost curve is <u>not</u> the same as its labor supply curve. The monopsony's MFC curve will be twice as steeply upward sloping as its labor supply curve.

**Example 6:** Monopso Company is a monopsony employer of labor. The table and the graph below illustrate the labor supply curve and MFC curve for Monopso Company.

| Wage Rate | Labor Quantity | Factor Cost | MFC |
|---|---|---|---|
| $7 | 0 | $0 | X |
| 8 | 1 | 8 | $8 |
| 9 | 2 | 18 | 10 |
| 10 | 3 | 30 | 12 |
| 11 | 4 | 44 | 14 |
| 12 | 5 | 60 | 16 |

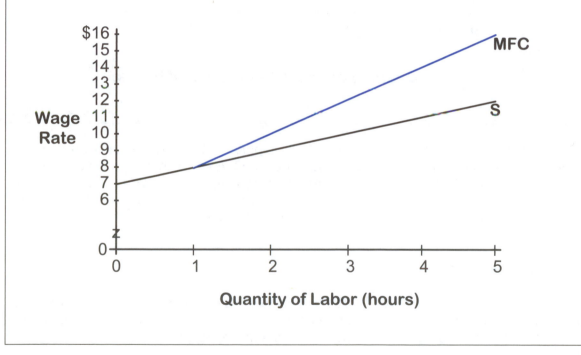

Notice from the graph that the slope of the labor supply curve is 1, and that the slope of the MFC curve is 2.

## Profit-Maximization for a Monopsony

A monopsony will attempt to employ the profit-maximizing quantity of labor. Thus, a monopsony will employ workers where MRP = MFC. The example on the next page illustrates profit-maximization for a monopsony.

**Example 7A:** On the graph below, MRP = MFC at 6,000 hours of labor. Thus, the monopsony will employ 6,000 hours of labor to maximize profit. The MRP and MFC are both $18 at 6,000 hours of labor. What wage rate will the monopsony pay? The labor supply curve indicates the wage rate that must be paid to attract different quantities of labor. To attract 6,000 hours of labor the monopsony will pay $6 per hour.

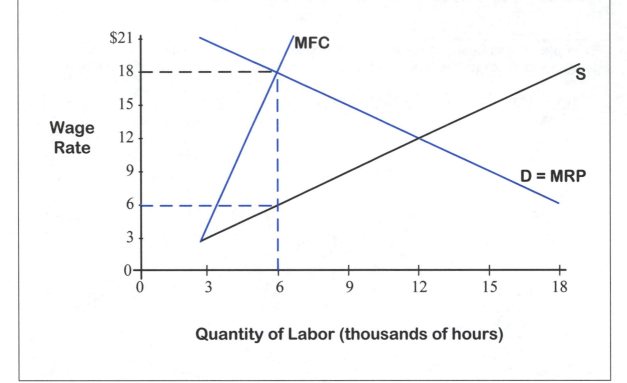

**Quantity of Labor (thousands of hours)**

How does the wage rate and quantity of labor employed by a monopsony compare to what a perfectly competitive labor employer would do? A perfectly competitive employer would hire where labor supply and demand intersect, which is at 12,000 hours of labor and a wage rate of $12 per hour. Thus, a monopsony will employ a lesser quantity of labor at a lower wage rate compared to a perfectly competitive employer.

### The Union and the Monopsony

What if a monopsony employer is confronted by a labor union across the bargaining table? If the union can convince the monopsony that the workers will strike unless their wage demands are met, the union can negotiate a higher wage.

**Example 7B:** Assume that the monopsony from Example 7A is negotiating with the union from Example 4B. The monopsony would like to employ 6,000 hours of labor at a wage of $6 per hour. But the union threatens to strike if the wage is less than $15 per hour. If the union can convince the monopsony that the workers will act on this threat, the labor supply curve will be horizontal at $15. With a horizontal labor supply curve, the MFC curve will also be horizontal at $15. As illustrated on the graph on the next page, the new wage rate will be $15 and the new quantity of labor employed will be 9,000 hours.

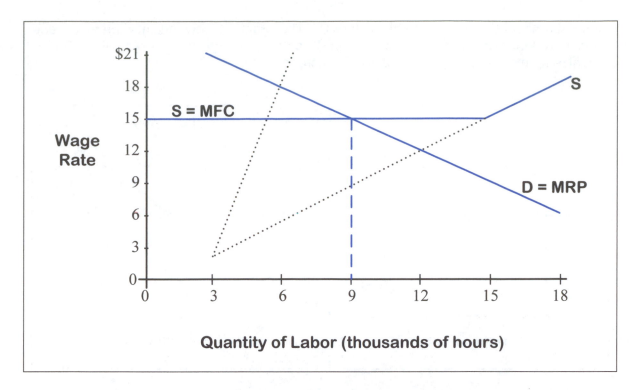

A union negotiating with a monopsony may be able to obtain both a higher wage <u>and</u> a greater quantity of labor employed. Workers employed by a monopsony employer have a strong incentive to form a union.

A union negotiating with a monopsony still faces a trade-off between wages and employment. In Example 7B, fewer workers would be employed if the union negotiated a wage of $16 per hour, and more workers would be employed if the union negotiated a wage of $14 per hour.

## Unions and Wages

Research indicates that unions increase the wages of union employees, but decrease the wages of nonunion employees.

**Example 8:** Research by Bernt Bratsberg and James F. Ragan, Jr. concluded that the union wage premium varies from 13% to 22%.

If a union successfully negotiates a higher wage for its members, fewer workers will be employed in the union market. This will mean an increase in the supply of labor in the nonunion market, decreasing the wages of nonunion employees.

**Example 9:** The two largest employers in Anytown are Factory A and Factory B. Both employ 500 workers, who do assembly line production. The workers at both factories earn similar wages. Then the workers at Factory A organize a union and negotiate a 20% pay increase.

The higher pay results in fewer workers employed at Factory A. Some of the displaced workers end up at Factory B, increasing the supply of labor available at Factory B, and thus decreasing the wage rate at Factory B.  The graphs below indicate the wage and quantity of labor employed at Factory A and Factory B <u>before</u> the workers at Factory A organize a union and negotiate a 20% pay increase.

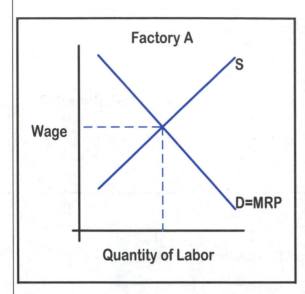

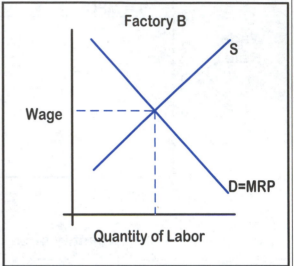

The graphs below indicate the wage and quantity of labor employed at Factory A and Factory B <u>after</u> the workers at Factory A organize a union and negotiate a 20% pay increase.

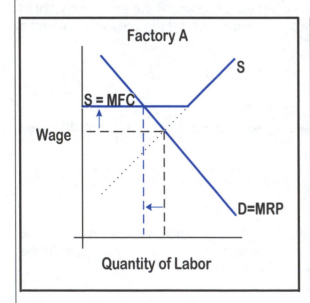

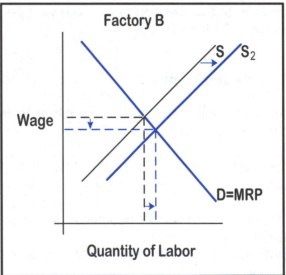

Higher union wages will also result in higher prices for union made products (or higher taxes to pay for union-produced government services).

> **Example 10:** If the autoworkers' union negotiates a higher wage rate for the autoworkers, automobile prices are likely to rise. If the firefighters' union negotiates a higher wage rate for the firefighters, taxes imposed by the municipal government are likely to rise.

## Unions and Productivity

The traditional view holds that unions hurt productivity due to:

1. **Strikes.** Strikes are much less common today than they were when union membership was greater. Still, strikes (and lockouts) result in lost production.

> **Example 11:** In 1952, there were 470 major work stoppages (strikes or lockouts). Major work stoppages involve 1,000 or more workers. The 470 major work stoppages resulted in 48.8 million workdays of idleness. In 2007, there were only 21 major work stoppages. Still, the 21 major work stoppages resulted in 1.3 million workdays of idleness. (Information from the Bureau of Labor Statistics)

2. **Unnecessary staffing requirements (featherbedding).** Unions often negotiate work rules designed to maximize employment, even at the expense of productivity.

> **Example 12:** A famous historical example of featherbedding occurred in the railroad industry. Long after railroads switched from coal-powered to diesel-powered engines, the union contracts required railroads to employ "firemen" (who shovel coal) on every train.

3. **Keeping willing employers and employees apart.** When a union negotiates a wage above equilibrium, it has the same effect as a price floor in the labor market. We saw in Chapter 3 that price controls are economically inefficient. Price controls eliminate exchanges that would be mutually beneficial to the buyer and the seller. Likewise, when a union negotiates a wage above equilibrium, it eliminates jobs that would be beneficial to both the employer and the employees.

An alternative view is that unions increase productivity. This view holds that unions increase productivity by:

1. **Providing union workers with a collective voice.** This results in greater worker satisfaction, less turnover, and a better trained workforce.

2. **Attracting higher quality workers.** Union jobs typically pay better than nonunion jobs and thus can attract higher quality workers. The workers will also be motivated to perform at a high level in order to keep their higher paying jobs.

## Questions for Chapter 25

### Fill-in-the-blanks:

1. A _____ _____ agreement requires union membership as a condition for employment.

2. A _____ _____ agreement requires employees to join the union within a specified time.

3. Right-to-work laws prohibit _____ shops.

4. _____ bargaining is where a union bargains with management on behalf of the workers.

5. _____ is a lone buyer in a factor market.


### Multiple Choice:

_____ 1. A union of plumbers is what type of union?
    a. craft union
    b. industrial union
    c. public employee union
    d. None of the above

_____ 2. Unionization rates:
    a. are about the same for private sector and public sector employees
    b. are three times higher for private sector employees than for public sector employees
    c. are over four times higher for public sector employees than for private sector employees
    d. None of the above

_____ 3. If a union negotiates a higher wage rate:
    a. generally, the number of union members employed will be unaffected
    b. generally, fewer union members will be employed
    c. generally, more union members will be employed

_____ 4. One of the three union goals is:
    a. reduce the elasticity of demand for union labor
    b. reduce the demand for union labor
    c. increase the supply of union labor
    d. Both a. and c. above

_____ 5. If a union reduces the elasticity of demand for union labor:
    a. the union will lose fewer jobs with any wage increase
    b. the union will have more bargaining power
    c. Both of the above
    d. Neither of the above

_____ 6. Labor unions would generally support legislation to:
    a. restrict imports
    b. restrict immigration
    c. increase the minimum wage
    d. All of the above

_____ 7. The Taft-Hartley Act:
    a. prohibited closed shops
    b. prohibited union shops
    c. required all states to enact right-to-work laws
    d. All of the above

_____ 8. In open shops:
    a. workers may choose to join the union or may choose to <u>not</u> join the union
    b. workers who choose to <u>not</u> join the union are still covered by the collective bargaining agreement
    c. unions have less bargaining power
    d. All of the above

_____ 9. For a monopsony:
    a. there is a downward sloping labor supply curve
    b. MFC is greater than the wage rate
    c. the wage will be higher than for a perfectly competitive employer
    d. All of the above

_____ 10. If a monopsony can employ 9 hours of labor at $12 per hour or 10 hours of labor at $13 per hour, the MFC of the 10$^{th}$ hour of labor is:
    a. $130
    b. $22
    c. $13
    d. $12

_____ 11. The traditional view holds that unions hurt productivity due to:
    a. keeping willing employers and employees apart
    b. unnecessary staffing requirements
    c. strikes
    d. All of the above

_____ 12. The alternative view holds that unions increase productivity by:
    a. providing union workers with a collective voice
    b. attracting higher quality workers
    c. increasing worker turnover
    d. Both a. and b. above

Refer to the graph below to answer questions 13. through 15.:

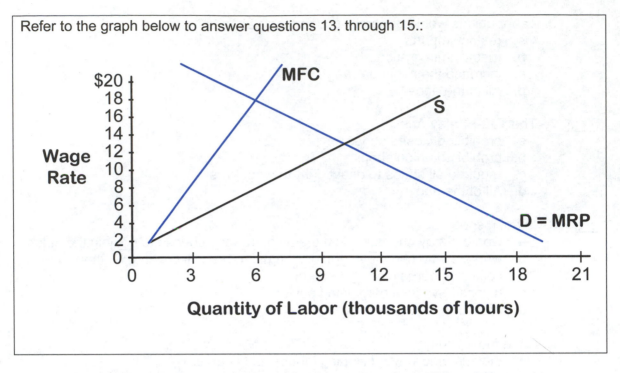

_____ 13. The quantity of labor employed by this monopsony will be:
   a.   3 thousand hours
   b.   6 thousand hours
   c.   9 thousand hours
   d.   10 thousand hours

_____ 14. The wage paid by this monopsony will be:
   a.   $18
   b.   $16
   c.   $12
   d.   $8

_____ 15. If the employees of this monopsony form a union and negotiate a wage rate of $15 per hour, the quantity of labor employed:
   a.   will increase
   b.   will decrease
   c.   will stay the same
   d.   Any of the above are possible

## Problems:

1.   List the three union goals.

2.  List three ways that unions can increase the demand for union labor.

3.  The graph below represents a labor market.  Then the workers form a union and
    threaten to strike if a wage less than $14 per hour is paid:
    (1)  Illustrate what this threat of a strike does to the labor supply curve.
    (2)  How many hours of labor will be employed at $14 per hour?

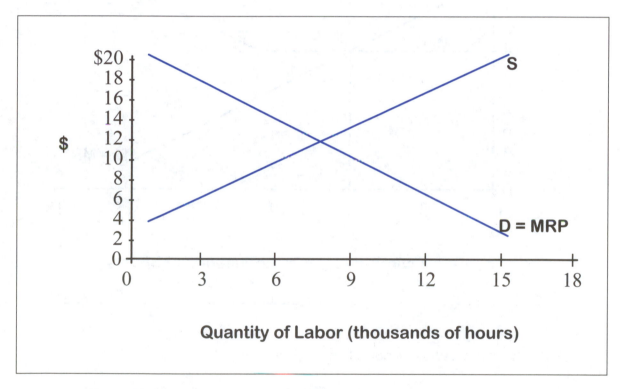

Quantity of Labor (thousands of hours)

**Answers for Chapter 25**

**Fill-in-the-blanks:**   1. closed shop          4. Collective
                          2. union shop           5. Monopsony
                          3. union

**Multiple Choice:**   1. a.          6. d.          11. d.
                       2. c.          7. a.          12. d.
                       3. b.          8. d.          13. b.
                       4. a.          9. b.          14. d.
                       5. c.         10. b.          15. a.

**Problems:**

1. All unions will tend to have three goals:
   (1) Reduce the elasticity of demand for union labor
   (2) Increase the demand for union labor
   (3) Decrease the supply of union labor

2. Unions can increase the demand for union labor by:
   (1) Increasing product demand
   (2) Increasing the MPP of union labor
   (3) Increasing the prices of substitute factors

3. (1)

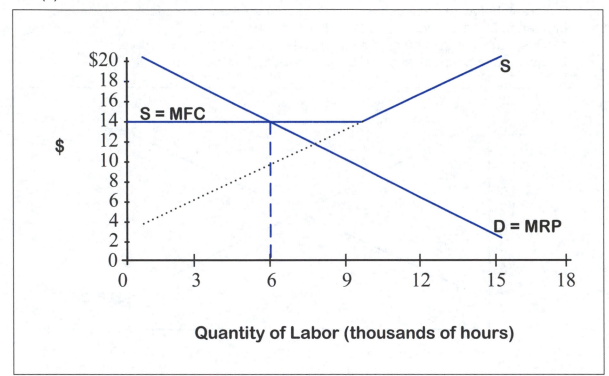

**Quantity of Labor (thousands of hours)**

   (2) Six thousand hours of labor will be employed

# Chapter 26  Interest, Present Value, Rent, and Profit

This chapter examines four topics related to factor markets; interest, present value, economic rent, and economic profit.

**Interest** – the payment for the use of loanable funds.

Interest is the payment received by savers for making loanable funds available. Interest is the payment made by borrowers to use loanable funds. The interest rate is determined by the supply of and the demand for loanable funds.

## The Loanable Funds Market

The supply of loanable funds comes from households that save (do not consume) part of their income. Household saving is motivated by the desire to accumulate wealth for retirement or for major future expenditures (e.g. a down payment on a house, college education, etc.). Household saving is also motivated by the desire to earn interest on savings. The interest earned will allow for greater consumption in the future.

> **Example 1:** Sanjiv Saver puts $10,000 in savings in Year 1. Sanjiv earns a 4% real interest rate on the savings for twenty years. Sanjiv's savings will now have 119% more buying power. Sanjiv can use this increased buying power to help finance his retirement, for a major purchase (e.g. down payment on a house), or for other consumption.

The quantity of household saving will be directly related to the interest rate. As the interest rate increases, the quantity of household saving will increase. Thus, the savings supply curve (or loanable funds supply curve) will be upward sloping, as illustrated on the graph in Example 2 below:

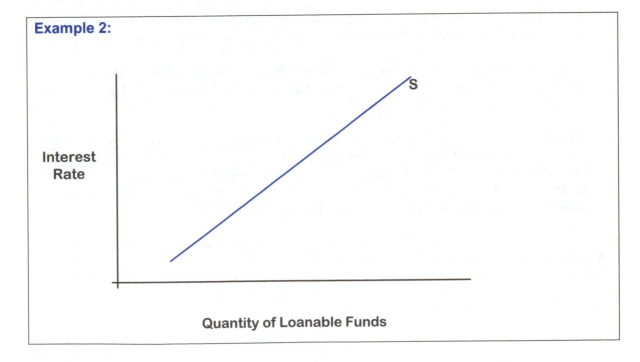

**Example 2:**

Interest Rate (vertical axis), Quantity of Loanable Funds (horizontal axis), S (supply curve)

The private demand for loanable funds comes from:

1. **Consumers, who have a positive rate of time preference.** A positive rate of time preference means consumers prefer earlier consumption to later consumption. This positive rate of time preference causes people to be willing to borrow (and pay interest) in order to consume now rather than later.

   Current consumption, financed by borrowing, is more expensive than future consumption, financed by accumulated savings.

   > **Example 3:** Imelda wants to buy a $2,000 sofa. Rather than waiting until she can accumulate $2,000 in savings, Imelda purchases the sofa and makes monthly payments, including interest, for four years. By the time Imelda has paid for the sofa, it has cost her $2,642.27. But Imelda is happy because she has a high rate of time preference.

   People with a higher rate of time preference will be willing to pay a higher interest rate in order to borrow for current consumption. People with a lower rate of time preference will only borrow for current consumption at lower interest rates. The consumer demand for loanable funds will be inversely related to the interest rate. The lower the interest rate, the greater the quantity of loanable funds demanded by consumers.

   For more on consumer saving and spending behavior, see the book review in the appendix at the end of the chapter.

2. **Business firms, which wish to invest in physical capital.** Investing in physical capital can increase a business firm's productivity. The increased productivity can add to a firm's profits by increasing the firm's revenue or by decreasing the firm's production costs.

   The rate of return from the investment is calculated as the additional annual profits generated by the investment divided by the cost of the investment (see Chapter 6).

   Investing in physical capital may require the use of loanable funds. Interest is the payment for the use of loanable funds, and ultimately for the use of the physical capital financed by the loanable funds.

   We learned in Chapter 6 that an investment in physical capital will be made only if the expected rate of return from the investment exceeds the interest rate that must be paid to finance the investment. The investment demand for loanable funds will be inversely related to the interest rate. The lower the interest rate, the greater the quantity of loanable funds demanded by business investors.

Both consumer demand and investment demand for loanable funds will be inversely related to the interest rate. Thus, the loanable funds demand curve will be downward sloping, as illustrated on the graph in Example 4 on the next page. The graph also shows the equilibrium interest rate, where the quantity demanded of loanable funds equals the quantity supplied of loanable funds.

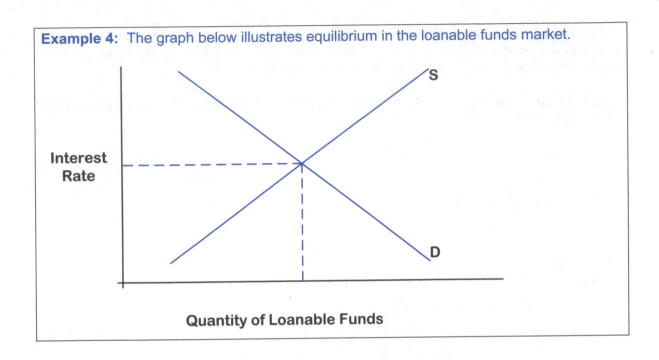
Investment demand for loanable funds will increase or decrease depending on the expected rates of return from the investment in physical capital. (See the explanation on page 6-3.)

An increase in expected rates of return would increase investment demand (shift the loanable funds demand curve to the right). This would result in a new equilibrium at a higher interest rate and a greater quantity of saving and borrowing. See $D_2$ on the graph in Example 5A below.

**Example 5A:** The graph below illustrates the effect of an increase ($D_2$) in expected rates of return from investment.

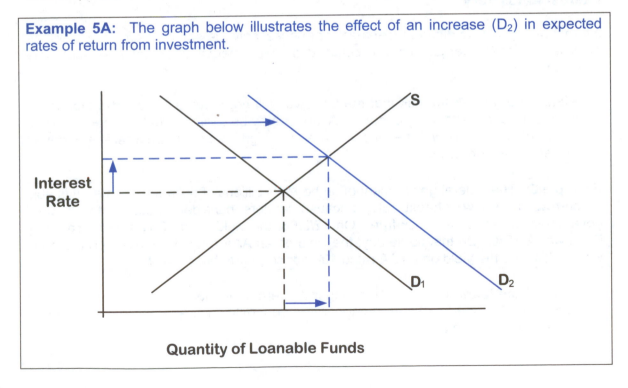

A decrease in expected rates of return would decrease investment demand. This would result in a new equilibrium at a lower interest rate and a lesser quantity of saving and borrowing. See $D_3$ on the graph in Example 5B below.

---

**Example 5B:** The graph below illustrates the effect of a decrease ($D_3$) in expected rates of return from investment.

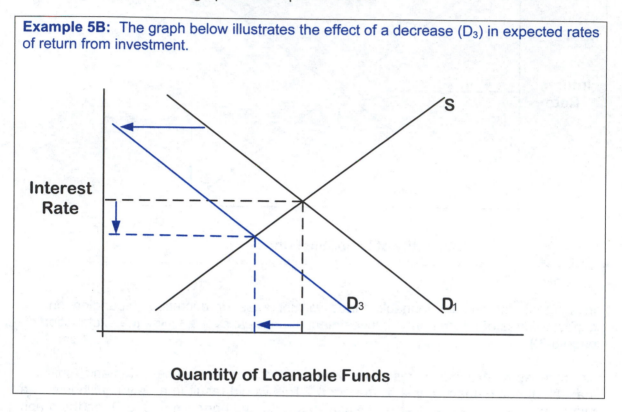

**Quantity of Loanable Funds**

---

## Interest Rates Vary

Interest rates paid on different loans are <u>not</u> necessarily the same. Some loans will be made at a higher interest rate and some at a lower interest rate. Interest rates vary depending on:

1. **Risk.** The greater the risk that the borrower will <u>not</u> repay the loan, the higher the interest rate the lender will demand. A lender may be willing to make a loan to a high risk borrower, but only if the lender can earn a high enough interest rate on the loan to justify the high risk.

---

**Example 6:** The federal government often borrows billions of dollars at a time. It is able to borrow at a low interest rate, because lenders consider loans to the federal government as essentially risk-free. On 12/2/08, the yield on a 10-year U.S. Treasury Bond was 2.75%. On that same day, the yield on an AAA rated 10-year corporate bond was 4.62% and the yield on an AA rated 10-year corporate bond was 5.91%.

---

2. **Term of the loan.** Generally, the longer the term of the loan, the higher the interest rate. For instance, a 30-year mortgage will generally have an interest rate about .5 percent higher than a 15-year mortgage.

> **Example 7:** On 11/17/08, the yield on a 10-year U.S. Treasury Bond was 3.783%. On that same day, the yield on a 3-year U.S. Treasury Bond was 1.800%.

3. **Relative cost of making the loan.** The cost to process a small loan may be the same as the cost to process a large loan. But the cost of processing the small loan is greater relative to the size of the loan. The greater the relative cost of making the loan, the higher the interest rate.

> **Example 8:** Ardell and Bertha both want to take out 5-year personal loans from 1st Bank. Ardell's loan is for $500,000 and Bertha's loan is for $5,000. The cost to the bank of making (processing) the two loans may be about the same. Assuming that both loans have the same risk, Ardell's loan will have a lower interest rate. The relative cost of making Ardell's loan will be less than the relative cost of making Bertha's loan.

## Real Interest Rate

The rate of interest that reflects the true cost of borrowing and the true gain from lending is the real interest rate.

**Real interest rate** – nominal interest rate minus the rate of inflation.

> **Example 9:** Arlene agrees to loan $10,000 to Professor at a nominal (named, stated) interest rate of 10%. The rate of inflation is 3%. What is the real interest rate on the loan? Answer; 7% (The 10% nominal interest rate minus the 3% rate of inflation).

## Present Value

What makes an asset valuable? An asset is valuable because we expect a future benefit from the asset. For a business asset, the future benefit is usually an amount of income or a stream of income to be received in the future. But income to be received in the future is not the same thing as income received today.

There is a time value to money. If we have money today, we can consume today. Current consumption is more valuable than future consumption and earlier consumption is more valuable than later consumption, because consumers have a positive rate of time preference.

Another reason that money received today is more valuable than money to be received in the future is interest. If we have the money today, we can invest the money and earn interest. This will give us a larger amount of money in the future. The sooner that we have the money to invest, the more money that we will have in the future.

An asset is valuable because we expect the asset to generate future income. The value of the asset today depends on the present value of that future income. Thus, the present value of an asset is the discounted value today of the income stream associated with the asset.

To compute the present value of a future amount, we use the formula below. In the formula, **F** is the future amount, **i** is the interest rate that we believe we could earn if we had the future amount today, and **n** is the number of years we have to wait to receive the future amount.

$$PV = F \div (1 + i)^n$$

---

**Example 10A:** Arlene can invest in an asset today that she can sell in one year for $5,000. What is the present value of $5,000 to be received one year from today, assuming Arlene could earn 5% interest if she had the money today?

$$PV = F \div (1 + i)^n = \$5,000 \div (1 + .05)^1 = \$5,000 \div (1.05)^1 = \$5,000 \div 1.05$$
$$= \$4,761.90$$

---

One factor that affects the present value of future income is the interest rate. The higher the interest rate that could be earned if a person had the money now, the more potential earnings the person is sacrificing by having to wait for the money. Thus, the higher the interest rate, the lower the present value of the future income.

---

**Example 10B:** Same facts as Example 10A, except that Arlene could earn 12% interest if she had the money today. What is the present value?

$$PV = F \div (1 + i)^n = \$5,000 \div (1 + .12)^1 = \$5,000 \div (1.12)^1 = \$5,000 \div 1.12$$
$$= \$4,464.29$$

---

Another factor that affects the present value of future income is the number of years until the future income is to be received. The longer the time until the future income is to be received, the lower the present value of the future income.

---

**Example 10C:** Same facts as Example 10B, except that Arlene has to wait eight years to receive the future income. What is the present value?

$$PV = F \div (1 + i)^n = \$5,000 \div (1 + .12)^8 = \$5,000 \div (1.12)^8 = \$5,000 \div 2.476$$
$$= \$2,019.39$$

---

In evaluating an investment opportunity, the present value of expected future returns is compared to the current cost.

---

**Example 10D:** Arlene can invest in an asset today that she can sell in five years for $5,000. Arlene can buy the asset today for $3,600. Assuming Arlene could earn 7% interest if she had the money today, is this a good investment? No. The asset is only worth $3,564.81, as computed below:

$$PV = F \div (1 + i)^n = \$5,000 \div (1 + .07)^5 = \$5,000 \div (1.07)^5 = \$5,000 \div 1.4026$$
$$= \$3,564.81$$

---

## Economic Rent

Chapter 2 introduced the concept of producer's surplus. Producer's surplus is the difference between the lowest price that a seller of a good is willing to accept and the price actually received. Economic rent is a similar concept for factors of production.

**Economic rent** – payment to a factor in excess of opportunity costs.

---

**Example 11:** Professor wants to hire 10 students to participate in a research project. When Professor offers to pay $20 per student, only two students are willing to participate in the project. The supply of students is indicated on the supply schedule and the supply curve below:

| Payments | Quantity of Students |
|----------|----------------------|
| $20 | 2 |
| 30 | 4 |
| 40 | 6 |
| 50 | 8 |
| 60 | 10 |

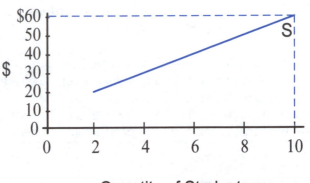

Quantity of Students

To attract 10 students to the project, Professor has to pay each student $60. The first two students, who were willing to supply their labor for $20, are receiving economic rent of $40. For the group of students, the economic rent is the area above the supply curve and below the payment amount ($60).

---

There is often a connection between the payment to a factor and the price of what the factor produces.

---

**Example 12A:** The head football coach at Local High School is paid $55,000 per year, and tickets to the high school games are $5. The head football coach at State University is paid $2 million per year, and tickets to the university games are $75.

---

Does the high salary of the university coach cause the high ticket prices to the university's games? No. The cause and effect runs in the other direction. The high ticket prices cause the high salary. If economic rent for a factor is high, it is because the demand for what the factor produces is high.

---

**Example 12B:** If the head football coach at State University agrees to coach for free during the upcoming season, would the university lower its ticket prices? Not if the stadium sells out at $75 per ticket.

---

## Functions of Economic Rent

Though economic rent is a payment in excess of opportunity costs, it is not an unnecessary payment. Economic rent performs two functions:

**1. Economic rent allocates resources to their most valuable use.**

> **Example 13A:** General Horatio Ordnance retires after a distinguished military career. General Ordnance hopes to pursue a new career as a public speaker. He decides to make five public speaking appearances each month. He receives offers for two hundred speaking appearances each month. He accepts the speaking engagements that pay the most. The General's desire for economic rent allocates his labor to its most valuable use.

**2. Economic rent provides incentive for resource owners to develop the productivity of their resources.**

> **Example 13B:** General Ordnance proves to be a very poor public speaker. Soon the fees offered to him drop to a low level. General Ordnance trains with a public speaking coach, and develops into a dynamic speaker. The fees offered to General Ordnance rise to a high level. The General's desire for economic rent provided the incentive for the General to improve the productivity of his labor.

## Economic Profit

Economic profit is the difference between total revenue and total costs, including both explicit and implicit costs. We saw in Chapter 21 that it is difficult for a perfect competitor to earn economic profit in the long run. Economic profit tends to attract new competitors into a market, driving market price down, and eliminating economic profit. But a firm may be able to tap into a source of economic profit.

There are four sources of economic profit:

**1. Arbitrage.** Arbitrage refers to buying at a low price in one market and selling at a higher price in another market. Arbitrage opportunities tend to be short-lived, as entrepreneurs rush in to take advantage of them.

> **Example 14:** A hurricane is forecast to strike Savannah, Georgia within 48 hours. The price of plywood in Savannah triples. Abby Arbitrager buys plywood in Atlanta at its normal price and ships it to Savannah where she sells it, earning economic profit.

**2. Uncertainty.** Most people prefer certain income to uncertain income. A person may be willing to accept greater uncertainty, if there is a chance of greater than normal profit.

> **Example 15:** Carlos is a chef at an upscale restaurant. Carlos is paid $60,000 per year. If Carlos quits his job and starts his own restaurant, he may earn more as a risk-taking entrepreneur than he does as an employee. But he also may earn much less if his restaurant fails.

3. **Innovation.** An entrepreneur who is innovative (develops new products, more efficient production techniques, etc.) can earn an economic profit. It is difficult to continue to be an innovative entrepreneur, because one's competitors are also trying to be innovative.

> **Example 16:** Farmer Reuben Goldberg designs an elaborate and time-saving system for gathering the eggs laid by his 10,000 hens. Farmer Goldberg's innovation may enable him to earn an economic profit.

4. **Monopoly profits.** If a firm can establish and maintain a monopoly position, it may be able to earn an economic profit in both the short run and the long run.

> **Example 17:** Kathleen "Kitty" Russell is the owner of the Long Branch Saloon, the only drinking establishment in Dodge City. Because of Kitty's influence with the town council, no other licenses to serve alcohol are granted in Dodge City. Kitty's monopoly position will allow her to earn economic profit.

## Profit as a Signal

Profit acts as a signaling device in a market economy. Profit attracts entrepreneurs and resources into markets of growing consumer demand.

> **Example 18:** A hurricane is forecast to strike Savannah within 48 hours. The demand for plywood dramatically increases. Plywood sellers respond to the increased demand by increasing the price of plywood dramatically. The profit for plywood sellers skyrockets. Should this type of "price gouging" be allowed? Yes! The high profit will signal entrepreneurs to ship plywood to Savannah, which is where it is most needed.
>
> Plywood will continue to be shipped to Savannah as long as economic profit is available. If the city of Savannah passes an ordinance prohibiting price increases due to hurricanes, the price of plywood will not rise, the profit in the plywood industry will not increase, and entrepreneurs will have no motivation to ship plywood to Savannah. And residents of Savannah will be unable to buy the plywood that they need.

## Appendix: Book Review – "Nudge"

In their 2008 book "Nudge", Richard Thaler and Cass Sunstein introduce the idea of designing choice architecture to nudge people toward better decision making.

According to "Nudge", we humans often make poor decisions because we are prone to various biases in our thinking. We make many decisions and don't want to spend large amounts of time carefully analyzing every decision. So we rely on simple rules of thumb for many of our decisions. Unfortunately, our rules of thumb may lead us to make poor decisions, especially when the decisions are complicated, arise infrequently, do not provide prompt feedback, and test our self-control.

Well-designed choice architecture can help people to make decisions that will make their lives longer, healthier, and better. **Choice architecture** is the context in which people make decisions.

> **Example 19:** If a school cafeteria places desserts as the first item available, students will eat more dessert (and less of healthier foods) than if the school cafeteria places desserts as the last item available.

The book describes the nudging approach as "libertarian paternalism". It is paternalistic in that it argues for efforts in both the private and the public sector to steer people's choices in directions that will improve their lives. It is libertarian in that it insists that people should be free to do what they like. The policies of libertarian paternalism are intended to maintain or increase freedom.

One area where humans regularly make poor decisions is in saving. Most people fear that they are saving too little, and often make resolutions to increase their savings rate. But then they don't.

A number of biases contribute to the low savings rate. One is "status quo bias". It is easier to leave things the way they are than to make a change. This is why so many people never change the original ring tone on their cell phone. And why so many people fail to join their company's 401(k) plan when they become eligible, even if their company offers to match their contributions.

One way to overcome the tendency of "status quo bias" to limit savings is to change the choice architecture. Most company 401(k) plans are "opt-in" plans. The employees have to take positive steps to join the plan. Many employees never get around to joining. The default option is to not join. If the choice architecture is changed so that the 401(k) plan is "opt-out" (each employee is automatically enrolled in the plan and must take positive steps to leave the plan), a much higher percentage of employees will be in the plan.

Another bias that contributes to the low savings rate is "loss aversion". People feel the pain of a loss more strongly than they feel the pleasure of a gain. As a result, people have a strong aversion to seeing their paychecks get smaller. But if a person chooses to increase their savings rate from 2% to 10% today, their paycheck will get smaller.

One way to overcome "loss aversion" is with a program called Save More Tomorrow. Employees commit today to increase their saving contribution in the future by some percentage of future raises.

> **Example 20:** Reluctant Saver is currently contributing nothing to his company's 401(k) plan. Under a Save More Tomorrow plan, Reluctant commits to contributing half of any future pay raises to his 401(k) plan. If Reluctant receives annual pay increases averaging 4% for the next five years, his saving rate will have increased to 10%. And his paycheck will still increase with each pay raise.

If a Save More Tomorrow plan is also made the default option, a high percentage of employees is likely to choose this option (or at least fail to opt-out of it). As a result, savings rates rise.

The book suggests that well-designed choice architecture can nudge people toward better decisions in a variety of other areas, including investment strategy, debt management, health insurance, and energy consumption.

## Appendix: Present Value Table

One factor that affects the present value of future income is the interest rate. The higher the interest rate that could be earned if a person had the money now, the lower the present value of the future income.

Another factor that affects the present value of future income is the number of years until the future income is to be received. The longer until the future income is to be received the lower the present value of the future income.

The table below shows the present value of $1,000 of future income to be received at different numbers of years in the future and at a variety of interest rates. The table illustrates that if either the length of time until the income is to be received increases or the interest rate increases, the present value of the future income decreases.

| | Present Value of $1,000 to be Received in the Future | | | | |
|---|---|---|---|---|---|
| Years in the Future | Interest Rate | | | | |
| | 3% | 5% | 7% | 10% | 15% |
| 1 | $970.87 | $952.38 | $934.58 | $909.09 | $869.57 |
| 2 | 942.60 | 907.03 | 873.44 | 826.45 | 756.14 |
| 3 | 915.14 | 863.84 | 816.30 | 751.32 | 657.52 |
| 4 | 888.49 | 822.70 | 762.90 | 683.01 | 571.75 |
| 5 | 862.61 | 783.53 | 712.99 | 620.92 | 497.18 |
| 6 | 837.48 | 746.22 | 666.34 | 564.47 | 432.33 |
| 7 | 813.09 | 710.68 | 622.75 | 513.16 | 375.94 |
| 8 | 789.41 | 676.84 | 582.01 | 466.51 | 326.90 |
| 9 | 766.42 | 644.61 | 543.93 | 424.10 | 284.26 |
| 10 | 744.09 | 613.91 | 508.35 | 385.54 | 247.19 |
| 15 | 641.86 | 481.02 | 362.45 | 239.39 | 122.89 |
| 25 | 477.61 | 295.30 | 184.25 | 92.30 | 30.38 |
| 50 | 228.11 | 87.20 | 33.95 | 8.52 | .92 |

## Questions for Chapter 26

### Fill-in-the-blanks:

1. _____ is the payment for the use of loanable funds.

2. The _____ interest rate is the nominal interest rate minus the rate of inflation.

3. _____ _____ is payment to a factor in excess of opportunity costs.

4. _____ refers to buying at a low price in one market and selling at a higher price in another market.

## Multiple Choice:

_____ 1. The supply of loanable funds:
  a. comes from households that save part of their income
  b. results from the desire to accumulate wealth for retirement or for major future expenditures
  c. is directly related to the interest rate
  d. All of the above

_____ 2. Positive rate of time preference means that:
  a. consumers prefer to postpone consumption until the future
  b. consumers will be willing to borrow (and pay interest) in order to consume now rather than later
  c. Both of the above
  d. Neither of the above

_____ 3. An increase in expected rates of return would lead to:
  a. a decrease in the demand for loanable funds
  b. a decrease in the equilibrium interest rate
  c. an increase in the quantity of borrowing
  d. All of the above

_____ 4. Generally, interest rates will be lower on loans:
  a. that have low risk
  b. that have a short term
  c. that have a small relative cost to make
  d. All of the above

_____ 5. The real interest rate:
  a. reflects the true cost of borrowing and the true gain from lending
  b. is the nominal interest rate plus the rate of inflation
  c. Both of the above
  d. Neither of the above

_____ 6. If the nominal interest rate is 9% and the real interest rate is 4%, the rate of inflation is:
  a. 4%
  b. 5%
  c. 9%
  d. 13%

_____ 7. Money received today is more valuable than money to be received in the future:
  a. because consumers prefer to postpone consumption until the future
  b. because money received today can be invested to earn interest
  c. Both of the above
  d. Neither of the above

_____ 8. The present value of $10,000 to be received two years from today, assuming an interest rate of 4% is:
   a. $10,000
   b. $9,259
   c. $9,246
   d. $9,200

_____ 9. The present value of $10,000 to be received two years from today, assuming an interest rate of 11% is:
   a. $8,100
   b. $8,116
   c. $8,197
   d. $10,000

_____ 10. The present value of $10,000 to be received six years from today, assuming an interest rate of 11% is:
   a. $5,346
   b. $6,452
   c. $8,247
   d. $18,704

_____ 11. Howie is a disc jockey. He loves his job and would be willing to work at it for $20,000 per year. He makes $350,000 per year.
   a. Howie receives $350,000 of economic rent
   b. Howie receives $330,000 of economic rent
   c. Howie receives no economic rent, he is worth $350,000 to his employer

_____ 12. Howie (from problem 11. above) has the highest rated radio show in his market. Advertising rates for Howie's show are very expensive. The high advertising rates:
   a. are caused by Howie's high salary
   b. are the cause of Howie's high salary
   c. are caused by the high ratings for the show
   d. Both b. and c. above

_____ 13. Economic rent:
   a. is an unnecessary payment
   b. allocates resources to their most valuable use
   c. provides incentive for resource owners to develop the productivity of their resources
   d. Both b. and c. above

_____ 14. The sources of economic profit include:
   a. arbitrage
   b. innovation
   c. earning a normal return on very productive resources
   d. Both a. and b. above

_____ 15. In a market economy, profit:
   a. acts as a signaling device
   b. attracts entrepreneurs and resources into markets of growing consumer demand
   c. is an unnecessary payment
   d. Both a. and b. above

_____ 16. An increase in home burglaries would lead to:
   a. increased consumer demand for home security systems
   b. increased profits in the home security business
   c. an increased number of workers in the home security business
   d. All of the above

_____ 17. According to the book "Nudge", choice architecture:
   a. is the context in which people make decisions
   b. can be designed to "nudge" people toward good decisions
   c. Both of the above
   d. Neither of the above

_____ 18. According to the book "Nudge", the best way to improve people's decisions:
   a. is for the government to mandate that certain decisions be made
   b. is for the government to severely punish unapproved decisions
   c. Both of the above
   d. Neither of the above

_____ 19. The present value of $1,000 to be received fifteen years in the future, assuming an interest rate of 7% is:
   a. $508.35
   b. $481.02
   c. $362.45
   d. $258.42

## Problems:

1. List and explain the two sources of private demand for loanable funds.

2. What is the present value of $75,000 to be received five years from today, assuming an interest rate of 6%.

3. List the functions that economic rent performs.

4. List the four sources of economic profit.

**Answers for Chapter 26**

**Fill-in-the-blanks:**   1. Interest
2. real
3. Economic rent
4. Arbitrage

**Multiple Choice:**

| | | |
|---|---|---|
| 1. d. | 8. c. | 15. d. |
| 2. b. | 9. b. | 16. d. |
| 3. c. | 10. a. | 17. c. |
| 4. d. | 11. b. | 18. d. |
| 5. a. | 12. d. | 19. c. |
| 6. b. | 13. d. | |
| 7. b. | 14. d. | |

**Problems:**

1. The private demand for loanable funds comes from:
   (1) Consumers, who have a positive rate of time preference. A positive rate of time preference means consumers prefer earlier consumption to later consumption. This positive rate of time preference causes people to be willing to borrow (and pay interest) in order to consume now rather than later.
   (2) Business firms, which wish to invest in physical capital. Investing in physical capital can increase a business firm's productivity. Investing in physical capital may require the use of loanable funds.

2. $PV = F \div (1 + i)^n = \$75,000 \div (1 + .06)^5 = \$75,000 \div (1.06)^5 = \$75,000 \div 1.3382 = \$56,044.36$

3. Economic rent performs two functions:
   (1) Economic rent allocates resources to their most valuable uses
   (2) Economic rent provides incentive for resources owners to develop the productivity of their resources

4. The four sources of economic profit are:
   (1) Arbitrage
   (2) Uncertainty
   (3) Innovation
   (4) Monopoly profits

# Chapter 27  Market Failure

The basic economic problem is scarcity. Human wants are unlimited. Resources are limited. The basic goal in dealing with the problem of scarcity is to produce as much consumer satisfaction as possible with the limited resources available. To achieve this goal, society must use its limited resources as efficiently as possible.

Private markets generally work very well. Private markets produce in response to consumer demand. Private producers are motivated to produce the goods and services that will maximize consumer satisfaction, and to do so at the lowest opportunity cost, in order to maximize profits.

As demand or supply change, the equilibrium price in a private market will adjust to eliminate any surplus or shortage. And private markets function based on the voluntary actions of consumers and producers. Private markets allow for maximum individual freedom.

But private markets are not flawless. Private markets do not always produce the most efficient quantity of output.

**Economic efficiency rule** – produce the quantity of output where marginal social benefit equals marginal social cost.

Chapter 21 introduced the economic efficiency rule. In Chapter 21, we saw that perfectly competitive markets generally produce the optimal (economically efficient) quantity of output.

In a perfectly competitive market, the firm's goal of profit-maximization coincides with society's goal of economic efficiency. A perfect competitor will maximize profits by producing the quantity of output where marginal revenue equals marginal cost. This will also be the quantity where price equals marginal cost and thus (assuming no externalities), where marginal social benefit equals marginal social cost.

Chapters 22 and 23 illustrated that when a market is not perfectly competitive (e.g. monopoly, monopolistic competition, and oligopoly), it will not produce the optimal (economically efficient) quantity of output. This is an example of market failure.

**Market failure** – occurs when the market does not produce the optimal quantity of output.

One cause of market failure is a lack of perfect competition. The inefficiency resulting from a lack of perfect competition was discussed in Chapters 22 and 23. In Chapter 22, we saw that the deadweight loss caused by monopoly is the area between the demand curve and the marginal cost curve for the amount of underproduction.

---

**Example 1:** The deadweight loss for Monop Company, a monopoly, is illustrated in Chapter 22 on page 22-8.

---

Government regulation of natural monopoly in order to increase economic efficiency will be discussed in Chapter 29. This chapter illustrates other causes of market failure.

## Externalities

When goods are produced and consumed, private benefits and private costs are generated. Sometimes benefits and costs are generated that are external to the private producer and consumer. These benefits and costs are called externalities.

**Externality** – a benefit or a cost of an activity that affects third parties.

When an external benefit or an external cost is generated, the private market will fail to produce the optimal (economically efficient) quantity. When an external benefit is generated, the private market equilibrium will be less than the optimal quantity. When an external cost is generated, the private market equilibrium will be greater than the optimal quantity.

Over the next few pages, we will see how external benefits and costs cause the private market equilibrium to differ from the optimal quantity.

## Private Market Equilibrium

Chapter 18 indicated that private market demand depends on the marginal utility consumers expect to receive from consumption. In this chapter, we will refer to the marginal utility of consumers as marginal private benefit (MPB). Marginal private benefit will decrease as more units are consumed due to the law of diminishing marginal utility.

Private market supply depends on the marginal cost of production incurred by the producers. In this chapter, we will refer to the marginal cost of producers as the marginal private cost (MPC). Marginal private cost will increase as more units are produced due to the law of diminishing marginal returns.

Private market equilibrium will occur where the private market demand curve intersects with the private market supply curve (where marginal private benefit equals marginal private cost).

---

**Example 2A:** The table below indicates marginal private benefit and marginal private cost for different quantities of output. The graph on the next page illustrates that private market equilibrium (where MPB = MPC) occurs at a quantity of 4 units and a price of $45.

| Quantity | Marginal Private Benefit | Marginal Private Cost |
|----------|--------------------------|-----------------------|
| 1 | $75 | $15 |
| 2 | 65 | 25 |
| 3 | 55 | 35 |
| 4 | 45 | 45 |
| 5 | 35 | 55 |
| 6 | 25 | 65 |
| 7 | 15 | 75 |

---

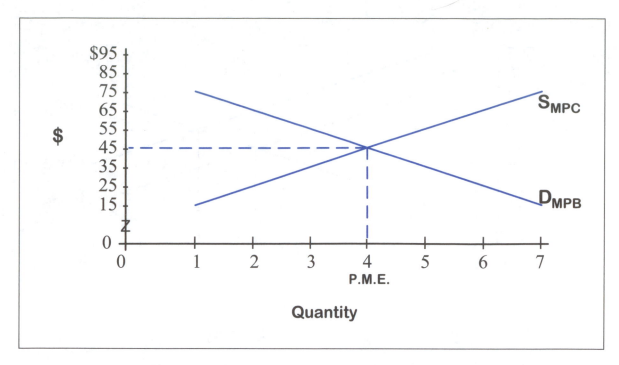

Private market equilibrium (P.M.E.) occurs where MPB = MPC. If there are no external benefits, marginal private benefit and marginal social benefit are the same. If there are no external costs, marginal private cost and marginal social cost are the same. Thus, if there are no externalities, the private market equilibrium (where MPB = MPC) is also the optimal quantity (where MSB = MSC).

## External Benefit

If a market generates an external benefit, the private market will underproduce compared to the optimal quantity. Marginal social benefit will be equal to marginal private benefit plus marginal external benefit.

**Example 2B:** Assume the same facts as Example 2A, except that now the market generates an external benefit of $20 for each unit consumed. The table below indicates marginal private cost (MPC), marginal private benefit (MPB), marginal external benefit, and marginal social benefit (MSB) for different quantities of output.

The graph on the next page illustrates that private market equilibrium (where MPB = MPC) occurs at a quantity of 4 units and a price of $45. The optimal quantity (where MSB = MSC) occurs at 5 units, which corresponds to a price of $55.

| Quantity | MPC | MPB | Marginal External Benefit | MSB |
|----------|------|------|---------------------------|------|
| 1 | $15 | $75 | $20 | $95 |
| 2 | 25 | 65 | 20 | 85 |
| 3 | 35 | 55 | 20 | 75 |
| 4 | 45 | 45 | 20 | 65 |
| 5 | 55 | 35 | 20 | 55 |
| 6 | 65 | 25 | 20 | 45 |
| 7 | 75 | 15 | 20 | 35 |

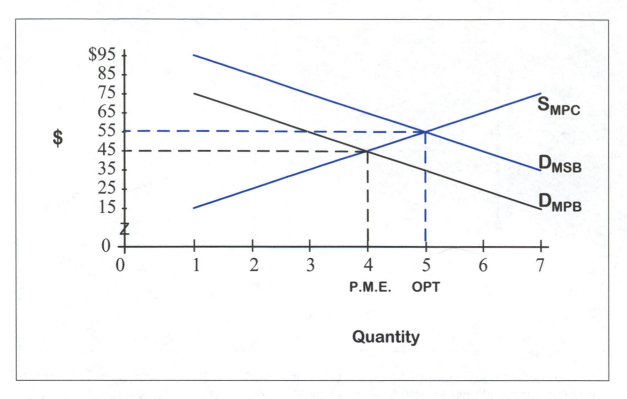

With an external benefit, the private market equilibrium (where MPB = MPC) will be less than the optimal quantity (where MSB = MSC).

### External Cost

If a market generates an external cost, the private market will overproduce compared to the optimal quantity. Marginal social cost will be equal to marginal private cost plus marginal external cost.

**Example 2C:** Assume the same facts as Example 2A, except that now the market generates an external cost of $20 for each unit produced. The table below indicates marginal private benefit (MPB), marginal private cost (MPC), marginal external cost, and marginal social cost (MSC) for different quantities.

The graph on the next page illustrates that private market equilibrium (where MPB = MPC) occurs at a quantity of 4 units and a price of $45. The optimal quantity (where MSB = MSC) occurs at 3 units, which corresponds to a price of $55.

| Quantity | MPB | MPC | Marginal External Cost | MSC |
|---|---|---|---|---|
| 1 | $75 | $15 | $20 | $35 |
| 2 | 65 | 25 | 20 | 45 |
| 3 | 55 | 35 | 20 | 55 |
| 4 | 45 | 45 | 20 | 65 |
| 5 | 35 | 55 | 20 | 75 |
| 6 | 25 | 65 | 20 | 85 |
| 7 | 15 | 75 | 20 | 95 |

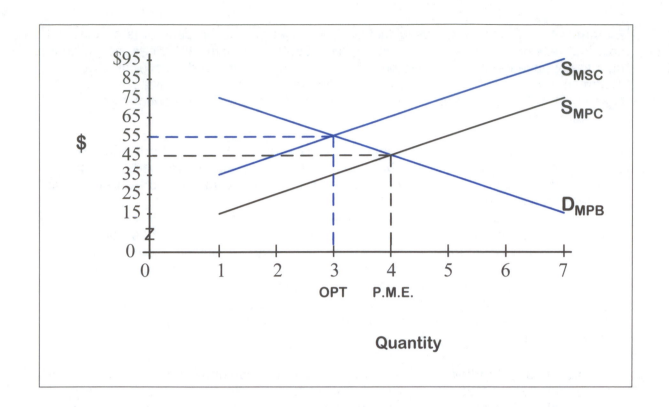

With an external cost, the private market equilibrium (where MPB = MPC) will be greater than the optimal quantity (where MSB = MSC).


## Controlling Externalities

There are four methods for controlling externalities. Three of these methods involve internalizing the externality (changing the external benefit or cost into a private benefit or cost to the person generating it).


## Internalizing Externalities:

1. **Persuasion.** Generally, a person generating an external benefit or cost does <u>not</u> take it into account in his or her consumption or production decision. Persuasion may cause the person to consider the external effect of his or her actions.

> **Example 3:** To encourage the consumption of flu shots, the local health department produces public service announcements stating, "Remember to buy your flu shot. The life you save may be your grandmother's." To discourage littering, the state government of Oklahoma produces public service announcements admonishing, "Don't lay that trash on Oklahoma."

2. **Establishing private property rights and reaching voluntary agreements.** Externalities often occur where property rights are <u>not</u> clearly established. For example, public property (owned by everybody) is much more likely to be littered on than private property (owned by a specific person).

**Example 4:** Nguyen produces widgets. The widget production generates an external cost that falls on Vu, imposing a cost on Vu of $500 per month. If Vu has the property right to <u>not</u> have the cost imposed on him, Vu can sue Nguyen and recover the $500 per month in damages caused by Nguyen's production. This internalizes the cost to Nguyen. It will cost Nguyen $500 per month in damages to Vu to continue generating the external cost.

If Nguyen has the property right to impose this cost on Vu, Vu can offer to pay Nguyen $500 per month to <u>not</u> generate the external cost. This also internalizes the cost to Nguyen. It will cost Nguyen $500 per month in foregone payment from Vu to continue generating the external cost.

If Nguyen's benefit from generating the external cost is greater than Vu's benefit from avoiding it ($500 per month), Nguyen will go ahead and generate the cost (paying the damages or turning down the offered payment). If Vu's benefit from avoiding the external cost ($500 per month) exceeds Nguyen's benefit from generating it, Nguyen will <u>not</u> generate the cost. Whichever party is assigned the property rights, a more efficient solution can be worked out. This is the Coase Theorem (developed by economist Ronald Coase).

3. **Taxes and subsidies.** To internalize an external benefit, a subsidy equal to the marginal external benefit could be offered to the consumers. To internalize an external cost, a tax equal to the marginal external cost could be imposed on the producers. To achieve the optimal quantity of output, the tax (or subsidy) needs to be equal to the external cost (or benefit).

**Example 5:** In Example 2B, a $20 subsidy to consumers would shift the private market demand curve to the right, making it the same as the demand curve based on MSB. In Example 2C, a $20 tax on producers would shift the private market supply curve to the left, making it the same as the supply curve based on MSC.

### Government Regulation of Externalities

Externalities can also be controlled through government regulation of the externality producing activity. If production of a good generates an external cost (e.g. pollution), the government can mandate certain types of producer behavior (e.g. pollution control devices must be used).

If consumption of a good generates an external benefit (e.g. a flu shot), the government can mandate certain types of consumer behavior (e.g. everyone must get a flu shot).

Unfortunately, government regulation of externalities may result in costs that exceed benefits, because:

1. Regulations are generally imposed on a blanket basis (or "one size fits all").

**Example 6:** Government regulations require all new cars to be equipped with catalytic converters. A catalytic converter converts harmful compounds in automobile exhaust (e.g. carbon monoxide) into less harmful compounds (e.g. carbon dioxide). Catalytic converters, which add to the cost of each new car, may benefit more than they cost for cars driven in heavily populated areas, but almost certainly cost more than they benefit for cars driven in rural areas.

2. Regulations are sometimes imposed without careful comparison of costs and benefits.

**Example 7:** The Endangered Species Act of 1973 has a purpose to "provide a means whereby the ecosystems upon which endangered species and threatened species depend may be conserved." The Act does not provide for a comparison of costs and benefits in the effort to protect endangered species. According to Lon Peters of the Cascade Policy Institute, the Northwest Planning Council has spent $150-200 million per year to protect salmon in the Columbia River Basin. In contrast, the value of the harvested salmon at the dock is around $15 million per year.

3. Regulations impose costs on the economy. These costs include the costs of the regulatory agencies, the costs to the regulated firms of complying with the regulations, the inefficiency costs if the regulations reduce competition, and the costs of unintended consequences of the regulations. The costs of government regulations will be examined in more detail in Chapter 29.

## Pollution Control

Production of goods and services often results in undesired byproducts (noise, odors, solid waste, etc.). We call these undesired byproducts pollution.

**Pollution** – any undesired byproduct of production.

Pollution is a type of external cost. As such, the private market will tend to produce more pollution than is optimal.

The ideal level of pollution is usually not zero. Since pollution is a byproduct of production, to achieve zero pollution would usually require completely eliminating valuable production. The cost of reducing pollution to zero is usually greater than the benefit of achieving zero pollution.

The optimal quantity of any activity occurs where marginal social benefit equals marginal social cost. Pollution control should be pursued up to the point where the MSB of control equals the MSC of control. The optimal level of pollution control will usually not result in zero pollution.

Typically, the MSB of pollution control will initially be high, and will decline as more pollution control is pursued. The MSC of pollution control will initially be low, and will increase as more pollution control is pursued.

**Example 8:** Assume that the table and the graph on the next page illustrate the MSB and the MSC of different quantities of pollution control. The optimal quantity of pollution control occurs at a quantity of 5 units of pollution control (where the MSB of pollution control equals the MSC).

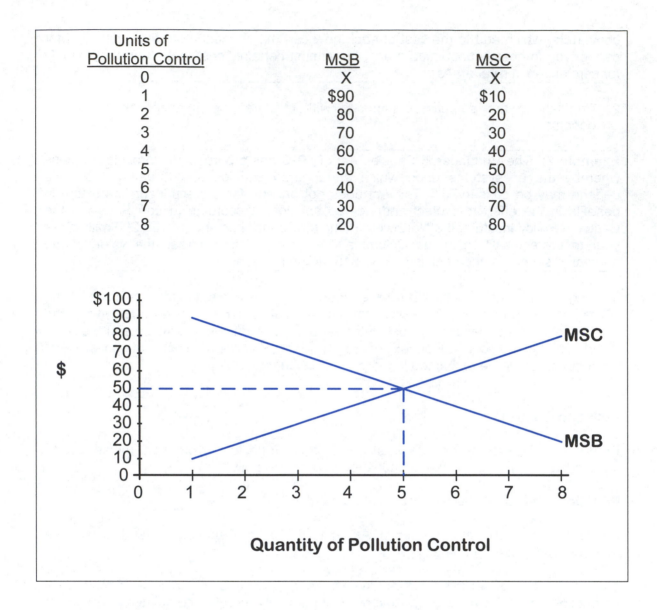

| Units of Pollution Control | MSB | MSC |
|---|---|---|
| 0 | X | X |
| 1 | $90 | $10 |
| 2 | 80 | 20 |
| 3 | 70 | 30 |
| 4 | 60 | 40 |
| 5 | 50 | 50 |
| 6 | 40 | 60 |
| 7 | 30 | 70 |
| 8 | 20 | 80 |

**Quantity of Pollution Control**

Historically, the government has relied primarily on two methods of pollution control:

1. **Regulatory standards.** The government mandates that certain types of pollution control must be used, or that certain targets for pollution reduction must be met. As discussed earlier in this chapter, government regulation may result in costs that exceed benefits.

2. **Market environmentalism.** The general theory of market environmentalism is to achieve environmental goals through the use of the market. This will hopefully allow for pollution control at the lowest possible cost.

**Example 9:** Highcost Company and Lowcost Company are discharging biodegradable waste into a lake. Highcost Company is discharging 200 units of waste per year and Lowcost Company is also discharging 200 units of waste per year. The government determines that an acceptable annual discharge into the lake is a total of 300 units of biodegradable waste per year. Under a regulatory standards approach, the government might mandate that each company must reduce waste discharge by 50 units. Under a market environmentalism approach, the government might issue marketable pollution permits to each company allowing for waste discharge of 150 units. The table below shows the cost of waste reduction for each company.

|  | Highcost Company | Lowcost Company |
|---|---|---|
| Cost of Reducing Waste per Unit | $5,000 | $1,000 |

Under the regulatory standard, Highcost Company would incur a cost of $250,000 to reduce waste by 50 units and Lowcost Company would incur a cost of $50,000 to reduce waste by 50 units. The total cost to reduce waste by 100 units is $300,000.

Under market environmentalism, Highcost Company would buy 50 units of pollution permits from Lowcost Company. Lowcost Company would incur a cost of $100,000 to reduce waste by 100 units. Highcost Company would <u>not</u> have to reduce waste. The total cost to reduce waste by 100 units is $100,000.

## Public Goods

Most of the goods that we produce and consume are private goods. **Private goods** are rivalrous in consumption and excludable. Some goods that we demand are public goods.

**Public goods** – nonrivalrous in consumption and nonexcludable.

A good is rivalrous in consumption if consumption by one person prevents or interferes with consumption by another person.

> **Example 10:** Professor eats the last three slices of leftover pizza. Professor's three kids are upset that there is no pizza left for them. Pizza is a rivalrous good.

A good is nonrivalrous in consumption if consumption by one person does <u>not</u> hinder consumption by others.

> **Example 11:** Professor sits on his patio and watches a beautiful sunset. Professor's kids do <u>not</u> complain that he is "watching up all the sunset". A sunset is a nonrivalrous good.

A good is excludable if nonpayers can easily be excluded from consuming the good.

> **Example 12:** Professor craves a candy bar from the vending machine. But Professor has no money (a painfully common occurrence). Professor will be excluded from consuming a candy bar. A candy bar is an excludable good.

A good is nonexcludable if nonpayers cannot easily be excluded from consuming the good.

> **Example 13:** Professor fails to pay his income taxes. (Note to IRS: Only kidding!) Professor will be just as protected by national defense as those who pay their taxes. National defense is a nonexcludable good.

A private market will produce private goods because the producer can easily exclude nonpayers from consumption. People who want to consume the good will have to pay for consumption. This allows the private producer to generate income to attempt to cover production costs (and maybe even earn a profit).

A private market will <u>not</u> produce public goods because the producer cannot easily exclude nonpayers from consumption. Once the public good is produced, people who want to consume the good will <u>not</u> have to pay for consumption. Thus, the private producer cannot earn income to attempt to cover production costs.

Because a public good is nonexcludable, consumers can obtain the benefit of the good without paying for it. This is the free rider problem. Thus, public goods must be produced by the government. The government (through taxation) can compel consumers of a public good to help pay to cover production costs.

## Common Goods

Private goods are rivalrous in consumption and excludable. Public goods are nonrivalrous and nonexcludable. A third possibility is common goods.

**Common goods** – rivalrous in consumption and nonexcludable.

A common good is rivalrous in consumption. Consumption by one person prevents or interferes with consumption by another person.

> **Example 14:** Lake Springfield is home to a rare and exotic breed of fish called the Monty. The Monty is orange and has three-eyes. If Homer fishes ten Montys from Lake Springfield, this reduces the number of Montys available for others to catch.

A common good is nonexludable. Nonpayers cannot easily be excluded from consuming the good.

> **Example 15:** Fishing in Lake Springfield has never been subject to restrictions. The lake has never been popular for fishing. People complain that the fish taste funny. So there has never been a reason to incur the cost of placing limitations on how many fish any one person can catch from the lake. There were never so many fish removed from the lake to significantly affect the fish population.

Because a common good is nonexcludable, consumers will tend to overconsume the good.

**Example 16:** Due to the publicity it receives from a popular television show, the Monty has become a valuable fish. Aquariums will pay hundreds of dollars for each one. Unfortunately, Montys are unable to reproduce in any environment other than Lake Springfield. Something in the water. Ideally, the Monty would be fished out of Lake Springfield no faster than it can reproduce and sustain its population. If Lake Springfield were privately owned, its owner would be motivated to avoid overfishing. But since the lake is a common good, each person who fishes the lake will be motivated to catch all the Montys that they can before someone else catches them all. The Monty will be fished to extinction.

The tendency to overconsume common goods is called the "tragedy of the commons". Historical examples include the hunting to extinction of the passenger pigeon (which was once the most common bird in North America) and the hunting to near-extinction of the American Bison. Other examples include traffic congestion, overfishing the oceans, overcrowded National Parks, and environmental degradation.

The tragedy of the commons can be analyzed as an externality problem. Each person who consumes a common good is receiving a private benefit and generating both a private cost and an external cost (the reduction of the amount of the common good available for others to consume). As long as the marginal private benefit exceeds the marginal private cost, the person will continue to consume.

**Example 17:** As long as the benefit to Homer of catching one more Monty from Lake Springfield exceeds the cost to Homer, he will continue to catch more Montys. He will ignore the external cost that he is imposing on others.

The tragedy of the commons can also be analyzed as a type of prisoners' dilemma.

**Example 18:** All of the people fishing for Montys in Lake Springfield would benefit if they could agree to limit their catch in order to sustain the Montys in the lake. However, each person's dominant strategy is to catch as many Montys as possible, whether other people stick to the agreement or break it.

One way to solve the tragedy of the commons is to turn the common good into a privately owned good.

**Example 19:** If Lake Springfield were privately owned, its owner would be motivated to avoid overfishing in order to sustain the population of Montys.

**Example 20:** According to the USDA, about 35 million cattle are slaughtered in the U.S. each year. Yet there is no concern that cows will become extinct.

Another way to solve the tragedy of the commons is by government regulation or taxation to prevent overconsumption.

**Example 21:** The city of Springfield can place a limitation of the number of Montys that can be fished out of Lake Springfield each year. The most economically efficient approach would be to auction off Monty fishing licenses to the high bidder. That would ensure that the limited supply of Montys would go to the user with the most valuable use.

## Asymmetric Information

Another source of market failure is asymmetric information. One party to an exchange may have information that the other party doesn't have. Asymmetric information may result in a market producing more or less than the optimal quantity.

> **Example 22:** Fifty years ago, tobacco companies knew a lot more about the dangers of cigarette smoking than the average cigarette smoker knew.

Asymmetric information may result in adverse selection. When adverse selection occurs, the party lacking information will be confronted by a different selection than expected.

> **Example 23:** If an auto insurance company charges "one rate" for all drivers, the company may expect a normal selection of drivers to apply for a policy. But the actual selection will consist mainly of "high risk" drivers.

Asymmetric information may result in moral hazard. Moral hazard occurs when one party to an exchange changes his or her behavior after the exchange in a way unexpected by and detrimental to the other party.

> **Example 24:** After drivers acquire an auto insurance policy, their driving habits may deteriorate since their personal risk of loss from an auto accident is reduced.

Economists disagree on how severe a problem is created by asymmetric information. Some economists see asymmetric information as a major flaw in the market system and believe that the less informed party (usually the consumer) suffers large losses as a result.

Other economists argue that information is usually available, though at a cost. They assert that the decision as to how much information to acquire is best left to the consumer.

> **Example 25:** Barney is in the market for a used car. Barney is a big guy and often suffers from alcohol-induced clumsiness, so he is looking for a car that is roomy and easy to climb into and out of. Moe owns a used car that is roomy and easy to climb into and out of. Moe knows a lot about the car's history for reliability. Barney does <u>not</u>. This asymmetric information may cause Barney to buy a car that he would not want or to agree to pay a price that is more than he would be willing to pay if he were better informed.
>
> However, Barney has the option of acquiring more information. He can take the car to a trusted mechanic to have it checked out. He can research the reliability of cars of the same make and model. He can pay for a service that will give him a history of the car. Barney will decide how much cost he is willing to incur to increase the information he has about the car.

## Questions for Chapter 27

### Fill-in-the-blanks:

1. Market _____ occurs when the market does <u>not</u> produce the optimal quantity of output.

2. A(n) _____ is a benefit or a cost of an activity that affects third parties.

3. _____ is any undesired byproduct of production.

4. _____ goods are rivalrous in consumption and excludable.

5. _____ goods are nonrivalrous in consumption and nonexcludable.

6. _____ goods are rivalrous in consumption and nonexcludable.

### Multiple Choice:

_____ 1. The economic efficiency rule requires production of the quantity of output where:
   a. profit is maximized
   b. marginal social benefit is maximized
   c. marginal social benefit equals marginal social cost
   d. the excess of marginal social benefit over marginal social cost is maximized

_____ 2. If an external benefit is generated, the private market equilibrium will be:
   a. less than the optimal quantity
   b. greater than the optimal quantity
   c. equal to the optimal quantity

Answer questions 3. through 5. by referring to the following table, which represents the relationships between MPC, MPB, marginal external benefit, and MSB for different quantities.

| Quantity | MPC | MPB | Marginal External Benefit | MSB |
|---|---|---|---|---|
| 1 | $20 | $65 | $30 | $95 |
| 2 | 30 | 60 | 30 | 90 |
| 3 | 40 | 55 | 30 | 85 |
| 4 | 50 | 50 | 30 | 80 |
| 5 | 60 | 45 | 30 | 75 |
| 6 | 70 | 40 | 30 | 70 |
| 7 | 80 | 35 | 30 | 65 |
| 8 | 90 | 30 | 30 | 60 |

_____ 3. What is the private market equilibrium quantity?
   a.  3
   b.  4
   c.  5
   d.  6

_____ 4. What is the optimal quantity?
   a.  4
   b.  5
   c.  6
   d.  7

_____ 5. What government policy would cause the market to achieve the optimal quantity?
   a.  impose a tax of $30 on producers
   b.  pay a subsidy of $30 to consumers
   c.  require all consumers to buy the product
   d.  do nothing

_____ 6. Internalizing an externality means:
   a.  the government prohibits the production of external costs
   b.  the government requires production of external benefits
   c.  changing the external benefit or cost into a private benefit or cost to the person generating it
   d.  Both a. and b. above

_____ 7. Which of the methods of controlling externalities does not involve internalizing externalities?
   a.  persuasion
   b.  government regulation
   c.  taxes and subsidies
   d.  establishing private property rights and reaching voluntary agreements

_____ 8. When using taxes and subsidies to internalize externalities:
   a.  a tax is imposed to internalize an external cost
   b.  a subsidy is paid to internalize an external benefit
   c.  the tax or subsidy needs to be equal to the external cost or benefit
   d.  All of the above

_____ 9. The optimal quantity of pollution control is the quantity of pollution control:
   a.  which eliminates pollution
   b.  where the MSB of control equals the MSC of control
   c.  set by government regulators
   d.  All of the above

_____ 10. A public good:
   a.  is rivalrous in consumption and excludable
   b.  is nonrivalrous in consumption and nonexcludable
   c.  must be produced by government
   d.  Both b. and c. above

_____ 11. The private market:
    a. tends to overproduce public goods because they are nonrivalrous
    b. can produce public goods more effectively than the government can
    c. fails to produce public goods because of the free rider problem
    d. earns excessive profit on public goods

_____ 12. A common good:
    a. is rivalrous in consumption and excludable
    b. is nonrivalrous in consumption and nonexcludable
    c. will tend to be overconsumed
    d. Both a. and c. above

_____ 13. A common good:
    a. is a type of externality problem
    b. is a type of prisoners' dilemma
    c. Both of the above
    d. Neither of the above

_____ 14. The tragedy of the commons can be solved by:
    a. turning the good into a public good
    b. government regulation or taxation to prevent overconsumption
    c. Both of the above
    d. Neither of the above

_____ 15. Jerolyn signs up for a computer dating service. She is disappointed when she finds that an unusually high percentage of the men who send her emails are, in her opinion, "computer nerds". This is an example of:
    a. Moral hazard
    b. Adverse selection
    c. Both of the above
    d. Neither of the above

_____ 16. Jerolyn finally meets a caring, considerate, hard working man through the computer dating service. Soon after they marry, he becomes uncaring, inconsiderate, and lazy. This is an example of:
    a. Moral hazard
    b. Adverse selection
    c. Both of the above
    d. Neither of the above

_____ 17. Consumers:
    a. usually have less information about a product than the seller
    b. usually can gain more information if they are willing to pay the cost of obtaining the additional information
    c. Both of the above
    d. Neither of the above

**Problems:**

1. Explain why the ideal level of pollution is usually <u>not</u> zero.

2. Explain the difference between a rivalrous good and a nonrivalrous good and give an example of each.

3. Explain why a private market will <u>not</u> produce public goods.

4. Based on the information on the table on the next page:
   (1) Graph the private market demand curve
   (2) Graph the private market supply curve
   (3) Indicate the private market equilibrium price and quantity
   (4) Graph the supply curve based on MSC
   (5) Indicate the optimal price and quantity

| Quantity | MPB | MPC | Marginal External Cost | MSC |
|----------|------|------|------------------------|------|
| 1 | $120 | $30 | $30 | $60 |
| 2 | 105 | 45 | 30 | 75 |
| 3 | 90 | 60 | 30 | 90 |
| 4 | 75 | 75 | 30 | 105 |
| 5 | 60 | 90 | 30 | 120 |
| 6 | 45 | 105 | 30 | 135 |

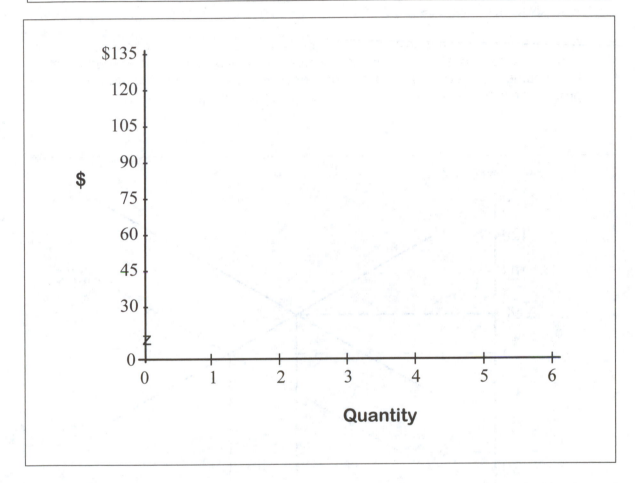

## Answers for Chapter 27

**Fill-in-the-blanks:**

| | |
|---|---|
| 1. failure | 4. Private |
| 2. externality | 5. Public |
| 3. Pollution | 6. Common |

**Multiple Choice:**

| | | |
|---|---|---|
| 1. c. | 7. b. | 13. c. |
| 2. a. | 8. d. | 14. b. |
| 3. b. | 9. b. | 15. b. |
| 4. c. | 10. d. | 16. a. |
| 5. b. | 11. c. | 17. c. |
| 6. c. | 12. c. | |

**Problems:**

1.  Pollution is any undesired byproduct of production. Since pollution is a byproduct of production, to achieve zero pollution would usually require completely eliminating valuable production. The cost of reducing pollution to zero is usually greater than the benefit of achieving zero pollution.

2.  A good is rivalrous in consumption if consumption by one person prevents or interferes with consumption by another person. A good is nonrivalrous in consumption if consumption by one person does <u>not</u> hinder consumption by others. A sandwich is a rivalrous good. A sunset is a nonrivalrous good.

3.  A private market will <u>not</u> produce public goods because the producer cannot exclude nonpayers from consumption. Once the public good is produced, people who want to consume the good will <u>not</u> have to pay for consumption. Thus, the private producer cannot earn income to attempt to cover production costs.

4.

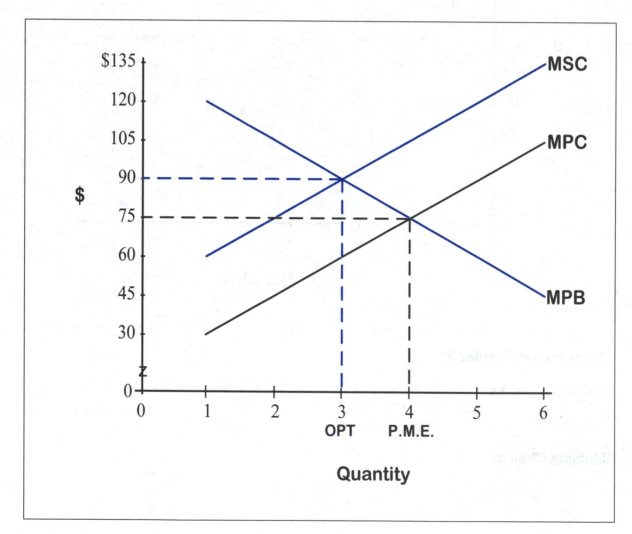

# Chapter 28  Public Choice and Government Failure

The basic economic problem is scarcity.  Human wants are unlimited.  Resources are limited.  The basic goal in dealing with the problem of scarcity is to produce as much consumer satisfaction as possible with the limited resources available.  In the U.S. economy, this goal is pursued primarily through private markets.

Private markets operate through the individual decision making of consumers and producers.  We saw in Chapter 3 that private markets generally produce the optimal quantity of output (where marginal social benefit equals marginal social cost).

However, we saw in Chapters 22 and 23 that a lack of perfect competition can lead to economic inefficiency.  We will see in Chapter 29 that government action can improve economic efficiency in the case of natural monopoly.

We saw in Chapter 27 that other sources of market failure can occur (e.g. externalities, public goods, common goods, asymmetric information).  In these cases of market failure, government action may result in a more efficient outcome.

> **Example 1:**  We saw in Chapter 27 that government action (e.g. taxes and subsidies) can improve economic efficiency when externalities occur.

Government action is also necessary to establish the legal environment that allows private markets to operate.  For private markets to operate, private property rights must be established and protected.  Government action is necessary to provide national defense, police protection, the judicial system, etc., in order that private property rights may be established and protected.

The government may also act outside these areas of obvious need.  Many production and distribution decisions in the U.S. economy are made on a collective basis in the public sector (by government).  **Public choice theory** applies economic principles to public sector decision making.

Government action may result in a more efficient allocation of resources (e.g. by solving a market failure).  But government action also may result in a less efficient allocation of resources.

**Government failure** – occurs when government action results in a less efficient allocation of resources.

This chapter examines public choice theory and the sources of government failure.

Participants in the public sector decision making process include voters, candidates for public office, elected officials, special-interest groups, and government bureaus.  What will motivate the various participants in the public sector?

The primary motivation of participants in the public sector is assumed to be the same as the primary motivation in the private sector; self-interest.

## Voters

In the public sector, voters are similar to consumers in the private sector. Consumers vote (with their dollars) for the goods and services that they want. Voters vote for the political policies that they favor.

However, consumers in the private sector can usually express their desires much more specifically than voters can. A consumer can purchase exactly the utility-maximizing combination of goods affordable with that consumer's income.

Voters cannot vote for the exact political policies that they favor. A voter can only express his or her preference from the <u>available</u> candidates or other political choices (e.g. a bond issue vote). Even then, the voter will not receive his or her preference unless the majority of voters agree with that preference. Thus, people are likely to be more satisfied with the choices that they can make as consumers than with the choices that they can make as voters.

> **Example 2:** When Lynda goes to Mazzio's she can order the exact pizza that she wants, maybe thin crust with black olives and mushrooms. But when Lynda steps into a voting booth, she usually can choose between only two candidates, neither of whom may be her idea of the perfect candidate. Lynda is likely to be more satisfied with the choices she can make as a consumer than with the choices she can make as a voter. What if Mazzio's offered only two choices in pizza, maybe sausage with onions or pepperoni with green peppers? Would Lynda be as happy with either of those choices as she would be if she could pick exactly what she wanted?

People are not likely to be perfectly satisfied with the choices available to them as voters. Will people be well informed about the candidates and issues when they have an opportunity to vote? For that matter, will most people even choose to vote?

## Low Voter Turnout

One of the characteristics of elections in the U.S. is low voter turnout. Even for a highly publicized presidential election, typically only a little more than one-half of the voting-age population actually votes. In a less publicized election, like a local school board election or a bond issue vote, a much smaller percentage is likely to vote.

> **Example 3:** The New York City school board election of 1999 had a voter turnout of 2%.

Why the low voter turnout?

We assume that voters (and non-voters) are primarily motivated by self-interest. Low voter turnout in political elections occurs because many potential voters see the costs of voting as greater than the benefits. The costs of voting are generally fairly small. A person gives up a bit of his or her time, drives to the polling place, waits in line for a few minutes, reads the ballot and then votes. Surely the benefits of voting will outweigh such minor costs.

But what are a person's benefits of voting?  The basic purpose of voting is to affect the outcome of the election; to cause the voter's desired candidate to win.  But what is the likelihood of one person's vote actually deciding the outcome of a major election?  Extremely small.

> **Example 4:**  According to a "Slate" magazine article by economist Steven Landsburg, the odds of any one person casting the deciding vote in a presidential election are much worse than a person's odds of winning the Powerball jackpot.  Quoting Landsburg: "…it's hard to argue that voting is a good use of your time.  Instead of waiting in line to vote, you could wait in line to buy a lottery ticket, hoping to win $100 million and use it to advance your causes—and all with an almost indescribably greater chance of success than you'd have in the voting booth."

If the only benefit a person anticipates from voting is the chance to affect the outcome of the election, that person will probably <u>not</u> vote.  That person will probably see the costs of voting as greater than the benefits of voting.

Many people do vote.  The people who do vote are apparently anticipating benefits (e.g. the opportunity to express their opinion, personal satisfaction from participating in the election, etc.) other than the chance to affect the outcome of the election.


## Rational Ignorance

Ignorance means lack of knowledge, being uninformed.  All people are ignorant about many things.  (Can you name the moons of Jupiter in alphabetical order?  Can you name the members of the Federal Reserve Board of Governors?  Neither can I.)  People rationally choose to remain ignorant about most subjects.  It is rational to remain ignorant if the cost of gaining the information is greater than the benefit of having the information.

Consumers are motivated to gather information before making a purchase.  There may be a significant benefit to being well-informed before making a specific private purchase.  Consumers will <u>not</u> have perfect information.  Perfect information is too costly.  But a consumer making a major purchase (e.g. house, car, college education) may become quite well-informed before making that purchase.

Will voters be as well-informed before casting a vote in a political election?  What is the benefit of being well-informed about political issues?  Does the well-informed person's vote count more than the ill-informed person's vote?  No. The well-informed person's vote is highly unlikely to affect the outcome of the election.  Thus, most voters will <u>not</u> be well-informed about political issues because they will rationally choose to remain ignorant.

In his book, "The Myth of the Rational Voter: Why Democracies Choose Bad Policies", economist Bryan Caplan asserts that voters are not just rationally ignorant, but are systematically biased in favor of mistaken views.  This book is reviewed in an appendix at the end of the chapter.

Low voter turnout and rational voter ignorance may result in government failure.

## Candidates and the Median Voter Model

A wide range of persons choose to become candidates for public office. But these candidates seem to behave in similar patterns. Why do candidates who are often very different in political opinions, backgrounds, personalities, etc. seem to behave so much alike? The median voter model provides an explanation.

The median voter model suggests that the median voter (the one in the middle) must be captured to achieve a majority vote. If two candidates are on opposite sides of an issue, or on the same side, the candidate closer to the median position will capture the median voter and the majority of the votes.

---

**Example 5:** If Candidate Waffle realizes that Candidate Waver is positioned closer to the median voter, Candidate Waffle will want to move closer to the median position. If Candidate Waver realizes that Candidate Waffle is now positioned closer to the median voter, Candidate Waver will want to move closer to the median position.

---

The median voter model predicts that a candidate will behave in certain predictable ways in his or her pursuit of the median voter:

1. **Aim for a middle-of-the-road position.** A candidate who is too far from the middle-of-the-road will lose the median voter to his or her opponent. A candidate may stake out a fairly extreme position during the nomination process, in order to appeal to the most committed members of the candidate's party. But after receiving the nomination, the candidate will want to move toward the median position.

2. **Label his or her opponents as extremists.** At the same time that Candidate Waffle tries to move toward the middle, Candidate Waffle will try to portray Candidate Waver as on the fringe, and out of touch with the desires of the average voter.

3. **Adjust his or her positions in response to polls.** Candidates will take polls to try to determine what the median voter wants. Candidates may have to change their positions on issues in order to get more in tune with the median voter.

4. **Speak in general rather than specific terms.** To appeal to the median voter, candidates will speak in general terms in favor of goals that the median voter will support (e.g. a strong economy, efficient government, better education, crime reduction, etc.).

   Candidates will try to avoid revealing specific details about how they might plan to accomplish these popular goals (e.g. free trade agreements, closure of redundant military bases, tuition vouchers, construction of new prisons, etc.), to avoid offending voters who might disagree with the specifics.

Policies favored by the median voter (who likely will be ill-informed on most issues) will not necessarily be the most economically efficient policies. The candidates' pursuit of the median voter may result in government failure.

## Elected Officials

Once a candidate is elected to public office, what will he or she do? An elected official may have a strong desire to support policies that will benefit the general public by increasing economic efficiency or promoting long term economic growth. But will an elected official actually support such policies?

## Elected Officials and Short Run Focus

Elected officials tend to have a strong desire to remain elected officials. Thus, an elected official will tend to focus on winning the next election. An elected official will naturally support policies that improve his or her chances of winning the next election, and will naturally oppose policies that harm his or her chances of winning the next election.

Thus, an elected official will tend to support policies that yield benefits in the short run (before the next election) and impose costs in the long run (after the next election). This will be true even if the long run costs of the policies exceed the short run benefits.

Likewise, an elected official will tend to oppose policies that impose costs in the short run and yield benefits in the long run. This will be true even if the long run benefits of the policies exceed the short run costs.

The short run focus of elected officials can lead them to support policies that are economically inefficient (impose costs that exceed benefits) and to oppose policies that are economically efficient (yield benefits that exceed costs). Thus, the short run focus of elected officials can lead to government failure.

## Elected Officials and Special-Interest Groups

Elected officials tend to have a strong desire to remain elected officials. Thus, an elected official will tend to focus on winning the next election. To improve his or her chances of winning the next election, an elected official will be responsive to the goals of special-interest groups.

A special-interest group is a group of people who are especially interested in a particular governmental policy. Usually, the group is strongly affected by the policy. Teachers will be especially interested in the government's education policy. Peanut farmers will be especially interested in the government's peanut subsidy policy. College students will be especially interested in a proposed tuition tax credit.

A special-interest group is usually very small in size compared to the total population. This small size can actually increase the political influence of the special-interest group. A special-interest group will support policies that yield a concentrated benefit for the members of the interest group, and impose a cost that is usually dispersed over a large number of other people. Or a special-interest group will oppose policies that impose a concentrated cost on the members of the interest group, and yield a benefit that is usually dispersed over a large number of other people.

The concentrated benefits or costs experienced by the special-interest group will cause the interest group to act in certain ways that will increase the interest group's political influence. The dispersed benefits or costs experienced by other people (outside the interest group) will cause them to act in ways that increase the interest group's political influence.

The influence of special-interest groups is increased by:

1. **Low voter turnout.** Low voter turnout in political elections increases the influence of the people who do vote. Special-interest group members (expecting a concentrated benefit or cost) are likely to have a high voter turnout. Other people (expecting only dispersed benefits or costs) are likely to have a low voter turnout.

> **Example 6:** A vote on a bond issue to provide funding for the local library system is held. Library employees will be especially interested in the outcome of this vote. Library employees make up a tiny percentage of eligible voters. But library employees have a voter turnout of nearly 100%. Other eligible voters have a very low voter turnout. So the special-interest group (library employees) has a greater influence due to the low voter turnout by most voters.

2. **Rational ignorance.** Special-interest group members (expecting a concentrated benefit or cost) will be well-informed about the issue of concern to the interest group. Other people (expecting only dispersed benefits or costs) will likely be ill-informed about the issue of concern to the interest group.

> **Example 7:** Elected Official Cater is deciding how to vote on an upcoming issue. A vote one way will benefit a special-interest group. The group will be well-informed about how Elected Official Cater votes on this issue, and may reward Elected Official Cater for a favorable vote with campaign contributions and other support. A vote the other way will yield a dispersed benefit to the general public. The general public will be ill-informed about how Elected Official Cater votes on this issue, and probably won't support or oppose Elected Official Cater based on this particular vote. Elected Official Cater will likely respond to the special-interest group on this issue.

3. **Lobbying.** Special-interest group members (expecting a concentrated benefit or cost) are likely to contribute money to hire lobbyists to try to persuade elected officials to vote a specific way on "their" issue. This lobbying is a type of rent seeking. (We discussed the socially wasteful nature of rent seeking in Chapter 22.) Other people (expecting only dispersed benefits or costs) are unlikely to lobby elected officials about the issue. The number of registered lobbyists indicates that special-interest groups do a lot of lobbying.

> **Example 8:** According to a study taken in 2005 by the Center for Public Integrity, there were over 39,000 registered lobbyists working at the state government level. That's over 5 lobbyists for each state legislator. According to the Washington Post, in 2005 there were nearly 35,000 registered lobbyists in Washington D.C., or about 65 lobbyists for each member of Congress.

There is nothing inherently wrong with special-interest groups. Any person has a right to be especially interested in a policy that will strongly affect that person. There is nothing wrong with voting, being well-informed, or lobbying for specific policies. However, policies that benefit special-interest groups may be harmful to the general public.

Because of special-interest group influence, elected officials will tend to favor policies that yield concentrated benefits and impose dispersed costs. This will be true even if the dispersed costs exceed the concentrated benefits (e.g. farm subsidies). Likewise, elected officials will tend to oppose policies that yield dispersed benefits and impose concentrated costs. This will be true even if the dispersed benefits exceed the concentrated costs (e.g. free trade agreements).

Special-interest group influence can lead elected officials to support policies that are economically inefficient (impose costs that exceed benefits) and to oppose policies that are economically efficient (yield benefits that exceed costs). Thus, special-interest group influence can lead to government failure.

## A Congressional District as a Special-Interest Group

A congressional district can be a special-interest group. The residents of a congressional district may be especially interested in a particular governmental policy. The people of Michigan may strongly favor restrictions on imported automobiles. The elected representatives from Michigan will feel strong pressure to enact legislation restricting imported automobiles.

How will the Michigan legislators gain enough votes to pass the legislation beneficial to Michigan? Legislators often trade votes in order to pass legislation beneficial to their own districts. (The elected representatives from Michigan may offer to vote in favor of subsidies for peanut farmers in exchange for the votes of Georgia representatives in favor of restrictions on imported automobiles.) This vote trading is commonly called **logrolling**.

Logrolling often leads to "pork barrel" legislation. **Pork barrel legislation** benefits a particular geographic region (e.g. a congressional district) and is paid for by taxpayers (and/or consumers) from a larger geographic region (e.g. the entire nation).

**Example 9A:** In 2008, Citizens Against Government Waste (CAGW) identified 11,610 federal government pork barrel projects, with a combined cost of $17.2 billion. Since 1991, CAGW has identified a total of $271 billion in pork barrel spending.

**Example 9B:** In 2008, CAGW identified Senator Thad Cochran (R-Mississippi) as the leader in pork barrel spending. Senator Cochran was credited by CAGW with garnering a total of $892.2 million in pork barrel spending for Mississippi, including;
   (1) $35.5 million for the National Center for Critical Information Process and Storage
   (2) $25 million for Delta Health Alliance
   (3) $19.7 million for Yazoo Basin – Delta Headwaters Project
   (4) $14.1 million for Department of Defense Corrosion Program
   (5) $12.8 million for Yazoo Basin – Upper Yazoo Projects
   (6) $10.8 million for Sustainable Energy Research Center at MSU
   (7) $7.5 million for Center for Marine Aquaculture
   (8) $5.4 million for Jackson County Water Supply Project

> **Example 9C:** In 2008, CAGW credited eleven senators with garnering at least $300 million in pork barrel spending for their home states. Sixty-eight senators garnered at least $100 million for their home states.

Pork barrel legislation is an example of concentrated benefits and dispersed costs. Pork barrel legislation is economically efficient to the region that benefits (the legislation benefits that region more than it costs that region), but is often economically inefficient overall (has total costs greater than total benefits).

## Government Bureaus

The policies enacted by legislators must be carried out by someone. The actual functioning of government is usually through government bureaus. Bureaucracies are often criticized as unresponsive, costly, hindered by excessive rules (red tape), prone to "empire-building", etc.

In the private sector, the competitive, profit-seeking nature of private business may serve to restrict bureaucratic inefficiency. In the public sector, these restrictions on bureaucratic inefficiency do not exist.

Government bureaus are likely to be very inefficient because:

1. **They have no profit motive.** A private business firm is generally assumed to pursue profit-maximization. But a government bureau has no profit motive. With no profit motive, a government bureau will be motivated to spend all of its funding. To end a budget year with leftover funding would likely result in decreased funding for the next year. The lack of profit motive also leads government bureaus to be less concerned about minimizing costs than a private business firm would be.

2. **They have no owner.** Private business firms have owners who have an incentive to monitor the efficiency of the firm. Government bureaus belong to "all the people". But none of the people have an owner's incentive to monitor the efficiency of the bureau. The leaders of the bureau may be able to manage it to suit their own interests. This is an example of the principal-agent problem discussed in Chapter 19.

3. **They usually face no competition.** Private business firms are compelled by competitive pressure to be responsive to consumer demand. This responsiveness to consumer demand leads to greater consumer satisfaction. Government bureaus usually face no competition, and thus do <u>not</u> have to be very responsive to consumer demand. Nor do government bureaus face competitive pressure to minimize costs of production.

4. **They seek to grow.** Government bureaucrats are motivated to work for the expansion of their programs. A government bureau is a special-interest group in favor of its own continued existence and growth. Thus, once a government bureau is created, it is politically difficult to eliminate or even to shrink the bureau.

The inefficiency of government bureaus can lead to government failure.

## Other Sources of Government Failure

Government failure occurs when government action results in a less efficient allocation of resources. Some of the sources of government failure have already been discussed in this chapter:

1. Voter flaws.
2. Candidates' pursuit of the median voter.
3. Short run focus of elected officials.
4. Special-interest group influence.
5. Government bureau inefficiency.

There are other sources of government failure:

1. **Difficulty in measuring the marginal social benefit and the marginal social cost of government spending.** In a private market, marginal social benefit is measurable (by the price that consumers are willing and able to pay) and marginal social cost is measurable (by the marginal cost of production to producers). In a competitive private market, equilibrium will tend to occur where price and marginal cost are equal, and thus where marginal social benefit and marginal social cost are equal. This is the economically efficient quantity of output.

   But with government spending, benefits and costs usually have to be estimated by government officials. The government officials preparing the estimates often have a self-interest in over-estimating the benefits and under-estimating the costs of government spending. Thus, government spending will tend to be inefficiently large (where marginal social cost exceeds marginal social benefit).

   **Example 10:** Boston's Central Artery/Tunnel, also known as "The Big Dig", was originally estimated to cost $2.6 billion. The actual cost of the project turned out to be nearly $15 billion. The project also took over 5 years longer than projected.

2. **Taxes collected do _not_ reflect the full cost of a government program.** Two types of costs are incurred when the government collects taxes and uses resources to provide goods and services:

   a. The opportunity cost of the resources used. If the government buys resources in the market, the price paid indicates the opportunity cost. If the government does not pay the market price (e.g. drafts personnel for the military), the opportunity cost may be much higher than the price paid by the government for the resources.

   **Example 11:** When Elvis Presley was drafted into the military in the late 1950s, his military paycheck did _not_ reflect the full opportunity cost to society of using his labor for military purposes instead of for entertainment purposes.

   b. The excess burden of the tax. (For a detailed discussion of excess burden, refer to Chapter 13.) The excess burden is the amount that the burden imposed by a tax exceeds the funding provided by the tax. The sources of excess burden include;

(1) The cost for the government to collect the tax.
(2) The cost for the taxpayers to comply with the tax.
(3) The deadweight loss of the tax.

3. **The inefficiencies caused by income redistribution.** Special-interest group theory suggests that there will be political support for income redistribution programs. Income redistribution programs will usually yield concentrated benefits for the recipients of the redistribution, and will impose costs dispersed over a larger group of taxpayers. Income redistribution causes economic inefficiency because:

   a. Income redistribution reduces the reward for productive behavior and reduces the punishment for unproductive behavior. The reward for productive behavior is high income. The punishment for unproductive behavior is low income. Income redistribution reduces higher incomes in order to supplement lower incomes.

   b. Income redistribution encourages socially wasteful rent seeking. We discussed the socially wasteful nature of rent seeking in Chapter 22.

   c. Income redistribution leads to higher tax rates. Higher tax rates increase the excess burden of taxation. (See Chapter 13.)

4. **Unintended consequences of government policies.** Policies intended to accomplish a desirable goal may have unintended consequences that are undesirable.

> **Example 12:** Cities often impose rent controls intended to make housing more affordable for those with lower incomes. But rent controls tend to reduce the quantity of housing supplied. As a result, cities that impose rent controls tend to experience an increase in homelessness.

5. **Majority voting may be economically inefficient.** Government policies are generally enacted by majority rule. What is good for the majority may be economically efficient, or it may be economically inefficient. The loss imposed on the minority may exceed the benefit to the majority.

> **Example 13:** Mike, Ted, and Gwyneth are deciding by majority vote where to eat lunch. Mike and Ted slightly prefer The Sizzlin' Steak over Veggies Are Us. Gwyneth strongly detests The Sizzlin' Steak and strongly prefers Veggies Are Us. By majority vote, they will choose The Sizzlin' Steak, even though the loss imposed on Gwyneth by this choice exceeds the benefit received by Mike and Ted.

6. **Government may stand in the way of creative destruction.** Economist Joseph Schumpeter coined the phrase **creative destruction** to describe the short run upheaval caused by the development of new technology.

   Creative destruction will impose concentrated costs (on the producers using outdated technology) and will yield dispersed benefits (to all who will benefit from the new technology). Standing in the way of creative destruction will yield concentrated benefits (to the producers using outdated technology) and will impose dispersed costs (on all who would benefit from the new technology).

Elected officials will tend to favor policies that yield concentrated benefits and impose dispersed costs. Thus, government may stand in the way of creative destruction. Blocking creative destruction is economically inefficient. Though creative destruction may mean upheaval and dislocation in the short run, in the long run it leads to economic growth.

7. **Government suffers from the principal-agent problem.** The principal-agent problem was introduced in Chapter 19. Elected officials and other government employees are agents of the people, and charged to act in the best interest of the people. But government employees may pursue their own interests (e.g. re-election, a larger budget for their bureau, etc.) at the expense of the best interest of the people.

### Appendix: Book Review – "The Myth of the Rational Voter"

In 2007, economist Bryan Caplan published "The Myth of the Rational Voter: Why Democracies Choose Bad Policies". In this book, Caplan asserts that voters are not just rationally ignorant, but are systematically biased in favor of mistaken views.

In theory, policies that are harmful to the best interest of society should not occur in a democracy. The majority of voters would not vote in favor of socially harmful policies, nor would they vote in favor of elected officials who enacted socially harmful policies. Yet socially harmful policies (e.g. trade restrictions) often do occur in democracies. Typically, these socially harmful policies have been blamed on rational voter ignorance and the influence of special-interest groups.

But Caplan asserts that democracy delivers socially harmful policies because it gives the voters what they want. Voters are worse than ignorant. They are irrational. They embrace a number of economic misconceptions and thus consistently favor economic policies that are harmful to the best interest of society.

Voter ignorance has been recognized for decades. It no longer shocks voter analysts that over half of Americans cannot name their congressional representative, or that voters believe that foreign aid consumes a much larger share of the federal budget than it actually does.

But economists have assumed that voter ignorance is not necessarily harmful. It is assumed that voters will not make systematic errors, but rather random errors. The random errors of the uninformed voters will cancel each other out and the few informed voters will determine the outcome.

---

**Example 14:** A vote is being held on an economic policy. Policy X is a good policy and Policy Y is a bad policy. Assume that 98% of voters are uninformed and 2% are well-informed. The uninformed voters are not biased toward one policy or the other and thus tend to vote randomly. Half of the uninformed voters vote for Policy X and half vote for Policy Y. Thus, each policy has received 49% of the total vote. Then the well-informed voters vote. They will all vote in favor of the good policy (Policy X). Thus, the good policy will win by a 51% to 49% majority. And the fact that 98% of the voters were uninformed has done no harm.

---

But what if the majority of voters are not just uninformed, but are systematically biased in favor of mistaken views? Then the majority of voters may vote in favor of socially harmful policies and in favor of elected officials who enact socially harmful policies. This is precisely what happens, according to Caplan.

According to Caplan, the vast majority of voters are noneconomists, and noneconomists are biased toward four common misconceptions:

1. **Antimarket bias.** This is a tendency to underestimate the economic benefits of the market mechanism. Noneconomists fail to comprehend that profit-seeking businesses in a competitive market will generally produce socially beneficial outcomes. Economists recognize that the goal of profit-maximization causes firms to be responsive to consumer demand and to produce efficiently. (See Chapter 19.)

   Noneconomists tend to see profits as simply a transfer to the businesses and fail to see the beneficial incentives that profits provide. (See Chapter 26.) Noneconomists also fail to comprehend how market-determined prices efficiently allocate resources and goods. They tend to see monopoly and conspiracy behind price movements.

2. **Antiforeign bias.** This is the tendency to underestimate the economic benefits of interaction with foreigners. Noneconomists usually can comprehend the mutual benefits of specialization and trade on a local or national level. But when the trade crosses national boundaries, noneconomists assume that trade is a zero-sum game. If Japan is benefiting by selling Toyotas to America, America must be losing.

3. **Make-work bias.** This is the tendency to underestimate the economic benefits of conserving labor. Noneconomists tend to have mixed feelings about technological advances that destroy jobs and to absolutely oppose downsizing and outsourcing. Economists recognize that labor is a valuable limited resource and that society benefits from conserving labor. The misconception that job destruction is harmful rests on the idea that employment, not production, is the source of prosperity. (For more on job destruction and economic growth, see Chapter 4.)

4. **Pessimistic bias.** This is the tendency to overestimate the severity of economic problems and underestimate the (recent) past, present, and future performance of the economy. Noneconomists tend to exaggerate the threat posed by current economic problems, e.g. recession, budget deficits, rising gasoline prices, etc. Noneconomists also tend to be pessimistic overall, failing to recognize the magnitude of past economic improvements and the strong likelihood that the positive trend will continue.

> **Example 15A:** When noneconomists are asked how much the standard of living has increased since 1900, the average answer is 50 percent. The actual increase is much greater, about 8-fold.

> **Example 15B:** When noneconomists are asked what will happen to the standard of living in the next generation, they tend to predict economic stagnation.

Given these four misconceptions, it is not surprising that democracies often choose bad policies. Caplan asserts that noneconomists are more rational when they make choices as consumers than when they make choices as voters. Caplan suggests that more economic decisions should be left to the market instead of the political process.

## Questions for Chapter 28

### Fill-in-the-blanks:

1. _____ _____ theory applies economic principles to public sector decision making.

2. _____ _____ occurs when government action results in a less efficient allocation of resources.

3. Vote trading in order to pass legislation is commonly called _____ .

4. _____ _____ legislation benefits a particular geographic region and is paid for by taxpayers (and/or consumers) from a larger geographic region.

5. _____ destruction is the short run upheaval caused by the development of new technology.

### Multiple Choice:

_____ 1. Low voter turnout occurs because:
   a. many potential voters underestimate the effect of their one vote
   b. many potential voters see the costs of voting as greater than the benefits
   c. many potential voters don't realize how much they benefit from voting
   d. All of the above

_____ 2. Voters may be rationally ignorant about political issues because they:
   a. don't realize how much they benefit from voting
   b. underestimate the effect of their one vote
   c. believe that the cost of gaining the information is greater than the benefit of having the information
   d. All of the above

_____ 3. The median voter model predicts that a candidate will do all of the following, except:
   a. label his or her opponents as extremists
   b. adjust his or her positions in response to polls
   c. speak in specific rather than general terms
   d. aim for a middle-of-the-road position

_____ 4. Policies favored by the median voter:
   a. will not necessarily be the most economically efficient policies
   b. will likely be favored by candidates
   c. Both of the above
   d. Neither of the above

5. An elected official will:
   a. tend to favor policies that yield benefits in the short run and impose costs in the long run
   b. tend to favor policies that impose costs in the short run and yield benefits in the long run
   c. Both of the above
   d. Neither of the above

6. Special-interest groups:
   a. are more likely to be well-informed about "their" issue than the general public
   b. may consist of a congressional district
   c. may support policies that are harmful to the general public
   d. All of the above

7. An elected official will:
   a. tend to favor policies that yield concentrated benefits and impose dispersed costs
   b. tend to oppose policies that yield dispersed benefits and impose concentrated costs
   c. improve his or her chances of re-election by being responsive to special-interest groups
   d. All of the above

8. Logrolling:
   a. occurs when legislators trade votes in order to pass legislation beneficial to their own districts
   b. often leads to pork barrel legislation
   c. Both of the above
   d. Neither of the above

9. Pork barrel legislation:
   a. benefits a particular geographic region
   b. is economically efficient to the region that it benefits
   c. is often economically inefficient overall
   d. All of the above

10. Government bureaus are likely to be very inefficient because:
    a. they are overly concerned with profit-maximization
    b. they face intense competition
    c. they seek to fulfill their mission and then dissolve
    d. None of the above

11. Government failure may occur due to:
    a. short run focus of elected officials
    b. special-interest group influence
    c. difficulty in measuring the marginal social benefit and the marginal social cost of government spending
    d. All of the above

_____ 12. The costs incurred when the government collects taxes and uses resources to provide goods and services include:
   a. the opportunity cost of the resources used
   b. the excess burden of the tax
   c. Both of the above
   d. Neither of the above

_____ 13. Income redistribution:
   a. reduces the reward for productive behavior
   b. encourages socially wasteful rent seeking
   c. leads to higher tax rates
   d. All of the above

_____ 14. Elected officials and government employees:
   a. are agents of the people
   b. always act in the best interest of the people, even at the expense of their own interest
   c. Both of the above
   d. Neither of the above

_____ 15. Government failure may occur because:
   a. majority voting is always economically efficient
   b. government will tend to promote "creative destruction"
   c. government suffers from the principal-agent problem
   d. All of the above

_____ 16. According to Bryan Caplan:
   a. voters have a good understanding of what economic policies will benefit society
   b. more economic decision making should be transferred from the market economy to the democratic political process
   c. Both of the above
   d. Neither of the above

_____ 17. According to Bryan Caplan, democracy delivers socially harmful policies because:
   a. elected officials refuse to be responsive to the desires of voters
   b. it gives the voters what they want
   c. Both of the above
   d. Neither of the above

_____ 18. When Vonda Voter hears that Widgetworks, Inc. is downsizing 5,000 employees as it adopts new technology, she says, "What a waste of labor! The economy just keeps getting worse." According to Bryan Caplan, Vonda has:
   a. make-work bias
   b. pessimistic bias
   c. Both of the above
   d. Neither of the above

## Problems:

1. Explain why most voters choose to remain rationally ignorant about political issues.

2. If a certain policy will yield small benefits in the short run and will impose larger costs in the long run, is an elected official likely to support that policy?

3. List and explain the three factors that increase the influence of special-interest groups.

4. What is creative destruction and why might the government stand in the way of creative destruction?

5.  According to "The Myth of the Rational Voter", what four common misconceptions are noneconomists biased toward?

## Answers for Chapter 28

**Fill-in-the-blanks:**

| 1. Public choice | 4. Pork barrel |
| 2. Government failure | 5. Creative |
| 3. logrolling | |

**Multiple Choice:**

| 1. b. | 7. d. | 13. d. |
| 2. c. | 8. c. | 14. a. |
| 3. c. | 9. d. | 15. c. |
| 4. c. | 10. d. | 16. d. |
| 5. a. | 11. d. | 17. b. |
| 6. d. | 12. c. | 18. c. |

## Problems:

1.  It is rational to remain ignorant if the cost of gaining information is greater than the benefit of having the information.  There is little direct benefit of being well-informed about political issues. The well-informed person's vote is no more likely to affect the outcome of an election than the poorly-informed person's vote.

2.  An elected official will want to support policies that will improve his or her chances of winning the next election.  Thus, an elected official will tend to favor policies that yield benefits in the short run and impose costs in the long run, even if the long run costs exceed the short run benefits.

3.  The influence of special-interest groups is increased by:
    (1) Low voter turnout.  Low voter turnout in political elections increases the influence of people who do vote.  Special-interest group members are likely to have a high voter turnout.
    (2) Rational ignorance.  The average voter will be poorly informed about most issues.  Special-interest group members will be well-informed about the issue of concern to the group.
    (3) Lobbying.  Special-interest group members are likely to contribute money and hire lobbyists to lobby elected officials to vote a specific way on "their" issue.

4. Creative destruction is the short run upheaval caused by the development of new technology. Standing in the way of creative destruction will yield concentrated benefits (to the producers using outdated technology) and impose dispersed costs (on all of society that would benefit from the new technology). Elected officials will tend to favor policies that yield concentrated benefits and impose dispersed costs. Thus, government may stand in the way of creative destruction.

5. Noneconomists are biased toward four common misconceptions:
   (1) Antimarket bias. This is the tendency to underestimate the economic benefits of the market mechanism.
   (2) Antiforeign bias. This is the tendency to underestimate the economic benefits of interaction with foreigners.
   (3) Make-work bias. This is the tendency to underestimate the economic benefits of conserving labor.
   (4) Pessimistic bias. This is the tendency to overestimate the severity of economic problems and underestimate the (recent) past, present, and future performance of the economy.

# Chapter 29  Government Regulation of Business

The basic economic problem is scarcity.  Human wants are unlimited.  Resources are limited.  The basic goal in dealing with the problem of scarcity is to produce as much consumer satisfaction as possible with the limited resources available.  In the U.S. economy, this goal is pursued primarily through private markets.

Private markets have many positive attributes.  We saw in Chapter 3 that in a private market the market price will automatically adjust to equilibrium, eliminating any surplus or shortage.  A competitive private market generally reaches equilibrium at the most efficient quantity of output (where marginal social benefit and marginal social cost are equal).

In a private market, the equilibrium quantity is generally the quantity that maximizes the net benefit of having the market available (i.e. maximizes the sum of consumer's surplus and producer's surplus).

In private markets, competition forces producers to respond to consumer demand.  And competition forces private market producers to use their limited resources efficiently.  Production will be allocated to the producers who can achieve the lowest cost of production.

Private markets also contribute to maximum individual freedom.  In private markets, consumers are free to pursue their self-interest (utility-maximization).  And producers are free to pursue their self-interest (profit-maximization).

But private markets are not flawless.  We saw in Chapter 27 that market failure occurs when the market does not produce the optimal quantity of output.  Market failure may occur for various reasons (lack of perfect competition, externalities, public goods, asymmetric information, etc.).

Government regulation of business may be aimed at correcting market failure and improving economic efficiency.  An example of this is government regulation of natural monopoly.

## Government Regulation of Natural Monopoly

Natural monopoly was introduced in Chapter 22.  Natural monopoly results from extreme economies of scale.

Economies of scale exist when, as the scale of production is increased, average costs of production decrease.  Economies of scale usually occur when fixed costs are very large (e.g. the cost of running natural gas lines throughout a city).  Once the fixed costs are incurred, average total cost will decrease over a large range of output.

If average total cost decreases over the entire market demand for an industry, the industry will be a natural monopoly.

**Natural monopoly** – an industry in which economies of scale are so important that only one firm can survive.

---

**Example 1:** If the annual market demand for widgets is 100,000 and the most efficient factory is one large enough to produce 100,000 widgets per year, the widget market is a natural monopoly market. Only one firm will be able to survive in the market.

If more than one firm initially enters the widget market, whichever firm gains the largest market share will have a competitive advantage over all the other (smaller) firms in the market.

The largest firm will be operating at a lower average cost of production, since it is producing at a lower point on the downward sloping average total cost curve. It will be able to charge a lower price and will thus gain additional market share. The increased market share will increase its cost advantage over the other firms.

Eventually, the larger firm will drive the smaller firms out of the market. Only one firm will survive in a natural monopoly market.

---

A natural monopoly may be regulated by government or may be unregulated. An unregulated natural monopoly would attempt to maximize profits. Profit-maximization would be achieved by following the profit-maximization rule for producing output (produce the quantity of output where marginal revenue equals marginal cost).

Unfortunately, the profit-maximizing quantity of output is <u>not</u> the same as the optimal (most efficient) quantity of output. The profit-maximizing quantity of output (the quantity of output where marginal revenue equals marginal cost) is less than the optimal quantity of output (the quantity of output where marginal social benefit equals marginal social cost).

The optimal quantity of output occurs where price equals marginal cost. As we saw in Chapter 21, the quantity where price equals marginal cost is also the quantity (assuming no externalities) where marginal social benefit equals marginal social cost.

If an unregulated natural monopoly produces the profit-maximizing quantity, this will cause a deadweight loss. The deadweight loss is equal to the area between the demand curve and the marginal cost curve for the quantity of underproduction.

The quantity of underproduction is the amount that the profit-maximizing quantity of output (where marginal revenue equals marginal cost) is less than the optimal quantity of output (where price equals marginal cost).

---

**Example 2A:** The graph on the next page illustrates the demand curve (D), the marginal revenue curve (MR), the average total cost curve (ATC), and the marginal cost curve (MC) for a natural monopoly. (Note that the average total cost decreases over the entire market demand.) If this natural monopoly is unregulated, it will attempt to maximize profits. The profit-maximizing quantity of output (labeled $Q_{UN}$) occurs where marginal revenue equals marginal cost.

---

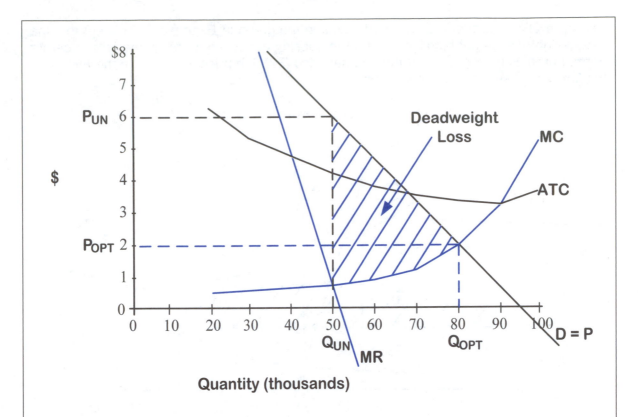

The profit-maximizing quantity of output (where MR equals MC) is 50,000 units. The profit-maximizing price (labeled $P_{UN}$) is indicated by the demand curve, and is $6. To sell 50,000 units of output, the firm can charge a price of $6. At the profit-maximizing quantity, the price ($6) is greater than the average total cost (slightly more than $4), and thus the firm would earn an economic profit.

The optimal quantity of output (labeled $Q_{OPT}$) occurs where price equals marginal cost (and thus where marginal social benefit equals marginal social cost). The optimal quantity of output is 80,000 units.

The deadweight loss is highlighted on the graph and is equal to the area between the demand curve and the marginal cost curve for the quantity of underproduction. The quantity of underproduction is the amount that the profit-maximizing quantity of output (50,000 units) is less than the optimal quantity of output (80,000 units).

The optimal quantity of output (80,000 units) occurs where price equals marginal cost. At this quantity of output, the price that the firm can charge (indicated by the demand curve) will be $2.

This optimal price (labeled $P_{OPT}$) would result in the firm suffering an economic loss. The optimal price ($2) is less than the average total cost (over $3). To keep the firm operating at this price would require a government subsidy to the firm to eliminate the economic loss.

**Example 2B:** The graph below is identical to the graph in Example 2A, except that the deadweight loss is <u>not</u> highlighted and the subsidy necessary to allow the firm to earn a normal profit is highlighted. At the optimal price ($2), the price is less than the ATC, and the firm would suffer an economic loss.

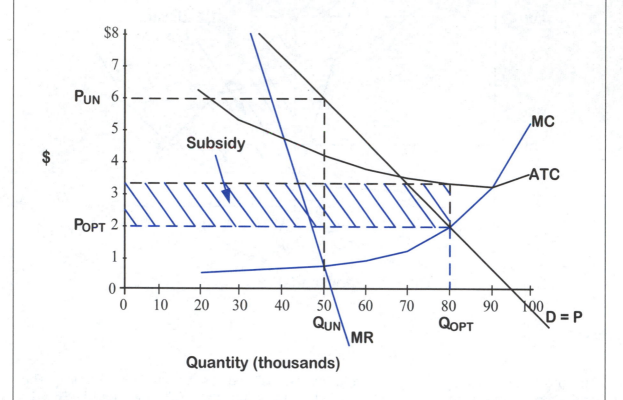

To keep the firm operating at the optimal price would require a government subsidy to allow the firm to earn at least zero economic profit (a normal profit). The subsidy necessary to allow the firm to earn at least a normal profit would equal the area between the ATC and the optimal price ($2) for the optimal quantity (80,000 units). The subsidy is highlighted on the graph above.

It is politically problematic to subsidize a natural monopoly. Voters may not approve of tax dollars being transferred to "a big rich corporation". Thus, natural monopolies are often regulated to earn zero economic profit (a normal profit or a normal rate of return).

Regulating a natural monopoly to earn zero economic profit leads to problems:

1. **The natural monopoly lacks incentives to control costs.** If costs of production are reduced, the natural monopoly may temporarily earn economic profit. But the price will soon be adjusted downward by the regulators in order to restore the natural monopoly to a position of zero economic profit.

   If costs of production increase, the natural monopoly may temporarily suffer economic loss. But the price will soon be adjusted upward by the regulators in order to restore the natural monopoly to a position of zero economic profit.

The natural monopoly does not significantly benefit from reducing its costs of production. And the natural monopoly does not significantly suffer if its costs of production increase. Thus, the natural monopoly lacks incentives to control costs.

2. **The regulators may not be able to obtain accurate information.** The regulators will have to rely primarily on cost information provided by the regulated natural monopoly. The natural monopoly will have a self-interest in overstating production costs (in order to receive price increases). The regulators may not be highly motivated to search for accurate information.

## Theories of Regulation

Government regulation of business often does not appear to be aimed at correcting market failure. Government regulations extend into many areas unrelated to controlling monopoly behavior, or adjusting for externalities, or other obvious sources of market failure. Government regulations also tend to be very detailed and specific instead of general. This raises two questions: Why does the government regulate business activity to the extent that it does? Why does the government regulate business activity in the way that it does?

Three theories of regulation have been developed:

1. **Public interest theory.** The public interest theory of regulation holds that regulation serves the public interest (promotes the general welfare). This theory assumes that elected officials (who ultimately control regulations) are motivated to always act in ways that serve the public interest. Our study of Chapter 28 would make us question this assumption.

   We saw in Chapter 28 that elected officials will often be responsive to special-interest groups. Special-interest groups may influence legislators to support government regulations that are harmful to the public interest (e.g. trade restrictions). A great deal of government regulation does not seem to be serving the public interest.

2. **Capture theory.** The capture theory of regulation holds that the regulatory agency will be captured (controlled) by the industry being regulated. The regulators may have previously worked in the industry that they are now regulating. They may return to work in that industry after they leave the regulatory agency.

   The firms in the regulated industry have a special interest in the policies of the regulatory agency, and are likely to remain well-informed about the policies of the agency and to lobby the agency for policies beneficial to the industry. The general public is unlikely to lobby the agency, or to be well-informed about the agency's policies.

   If the regulated industry captures the regulatory agency, the agency is likely to impose regulations that serve the best interests of the regulated industry. Regulations have often been used to protect the regulated firms from competition.

> **Example 3:** Between 1938 and 1978, the federal government regulated prices and routes in the interstate airline industry. The regulatory agency divided markets and limited price competition, much as a cartel would. The regulatory agency also controlled the entry of new competitors into the interstate airline industry. During the forty year period of government regulation, <u>no</u> new carriers were permitted to enter the interstate airline market.

3. **Public choice theory.** The public choice theory of regulation holds that regulation serves the best interests of the government regulators. Regulators would naturally tend to create regulations that would serve their own self-interest. Regulators would favor a regulatory approach that led to more regulatory power and a growing budget for the regulatory agency.

Regulatory agencies often choose a "micromanagement" approach to regulation. Micromanagement (managing the details as well as the big picture) would increase regulatory power, would require a larger regulatory staff, and would require a larger regulatory budget compared to a "macromanagement" (focusing on the big picture) approach. Regulatory micromanagement results in businesses being subject to an enormous amount of highly detailed government regulation.

> **Example 4:** The Federal Register records all of the regulations that the federal government imposes on businesses. The 2007 Federal Register contains 74,408 pages.

## Costs of Regulations

Regulations may benefit the general public (e.g. cleaner air and water,) or the regulated industry (e.g. protection from competition) or the regulatory agency (e.g. a bigger agency budget). But regulations also impose costs on the economy:

1. **Costs of the regulatory agency.** Environmental regulations require an Environmental Protection Agency to enforce them. The EPA has 17,000 employees. The salaries of those employees, as well as other costs to operate the agency, are paid by the taxpayers. The table below shows the annual budgets for some of the larger federal regulatory agencies for fiscal year 2007.

| Regulatory Agency | Annual Budget |
|---|---|
| Environmental Protection Agency | $8,259 million |
| Small Business Administration | 1,175 million |
| Securities and Exchange Commission | 877 million |
| Employment Standards Administration | 720 million |
| Occupational Safety and Health Administration | 484 million |
| Federal Communications Commission | 440 million |
| Equal Employment Opportunity Commission | 329 million |
| Mine Safety and Health Administration | 288 million |
| Federal Energy Regulatory Commission | 227 million |
| Federal Trade Commission | 220 million |
| Antitrust Division of the Department of Justice | 148 million |
| Consumer Product Safety Commission | 63 million |

The costs of regulatory agencies have been increasing. According to research by economist W. Mark Crain, federal regulatory agency budgets increased by 88 percent (in constant dollars) between 1990 and 2004. Staffing levels for federal regulatory agencies increased by 56 percent over this time period.

2. **Costs to the regulated firms of complying with the regulations.** A company may incur costs to install pollution abatement equipment required by the EPA as well as costs to complete paperwork required by the EPA. The company may also incur costs to comply with regulations created by the Employment Standards Administration, the Occupational Safety and Health Administration, the National Labor Relations Board, the Equal Employment Opportunity Commission, the Federal Trade Commission, etc.

The cost of complying with the various regulations adds to the company's cost of production, and is ultimately paid by the consumers of the company's products.

---

**Example 5:** Research by economist W. Mark Crain estimated the costs of complying with federal regulations at $1.1 trillion in 2004. These costs fell disproportionately on small businesses (businesses with fewer than 20 employees).

---

3. **Inefficiency costs if the regulations reduce competition.** Regulation often reduces competition in the regulated industry. Competition enhances economic efficiency (see Chapter 21). A lack of competition leads to higher prices for consumers.

---

**Example 6:** After the deregulation of the airline industry in 1978, the increased competition in the airline industry led to lower prices. Research estimated a savings to consumers of $12 billion per year because the deregulation increased competition.

---

4. **Costs of unintended consequences of regulations.** Regulations intended to accomplish a desirable goal may have unintended consequences that are undesirable. The regulation of the airline industry from 1938 to 1978 was not intended to increase fatalities from auto accidents, but it did.

---

**Example 7:** The regulation of the airline industry led to higher prices for air travel. This increased auto travel. Air travel is much safer than auto travel. Deregulation of the airline industry lowered the cost of air travel, leading to more air travel and less auto travel. Research by Richard McKenzie indicated that airline deregulation caused a reduction in auto fatalities of nearly 1,700 per year. Thus, the regulation of the airline industry (from 1938 to 1978) resulted in many thousands of additional fatalities from auto accidents.

---

Another example of unintended consequences of government regulations involves the Americans with Disabilities Act (ADA), enacted in 1990.

---

**Example 8:** One of the intended purposes of the Americans with Disabilities Act is to guarantee equal opportunities in employment for individuals with disabilities. Toward this end, the ADA requires employers to make reasonable accommodation to the known physical and mental limitations of otherwise qualified individuals with disabilities. However, in his book "Disabling America", Greg Perry asserts that by requiring

---

employers to provide "reasonable accommodation" for disabled workers, the ADA has greatly increased the cost of employing disabled workers. Thus, regulation intended to provide greater employment opportunities for disabled workers has the unintended consequence of discouraging the employment of disabled workers.

## Deregulation

Deregulation will usually result in lower prices due to increased competition. The savings to consumers following airline deregulation was mentioned previously in this chapter. Lower prices also followed deregulation in telecommunications, banking, natural gas, trucking, and railroads.

**Example 9A:** The Staggers Rail Act of 1980 deregulated railroad freight operations. According to the Association of American Railroads, real operating costs per ton-mile decreased by 69 percent between 1980 and 2002, and real rail rates decreased by 65 percent over this time period.

**Example 9B:** The Motor Carrier Act of 1980 partially deregulated the trucking industry. The Brookings Institution estimated the savings resulting from the increased competition in the trucking industry at $20 billion per year.

Deregulation will also eliminate the cost to taxpayers of paying for the regulatory agency and the cost to consumers of paying for the compliance costs of the regulations.

However, deregulation can be politically difficult to accomplish. Regulation will benefit someone (if only the regulatory agency). Those who benefit from the regulation will act as a special-interest group to fight against deregulation.

## Appendix: Antitrust Law

We saw in Chapter 21 that perfect competition is the ideal market structure. In Chapters 22 and 23, we saw that monopoly, monopolistic competition, and oligopoly are inefficient. It is not possible for all markets to be perfectly competitive. Economies of scale may require firms to be relatively large in order to operate at the most efficient size.

**Example 10:** The annual market demand for widgets is 100,000 units and the most efficient factory is one large enough to produce 25,000 widgets per year. To achieve the most efficient size, each firm in the widget market will need to capture 25% of the market. A small number of large firms will be more cost efficient than would a large number of small firms.

In the extreme example of economies of scale, natural monopoly, only one firm can survive. As we saw earlier in this chapter, natural monopolies are usually subject to direct government regulation. The regulation is intended to allow the natural monopoly to take advantage of economies of scale, while moving the quantity of production nearer to the optimal quantity.

The degree of economic inefficiency in monopolistic competition and oligopoly tends to be much smaller than in monopoly. But firms in these market structures have an incentive to try to establish cartel agreements with their competitors, or otherwise attempt to monopolize the market. They may agree with their competitors to fix prices, divide up markets, merge their competing companies, or otherwise reduce the level of competition in the market.

Attempts to monopolize or reduce the competition in a market can increase the economic inefficiency in the market. Antitrust law is intended to prohibit attempts to monopolize markets or to engage in anti-competitive behavior.

**Antitrust law** – legislation intended to prohibit attempts to monopolize markets or to engage in anti-competitive behavior.

The first federal antitrust legislation was the Sherman Act, enacted in 1890. Section 1 of the Sherman Act prohibits contracts, combinations, and conspiracies in restraint of trade (in other words, prohibits agreements to avoid competition). Section 2 of the Sherman Act prohibits persons from monopolizing, or attempting to monopolize, a market.

The Supreme Court has interpreted the Sherman Act as only prohibiting behavior that underlying restrains trade. Certain actions are held to always be unreasonable restraints of trade and thus are illegal per se. For instance, a price-fixing agreement between competing firms is a per se violation of Section 1 of the Sherman Act.

> **Example 11:** Darla's Delectable Donuts and Ben's Bakery agree to increase their prices by 15 percent. This is a price-fixing agreement between competing firms and is a per se violation of the Sherman Act.

Other actions are held not to be per se violations of the Sherman Act, and are judged under the "rule of reason". For instance, a vertical restraint on distribution is an agreement between a producer and a distributor that the distributor will not market the producer's products outside the distributor's assigned region.

> **Example 12:** Janelle's Juice Company wants to establish a strong network of distributors to distribute its juice products. Janelle's requires its distributors to agree that they will not market Janelle's products outside their assigned regions. This is a vertical restraint on distribution and will be a violation of the Sherman Act only if it unreasonably restrains trade.

The Sherman Act was seen by many as being too general to effectively prevent anticompetitive behavior. The Clayton Act, enacted in 1914, prohibits certain specific actions if the effect of the actions is to "substantially lessen competition or tend to create a monopoly".

Section 3 of the Clayton Act restricts tying agreements and exclusive dealing agreements. In a tying agreement, a seller refuses to sell one product to a buyer unless the buyer agrees to buy a second product. In an exclusive dealing agreement, a producer refuses to sell a product to a retailer unless the retailer agrees to deal only in the producer's product.

Section 7 of the Clayton Act restricts mergers. A merger is the combining of two separate companies into one. Mergers are usually accomplished by one company purchasing the common stock or the assets of another company.

Whether a proposed merger will be judged to substantially lessen competition or tend to create a monopoly depends largely on the type of merger proposed:

1. **Horizontal merger** – a merger of firms competing in the same product market.

2. **Vertical merger** – a merger of firms in the same industry, but not at the same stage in the production process.

3. **Conglomerate merger** – a merger of firms that are not in the same industry.

**Example 13:** A merger of General Motors and Ford Motor Company would be a horizontal merger. A merger of General Motors and Goodyear Tire and Rubber Company would by a vertical merger. A merger of General Motors and Tonka Toys would be a conglomerate merger.

The type of merger that is most likely to be opposed by the federal government is a horizontal merger. Factors that are considered in determining whether a proposed horizontal merger will be opposed include:

1. Is the market already highly concentrated?
2. Will the proposed merger significantly increase the concentration in the market?
3. Is the proposed merger necessary to prevent one of the merging firms from failing?
4. Will the proposed merger allow the new company to compete more effectively with larger firms in the market?
5. Will the proposed merger allow the new company to operate more efficiently?

The Federal Trade Commission Act, enacted in 1914, prohibits unfair methods of competition and established the Federal Trade Commission to enforce antitrust laws.

Today, the antitrust laws are enforced by the Federal Trade Commission and by the Antitrust Division of the Department of Justice. Also, private parties who suffer damages caused by antitrust violations may sue the violator and recover three times the damages proved.

Antitrust law has proven to be controversial. The interpretation and enforcement of antitrust law varies from one presidential administration to the next. The antitrust law can sometimes serve to protect less efficient producers from competition with more efficient producers.

Nonetheless, antitrust law is necessary to restrict anti-competitive behavior (price-fixing, cartel agreements, etc.) which would be likely to occur in oligopolistic markets. As Adam Smith wrote in "An Inquiry into the Nature and Causes of the Wealth of Nations", "People of the same trade seldom meet together…but the conversation ends in a conspiracy against the public, or in some diversion to raise prices."

## Questions for Chapter 29

### Fill-in-the-blanks:

1. _____ _____ is an industry in which
   economies of scale are so important that only one firm can survive.

2. _____ _____ is legislation intended to prohibit
   attempts to monopolize markets or to engage in anti-competitive behavior.

3. A _____ merger is a merger of firms competing in the same
   product market.

4. A _____ merger is a merger of firms in the same industry, but
   not at the same stage in the production process.

5. A _____ merger is a merger of firms that are not in the same
   industry.


### Multiple Choice:

_____ 1. For a natural monopoly market:
   a. average total cost decreases over the entire market demand for the
      industry
   b. if more than one firm initially enters the market, whichever firm gains the
      largest market share will have a competitive advantage over all the other
      firms in the market
   c. the largest firm will be operating at a lower average cost of production,
      since it is producing at a lower point on the downward sloping average
      total cost curve
   d. All of the above

_____ 2. If a natural monopoly is unregulated, it will produce the quantity of output
   where:
   a. marginal revenue equals marginal cost
   b. price equals marginal cost
   c. price equals ATC
   d. ATC is minimized

_____ 3. If a natural monopoly is regulated to produce the optimal quantity of output, it
   will produce where:
   a. marginal revenue equals marginal cost
   b. price equals marginal cost
   c. price equals ATC
   d. ATC is minimized

_____ 4. If a natural monopoly is regulated to earn zero economic profit, it:
   a.  may lack incentives to control costs
   b.  will produce the optimal quantity
   c.  will require a government subsidy to stay in business
   d.  Both b. and c. above

Answer questions 5. through 8. by referring to the graph below:

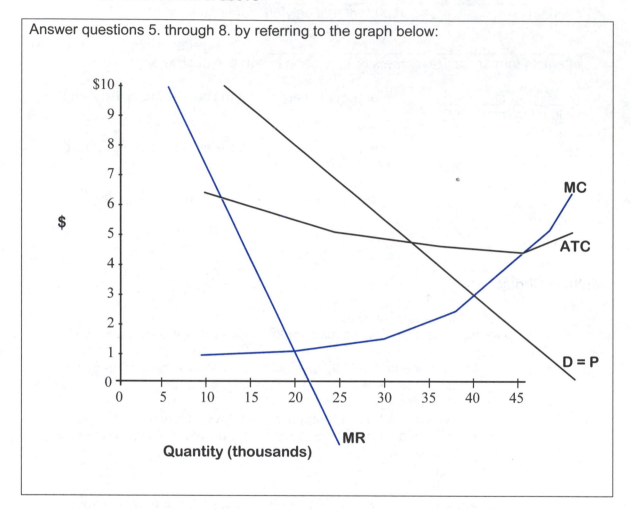

_____ 5. If this natural monopoly is not regulated, how many units of output will it produce?
   a.  15 thousand
   b.  20 thousand
   c.  33 thousand
   d.  40 thousand

_____ 6. If this natural monopoly is not regulated, what price will it charge?
   a.  $3
   b.  $5
   c.  $8
   d.  $10

_____ 7. If this natural monopoly is regulated to produce the optimal quantity, what quantity will it produce?
   a. 15 thousand
   b. 20 thousand
   c. 33 thousand
   d. 40 thousand

_____ 8. If this natural monopoly is regulated to produce the optimal quantity, what price will it charge?
   a. $3
   b. $5
   c. $8
   d. $10

_____ 9. The public choice theory of regulation holds that regulation serves the best interests of:
   a. the general public
   b. the regulated industry
   c. the government regulators

_____ 10. The capture theory of government regulation assumes that:
   a. the general public will lobby the regulatory agency for policies beneficial to the general public
   b. the regulated industry is unlikely to lobby the regulatory agency for policies beneficial to the regulated industry
   c. Both of the above
   d. Neither of the above

_____ 11. The costs of government regulations include:
   a. the costs to the regulated firms of complying with the regulations
   b. the inefficiency costs if regulations reduce competition
   c. the costs of the regulatory agencies
   d. All of the above

_____ 12. Between 1990 and 2004:
   a. federal regulatory budgets decreased (in constant dollars)
   b. staffing levels for federal regulatory agencies decreased due to deregulation
   c. Both of the above
   d. Neither of the above

_____ 13. In 2007, the budget for the Equal Employment Opportunity Commission was:
   a. $220 million
   b. $288 million
   c. $329 million
   d. $440 million

_____ 14. The cost of complying with government regulations:
  a.  adds to the company's cost of production
  b.  ultimately is paid by the consumers of the product
  c.  was estimated at $1.1 trillion for 2004
  d.  All of the above

_____ 15. The federal government's regulation of the airline industry from 1938 to 1978:
  a.  cost consumers billions of dollars in higher ticket prices
  b.  decreased the amount of air travel and increased auto travel
  c.  resulted in thousands of additional fatalities from auto accidents
  d.  All of the above

_____ 16. Deregulation:
  a.  will usually result in lower prices due to increased competition
  b.  will be fought by special-interest groups that benefit from the regulation
  c.  Both of the above
  d.  Neither of the above

_____ 17. The Sherman Act:
  a.  prohibits contracts, combinations, and conspiracies in restraint of trade
  b.  prohibits persons from monopolizing, or attempting to monopolize, a market
  c.  Both of the above
  d.  Neither of the above

_____ 18. An agreement between competing firms to fix the price of their products:
  a.  would be illegal as a per se violation of the Sherman Act
  b.  would be judged under the "rule of reason"
  c.  would be illegal only if the agreed-upon price were unreasonably high
  d.  Both b. and c. above

_____ 19. The antitrust laws are enforced by:
  a.  the Federal Trade Commission
  b.  the Antitrust Division of the Department of Justice
  c.  private lawsuits brought by injured parties against antitrust violators
  d.  All of the above

## Problems:

1.  Explain the two problems regulating a natural monopoly to earn zero economic profit will lead to.

2.  Explain the capture theory of government regulation.

3.  Explain the public choice theory of government regulation.

4.  List the four types of costs imposed on the economy by government regulations.

5.  How are the antitrust laws enforced?

## Answers for Chapter 29

**Fill-in-the-blanks:**
1. Natural monopoly
2. Antitrust law
3. horizontal
4. vertical
5. conglomerate

**Multiple Choice:**

| | | |
|---|---|---|
| 1. d. | 8. a. | 15. d. |
| 2. a. | 9. c. | 16. c. |
| 3. b. | 10. d. | 17. c. |
| 4. a. | 11. d. | 18. a. |
| 5. b. | 12. d. | 19. d. |
| 6. c. | 13. c. | |
| 7. d. | 14. d. | |

## Problems:

1. Regulating a natural monopoly to earn zero economic profit will lead to problems:
   (1) The natural monopoly lacks incentives to control costs. If costs of production are reduced (or increase), the natural monopoly may temporarily earn economic profit (or loss). But the price will soon be adjusted down (or up) by the regulators to restore zero economic profit.
   (2) The regulators may <u>not</u> be able to obtain accurate information. The regulators will have to rely primarily on cost information provided by the regulated natural monopoly. The natural monopoly will have a self-interest in overstating production costs (in order to obtain price increases).

2. The capture theory of government regulation holds that the regulatory agency will be captured by the industry being regulated. If the regulated industry captures the regulatory agency, regulations can be used to exclude competition from the industry.

3. The public choice theory of government regulation holds that regulation serves the best interests of the government regulators. Regulators would favor a regulatory approach that led to more regulatory power and a growing budget for the regulatory agency.

4. Government regulations impose costs on the economy:
   (1) Costs of the regulatory agency
   (2) Costs to the regulated firm of complying with the regulations
   (3) Inefficiency costs if the regulations reduce competition
   (4) Costs of unintended consequences of regulations

5. Antitrust laws are enforced by the Federal Trade Commission and by the Antitrust Division of the Department of Justice. Also, private parties who suffer damages caused by antitrust violations may sue the violator and recover three times the damages proved.

# Chapter 30  Agriculture

The basic economic problem is scarcity.  Human wants are unlimited.  Resources are limited.  The basic goal in dealing with the problem of scarcity is to produce as much consumer satisfaction as possible with the limited resources available.

For most of recorded history, the majority of resources have been devoted to food production.  In less developed countries, food production still requires a large percentage of the available resources.

In developed countries, agricultural productivity has increased greatly.  Thus, food production has required a steadily shrinking percentage of the available resources in developed countries.

---

**Example 1:**  The table below indicates per capita GDP for five developed countries and for five less developed countries.  The table also details, for each country, the percentage of the labor force devoted to agriculture.  The information is for 2007, and is from the "CIA World Factbook".

| Nation | per capita GDP | % of Labor Force in Agriculture |
|---|---|---|
| Canada | 38,400 | 2% |
| Australia | 36,300 | 4% |
| Sweden | 36,500 | 2% |
| France | 33,200 | 4% |
| Spain | 30,100 | 5% |
| India | 2,700 | 60% |
| Vietnam | 2,600 | 56% |
| Nigeria | 2,000 | 70% |
| Bangladesh | 1,300 | 63% |
| Ethiopia | 800 | 80% |

---

The decrease in the percentage of resources devoted to food production has freed resources for other types of production.  The increasing production of clothing, housing, transportation, medical care, education, recreation, etc. has been made possible by increases in agricultural productivity.

## Good News about U.S. Agriculture

Agricultural markets are among the most competitive of all U.S. markets.  Most agricultural markets are very large.  Most agricultural markets have a large number of relatively small producers.

---

**Example 2:**  In 2000, there were about 2 million farms in the U.S. containing about 943 million acres of agricultural land.  Each year, U.S. farmers plant about 80 million acres of corn, about 13 million acres of cotton, about 75 million acres of soybeans, and about 60 million acres of wheat.  The average farm is between 400 and 500 acres.

---

Agricultural producers are producing essentially identical products to those of their competitors. Most producers have no market power (ability to affect market price) and must compete in terms of productivity and cost efficiency. Productivity and cost efficiency have been improving in agriculture.

---

**Example 3:** The table below details yields per acre for seven important agricultural commodities for 1954 and 2004, and indicates the percentage increase in the yield per acre over this fifty year period. Information is from the USDA National Agricultural Statistics Service.

| Commodity | 1954 Yield per acre | 2004 Yield per acre | Percentage increase |
|-----------|---------------------|---------------------|---------------------|
| Corn | 39.4 bushels | 160.4 bushels | 307% |
| Cotton | 341 pounds | 855 pounds | 151% |
| Oats | 34.8 bushels | 64.7 bushels | 86% |
| Peanuts | 727 pounds | 3,076 pounds | 323% |
| Rice | 2,517 pounds | 6,988 pounds | 178% |
| Soybeans | 20 bushels | 42.2 bushels | 111% |
| Wheat | 18.1 bushels | 43.2 bushels | 139% |

---

Given these desirable characteristics, one might expect little or no government intervention in agricultural markets. But the opposite is true. The federal government has played a large role in agricultural markets for many decades. The nature of the federal government's farm policies is one of the main topics in this chapter.

The federal government's farm policies have been aimed at helping farmers deal with their long run problem (falling farm prices and total revenue) and with their short run problem (unstable farm prices and total revenue). We will look at the farmers' long run problem first.

## The Long Run Problem for Farmers

The long run problem for farmers is that farm prices and total revenue have generally been falling.

---

**Example 4:** The table below details real prices for seven important agricultural commodities in 1954 and in 2004. For each commodity, the real price fell. The prices are stated at the 2004 price level. Information is from the USDA National Agricultural Statistics Service.

| Commodity | 1954 Price | 2004 Price |
|-----------|------------|------------|
| Corn | $10.04/bu. | $2.06/bu. |
| Cotton | $2.36/lb. | $.72/lb. |
| Oats | $5.01/bu. | $1.48/bu. |
| Peanuts | $.86/lb. | $.19/lb. |
| Rice | $32.09/cwt. | $7.33/cwt. |
| Soybeans | $17.27/bu. | $5.74/bu. |
| Wheat | $14.89/bu. | $3.40/bu. |

---

Farm prices and total revenue have generally been falling due to:

1.  **Increasing productivity in agriculture.** Productivity in agriculture has been increasing faster than productivity in the overall economy. Labor productivity in agricultural has increased by nearly 500 percent since 1929. Even farm animals have become more productive.

---

**Example 5:** In the last 50 years, annual milk output by the typical dairy cow has more than tripled.

---

As productivity in a particular agricultural market increases, the supply curve in the market shifts to the right. If the supply curve shifts to the right faster than the demand curve for the good shifts to the right, the equilibrium price falls. This has generally been the case for farm products.

2.  **Demand for farm products is income inelastic.** Income elasticity of demand measures the responsiveness of consumers to changes in income. If real income doubles, will the demand for farm products double? No. As real income has increased, demand for farm products has increased much more slowly. As a result, agricultural productivity has generally increased faster than the demand for farm products and the supply of farm products has generally increased faster than the demand.

3.  **Demand for farm products is price inelastic.** Price elasticity of demand measures consumer responsiveness to changes in price. If the price for a farm product decreases by 50%, will the quantity demanded of the farm product increase by 50%? No. Thus, as the supply of farm products has increased faster than the demand, price has decreased more than quantity has increased.

The long run problem for farmers is that farm prices and total revenue have generally been falling, as illustrated in Example 6 below. As farm productivity increases faster than demand, fewer farmers are required to meet demand. Less efficient farmers are unable to survive in the market as the price decreases. The number of farmers decreases over time. This is bad news for farmers, but good news for the economy.

The basic economic problem is scarcity. Society wants to produce all goods (including food) with as few resources as possible. Resources that are no longer needed to produce food are made available to produce other goods.

---

**Example 6:** Assume that the graph on the next page illustrates the market for a farm product. Initially, demand for the product is $D_1$, supply of the product is $S_1$, the equilibrium price is $5, and the equilibrium quantity is 3,000 units. The total revenue (price x quantity) of farmers in the market is $15,000. Over time, agricultural productivity increases and the supply of the product increases to $S_2$, the demand for the product increases (though less than the supply) to $D_2$. The equilibrium price falls to $3 and the equilibrium quantity is 4,000 units. The total revenue of farmers in the market is now only $12,000. Both price and total revenue have fallen.

---

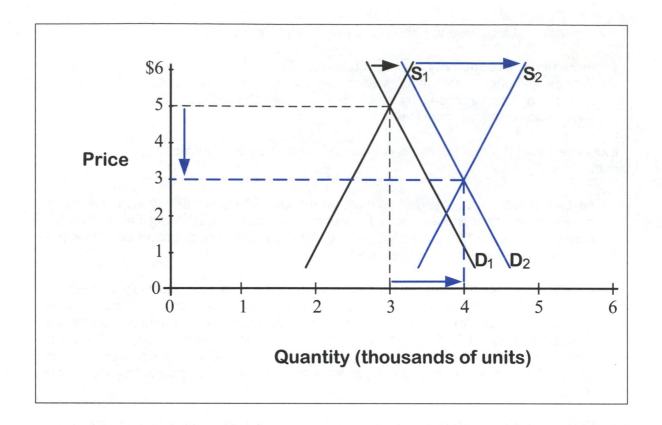

## The Short Run Problem for Farmers

In the short run, farm prices and total revenue tend to be unstable. This creates a problem for even the more efficient farmers, who may suffer losses if they guess wrong about future farm prices. Remember that the demand for farm products is price inelastic. Unpredictable supply combined with inelastic demand leads to unstable prices and total revenue.

The supply of farm products is unpredictable. Good weather may cause bumper crops. Bad weather may cause decreased production.

**Example 7:** In the long run, agricultural productivity has been increasing. In the short run, productivity can fluctuate, often tied to weather conditions. From 1987 to 1988, corn yields decreased by 29% per acre, and corn prices increased by 31%. From 2003 to 2004, corn yields increased by 13% per acre, and corn prices decreased by 15%.

When the supply changes, equilibrium price and quantity will change. Since the demand for farm products is price inelastic, price will change more than quantity.

**Example 8:** Assume that the graph on the next page illustrates the market for a farm product. Initially, supply of the product is $S_1$, demand for the product is D, the equilibrium price is $5, and the equilibrium quantity is 3,000 units. The total revenue of farmers in the market is $15,000. The next year, exceptionally good weather occurs, the supply of the product increases to $S_2$ and the demand remains at D. The equilibrium price falls to $3 and the equilibrium quantity is 3.500 units. The total revenue of farmers in the market is now only $10,500.

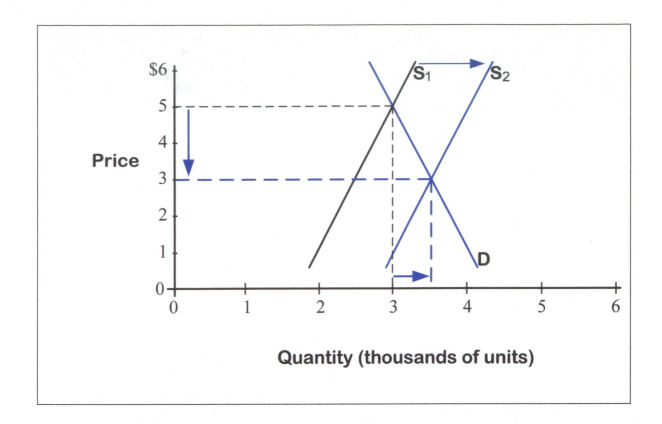

## Traditional Farm Policies

For the last 75 years or so, the federal government has intervened in agricultural markets, generally trying to maintain prices above free market equilibrium. For most of this time period, the federal government has relied mainly on three traditional farm policies:

1. **Price supports.** A price support program establishes a price floor above the equilibrium price for the farm product. At the floor price, quantity supplied exceeds quantity demanded, resulting in a surplus.

   To maintain the floor price, the government must buy the surplus. The government cannot re-sell the surplus. To do so would depress the price, defeating the purpose of the price floor.

   The government may be able to give away a limited amount of the surplus. But the surplus must be given only to parties who would not otherwise buy the product and who will not turn around and re-sell the product. Otherwise, the giveaway will depress the price. Generally, the government stores the surplus.

   This policy is costly to taxpayers (who pay to buy and store the surplus) and to consumers (who pay the higher floor price for the product).

**Example 9A:** Assume that the graph below illustrates the market for a farm product. The equilibrium price is $4, and the equilibrium quantity is 1,600 units. The government establishes a support price (floor) at $6. At this price, the quantity supplied is 2,000 units and the quantity demanded is 1,200 units. This results in a surplus of 800 units. The cost for the government to purchase the surplus is $4,800 ($6 x 800 units).

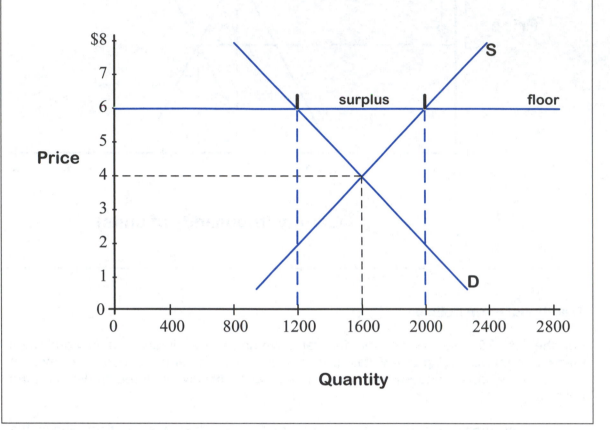

2. **Supply restricting policies.** Various programs have either required farmers to reduce supply, or paid farmers to reduce supply. When the supply is reduced, the equilibrium price is increased.

    This policy is costly to consumers (who pay a higher price for the product) and to taxpayers (if farmers are paid to reduce supply).

**Example 9B:** Assume that the graph on the next page illustrates the market for a farm product. The initial equilibrium is at a price of $4 and a quantity of 1,600 units. The government uses supply restricting policies to reduce supply from $S_1$ to $S_2$. The new equilibrium price is $6 and the new equilibrium quantity is 1,200 units.

The effect on consumers is the same as for the price floor in Example 9A (1,200 units are purchased at $6). The cost to taxpayers will be less than for the price floor, because it will cost less to pay farmers to <u>not</u> produce than to pay them to produce a surplus crop.

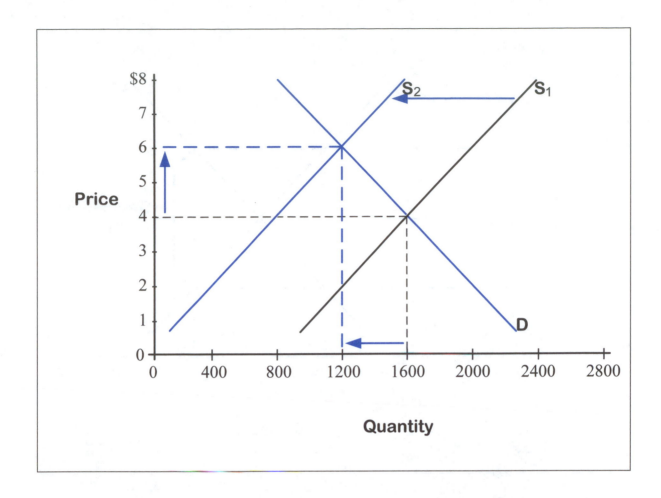

3. **Target prices.** With target prices, the government establishes a target price for the farm product. If the market price is less than the target price, the government pays a deficiency payment to the farmers to make up the difference between the target price and the market price. This policy is costly to taxpayers (who pay the deficiency payment).

**Example 9C:** Assume that the graph on the next page illustrates the market for a farm product. The initial equilibrium price is $4, and the equilibrium quantity is 1,600 units. The government establishes a target price of $6. At this price, quantity supplied increases to 2,000 units.

Since there is no price floor in place, the market price is free to adjust downward to achieve equilibrium. The market price will fall to $2 in order to achieve a quantity demanded equal to the quantity supplied (2,000 units).

There is no surplus, but the government must make a deficiency payment to farmers of $4 per unit. The cost of the deficiency payment is $8,000 ($4 x 2,000 units).

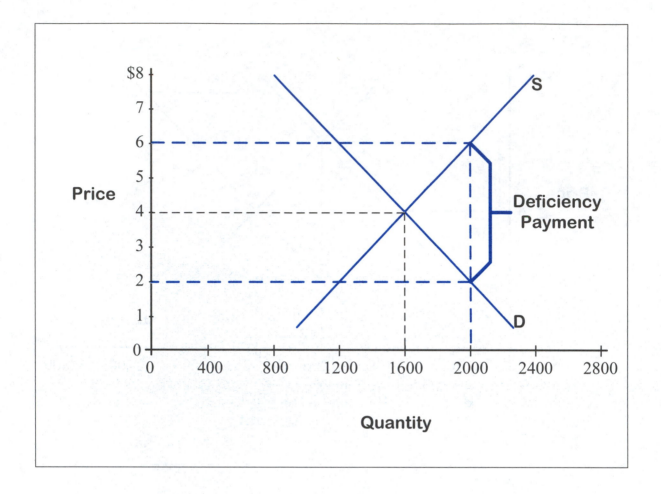

## The FAIR Act of 1996

In 1996, the Federal Agricultural Improvements and Reform (FAIR) Act was enacted. The Act was an attempt to reduce the federal government's role in subsidizing farmers, and to eventually eliminate most government subsidies to farmers.

The Act eliminated supply restrictions and target prices. These were replaced by production flexibility contract payments (a type of direct subsidy). Farmers receiving production flexibility contract payments were allowed to grow any crop (except for certain fruits and vegetables).

The subsidies under the FAIR Act were scheduled to decrease in size each year, eventually ending completely after 2002. Instead extra subsidy payments were made in 1998, 1999, 2000, and 2001.

Under the FAIR Act, farmers could still receive price supports. The price supports were received through nonrecourse commodity loans from the Commodity Credit Corporation (CCC). The CCC would make loans to farmers, with the farmers pledging their crops as collateral. If the market value of the crop fell below the loan value set by the CCC, the farmer would default on the loan. The effect was that the CCC "bought" the crop for its loan value. Thus, the loan value acted as a price floor in the market.

Under the FAIR Act, import restrictions on certain farm products (e.g. sugar, peanuts) continued. Import restrictions benefit domestic farmers at the expense of domestic consumers. As discussed in Chapter 16, import restrictions are a very inefficient way to redistribute income.

Import restrictions on farm products also impose a loss on foreign farmers, as will be discussed in an appendix at the end of the chapter.

The FAIR Act was supposed to gradually phase out the government's role in subsidizing farmers. The Act was intended to provide a transition period for farmers to move from government-subsidized farming to free market farming. Government subsidies were scheduled to end after 2002. Instead, in 2002, the federal government enacted the Farm Security and Rural Investment Act of 2002

## The Farm Security and Rural Investment Act of 2002

The Farm Security and Rural Investment Act of 2002 renewed the federal government's major role in agricultural markets. The Act provided larger subsidies to farmers than provided by the FAIR Act. Subsidies were provided largely through three programs:

1. **Direct payments.** These are fixed payments to producers of eligible crops (corn, wheat, rice, upland cotton, barley, grain sorghum, soybeans, other oilseeds, and peanuts). These direct payments are similar to the production flexibility contract payments provided under the 1996 Act.

2. **Counter-cyclical payments.** The 2002 Act establishes target prices for the same crops eligible for direct payments. Counter-cyclical payments are similar to the deficiency payments provided under traditional target prices.

3. **Nonrecourse commodity loans.** These have the effect of establishing a price floor for the commodity. To minimize the surplus that the government must purchase, the marketing loan program allows farmers to repay the commodity loans at less than the loan rate if the world price for the commodity drops below the loan rate. The marketing loan program causes the nonrecourse commodity loan program to have a similar effect to counter-cyclical payments.

The Act also provided certain restrictions on imports (e.g. sugar) and subsidies for exports (e.g. the Export Enhancement Program and the Dairy Export Incentive Program).

The Act was expected to cost taxpayers about $19 billion per year. The Act would also cause higher food prices for consumers. The cost to consumers in higher food prices was estimated at about $27 billion per year.

## The Food, Conservation, and Energy Act of 2008

The Food, Conservation, and Energy Act of 2008 continued the federal government's major role in agricultural markets. The Act continued the three major subsidy programs provided in the Farm Security and Rural Investment Act of 2002: direct payments, counter-cyclical payments, and nonrecourse commodity loans.

The Act also created a new Average Crop Revenue Election (ACRE) program. Beginning in 2009, farmers will have the option of participating in the ACRE program, but will have to agree to a 20 percent reduction in direct payments and a 30 percent reduction in loan rates. Participants in the ACRE program will be eligible for a state-based revenue guarantee. The revenue guarantee will be based on the acres planted by the farmer and is equal to 90 percent of the product of the state average yield factor times the national average price for the previous two years for the commodity.

The Act also provided more funding for food assistance programs, conservation and farmland protection programs, and renewable energy development programs.

President Bush vetoed the 2008 Farm Bill, citing its high cost, market distortions, numerous earmarks, and continuing subsidies for wealthy farmers. Congress easily overrode the President's veto.

## Some Comments on the Government's Agricultural Policies

It is hard, from an economic standpoint, to find anything good to say about the federal government's farm policies. On the negative side, the federal government's farm policies are economically inefficient, misallocating resources. The higher food prices caused by the government's farm policies amount to a hidden (and very regressive) tax on consumers.

The federal government's farm policies exemplify successful rent seeking by a powerful special-interest group. The federal government's farm policies are essentially welfare payments received mainly by the relatively richer farmers and paid for by both taxpayers and consumers.

> **Example 10:** According to a USDA survey, in 2000, small farms (average farm revenue of $15,000) made up 62% of total farms and received 13% of total government payments. Mid-size farms (average farm revenue of $99,000) made up 30% of total farms and received 40% of total government payments, and large farms (average farm revenue of $625,000 and average household net worth of $1.3 million) made up 8% of total farms and received 47% of total government payments.

The percentage of government payments received by large farms has been increasing in recent years.

> **Example 11:** According to the USDA, the share of commodity program payments received by farms with annual sales under $100,000 decreased from 31.5% in 1989 to 18.4% in 2003. The share of commodity program payments received by farms with annual sales of over $500,000 increased from 12.7% in 1989 to 31.8% in 2003. (Sales are measured in 2003 dollars.)

There are two good things that we can say about the federal government's farm policies:

1. **They are not as bad as the farm policies of many other countries.** Many other countries subsidize their farmers even more heavily than the U.S. subsidizes it farmers.

> **Example 12:** For 2004, the Organisation for Economic Co-operation and Development estimated that, for the United States, 18% of the value of farm production came from government support. The percentage of the value of farm production coming from government support was 33% for the European Union, 56% for Japan, and 68% for Norway and Switzerland.

2. **They don't work.** The less efficient farmers still eventually go broke. The amount of resources devoted to agriculture still eventually decreases. These things must happen in order for the limited resources to be allocated to their most valuable uses.


## Appendix: Effect of Developed Countries' Farm Policies on LDCs

As noted in Example 12, governments in developed countries typically provide heavy financial support for their farmers. The U.S., the European Union, and Japan support their farmers with a variety of subsidies and import restrictions. These policies are not only harmful to the domestic economies of the developed countries, they also have a detrimental effect on less developed countries.

When the governments of developed countries subsidize their farmers, production of farm products increases and price falls. This puts farmers in less developed countries at a disadvantage. From the perspective of farmers in less developed countries, the developed countries are "dumping" farm products on their markets, driving the farmers in less developed countries out of business.

When the governments of developed countries restrict imports of agricultural products (e.g. rice in Japan, sugar in the U.S. and the European Union), farmers in less developed countries are shut out of these markets.

Governments of less developed countries are naturally unhappy with the farm policies of developed countries. These farm policies have been a stumbling block in World Trade Organization negotiations to reduce trade restrictions. Governments of less developed countries are hesitant to reduce their trade restrictions on manufactured goods and agricultural commodities when the governments of developed countries are unwilling to reduce their farm support policies.

The Doha round of World Trade Organization negotiations began in 2001. At a number of different venues over the subsequent years, the negotiations have repeatedly been stymied by the unwillingness of developed countries to significantly reduce their farm support payments.

**Multiple Choice:**

_____ 1. Most agricultural markets:
   a. have a large number of relatively small producers
   b. have seen improving productivity and cost efficiency
   c. Both of the above
   d. Neither of the above

_____ 2. Farm prices and total revenue have generally been falling because:
   a. productivity in agriculture has been increasing
   b. demand for farm products is income elastic
   c. demand for farm products is price elastic
   d. All of the above

_____ 3. As real income increases, demand for farm products:
   a. decreases
   b. increases less than income
   c. increases more than income

_____ 4. As farm productivity increases faster than demand:
   a. fewer farmers are required to meet demand
   b. the number of farmers decreases over time
   c. the decreasing number of farmers is good news for the economy because the basic economic problem is scarcity
   d. All of the above

_____ 5. A price support program:
   a. establishes a price floor for a farm product
   b. results in a surplus
   c. is costly to taxpayers and consumers
   d. All of the above

_____ 6. Policies that restrict the supply of farm products:
   a. benefit farmers by increasing prices
   b. hurt consumers by increasing prices
   c. often involve paying farmers to not produce
   d. All of the above

_____ 7. Target prices:
   a. establish a target price above equilibrium
   b. result in a surplus
   c. cause a higher price for consumers
   d. All of the above

Answer questions 8. through 11. by referring to the graph below:

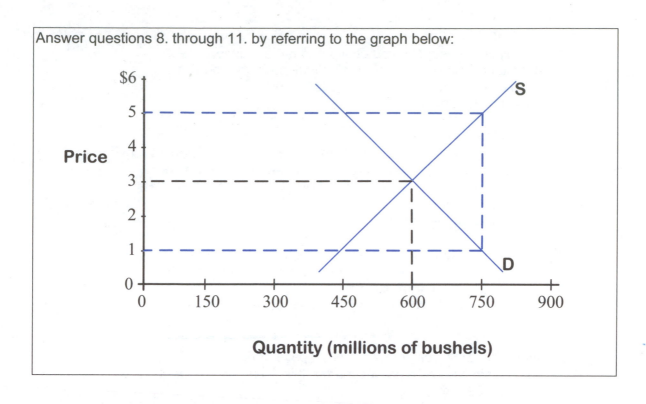

**Quantity (millions of bushels)**

_____ 8. If the government establishes a price floor at $5, how many bushels will the government need to purchase?
    a. 750 million bushels
    b. 300 million bushels
    c. 150 million bushels
    d. None, no surplus will result

_____ 9. If the government establishes a price floor at $5, how much will it cost the government to purchase the surplus?
    a. $3750 million
    b. $1500 million
    c. $750 million
    d. None, no surplus will result

_____ 10. If the government establishes a target price of $5, how many bushels will the government need to purchase?
    a. 750 million bushels
    b. 300 million bushels
    c. 150 million bushels
    d. None, no surplus will result

_____ 11. If the government establishes a target price of $5, how much will the total deficiency payment to farmers be?
    a. $3000 million
    b. $1500 million
    c. $750 million
    d. None, no deficiency payment will be necessary

Agriculture

_____ 12. The FAIR Act of 1996:
  a. eliminated supply restrictions and target prices
  b. did <u>not</u> eliminate import restrictions on farm products
  c. did <u>not</u> eliminate price supports
  d. All of the above

_____ 13. The FAIR Act of 1996:
  a. was intended to provide a transition period for farmers to move from government-subsidized farming to free market farming
  b. succeeded in removing the government from farm markets
  c. Both of the above
  d. Neither of the above

_____ 14. The Farm Security and Rural Investment Act of 2002:
  a. put an end to government intervention in farm markets
  b. drastically cut farm subsidies
  c. was expected to cost taxpayers about $19 billion per year
  d. All of the above

_____ 15. Under the 2002 Act, counter-cyclical payments:
  a. are similar to the production flexibility contract payments provided under the 1996 Act
  b. are similar to the deficiency payments provided under traditional target prices
  c. establish a price floor for the commodity
  d. All of the above

_____ 16. The Food, Conservation, and Energy Act of 2008:
  a. drastically cut farm subsidies
  b. continued the federal government's major role in agricultural markets
  c. was supported by President Bush as "fiscally responsible"
  d. All of the above

_____ 17. The federal government's farm policies:
  a. are an example of rent seeking
  b. pay benefits received mainly by small farms
  c. Both of the above
  d. Neither of the above

_____ 18. The federal government's farm policies:
  a. provide the largest subsidies to farmers of any country on earth
  b. permit the less efficient farmers to avoid going broke indefinitely
  c. Both of the above
  d. Neither of the above

_____ 19. Farm policies in developed countries:
  a. benefit the domestic economies of the developed countries
  b. benefit farmers in less developed countries
  c. have been a stumbling block in World Trade Organization negotiations to reduce trade restrictions
  d. All of the above

**Problems:**

1. What is the long run problem for farmers?

2. If the government establishes a price support program for a farm product, who pays for this program?

3. If the government pays farmers to reduce the supply of a farm product, who pays for this supply restricting policy?

4. If the government establishes a target price for a farm product, who pays for this policy?

## Answers for Chapter 30

**Multiple Choice:**

| | | |
|---|---|---|
| 1. c. | 8. b. | 15. b. |
| 2. a. | 9. b. | 16. b. |
| 3. b. | 10. d. | 17. a. |
| 4. d. | 11. a. | 18. d. |
| 5. d. | 12. d. | 19. c. |
| 6. d. | 13. a. | |
| 7. a. | 14. c. | |

## Problems:

1. The long run problem for farmers is that farm prices and total revenue have generally been falling. As farm productivity increases faster than demand, fewer farmers are required to meet demand. Less efficient farmers are unable to survive in the market as the price drops. The number of farmers decreases over time.

2. A price support program is costly to taxpayers (who pay to buy and store the surplus) and to consumers (who pay the higher floor price for the product).

3. This policy is costly to taxpayers (who pay the farmers to reduce supply) and to consumers (who pay a higher price for the product).

4. This policy is costly to taxpayers (who pay the deficiency payment).

# Chapter 31  Income Distribution and Redistribution

The basic economic problem is scarcity.  Human wants are unlimited.  Resources are limited.  The basic goal in dealing with the problem of scarcity is to produce as much consumer satisfaction as possible with the limited resources available.  Two elements are necessary to achieve this goal:

1.  Producing as much as possible of the combination of goods that provides the greatest consumer satisfaction.

2.  Achieving the distribution of income that will yield the greatest total utility for society.

A market economy is ideal for accomplishing the first element.  But the unequal distribution of income in a market economy will probably <u>not</u> yield the greatest utility for society.  This chapter examines income distribution and redistribution.

## Some Income Distribution Facts

Ask the average person what U.S. GDP is, and they are unlikely to know with any precision.  Ask the same person what their own income is, and they are likely to know very precisely (though they may not be willing to reveal it).  Most people are less concerned about National Income than they are about their own income.  Most people care less about the size of the whole economic pie than about the size of their slice.

In a market economy, income is distributed based on the productivity of resources.  The resources owned by different households are <u>not</u> all of the same productivity.  So the income distribution is unequal.  But just how unequal is income distribution in the U.S.?

The table below shows the share of total money income received by different groups of households, ranging from the Lowest Income 20% of households to the Highest Income 20% of households, for the year 2007.  The table also shows the income range for each Household Income Group.  The information is from the U.S. Census Bureau.

| Household Income Group | Percentage of Total Money Income | Income Range |
|---|---|---|
| Lowest 20% | 3.4% | $0 – 20,291 |
| Second 20% | 8.7% | $20,291 – 39,100 |
| Third 20% | 14.8% | 39,100 – 62,000 |
| Fourth 20% | 23.4% | 62,000 – 100,000 |
| Highest 20% | 49.7% | 100,000 and up |

The table above shows that the Highest Income 20% of households have over 14 times the share of total money income as the Lowest Income 20% of households.  (49.7 ÷ 3.4 = 14.6)

## Economic Mobility

There is significant economic mobility in the U.S. economy. We should not assume that the Household Income Groups consist of the same households over time. Over a typical ten year period, fewer than half of the households in the Lowest Income 20% will remain in that Group. Most will move up to one of the four higher Income Groups.

## The Lorenz Curve

The degree of income inequality can be expressed with a Lorenz curve. A **Lorenz curve** contrasts the actual distribution of income with perfect equality.

The graph below shows the actual distribution of money income for 2007 and the line of perfect equality. If income was distributed with perfect equality, 20% of the households would have 20% of the income, 40% of the households would have 40% of the income, etc.

In actuality, the Lowest Income 20% of households have 3.4% of total money income, the Lowest Income 40% of households have 12.1% of total money income, etc. The gap between the line of perfect equality and the actual distribution curve indicates the degree of income inequality.

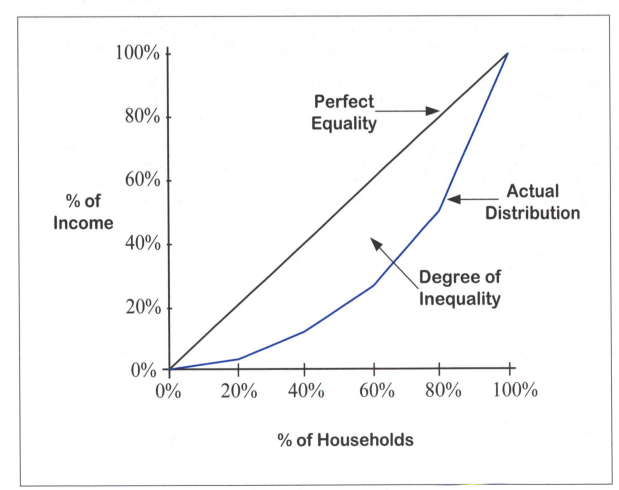

The distribution of income has been growing more unequal in recent decades.

> **Example 1:** In 1971, the Highest Income 20% of households had only about 11 times the share of total money income as the Lowest Income 20% of households (43.5% versus 4.1%).

The increase in income inequality in recent decades was due largely to increased immigration. Between 1970 and 2005, the foreign-born population in the U.S. increased from 9.6 million to 35.7 million. The percentage of the U.S. population that is foreign-born increased from 4.7% in 1970 to 12.4% in 2005.

Immigrants have a median annual income about 15% lower than native-born Americans. Thus, the increased number of immigrants reduces the median income at the bottom of the income scale and widens the gap between the top and bottom Income Groups.

## Overstating the Degree of Income Inequality

The distribution of money income expressed on the previous page overstates the actual degree of income inequality in two ways. First, the distribution of money income does not take into account the effect of taxes paid or of in-kind transfer payments received. Money transfer payments (e.g. social security benefits, unemployment compensation) are included in money income. In-kind transfer payments (e.g. food stamps, medical assistance) are not included in money income.

Income is more equally distributed after taking taxes and in-kind transfer payments into account. Higher income households pay a higher percentage of income in taxes. In-kind transfer payments are received disproportionately by lower income households. After taking taxes and in-kind transfer payments into account, the Highest Income 20% of households have about 10 times the income share of the Lowest Income 20%.

The second way that the distribution of money income expressed on the previous page overstates the actual degree of income inequality is by focusing on income distribution at a point in time (e.g. 2007) rather than over the course of a lifetime. Income is distributed more equally over the course of a lifetime than at a point in time.

Many people in the Lowest Income 20% of households are young people at the start of their careers. Most of these young people will move into higher Income Groups as their careers progress and they develop more human capital.

If career incomes were compared or if incomes were compared for households at the same career stage (e.g. compare 30-year-olds to 30-year-olds, 50-year-olds to 50-year-olds, etc.), the gap between the highest and lowest Income Groups would be much smaller.

## Distribution of Wealth

In one way, the distribution of money income understates the inequality problem. The terms "rich" and "poor" refer to wealth distribution rather than to income distribution. The distribution of wealth is much more unequal than the distribution of income.

**Example 2:** In 2004, the top 20% of wealth holders had roughly 85% of total wealth. The bottom 20% of wealth holders had roughly 0% of total wealth.

The greater inequality in the distribution of wealth has two primary causes:

1. **Differences in savings rates.** High-income households typically have much higher savings rates than low-income households.

**Example 3:** The table below represents income, savings rate, and wealth for two persons. Max, a high-income person, has a higher savings rate than Minnie, a low-income person. The higher savings rate for Max means that there is a bigger gap in wealth accumulation between Max and Minnie than the gap in income. Max has 14 times as much income as Minnie, but 70 times as much wealth.

|  | Max | Minnie |
|---|---|---|
| Income | $140,000 | $10,000 |
| Savings Rate | 10% | 2% |
| Wealth Accumulation | $14,000 | $200 |

2. **Wealth distribution is measured at a point in time.** Wealth, like income (but to a greater degree), is distributed more equally over the course of a lifetime than at a point in time.

**Example 4:** If wealth were compared for households at the same career stage (e.g. compare 30-year-olds to 30-year-olds, compare 50-year-olds to 50-year-olds, etc.), the gap between rich and poor would be much smaller.

## Overstating the Inequality of Wealth Distribution

The inequality of wealth distribution is overstated in two ways. First, the distribution of wealth is measured at a point in time just like the distribution of income. Thus, wealth distribution compares persons at different career stages. Comparing the wealth of 60-year-olds to the wealth of 25-year-olds overstates the inequality of wealth distribution.

The second way that the inequality of wealth distribution is overstated is that the value of human capital is not included in measuring wealth. For most people, human capital is by far the most valuable asset owned. According to economist Gary Becker, human capital makes up 75% of the wealth in a modern economy.

**Example 5:** A 25-year-old recent graduate of Harvard Law School may have very little accumulated wealth in terms of physical assets. But a Harvard Law School degree is very valuable human capital.

## Causes of Continuing Income Inequality

There is a large degree of economic mobility in the U.S. economy. Many people who start out with a low income level eventually reach much higher income levels. Most people prefer higher income to lower income. If most people are striving for higher income, why don't all people eventually achieve equal income? Why is there continuing income inequality? There are six causes of continuing income inequality:

1. **Natural ability.** People differ in their natural abilities. Some people are born with a high level of natural ability in an area such as mathematics, or music, or athletics. A person with a high level of a marketable natural ability may earn higher income than a person with a lower level of that natural ability.

2. **Human capital.** People differ in their development of human capital. **Human capital** is developed ability that increases a person's productivity. Human capital is developed primarily through education and training and through work experience.

   Not all education and training provides the same value of human capital. A degree in chemical engineering may increase a student's earning power more than a degree in elementary education. Still, mean earnings increase as the education level increases.

**Example 6:** Fewer than 10 percent of households in the Lowest Income 20% include a person with a college degree. About 60 percent of households in the Highest Income 20% include a person with a college degree.

The table below shows the mean earnings for full-time workers with different education levels in 2007. The information is provided by the Census Bureau.

| Mean Earnings by Education Level for Full-time Workers Age 18-64 in 2007 | |
| --- | --- |
| Not a high school graduate | $27,792 |
| High school graduate | 37,492 |
| Some college | 44,633 |
| Bachelor degree | 66,558 |
| Advanced degree | 90,933 |

Not all work experience provides the same value of human capital. Fifteen years of experience as an attorney will likely increase a person's earning power more than fifteen years of experience as a truck driver.

Still, mean earnings increase over the average worker's career. The main reason that earnings increase over a typical career is the accumulation of human capital through work experience. The table on the next page shows the mean earnings for full-time workers of different age ranges in 2007. The information is provided by the Census Bureau.

| Mean Earnings by Age Range for Full-time Workers in 2007 | |
|---|---|
| 18-24 | $25,582 |
| 25-34 | 43,995 |
| 35-44 | 55,833 |
| 45-54 | 57,453 |
| 55-64 | 57,651 |

3. **Work and leisure choices.** People differ in the work and leisure choices that they make. Some choose to work longer hours or hold a second job. Others choose more leisure time.

**Example 7:** In 2006, for households in the Lowest Income 20%, only 15% of households included a full-time, year-round worker. 75% of households in the Highest Income 20% had at least two earners in the household.

The career path chosen, willingness to work overtime, travel extensively or relocate frequently are other aspects of work and leisure choices. Different work and leisure choices lead to different levels of income.

4. **Risk taking.** People differ in their willingness to take risks. Risk takers are more likely to rise to the top of the income scale or to sink to the bottom. Self-employed entrepreneurs make up a disproportionate share of society's millionaires and also make up a disproportionate share of those filing for bankruptcy.

**Example 8:** Less than 20 percent of the American labor force is self-employed. But nearly 70 percent of American millionaires are (or were) self-employed.

5. **Wrongful employment discrimination.** People differ in the degree that they suffer from wrongful employment discrimination. Employment discrimination is <u>not</u> necessarily wrongful. An employer may justifiably discriminate among employees on the basis of education, work experience, or any other characteristic related to worker productivity.

Wrongful employment discrimination occurs when employers make hiring, promotion, and pay decisions based on factors unrelated to worker productivity. There are two distinct viewpoints on the best way to reduce wrongful employment discrimination.

One viewpoint holds that wrongful employment discrimination can be reduced by making markets more competitive. In highly competitive markets, employers who discriminate based on factors unrelated to worker productivity will put themselves at a competitive disadvantage.

**Example 9A:** Remember from Chapter 24 that, according to the book "Moneyball", most major league teams used screening devices that did <u>not</u> accurately predict the productivity of players. The Oakland A's, by avoiding this type of wrongful employment discrimination, gained a competitive advantage.

> **Example 9B:** If an NFL team drafts players only from the team owner's alma mater, the team will _not_ be drafting the best players available. This wrongful employment discrimination will put the team at a competitive disadvantage.

Another viewpoint contends that increased government regulation of labor markets is necessary to reduce wrongful employment discrimination. This viewpoint assumes that markets will not be competitive enough to punish wrongful employment discrimination or that employers will be so biased against certain employee characteristics that they will willingly put themselves at a competitive disadvantage. This viewpoint also assumes that the government can distinguish which employee characteristics are related to productivity and which are not.

6. **Luck.** People differ in the kind of luck that they experience. If a person enjoys extremely good luck (e.g. wins the lottery), this good luck may result in high income. If a person incurs extremely bad luck (e.g. suffers a debilitating illness), this bad luck may result in low income. Most people are likely to experience a mixture of good luck and bad luck. For most people, luck probably won't have a large impact on income earning.

## Standards of Income Distribution

Different standards for determining income distribution exist. Most societies choose some variation or combination of the following two standards of income distribution:

1. **Marginal productivity standard (market).** In a market economy, income is distributed to resource owners based on the marginal productivity of their resources. This provides maximum incentive for productivity. Resource owners will have a self-interest in producing as much consumer satisfaction as possible. Resource owners will also be motivated to develop the productivity of their resources in the long run.

   In a market economy, the resource owners decide for themselves how to use their resources in the pursuit of their self-interest. Thus, the marginal productivity standard also provides maximum individual freedom.

   However, since resources can vary widely in their productivity, income may be distributed very unequally. This unequal distribution of income may _not_ produce maximum total utility for society. Theoretically, a dollar of income provides greater utility to a low-income person than to a high-income person. The marginal productivity standard does _not_ redistribute income to attempt to achieve greater total utility.

2. **Equality standard.** Under the equality standard, income is distributed equally. This may increase total utility for society. However, the quantity of total production is likely to fall since the equality standard breaks the market link between effort and reward. Achieving equality will require government redistribution of income. This government intervention will decrease individual freedom.

## Income Redistribution

In the U.S., the distribution of income is determined primarily by the marginal productivity standard. But a wide variety of government programs and policies redistribute income, generally making the distribution more equal than the result under the marginal productivity standard.

The basic justification for income redistribution is to increase total utility for society. The utility received by one person cannot be measured objectively. Utility cannot be scientifically compared for different persons. (See the discussion in Chapter 18.) However, it is reasonable to believe that a certain quantity of production will yield greater total utility for society if income is distributed more equally rather than less equally.

> **Example 10:** 50 coconuts are produced on Gilligan's Island. The Howells consume 45 of the coconuts, and the other 5 coconuts are divided among the rest of the group. The 50 coconuts will yield a certain amount of total utility distributed in this way. If the coconuts had been distributed more equally, they would probably yield more total utility.

However, when income redistribution takes place, the total quantity of production will be reduced. Income redistribution reduces the incentive for production, both in the short run and in the long run.

So, as is usual in economic decisions, there is a trade-off. Market determination of income distribution will likely create the greatest quantity of total production, but not the greatest total utility. Redistribution of income to achieve greater equality may increase total utility up to a point. But as the degree of income redistribution is increased, at some point the disincentive effect of income redistribution will decrease the total quantity of production so much that total utility decreases.

## Ideal Income Redistribution

The ideal degree of income redistribution cannot be objectively determined. Total utility for society cannot be objectively measured. And one must consider that individual freedom is a source of utility. Income redistribution efforts will infringe on individual freedom.

Identifying the ideal degree of income redistribution is impossible. But certain desirable characteristics of an income redistribution program can be identified. An ideal income redistribution program would:

1. **Transfer most <u>from</u> those with the highest income.** Theoretically, those with the highest income would lose the least amount of utility by having a portion of their income taxed away.

2. **Transfer most <u>to</u> those with the lowest income.** Theoretically, those with the lowest income would gain the greatest amount of utility by receiving a transfer of additional income.

3. **Interfere with private market decisions as little as possible.** We saw in Chapter 3 that private market decisions generally lead to economic efficiency. If private

market decisions are altered by tax and transfer considerations, a deadweight loss is created.

4. **Interfere with the incentive for productivity as little as possible.**  Income redistribution will reduce the incentive for productivity for both taxpayers and transfer recipients.  But as much incentive for productivity should be maintained as is possible.

5. **Provide as little opportunity for rent seeking as possible.**  Rent seeking (see Chapters 22 and 28) is socially wasteful.  To minimize rent seeking, income redistribution should not target specific groups, other than those with low income.

6. **Be as simple and inexpensive to administer as possible.**  The cost to administer an income redistribution program is a type of deadweight loss.

## Actual Income Redistribution

How does the actual income redistribution program in the U.S. compare with the ideal discussed above?  Not very well.  Specifically:

1. **The income that funds income redistribution is not necessarily transferred from those with the highest income.**  The federal personal income tax is a progressive tax.  But other taxes that fund income redistribution (e.g. social security taxes, property taxes, sales and excise taxes, etc.) are regressive.

   Some government policies that redistribute income (e.g. trade restrictions, agricultural subsidies) cause higher consumer prices.  Higher consumer prices are a more severe burden for lower income households than for higher income households.

2. **Most income redistribution transfers are not received by those with the lowest income.**  While some income redistribution programs target the low income (e.g. Temporary Assistance for Needy Families, food stamps, housing subsidies, Medicaid), the largest income redistribution programs (e.g. social security, Medicare, public education) transfer income largely to households above the poverty line.

3. **Income redistribution policies often interfere strongly with private market decisions.**  Policies that alter market prices (e.g. trade restrictions, agricultural subsidies) clearly cause economic inefficiency.

   People will also alter their private market decisions based on tax and transfer considerations.  As an example, labor force participation drops off dramatically when people reach the age of eligibility for social security benefits.  For another example, the availability of unemployment compensation often extends the length of unemployment.

4. **Income redistribution efforts have a strong disincentive effect on both taxpayers and transfer recipients.**  Taxpayers face high marginal tax rates, partially due to the broad scope of income redistribution efforts.

Transfer recipients often face a form of high marginal tax rates as well. Transfer payments received are reduced by a percentage (called the "reduction rate") of income earned. A transfer recipient who earns $1,000 of income may face a decrease in transfer benefits of $500 or more. That means a reduction rate of fifty percent or more.

5. **Income redistribution policies often are subject to rent seeking.** Trade restrictions and agricultural subsidies are clear examples. Political questions, such as the location of military bases and the distribution of federal funding for highways, often have a strong income redistribution element and are subject to rent seeking.

6. **The income redistribution program is very complex.** The complexity of the tax system was discussed in Chapter 13. The wide variety of "welfare" programs (Temporary Assistance for Needy Families, food stamps, housing subsidies, etc.) makes for a transfer program that is complex and expensive to administer.

## Negative Income Tax

Given the flaws in the current income redistribution program, could a better program be devised? Many economists favor a negative income tax as a replacement for the traditional "welfare" programs (e.g. Temporary Assistance for Needy Families, food stamps, housing subsidies, etc.) and for the broader redistribution programs (e.g. social security, Medicare, trade restrictions, agricultural subsidies, etc.).

A negative income tax would transfer income to low-income households. A basic support amount would be set (e.g. two-thirds of the poverty line) and then the support amount would be reduced by a fraction of income earned. At some level of income, support would be eliminated, and any additional income would be subject to the regular (positive) income tax.

---

**Example 11:** A negative income tax system is implemented. The basic support amount is set at two-thirds of the poverty line. The reduction rate is set at twenty-five percent, until support is eliminated. Income above the threshold where support is eliminated is taxed at fifteen percent.

The table below illustrates how such a negative income tax system would work. The table represents the support received by a family of three, assuming that the poverty line for a family of three is $16,500.

| Income | Support | Tax Paid | Total |
|--------|---------|----------|-------|
| $0 | $11,000 | $0 | $11,000 |
| 1,000 | 10,750 | 0 | 11,750 |
| 10,000 | 8,500 | 0 | 18,500 |
| 20,000 | 6,000 | 0 | 26,000 |
| 30,000 | 3,500 | 0 | 33,500 |
| 40,000 | 1,000 | 0 | 41,000 |
| 44,000 | 0 | 0 | 44,000 |
| 50,000 | 0 | 900 | 49,100 |
| 60,000 | 0 | 2,400 | 57,600 |

---

A negative income tax system would have a number of advantages over the current income redistribution program:

1. It would transfer most <u>from</u> those with the highest income.
2. It would transfer most <u>to</u> those with the lowest income.
3. It would interfere less with private market decisions.
4. It would interfere less with the incentive for productivity because it could be funded with lower marginal tax rates than are currently imposed and could use lower reduction rates than are currently used.
5. It would provide no apparent opportunity for rent seeking.
6. It would be simpler and less expensive to administer.

## Poverty

With unequal distribution of income, those households at the bottom of the income scale may <u>not</u> have enough income for an adequate standard of living. Such households are classified as living in poverty.

**Poverty** – a family whose income falls below a minimum necessary for an adequate standard of living is classified as living in poverty.

The amount of income necessary for an adequate standard of living varies by household size. For 2007, the poverty line for a family of four was about $21,200, and the poverty line for a family of three was about $16,500.

Poverty rates vary based on certain characteristics. Poverty rates tend to be higher for minority groups, single parent families, the young, and the poorly educated.

The table below illustrates some of these differences. The information is provided by the U.S. Census Bureau, and is for 2007.

| <u>Group</u> | <u>Percent in Poverty</u> |
|---|---|
| Total Population | 12.5% |
|  |  |
| By Race/Ethnic Group |  |
| White | 10.3% |
| African American | 24.3% |
| Hispanic | 20.6% |
|  |  |
| By Age |  |
| Under 18 years | 18.0% |
| 18 to 24 years | 17.3% |
| 25 to 44 years | 10.8% |
| 45 to 64 years | 8.5% |
| 65 years and over | 9.7% |
|  |  |
| By Type of Family |  |
| Married-couple | 4.9% |
| Single-parent; male | 13.6% |
| Single-parent; female | 28.3% |

High school dropouts have a poverty rate about 5 times higher than college graduates.

## Poverty and Economic Mobility

As discussed earlier in this chapter, there is significant economic mobility in the U.S. economy. The percentage of Americans living below the poverty line may change little from year to year, but the actual persons who are living in poverty change.

> **Example 12:** In an average ten year period, about a quarter of households will have income below the poverty line in at least one year. But fewer than 3% of households will have income below the poverty line for eight or more of the ten years.

## Four Keys to Achieving Financial Security

The U.S. economy is the largest in the world. The standard of living is among the highest in the world. Americans enjoy a relatively large amount of economic freedom and opportunity. Yet, many Americans fail to achieve financial security.

Financial security means different things to different people. For a college student, financial security might mean being able to pay one's bills as they come due.

For a person approaching retirement age, financial security might mean having sufficient sources of income (investments, pensions, etc.) to provide a comfortable lifestyle after retirement. Most people would like to achieve financial security, but many do not.

There are four keys to achieving financial security:

1. **Believe that you can achieve financial security.** Achieving financial security may not be easy. A college student, saddled with large student loans and facing additional years of education, may see no path to financial security. But it is possible even for a debt-burdened college student to eventually achieve financial security.

   Any person who enjoys reasonably good health and takes the necessary steps to achieve financial security can eventually achieve financial security. However, if a person believes that it is impossible to achieve financial security, that person will not take the steps necessary to achieve financial security.

2. **Invest in your human capital.** Investing in human capital is a way to increase one's earning power. Investing in human capital pays an even higher return today than it did in the past.

> **Example 13:** In 1974 male college graduates earned 27% more than male high school graduates. In 2007, male college graduates earned 92% more than male high school graduates.

   It is possible to achieve financial security with a low level of income. But it is much easier (and more pleasant) to achieve financial security from a higher level of income.

3. **Make good personal choices.** No one sets out to make bad personal choices. But people often do make choices that hinder their attempts to achieve financial security. Good personal choices are particularly crucial in three areas:

   a. **Health.** Maintaining good health is essential to achieving financial security. Health problems not only lower a person's quality of life, but also reduce income earning potential. Most workers reach their peak earnings relatively late in their careers. Poor health may prematurely end a career before financial security can be achieved.

   b. **Marriage.** A successful marriage is advantageous to achieving financial security. An unsuccessful marriage can be a severe hindrance to achieving financial security. Marrying wisely, with a commitment to having a successful marriage, is a big step toward achieving financial security.

   c. **Self-control.** Many high income persons have ended up in bankruptcy court because of a failure to exercise self-control in spending. Whatever a person's income level, one must be able to live within that income in order to achieve financial security.

4. **Get on the good side of compound interest. Compound interest** refers to interest paid on interest. Compound interest is the saver's best friend and the borrower's worst enemy, as illustrated in the examples below:

---

**Example 14A:** Starting at age 23, Saver puts $100 per month into a 401(k) savings plan. (The earnings on a 401(k) savings plan are not taxed until the earnings are withdrawn, usually at retirement.) Saver's contributions earn a 10% annual return. At age 67, Saver will have contributed a total of $52,800. Saver's investment will be worth $824,973 (over 15 times the amount of Saver's contributions), and Saver will be earning investment income of over $6,800 per month.

---

**Example 14B:** Length of time is crucial to the power of compound interest. Starting at age 45, Saver puts $200 per month into a 401(k) savings plan. Saver's contributions earn a 10% annual return. At age 67, Saver will have contributed a total of $52,800. Saver's investment will be worth $180,514 (about 3.4 times the amount of Saver's contributions).

---

**Example 14C:** Rate of return is also crucial to the power of compound interest. Starting at age 23, Saver puts $100 per month into a 401(k) savings plan. Saver's contributions earn a 5% annual return. At age 67, Saver will have contributed a total of $52,800. Saver's investment will be worth $186,247 (about 3.5 times the amount of Saver's contributions).

---

**Example 15:** Compound interest is also powerful at building debt. Starting at age 23, Borrower borrows $100 per month on a credit card that does not require a minimum payment. Borrower's interest rate is 12%. At age 67, Borrower will have borrowed a total of $52,800. Borrower's debt will total $1,547,060 (over 29 times the amount that Borrower has borrowed) and Borrower will be incurring interest on the debt of almost $15,500 per month.

---

## Appendix: Income Inequality around the World

The degree of income inequality in the U.S. was discussed earlier in the chapter. What about income inequality in the rest of the world? Some general comments can be made about the distribution of income in the rest of the world. But first we introduce a new measure of income inequality: the Gini coefficient.

The Gini coefficient was developed by Italian statistician Corrado Gini. The **Gini coefficient** is a measure of income inequality based on the Lorenz curve. The Gini coefficient is calculated as the ratio of the area indicating the degree of inequality and the area beneath the line of perfect equality. The Lorenz curve below illustrates the two areas.

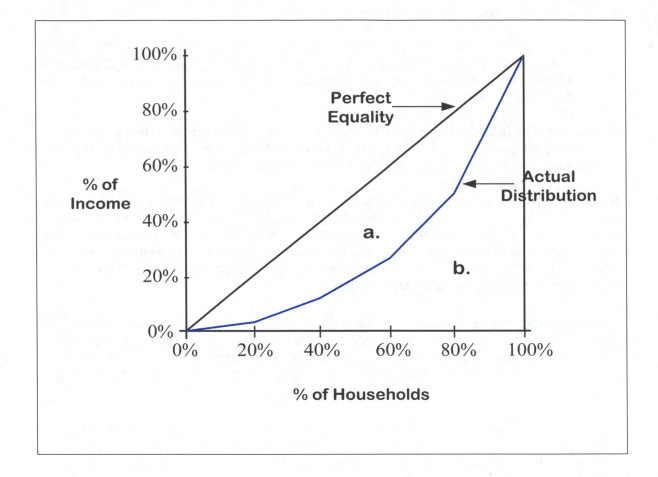

The area indicating the degree of inequality is the area between the line of perfect equality and the actual distribution curve. This area is identified by the letter a. The area beneath the line of perfect equality is the sum of area a. and area b. So the formula for the Gini coefficient is:

**Gini coefficient = a. ÷ (a. + b.)**

The higher the Gini coefficient, the greater the degree of income inequality.

Based on the Gini coefficients of various countries, some general comments can be made about income inequality around the world:

1.  The Gini coefficient for the United States is 45.

2.  The other members of the top five largest economies in the world have the following Gini coefficients:  China, 47; Japan, 38.1; India, 36.8; and Germany, 28.

3.  The Scandinavian countries have a low degree of income inequality.  Denmark, Finland, Norway, and Sweden have an average Gini coefficient of 25.

4.  The European Union has a lower degree of income inequality than the U.S.  The Gini coefficient for the European Union is 30.7.

5.  Less developed countries tend to have a higher degree of income inequality than developed countries.

6.  Some of the highest Gini coefficients are found in Latin America and Africa.

> **Example 16:**  Gini coefficients from selected African and Latin American countries:  Bolivia, 59.2; Botswana, 63; Brazil, 56.7; Central African Republic, 61.3; Chile, 54.9; Colombia, 53.8; Guatemala, 55.1; Honduras, 53.8; Lesotho, 63.2; Namibia, 70.7; Panama, 56.1; Paraguay, 56.8; South Africa, 65; and Zimbabwe, 50.1.

The Gini coefficients detailed above are from the CIA World Factbook.


## Questions for Chapter 31

### Fill-in-the-blanks:

1.  A _____ curve contrasts the actual distribution of income with perfect equality.

2.  _____ _____ is developed ability that increases a person's productivity.

3.  A family whose income falls below a minimum necessary for an adequate standard of living is classified as living in _____ .

4.  _____ interest refers to interest paid on interest.

5.  The _____ coefficient is a measure of income inequality based on the Lorenz curve.

**Multiple Choice:**

_____ 1. In a market economy:
   a. income is distributed based on the productivity of resources
   b. the resources owned by different households are <u>not</u> all of the same productivity
   c. Both of the above
   d. Neither of the above

_____ 2. In 2007, the Lowest Income 60 percent of households had about what percentage of total money income?
   a. 23.4%
   b. 26.9%
   c. 46.6%
   d. 60.0%

_____ 3. Households in the Lowest Income 20%:
   a. usually have at least one full-time, year-round worker
   b. usually remain in this Group for decades
   c. Both of the above
   d. Neither of the above

_____ 4. The degree of income inequality can be expressed with a:
   a. Laffer curve
   b. Lorenz curve
   c. Lector curve
   d. Philips curve

_____ 5. Income is more unequally distributed:
   a. than wealth
   b. today than it was 30 years ago
   c. at a point in time than over the course of a lifetime
   d. Both b. and c. above

_____ 6. Human capital can be acquired:
   a. only through education
   b. equally well on any job
   c. more on some jobs than others

_____ 7. Wrongful employment discrimination:
   a. occurs when employers make hiring, promotion, and pay decisions based on factors unrelated to worker productivity
   b. in competitive markets, puts the discriminating employer at a competitive disadvantage
   c. Both of the above
   d. Neither of the above

_____ 8. The marginal productivity standard of income distribution:
   a. provides maximum incentive for productivity
   b. requires government redistribution of income
   c. is based on the theory that a dollar of income provides greater utility to a poor person than to a rich person
   d. All of the above

_____ 9. Income redistribution:
   a. may increase total utility for society
   b. may decrease the total quantity of production so much that total utility for society decreases
   c. Both of the above
   d. Neither of the above

_____ 10. The largest income redistribution programs:
   a. are funded solely by highly progressive taxation
   b. pay benefits mainly to those below the poverty line
   c. Both of the above
   d. Neither of the above

_____ 11. Compared to the current income redistribution program, a negative income tax:
   a. would interfere more with private market decisions
   b. would be simpler and less expensive to administer
   c. would provide more opportunity for rent seeking
   d. All of the above

_____ 12. In 2007, the poverty line for a family of four was about:
   a. $16,500
   b. $21,200
   c. $25,300
   d. $35,000

_____ 13. In 2007, the poverty rate for single parent families headed by males was:
   a. about half the overall poverty rate
   b. about the same as for families headed by married couples
   c. about half the rate for single parent families headed by females
   d. All of the above

_____ 14. Poverty rates tend to be higher than average for:
   a. those 65 years and older
   b. those under 18 years
   c. Both of the above
   d. Neither of the above

_____ 15. In 2007, male college graduates earned _____ more than male high school graduates.
   a. 27%
   b. 49%
   c. 92%
   d. 123%

_____ 16.  Which of the following is correct?
   a.  the Gini coefficient is a measure of income inequality based on the
       Lorenz curve
   b.  developed countries tend to have a higher degree of income inequality
       than less developed countries
   c.  Both of the above
   d.  Neither of the above

_____ 17.  Which of the following countries has the highest degree of income inequality?
   a.  U.S.
   b.  India
   c.  Japan
   d.  Brazil


Problems:

1.  Explain the two primary causes that the distribution of wealth is more unequal than
    the distribution of income.

2.  Explain the two advantages of the marginal productivity standard of income
    distribution.

3. Explain the disadvantage of the marginal productivity standard of income distribution.

4. List the six characteristics of an ideal income redistribution program.

5. List the four keys to achieving financial security.

## Answers for Chapter 31

**Fill-in-the-blanks:**   1. Lorenz
2. Human capital
3. poverty
4. Compound
5. Gini

**Multiple Choice:**  1. c.       7. c.       13. c.
                      2. b.       8. a.       14. b.
                      3. d.       9. c.       15. c.
                      4. b.      10. d.       16. a.
                      5. d.      11. b.       17. d.
                      6. c.      12. b.

**Problems:**

1.  The greater inequality in the distribution of wealth has two primary causes:
    (1) Differences in savings rates.  High-income households typically have much
        higher savings rates than low-income households.
    (2) Wealth distribution is measured at a point in time.  Wealth, like income (but to a
        greater degree) is distributed more equally over the course of a lifetime than at a
        point in time.

2.  The marginal productivity standard of income distribution has two advantages:
    (1)  It provides maximum incentive for productivity.
    (2)  It provides maximum individual freedom.

3.  The marginal productivity standard may result in income being distributed very
    unequally.  This unequal distribution of income may <u>not</u> produce maximum total
    utility for society.  The marginal productivity standard does <u>not</u> redistribute income to
    attempt to achieve greater total utility.

4.  An ideal income redistribution program would:
    (1)  Transfer most <u>from</u> those with the highest income.
    (2)  Transfer most <u>to</u> those with the lowest income.
    (3)  Interfere with private market decisions as little as possible.
    (4)  Interfere with the incentive for productivity as little as possible.
    (5)  Provide as little opportunity for rent seeking as possible.
    (6)  Be as simple and inexpensive to administer as possible.

5.  The four keys to achieving financial security are:
    (1)  Believe that you can achieve financial security.
    (2)  Invest in your human capital.
    (3)  Make good personal choices.
    (4)  Get on the good side of compound interest.

# Glossary

**Absolute advantage** – when one nation can produce a good with greater productivity than another nation.

**Absolute economic growth** – an increase in Real GDP.

**Accounting profit** – the difference between total revenue and explicit costs.

**Actual money multiplier** – measures the change in the money supply for a given dollar change in monetary base.

**Adverse selection** – a party on one side of the market is confronted by a different selection than expected.

**Agent** – a person who agrees to act for the benefit of another, the principal.

**Aggregate demand (AD)** – the quantity demanded of all goods and services at different price levels.

**Aggregate supply** – the quantity supplied of all goods and services at different price levels.

**Antitrust law** – legislation intended to prohibit attempts to monopolize markets or to engage in anti-competitive behavior.

**Arbitrage** – buying at a low price in one market and selling at a higher price in another market.

**Asymmetric information** – one party to an exchange has information that the other party doesn't have.

**Automatic stabilizers** – taxes and transfer payments that automatically tend to move equilibrium Real GDP toward Natural Real GDP.

**Barriers to entry** – factors that block the entry of new firms into a market.

**Barter** – the direct exchange of goods.

**Budget constraint** – a curve showing the different combinations of two goods that a consumer can purchase with a certain amount of income.

**Budget deficit** – when government expenditures are greater than tax revenues.

**Budget surplus** – when tax revenues are greater than government expenditures.

**Capital** – produced goods that are used in the production of other goods.

**Cartel** – an organization through which members jointly make decisions about prices and production.

**Ceteris paribus (kā´ ter is - pair´ u bus)** – all other things held constant.

**Change in demand** – a shift in the demand curve caused by a change in one of the determinants of demand.

**Change in quantity demanded** – a movement along the demand curve caused by a change in price.

**Change in quantity supplied** – a movement along the supply curve caused by a change in price.

**Change in supply** – a shift in the supply curve caused by a change in the cost of production.

**Checkable deposits** – deposits in banks or other financial institutions on which checks can be written.

**Choice architecture** – the context in which people make decisions.

**Closed shop** – requires union membership as a condition for employment.

**Collective bargaining** – where a union bargains with management on behalf of the workers.

**Common goods** – rivalrous in consumption and nonexcludable.

**Comparative advantage** – when one nation can produce a good at a lower opportunity cost than another nation.

**Compound interest** – interest paid on interest.

**Conglomerate merger** – a merger of firms that are not in the same industry.

**Consumer's surplus** – the difference between the highest price a buyer is willing to pay and the price actually paid.

**Consumption function** – the curve showing the relationship between disposable income and consumption.

**Continued inflation** – when the price level increases at a high rate year after year.

**Contraction** – the phase of the business cycle when Real GDP is decreasing.

**Contractionary fiscal policy** – a decrease in government expenditures or an increase in taxation.

**Contractionary monetary policy** – a decrease in the money supply.

**Copyright** – a government granted monopoly on the production and sale of a creative work granted to the creator.

**Corporation** – an organization owned by stockholders that is considered a legal person, separate from its owners.

**Craft union** – a union made up of workers who practice the same craft.

**Creative destruction** – the short run upheaval caused by the development of new technology.

**Cross elasticity of demand** – measures the responsiveness of demand for one good to a change in price for another good.

**Crowding out** – occurs when increases in government spending lead to decreases in private spending.

**Currency** – consists of the coins and paper money issued by the federal government.

**Cyclical unemployment** – due to downturns in the business cycle.

**Deflation** – a decrease in the price level.

**Demand** – the willingness and ability of buyers to buy different quantities of a good at different prices.

**Demand schedule** – a table showing the different combinations of price and quantity demanded for a good.

**Determinants of demand** – the factors that change demand (shift the demand curve).

**Determinants of factor demand** – cause the marginal revenue product of a factor to increase or decrease.

**Determinants of labor supply** – factors that cause the labor supply curve to shift.

**Determinants of price elasticity of demand** – the factors that determine whether the demand for a good is elastic or inelastic.

**Determinant of supply** – the factor that changes supply (shifts the supply curve).

**Developed country** – has a relatively high per capita Real GDP.

**Diamond-water paradox** – the observation that essential goods are often lower priced than non-essential goods.

**Discount rate** – the interest rate the Fed charges banks that borrow reserves from it.

**Disposable income** – household income after taxes.

**Dominant strategy** – a strategy that always yields the best result regardless of the strategies of the other players.

**Dumping** – the practice of selling exports at a price below the price charged in the home market.

**Economic efficiency rule** – produce the quantity of output where marginal social benefit equals marginal social cost.

**Economic growth** – an increase in the productive capacity of an economy.

**Economic profit** – the difference between total revenue and total opportunity costs, both explicit and implicit.

**Economic rent** – payment to a factor in excess of opportunity costs.

**Economic system** – the way in which a society answers economic questions.

**Economics** – the study of how individuals and societies use their limited resources to try to satisfy their unlimited wants.

**Economies of scale** – exist when, as the scale of production is increased, average costs of production decrease.

**Elastic demand** – price elasticity of demand is greater than one.

**Elasticity** – a measure of the responsiveness of one variable to changes in another variable.

**Elasticity of demand for labor** – measures the responsiveness of employers to a change in the wage rate.

**Employed** – those with paying jobs.

**Employment discrimination** – occurs when employers make hiring, promotion, and pay decisions based on factors unrelated to worker productivity.

**Entrepreneurship** – the special skill involved in organizing labor, land, and capital for production.

**Equilibrium price** – the price where quantity demanded equals quantity supplied.

**Excess burden** – the amount that the burden imposed by a tax exceeds the funding provided by the tax.

**Excess reserves** – the excess of reserves over required reserves.

**Exchange rate** – the value of one nation's currency in terms of another nation's currency.

**Exchange rate effect** – when the price level decreases, interest rates will decrease, causing depreciation in the exchange rate for the dollar.

**Excludable good** – nonpayers can easily be excluded from consuming the good.

**Exclusive dealing agreement** – a producer refuses to sell a product to a retailer unless the retailer agrees to deal only in the producer's product.

**Expansion** – the phase of the business cycle when Real GDP is increasing.

**Expansionary fiscal policy** – an increase in government expenditures or a decrease in taxation.

**Expansionary monetary policy** – an increase in the money supply.

**Exports** – total foreign purchases of domestic goods.

**Externality** – a benefit or a cost of an activity that affects third parties.

**Fallacy of composition** – the idea that what is true for one must be true for the group.

**Fatalism** – the belief that the course of a person's life is determined by fate.

**Federal funds rate** – the interest rate one bank charges another bank to borrow reserves.

**Fiat money** – money by government decree or fiat.

**Financial intermediation** – the process by which banks make depositors' savings available to borrowers.

**Firm** – an entity that employs resources to produce goods and services.

**Fiscal policy** – changes in government expenditures and taxation to achieve macroeconomic goals.

**Fixed costs** – costs that do not vary with output.

**Free market** – a market in which price is free to adjust up or down in response to demand and supply.

**Frictional unemployment** – due to the time required to match workers with jobs.

**Game theory** – a method for analyzing strategic behavior.

**Gini coefficient** - a measure of income inequality based on the Lorenz curve.

**Government failure** – occurs when government action results in a less efficient allocation of resources.

**Graphs** – illustrate the relationship between two variables.

**Gross domestic product (GDP)** – the market value of all final goods and services produced annually.

**High dependency ratio** – a large percentage of the population consists of children and the elderly.

**Horizontal merger** – a merger of firms competing in the same product market.

**Human capital** – developed ability that increases a person's productivity.

**Imports** – total domestic purchases of foreign goods.

**Incentive** – changes the benefit or cost associated with an action.

**Income elasticity of demand** – measures the responsiveness of demand to a change in income.

**Indifference curve** – a curve showing different combinations of two goods that provide equal total utility to a consumer.

**Industrial policy** – government aid to those industries that have the greatest potential for future growth.

**Industrial union** – a union made up of workers in the same industry.

**Inelastic demand** – price elasticity of demand is less than one.

**Infant mortality rate** – the number of infants who die before reaching one year of age out of every 1,000 live births.

**Inferior goods** – goods for which income and demand are inversely related.

**Inflation** – an increase in the price level.

**Inflationary gap** – when Real GDP is greater than Natural Real GDP.

**Interest** – the payment for the use of loanable funds.

**Interest rate effect** – when the price level decreases, the demand for money will decrease, causing interest rates to decrease.

**Intermediate good** – a good that has not yet reached its final user, but rather is an input in the production of another good.

**Inverse relationship** – as the value of one variable increases, the value of the other variable decreases.

**Investment** – the acquisition of new physical capital.

**Keynesian monetary transmission mechanism** – the series of steps through which changes in the money supply affect Real GDP, according to Keynesian theory.

**Labor** – the physical and mental efforts that people contribute to production.

**Labor force** – the sum of the number of people employed plus the number unemployed.

**Labor union** – an organization of workers that represents all the eligible workers in negotiating with management over wages and other issues.

**Laffer curve** – indicates that lowering tax rates might actually increase tax revenues.

**Laissez-faire** – do nothing; the policy that the government should not interfere with the economy.

**Land** – the naturally occurring resources.

**Law of comparative advantage** – trade between nations is beneficial to both if there is a difference in opportunity costs.

**Law of demand** – the price and the quantity demanded of a good are inversely related.

**Law of diminishing marginal returns** – as larger amounts of a variable input are combined with fixed inputs, eventually the marginal physical product of the variable input declines.

**Law of diminishing marginal utility** – the marginal utility from consuming additional units of a good eventually declines.

**Law of increasing opportunity cost** – as production of a good increases, the opportunity cost of producing that good increases.

**Legal barriers to entry** – barriers to entry created by government action.

**Less developed country (LDC)** – has a relatively low per capita Real GDP.

**License** – a permit issued by the government authorizing a person to conduct a certain type of business.

**Liquid asset** – an asset that can be converted quickly into cash at a low transaction cost.

**Logrolling** – vote trading in order to pass legislation.

**Long run** – a period in which all inputs can be varied.

**Long-run equilibrium** – when Real GDP is equal to Natural Real GDP.

**Loopholes** – exclusions and exemptions from income, deductible expenses, and tax credits.

**Lorenz curve** – contrasts the actual distribution of income with perfect equality.

**M1** – consists of currency in circulation plus checkable deposits.

**M2** – consists of M1 plus small-denomination time deposits, savings deposits, and money market accounts.

**Macroeconomics** – the branch of economics that focuses on overall economic behavior.

**Marginal cost** – the change in total cost that results from producing an additional unit of output.

**Marginal factor cost (MFC)** – the additional cost from employing an additional factor unit.

**Marginal physical product (MPP)** – the change in output with one additional unit of output.

**Marginal propensity to consume (MPC)** – the slope of the consumption function.

**Marginal rate of substitution** – the quantity of one good that a consumer is willing to sacrifice to obtain a unit of another good.

**Marginal revenue** – the change in total revenue from selling one additional unit of output.

**Marginal revenue product (MRP)** – the change in total revenue from employing an additional factor unit.

**Marginal social benefit (MSB)** – the value (benefit) to society of the marginal unit of output.

**Marginal social cost (MSC)** – the cost to society of producing the marginal unit of output.

**Marginal utility** – the additional utility received from consuming an additional unit of a good.

**Market failure** – occurs when the market does <u>not</u> produce the optimal quantity of output.

**Market power** – the ability of a seller or a buyer to affect market price.

**Merger** – the combining of two separate companies into one.

**Microeconomics** – the branch of economics that focuses on the components of the economy.

**Misperception effect** – If the price level changes, both workers and producers may misperceive the effect of the change in the price level.

**Monetary base** – currency in circulation plus bank reserves.

**Monetary policy** – changes in the money supply to achieve macroeconomic goals.

**Money** – whatever is generally accepted as a medium of exchange.

**Money creation** – increases in checkable deposits made possible by fractional reserve banking.

**Monopolistic competition** – many sellers of similar products.

**Monopoly** – a firm that is the lone seller of a product with no close substitutes.

**Monopsony** – a lone buyer in a factor market.

**Moral hazard** – one party to an exchange changes his or her behavior in a way unexpected by and detrimental to the other party.

**Multiplier effect** – according to Keynesian theory, an initial change in Total Expenditures will lead to a multiplied change in Real GDP.

**Nash equilibrium** – the outcome when each game player has chosen their best strategy, assuming that all other players have also chosen their best strategies.

**National debt** – the total amount the federal government owes its creditors.

**National defense argument** – argument for trade restrictions that says that national defense concerns may require certain trade restrictions.

**National income** – total output measured as the sum of all payments to resource owners.

**Natural monopoly** – an industry in which economies of scale are so important that only one firm can survive.

**Natural Real GDP** – the quantity of total output that results in the natural unemployment rate.

**Natural unemployment rate** – the lowest unemployment rate that can be sustained without causing increasing inflation.

**Net exports** – exports minus imports.

**Net worth** – a firm's assets minus its liabilities.

**Nonexcludable good** – nonpayers cannot easily be excluded from consuming the good.

**Nonrivalrous good** – a good for which consumption by one person does not hinder consumption by others.

**Normal goods** – goods for which income and demand are directly related.

**Normative statements** – propose the way things ought to be.

**Oligopoly** – an industry dominated by a few mutually interdependent firms.

**One-shot inflation** – a one-time increase in the price level.

**Open market operations** – the Fed buying and selling U.S. government securities in the open market.

**Open shop** – workers may join the union, or may choose to not join the union.

**Opportunity cost** – the value of the best alternative surrendered when a choice is made.

**Partnership** – a firm owned and operated by two or more co-owners.

**Patent** – a government granted monopoly on the production and sale of an invention granted to the inventor.

**Peak** – the highest phase of the business cycle.

**Per capita economic growth** – an increase in per capita Real GDP.

**Per capita output** – a basic measure of standard of living, computed by dividing total output by the population.

**Perfect competition** – many sellers of identical products.

**Perfectly elastic demand** – the demand curve is horizontal.

**Perfectly inelastic demand** – quantity demanded is unchanged by a change in price.

**Pollution** – any undesired byproduct of production.

**Pork barrel legislation** – benefits a particular geographic region and is paid for by taxpayers (and/or consumers) from a larger geographic region.

**Positive rate of time preference** – consumers prefer earlier consumption to later consumption.

**Positive statements** – claim to describe the way things are.

**Poverty** – a family whose income falls below a minimum established for an adequate standard of living is classified as living in poverty.

**Present value of an asset** – the discounted value today of the income stream associated with the asset.

**Price ceiling** – a maximum legal price.

**Price discrimination** – occurs when a seller charges different prices to different buyers for the same good.

**Price elasticity of demand** – measures the relative sizes of the changes in quantity demanded and price.

**Price elasticity of supply** – measures the relative sizes of the changes in quantity supplied and price.

**Price floor** – a minimum legal price.

**Private goods** – rivalrous in consumption and excludable.

**Private market equilibrium** – occurs where marginal private benefit equals marginal private cost.

**Producer's surplus** – the difference between the lowest price a seller is willing to accept and the price actually received.

**Product differentiation** – the process of distinguishing a firm's product from similar products.

**Production possibilities frontier (PPF)** – represents the maximum combinations of two goods that an economy can produce.

**Productivity** – measured by the output produced per unit of input.

**Profit-maximization rule** – produce the quantity of output where marginal revenue equals marginal cost.

**Profit-maximization rule for employing factors** – employ additional factor units up to the quantity where marginal revenue product equals marginal factor cost.

**Progressive tax** – imposes higher tax rates on higher levels of income.

**Proportional tax** – imposes the same tax rate on all levels of income.

**Proprietorship** – a firm owned and operated by one individual.

**Public choice theory** – applies economic principles to public sector decision making.

**Public employee union** – a union made up of workers employed by the government.

**Public franchise** – the government grants one firm an exclusive right to provide a good or a service to a market.

**Public goods** – nonrivalrous in consumption and nonexcludable.

**Quota** – a legal limit on the quantity of a good that may be imported.

**Real GDP** – GDP adjusted for changes in the price level.

**Real interest rate** – the nominal interest rate minus the rate of inflation.

**Recessionary gap** – when Real GDP is less than Natural Real GDP.

**Regressive tax** – imposes higher tax rates on lower levels of income.

**Rent seeking** – when people use resources to manipulate public policy in order to redistribute income to themselves from others.

**Required reserves** – the minimum amount of reserves that a bank is legally required to hold against its deposits.

**Reserves** – vault cash plus bank deposits with the Fed.

**Resources** – the inputs that make production possible.

**Rivalrous good** – a good for which consumption by one person prevents or interferes with consumption by another person.

**Rule of 70** – a rule of thumb for calculating the approximate time required for any variable to double at a given growth rate.

**Say's Law** – supply creates its own demand.

**Scarcity** – the problem that human wants exceed the production possible with the limited resources available.

**Screening device** – a characteristic used by employers as the basis for hiring and promoting employees.

**Seignorage -** the profit derived by the issuer of money by issuing new money.

**Self-sufficiency** – a person uses their own resources to produce the goods and services that they want to consume.

**Shirking** – avoiding the performance of an obligation.

**Short run** – a period in which at least one input is fixed.

**Shortage** – when quantity demanded exceeds quantity supplied.

**Shutdown point** – occurs if price falls below average variable cost.

**Slope of a curve** – the ratio of the vertical change to the horizontal change as the graph is read from left to right.

**Special-interest group** – a group of people who are especially interested in a particular government policy.

**Sticky-price effect** – prices in a market economy can be slow to adjust.

**Sticky-wage effect** – wages in a market economy can be slow to adjust (especially downward).

**Structural unemployment** – workers do not have the skills required in available jobs.

**Subprime mortgage** – home loan given to a person who is considered a poor credit risk.

**Sunk cost** – a past cost that cannot be changed by current decisions.

**Supply schedule** – a table showing the different combinations of price and quantity supplied for a good.

**Supply shocks** – unusual events that affect the overall costs of production.

**Surplus** – when quantity supplied exceeds quantity demanded.

**Tariff** – a tax on an imported good.

**Technological advance** – the ability to produce more output per resource.

**Total Expenditures (TE)** – consists of four types of spending; consumption, investment, government purchases, and net exports.

**Trade deficit** – when a nation's imports exceed its exports.

**Trade restrictions** – government imposed limitations on international trade.

**Transaction costs** – the costs of bringing buyers and sellers together for exchanges.

**Transfer payments** – transfers of income from the government to households or businesses, not in exchange for goods, services, or resources.

**Trough** – the lowest phase of the business cycle.

**Tying agreement** – a seller refuses to sell one product to a buyer unless the buyer agrees to buy a second product.

**Underground production** – production that is unreported because it is illegal or because the producer is evading taxation.

**Unemployed** – those without paying jobs who are actively seeking employment.

**Unemployment rate** – the percentage of the labor force that is unemployed.

**Union shop** – requires employees to join the union within a specified time.

**Unitary elastic demand** – price elasticity of demand is equal to one.

**U.S. government securities** – debt instruments issued by the federal government.

**Utility** – a measure of the satisfaction received from the consumption of a good.

**Value of the marginal product (VMP)** – the value to society of the output produced by the marginal factor. Equal to the price of the product times the MPP of the factor.

**Variable costs** – costs that vary with output.

**Velocity of money** – the average number of times that a dollar is spent annually.

**Vertical merger** – a merger of firms in the same industry, but not at the same stage in the production process.

**Wealth (real balance) effect** – when the price level decreases, consumers are wealthier (their money balances have more buying power).

# Index